BUILDING IMAGINARY WORLDS

Mark J. P. Wolf's study of imaginary worlds theorizes world-building within and across media, including literature, comics, film, radio, television, board games, video games, the Internet, and more. *Building Imaginary Worlds* departs from prior approaches to the topic that focused mainly on narrative, medium, or genre, and instead considers imaginary worlds as dynamic entities in and of themselves. Wolf argues that imaginary worlds—which are often transnarrative, transmedial, and transauthorial in nature—are compelling objects of inquiry for Media Studies.

Chapters present:

- a theoretical analysis of how world-building extends beyond storytelling, the engagement of the audience, and the way worlds are conceptualized and experienced
- a history of imaginary worlds that follows their development over three millennia from the fictional islands of Homer's *Odyssey* to the present
- internarrative theory examining how narratives set in the same world can interact and relate to one another
- an examination of transmedial growth and adaptation, and what happens when worlds make the jump between media
- an analysis of the transauthorial nature of imaginary worlds, the resulting concentric circles of authorship, and related topics of canonicity, participatory worlds, and subcreation's relationship with divine Creation.

Building Imaginary Worlds also provides the scholar of imaginary worlds with a glossary of terms and a detailed timeline that spans three millennia and more than 1,400 imaginary worlds, listing their names, creators, and the works in which they first appeared.

Mark J. P. Wolf is Professor of Communication at Concordia University Wisconsin. He is the author of *Myst and Riven: The World of the D'ni*, editor of the two-volume *Encyclopedia of Video Games*, and co-editor with Bernard Perron of *The Video Game Theory Reader 1* and *2*, among other books.

BUILDING IMAGINARY WORLDS

The Theory and History of Subcreation

Mark J. P. Wolf

Routledge
Taylor & Francis Group

NEW YORK AND LONDON

First published 2012
by Routledge
711 Third Avenue, New York, NY 10017

Simultaneously published in the UK
by Routledge
2 Park Square, Milton Park, Abingdon, Oxon OX14 4RN

Routledge is an imprint of the Taylor & Francis Group, an informa business

© 2012 Taylor & Francis

Library of Congress Cataloging in Publication Data
Wolf, Mark J. P.
Building imaginary worlds: the theory and history of subcreation /
Mark J. P. Wolf.
p. cm.
Includes bibliographical references and index.
1. Creation (Literary, artistic, etc.) 2. Imaginary societies–Authorship.
3. Fiction–History and criticism–Theory, etc. I. Title.
PN56.C69W67 2013
801'.92–dc23   2012016677

ISBN: 978-0-415-63119-8 (hbk)
ISBN: 978-0-415-63120-4 (pbk)
ISBN: 978-0-203-09699-4 (ebk)

Typeset in Bembo
by Cenveo Publisher Services

DEDICATION

A. M. D. G.

CONTENTS

LIST OF FIGURES

ACKNOWLEDGEMENTS

This book has been in development longer than any other academic work of mine, and has afforded me some very enjoyable research. Portions of this material have appeared in other works and presentations over the years as it was developing, including the presentation "Subcreation: Imaginary Worlds and Embedded World-Views" solicited for the Cranach Institute Spring Speaker Series at Concordia University Wisconsin in 2002; the essay "The Subcreation of Transmedia Worlds" solicited by the editor of the Media Culture issue of *Compar(a)ison: An International Journal of Comparative Literature* of Fall of 2005; an invited keynote address entitled "A Brief History of Imaginary Worlds" given at the Virtual Worlds Best Practices in Education Conference, held on-line in *Second Life* in 2010; "World Gestalten: Ellipsis, Logic, and Extrapolation in Imaginary Worlds" solicited by the editor of *Projections* for the summer 2012 issue; and two papers given at conferences of the Society for Cinema and Media Studies (SCMS), "The Subcreation of Transmedia Worlds" in 2006, and "Video Games in the Imaginary World Tradition" in 2011. The material in these essays and presentations was from the research for this book, and I am grateful to their audiences for a chance to debut the material. For suggestions, answers to questions, and research assistance, I would also like to thank Angus Menuge, Douglas A. Anderson, Christian Himsel, Thomas Krenzke, Reid Perkins-Buzo, Brian Stableford, Christine R. Johnson, Sally Canapa, Gaylund Stone, Mark Hayse; manuscript reviewers Kevin Schut, Marie-Laure Ryan, and Henry Lowood; and all the other friends, colleagues, and students who brought things to my attention. For various permissions, I would like to thank Adrian Leskiw, Franco Maria Ricci, Mark

Bennett and the Mark Moore Gallery, James L. Dean, Richard Watson, Michael O. Riley, and A. K. Dewdney. I am also grateful for the enthusiasm and encouragement of Matthew Byrnie and Erica Wetter at Routledge. Thanks also to my wife Diane and my sons Michael, Christian, and Francis, who put up with me during the years while I was working on this book. And, as always, thanks be to God, the Creator of all subcreators.

INTRODUCTION

A map of the world that does not include Utopia is not worth even glancing at, for it leaves out the one country at which Humanity is always landing.

—Oscar Wilde, *The Soul of Man under Socialism*[1]

Like most Americans my age (with access to books), I spent a good deal of my youth in Baum's Land of Oz. I have a precise, tactile memory of the first Oz book that came into my hands. It was the original 1910 edition of The Emerald City. *I still remember the look and the feel of those dark blue covers, the evocative smell of dust and old ink. I also remember that I could not stop reading and rereading the book. But "reading" is not the right word. In some mysterious way, I was translating myself to Oz, a place which I was to inhabit for many years while, simultaneously, visiting other fictional worlds as well as maintaining my cover in that dangerous one known as "real". With* The Emerald City, *I became addicted to reading.*

—Gore Vidal, "The Oz Books"[2]

All my movies are about strange worlds that you can't go into unless you build them and film them. That's what's so important about film to me. I just like going into strange worlds.

—David Lynch, filmmaker[3]

Since the advent of daydreaming, imaginary worlds have drawn us away vicariously to fantastic realms culled from endless possibilities. The allure of such wayward speculation, conjuring new wonders, strange terrors, and the unexplored byways of beckoning vistas, has grown stronger over time along with our ability to render them into concrete forms, albeit mediated ones. Books, drawings, photographs, film, radio, television, video games, websites, and other media have opened portals through which these worlds grow in clarity and detail, inviting us to enter and tempting us to stay, as alive in our thoughts as our own memories of lived experience.

Yet, imaginary worlds, which rank among the most elaborate mediated entities, have been largely overlooked in Media Studies, despite a history spanning three millennia. Imaginary worlds are occasionally considered tangentially, either from the point of view of a particular story set in them, or a particular medium in which they appear, but in either case the focus is too narrow for the world to be examined as a whole. Often when a world is noticed at all, it is only considered as a background for stories set in it, rather than a subject of study in itself. At the same time, a world is more difficult to encapsulate in a description or analysis than a particular story, character, or situation, making it easier to overlook.

Imaginary worlds, built of words, images, and sounds, can be tremendous in size; for example, as of summer 2012, the *Star Trek* universe consisted of over 500 hours of television shows, 11 feature films, and hundreds of novels, not to mention several decades worth of video games, comic books, and other books including technical manuals, chronologies, and encyclopedias. And since it is an open-ended and still-growing universe, more *Star Trek* material appears every year. Worlds of this size, even closed ones that are no longer being added to (though they may still be adapted and interpreted), can often be difficult to see in their totality, and much time must be spent to learn enough about a world to get an overall sense of its shape and design. In this sense, an imaginary world can become a large entity which is experienced through various media windows; but quite often, no one window shows everything, and only an aggregate view combining a variety of these windows can give a complete sense of what the world is like and what has occurred there. Experiencing an imaginary world in its entirety, then, can sometimes be quite an undertaking.

Besides the amount of time required for their study, another reason for the scholarly neglect of imaginary worlds might be due to the ways that imaginary worlds differ from other media entities. First, the construction of most narrative media entities, be they novels, films, television programs, and so on, is usually strictly determined by the narrative line (or lines) they contain; that is to say, the determination of which details and events will appear is motivated by whether or not they advance the story, which is given primary importance in traditional storytelling. For works in which world-building occurs, there may be a wealth of details and events (or mere mentions of them) which do not advance the story but which provide background richness and verisimilitude to the imaginary world. Sometimes this material even appears outside of the story itself, in the form of appendices, maps, timelines, glossaries of invented languages, and so forth. Such additional information can change the audience's experience, understanding, and immersion in a story, giving a deeper significance to characters, events, and details. Audience members and critical approaches that center on narrative, then, may find such excess material to be extraneous, tangential, and unnecessary, while those that consider the story's world will find their experience enhanced.

Another way that imaginary worlds differ from traditional media entities is that they are often transnarrative and transmedial in form, encompassing books, films, video, games, websites, and even reference works like dictionaries, glossaries, atlases, encyclopedias, and more. Stories written by different authors can be set in the same world, so imaginary worlds can be transauthorial as well. Worlds that extend and expand across multiple media are now common, and a world may even become something of a brand name or franchise, with new stories, locations, and characters continually being added. In some cases, an imaginary world's opened-ended and work-in-progress nature can work against the sense of closure often desired for the purposes of analysis and scholarship; an essay written about the 1977 version of the film *Star Wars* may no longer apply to the 1981 re-release, the "Special Edition" re-release of 1997, the DVD version released in 2004, the Blu-Ray version released in 2011, or the 3-D version of the film promised for 2015 (and, probably, a 3-D home video version after that).

Finally, imaginary worlds may depend relatively little on narrative, and even when they do, they often rely on other kinds of structures for their form and organization (see Chapter 3). Imaginary worlds are, by their nature, an inter-disciplinary object of study, and thus likely to either fall between the cracks between disciplines and sub-disciplines or receive only a partial examination according to which features are considered salient according to the analytical tools being applied. Yet, the study of imaginary worlds is occurring in a variety of fields (such as philosophy, film studies, psychology, video game studies, economics, and religion) and the research regarding them is gradually converging, suggesting that the study of imaginary worlds can easily constitute its own subfield within Media Studies. I am hoping that this book will represent a step in that direction. Such a field of study is necessary, since visiting and creating imaginary worlds are likely to remain common and popular activities.

World-building as a Human Activity

Imaginary worlds are enjoyed not only by those who visit them, but also by those who invent them, and world-building activities often occur from a very young age onward. Little children enjoy building forts from couch cushions and blankets, and transforming spaces into imaginary places that they can physically enter into during their games of pretend and make-believe. As they get older, such play shifts to tabletop playsets where smaller physical spaces represent larger imaginary ones; pirate ships, space stations, LEGO cities, dungeons drawn on graph paper, and so on. Time is compressed as well as space; entire wars and the rise and fall of civilizations can occur in a single afternoon. Such play is removed even further from direct experience in the abstracted versions of events found in board games and the virtual and intangible worlds of video games. And even more common among adults are the imaginary worlds found in novels, films, and on television (which, of course, often extend to board games, video games, and other media as well). For many, the desire for imaginary worlds does not change over time, only the manner in which those worlds are constructed and experienced.

Some researchers have gone so far as to suggest that the building of imaginary worlds is something innate and even serves an evolutionary purpose. In *Literature and the Brain* (2009), Norman Holland summarizes the work of psychologists John Tooby and Leda Cosmides, stating their position in five points:

1. The ability to "simulate" situations (to imagine them without acting on them) has great value for humans both in survival and reproduction. This ability to simulate seems to occur innately in the human species. We evolved the "association cortices" in our large frontal lobes for just this purpose.
2. All cultures create fictional, imagined worlds. We humans find these imagined worlds intrinsically interesting.
3. Responding to imaginary worlds, we engage emotion systems while disengaging action systems.
4. Humans have *evolved special cognitive systems that enable us to participate in these fictional worlds. We can, in short, pretend and deceive and imagine, having mental states about mental states.*
5. We can separate these fictional worlds from our real-life experiences. We can, in a key word, *decouple* them.[4]

It seems only natural, then, that such abilities and activities would continue to develop beyond their basic initial purposes and into a form of art and even entertainment.

World-building, as a deliberate activity, can begin very early on in a person's life. Imaginary worlds built during early childhood are common enough that they have been dubbed "paracosms" in the field of psychology, and since the late 1970s, they have been the subject of a number of articles and books. As Michele Root-Bernstein writes in "Imaginary Worldplay as an Indicator of Creative Giftedness":

Early research explored ties between worldplay and later artistic endeavor. Recent study of gifted adults finds strong links, too, between worldplay and mature creative accomplishment in the sciences and social sciences. As many as 1 in 30 children may invent worlds in solitary, secret play that is hidden from ready view. Worldplay nevertheless figured tangentially in early studies of intellectual precocity. Improved understanding of the phenomenon, its nature and its potential for nurture, should bring childhood worldplay to the foreground as an indicator of creative giftedness.[5]

Many writers, including Hartley Coleridge (son of Samuel Taylor Coleridge), Thomas Penson de Quincey, the Brontë siblings (Emily, Anne, Charlotte, and Patrick), James M. Barrie, Isak Dineson, C. S. Lewis, Austin Tappan Wright, M. A. R. Barker, and Steph Swainton, invented paracosms during childhood, and some continued to develop them into adulthood. These early worlds were often the precursors for the imaginary worlds which they would invent and write about during their careers.

Imaginary worlds are sometimes very important to their creators and central to their own lives. L. Frank Baum's last words on his deathbed were reportedly "Now we can cross the Shifting Sands",[6] while the tombstone for J. R. R. Tolkien and his wife Edith contains their own names as well as those of Beren and Lúthien, the heroic husband and wife from *The Silmarillion* (1977). Another subcreator, Henry Darger (who, like Tolkien, was born in 1892, died in 1973, and worked on his imaginary world for decades), was a recluse whose life's work was writing about and illustrating his imaginary world, into which he even placed himself as a character. Some use imaginary worlds for healing; while recovering from a severe beating and a coma with injuries that include memory loss, Mark Hogancamp began his imaginary town of Marwencol as a form of therapy, and his photographs of it later led to a gallery show in Manhattan and the award-winning feature-length documentary *Marwencol* (2010). And even when an author is less closely associated with his or her imaginary world, it will still often occupy a central position within the author's *oeuvre*, and is usually the setting for multiple stories.

My own interest in imaginary worlds extends back into my childhood. Looking back, I can see that many of the things that interested me—drawing, architecture, film, building with LEGO, animation, adventure games, and the works of my favorite author, Tolkien—all had to do with various aspects of imaginary worlds. Born in 1967, I grew up in the 1970s during the time when table-top role-playing games and video games were gaining popularity, and cinematic special effects were being developed for world-building, most notably in *Star Wars* (1977). At the time, Tolkien's work exerted a strong influence over fantasy novels, fantasy art, role-playing games, and video games of the adventure genre, and these collectively had an effect on the culture in general. Amidst my own creative endeavors were drawing and writing, making stop-motion movies, and even designing graphics and programming games on my Texas Instruments TI99/4a home computer. I eventually went on to film school in college, beginning at the University of Wisconsin-Milwaukee and then transferring to the University of Southern California where I was accepted into the School of Cinema/Television (as it was called back then). While doing my Bachelor's degree in the Production side of the cinema school, I realized how much I enjoyed the analytical side of film and media studies, and went on to get a Master's degree in the Critical Studies side of the school, while doing a teaching assistant-ship in the Animation Department of the Production side. After that, a Ph.D.

seemed the way to go, and I completed mine in the spring of 1995. Since then, I have also completed two novels (one fantasy, one science fiction) and am looking for an agent and publisher for them.

I mention all of this because I was interested in building imaginary worlds, and did so in various media, before I was consciously aware of how much I also liked analyzing them. My interest in making imaginary worlds greatly informs the way that I look at and analyze imaginary worlds, since the maker's perspective helps to account for much of the shape of a world; even when one has an initial plan, much world-building ends up being the result of problem-solving and a good dose of serendipity. Only in retrospect did I see the research value of some of my past activities, and how they provided a good foundation for further study. Since then, my research has become more deliberate, and even my work in video game studies was initially done to better understand them as imaginary worlds, and as a part of the background research necessary for this book.

Imaginary worlds are an interdisciplinary subject and can be approached from many angles, but Media Studies, which acknowledges and accounts for the windows through which imaginary worlds are so often seen, provides the best basis for examining them as entities in and of themselves, laying a foundation for contributions from other disciplines. At the same time, as a convergence of concerns, methodologies, and interests from a variety of other fields (including literary theory, film and television studies, psychology, rhetoric, linguistics, semiotics, anthropology, sociology, and art history), Media Studies is still relatively new as a field, while the study of imaginary worlds has roots extending back more than a century.

Toward a Theory of Imaginary Worlds

Before the field of Media Studies existed in academia, the making of imaginary worlds was discussed and theorized by writers and poets like George MacDonald, J. R. R. Tolkien, Dorothy L. Sayers, and C. S. Lewis, and later discussed as a practice in "how-to" books on world-building for writers, like Orson Scott Card's *How to Write Science Fiction and Fantasy* (1990) or Stephen L. Gillett's *World-Building: A Writer's Guide to Constructing Star Systems and Life-Supporting Planets* (1995). Lin Carter's *Imaginary Worlds: The Art of Fantasy* (1973) was one of the first book-length studies devoted to examining imaginary worlds, though it was mainly limited to novels within the fantasy genre. Tolkien in particular thought about imaginary worlds and worked on them his entire adult life, revising and adding to his own subcreation, as the posthumous 12-volume *History of Middle-earth* series, which documents over five decades of his work on his world, can attest. It was from Tolkien's famous essay on imaginary worlds, "On Fairy-stories", that the term in the subtitle of this book was taken; "subcreation" was Tolkien's word for the making of imaginary worlds, the "sub" prefix designating a specific kind of creation distinct from God's *ex nihilo* creation, and reliant upon it (thus "sub", meaning "under").

As poets and novelists, the authors mentioned above were mainly practitioners creating their own worlds and theorizing what they were doing, resulting in analyses concerned with authorial invention and limitations, and the experience of the audience. From the 1960s onwards, fictional worlds were studied from a philosophical point of view, using "possible worlds" theory and modal logic, which consider the ontological status of fictional worlds, the nature of their functioning, and their relationship with the actual world. These ideas have been combined with literary theory, setting the foundation for the study of imaginary worlds. Philosophical writings on fictional worlds consider mainly questions of language, with most of their examples taken from literature, thereby neglecting imaginary worlds that are audiovisual in nature; Media Studies, then, must pick up where they have left off.

Of course, scholarly work exists examining such things as *The Lord of the Rings* (1954–1955), *Star Trek*, *Star Wars*, and the worlds of video games. However, most approaches tend to be, at their core, either medium-oriented (looking at a particular medium, and its form) or narrative-oriented (where the focus is on story, or content), or some combination of these. While the first approach considers the windows through which the world is seen, the second comes only a little closer by examining stories set in the world, rather than the world itself. Over the years, however, Media Studies approaches have been drawing ever closer to the *world* as an object of study. The notion of "media franchises", for example, appeared in the early twentieth century and dealt with more than a single medium or story, but it was more concerned with the commercial impetus behind the production of the world, which in earlier franchises was generally built around characters (for example, the studio film franchises built around Tarzan, Andy Hardy, Ma and Pa Kettle, Superman, and so on). Some of these franchises began to be transmedial as well, appearing in comic books, serials, animated shorts, radio dramas, and feature films.

Going beyond the idea of franchises, Marsha Kinder's notion of a "supersystem of entertainment", introduced in her book *Playing With Power in Movies, Television, and Video Games: From Muppet Babies to Teenage Mutant Ninja Turtle* (1991), began to acknowledge the transmedial nature that worlds often have, though it did not focus on the worlds themselves:

> A supersystem is a network of intertextuality constructed around a figure or group of figures from pop culture who are either fictional (like TMNT, the characters from *Star Wars*, the Super Mario Brothers, the Simpsons, the Muppets, Batman, and Dick Tracy) or "real" (like PeeWee Herman, Elvis Presley, Marilyn Monroe, Madonna, Michael Jackson, the Beatles, and most recently, the New Kids on the Block). In order to be a supersystem, the network must cut across several modes of image production; must appeal to diverse generations, classes, and ethnic subcultures, who in turn are targeted with diverse strategies; must foster "collectability" through a

proliferation of related products; and must undergo a sudden increase in commodification, the success of which reflexively becomes a media event that dramatically accelerates the growth curve of the system's commercial success.[7]

Like the idea of a franchise, the supersystem is mainly defined by commercial concerns, and the figures at the center of a supersystem do not need to have an entire world built around them. The "several modes of image production" requirement rules out purely literary worlds, while commodification and commercial success rule out other types of worlds. The notion of a supersystem does acknowledge that a "network of intertextuality" is needed, which worlds usually provide, and that these phenomena are often transmedial ones. However, not all supersystems qualify as worlds, and probably the majority of imaginary worlds would not be considered supersystems according to Kinder's criteria.

In *Hamlet on the Holodeck: The Future of Narrative in Cyberspace* (1997), Janet H. Murray moved closer to examining imaginary worlds by noting how they were being encouraged by new media and the changes in consumption due to them. Describing nonlinear, continuing stories which she calls "hyperserials", she writes:

> Probably the first steps toward a new *hyperserial* format will be the close integration of a digital archive, such as a Web site [*sic*], with a broadcast television program. Unlike the Web sites currently associated with conventional television programs, which are merely fancy publicity releases, an integrated digital archive would present virtual artifacts from the fictional world of the series, including not only diaries, photo albums, and telephone messages but also documents like birth certificates, legal briefs, or divorce papers. ... The compelling spatial reality of the computer will also lead to virtual environments that are extensions of the fictional world. For instance, the admitting station seen in every episode of *ER* could be presented as a virtual space, allowing viewers to explore it and discover phone messages, patient files, and medical test results, all of which could be used to extend the current story line or provide hints of future developments. ... In a well-conceived hyperserial, all the minor characters would be potential protagonists of their own stories, thus providing alternate threads within the enlarged story web. The viewer would take pleasure in the ongoing juxtapositions, the intersection of many lives, and the presentation of the same event from multiple sensitivities and perspectives.[8]

Murray's prediction has come true, and what she describes is significant in that it reflects the shift in audience attention from the central storyline to the world in which the story takes place, where multiple storylines can interweave in a web of story. This idea is taken a step further in Lev Manovich's notion of the "database narrative" discussed a few years later in his book *The Language of New Media* (2001). In a section entitled "Database and Narrative", Manovich writes:

> As a cultural form, the database represents the world as a list of items, and it refuses to order this list. ... Some media objects explicitly follow a database logic in their structure whereas others do not; but under the surface, practically all of them are databases. In general, creating a work in new media can be understood as the construction of an interface to a database. In the simplest case, the interface merely provides access to the underlying database. ... *The new media object consists of one or more interfaces to a database of multimedia material.* If only one interface is constructed, the result will be similar to a traditional art object, but this is an exception rather than the norm.
>
> This formulation places the opposition between the database and the narrative in a new light, thus redefining our concept of narrative. The "user" of a narrative is traversing a database, following links between its records as established by the database's creator.[9]

Here, the database viewed through one or more interfaces sounds very much like an imaginary world seen through various media windows; but "database" is defined much more broadly, and the ordering of data into a coherent *world* is not required.

Both Murray and Manovich conceive of multimedia works as generating spaces through which users can explore the content of imaginary worlds, each containing narrative (or at least informational) elements which add detail to the imaginary world. The distribution of stories over and across a variety of media is the idea behind what Henry Jenkins calls "transmedia storytelling", described in his book *Convergence Culture: Where Old and New Media Collide* (2006).[10] In a sense, imaginary worlds have always promoted convergence culture, since individual worlds have appeared through multiple media windows ever since those windows became available. Jenkins looks at how stories spill over from one media window to another and interconnect with other narratives set in a world:

> A transmedia story unfolds across multiple media platforms, with each new text making a distinctive and valuable contribution to the whole. In the ideal form of transmedia storytelling, each medium does what it does best— so that a story might be introduced in a film, expanded through television, novels, and comics; its world might be explored through game play or experienced as an amusement park attraction. Each franchise entry needs to be self-contained so you don't need to have seen the film to enjoy the game, and vice versa. Any given product is a point of entry into the franchise as a whole.[11]

In another section of the same essay, Jenkins discusses cult movies and what makes them different from other films, writing:

> Umberto Eco asks what, beyond being loved, transforms a film such as *Casablanca* (1942) into a cult artifact. First, he argues, the work must come to us as a "completely furnished world so that its fans can quote characters and episodes as if they were aspects of the private sectarian world." Second, the work must be encyclopedic, containing a rich array of information that can be drilled, practiced, and mastered by devoted consumers.
>
> The film need not be well made, but it must provide resources the consumers can use in constructing their own fantasies: "In order to transform a work into a cult object one must be able to break, dislocate, unhinge it so that one can remember only parts of it, irrespective of their original relationship to the whole." And the cult film need not be coherent: the more different directions it pushes, the more different communities it can sustain and the more different experiences it can provide, the better. We experience the cult movie, he suggests, not as having "one central idea, but many," as "a disconnected series of images, of peaks, of visual icebergs."[12]

The need for a "completely furnished world" emphasizes the world's importance, and its encyclopedic nature is another way of describing it as a database narrative. Eco's last point quoted here, that cult films do not have a central idea but many ideas in a disconnected series, further seems to be emphasizing the need for world-building beyond mere storytelling. Finally, Jenkins comments on the shift from story to world as well:

> More and more, storytelling has become the art of world-building, as artists create compelling environments that cannot be fully explored or exhausted within a single work or even a single medium. The world is bigger than the film, bigger than even the franchise—since fan speculations and elaborations also expand the world in a variety of directions. As an experienced screenwriter told me, "When I first started, you would pitch a story because without a good story, you didn't really have a film. Later, once sequels started to take off, you pitched a character because a good character could support multiple stories. And now, you pitch a world because a world can support multiple characters and multiple stories across multiple media." Different franchises follow their own logic: some, such as the *X-Men* (2000) movies, develop the world in their first installment and then allow the sequels to unfold different stories set within that world; others, such as the *Alien* (1979) films or George Romero's *Living Dead* (1968) cycle, introduce new aspects of the world with each new installment, so that more energy gets put into mapping the world than inhabiting it.[13]

Later in 2007, Jenkins would add a related comment in an article on his website:

> Most often, transmedia stories are based not on individual characters or specific plots but rather complex fictional worlds which can sustain multiple interrelated characters and their stories. This process of world-building encourages an encyclopedic impulse in both readers and writers. We are drawn to master what can be known about a world which always expands beyond our grasp. This is a very different pleasure than we associate with the closure found in most classically constructed narratives, where we expect to leave the theatre knowing everything that is required to make sense of a particular story.[14]

Recognizing that the experience of a *world* is different and distinct from that of merely a *narrative* is crucial to seeing how worlds function apart from the narratives set within them, even though the narratives have much to do with the worlds in which they occur, and are usually the means by which the worlds are experienced. David Bordwell has also noticed the growing popularity of world-building, writing:

> Less widespread, but becoming very striking in recent years, is what we may call "worldmaking". More and more films have been at pains to offer a rich, fully furnished ambience for the action. ... The minutiae accumulate into a kind of information overload. ... Layered worlds, complete with brand names and logos, became essential to science fiction, but the tactic found its way into other genres, too. Perhaps because 1970s location filming turned Hollywood away from spotless sets, filmmakers sought richly articulated worlds that were grimy. ... *Star Wars* signaled the marketing potential of massive detailing. Lucas remarked in 1977 that inventing everything from scratch—clothes, silverware, customs—created a "multi-layered reality" ... Story comprehension was now multidimensional: a novice could follow the basic plot, but she could enjoy it even more if she rummaged for microdata in the film or outside it.[15]

Other works, like Jesper Juul's book *Half-Real: Video Games between Real Rules and Fictional Worlds* (2005), Edward Castronova's *Synthetic Worlds: The Business and Culture of Online Games* (2005), and many of the essays in Pat Harrigan and Noah Wardrip-Fruin's *Third Person: Authoring and Exploring Vast Narratives* (2009), discuss imaginary worlds and world-building, albeit from different angles and for different purposes. The attitudes and ideas found in these works, and in the above-mentioned works of Kinder, Murray, Manovich, and Jenkins, are growing in the field of Media Studies; and certain subfields within it, like video game studies, encourage thinking about worlds as entities in and of themselves, instead of merely as backgrounds in which narratives occur.[16] One author,

Michael O. Riley, has already used this approach in his book *Oz and Beyond: The Fantasy World of L. Frank Baum* (1997), where he writes in the book's prologue:

> No study, however, has examined his fantasy solely from the standpoint of his Other-world or examined that Other-world as a whole. Understandably, because Oz is what Baum is best remembered for, the tendency has been to concentrate on his masterpiece, *The Wonderful Wizard of Oz*, or to deal with his Oz series without giving much emphasis to his non-Oz fantasies. Yet, Baum's Other-world includes much besides Oz, and Oz itself was not a static creation; it developed and changed over the course of the books in the series. Therefore, considering Oz only as an inert, unchanging imaginary world can lead to confusion and sometimes misunderstanding. ... My approach will be to examine each of Baum's relevant fantasies (whether book-length or short story), to analyze the glimpses of his Other-world, and to piece together a picture of the way in which that world emerged, was changed, was modified, or was enlarged from its beginning until Baum's death. I will also point out how that world and its development reflected the circumstances of Baum's life and his experiences of America. For the purposes of this study, all his works of fantasy are of equal importance, and there will be little attempt at critical evaluation of the books because some stories that critics count among his weakest from the standpoint of plot, characters, and theme are among his strongest from the standpoint of the development of his Other-world.[17]

Riley is right in suggesting that new criteria are needed for the examination of a world; the criteria used in more traditional literary criticism are not world-centered and constitute a different focus, one that leaves out much that is important to an analysis of world-building. In this book, then, I hope to combine approaches like Riley's with that of MacDonald, Tolkien, Jenkins, and other authors, into an integrated examination of imaginary worlds from a Media Studies perspective, looking at the history of their development and their structures, as well as other areas like internarrative construction, transmedial growth and adaptation, self-reflexivity, and authorship.

A focus on the worlds themselves, rather than on the individual narratives occurring within them or the various media windows through which those narratives are seen and heard, becomes more interesting the larger the world is that one is considering, and can provide a more holistic approach to analysis, especially when the worlds in question are transnarrative and transmedial ones. An examination of the experience of subcreated or secondary worlds also helps explain the disparity between the popular and critical reception of films like those of the *Star Wars* prequel trilogy. Whereas critics tend to be more interested in traditional categories like acting, dialogue, character development, and story for their critiques, audiences are often more concerned with the overall experience, especially of the world that they are being asked to enter vicariously. As Eco's comments (quoted earlier) on cult objects suggest, imaginary worlds invite audience participation in the form of speculation and fantasies, which depend more on the fullness and richness of the world itself than on any particular storyline or character within it; quite a shift from the traditional narrative film or novel. As Louis Kennedy wrote in *The Boston Globe* in a 2003 review of the *Matrix* franchise entitled "Piece of Mind: Forget about beginnings, middles, and ends. The new storytelling is about making your way in a fragmented, imaginary world":

> ... these movies aren't about the things we have spent our lives thinking movies are about—much less what older forms of storytelling, from theater to novels, are about. They don't care much about character development or plot. They don't care about starting at point A and moving neatly and clearly to point B, with the action motivated by and enriched by the believable, carefully portrayed needs and desires of the humans who enact it.
>
> But what they do care about, and deeply, is creating a world—a rich, multifaceted, and complex environment that the viewer can enter and explore in a variety of ways. ... We can critique the makers of the "Matrix" series, Larry and Andy Wachowski, for lots of things, but we should not fall into the trap of calling them bad storytellers. They aren't storytellers at all. They are worldmakers.[18]

There is no doubt that franchised entertainment, and entertainment in general, is moving more and more in the direction of subcreational world-building. Science Fiction and Fantasy have been major mass-market publishing genres for several decades now, and digital special effects technology has renewed both genres in cinema. Many of the top-grossing movies of all time take place in secondary worlds (such as Middle-earth, Hogwarts Academy, and the *Star Wars* galaxy). Video games worlds have become tough competition for the worlds of film and television, not to mention those of novels and comics. And subcreated worlds often span all of these media simultaneously.

For the writing of this book, I have had to find more generalized language that reflects the transmedial nature of so many worlds. The term "author" is used to include writers, filmmakers, game makers, and so on, whereas "audience" includes readers, viewers, listeners, and players. The media objects in which worlds appear, such as books, photographs, films, radio plays, comics, and video games, are collectively referred to as the "works" set in a world, which the audience "experiences" (by reading, watching, listening, playing, and so on). Thus, general statements can be made about a world and its use without being limited to specific media and media-related activities.

Imaginary worlds have been referred to in a number of ways, many of which appear throughout this book as well; as "subcreated worlds", "secondary worlds", "diegetic worlds", "constructed worlds", and "imaginary worlds". While these terms are sometimes used interchangeably, each term emphasizes different aspects of the same phenomenon. Tolkien's term "subcreated world" indicates the philosophical and ontological distinction between creation and subcreation (and the dependence of the latter on the former), while "secondary world" refers to a world's relationship with our own world, the "Primary World". The term "diegetic world" comes from narratology, and "constructed world" from popular culture, while "imaginary world" is perhaps the broadest and least technical term, and it appears the most often in this book, as a kind of default, unless a more specific term is required.

I have tried to acknowledge the wide range of worlds in different media by a variety of examples throughout this book, while at the same time I have taken many examples from those worlds that are the most widely known, including Tolkien's Arda (in which Middle-earth is found), the universes of *Star Wars* and *Star Trek*, and other popular worlds like those of Oz, *Myst*, and *The Matrix*. In addition to being the most familiar and accessible, they are also among the largest and most detailed and developed worlds, and therefore rife with examples of much of what I will be discussing.

This book is divided into seven chapters, and arranged to set a foundation in the first three chapters before proceeding to explorations of particular aspects of imaginary worlds in the latter four. Chapter 1 attempts to define imaginary worlds and lays the groundwork for a theoretical description of how they operate, such as the way world-building extends beyond storytelling, the engagement of the audience, and the way in which worlds are experienced. Chapter 2 is a history of imaginary worlds, following their development over three millennia from the fictional islands of Homer's *The Odyssey* to the present, looking at the new directions and uses for imaginary worlds especially in the past century or so. It also follows some of the ways conventions and tropes changed over time and how worlds adapted to new technologies and new media windows through which they could be experienced. Chapter 3 then examines the various infrastructures that are used both by authors and audiences to hold a world together, keeping track of all the relationships among thousands of elements, and also how these structures might relate to each other.

I have already mentioned how imaginary worlds are often transnarrative, transmedial, and transauthorial in nature, and these concerns are taken up in the rest of the book. Chapter 4 looks at narrative as a structuring device, as well as how multiple narratives set in a world can interact, resulting in what one might call internarrative theory. Other ideas, like retroactive continuity, multiverses, and interactivity are also considered in regard to narrative. Chapter 5 focuses on a particular kind of situation in which subcreation is itself a theme, resulting in self-reflexivity and subcreated subcreators. Chapter 6 grazes the surface of an enormous topic, that of transmedial growth and adaptation, and the demands they make on a world, as well as some of the processes that occur when worlds make the jump between media. Chapter 7 examines the transauthorial nature of imaginary worlds, the resulting concentric circles of authorship, and related topics of canonicity, participatory worlds, and subcreation's relationship with Creation. Finally, the book ends with a glossary of terms, and an Appendix which is a timeline offering a sampling of 1440 imaginary worlds produced across three millennia, along with the names of their authors and the works in which they made their first public appearance.

Imaginary worlds are diverse, dynamic, and often ongoing projects, and this book could easily have been many times the size that it is. Much remains to be done in the realm of subcreation studies, and hopefully this book can provide some framework for thinking about imaginary worlds, as well as a point of departure for those who will venture off, like the early explorers in traveler's tales, into explorations of how worlds grow and function and reflect our own world. And since our own Primary World has become a highly mediated one, with much of what we know about it coming through media rather than just direct experience, an understanding of how secondary worlds are experienced and imagined by people may also tell us something about the way in which we form a mental image of the world we live in, and the way we experience it and see our own lives intersecting with it.

1
WORLDS WITHIN THE WORLD

> *It was toward that point in space that I directed my thoughts, and, completely
> permeated by the reading and study of my Starian books, I crossed the Heavens faster
> than the speed of light; no longer did anything Terrestrial occupy my thoughts;
> I believed that I really was on a planet in the solar system of Star.*
>
> —Charles Ischir Defontenay, *Star (Psi Cassiopeia)*[1]

> *And then finally when you get far enough along in a thing, you feel as though you're
> living there—not just working at a painting, but actually working in that valley.
> You're there.*
>
> —Andrew Wyeth, painter[2]

> *Texts, media, are not just referential paths leading to worlds: to read a text or to look
> at a painting means already to inhabit their worlds.*
>
> —Thomas G. Pavel, literary theorist[3]

To give oneself over to a painting, novel, movie, television show, or video game is
to step vicariously into a new experience, into an imaginary world. This can be
as true for the author of the work as it is for the rest of the work's audience. And
when such works are well made, they can pull their audience in so skillfully that
not only is one's imagination stimulated without much conscious effort, but the
whole experience is a pleasurable one. Storytelling may be a part of it, but less
often acknowledged is the draw of the world itself, especially when that world is
substantially different from our own. Whether through verbal description, visual
design, sound design, or virtual spaces revealed through interaction, it is the world
(sometimes referred to as the storyworld or diegetic world) that supports all the

narratives set in it and that is constantly present during the audience's experience. And that experience may or may not include narrative; enjoyment of a world can be done for its own sake, for example, by interactively exploring the islands of *Riven* (1997), poring over floor plans and technical specifications in *Star Trek: The Next Generation Technical Manual* (1991), paging through the bizarre images and unreadable text of *Codex Seraphinianus* (1981), or contemplating Naohisa Inoue's paintings of his world called Iblard. To invite an audience to vicariously enter another world, and then hold them there awhile is, after all, the essence of *entertainment*, which traces its etymology to the Latin roots *inter* meaning "among", and *tenere* meaning "to hold".

How imaginary worlds work (when they are successful) depends on how they are constructed and how they invoke the imagination of the audience experiencing them. Worlds, unlike stories, need not rely on narrative structures, though stories are always dependent on the worlds in which they take place. Worlds extend beyond the stories that occur in them, inviting speculation and exploration through imaginative means. They are realms of possibility, a mix of familiar and unfamiliar, permutations of wish, dread, and dream, and other kinds of existence that can make us more aware of the circumstances and conditions of the actual world we inhabit.

The Philosophy of Possible Worlds

The notion that "things could have been otherwise than what they are" is the idea behind the philosophy of possible worlds, a branch of philosophy designed for problem-solving in formal semantics, that considers possibilities, imaginary objects, their ontological status, and the relationship between fictional worlds and the actual world. Possible worlds theory places the "actual world" at the center of the hierarchy of worlds, and "possible worlds" around it, that are said to be "accessible" to the actual world. These worlds are then used to formulate statements regarding possibility and necessity (that is, a proposition is "possible" if it is found in one of the worlds, and "necessary" if it is found in all of them). One philosopher, David Lewis, has even defended the extreme position that all possible worlds are as real as our own world, at least to their inhabitants.[4]

In the 1970s, philosophical ideas from possible-worlds semantics, speech-act theory, and world-version epistemology made their way into literary studies, to be used in the analysis of fictional worlds.[5] They also helped legitimize the notion that fiction can contain certain kinds of truth. One idea emerging from these writings is an appreciation for the fact that imaginary worlds can be represented at all. Philosopher Thomas G. Pavel calls realism "a remarkably courageous project" and writes:

> We confidently regard our worlds as unified and coherent; we also treat them as economical collections of beings, our fits of ontological prodigality

notwithstanding. Since coherence and economy may not stand up to scrutiny, we most often start by refraining from close examination. The worlds we speak about, actual or fictional, neatly hide their deep fractures, and our language, our texts, appear for a while to be transparent media unproblematically leading to worlds. For, before confronting higher-order perplexities, we explore the realms described by compendia and texts, which stimulate our sense of referential adventure and, in a sense, serve as mere paths of access to worlds: once the goal is reached, the events of the journey may be forgotten.[6]

Over the next few decades, a number of books applied possible worlds theory directly to the making of fictional worlds, most notably Nelson Goodman's *Ways of Worldmaking* (1978), Thomas G. Pavel's *Fictional Worlds* (1986), Lubomír Doležel's *Heterocosmica: Fiction and Possible Worlds* (1998), and Marie-Laure Ryan's *Possible Worlds, Artificial Intelligence, and Narrative Theory* (1991) and *Narrative as Virtual Reality: Immersion and Interactivity in Literature and Electronic Media* (2001). Goodman's book is concerned with how the worlds of science, art, and other practices are made and related to each other, and the conflicts and truth-value they contain, with fictional worlds touched upon mainly in the last chapters. Pavel's book narrows its focus to fictional worlds, their philosophical underpinnings, and their ontological status and relationship to the actual world, but is still cast in more general terms for the most part. Doležel makes the connections to literary theory more firmly, using more specific analyses and examples from literature. Like Pavel, he rejects philosophical notions that deny fiction's truth-value, or that do not allow for its unique position between actuality and unreality:

> The assertion that fictional texts have a special truth-conditional status does not mean that they are less actual than imaging texts of science, journalism, or everyday conversation. Fictional texts are composed by actual authors (storytellers, writers) using the resources of an actual human language and destined for actual readers. They are called fictional on *functional* grounds, as media for making, preserving, and communicating fictional worlds. They are stores of fictionality within the world of actuality, where the products of the writers' imaginations are permanently available to receptive readers. However distant—historically, geographically, culturally—they may be from the world-creating act, readers have a standing invitation to visit and use the immense library where imaginary realms are preserved.[7]

Doležel further develops the integration of possible worlds theory into narrative theory, looking at the functioning of one-person narrative worlds and multi-person worlds, the narrative modalities that shape the action occurring in them, and the way texts bring fictional entities into being.

Ryan's books go even farther with the application of possible worlds theory to narrative theory, and her work overlaps the most with Media Studies. In *Narrative as Virtual Reality*, Ryan considers how texts create worlds and immerse audiences in them, including the effects of the interactivity found in hypertext and video games and other forms of participatory interactivity in mediated realms, and even the "world" metaphor itself. Ryan considers immersion and interactivity and how they relate to each other as well as to literary texts, and much of the discussion has to do with the worlds in which texts are set and the reader's reconstruction of them during the reading process. She also considers different types of fictionality; in the second chapter of her book *Possible Worlds, Artificial Intelligence, and Narrative Theory*, Ryan identifies a series of accessibility relations that can exist between a fictional world and the actual world, looking at how they can share objects, chronological compatibility, natural laws, analytical truths, and linguistic compatibility. She shows how worlds can be devised that share some of these properties while not sharing others, devising a list of genres based on what is shared and what is not.

While the philosophy of possible worlds is a necessary starting point, it tends to lean more toward the abstract and the conceptual nature of imaginary worlds than practical particulars, and is more concerned with status and modes of being than with experience and design (although here Ryan is an exception, as her concerns coincide more with those of Media Studies). According to Doležel, fictional worlds are a particular kind of possible world, and are different from those of logic and philosophy; they are inevitably incomplete, heterogeneous in their macrostructure (worlds are composites of multiple domains), and constructs of textual poiesis (created by authors through literature or other media).[8] And, according to Nelson Goodman, "Fiction, then, whether written or painted or acted, applies truly neither to nothing nor to diaphanous possible worlds but, albeit metaphorically, to actual worlds. Somewhat as I have argued elsewhere that the merely possible—so far as admissible at all—lies within the actual, so we might say here again, in a different context, that the so-called possible worlds of fiction lie within actual worlds."[9]

Ryan is the most explicit in her descriptions of textual worlds, first summarizing how the concept of "world" involves a "connected set of objects and individuals; habitable environment; reasonably intelligible totality for external observers; field of activity for its members",[10] and then going on to describe the process by which a world emerges from a text:

> In the metaphor of the text as world, the text is apprehended as a window on something that exists outside of language and extends in time and space well beyond the window frame. To speak of a textual world means to draw a distinction between a realm of language, made of names, definite descriptions, sentences, and propositions, and an extralinguistic realm of characters, objects, facts, and states of affairs serving as referents to the

linguistic expressions. The idea of textual world presupposes that the reader constructs in imagination a set of language-independent objects, using as a guide the textual declarations, but building this always-incomplete image into a more vivid representation through the import of information provided by internalized cognitive models, inferential mechanisms, real-life experience, and cultural knowledge, including knowledge derived from other texts.[11]

Ryan refers mainly to written texts made of words, but her description could easily be enlarged to include imagery and sound as well (the transmedial nature of imaginary worlds is discussed in Chapter 6).

The philosophy of possible worlds provides a philosophical foundation for fictional worlds, and its application to narrative theory has helped to emphasize the role of the world in which a story takes place. However, in addition to focusing almost exclusively on narrative-based worlds, most philosophical writings look mainly at questions of language, taking their examples from literature, with far less examination of audiovisually-based worlds and their representation (for example, Goodman touches upon pictorial representation, mostly in contrast to linguistic representation, and only more recent works like Ryan's consider newer media like video games). Certainly, text is easier to deal with, since it is linear and made of discrete units, allowing quotation, dissection, and analysis to be done more easily than similar analyses of imagery and sound. Imagery and sound can both convey large amounts of information in a simultaneous fashion, and neither can be adequately described in purely verbal terms. Imagery and sound differ from text in their referential and mimetic abilities, and provide a much different experience for an audience, or for an author constructing a world; so practical concerns must be added to philosophical ones. For that, we must turn to a consideration of imaginary worlds from the point of view of building them and visiting them, found in the writings of authors who were both theoreticians and practitioners of world-making.

Imagination, Creation, and Subcreation

In the eighteenth century, the empirical philosophy represented by Hobbes, Locke, and Hume was the dominant force behind the conceptualization of the mind as a storehouse of information and a blank slate or *tabula rasa* to be written on by the senses. Imagination was seen as merely a function of memory, the recollection of decaying sensory data that was to be brought forth to mind after its objects were gone. For some philosophers, like William Duff and Dugald Stewart, imagination might be able to combine or associate ideas, but it was not seen as a truly creative force that could produce something new.[12] Poets like William Wordsworth and Samuel Taylor Coleridge began to challenge these ideas with a conception of imagination that was active and creative, and even present from the first moments of perception. Coleridge saw the active mind as one way in which human beings were made in God's image:

> Newton was a mere materialist—*Mind* in his system is always passive— a lazy Looker-on on an external World. If the mind be not *passive*, if it be indeed made in God's Image, and that too in the sublimest sense—the image of the Creator—there is ground for suspicion, that any system built on the passiveness of the mind must be false, as a system.[13]

Thus, for Coleridge, imagination was a divinely-appointed attribute, and as a result, even something of a sacred duty. As he wrote in a lecture of 1795:

> But we were not made to find Happiness in the complete gratification of our bodily wants—the mind must enlarge the sphere of its activity, and busy itself in the acquisition of intellectual aliment. To develope [sic] the powers of the Creator is our proper employment—and to imitate Creativeness by combination our most exalted and self-satisfying Delight. But we are progressive and must not rest content with present Blessings. Our Almighty Parent hath therefore given to us Imagination that stimulates to the attainment of *real* excellence by the contemplation of splendid Possibilities…[14]

The contemplation of possibilities, rather than the recollection or reconstruction of sensory data, meant a different type of imagination from that which was traditionally conceived. In his examination of imagination, Coleridge went on to make a distinction between these two types of imagination, based on their subject matter and function:

> The IMAGINATION then I consider either as primary, or secondary. The primary IMAGINATION I hold to be the living Power and prime Agent of all human Perception, and as a repetition in the finite mind of the eternal act of creation in the infinite I AM. The secondary Imagination I consider as an echo of the former, co-existing with the conscious will, yet still as identical with the primary in the *kind* of its agency, and differing only in *degree*, and in the *mode* of its operation. It dissolves, diffuses, dissipates, in order to recreate: or where this process is rendered impossible, yet still at all events it struggles to idealize and to unify. It is essentially *vital*, even as all objects (*as* objects) are essentially fixed and dead.[15]

The Primary Imagination is what allows us to coordinate and interpret our sensory data, turning them into perceptions with which we make sense of the world around us. The Secondary Imagination "dissolves, diffuses, dissipates" the concepts and elements of the world around us so as to recreate something new with them. So the use of the Primary Imagination occurs, for the most part, unconsciously, as we conceptualize the world around us and our place in it, while the use of the Secondary Imagination, by contrast, is conscious and deliberate, not done merely out of habit or necessity but as a creative act.

But the Secondary Imagination needs limitations to function properly and usefully. Used to its fullest extent, the Secondary Imagination can result in the construction of an entire imaginary world, be it a city, island, country, or planet. Such a world, though, as a whole, cannot be just a random jumble of made-up things if it is to be believable enough to engage an audience. In "The Fantastic Imagination", the Introduction to *The Light Princess and Other Fairy Tales* (1893), Scottish author George MacDonald began to examine how Secondary Imagination is necessarily shaped by laws when it is used to form an internally consistent world:

> The natural world has its laws, and no man must interfere with them in the way of presentment any more than in the way of use; but they themselves may suggest laws of other kinds, and man may, if he pleases, invent a little world of his own, with its own laws; for there is that in him which delights in calling up new forms—which is the nearest, perhaps, he can come to creation. When such forms are new embodiments of old truths, we call them products of the Imagination; when they are mere inventions, however lovely, I should call them the work of Fancy; in either case, Law has been diligently at work.
>
> His world once invented, the highest law that comes next into play is, that there shall be harmony between the laws by which the new world has begun to exist; and in the process of his creation, the inventor must hold by those laws. The moment he forgets one of them, he makes the story, by its own postulates, incredible. To be able to live a moment in an imagined world, we must see the laws of its existence obeyed. Those broken, we fall out of it. The imagination in us, whose exercise is essential to the most temporary submission to the imagination of another, immediately, with the disappearance of Law, ceases to act. ... A man's inventions may be stupid or clever, but if he does not hold by the laws of them, or if he makes one law jar with another, he contradicts himself as an inventor, he is no artist. He does not rightly consort his instruments, or he tunes them in different keys. ... Obeying law, the maker works like his creator; not obeying law, he is such a fool as heaps a pile of stones and calls it a church.
>
> In the moral world it is different: there a man may clothe in new forms, and for this employ his imagination freely, but he must invent nothing. He may not, for any purpose, turn its laws upside down. He must not meddle with the relations of live souls. The laws of the spirit man must hold, alike in this world and in any world he may invent. It were no offence to suppose a world in which everything repelled instead of attracted the things around it; it would be wicked to write a tale representing a man it called good as

always doing bad things, or a man it called bad as always doing good things: the notion itself is absolutely lawless. In physical things a man may invent; in moral things he must obey—and take their laws with him into his invented world as well.[16]

Once an imaginary world's initial differences from the actual world are established, they will often act as constraints on further invention, suggesting or even requiring other laws or limitations that will define a world further as the author figures out all the consequences of the laws as they are put into effect (how laws form an underlying logic that shapes a world is the subject of a section later in this chapter). MacDonald's work would also inspire another author, who produced one of the most successful secondary worlds ever created: J. R. R. Tolkien's Arda, in which lies the lands of Middle-earth. Like MacDonald, Tolkien also theorized about what he was doing.

Following Coleridge and MacDonald, Tolkien further refined and combined their ideas, applying them to the building of imaginary worlds. In his 1939 Andrew Lang lecture, a more developed version of which appeared in print as "On Fairy-stories" in 1947 and again in a revised version of 1964, Tolkien discussed authorial invention and extended the idea of Primary and Secondary Imagination to the worlds to which they refer. He referred to the material, intersubjective world in which we live as the Primary World, and the imaginary worlds created by authors as secondary worlds. Tolkien's terms carefully sidestep the philosophical pitfalls encountered with other terms like "reality" and "fantasy", while also indicating the hierarchical relationship between the types of worlds, since secondary worlds rely on the Primary World and exist within it.

As a philologist, ever careful with words, Tolkien realized that the ontological differences between the Primary World and secondary worlds were enough that a similar distinction should be made when referring to their creation. Like Coleridge, Tolkien saw Imagination as a Divine attribute shared by humans, and creativity and the desire to create as one of the main ways human beings were created in the image of God (an idea also found in Nikolai Berdyaev's *The Destiny of Man* (1931), in which he wrote, "God created man in his own image and likeness, i.e., made him a creator too, calling him to free spontaneous activity and not to formal obedience to His power. Free creativeness is the creature's answer to the great call of its creator."[17]). Since human beings are created in the image of God, they also have a desire to create, but the creative activity by which a secondary world is made differs in both degree and kind from God's *ex nihilo* ("from nothing") creative power used to bring the Primary World into being. Thus, Tolkien termed the making of a secondary world "subcreation", meaning "creating under", since human beings are limited to using the pre-existing concepts found in God's creation, finding new combinations of them that explore the realm of possibilities, many of which do not exist in the Primary World.[18] Thus, a "subcreator" is a specific kind of author, one who very deliberately builds an imaginary world, and does so for reasons beyond that of merely providing a backdrop for a story.

"Subcreation", as a noun, refers to both *process* and *product* and suggests their inseparable nature, just as Tolkien saw language and idea as inseparable. For Tolkien, language was the main means of subcreation, which was made possible by the separation of the adjective from the noun:

> When we can take green from grass, blue from heaven, and red from blood, we have already an enchanter's power—upon one plane; and the desire to wield that power in the world external to our minds awakes. It does not follow that we shall use that power well upon any plane. We may put a deadly green on a man's face and produce a horror; we may make the rare and terrible blue moon to shine; or we may cause woods to spring with silver leaves and rams to wear fleeces of gold, and put hot fire into the belly of the cold worm. But in such "fantasy", as it is called, new form is made. ... Man becomes a subcreator.[19]

Subcreation, then, involves new combinations of existing concepts, which, in the building of a secondary world, become the inventions that replace or reset Primary World defaults (for example, new flora and fauna, new languages, new geography, and so forth). The more one changes these defaults, the more the secondary world becomes different and distinct from the Primary World. It is not surprising, then, that secondary worlds will in many ways resemble the Primary World; not only because it is the source of material, but also because it is this familiarity that lets us relate to a secondary world, especially to its characters and their emotions. Secondary worlds, then, have the same default assumptions as does the Primary World, except where the author has indicated otherwise.

Like MacDonald, Tolkien was also interested in a secondary world's effects on those who enter it, and how such effects take place. Starting with the audience's state of mind and Coleridge's ideas of "willing suspension of disbelief" and "poetic faith", Tolkien suggested that it was a new form of belief, not disbelief, that was needed:

> That state of mind has been called "willing suspension of disbelief". But this does not seem to me a good description of what happens. What really happens is that the story-maker proves a successful "subcreator". He makes a Secondary World which your mind can enter. Inside it, what he relates is "true": it accords with the laws of that world. You therefore believe it while you are, as it were, inside. The moment disbelief arises, the spell is broken; the magic, or rather art, has failed. You are then out in the Primary World again, looking at the little abortive Secondary World from outside. ... then disbelief must be suspended. ... But this suspension of disbelief is a substitute for the genuine thing...[20]

Tolkien goes on to call this necessary belief "Secondary Belief", which is the additional belief pertaining to the secondary world in question, rather than merely a suspension of our knowledge as to how that secondary world exists in the Primary World; that is, we imagine what the world would be like if it really existed, instead of simply ignoring the fact that it is only a story told in a book (or in other media). Secondary Belief relies on a secondary world's completeness and consistency, topics discussed later in this chapter.

In its broadest sense, subcreation covers more than just ideas, conceptual inventions, and imaginary worlds; it could also include the physical works of human beings in the world, since things like automobiles, violins, turpentine, scimitars, and chocolate chip cookie dough ice cream did not exist in the Primary World before human beings invented them. However, this sense is far too broad to be useful here, and Tolkien's use of the term typically restricted it to the development of secondary worlds. Likewise, every story is set in a world; but some storyworlds have a closer resemblance to the Primary World, or are more integrated into the Primary World, while others are more isolated or detached from the Primary World. Some worlds are more detailed and developed, while others rely heavily on existing Primary World defaults, with only a minimal amount of invention. Thus, fictional worlds can be placed along a spectrum based on the amount of subcreation present, and what we might call the "secondariness" of a story's world then becomes a matter of degree, varying with the strength of the connection to the Primary World.

Degrees of Subcreation

Just as fictional worlds are a subset of possible worlds, secondary worlds are a subset of fictional worlds, since secondary worlds are necessarily different enough (and usually detached or separated in some way) from the Primary World to give them "secondary" status. To qualify something as a secondary world, then, requires a fictional *place* (that is, one that does not actually appear in the Primary World); but a *place* is not always a *world*. The term "world", as it is being used here, is not simply geographical but *experiential*; that is, everything that is experienced by the characters involved, the elements enfolding someone's life (culture, nature, philosophical worldviews, places, customs, events, and so forth), just as *world*'s etymological root word *weorld* from Old German refers to "all that concerns humans", as opposed to animals or gods. Often, this kind of world does involve geographic isolation, as in the "lost worlds" found in literature; islands, mountain valleys, underground kingdoms, or other places that are uncharted and difficult to find or travel to. In order for a world to be "secondary", it must have a distinct border partitioning it from the Primary World, even when it is said to exist somewhere in the Primary World (or when the Primary World is said to be a part of it, as in the case of the *Star Trek* universe containing Earth). A secondary world is usually connected to the Primary World in some way, but, at the same time, set apart from it enough to be a "world" unto itself, making access difficult (the ways that secondary worlds are connected to the Primary World is examined in a section later in this chapter). The secondary world's remoteness and the difficulty of obtaining entry into it make the world more believable, because it becomes like any other place that the audience has heard of but is not likely to have experienced in person due to its remoteness or lack of accessibility, such as Tibet, Tuva, the depths of the African or Amazonian jungles, the interior of a volcano, or the bottom of the ocean. Lack of accessibility can also be due to lack of information; for example, Lake Wobegon does not appear on maps due to incompetent surveyors, according to its history.

The nature of the borders separating a secondary world from the Primary World depends on the secondary world's location and size, and points of entry for passage between the two are often very limited. The parameters of secondary worlds vary greatly, from whole universes to small towns or villages that fully encompass its characters' world. Moving down from the large end of the scale, we find multiverses or parallel universes that contain or are somehow connected to our own; entire galaxies that are separate from our own but still in the same universe (like the *Star Wars* galaxy); series of planets, which may include Earth among them (as in the worlds of *Dune* or *Star Trek*); Earth itself, but with alternate histories or imaginary time periods (like Robert E. Howard's Hyborian Age or J. R. R. Tolkien's First, Second, and Third Ages) or Earth in the future (as in *The Matrix* series); imaginary continents of the real Earth (like Robert E. Howard's Thuria, George R. R. Martin's Westeros, or Austin Tappan Wright's Karain Continent); imaginary countries set in real continents (like Leo McCarey's Freedonia, Meg Cabot's Genovia, Lia Wainstein's Drimonia, Samuel Butler's Erewhon, or Norman Douglas's Crotalophoboi Land); and finally, imaginary cities, settlements, or towns (like Edgar Rice Burroughs's Ashair, Paul Alperine's Erikraudebyg, or Lerner and Loewe's Brigadoon). A single city or town can qualify as a world unto itself if it is secluded enough from its surroundings so as to contain most of its inhabitants' experiences; Ashair is set deep inside a volcano, Erikraudebyg is surrounded by mountains, and Brigadoon only appears once in a while and its inhabitants are not allowed to leave. Obviously, many fictional cities are less isolated; Stephen King's Castle Rock, John Updike's Eastwick, and Garrison Keillor's Lake Wobegon, for example, are much closer to towns of the Primary World, both geographically and conceptually, and arguably far less "secondary" than the other examples mentioned above. Only a more inclusive definition of secondary world would include them, and then only because their authors have set multiple stories in them and developed them to a greater degree than most fictional towns or cities.

A world's "secondariness" depends on the extent to which a place is detached from the Primary World and different from it, and the degree to which its fictional aspects have been developed and built (including such things as how many stories are set there, whether the place has been mapped, and how much its history has been developed). For example, Leo Tolstoy's *War and Peace* (1869) could not really be said to contain a secondary world, since its main action is set in the Primary World, in Russia, during a real historical period, even though it includes fictional characters, events, and places (such as characters' homes and estates). On the other hand, even though L. Frank Baum's *The Wonderful Wizard of Oz* (1900) begins and ends in the Primary World (in Kansas), the majority of its action takes place in the land of Oz, which clearly is part of a secondary world. However, what about the Los Angeles of 2019 depicted in *Blade Runner* (1982)? While Los Angeles is part of the Primary World, the city depicted in the movie contains a great deal of invention not found in the actual Los Angeles and is a place very different from the Primary World. *Blade Runner*'s Los Angeles is as much a constructed environment as Oz, yet it depicts a Primary World location, set in an alternate version of 2019 (released in 1982), in which replicants, artificial animals, flying cars, and gigantic buildings not only exist but are common. Such examples demonstrate that rather than having a strict delineation between Primary and secondary worlds, we have something of a spectrum connecting them, just as "fiction" and "nonfiction" are not as mutually exclusive as they may first appear.

As secondariness is a matter of degree, it may be more useful to arrange fictional worlds along a spectrum of attachment to, or reliance on, the Primary World (as we know it) and its defaults; from those closest to the Primary World, to the secondary worlds that are the farthest from it (that contain the highest degree of subcreation). On the Primary World end of the spectrum would be nonfictional autobiography, which claims as its subject an individual's actual lived experience, as told by that individual. Here, we have actual events involving actual characters and actual places; but in even the most careful autobiography, some reconstruction of events occurs (either consciously or unconsciously) due to imperfections of memory, and thus an element of fiction enters into the world depicted.[21] Biography and historical documentary, which recounts events and experiences of others, adds more speculation into the mix; and openly speculative documentary, which questions its own material and often foregoes the truth-claims found in traditional documentary, may even suggest multiple versions of events or possibilities.

Moving down the spectrum, historical novels (or films) leave the realm of documentary, creating fictional versions of actual events, characters, and places. For example, in Tolstoy's *War and Peace*, Napoleon invades Russia, Moscow is burned, and the French are eventually forced to retreat; but on a smaller scale, characters and places (like Pierre and Nicolai, and their estates) are invented, and even Napoleon has fictional actions and dialogue attributed to him. While such novels may try to remain true (at least in spirit) to history, they will necessarily invent some characters and places as well, though often in a way that disrupts the continuity of the Primary World as little as possible. As we move further down the spectrum, the notion of "historical", or even "realistic", applies less and less, as stories increasingly replace or reset Primary World defaults, even though the stories are still ostensibly set within the Primary World. Here we find what we might call "overlaid worlds"; for example, the stories involving Spider-man (a.k.a. Peter Parker) are set in a version of New York City in which Spider-man and the super-villains he fights remain conspicuously in the public eye, both in person and in the media. In such cases, fictional elements are overlaid onto a real location, but without separating a secondary world from the Primary World.

In all of the cases mentioned so far, story events occur in places that are a part of, or are closely associated with, the Primary World. Such fictional locations are designed to be typical of the kinds of places that they represent; for example, Tara in Margaret Mitchell's *Gone with the Wind* (1936) is designed to be a typical Southern plantation during the Civil War era. Characters who live at or visit Tara are not really leaving the Primary World, they are still in the midst of it. Nevertheless, fictional places can be designed to be set apart, even detached, from the Primary World, so that there is more of a distinct boundary between them; although such a boundary, too, is a matter of degree. As places are set farther away from populated and well-known areas, their remoteness and inaccessibility begin to isolate them from the Primary World, making them into separate or secondary worlds. Uncharted islands, desert cities, hidden mountain kingdoms, underground realms, and other planets are also often populated with inhabitants who never leave them, and who do not know of the Primary World as we know it. Customs, languages, cultures, and even flora and fauna can diverge from those of the Primary World, and become almost completely independent of them. The greater the amount of such invention occurs in a world, the more "secondary" it becomes when compared with the Primary World.

Detachment or separation from the Primary World can also occur temporally; worlds set in the ancient (or even imaginary) eras of the past, or in the unknowable future, can also be made to differ from the known Primary World (as hinted in author L. P. Hartley's claim that "The past is a foreign country; they do things differently there."[22]). For stories set in the future, greater temporal distance usually results in more Primary World defaults being changed; stories set in the near-future can be similar enough to the Primary World to be merely overlaid worlds, whereas far-future stories usually depict an Earth very different and alien from our own.

Secondary worlds that differ the most from the Primary World contain the most subcreation, and are thus the kinds of worlds most discussed in this book, and to which its focus will be narrowed: secondary worlds that are geographically distinct from the Primary World (even when they are said to exist somewhere on Earth), and those that are used for stories whose action occurs mainly within a secondary world, even though those stories' characters may come from, return to, or otherwise visit the Primary World. These worlds, in their isolation and uniqueness, are complex entities, wide-ranging in their variety, sometimes made for no other reason than to create vicarious experiences for their audiences, and interesting in their own right apart from the stories that they often contain.

Thus, before embarking on examinations of these worlds, it will first be useful to examine how they are related to, and differ from, the stories that occur in them.

Story vs. World: Storytelling and World-building

Worlds often exist to support the stories set in them, and they can even have stories embedded in them, for example, in "environmental storytelling" as described by theme park designer Don Carson.[23] Yet, while the telling of a story inevitably also tells us about the world in which the story takes place, storytelling and world-building are different processes that can sometimes come into conflict. One of the cardinal rules often given to new writers has to do with narrative economy; they are told to pare down their prose and remove anything that does not actively advance the story. World-building, however, often results in data, exposition, and digressions that provide information about a world, slowing down narrative or even bringing it to a halt temporarily, yet much of the excess detail and descriptive richness can be an important part of the audience's experience.[24] World information that does not actively advance the story may still provide mood and atmosphere, or further form our image of characters, places, and events. A compelling story and a compelling world are very different things, and one need not require the other. For example, as Oz scholar Michael O. Riley writes of L. Frank Baum's works, "stories that critics count among his weakest from the standpoint of plot, characters, and theme are among his strongest from the standpoint of the development of his Other-world."[25] At the same time, it is usually story that draws us into a world and holds us there; lack of a compelling story may make it difficult for someone to remain vicariously in a secondary world.

Since stories involve time, space, and causality, every story implies a world in which it takes place. Worlds can exist without stories, but stories cannot exist without a world. As Doležel describes it:

> Fictional semantics does not deny that the story is the defining feature of narrative but moves to the foreground the macrostructural conditions of story generation: stories happen, are enacted in certain kinds of possible worlds. The basic concept of narratology is not "story," but "narrative world," defined within a typology of possible worlds.[26]

Yet, while a story takes place in a world, it need not show us very much of that world (though stories set in a secondary world are set there for a reason, typically tied to the uniqueness of the secondary world; the story simply could not be set in the Primary World, or else it would be). A world can have multiple stories set in it, and need not be dependent on any particular story for its existence. However, story and world usually work together, enriching each other, and if an author has been careful in the construction of a story, the world will appear to exist beyond the immediate events, locations, and characters covered in the story.

Therefore, while all stories are set in some kind of world, what I will refer to here as a "traditional" story is a narrative work in which world-building generally does not occur beyond that which is needed to advance the story, as opposed to narrative (or even nonnarrative) works whose worlds are deliberately built beyond the immediate needs of whatever narrative material may be present.

World-building is often something that occurs as a background activity, allowing storytelling to remain in the foreground of the audience's experience. At times, however, world-building may overtake storytelling. Due to secondary worlds' differences, subcreative works often exhibit an "encyclopedic impulse" for explanatory interludes; points at which the narrative halts so that information about the world and its inhabitants can be given. Descriptions of landscapes, peoples, customs, backstories, and philosophical outlooks are given either by the main character directly to the audience if a story is told in first person, or experienced by the main character and the audience together (with the main character as a stand-in for the audience), with expository passages in which other characters introduce lands and peoples. In worlds designed primarily for entertainment (like James Cameron's Pandora in *Avatar* (2009)), for satirical purposes (like Samuel Butler's Erewhon), for the purpose of scientific speculation (like A. K. Dewdney's Planiverse), or for thought experiments of a philosophical nature (like those of Alan Lightman's *Einstein's Dreams* (1992)) or a political or social nature (like Thomas More's Utopia), exposition regarding the peculiarities of a secondary world can completely overtake narrative, reducing it to little more than a frame story or a means of moving through and joining together the various descriptions of aspects of the world. In many video games, narrative also becomes a way of providing a context for the games' action; in particular, adventure games and games with a three-dimensional environment often emphasize exploration and navigation of the game's world, making them an important part of the player's experience.

Nor does a subcreated world have to be built along a single, main storyline at all. If the encyclopedic impulse for explanatory interludes is taken a step further, a series of fragments can form an aggregate picture of a world and the culture and events within it. In her novel *Always Coming Home* (1985), Ursula K. LeGuin describes the Kesh, the people who live in the Valley, through a variety of narrators and an assortment of brief stories, fables, poems, artwork, maps, charts, archaeological and anthropological notes and brief essays, all without a main character or central storyline (a woman named Stone Telling comes closest to being a main character, but her story only covers a fraction of the book). There are even extreme cases in which documentation takes the place of narrative completely, for example, Luigi Serafini's *Codex Seraphinianus*, a profusely illustrated 360-page book written in an untranslated made-up language that is designed to look like a scientific treatise describing the flora, fauna, inventions, and civilizations of an unnamed imaginary world. With an unreadable text, one can only browse and speculate, with each page adding to the experience of the world depicted (see Figure 1.1).

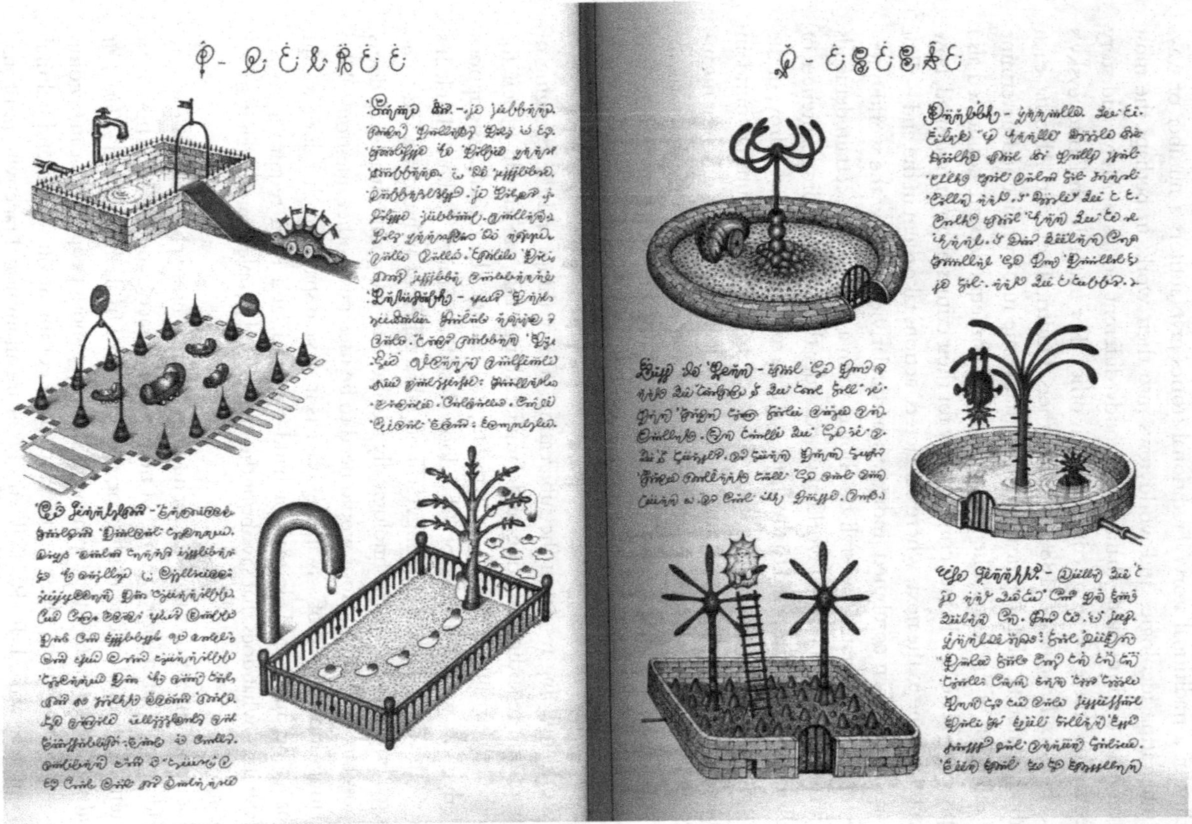

FIGURE 1.1 An example of world documentation without narrative: typical pages from the enigmatic *Codex Seraphinianus* (1981) by Luigi Serafini. (Image courtesy of Luigi Serafini, *Codex Seraphinianus*, Milano, Franco Maria Ricci, First Edition, 1981.)

The political, social, and philosophical thought experiments in the worlds mentioned earlier are also examples of how the subcreator of a world has more strategies available for the embedding of worldviews into a work than does the author of a traditional story. Traditional stories give authors a number of ways of integrating ideologies and worldviews into their work; in perhaps the most commonly used method, characters embody different points of view, and story events cause these views to confront each other. For example, in Dostoyevsky's *The Brothers Karamazov* (1880), the brothers Dmitri, Ivan, and Alyosha each embody different philosophical outlooks that come into conflict and determine the direction of the story. The way actions and consequences are connected also imply a worldview; whether criminals pay for their crimes or go unpunished, how events lead one to the next, where characters' actions take them in the end—all of these things, when combined, indicate a particular view of how the world operates, or should operate. And stylistic choices form a work, make certain demands on an audience, and imply a worldview: consider the long, rambling sentences of William Faulkner compared to the short, staccato sentences of James Ellroy; or the long takes of a Miklós Jancsó film compared to the quick cutting found in so many contemporary action films; each imbues its material with different meanings and changes its effect on the audience. For most authors, the tools of traditional storytelling are sufficient for the expression of ideas embedded in their works; but some require tools and strategies that are only available through world-building.

World-building results in the subcreation of new things and the changing of assumptions regarding existing and familiar things that are usually taken for granted. Even simple changes in wording can change the default assumptions underlying a world. Instead of "the door closed", consider Robert Heinlein's use of "the door dilated".[27] It suggests not only a different architecture and technology, but also a society technologically advanced to the point where such doors are possible. *Why* such a door would need to be used raises other questions: Why a dilating door instead of a swinging one? Is it to save space? Such a door would probably be automated, instead of hand-operated, and even require a power source; if so, what does that say about the culture and people from which it arises? And so on.

Nor does invention end with technology; besides using characters to embody worldviews, a subcreator can invent new cultures, races, and species whose very existence can imply certain ideas or outlooks. In Ursula K. LeGuin's *The Left Hand of Darkness* (1969), the Gethen are an androgynous people who can become either male or female, allowing the author to comment on sexism and cultural biases in new ways. J. R. R. Tolkien's Elves are an immortal race who must stay in Arda (the world) until it ends, and they come to envy Men their mortality, allowing for extended commentary regarding Death and Immortality, the main theme of *The Lord of the Rings*. The culture and customs of Samuel Butler's Erewhonians are a satirical reflection of nineteenth-century Britain, though the analogies are not made explicit. By changing the defaults of the Primary World, especially in playful ways that reveal and reverse audience expectations, secondary worlds can make strange the familiar by exploring alternatives to the ordinary.

That secondary worlds often differ markedly from the Primary World has led some people to consider them "unrealistic", which is to miss the point of most secondary worlds. While secondary worlds may represent strange and fantastic alternative worlds, to automatically claim that they are "escapist" (with the term being applied pejoratively) is to do them an injustice. Tolkien himself dealt with such accusations, writing:

> ... it is plain that I do not accept the tone of scorn or pity with which "Escape" is now so often used: a tone for which the uses of the word outside literary criticism give no warrant at all. In what the misusers are fond of calling Real Life, Escape is evidently as a rule very practical, and may even be heroic. In real life it is difficult to blame it, unless it fails; in criticism it would seem to be the worse the better it succeeds. Evidently we are faced by a misuse of words, and also a confusion of thought. Why should a man be scorned if, finding himself in prison, he tries to get out and go home? Or if, when he cannot do so, he thinks and talks about other topics than jailers and prison-walls? The world outside has not become less real because the prisoner cannot see it. In using escape in this way the critics have chosen the wrong word, and, what is more, they are confusing, not always by sincere error, the Escape of the Prisoner with the Flight of the Deserter.[28]

When one considers that the stories set in many secondary worlds often include oppression, conflict, war, and dark times for their characters, it soon becomes clear that these are not worlds that someone would want to physically escape to, much less reside in.

Having examined how worlds are distinct from the stories set in them, and how "secondariness" is a matter of degree, we may now turn to the three main properties needed to produce a secondary world, hold it together, and make it distinct from the Primary World.

Invention, Completeness, and Consistency

If a secondary world is to be believable and interesting, it will need to have a high degree of invention, completeness, and consistency. Of course, no secondary world can be as complete as the Primary World, inconsistencies are increasingly likely as a world grows, and no world can be the product of invention to the point that there is no longer any resemblance to the Primary World. Nevertheless, unless an effort is made in all of these directions, the resulting subcreation will fail to create the illusion of an independent world. Without enough invention, you will have something set in the Primary World, or something quite close to it: our world with vampires or aliens added, or some new technology, or some strange occurrence that sets the story in motion; but not a world unique, different, and set apart from our own. Without an attempt at completeness, you have the beginnings of expansion beyond the narrative, but not enough to suggest an independent world; too many unanswered (and unanswerable) questions will remain which together destroy the illusion of one. And without consistency, all the disparate and conflicting pieces, ideas, and designs will contradict each other, and never successfully come together to collectively create the illusion of another world.

At the same time, as each of these three properties grows, world-building becomes more challenging. The more complete a world is, the harder it is to remain consistent, since additional material has to be fit into existing material in such a way that everything makes sense. Completeness also demands more invention, as more of the world is revealed. The more invention a world contains, the more difficult it is to keep everything in that world consistent, since every Primary World default that is changed affects other aspects of the world, and those changes in turn can cause even more changes. Likewise, consistency will limit what kind of invention is possible as a world grows. Therefore, all three properties must be considered simultaneously as the world takes shape and develops.

Invention

Invention can be defined as the degree to which default assumptions based on the Primary World have been changed, regarding such things as geography, history, language, physics, biology, zoology, culture, custom, and so on. These differences, obvious markers indicating a work's status as fiction, must be carefully presented (in the case of audiovisual media, designed and constructed as well) to be believable. Credibility is not only a matter of their technological construction (laughable failures in this area include the bad special effects in B-movies), but also their design, which must incorporate a certain logic to seem real and practical, instead of merely fanciful or random. Believable design is especially important for genres like fantasy and science fiction, which typically contain more invention than other genres. Tolkien recognized this need, writing:

> Fantasy, of course, starts out with an advantage: arresting strangeness. But that advantage has been turned against it, and has contributed to its disrepute. Many people dislike being "arrested". They dislike any meddling with the Primary World, or such small glimpses of it as are familiar to them. They, therefore, stupidly and even maliciously confound Fantasy with Dreaming, in which there is no Art; and with mental disorders, in which there is not even control: with delusion and hallucination. ... Fantasy also

has an essential drawback: it is difficult to achieve. Fantasy may be, as I think, not less but more subcreative; but at any rate it is found in practice that "the inner consistency of reality" is more difficult to produce, the more unlike are the images and the rearrangements of primary material to the actual arrangements of the Primary World. It is easier to produce this kind of "reality" with more "sober" material. Fantasy thus, too often, remains undeveloped; it is and has been used frivolously, or only half-seriously, or merely for decoration: it remains "fanciful". Anyone inheriting the fantastic device of human language can say *the green sun*. Many can then imagine or picture it. But that is not enough—though it may already be a more potent thing than many a "thumbnail sketch" or "transcript of life" that receives literary praise.

To make a Secondary World inside which the green sun will be credible, commanding Secondary Belief, will probably require labour and thought, and will certainly demand a special skill, a kind of elvish craft. Few attempt such difficult tasks. But when they are attempted and in any degree accomplished then we have a rare achievement of Art: indeed narrative art, story-making in its primary and most potent mode.[29]

The degree and depth to which something is invented depends on the skills of the subcreator and the needs of the work. Invention will inevitably play a crucial role in whatever story is present; otherwise, there would be no need for invention and the story could simply be set in the Primary World. Even if the world exists for its own sake, with story added as a mere structuring device, the ideas behind the changes of Primary World defaults will dictate the degree to which they are changed.

We can divide Primary World default changes (in which invention occurs) into four distinct realms, each of which affects the design of a world on a different level. The first involves changes in the *nominal* realm, in which new names are given for existing things. Very little in the way of world defaults is changed in such a case, although new language may be invented. New names may call attention to different aspects of familiar things, or even define new concepts, since language bears an inherent cultural worldview within it (another tool available to the subcreator). Almost every world features new names, but usually more than just names are changed, since a new language usually implies a new culture.

The most changes to be found are in the next level, the *cultural* realm, which consists of all things made by humans (or other creatures), and in which new objects, artifacts, technologies, customs, institutions, ideas, and so forth appear. In addition to these, authors have invented new countries and cultures, new institutions and orders (like the Jedi, Bene Gesserit, or the Aes Sedai), and even new concepts, like J. R. R. Tolkien's "mathom" or Philip K. Dick's "kipple".[30] The use of fictional cultures allows an author to comment on existing cultures by contrast, and create hypothetical situations without the limitations and connotations that would come with the use of an existing culture. At the same time, fictional cultures are often modeled after real cultures, using different combinations of their traits that an audience might find familiar, but in new configurations, some which play with stereotypes and audience expectations in interesting ways (like the androgynous Gethen of LeGuin's *The Left Hand of Darkness* mentioned earlier, or the Tassulians of C. I. Defontenay's *Star* (1854) who are all hermaphrodites). Cultures like the Gethen and the Tassulians rely on new species of beings, which brings us to the boundary of culture and nature.

The third level is the *natural* realm, which includes not only new landmasses (or other places like underground regions), but new kinds of plants and animals, and new species and races of creatures. The unique aspects of these creatures are often crucial for the role they play in their world and its stories; for example, the Hobbits in *The Lord of the Rings* or the sandworms in *Dune*. Invention in this area sometimes extends beyond individual species of plants and animals to entire ecosystems that integrate a number of them together (as in the film *Avatar* (2009)). Because this level goes deeper than that of cultural things, invention in the natural realm must either rely on convention (for example, well-known fictional animals like unicorns, dragons, and griffins) or attempt to have some plausible explanation relating to biology and zoology if some degree of verisimilitude is desired (which it may not be). On a small scale, invention in the natural realm proposes new flora and fauna, while on a larger scale, it may propose new planetary forms, such as the worlds of Larry Niven's *Ringworld* series or Terry Pratchett's *Discworld* series, which have planets shaped like rings and discs, respectively.

The deepest level is the *ontological* realm itself, which determines the parameters of a world's existence, that is, the materiality and laws of physics, space, time, and so forth that constitute the world. For example, the worlds of Edwin Abbott's *Flatland* (1884) and A. K. Dewdney's *The Planiverse* (1984) are both set in two-dimensional universes very different from our own, and in both cases, their books are dominated by the encyclopedic impulse described earlier, using narrative as little more than a vehicle to explain their worlds. Alan Lightman's *Einstein's Dreams* also features vignettes of universes in which time and space behave differently, and reflects philosophically on each one. A number of common science fiction conventions, including faster-than-light travel, other dimensions, time travel, and wormholes used for interstellar travel, usually imply laws of physics that are different from those currently understood, but the full consequences of such differences are typically not carried out in the design of the world. In the few instances where this does happen (as in *The Planiverse*), the world necessarily takes center stage and narrative becomes little more than a frame story used for advancing the exploration (and explanation) of the world. As such, relatively few books subcreate at this depth.

Of these four levels, the first two involve things more easily changed by humans (or other creatures), while the last two are usually far more difficult to shape or control.[31] The second and third, covering culture and nature, have the greatest balance between familiar Primary World defaults and new subcreated ones. This seems to be the best combination for Secondary Belief as well. All invention that occurs in a world must remain analogous, in some way, to the Primary World in order to be comprehensible (unless, of course, if the whole point is that something is *not* able to be understood, like the sentient sea in Stanisław Lem's *Solaris* (1961), which the story's scientists know is intelligent even though they are unable to find a way to communicate with it).

Successful invention may spill over into other worlds; objects and ideas that prove useful or solve narrative problems can appear in multiple worlds and even become generic conventions. Faster-than-light spaceships, laser guns, magical swords, incantations, wormholes, changelings, anti-gravity technology, elves, dragons, clones, force fields, sentient robots, and other tropes of science fiction and fantasy have all transcended their worlds of first appearance to become familiar and acceptable conventions that need little explanation or justification when they appear in a new world, provided the work they appear in is of the right genre. (Some things, though, have been overused to the point of becoming clichés; those of the Fantasy genre are brilliantly collected in Diana Wynne Jones's book *The Tough Guide to Fantasyland* (1996).)

However, there are certain areas in which invention usually does *not* occur, because it would be detrimental to narrative and the audience's experience. In order for a world to be taken seriously, audiences have to be able to relate to a world and its inhabitants, comparing their situations to similar ones in the Primary World. As a result, we rarely find stories based on non-humanoid characters like amoebas or gasbags living in Jupiter's atmosphere; and when we do, they are inevitably anthropomorphized to make their experiences relatable (like the lives of the rabbits in Richard Adams's *Watership Down* (1972)). Worlds must also retain some form of causality, concepts of good and evil, and emotional realism. Without causality, narrative is lost. The way that events are connected by causality may change greatly, but causality must be present for actions to have foreseeable consequences and for events to cohere into a narrative form. Likewise, what cultures consider to be good and evil may vary, but the concepts themselves must be present, as they are in all human cultures. Without them one would have not only lawlessness, but all narrative would become pointless, since it would no longer matter what characters did or what happened to them (as discussed in the MacDonald quote given earlier). Finally, emotional realism is necessary for character identification. Emotions may be differently expressed or even be suppressed (as they are for *Star Trek*'s Vulcans), but they must be present in character interactions. A lack of emotional realism will make empathy difficult, severely limiting or even eliminating identification with the world's characters.

In order to maintain audience interest, invention must take audience knowledge into account and attempt to avoid implausibilities that could disrupt a world's believability. Even though audiences know something is not real, Secondary Belief is easier to generate if the proposed inventions fit in with what the audience knows (or does not know) about the Primary World. A story set on another planet does not contradict any known facts, since we do not know what life there may be on other planets. Likewise, a fictional island in the South Pacific we can reasonably accept, because few people can claim to know all the islands in the Pacific. However, invention that conflicts with what the audience already knows is harder to accept; for example, a fictional U.S. state would make Secondary Belief more difficult for an American audience who know the 50 states than for a foreign audience who did not. Likewise, a fictional African country may be easier for an audience to accept than a fictional North American country, simply because there are more African countries and fewer people who can name all of them.[32] In 1726, Jonathan Swift could claim Brobdingnag to be located on a peninsula off the California coast, because his audience was European and far less familiar with the lands across the ocean that were still being explored (and, of course, because he was writing a satire). If invention blatantly contradicts what we already know, it can only work in a lighthearted fashion (like the fictional U.S. states of Missitucky in the Broadway musical *Finian's Rainbow* (1947) and Michisota in Lisa Wheeler's children's book *Avalanche Annie: A Not-So-Tall Tale* (2003)); or as an alternate reality or a thinly veiled version of a real place (like Sinclair Lewis's Gopher Prairie, based on Sauk Centre, Minnesota; Leo Edwards's Tutter, based on Utica, Illinois; or William Faulkner's Yoknapatawpha County, believed to be a version of Lafayette County, Mississippi); or as a composite that typifies a kind of state without referencing any particular real one (for example, the Colorado-like state of Fremont in James Michener's *Space* (1982) or Winnemac, the half-midwestern, half-eastern state in the novels of Sinclair Lewis). Fictional counties, cities, and towns, however, are easier to accept, because there are so many real ones, that quite likely no audience member will know them all (though the invention may seem contrived if one happens to live right where the fictional place is supposed to be).

Invention, then, is what makes a secondary world "secondary". Despite the initial freedom that a subcreator seems to have when inventing, each invention and changed default places limitations on further directions the world can develop in, making systems of integrated inventions more difficult, the more completely one has invented a world.

Completeness

Imaginary worlds are inevitably incomplete; Lubomír Doležel has even suggested that incompleteness is "a necessary and universal feature" of fictional worlds, and one of the main ways they differ from the actual world.[33] True completeness is impossible; so *completeness*, then, refers to the degree to which the world contains explanations and details covering all the various aspects of its characters' experiences, as well as background details which together suggest a feasible, practical world. Stories often have very incomplete worlds, and world detail beyond what is necessary to tell the story is often considered extraneous. However, if a world is to be important to an author or audience, to be the setting of a series of stories or a franchise, or just be compelling enough that an audience will want to vicariously enter the world, then completeness—or rather, *an illusion of completeness*—will become one of the subcreator's goals (with the exception of enigmas and deliberate gaps that arouse speculation, which are discussed toward the end of this chapter). As Tom Shippey puts it in *The Road to Middle-earth* (2003), "the more *unnecessary* details are put in, the more lifelike we take fiction to be."[34]

While stories require a certain degree of completeness to be convincing and satisfying, including such things as well-rounded multi-dimensional characters and sufficient backstory to explain motivation, worlds need additional information to appear fully developed and convincingly feasible. To begin with, characters must have some source of food, clothing, and shelter to survive, and come from some kind of culture. On a larger scale, communities will likely need some form of governance, an economy, food production, a shared form of communication, defense against outsiders, and other such things. Some things may be central to the story, while others may only be in evidence in background details, with just enough hints provided for the audience to answer basic questions concerning a character's subsistence and livelihood. Even questions left unanswered will not disturb an audience if there is enough information present for them to piece together or at least speculate as to what the answer might be. So long as audiences do not find their questions *unanswerable*, the world will appear to be sufficiently complete. It may take some work to gather and relate the relevant details in order to answer a particular question; but such effort is exactly what many fans enjoy, and such activities fuel debate and further speculation about a world.

For example, we might question the feasibility of the desert settlements on the planet Tatooine, as seen in Episodes I, II, III, IV, and VI of the *Star Wars* films, beginning with basics like food and water. We are told that Owen Lars runs a moisture farm, with vaporators that collect water from the atmosphere. In some shots, there are clouds in the sky, so water vapor is present (and the clouds seen in Episode IV were actually present over Tunisia when the film was shot, so it is realistic). So they have water, but is there enough? While the Lars homestead appears to be in a remote and unpopulated area, Mos Eisley and Mos Espa are relatively large cities; this can be seen in the various street scenes and establishing shots. Even if there is enough water, what about Tatooine's food supply? There appear to be no farms, and certainly not enough moisture for growing crops (though in Episode II we are told that Shmi used to pick mushrooms off of the vaporators). No trees of any kind are seen anywhere, and very little greenery appears, except for a few small houseplants on the Lars Homestead, and a bit of greenery growing in the background of two shots in Episode IV when Luke leaves with C-3P0 to find R2-D2 (see Figure 1.2).

Yet, we see meals being eaten in people's homes on Tatooine in Episodes I, II, and IV. Where does the food come from? One clue might be found in the

FIGURE 1.2 Evidence of plant life on Tatooine. In the top image alone, one can find nine instances of plant life growing in the Lars homestead. In the center image, Aunt Beru holds a large vegetable (actually fennel) which she uses for cooking. In the bottom image, one can see a fringe of greenery growing in the valley along the path over which Luke's landspeeder passes as Tusken Raiders watch from above. All images from *Star Wars Episode IV: A New Hope* (20th Century Fox, 1977).

merchants' stalls in the streets of Mos Espa. In Episode I, Jar Jar Binks steals a froglike gorg from one stall, where many more are hanging. Are these animals imports from other planets, or are they native? In an exterior shot of Jabba the Hutt's palace in Episode VI, we see another larger creature shoot out its tongue and eat a smaller creature. And there are much larger animals on Tatooine as well; for example, a herd of banthas are seen in Episode VI, and dewbacks are seen in Episodes I and IV. Dewbacks are creatures large enough to ride, and banthas are the size of elephants. So how do these desert creatures survive? Larger animals can eat smaller ones, but at some point in an ecosystem the animals need plants to eat, and some source of water. Some plant life is indicated: in Episode IV, Luke's Aunt Beru is seen putting a vegetable of some kind into a blender-like machine; in Episode I there is a bowl of fruit on the table in the Skywalker hovel; and in Episode II, when Shmi Skywalker is a captive of the Tusken Raiders, she is tied to a frame made of thick wooden branches inside a hut. Where do the vegetables, fruit, and wood come from? We might suppose that there are other areas of Tatooine that are vegetated, but all shots of the planet from space do not show any green or blue areas (though we do not see all of the planet's surface in these shots).

If we suppose that Tatooine's food is imported from other planets, what does this mean for the planet's economy? What exports might they have to balance trade? Such questions are better answered for the planet Arrakis in Frank Herbert's *Dune* series. Arrakis, also known as Dune, is a desert planet whose main export is the expensive spice called *melange*, which is produced by Dune's sandworms and required by Guild Navigators for interstellar travel (which is only possible using the spice). The valuable spice gives Dune political importance, and helps make the planet economically feasible in the process, since whoever controls the planet controls spice production. Herbert even includes a short section at the back of *Dune* (1965) entitled "The Ecology of Dune". Could Tatooine be similar? At one point in Episode IV, Luke, believing what his Uncle Owen has told him, says that his father "was a navigator on a spice freighter", which sounds very much like *Dune*. In the background of a desert shot in Episode IV, we can see a long skeleton of what appears to be a snake-like animal, that could have been inspired by *Dune*'s sandworms (the central part of the Sarlaac also looks a bit like one; and sandworms on Tatooine are mentioned in the short story "Sandbound on Tatooine" by Peter M. Schweighofer, and in the video game *Super Star Wars* (1992) for the Super Nintendo Entertainment System). Finally, the sector that Tatooine is in is called *Arkanis*, which is very close to *Arrakis*, suggesting that Tatooine's design may have been influenced by *Dune*.[35]

Therefore, the movies are somewhat inconclusive about food and plant life on Tatooine. If we go beyond the movies into the *Star Wars* "Expanded Universe", which includes media beyond the films, we find that there are a few native plants on Tatooine. The plants growing at the Lars homestead are "funnel flowers" (first identified as such in *The Illustrated Star Wars Universe* (1995)); according to Barbara

Hambley's 1995 book *The Children of the Jedi*, "deb-debs" are sweet fruits grown in oases; and "hubba gourds" appear in a few works, their first appearance being in the short story "Skin Deep: The Fat Dancer's Tale" by A. C. Crispin.[36] Also, the *Star Wars* Wiki database, *Wookieepedia*, tells us that the gorg seller in Episode I is named Gragra, and that she "was a Swokes Swokes gorgmonger that worked in the marketplace of Mos Espa" who "grew her food in a sewer zone underneath Mos Espa."[37] The additional details do not fully answer our questions, and even raise questions of their own, but they do hint at what solutions there might be.[38]

While this example requires information to be drawn from several sources and combined, for fans familiar with a franchise, such an activity makes use of their specialized knowledge (rewarding them for the time and effort they have invested the franchise) and their gap-filling may occur more quickly and automatically than audience members with less familiarity, resulting in a different experience of the world. In this particular case, we can even see how knowledge of multiple worlds (in this case, those of *Star Wars* and *Dune*) can influence the process of extrapolation. While casual audience members only interested in following a narrative will not actively piece together such world data or pursue them in different venues, they can still get a sense of how well a world seems to be fleshed out and revealed, and this may affect the reception of the work as a whole (see the discussion of world gestalten in the following text).

The completeness of a world is what makes it seem as though it extends far beyond the story, hinting at infrastructures, ecological systems, and societies and cultures whose existence is implied but not directly described or clearly shown. Likewise, a sense that a world has a past history is also necessary for it to seem complete. Tolkien was very aware of the need for an implied background and history, writing about *The Lord of the Rings* in two of his letters:

> It was written slowly and with great care for detail, and finally emerged as a Frameless Picture: a searchlight, as it were, on a brief episode in History, and on a small part of our Middle-earth, surrounded by the glimmer of limitless extensions in time and space.[39]

> Part of the attraction of The L. R. [*The Lord of the Rings*] is, I think, due to the glimpses of a large history in the background: an attraction like that of viewing far off an unvisited island, or seeing the towers of a distant city gleaming in a sunlit mist. To go there is to destroy the magic, unless new unattainable vistas are again revealed.[40]

The "glimpses of a large history" that result in a "Frameless Picture" aid the illusion of completeness, and the feeling of the unexhausted, or better still, inexhaustible, landscape of the world keeps it fresh for exploration and speculation (a topic covered later in this chapter).

Apart from direct exposition, there are many ways of indicating the existence of a past history, from extended backstories to the inclusion of ruins and legends, to more subtle things, like the condition of objects. When *Star Wars* (1977) was first released, it was noted for the way it portrayed a lived-in universe; vehicles and equipment had dirt, scratches, rust, and other grit that contributed to a "used" appearance with the wear-and-tear of a past history. Such silent evidence of a past can now be found in any visual medium, and has become an important part of building mood and atmosphere in the worlds in which it appears.

Completeness varies along with the effect the author desires; for example, some postmodern texts will revel in their incompleteness and foreground it. Whatever the case, the completeness of a secondary world determines in large part how believable a world will be, but the depth and detail added to a world must be done carefully if contradiction is to be avoided. A feeling of completeness will only be possible if the world also has an inner consistency that holds all of its many details together in agreement.

Consistency

Consistency is the degree to which world details are plausible, feasible, and without contradiction. This requires a careful integration of details and attention to the way everything is connected together. Lacking consistency, a world may begin to appear sloppily constructed, or even random and disconnected. Consistency may provide the most restraints for a subcreator, since it involves the interrelationship of the various parts of the world, and is one of the main ways that a secondary world attempts to resemble the Primary World.

The likelihood of inconsistencies occurring increases as a world grows in size and complexity, but it is also important to note *where* inconsistencies occur when they do, to determine how damaging to credibility they will be. Inconsistencies can occur in the main storyline, secondary storylines, background details, world infrastructure, or world mechanics. Inconsistencies in the storylines distract and disrupt the audience's mental image of the story as they follow it, especially if they occur in the main storyline driving the work along; inconsistencies in secondary storylines may have a less harmful effect, but will still weaken the overall impression of the work. Background details that are not crucial to the story can tolerate more inconsistency, especially if they go relatively unnoticed, or if they are not actively used in any of the storylines. World infrastructure and world mechanics are even further in the background, and both are usually present in only partial representations; for instance, the economic system or ecological systems of the world and the way they function and operate (like the question of food and water on Tatooine). Inconsistencies in these areas are usually far less noticeable, as their constituent parts (the facts that are in conflict) may be spread out throughout the story or the world, and would need to be considered together for any contradiction to be noticeable.

Consistency is necessary for a world to be taken seriously, but of course, not all worlds ask to be taken seriously. Some, like Springfield, the town where *The Simpsons* (1989–present) is set, use inconsistencies as a source of humor, or merely place the desire for variety and humor above the need to be consistent.

Springfield's geography is always changing, as is the Simpson family's own history. In the episode "Lisa's First Word" from season 4, we learn that Lisa was born during the 1984 Summer Olympics, while the episode "That '90s Show" from season 19 features Homer and Marge when they were dating, without any kids, in the 1990s. And of course, the entire Simpson family has remained the same age for the 20+ years the show has been around. Likewise, super-spy James Bond has remained roughly the same age over more than four decades of films, while the world around him keeps pace with the times.

Nevertheless, consistency is often taken seriously, even as a world grows to an enormous size. Leland Chee, the continuity database administrator for Lucas Licensing, maintains a *Star Wars* database of over 30,000 entries on all the characters, places, weapons, vehicles, events, and relationships from the *Star Wars* universe. The database was not started until the late 1990s, after two decades worth of *Star Wars* material had been released, resulting in the organization of several levels of canonicity (see Chapter 7) in an attempt to deal with the inconsistencies. Since then, Chee's office has become the force behind *Star Wars* consistency, as movies, TV series, games, toys, and other merchandise can be compared with and integrated into the franchise's existing world information. The *Star Trek* universe, however, spread over an even longer time period beginning with the original series in 1966, has hundreds of television episodes, novels, games, an animated TV series, and more material to coordinate. Stylistic inconsistencies between The Original Series and the later series (of the 1980s, 1990s, and 2000s) are occasionally even noticed by characters within the *Star Trek* universe itself. For its time travel story, one episode of *Deep Space Nine*, season 5, "Trials and Tribble-ations", composites its characters into footage from The Original Series season 2 episode, "The Trouble with Tribbles", and was broadcast to coincide with *Star Trek*'s thirtieth anniversary. The *DS9* characters dress in period costumes, comment on the difference of styles, and in one scene, the differences in the design of the Klingons' makeup are foregrounded. In The Original Series, Klingons looked much more like humans, with a minimum of makeup to suggest their foreignness, while in later series the Klingons' features, particular the forehead ridges, were much more pronounced. Since Worf, one of the time-traveling *DS9* characters, was a Klingon of the later design, the differences were particularly noticeable. This was acknowledged when another *DS9* character, the human O'Brien, sees the older style of Klingons and asks about the difference, to which Worf replies, "They *are* Klingons … and it is a long story." When pressed, he adds, "We do not discuss it with outsiders." Years later, two episodes of *StarTrek: Enterprise* ("Affliction" and "Divergence") would explain the differences as the result of a virus, which caused the physical changes as well as a change in the Klingons' temperament and disposition.[41]

Discussions of canonicity and speculation as to how inconsistencies might be resolved can be found on various Internet forums for a variety of franchises.

What is interesting is the degree to which fan communities want to see inconsistencies resolved; although they would seem to threaten the believability of a world more than the lack of completeness or invention, inconsistencies are treated by these fans as though they are merely gaps in the data, unexplained phenomena that further research and speculation will sort out and clear up. In some cases they are, while other inconsistencies are too incongruous to explain and too damaging to be left alone. Sometimes gaps must be filled before the conflicting information surrounding them makes it impossible to fill them; at this point, someone authorized by the franchise must step in and figure out how to reconcile multiple sources and bring them into agreement. For example, *Star Wars* fans always wondered what the floor plan of the *Millennium Falcon* was, and the exact size of the spaceship. A ten-page article on the topic appeared on Starwars.com in 2008, which explained:

> Despite repeated efforts by scholars, artists and fans, the interior of the *Millennium Falcon* eluded definitive mapping. Artists Chris Reiff and Chris Trevas finally cracked the puzzle that is the *Falcon* in the 2008 boxed set from DK Books, *Star Wars Blueprints: The Ultimate Collection*. … Hindering attempts at defining the *Falcon*'s true specs were the flexible requirements of filmmaking, which often favored cost-saving cheats rather than to-the-rivet accuracy in the ship's various depictions. Even the most basic question did not produce a simple answer: how big is the *Falcon*?
>
> If one were to use the studio interior sets seen in Episode IV and Episode V as a foundation of scale, it became apparent that they simply could not fit comfortably within the *Falcon*'s exterior dimensions as defined by the ILM models. If the cockpit indicated a certain size, then the hull height meant Han, and especially Chewie, would have to crouch to walk around the crew compartments. Furthermore, the full-sized *Falcon* exterior built for *The Empire Strikes Back* was, in actuality, about 75–80 percent of its intended true size, if one were to make an imaginary blow-up of the ILM miniature to the appropriate dimensions.
>
> Years of expanded universe publishing used an estimate of 87.6 feet (26.7 meters) as the *Falcon*'s official length, but Reiff and Trevas discovered that that would be an impossibility. Using a 1976 scale illustration by visual effects art director Joe Johnston as a foundation, and comparing the known lengths of X- and Y-wing fighters, they came up with a measurement of about 110 feet (33.5 meters). Unfortunately, Johnston's sketch was *too* sketchy for it to produce an accurate measurement.
>
> Trevas and Reiff used their blueprints to further refine the Johnston-scaled *Falcon* and came up with a surprising number. "The first time we measured, it very nearly came out to 113.8 feet," says Reiff. "When I suggested we use that length, Lucasfilm thought it would sound like we

made it up." That measurement, you see, looks an awful lot like an Easter Egg reference to *THX 1138*. The artists instead rounded up to 114 feet.[42]

The article goes on to relate how Rieff and Trevas used a variety of other sources to map the *Falcon*: images from freeze-framed HD copies of the films for interior and exterior layouts, control panel designs, maps of the underside lights, gun placements, hatches, doors, and landing gear; measurements of the sets built for the films; various scale models and props; the *Star Wars* Radio Drama (which described several escape pods); West End Games's 1987 *Star Wars Sourcebook* floor plans; Shane Johnston's drawings of the *Falcon*'s interior in *Starlog's Star Wars Technical Journal* published in 1993; Wizards of the Coast floor plans (which showed the location of the ship's bathroom); a 1997 cut-away poster illustration from SciPubTech; an expansive exploded view by Hans Jenssen in DK Books's *Star Wars: Incredible Cross Sections* (1997); a three-dimensional walkthrough from the CD-ROM *Behind the Magic* (1998); Timothy Zahn's novel *Allegiance* (2007); and the fact that a hyperdrive had to be included and fit into the overall design. At least in the case of *Star Wars*, the amount of effort put into answering such questions and restoring consistency can sometimes equal that of actual historical researchers establishing facts and revising earlier claims as new data conflicts with them.

Occasionally, franchise creators will even go back and alter earlier works to make them consistent with later ones, a process now referred to as "retroactive continuity" or "retcon" (see Chapter 4). Famous examples of retconning include J. R. R. Tolkien revising *The Hobbit* (1937) to bring it into alignment with *The Lord of the Rings* (since the Ring did not originally have many of the properties it was given later), or George Lucas's many alterations to the *Star Wars* re-releases. While controversial among fan communities, retcon is more common in superhero comic books, and sometimes attempts are made to explain it away through the use of time travel, alternate universes, dreams, and other questionable techniques. And one can find lighthearted approaches toward it as well; on the British TV show *Torchwood*, a drug used to erase memories is called "Retcon".[43]

The death of an author who leaves works unfinished can also result in inconsistencies, which may or may not be reconcilable by those who carry on his work. While the Tolkien Estate does not approve of or allow new works set in Middle-earth to be written by other authors, it does allow Tolkien's own unpublished material to appear, including multiple drafts of his works, sometimes resulting in partial and even conflicting versions of stories. In the foreword to *The Silmarillion* (1977), Christopher Tolkien wrote:

> On my father's death it fell to me to try to bring the work into publishable form. It became clear to me that to attempt to present, within the covers of a single book, the diversity of materials—to show *The Silmarillion* as in truth a continuing and evolving creation extending over more than half a

century—would in fact lead only to confusion and the submerging of what was essential. I set myself therefore to work out a single text, selecting and arranging in such a way as seemed to me to produce the most coherent and internally self-consistent narrative. ... A complete consistency (either within the compass of *The Silmarillion* itself or between *The Silmarillion* and other published writings of my father's) is not to be looked for, and could only be achieved, if at all, at heavy and needless cost.[44]

Arda, Tolkien's subcreated world in which Middle-earth appears, is one of the largest and most detailed worlds ever made by a single author. It is amazing how consistent it is, given its expansiveness, fine level of detail, and span of more than 6,000 years. Yet, some inconsistencies still remain, though they are usually what we might call "aggregate inconsistencies", things that are not readily noticeable unless one combines several facts which one would not normally consider together, and which would go unnoticed by casual readers. For example, in *The Hobbit*, there is the question of Bilbo and Gollum and their ability to understand each other when they meet under the mountain. Gollum, or Sméagol as he was known (as we later learn in *The Lord of the Rings*), originally came from a different variety of hobbits, the Stoors, who lived in another region of Middle-earth. As Tolkien explained in a draft of a letter to A. C. Nunn:

> With the remigration of the Stoors back to Wilderland in TA 1356, all contact between this retrograde group and the ancestors of the Shirefolk was broken. More than 1,100 years elapsed before the Déagol–Sméagol incident (c. 2463). At the time of the Party in TA 3001, when the customs of the Shire-folk are cursorily alluded to insofar as they affect the story, the gap of time was nearly 1,650 years.
>
> All hobbits were slow to change, but the remigrant Stoors were going back to a wilder and more primitive life of small and dwindling communities; while the Shire-folk in the 1,400 years of their occupation had developed a more settled and elaborate social life, in which the importance of kinship to their sentiment and customs was assisted by detailed traditions, written and oral.[45]

Even though "hobbits were slow to change", the two groups were on markedly different paths of development, and the passage of over 1,500 years would surely find them so different that it is hard to believe that their language would remain so unchanged that Bilbo and Gollum could communicate without any difficulty. Considering Tolkien's careful treatment of language (and language change) throughout his work, it is surprising that such a discrepancy exists; but to notice the inconsistency, one must integrate information from *The Hobbit*, *The Lord of the Rings*, and *The Letters of J. R. R. Tolkien*. If *The Hobbit* is considered alone, there appears to be no discrepancy.

As worlds grow in size and detail, aggregate inconsistencies become more likely, but in many cases, they are so spread out, requiring so many disparate facts to be considered together, that they are more likely to go unnoticed. Yet, fans are often very knowledgeable about their favorite franchises, and even enjoy catching such inconsistencies and trying to explain and reconcile them with their own theories.[46] And this kind of activity requires one to be thoroughly immersed in the world in question.

Immersion, Absorption, and Saturation

Much has been written about "immersion" in regard to a user's experience with new media.[47] The term is typically used to describe three different types of experiences, which exist along a spectrum. On one end, there is the *physical* immersion of user, as in a theme park ride or walk-in video installation; the user is physically surrounded by the constructed experience, thus the analogy with immersion in water. Moving away from the surrounding of the entire body, there is the *sensual* immersion of the user, as in a virtual-reality-driven head-mounted display that covers the user's eyes and ears. While the user's entire body is not immersed, everything the user sees and hears is part of the controlled experience; another example, a step further down the spectrum, would be the watching of a movie in a darkened theater, or a video game with a three-dimensional space through which the player's avatar moves; in such cases, the audience vicariously enters a world through a first-person point of view or an on-screen avatar. Finally, on the other end of the spectrum is *conceptual* immersion, which relies on the user's imagination; for example, engaging books like *The Lord of the Rings* are considered "immersive" if they supply sufficient detail and description for the reader to vicariously enter the imagined world.

It is also interesting to note how certain media, like newspaper and radio, are usually *not* considered immersive, even though a newspaper, when opened in front of the reader, fills more peripheral vision than does a book or television screen, and music on the radio literally surrounds a listener physically with sound waves. Part of the reason these media are usually not considered immersive is that neither is likely to provide the kind of vivid experience of going elsewhere, into a different place, that one can find in other more "immersive" media.[48] Thus, it would seem that an imaginary world is an aid to conceptual immersion. The metaphor of "immersion", the further it moves away from actual, physical immersion, becomes less of an analogy of what is happening, and only covers the first step of the experiencing of an imaginary world. In some of the examples of immersion described above, one might be "immersed", but cease to be much more than that. A theme park ride will successfully physically immerse someone, but may still be uninvolving mentally and emotionally. A virtual space seen through a head-mounted display may likewise dominate a person's sensory registers, but fail to interest a person beyond merely looking around.

On the other hand, for conceptual or emotional immersion to occur, the audience must be fully engaged with the work at hand; thus, to speak only of "immersion" is not enough, and an additional liquid metaphor is needed; that of *absorption*.[49]

Absorption differs from immersion in that it is a two-way process. In one sense, the user's attention and imagination is absorbed or "pulled into" the world; one willingly opens a book, watches a screen, interacts with a game world, and so forth. At the same time, however, the user also "absorbs" the imaginary world as well, bringing it into mind, learning or recalling its places, characters, events, and so on, constructing the world within the imagination the same way that that memory brings forth people, events, and objects when their names are mentioned. Thus, we are able to mentally leave (or block out) our physical surroundings, to some degree, because details of the secondary world displace those of the Primary World while we are engaged with it. As psychologist Norman Holland describes it:

> We humans have a finite amount of attention or "psychic energy." Attention is a way of focusing that limited energy on what matters. If we concentrate on one thing, an important thing, we pay less attention to other things. Those other things become unconscious (or, more accurately, "preconscious" in Freud's term). If we use more energy and excitation in one prefrontal function, following the play or story, we have less energy available for other prefrontal functions, like paying attention to our bodies or to the [Primary] world around that play or story.[50]

Since details of the secondary world displace those of the Primary World in the audience member's attention, the more details the secondary world asks the audience to keep in mind (especially details important to the understanding and enjoyment of the story), the more "full" the audience's mind is of the secondary world, and the more absorbing the experience of it becomes (the challenge of remembering and integrating a wealth of detail can make absorption similar to Mihaly Csíkszentmihályi's notion of "flow", another liquid metaphor).

Thus, we can add a third liquid metaphor to complete the process; that of *saturation*.[51] When there are so many secondary world details to keep in mind that one struggles to remember them all while experiencing the world, to the point where secondary world details crowd out thoughts of the immediate Primary World, saturation occurs (as in the quote from Defontenay's *Star* (1854) given at the start of this chapter). Saturation is the pleasurable goal of conceptual immersion; the occupying of the audience's full attention and imagination, often with more detail than can be held in mind all at once. And some worlds do require a great deal of attention, concentration, and memory, if one is to appreciate all the nuances and subtleties that an author can offer. *The Silmarillion*, for example, includes an "Index of Names" listing 788 entries for all the characters, places, titles, and terms used in the book.[52] To make matters even more difficult, certain characters have multiple names (Túrin, for example, is also known as Neithan, Gorthol, Agarwaen, Mormegil, Thurin, Wildman of the Woods, and Turambar), and several names are shared by more than one character, place, or thing (for example, Celeborn, Elemmirë, Gelmir, Gorgoroth, Lórien, Minas Tirith, Míriel, and Nimloth all refer to more than one person or place). And Tolkien's names almost always carry meaning as well; after the "Index of Names" is an appendix entitled "Elements in Quenya and Sindarin Names" that lists 180 root words and their meanings, from which the majority of the 788 entries in the "Index of Names" are formed. Many of the book's characters are related in elaborate family trees, and these relationships often play an important role in the stories. Throughout the book, various events are alluded to long after they have occurred, or are foretold long before they occur, requiring the reader to remember a good deal in order to understand the events and motivations behind them. And *The Silmarillion*, in turn, acts as a backdrop and backstory for *The Lord of the Rings*, which frequently alludes to its material and, in a sense, is *The Silmarillion*'s climax and conclusion. For example, Aragorn is distantly related to Beren, whose romance with Lúthien mirrors Aragorn's romance with Arwen; and Aragorn is also the heir of Isildur, whose weakness and fate he hopes will not match his own. While one can read and enjoy *The Lord of the Rings* without having read *The Silmarillion*, knowledge of *The Silmarillion* adds to the story's depth and nuance, enhancing the reader's pleasure and understanding.

Saturation can affect one's experience of an imaginary world in other ways as well. In many video games, especially those of the adventure game genre, players must be able to remember a wealth of details about the game's imaginary world in order to put together its backstory and solve puzzles, both of which are often needed to win the game (as in *Riven* (1997)). The worlds of the largest massively multiplayer on-line role-playing games (MMORPGs), with their vast territories, millions of player-characters, and ongoing events, are too large for any player to know in their entirety, allowing even the most hardcore players to achieve saturation.

Worlds offering a high degree of saturation are usually too big to be experienced completely in a single sitting or session. The amount of detail and information must be great enough to overwhelm the audience, imitating the vast amount of Primary World information which cannot be mastered or held in mind all at once. This overflow, beyond the point of saturation, is necessary if the world is to be kept alive in the imagination. If the world is too small, the audience may feel that they know all there is to know, and consider the world exhausted, feeling there is nothing more to be obtained from it. A world with an overflow beyond saturation, however, can never be held in the mind in its entirety; something will always be left out. What remains in the audience's mind then, is always changing, as lower levels of detail are forgotten and later re-experienced and re-imagined when they are encountered again. For example, someone can read Tolkien's works in grade school, high school, college, and later; and with each re-reading, the reader will notice new things, make new connections, and re-imagine events and characters due to the reader's own changed level of maturity and experience. While this can also occur with smaller works that do not reach the same levels of saturation or overflow, it is those that do that provide more interesting re-visioning, as forgotten details return in new imagined forms, and new configurations of detail and information inhabit the reader's mind. Even in the case of visual media like film and television, where images and sounds are concrete and fixed, the way we imagine the unseen parts of the world may change with each viewing. We may ask different questions and focus on different aspects that we had not previously considered, resulting in a different experience insofar as our speculation and imagination is concerned. These differences arise due to the way we complete narrative and world gestalten, which also depends on our own previous experience.

World Gestalten: Ellipsis, Logic, and Extrapolation

The reader makes implicit connections, fills in gaps, draws inferences and tests out hunches; and to do this means drawing on a tacit knowledge of the world in general and of literary conventions in particular. The text itself is really no more than a series of "cues" to the reader, invitations to construct a piece of language into meaning. ... Without this continuous active participation on the reader's part, there would be no literary work at all.

—Terry Eagleton, literary theorist[53]

The automatic filling in of gaps by an observer was first noted in Gestalt psychology, which began in the early twentieth century and saw the whole as being more than the sum of its parts. In particular, the gestalt principles of emergence, reification, good continuity, closure, and *prägnanz* all have to do with how the human perceptual system organizes sensory input holistically, automatically filling in gaps, so that the whole contains percepts that are not present in the individual parts from which it is composed. While a few principles have been applied to sound, most Gestalt principles apply to vision, and the way one perceives and completes an image, adding details, connections, or forms that are not actually present.

As the Eagleton quote in the preceding text suggests, the idea of the gestalt can be usefully applied not just to the *perceptual* realm, but the *conceptual* realm as well. For example, in classical Hollywood film continuity, when we see a person drive off in a car in one scene and arrive at a different location in the next scene, we automatically assume they have driven from one place to another; a *narrative gestalt* occurs, as the departure and arrival together suggests a journey we have not seen. Like visual gestalten, narrative gestalten occur automatically and seemingly without much conscious effort on the part of the viewer, provided the viewer is familiar with the cinematic storytelling conventions being used.

Biographical films like *Gandhi* (1982) and *The Last Emperor* (1987) may cover several decades of someone's life in only a few hours, resulting in a staggering amount of omission and ellipsis, and yet such stories, if they are well constructed and include the right events, can seem complete and comprehensible.

Likewise, we can go one step further and suggest the idea of *world gestalten*, in which a structure or configuration of details together implies the existence of an imaginary world, and causes the audience to automatically fill in the missing pieces of that world, based on the details that are given. Psychologists have already considered how our imagination constructs our own internal version of the real world (as in Steven Lehar's book *The World in Your Head: A Gestalt View of the Mechanism of Conscious Experience* (2002)) but the same processes can, to a degree, be applied to our imagining of secondary worlds as well (as Norman Holland demonstrates in *Literature and the Brain*).[54]

Naturally, the gaps existing in world information overlap considerably with gaps in the narrative. Narrative theory attempts to answer how narrative gaps work and how the audience tries to fill them. In *Narration and the Fiction Film* (1985), David Bordwell uses the Russian formalist notions of "fabula" (the story we construct from the causal, spatial, and temporal links that a narrative provides) and the "syuzhet" (how the film arranges and presents the fabula) when discussing how narrative gaps are filled:

> The analysis of narration can begin with the syuzhet's tactics for presenting fabula information. We must grasp how the syuzhet manages its basic task—the presentation of story logic, time, and space—always recalling that in practice we never get ideally maximum access to the fabula. In general, the syuzhet shapes our perception of the fabula by controlling (1) the quantity of fabula information to which we have access; (2) the degree of pertinence we can attribute to the presented information; and (3) the formal correspondences between syuzhet presentation and fabula data.
>
> Assume that an ideal syuzhet supplies information in the "correct" amount to permit coherent and steady construction of the fabula. Given this hypostatized reference point, we can distinguish a syuzhet which supplies too little information about the story and a syuzhet which supplies too much: in other words, a "rarefied" syuzhet versus an "overloaded" one.[55]

If only narrative is considered, most subcreated worlds would be considered to have an overloaded syuzhet, since much of the world information supplied in a narrative may be considered excess beyond what is needed to tell the story. However, we can extend the notions of fabula and syuzhet to the world that is presented and the way it is constructed in the mind of the audience. If the world is considered instead of merely the narrative set in the world, the reference point for the ideal syuzhet must change; the ideal syuzhet would have to provide enough information for the audience to be able to feel that an independent world appears to exist, and to have some sense of its infrastructure, cultures, geography, history, and so forth. Thus, what might appear to be "excess" from a narrative-oriented point of view, may prove to be necessary from a world-oriented point of view.

If, during fabula construction, a narrative is constructed from causal, spatial, and temporal linkages, from what is a world constructed? Similar systems of relationships hold a world's elements together and define its structure; maps (spatial links), timelines (temporal links), histories and mythologies (causal links), and other systems such as genealogical relationships, and those involving nature, culture, language, and society (these structures are the topic of Chapter 3). When a large enough number of elements from these systems are combined in a consistent fashion, a kind of "world logic" starts to form, by which one can see how a world works and how its various systems are interrelated. This logic may cover everything from social customs to the laws governing magic or the limitations of technology, to even laws of physics that differ from those of the Primary World, which all help to establish the ontological rules of the secondary world. Following the Gestalt principle of "good continuation", structures like maps and timelines may suggest how gaps are to be filled by laying out places or events that allow the audience to figure out what lies between them (for example, terrain that changes from rain forest to desert cannot do so abruptly; the landscape in between them must gradually transform). World events likewise can be elided with enough information given so that the gradual shift from one state to another can be reconstructed in the audience's imagination, just as in a narrative we are given the turning points in a character's life from which a character arc can be plotted. When Primary World defaults can be used to fill in such areas, the author can leave such information to be extrapolated by the audience; for example, city-scapes in alien worlds often rely on similarities with Primary World cityscapes in their structure and functioning, despite the fantastic architecture and grand scale that often set them apart from Primary World cities. Differences are highlighted while similarities are taken for granted, resulting in an emphasis on the uniqueness of the secondary world, while still keeping it relatable to an audience.

World logic, which itself is part of the world's fabula, gives the audience the evidence and solid ground which enables them to speculate and extrapolate, filling in the gaps and completing the gestalten needed for the illusion of a secondary world. A world's logic does not need to be so rigorous as to fill every gap definitively; there will always be room for ambiguity, especially in word-based media that leave visualization to its readers' imagination. For example, Douglas A. Anderson's book, *The Annotated Hobbit* (1986; revised edition, 2002) is replete with illustrations from translations of *The Hobbit* from around the world, which together form a wide gamut of illustration styles and character designs, all based on the same novel.[56]

Once a world is developed enough, even its author can become beholden to a world's logic and the rules that result from it. This is why one often hears that a story begins "writing itself" or that characters seem to take on lives of their own and end up saying or doing things the author had not planned (while stuck during the writing of one of his Oz novels, L. Frank Baum once complained that characters would not do what he wanted them to do[57]). At such a point, the world's logic has begun to shape and limit further additions to the world, occasionally even suggesting things the author had not considered previously. In a letter of 1956, Tolkien wrote that:

> I have long ceased to *invent* (though even patronizing or sneering critics on the side praise my "invention"): I wait until I seem to know what really happened. Or till it writes itself. Thus, though I knew for years that Frodo would run into a tree-adventure somewhere far down the Great River, I have no recollection of inventing Ents. I came at last to the point, and wrote the "Treebeard" chapter without any recollection of previous thought: just as it now is. And then I saw that, of course, it had not happened to Frodo at all.[58]

Such inventions can even work against an author's narrative goals, as world logic begins to drive the narrative. While working on *The Lord of the Rings* in 1944, Tolkien wrote his son Christopher about how a new, initially unwanted character was holding back his work:

> A new character has come on the scene (I am sure that I did not invent him, I did not even want him, though I like him, but there he came walking into the woods of Ithilien): Faramir, the brother of Boromir—and he is holding up the "catastrophe" by a lot of stuff about the history of Gondor and Rohan (with some very sound reflections no doubt on martial glory and true glory): but if he goes on much more a lot of him will have to be removed to the appendices—where already some fascinating material on the hobbit Tobacco industry and the Languages of the West have gone.[59]

Not only does Faramir appear as a character needed by the story, he also personifies the encyclopedic impulse, through his exposition regarding Gondor and Rohan. Tolkien's reaction, threatening to remove the exposition to the appendices, shows the potential tension between story and world concerns.

World data may slow narrative progress or halt it momentarily, but it also enriches narrative by giving it more of a context and background depth. Yet, no matter how much of a world is documented, there is never enough invented material to fill all the gaps that exist; nor is any world invented so completely that they could be. Where the world's own logic does not dictate specific answers, gaps are usually filled with Primary World defaults; in other words, unless we are told otherwise, we expect the laws of physics in a secondary world to be the same as those of the Primary World, and expect that the secondary world's social, political, or economic structures will operate in a similar fashion as those that exist (or used to exist) in the Primary World. For example, the Anglo-Saxons serve as the model for Tolkien's Riders of Rohan, in their poetry, names, and customs. This makes them more believable and gives them an underlying logic that connects the various aspects of their culture. While the casual reader may not have any background in Anglo-Saxon history, their cultural logic remains, adding consistency and aiding in the filling of gaps.[60] Kendall Walton calls this gap-filling using Primary World defaults the "reality principle",[61] while Marie-Laure Ryan calls it the "principle of minimal departure", writing:

> We construe the world of fiction and of counterfactuals as being the closest possible to the reality we know. This means that we will project upon the world of the statement everything we know about the real world, and that we will make only those adjustments which we cannot avoid.[62]

As mentioned earlier, this is one feature that makes some books, like *The Lord of the Rings*, so popular for re-reading; because at different stages of one's life, one's understanding of the world, and thus its defaults, may differ considerably, so that each time we read the book we fill in the gaps differently, creating a new experience of the world even though the book itself has not changed, but rather because the reader has changed since his or her last reading.

The more detail one is given about a world, the more gestalten can operate, since the gaps to be filled will be smaller and thus more easily closed by extrapolation. And the easier they are to close, the more automatically and unconsciously the audience will close them, resulting in a greater illusion of an independently existing world. Larger gaps can be closed too, but with a conscious effort on the part of the audience, who must actively consider how to close them; an activity that can be a pleasurable one if the audience feels that the author has already considered the gaps in question and accounted for them somehow. Even in the case of an apparent inconsistency, audience members may try to resolve a gap in order to defend the consistency of a world which they are fond of. Consider, for example, British theoretical astrophysicist Dr. Curtis Saxton's thoughtful explanation as to why we can hear the spaceships in *Star Wars* even though sound does not travel in space:

> Sound does not propagate in space. ... Therefore it becomes difficult and important to explain how it is that the crews of starships and starfighters are apparently able to hear the movement of nearby vessels and beam weapons. Several qualities need to be accommodated:
>
> 1. Crew actually hear these phenomena; they behaviorally respond as if to audio stimuli.
> 2. Nearby weapon beams sound louder than distant ones.
> 3. A nearby starship sounds louder than a distant one.
> 4. The sound characterises the model of starship.
> 5. A passing starship exhibits a Doppler shift of pitch, according to relative velocity.

The most plausible explanation is that the sound is produced inside the cockpit of each starship for the benefit of crew. External radiation sensors of various kinds are linked to audio systems of the cockpit in order to provide the pilot with audible cues to the proximity of other starships and energetic phenomena, operating like a glorified Geiger-counter. A greater rate of particle detections occurs when the source is more powerful or closer; each of these contributes an audible click on internal speakers, millions of pulses received combine to give a sound which characterizes the emission spectrum of the passing starship.

This is an efficient use of the pilot's senses to convey vital information; the pilot's sight is likely to be preoccupied with controls and visual displays. As a technology, it also has the strength of appealing to basic human intuitions about how the physical world operates.

An alternative explanation for the sounds involves the starships' shields. All space vessels operating beyond the protection of the atmosphere and magnetosphere of a planet require at least some shielding to protect them from solar wind particles, etc. It therefore seems possible that disturbances to the shields could be indirectly but physically felt through the hull or the generators. The radiation from blaster shots or nearby sublight engines may cause resonant vibrations, heard inside the ship as sounds.

An important quote has been discovered in the *A New Hope* radio play that conclusively proves that the "sounds in space" really are just auditory sensor feedback provided to crew inside a ship. This does not rule out the possibility of some kinds of shield disturbances may have audible effects, but it does indicate that the sounds heard in the movies are primarily a product of sensor systems. As Han Solo explains to Luke Skywalker [ANHRD: 286–287]:

> Your sensors'll give you an audio simulation for a rough idea of where those fighters are when they're not on your screen. It'll sound like they're right there in the turret with you.

From the evidence of the movies, it seems that major warships dispense with this effect, which is how the Executor, Home One, and star destroyer command bridges maintain such a pure and clinical atmosphere. Of course, the ships' gunners, helmsmen and other crew who are immediately and directly concerned with outside action may have auditory sensor data fed into their helmets and headsets.[63]

This extended discussion, both serious and playful in nature, demonstrates the importance of consistency in the gap-filling process, and the degree of speculation it can involve.

Of course, the casual audience member who merely wishes to follow a narrative and discover its outcomes will probably never experience many of the world gestalts available to those for whom a vicarious experience of the world is as important (or more) as the understanding of the narrative. (Likewise, a single viewing or reading is usually enough for someone interested only in story, whereas someone interested in the world and its structures will probably return to a work multiple times in order to focus on details and the various links between world data.) However, for those who do care, the vicarious experience of a world is strengthened through transnarrative and transmedial references, all of which are unified by the world into an overarching experience (provided all the various details are in agreement, of course).

Even for the casual audience member, many world gaps are filled unconsciously (like the gaps of perceptual psychology), giving the feeling of a fully-rendered complete world with little effort on the part of the audience; for example, in movies when locations are seen from multiple angles, a viewer will typically automatically combine the images into a three-dimensional composite structure, even though the images may actually be a combination of live-action sets, models, and computer-generated imagery (this process is similar to what Irvin Rock refers to as "unconscious inference" in *The Logic of Perception* (1983)[64] and can also be seen as an extension of the Gestalt principle of *invariance*). While unconscious inferences of this kind may be enough to give the casual viewer enough of a sense of a world's completeness to keep him or her from being distracted from following the narrative, viewers more interested in the vicarious experience of the world may further question a world's feasibility and look to data beyond what is needed by the narrative, where larger gaps need to be filled in with conscious effort (as in the earlier example regarding food and water on Tatooine).

Apart from the visual and auditory gestalten that occur when a story or world is presented in audiovisual media, extrapolation can be divided into three types: the completion of narrative gestalts, gap-filling using Primary World defaults, and gap-filling using secondary world defaults. The first two of these we have already examined, and both are general processes used across all fictional worlds. The third, however, involves the particular defaults of a specific secondary world, which the audience must learn in order to fill in gaps. This includes such things as customs, design styles, languages, and so on, that are often introduced without explanation and left for the audience to figure out either directly, from the information given, or indirectly, from the context formed by events as the world unfolds (for example, avid *Star Trek* viewers are familiar with starship layouts and their interior design styles, allowing them to imagine ship interiors even when they are not shown). Thus, while Primary World defaults and narrative gestalts can function right from the beginning of the audience's encounter with a world, the defaults of a secondary world must be learned over time through exposure to, and experience of, a secondary world, occasionally with conscious effort on the audience's part (in some cases, sources like glossaries and appendices can provide direct explanations and details).

This leads to the question of what details need to appear and what can be left to the imagination. Secondary world defaults are what define a secondary world and delineate its difference from the Primary World, so they form the foundation of what must be included. Once enough of them have been given to establish the world's logic, the author may begin to leave things to be extended, inferred, or extrapolated by the audience, so that detail appears to continue beyond what has actually been given; as Tolkien puts it, "a Frameless Picture: a searchlight, as it were, on a brief episode in History ... surrounded by the glimmer of limitless extensions in time and space."[65] The necessary details, then, are those that form the very structures by which subcreated worlds are held together (and which are the subject of Chapter 3). Beyond these, an author may add additional details to fill out and embellish the world, suggest unexplored horizons, and engage the imagination. In audiovisual media, these may be small details in the background that reward the observant spectator with additional world data (see Figure 1.3).

FIGURE 1.3 World details in *Star Wars Episode II: Attack of the Clones* (20th Century Fox, 2002). Staging in depth results in suggestive glimpses of distance objects and locations (top), while background details and events reveal further consequences of story events, like the flying droids seen outside Padmé's apartment that replace the window which was broken during the attack of the night before (bottom).

Such details would have to be described in a novel rather than simply remaining in the background; audiovisual media such as movies, then, have an advantage when it comes to world-building insofar as they can depict things in the background without calling attention to them, letting viewers find them during subsequent viewings after the narrative has been exhausted.

Secondary world defaults can be rigidly defined, or room can be left for audience interpretation. There is a tendency, especially in word-based media that leave visualization of a world to the audience's imagination, for Primary World defaults to "normalize" secondary world defaults to some degree. Two examples of this "normalizing tendency" can be found in Tolkien's work. When Gandalf is first introduced in *The Hobbit*, he is described as having "long bushy eyebrows that stuck out farther than the brim of his shady hat."[66] And in *The Lord of the Rings*, Frodo leaves Hobbiton with the Ring a day after his fiftieth birthday. Despite these facts, Gandalf, when he is visualized (either in illustrations or in films) is rarely depicted with eyebrows extending so far out, nor is Frodo depicted as looking 50 years old. While the Ring is partly responsible for Frodo's youthful appearance,[67] the other hobbits of the Fellowship are also typically portrayed to be younger (perhaps all in their twenties, like the four actors portraying them in Peter Jackson's film adaptations), even though when the four hobbits begin their journey Sam is 35, Merry is 36, and Pippin is 28. Thus, while the description of Gandalf's eyebrows create a certain feeling about him when he is introduced, to actually depict (or constantly imagine) Gandalf to have eyebrows of that size would make him see comic, so the initial description is more likely to be treated as hyperbole as opposed to a literal description. Likewise, the hobbits' initial innocence and relative inexperience, along with their short height, make them seem more youthful than they actually are, since these aspects are more strongly emphasized by the narrative than their ages are. Primary World defaults, then, can temper strange or unusual details and subtly adjust one's image of the secondary world to be more in line with what may be considered more "realistic".

A world's inventions and changed defaults can be revealed suddenly or gradually, and can be explained directly, deliberately left unexplained, or left to the audience to figure out through context. An example of meaning given through context can be found on the first page of Frank Herbert's *Dune*, when an old crone comes to see Paul Atreides and it is said of her that, "Her voice wheezed and twanged like an untuned baliset." Without defining "baliset", the audience can infer it is a musical instrument, because it can be tuned. In addition, the analogy also describes the sound from what may be the character's point of view (Paul may think her voice sounds like a baliset) which in turn reveals that music is a part of the world's culture, and perhaps also among the character's interests.

Inferences can also be very subtle and require the connecting of small details. For example, it is never stated directly that Tolkien's Elves have pointed ears, but the similarity between the Quenya words for "leaf" and "ear" suggest such a shape. As Douglas A. Anderson writes:

> In his notes on the stem LAS[1] from *lasse = "leaf" and LAS[2] "listen" (*lasse = "ear"), Tolkien noted the possible relationship between the two in that Elven "ears were more pointed and leaf-shaped" than human ones.[68]

Although some questions can be answered by information in ancillary materials, much room is left for speculation. While incompleteness is not desirable in certain areas necessary for comprehension of the story or the world, room for speculation in other areas is a valuable asset to an imaginary world, as this is where the audience's imagination is encouraged and engaged.

Catalysts of Speculation

> *I've put in so many enigmas and puzzles that it will keep the professors busy for centuries arguing over what I meant, and that's the only way of insuring one's immortality.*
>
> —James Joyce, on his novel *Ulysses*[69]

As Joyce realized, a work's immortality depends on whether or not it remains discussed by others. For a world, this can mean speculation in the areas where extrapolation attempts to reach: mysterious aspects and open-ended questions (not without clues, perhaps) that allow speculation to continue after the works are consumed. Deliberate gaps, enigmas, and unexplained references help keep a work alive in the imagination of its audience, because it is precisely in these areas where audience participation, in the form of speculation, is most encouraged. Some of the most successful world-builders have realized this. In a letter of 1954, Tolkien wrote:

> As a story, I think it is good that there should be a lot of things unexplained (especially if an explanation actually exists); and I have perhaps from this point of view erred in trying to explain too much, and give too much past history. Many readers have, for instance, rather stuck at the Council of Elrond. And even in a mythical Age there must be some enigmas, as there always are. Tom Bombadil is one (intentionally).[70]

And in another letter of 1965, referring to Gandalf's departure from the Grey Havens at the end of the book, Tolkien wrote:

> I think Shadowfax certainly went with Gandalf, though this is not stated. I feel it is better not to state everything (and indeed it is more realistic, since

in chronicles and accounts of "real" history, many facts that some enquirer would like to know are omitted, and the truth has to be discovered from such evidence as there is.[71]

The same is apparently felt by George Lucas:

> The careful tending of the *Star Wars* continuity has yielded great wealth, but the key to a productive farm is to leave some fields fallow. A complete Holocron would leave little room for fantasy—for fans who, as [*Henry*] Jenkins says, "love unmapped nooks and crannies, the dark shadows we can fill in with our imagination."
> That's something that GWL [*George Walton Lucas*] understands. For instance, the origins of the Jedi master Yoda, his species, and his home planet are off-limits. The backstory isn't even in the Holocron. "It doesn't exist, except maybe in George's mind," [*Leland*] Chee says. "He feels like, 'You don't have to explain everything all the time. Let's keep some mystery.'"[72]

Of course, every subcreated world has gaps, so speculation is always possible; but the difference here is that a successful secondary world is one an audience *wants* to extrapolate. Before speculation occurs, curiosity must be aroused, and it will only be aroused if there is the possibility that a correct, or at least plausible, answer is thought to exist somewhere. While completeness can never be achieved, a *sense of completeness* can, which gives the impression that all questions could, in theory, be answered, even though they are not. For the areas of a world in which speculation is encouraged, the ideal balance of information is one in which enough information is provided to support multiple theories, but not enough to prove any one theory definitively. The ability to debate and find new ways to answer questions can keep a world fresh, especially if it is a "closed" world for which authorized additions are no longer being made (see Chapter 7). For "open" worlds which are still being built, speculation may lead to new works that attempt to answer questions in more detail, either by the world's originator, by those authorized to add to it, or even by unauthorized fan additions.

Another catalyst for speculation occurs when a world's originator dies leaving unfinished work. Much of Tolkien's work was unpublished at the time of his death, and has appeared posthumously in *The Silmarillion* (1977), *Unfinished Tales* (1980), the 12-volume *History of Middle-earth* series (1983–1996), and *The Children of Húrin* (2007), all edited by his son Christopher Tolkien. Frank Herbert left the seventh and final novel of his *Dune* series unfinished in outline form when he died in 1986, and his son Brian (along with Kevin J. Anderson) used this outline to produce two more Dune novels, *Hunters of Dune* (2006) and *Sandworms of Dune* (2007), as well as a number of prequel novels. Thus, the desire to see gaps filled and unfinished material published can help stimulate the circles of authorship that can extend out from around a world's originator (see Chapter 7).

As suggested in the second Tolkien quote, regarding Shadowfax, deliberate gaps, enigmas, and unexplained references add to a world's verisimilitude by making it more like the Primary World, where ambiguity and missing pieces often remain in the search for knowledge, requiring what poet John Keats called "Negative Capability"; that is, "when a man is capable of being in uncertainties, mysteries, doubts, without any irritable reaching after fact and reason".[73] Negative Capability is almost always a necessity in the enjoyment of subcreated worlds, since much of a world typically remains unrevealed, unexplained, or ambiguous (like whether balrogs have wings or not).[74] The more information that an author gives of a secondary world, the more that can be ellipsized, or left vague. Speculation is more likely to occur in a near-complete world than a very incomplete one, because the possibility of completion seems much closer and attainable; smaller gaps are more likely to be bridged than larger ones. Authors, then, cannot rely on speculation occurring unless their worlds are substantial enough to generate theories for their completion.

Yet, despite all the elaborate details that can be included in a world, one important detail—its exact location—is often left purposely vague, although at the same time, there is usually some link connecting the secondary world back to the Primary World.

Connecting the Secondary World to the Primary World

The boundaries between a secondary world and the Primary World are usually very distinct (so long as the former does not already contain the latter, as in *Star Trek*), and they are important, as they determine who comes and goes into the secondary world. Getting to a secondary world often takes some effort, and many secondary worlds have a kind of "no-man's-land" or area[75] surrounding them which further separates the secondary world from the Primary World, including oceans (around islands), deserts, mountains, and other unoccupied lands that serve as a buffer zone, helping to hide the location (secondary worlds are often hard to find and enter). This buffer zone could also be outer space itself, or the layers of earth covering an underground realm. The buffer zone surrounding a secondary world may also help explain why it is as isolated as it is, and how it has remained separate from the Primary World, and why it is different from it. A buffer zone can also make it difficult for someone to leave the secondary world as well, either because crossing it requires a vehicle of some sort that the character does not have, because an exit cannot be found, or because the world's inhabitants will not permit visitors to leave once they have entered the secondary world. In any event, the connection to the Primary World, when it exists, is one that is carefully considered and controlled.

All secondary worlds reflect or resemble the Primary World in some way; otherwise, we would not be able to relate to them. As Tolkien puts it, "Fantasy does not blur the sharp outlines of the real world; for it depends on them."[76]

Secondary worlds are, to some degree, versions or variations of our own world. Likewise, the main character in stories set in secondary worlds is often a very ordinary sort of person with whom an audience can easily relate, seeing as they are experiencing the new world vicariously through the main character. As C. S. Lewis describes it:

> Every good writer knows that the more unusual the scenes and events of his story are, the slighter, the more ordinary, the more typical his persons should be. Hence Gulliver is a commonplace little man and Alice a commonplace little girl. If they had been more remarkable they would have wrecked their books. The Ancient Mariner himself is a very ordinary man. To tell how odd things struck odd people is to have an oddity too much: he who is to see strange sights must not himself be strange. He ought to be as nearly as possible Everyman or Anyman.[77]

The need for distance and a distinct border around a secondary world, which helps to constitute its secondariness from the Primary World, has already been discussed. Uncharted islands, hidden underground kingdoms, lost worlds hidden in the mountains; these were the settings for most worlds before authors began to situate them on distant planets in other star systems. Wherever they might be located, we are usually given some indication of where they are in relation to where we are, providing a spatial link between worlds, though it is usually a very difficult and treacherous one to cross. Other stories take place in the past or future, connected to us but inaccessible to travelers (except, of course, time travelers).

From early on, framing devices were often employed which linked secondary worlds to the Primary World. In earlier works, in which the secondary world has an earthly location in some unexplored region, the main character often must sail a great distance, or climb through mountain passes or down into elaborate cave systems in order to reach these places. Later stories would find magical, supernatural, or technological means of transporting main characters from the Primary World into a secondary world, whether Alice into Wonderland, Dorothy into Oz, or Neo into the Matrix. Some later stories dispense with framing devices, but the connection to the Primary World remains; stories set in space often include Earth, though on the margins of the story (as in *Star Trek* or *Dune*). *Star Wars*, for example, begins each episode with "A long time ago, in a galaxy far, far away", connecting us both spatially and temporally (albeit very tenuously) with the galaxy we are about to see. Temporal connections are also important; many stories are set in the distant past or the future, out of reach but somehow linked to our place in history, even if alternate histories or imagined time periods are invented. In most cases, there is no narrative need to do this (and not all worlds have these links), but such links appear often enough to suggest that many authors still feel that some spatiotemporal linkage to the audience's experience in the

Primary World helps them relate better to the secondary world, from which they would otherwise be completely detached.

The necessity of linking secondary worlds to the Primary World has lessened over time, however, as audiences have grown accustomed to stranger and more alien worlds. From uncharted islands and underground kingdoms, to planets in outer space, to worlds with no discernable spatiotemporal connection to our own, the range of examples of secondary worlds has grown along with their numbers over time. Their popularity has also increased, especially during the latter half of the twentieth century, and demand for them is still growing; but to fully understand the direction of their development, we must next turn to their history, which reaches back across three millennia and is the topic of the next chapter.

2

A HISTORY OF IMAGINARY WORLDS

> *To confront objects which do not exist as though they existed and to be influenced by them, to believe that they do exist, is not this, since no harm can come of it, a suitable and irreproachable means of providing entertainment?*
>
> —Philostratos the Younger, third century AD[1]

> *I have neither power, time, nor occasion to conquer the world as Alexander and Caesar did; yet rather than not to be mistress of one, since Fortune and the Fates would give me none, I have made a World of my own: for which no body, I hope, will blame me, since it is in every ones power to do the like.*
>
> —Margaret Cavendish, writing about her Blazing-World, in 1666[2]

Before examining how imaginary worlds came about, we might ask *why* they came about; why did authors find it necessary to invent other worlds? Usually, the answer lies in the changing of Primary World defaults, to amaze, entertain, satirize, propose possibilities, or simply make an audience more aware of defaults they take for granted. Just like stories of foreign lands, stories set in imaginary worlds provide the bizarre and exotic, without the need to travel and without needing to be limited to what actually exists.

Secondary worlds make us look differently at the Primary World, and are often used to comment on it. A look at the history of imaginary worlds shows how closely tied they are to the times in which they appear, in their positioning and location, their design, aesthetics, themes, and their structure and purpose, as well as the stories told in them. At the same time, however, secondary worlds often differ greatly from the Primary World, making us more aware of its default assumptions. And as time went on, more and more of these defaults could be changed, as the imaginary-world tradition developed its own conventions and solutions to world-building problems.

Exploring the history and development of subcreated worlds is an ambitious venture that intersects with the history of literature, painting, film, television, animation, comic strips and comic books, video games, and other visual arts, crisscrossed with the history of exploration, utopias, fantasy, science fiction, playsets, board games, role-playing games, interactive fiction, special effects, and computer graphics. Even summaries of these histories is well beyond the scope of this chapter; only their highlights, insofar as they touch upon the development of imaginary worlds, will be given.[3] Nor is there room for detailed descriptions of all the worlds discussed here; but a sense of their place in history and contribution to it will be attempted. From a few fictional islands used as stopping points for travelers to enormous universes which are the work of hundreds of people over several decades and worlds so vast that no individual can possibly experience them in their entirety, imaginary worlds have a long and interesting history, which begins with the first indications of the presence of a world beyond the immediate locale in which a story takes place.

Transnarrative Characters and Literary Cycles

Perhaps the simplest literary indication that a world exists beyond the details needed to tell a particular story is a transnarrative character. A character who appears in more than one story links the stories' worlds together by being present in them, and the character's presence in multiple stories suggests that there is more to the character than what any single story reveals. When multiple characters, objects, and locations from one story appear in another story, the world in which they all appear becomes larger than either story, and the audience begins to build up expectations based on their previous knowledge, and may begin to fill in the gaps between stories, imaginatively adding to the world.

The first transnarrative characters were actual historical figures, like King Nebuchadnezzar II of Babylon, who appears in or is mentioned in several books of the Old Testament (the Second Book of Kings, the First and Second Books of Chronicles, Ezra, Nehemiah, Esther, Jeremiah, and Daniel) as well as other historical texts (like Book VIII of Claudius Josephus' *Antiquities of the Jews*). The world in which these historical figures appeared was the Primary World, and the veracity of stories from different sources about the same characters could be determined by comparing details like the characters' appearance and behavior to see if they were consistent from one story to the next. In the case of fiction, multiple stories about the same characters could help create the illusion of an existence independent of any individual story; thus, transnarrative fictional characters could seem more real than those that only appeared in a single story.

Multiple stories centered around a transnarrative character sometimes result in a literary cycle, which can further develop the world beyond the needs of any specific story. Often an ensemble of characters as well as a network of locations is shared by the stories of a literary cycle, like those surrounding the Trojan War, or King Arthur and the Knights of the Round Table, or Robin Hood. Literary cycles are such that multiple authors may add stories many years apart, making use of an audience's familiarity with the characters and situations of earlier stories in the cycle. To some extent, literary cycles can be seen as precursors of media franchises, wherein a series of works, sometimes produced by multiple authors, features the same characters, objects, and locations. Today's media franchises differ from literary cycles in the way they are deliberately constructed and built upon, often with a framework in mind that encompasses the characters and events of multiple stories or works before they are produced. Likewise, today fictional characters are usually considered the intellectual property of their authors, and unauthorized stories are seen as noncanonical or apocryphal. In any event, transnarrative characters grow as more of their experiences are related and the world they inhabit grows along with them.

Nevertheless, the worlds of transnarrative characters, literary cycles, and media franchises can be set in the Primary World, without a separate, developed secondary world of their own. The move from stories set in Primary World locations to those whose action occurs mainly in well-developed fictional places of considerable size and complexity was one that required reasons for imagining new worlds. The degree to which a world was developed depended on that need, as well as the seriousness with which the design of the world was undertaken. Thus, we find the roots of secondary worlds extending back into Classical Antiquity.

The Mythical and Unknown World

Fantastic places have always gained more credibility by being set in remote or little-known areas of the world where their existence is harder to disprove. In classical antiquity, the inhabitants of the area surrounding the Mediterranean Sea knew relatively little about the world beyond their realms; the oceans, and the land masses that lay to the far north and west, were largely unexplored by them, so they proved fertile ground for the imagination. Likewise, almost every culture had some kind of afterlife destinations or Underworld, such as Hades, the Elysian Fields, Annwn, Toonela, Yum Gan, Uku Pacha, the Fortunate Isles, Adlivun, Hawaiki, and Xibalba, all of which were thought to exist somewhere underground or beyond the horizon, in unknown parts of the world. Moreover, what was known or guessed varied greatly from place to place, as myth and legend were closely interwoven with everyday life. Belief in the pantheons of Greek and Roman gods, legends of heroic figures whose deeds transcended what was humanly possible, and tales passed on orally (growing more elaborate as they traveled), all combined to create a fantastic vision of the world, where the real and the unreal intermixed considerably.

A good example of this can be found in the *Odyssey*. From antiquity to the present day, scholars have tried to map the fictional islands visited by Odysseus and the routes between them onto real locations ranging from the Aegean Sea to as far away as the Atlantic Ocean; that debates concerning the status of the story's geography have continued for so long is a testament to its liminality.[4] The uncharted islands visited or mentioned in the *Odyssey* include Pharos, Ogygie, Scherie, the island of the Cyclops, the island of the Lotus-eaters, the floating island of Aeolus, Aeaea, the island of the Sirens, the island of Helios, Syrie, and Ithaca (whether Homer's Ithaca is the same as the real island of Ithaca is still a matter of debate). In the story, these islands are experienced directly by Odysseus, or described by him or by other characters (Menelaus describes Pharos, and Eumaeus describes Syrie), an example of the two main strategies of easing the burden of exposition created by imaginary worlds. As mentioned earlier, stories involving imaginary worlds often have more information to convey than stories set in a familiar part of the Primary World, since more Primary World defaults have been reset. A main character who is a traveler experiencing the imaginary world for the first time becomes a stand-in for the audience who experiences the world through him or her. Likewise, tales told by other characters are first-person experiences that perform a similar function within the diegesis. From the *Odyssey* onward, these two methods appear in a majority of stories set in secondary worlds, with the *Odyssey* becoming an influential model for subcreators in the centuries that followed.

Another method of introducing an imaginary world is to describe it directly, without recourse to a narrative. A number of historical works of antiquity also contain descriptions of imaginary realms. Herodotus' *Histories* describes the Arimaspi, and includes the author's own doubts about them:

> The northern parts of Europe are very much richer in gold than any other region: but how it is procured I have no certain knowledge. The story runs that the one-eyed Arimaspi purloin it from the griffins; but here too I am incredulous, and cannot persuade myself that there is a race of men born with one eye, who in all else resemble the rest of mankind. Nevertheless it seems to be true that the extreme regions of the earth, which surround and shut up within themselves all other countries, produce the things which are the rarest, and which men reckon the most beautiful.[5]

Other imaginary lands mentioned in ancient histories include the island of Thule in Pytheas' *On the Ocean*, the island of Pankhaia in Diodorus Siculus' *Bibliotheca Historia*, the island of Anostus in Claudius Aelianus' *Varia Historia*, Mount Kunlun in the ancient Chinese text *The Book of the Mountains and the Sea*, and the Southwest Wilderness region of China in Tung-Fang Shuo's *Book of Deities and Marvels*. In *Inventum Natura* and *Naturalis Historia*, Pliny the Elder mentions the Arimaspi and several other imaginary lands: Ear Islands, home of the Auriti, a people with very large ears; Hyperborea, a land of happiness and long life in the far north; and the land of the Blemmyae, a race of headless people whose eyes and mouths are on their chests. Many of these lands and their fantastic inhabitants appeared in the writings of multiple authors, thereby making them more like real historical entities that existed beyond the imaginings of an individual author.

With so much of the world unexplored, entire continents could be proposed and considered. Plato wrote of Atlantis, and in the east, Tung-Fang Shuo wrote of Hsuan in *Accounts of the Ten Continents*. Whether or not such places really existed was something only explorers could disprove, so legends could persist for centuries (some, like the sunken Atlantis, even to the present day). Terra Australis, a great continent supposedly in the southern oceans, appeared in various works into the seventeenth and eighteenth centuries. In *Renaissance and Reformation*, author James Patrick summarizes the history of *Terra Australis*:

> *Terra Australis*, the great southern continent, filled the earth's remotest and most mysterious regions in the popular imagination. A southern *Terra Incognita* ("unknown land") was included on the world map detailed by the second-century Greek geographer Ptolemy, whose works were rediscovered in the fifteenth century. Ptolemy accepted the theory put forward by Aristotle (384–322 BCE) that, since the earth was symmetrical, there must exist frozen lands in the south to balance those of the north. On a 1569 world map drawn by the great Flemish cartographer Gerardus Mercator, a huge *Terra Australis* (the Latin words literally mean "southern landmass") fills the world's southern extremity. Not until James Cook's circumnavigation of Antarctica in the late eighteenth century was the myth of *Terra Australis* finally exploded.[6]

Another imaginary-world tradition that can trace its roots to antiquity is the utopia. The Kallipolis, the ideal city of Plato's *Republic*, is a secondary world used as a philosophical thought experiment, a world in which the foundation and parameters of a human society are reset and used to debate what would happen if people were to live a certain way. Plato not only describes what he thinks a perfect society would be like (establishing what would later become the utopian tradition), but in Book VIII of his dialogue, he also describes the decay of an imperfect state from an aristocracy to a timocracy, to a plutocracy, to a democracy which grows increasingly chaotic and finally falls into tyranny, thus describing what would later be called a dystopia. Plato's city is perhaps the first imaginary world whose societal structure was given serious consideration and described in detail. It is also among the earliest secondary worlds created for reasons beyond that of providing a backdrop for a story, and thus is more of interest in and of itself as a world.

The final use of secondary worlds to develop in classical antiquity was that of satire. The island of Meropis, in the text *Philippica* by Theopompos of Chios, is a parody of Plato's Atlantis, with everything exaggerated, like the continent's size and the size and number of its people, beyond Plato's claims for his continent.

Another world made for comic effect is Aristophanes's city of Nephelokokkygia or "Cloudcuckooland", in his comedy *The Birds*. In it, the two main characters, Pisthetairos and Euelpides, join the kingdom of the birds who take over a city and build a giant wall around it. The city becomes the center of worship, the gods send Poseidon and Hercules to negotiate, and eventually Pisthetairos marries Zeus' maid Basileia and goes to join the gods.

The most sophisticated and elaborate satire of antiquity to make use of a secondary world came late in the classical period, in the second century AD. Lucian of Samosata's *True History* parodies travelers' tales and histories and their literary form and style with a variety of imaginary places and cultures, and which, in his "Introduction", he openly admits is untrue:

> I am myself vain enough to cherish the hope of bequeathing something to posterity; I see no reason for resigning my right to that inventive freedom which others enjoy; and, as I have no truth to put on record, having lived a very humdrum life, I fall back on falsehood—but falsehood of a more consistent variety; for I now make the only true statement you are to expect—that I am a liar. This confession is, I consider, a full defence against all imputations. My subject is, then, what I have neither seen, experienced, nor been told, what neither exists nor could conceivably do so. I humbly solicit my readers' incredulity.[7]

Lucian recognizes that "falsehood of a more consistent variety" is necessary for verisimilitude especially when the fantastic is presented. Even though he clearly does not intend his story to be believed, he provides many details and writes in a style that makes the work sound like the histories of the period, parodying their style as well as content. He describes strange island worlds, including the island of Galatea made of cheese which has fruit-covered vines that give milk; Cork Island whose inhabitants have feet of cork and can walk on water; Cabbalusa where they find women with asses' hooves; Lampton, whose inhabitants are speaking lamps, and even Aristophanes's Cloudcuckooland. The travelers also visit the Elysian Plain and meet Homer, Socrates, Pythagoras, and other historical figures. In one of the longer sections of the story, Lucian describes a war of enormous scale between the Moonites who live on the Moon and the Sunites who live on the Sun, and then goes on to describe the Moonites' culture in detail. The voyage to the moon is also described; the narrator's ship encounters a waterspout which sends it sailing into space for eight days, until they cast anchor on the moon. This interplanetary journey, probably the first in literature, and other elements of the story, such as encounters with alien cultures, have led some to consider *True History* as the first story of the science fiction genre. As S. C. Fredericks writes:

> Because of its powerful mimetic dimension his narrative must not be reduced solely to being satire nor to being a sequence of literary parodies.

Like a modern SF [*science fiction*] writer, Lucian takes the sciences and other cognitive disciplines available to him and pictures alternate worlds which can dislocate the intellects of his readers in such a way as to make them aware of how many of their normal convictions about things were predicated upon cliché thinking and stereotyped response—in areas as diverse as religious belief, aesthetic judgment, and philosophical theory. The "places" visited by the protagonist–narrator are, therefore, intellectual loci, and much more of Lucian's geography is figurative then [*sic*] literal. We really travel with the narrator through a sequence of conceptions and speculations which comment satirically and critically on men's habits of mind in the real world.[8]

Lucian's works, including *True History*, were revived during the Renaissance, enjoying great popularity and influencing writers including Thomas More, Desiderius Erasmus, Ludovico Ariosto, and François Rabelais (More and Erasmus also translated Lucian's work into Latin).[9] Many of these authors would go on to create their own secondary worlds.

By the end of the age of classical antiquity, secondary worlds had already appeared in several of the literary modes that make use of them: tall tales, histories, satires, thought experiments (which include utopias and dystopias), and descriptions of proposed places thought to already exist (like Atlantis or the Elysian Fields). These forms would each develop into a tradition over time, with later works often referencing earlier ones (Lucian's inclusion of Aristophanes's Cloudcuckooland may be the first time an author has connected another author's secondary world to his own).

Over the centuries that followed, Greek and Roman mythology became a part of the "Matter of Rome" in Medieval European literature, alongside other cycles and legends, including the Arthurian legends (the "Matter of Britain"), the legends in the cycles of Charlemagne, Roland, and Guillaume d'Orange (collectively known as the "Matter of France"), and the Mabinogion of Welsh mythology. Many of these stories contained fantastic elements, if not imaginary places, and would provide material for later authors who would continue the cycles and locate them in imaginary worlds.

The early Middle Ages saw the production of secondary worlds continue in the modes established by the ancients. St. Augustine's *City of God* described a utopia not to be found on Earth, and centuries later Dante Alighieri envisioned what heaven, purgatory, and hell might be like in his *Divine Comedy*. Legendary places remained on maps, like the island of Hy Brasil mentioned in Angelinus Dalorto's 1325 thesis *L'Isola Brazil*. Fictional fantastic islands appeared in literature, like Brissonte and Polyglot in *Liber monstrorum de diversis generibus* from around the eighth century, or the desert islands that provided the settings for two eleventh-century Islamic novels, Ibn Tufail's *Hayy ibn Yaqdhan* (in Latin, *Philosophus Autodidactus*), a thought experiment about a feral child rasied by a gazelle on an island, and Ibn al-Nafis' *Al-Risalah al-Kamiliyyah fil Siera al-Nabawiyyah* (*Theologus Autodidactus*), about a feral child found by castaways and taken back to civilization.[10] Another Islamic work, completed around the fourteenth century, *The Book of One Thousand and One Nights* (known in the West as *The Arabian Nights*) contains stories which include an underwater society, the ancient lost "City of Brass", and travel to other worlds. Comedic uses of secondary worlds also continued, as in the anonymously authored *Aucassin et Nicollette* from late-thirteenth-century France which featured the kingdom of Torelore, where the king is pregnant, the Queen leads the troops, and wars are fought with rotten fruit, cheese, and other food items.

The secondary worlds produced during these times ranged in their scope and seriousness, but few of them contained the level of detail and verisimilitude needed to compete with Primary World settings. Of course, competition with the real world was usually not a goal; even proposed continents that cartographers included did not have the detail of actual landmasses since they remained undiscovered. However, by the end of the Medieval period, new inspiration for the creation of secondary worlds would spur their production and demand a greater degree of detail and verisimilitude, as audience began reading travelers' tales of actual journeys undertaken by explorers seeking new worlds during the Age of Exploration.

Travelers' Tales and the Age of Exploration

The intermixing of fiction and nonfiction continued through Medieval times and into the Renaissance as a genre of literature known sometimes as "travelers' tales" or "travel writing". The premise of each work is a traveler, traveling in lands foreign to the reader, who narrates his adventures and especially the strange sights he sees along the way, including new countries and their peoples and cultures. Although some works were deliberately intended as fiction, even the journals of actual travelers could contain exaggeration or fantastic elements resulting from either the difficulty in verbally describing the new things or descriptions resulting from misperceptions of them; Marco Polo described the rhinoceros as a "unicorn" because of its large single horn, and descriptions of headless men with faces on their chests is said to have perhaps been a misperception of natives with their shoulders raised high around their heads. As travelers' tales related stories of distant lands, little verification was available to readers, apart from tales by other travelers to the same lands; and some places believed to be real, like El Dorado, the mythical city of gold, would themselves become the inspiration for expeditions.

Although tales of travels had always existed, a landmark of travel writing that would redefine the genre was produced by the explorer Marco Polo. During his imprisonment by the Genoese in 1298, Polo dictated stories about his travels in Asia and China, and the resulting book, *Il Milione*, later known as *The Description of the World* or *The Travels of Marco Polo*, was very successful, and later led to Polo to write a new edition between 1310 and 1320. Polo's book would become the main source of information on the Far East for Europeans, and a later inspiration to Christopher Columbus. Besides inspiring exploration, the book also had its imitators, most notably the fictional work *The Book of Sir John Mandeville* from c. 1357. Mandeville's *Book* attained great popularity in Europe and by the 1470s there were versions in English, French, Anglo–Norman French, German, Flemish, Czech, Castilian, Aragonese, Latin, Italian, Danish, and Gaelic, and 72 editions of the book were printed during the fifteenth and sixteenth centuries.[11]

As exploration increased, more travelers' tales appeared, and their audience grew as well. As Rosemary Tzanaki writes in *Mandeville's Medieval Audiences*:

> New knowledge of the East was also flowing in during the thirteenth cen-
> tury, following the conquest of Constantinople and the opening of routes
> via the Black Sea, and in particular because of the stability and security of
> Central Asia following the Mongol invasion. A new East was soon to
> appear through the works of travelers like John of Plano Carpini, William
> of Rubruck and Odoric of Pordenone, among the first to journey to the
> Tartar Empire. Marco Polo also benefited from the more secure trade
> routes to China. By Mandeville's time, Mamluk expansion and the conver-
> sion of the Khans of the Golden Horde to Islam had reduced the Christian
> access to the East once more, but this only served to increase interest in
> those lands. Pilgrim itineraries to the Holy Land were also becoming ever
> more popular. It was in this climate of geographical enthusiasm and curios-
> ity that the *Book* was written.[12]

The Book of Sir John Mandeville mixes factual travel information, which scholars have identified as being copied from the works of others, with fictional fantastic locations and peoples. Among them are the kingdom of Amazony "whereas dwelleth none but women"; the kingdom of Salmasse with its venomous trees; the kingdom of Talonach where fish come on land to worship the king, who has over a thousand wives; the land of Raso where men are hung if they get sick; the island of Macumeran where the people have heads like hounds; the island of Silo with its four-legged serpents, two-headed geese, and white lions; and the island of cyclopses (see Figure 2.1). Several of the peoples he describes, like the Blemmyae and a race of one-legged men, seem to be taken from Pliny, and scholars have identified many other sources from which the author (who may or may not have been called Mandeville) compiled and copied his stories. Such fantastic tales and places made the book popular, and Sir Henry Yule, writing in his 1871 work *The Book of Ser Marco Polo*, compared its popularity to that of Polo's book:

> And from the greatest frequency with which one encounters in catalogues
> both MSS. and early printed editions of Sir John Maundeville [*sic*], I should

FIGURE 2.1 Examples of the 119 woodcut images that accompanied the 1481 edition of *The Book of John Mandeville* (circa 1357): a cockodrill of Silha (top left); an ox-headed man (top, right); the two-headed wild geese of Silha (center, left); a Blemmyae (center, right); a giant cyclops (bottom, left); and an Ethiopian with one foot (bottom, right).

suppose that the lying wonders of our English knight had a far greater popularity and more extensive diffusion than the veracious and more sober marvels of Polo. In Quaritch's last catalogue (November, 1870) there is only one *old* edition of Polo; there are nine of Maundeville. In 1839 there were nineteen MSS. of the latter catalogued in the British Museum Library. There are now only five of Marco Polo. At least twenty-five editions of Maundeville, and only five of Polo were printed in the fifteenth century.[13]

The texts' popularity is not necessarily an indication that they were believed to be true; even Polo encountered much disbelief in his stories. At the same time, however, books like Polo's provided a new level of detail and verisimilitude for authors of secondary worlds to imitate, and made the role of the main character more important in achieving such an effect. As Tzanaki writes:

> ...the author's authority is based not on the written *authoritas* of his stories but on his traveller-*persona* of Sir John. As Rubiés and Elsner have discussed, "after Marco Polo the authority of the traveller replaced that of the book; the book was only authoritative if the traveller whose report it contained was authoritative too". The author of the *Book* accordingly created a traveller with a consistently developed personality to give his unacknowledged compilation a voice. Although we now know he never truly existed, "Sir John Mandeville" contributed immensely to the *Book*'s reception by linking the accounts he used and constantly reinforcing their veracity. ... "Sir John Mandeville" constantly inserts personal comments into the narrative, describing his experiences (he has been in the service of both the Sultan of Egypt and the Emperor of Cathay) and stressing that he has seen many wonders with his own eyes. ... In inspired displays of verisimilitude, the author of the *Book* even makes "Mandeville" deny seeing some marvels in order to lend greater credence to his other assertions. He cheekily explains the omission of some lands and "diverse things" by saying that he wants to leave something for others to record.[14]

In stories of the travelers' tales genre, the story's world and its uniqueness is, to some degree, the main reason for the tale itself, and its main character is the vehicle by which the audience is vicariously transported to that world. The central importance given to the story's world and its oddities is evident when the travelers' tales genre is compared to another genre of the time that made use of imaginary locations: knight-errantry tales, like Thomas Mallory's *Le Morte d'Arthur* (1485) or the influential Spanish *Amadis de Gaula* (1508) of unknown authorship. Although fictional settings appear, the emphasis in these stories is usually on character and action, which one would expect in tales of chivalry. For example, Matteo Maria Boiardo's *Orlando Innamorato* ("Orlando in Love", left unfinished at the time of his death in 1494 and published the following year) mentions the city of Albracca and the kingdoms of Sericana, Aronda, Orgagna, Baldacca, Damogir, Lissa, and the Distant Isles, but develops them very little if at all, and some locations mentioned are never even visited. Its sequel, Ludovico Ariosto's *Orlando Furioso* ("Orlando Enraged", 1516), one of the longest poems in Western literature at over 38,000 lines, continues the tale, adding lands, including Alcina's Island, Ebuda, and Nubia, as well as Astolpho's journey to the moon with St. John to find a cure for Orlando's madness. The moon is the one location described in detail, but it is mostly a landscape of symbolic imagery rather than a habitable place. As chivalric notions declined, so did knight-errantry tales, until they were parodied in works like Cervantes' *Don Quixote* (*El ingenioso hidalgo Don Quixote de La Mancha*, 1605 and Part II in 1615), which included Barataria, a fictional island within the story, the governorship of which is promised to Sancho Panza.

Travel writing, both fictional and nonfictional, could also comment on current affairs in politics, through allegories, utopias (discussed in the next section), or satire, and often employed the travelers' tales format which introduced worlds through the explorer's eyes and used them as parodies of existing societies or outlandish tall tales.[15] The books of François Rabelais' bawdy Gargantua and Pantagruel series (appearing 1532–1564), about a father and son who are both giants, introduce a variety of worlds, mostly in the form of islands. Perhaps the most outrageous world presented in his work is the country of Aspharage, located in Pantagruel's mouth:

> I passed amongst the rocks, which were his teeth, and never left walking till I got up on one of them; and there I found the pleasantest places in the world, great large tennis courts, fair galleries, sweet meadows, store of vines, and an infinite number of banqueting summer outhouses in the fields, after the Italian fashion, full of pleasure and delight, where I stayed full four months, and never made better cheer in my life as then. After that I went down by the hinder teeth to come to the chaps. But in the way I was robbed by thieves in a great forest that is in the territory towards the ears. Then, after a little further travelling, I fell upon a pretty petty village— truly I have forgot the name of it—where I was yet merrier than ever, and got some certain money to live by. Can you tell how? By sleeping. For there they hire men by the day to sleep, and they get by it sixpence a day, but they that can snort hard get at least ninepence. How I had been robbed in the valley I informed the senators, who told me that, in very truth, the people of that side were bad livers and naturally thievish, whereby I perceived well that, as we have with us the countries Cisalpine and Transalpine, that is, behither and beyond the mountains, so have they there the countries Cidentine and Tradentine, that is, behither and beyond the teeth. But it is far better living on this side, and the air is purer. Then I began to think that it is very true which is commonly said, that the

one half of the world knoweth not how the other half liveth; seeing none before myself had ever written of that country, wherein are above five-and-twenty kingdoms inhabited, besides deserts, and a great arm of the sea. Concerning which purpose I have composed a great book, entitled, The History of the Throttias, because they dwell in the throat of my master Pantagruel.[16]

While satires, similar to knight-errantry tales, presented worlds which were different enough to be overtly fictional, or were at the very least not intended to deceive, other imaginary places were more readily combined with actual ones. Maps would feature them, sometimes with names that indicated their questionable status (such as *Terra Incognita*), sometimes as newly discovered lands, and sometimes as named lands with specific geography and detailed coastlines, as though there was no question as to their existence. Some fictional lands were misrepresentations of other places; the island known as Thule was probably Iceland, and the island of Estotiland may have been Labrador or Nova Scotia. Other lands remained on maps until disproven by further exploration. For example, Antillia, an island believed to exist in the Atlantic ocean somewhere west of Portugal, appeared on maps including the chart made by Zuane Pizzigano around 1424, maps made by Genoese Beccario, Andrea Bianco, Grazioso Benincasa, and many others throughout the 1400s, and Christopher Columbus even planned to stop at Antillia on his way across the ocean in 1492. As knowledge of the ocean grew, Antillia shrank and finally disappeared from maps around 1587.[17]

As more travelers journeyed and returned, maps grew more complete and accurate, and more travel literature appeared. With multiple authors writing about the same areas, not only were more facts available, but stories could be compared for consistency and checked with other sources. This in turn would change the nature of travel literature itself. According to Nathalie Hester:

> When foreign lands were less or barely known, travel writing was esteemed above all as a container of invaluable and rare information… Later on, as more travelers roamed the globe and facts and data became increasingly accessible, travelers dedicated more of their exploratory energies to new ways of narrating their journeys. In the late sixteenth and seventeenth centuries, many… began focusing more on their roles as narrators and protagonists and on developing their own poetics of travel writing. In short, a more personalized narrative of travel became as much a subject of investigation as the factual elements of the journey itself.[18]

As travel narratives grew more personalized and audiences more sophisticated, imaginary worlds had to keep pace with them. It was no longer enough to merely describe a world's inhabitants; interaction with them was needed, and more detail as to their societies, customs, and cultures was necessary to match the increased verisimilitude found in nonfictional travel writing. Maps were sometimes included to give a visual dimension to imaginary places; for example, Fr. Zacharie de Lisieux's *Relation du pays de Jansénie, où il est traité des singularitez qui s'y trouvent, des coustumes, Moeurs et Religion des habitants* (1660), a satire on Jansenism, had a map of the country (an oblique one, showing buildings and people in a land-scape) added to its English translation in 1668; and Swift's *Gulliver's Travels* (1726) had maps of its islands, even though both works were not intended to be taken as true stories.

However, some authors hoped their imaginary places would be taken as real. In his book *Travelers and Travel Liars 1660–1800*, Percy Adams identifies three types of travel writing: true tales of travels, fictional tales that were intended to be seen as such, and fictional tales which were passed off as real by their authors (who Adams calls "travel liars"). Adams' book is most concerned with the third group, of whom he writes:

> And they have been important, so important that one of them caused the newspapers of the world to use up a small river of ink reporting a race of nine-foot giants in Patagonia; so important that another team of them could persuade the Academy of Sciences in Paris to spend hours discussing a spurious Northwest Passage; so important that historians quoted them; cartographers changed maps to conform to them, wits like Voltaire used them, readers were entertained by them, and philosophers like Buffon depended on them.[19]

These "travel liars" plagiarized existing travel accounts (even some written by other liars), and did research using books like the *Atlas Geographus* of 1717 to give their stories the verisimilitude they needed. While many kept their imaginary voyages confined to real locations in order to make their claims sound more plausible, others ventured into imaginary places, the details of which were made as realistic as possible. The contribution of "travel liars" to secondary worlds was an increase in the kind of detail that made locations seem real, moving both "travel lies" and fiction in the direction of worlds that were richer and fuller than the mere glimpses and outrageous descriptions found in earlier works.

Due to their similarities, it is sometimes difficult to completely separate "travel lies" from works that were not intended to deceive; partly because some authors' motives were not always entirely clear, some critics recognized hoaxes early on, and some readers believed stories which were intended as fiction. Both types of writing could aspire to verisimilitude, if not to realism, while still emphasizing the fantastic and exotic; and both took place in remote and inaccessible places, such as lands in the Americas which remained unexplored, or in the south seas, or in *Terra Australis* (for example, Joseph Hall's *Mundus alter et idem, sive Terra Australis ante hac semper incognita* (1605), Gabriel Foigny's *Les Aventures De Jacques Sadeur* (1676), or Denis Vairasse D'Allais' *Histoire des Sevarambes* (five volumes in the 1670s)).

The secondary worlds of these stories ranged along the spectrum from fantastic to realistic, since even authors who did not intend to deceive could still try to be as convincing as possible without resorting to the same truth-claims as travel lies.

The most popular and influential book of the travelers' tale genre, and also one categorized by Adams as a "travel lie", was Daniel Defoe's *Robinson Crusoe* (1719) (see the Appendix for the full titles of this book and others mentioned in this chapter). *Robinson Crusoe* became one of the most reprinted books in the English language, and had so many imitators that they became a genre unto themselves, known as "robinsonades", and books of a similar nature published before Defoe's came to be called "prerobinsonades" (including Henry Neville's novel *The Isle of Pines* (1668), about George Pines, who is shipwrecked on a deserted island along with four women; after 59 years, due to their polygamous behavior, the island has a population of 1,789). Existing stories were even repackaged with new titles that had "Robinson" in them; as Philip Babcock Gove writes:

> When authors could not supply the demand, publishers did not hesitate to rechristen fictitious heroes already flourishing. Thus, among a score, *Gil Blas* (1715) became *Der spanische Robinson* (1726), *Krinke Kesmes* (1708) became *Der holländische Robinson* (1721), and *François Leguat* (1707) became *Der französische Robinson* (1723). Even supposedly true voyage-accounts were not exempt; Antonio Zucchelli's *Relazioni del viaggio e missione di Congo* (1712) became *Der geistliche Robinson* (1723).[20]

Gove also mentions a bibliography compiled by Hermann Ullrich that lists 196 English editions of Robinson Crusoe, along with 110 translations, 115 revisions, and 277 imitations.[21]

As secondary worlds go, Crusoe's Island is small, but depicted very realistically and in great detail; its low degree of invention helps to explain its believability and the ease with which it was imitated. Crusoe, and much later Friday, are the island's only human inhabitants (the cannibals and Spaniards being merely visitors), and the island's small size becomes evident early on, when Crusoe looks out over it:

> My next work was to view the country, and seek a proper place for my habitation, and where to stow my goods to secure them from whatever might happen; where I was, I yet knew not, whether on the continent or an island, whether inhabited, whether in danger of wild beasts or not. There was a hill not above a mile from me, which rose up very steep and high, and which seemed to over-top some other hills, which lay as in a ridge from it northward; I took out one of the following pieces, and one of the pistols, and an horn of powder, and thus armed I travelled for discovery up to the top of that hill, where after I had with great labour and difficulty got to the top, I saw my fate to my great affliction, viz. that I was on an

island environed every way with the sea, no land to be seen, except some
rocks which lay a great way off, and two small islands less than this, which
lay about three leagues to the west.[22]

Unlike most travelers who are merely passing through the lands they describe,
Crusoe lives on the island for 28 years and comes to know it well. *Robinson Crusoe*,
then, earns its place in the history of secondary worlds based not on the size of
its world, but on the degree to which Defoe developed it and the number
of imitators it inspired.

Seven years later another influential book appeared, with fantastic inhabited
lands and their cultures; Jonathan Swift's innovative satire, *Gulliver's Travels*
(1726). In it, detailed accounts are given of the islands of Lilliput, Blefuscu,
Balnibarbi, Luggnagg, Glubbdubdrib, the island of the Houyhnhnms, the flying
island of Laputa, and the peninsula of Brobdingnag, as well as the cultures of their
peoples, and even how the human Gulliver appears from their point of view. As
a result, the cultures depicted are well-rounded, and we are even given glimpses
of their history; for example, the backstory behind the conflict between the
Lilliputians and the Blefuscudians, which has to do with how they break their
eggs. Swift even suggests Lilliputian culture extends beyond the book, stating:

> But I shall not anticipate the Reader with farther Descriptions of this Kind,
> because I reserve them for a greater Work, which is now almost ready for
> the Press; containing a general Description of this Empire, from its first
> Erection, through a long Series of Princes, with a particular Account of
> their Wars and Politiks, Laws, Learning, and Religion; their Plants and
> Animals, their peculiar Manners and Customs, with other Matters very
> curious and useful; my chief Design at present being only to relate such
> Events and Transactions as happened to the Publick, or to my self, during
> a Residence of about Nine Months in that Empire.[23]

Like no other book before it, *Gulliver's Travels* struck a balance between
fantastic elements and realistic description, allowing the reader to picture things
vividly no matter how strange they may be. For example, Swift gives a lengthy
explanation of how the flying island of Laputa stays aloft and is steered, raised, and
lowered, as well as why it cannot drift away from the island of Balnibarbi over
which it flies, and the consequences of immortality experienced by the *Struldbruggs*
of Luggnugg. Descriptions of architecture, language, customs, landscapes, and
other attention to detail surpassed the verisimilitude found in other satires, and
equaled that of other long fiction of the time like *Crusoe*, setting a new standard
for literary secondary worlds.

As the eighteenth century drew on, island worlds continued to appear, in
dozens of imitations, robinsonades, and unauthorized sequels to *Gulliver's Travels*,
along with more original places like Cacklogallinia, a land of giant chickens and

other birds, in Samuel Brunt's *A Voyage to Cacklogallinia* (1727), a satire inspired by the South Sea Bubble of 1720 and the economic conditions surrounding it. The island of Cantahar, from De Varennes de Mondasse's *La Découverie De L'Empire De Cantahar* (1730), had new species including the dangerous *picdar*, the lazy *igriuo*, and the *tigrelis* used to pull carriages. Countries in unexplored continental interiors also appeared, like Drexara, a region in North America and home to a savage Indian tribe, from Abbé Antoine François Prévost's *Le Philosphe anglois, ou Histoire de Monsieur Cleveland* (1731); or Mezzorania, an African country where there is no competition or egoism, from Simon Berington's *The Memoirs of Sigr. Gaudentio di Lucca* (1737).

As more of the world became known and mapped, some authors found a new place to locate their worlds that was not only difficult for explorers to reach but would also not appear on maps: underground, deep beneath the earth's surface. This choice of location may have been influenced by nonfiction works like Athanasius Kircher's *Mundus Subterraneus* (1665), which suggested that the earth's interior contained channels and fire chambers. Earlier underground worlds were either more mythical or allegorical in nature, like Hades or the circles of Hell described in Dante's *Divine Comedy*. Hans Jakob Christoffel von Grimmelshausen's *Der abenteuerliche Simplicissimus Teusch* (1668), sometimes claimed to be the first adventure novel written in German, includes a journey to "Centrum Terrae", a kingdom deep inside the earth, reached through lakes and waterways. The place is inhabited by mortal water-spirits or "sylphs" and their king, and it is only through the use of a magic stone that the story's main character, Simplicissimus, is able to travel there:

> Meanwhile there rose up here and there more of such water-spirits, like diving birds, all looking upon me and bringing up again the stones I had cast in, which amazed me much. And the first and chiefest among them, whose raiment shone like pure gold and silver, cast to me a shining stone of bigness of a pigeon's egg and green and transparent as an emerald, with these words: "Take thou this trinket, that thou mayst have somewhat to report of us and of our lake." But scarce had I picked it up and pocketed it when it seemed to me the air would choke or drown me, so that I could not stand upright but rolled about like a ball of yarn, and at last fell into the lake. Yet no sooner was I in the water than I recovered, and through the virtue of the stone I had upon me could breathe in water instead of air: yea, I could with small effort float in the lake as well as could the water-spirits, yea, and with them descended into the depths; which reminded me of nothing so much as of a flock of birds that so descend in circles from the upper air to light upon the ground.[24]

Because Centrum Terrae is inhabited by spirits and uninhabitable by humans, it has as much in common with Dante's metaphysical places as it does with the other physical places visited by Simplicissimus, in some ways bridging the gap between the two types of worlds.

After 1700, underground worlds took on more solidity and became like other earthly locations ripe for exploration. The country of Rufsal, in Simon Tyssot de Patot's *La Vie, Les Aventures, & le Voyage de Groenland Du Révérend Père Cordelier Pierre De Mesange* (1720), had four underground cities with its entrance near the North Pole; earlier "Hollow Earth" theories often suggested that entrances would be near the poles.[25] Rufsal is probably the earliest instance of a "Hollow Earth" in fiction, a subgenre of literature that continues to the present.[26]

Along with the new setting for secondary worlds came new world-building problems and practical concerns like lighting, oxygen, food production, and how the inhabitants came to live there. Over the years, authors have found a variety of solutions to such problems. For example, regarding lighting: Rufsal is lit by a mysterious fireball; Baron Ludvig Holberg's Nazar (from *Nicolai Klimii Iter Subterraneum Novam Telluris Theoriam* (1741)) and Edgar Rice Burroughs's Pellucidar are both lit by subterranean suns inside the hollow earth (individual homes in Nazar are lit by luminous creatures called *sweecoes*); the creatures that live underneath Anderson's Rock in Ralph Morris' *A Narrative of the Life and Astonishing Adventures of John Daniel* (1751) live near the surface and catch "oil-fish" which give them the oil which they use to light their underground homes; and Rand and Robyn Miller's underground cavern of the D'ni is lit by a lake inhabited by bioluminescent plankton. In some cases, a world's inhabitants were designed for subterranean life, like the burrowing half-man, half-worm Worm-men of Trisolday, in Charles Fieux de Mouhy's *Lamékis* (1735). And there are also the Megamicroes, who live underground *within* an underground world; in Giacomo Girolamo Casanova di Seingalt's *Icosaméron* (1788), Protocosmo is an island floating on a muddy layer of the concave interior of the hollow earth, which is lit by a globe in the earth's center, and the Megamicroes live underground on the island itself. Subterranean worlds would continue to appear in the works of Jules Verne, Edgar Rice Burroughs, and others, representing a step toward more imaginative worlds with their own unique problems of feasibility for authors to solve, and worlds less like existing earthly foreign cultures than surface-based imaginary worlds had been.

Also during the 1700s, an increasing number of worlds, both above and below ground, appeared in stories in which the world itself was given more emphasis than the travels that brought characters to and from the world. Descriptions of languages, laws, and customs would be related during the main character's extended stay, like Peter Wilkins' many years living with the flying Glumms and Gawreys of Sass Doorpt Swangeanti (the Great Flight Land) in Robert Paltock's *The Life and Adventures of Peter Wilkins* (1751). Wilkins interacts with the world he enters to an exceptional degree unusual for the time; he marries one of the native women and starts a family with her, stops an attempt to overthrow the kingdom, brings about a technological revolution by introducing European technology, and persuades the kingdom to abolish slavery, all before his wife dies and he decides to return to England in his old age.

Besides the main character's narration in these stories, natives would also appear and explain their worlds directly. Occasionally, such details about a world and its wonders proved to be prophetic. In Giphantie, the land of Charles François Tiphaigne de la Roche's 1760 book of the same name (which was an anagram of Tiphaigne), there is a scene in which the main character is told how pictures are made:

> You know, that rays of light reflected from different bodies form pictures, paint the image reflected on all polished surfaces, for example, on the retina of the eye, on water, and on glass. The spirits have sought to fix these fleeting images; they have made a subtle matter by means of which a picture is formed in the twinkling of an eye. They coat a piece of canvas with this matter, and place it in front of the object to be taken. The first effect of this cloth is similar to that of a mirror, but by means of its viscous nature the prepared canvas, as is not the case with the mirror, retains a fac-simile of the image. The mirror represents images faithfully, but retains none; our canvas reflects them no less faithfully, but retains them all. This impression of the image is instantaneous. The canvas is then removed and deposited in a dark place. An hour later the impression is dry, and you have a picture the more precious in that no art can imitate its truthfulness.[27]

This prediction of photography, made 66 years before the first permanent photograph was made by Joseph Nicéphore Niépce in 1826, shows how the imaginative potential of secondary worlds can foreshadow technological advances, and such speculation would especially be taken up in the genre of science fiction (discussed later in this chapter).

Although the travelers' tale genre would decline in the early 1800s, the framing device of using journeys to and from a world to bookend the visit to that world would never fall out of use. Nevertheless, the importance of such journeys and the amount of time spent describing them would shrink as the emphasis shifted to the world itself, which was beginning to take center stage as the location where most of the story took place. Eventually, when such framing devices were no longer needed and main characters could be inhabitants of a world instead of merely visitors to them, the main character's journey of exploration could take place entirely within the world itself, as the character moved from the world's margins to its center, learning about the world along with the audience. For example, Tolkien's hobbits leave the Shire and learn about Middle-earth en route to Gondor and Mordor; Luke Skywalker leaves Tatooine to join the conflict between the Rebel Alliance and the Empire; and Neo leaves his desk job to discover what the Matrix is. These journeys are not unlike the traveler's journeys in earlier works, but they take place entirely within their secondary worlds.[28]

By the start of the nineteenth century, secondary worlds had become more detailed as authors sought to answer more questions about their worlds. With every answer, however, came further questions about how the worlds worked, particularly their social, cultural, and technological aspects. As the prediction of photography cited in the preceding text illustrates, imaginative inquiry into technological possibilities was growing and would soon eclipse travel literature in the public imagination as the Industrial Age began producing new scientific and industrial marvels. According to Adams:

> ...the great age for such literature was over with the advent of the steam-boat and the steam locomotive, when real travelers became so numerous that false ones were both less necessary and more easily exposed. But the fireside travelers of the eighteenth century continued to exert their influence. ... The historical and adventure novels, from Smollett's *Roderick Random* to Cooper's *Afloat and Ashore* to Waltari's *The Egyptian*, have learned from the school of Defoe that by applying the tools of the scholar they can add color, concreteness, and verisimilitude to the lands where their heroes go.[29]

Imaginary worlds did more than influence fiction writing, they also helped people grow more aware of the default assumptions of their own worldviews, as well as their ethnocentrism. As Adams writes:

> But the influence went beyond belles-lettres. In a period when tolerance, democracy, and relativity became important, no thinker or historian could do without the voyagers, who taught that each nation had a distinctive, even appropriate, way of life. They inspired studies in comparative religion, comparative natural history, and comparative government. Although their great wealth of illustrative material has sometimes caused historians to decry their lack of "ideas", the ratio of original thinkers among them was no doubt as high as it was for any class of writers.[30]

While travelers' tales wrought visions of remote and exotic locales which they later sought to flesh out into societies and cultures, another concurrent branch of literature used secondary worlds to construct imaginary societal structures, at first abstractly and later with increasing attention to their aesthetic dimension and concrete details: the literature of utopias and dystopias.

Utopias and Dystopias

While the imaginary worlds of travelers' tales focused mainly on their inhabitant's customs, aesthetics, and cultural differences, utopic fiction of the same period concentrated more on the social, political, and economic structures of the worlds they described. Of course, much overlap exists between the two strands of literature, since a utopia can be a traveler's destination. As Gove writes:

> The imaginary voyage frequently offers a double opportunity to the utopist. The voyager's native guide—the conventional figure who teaches him the language and explains the customs—usually relates the story of the founding of his commonwealth; if the people are descended from Europeans, then their origins involve an earlier voyage and shipwreck. So the utopist, perhaps not artistically interested in writing fiction at all, finds in the imaginary voyage the readiest vehicle, especially in the seventeenth and eighteenth centuries, for his optimism and enjoyment of vicarious justice.[31]

Travel appears in early utopic fiction, but the journeys to the utopia and back to Europe are relegated to a thin framing device that brackets the description of the utopia, which is often nonnarrative in form and more typically a social proposal or thought experiment than a story.

The utopic tradition can be traced back to antiquity (including such things as the Garden of Eden and Hesiod's Golden Age), with Kallipolis, the ideal city of Plato's *Republic*, the most detailed and sophisticated example from ancient times. As it includes an analysis of a society falling into tyranny, *Republic* also anticipates the idea of a *dystopia* (or "bad place"; the term itself would not appear until the 1860s), although the difference between a utopia and dystopia largely depends on the point of view of what someone considers desirable for a society; in Kallipolis, for example, all music, art, literature, painting, and architecture must conform to standards set by the State and serve its interests, a state of affairs many would consider dystopic. As such, both utopias and dystopias will be considered here in tandem.

Like travelers' tales, early utopias were an extension of speculation regarding the new lands being explored, and were set in their vicinity. According to historians Frank E. Manuel and Fritzie P. Manuel:

> Much of Western utopia can be related to the acquisition of the known visible world by the peoples of the peninsula of Europe. ... Imaginary societies are situated along the general path of actual conquests, discoveries, and explorations. In the wake of Alexander's drive to the heart of Asia, Euhemerus, a Hellenistic Greek, found a good order of society on Panchaïa, an island on the Indian Ocean. The trader Iambulus, probably a Syrian metic, abandoned to the sea by his Ethiopian captors as a sacrificial offering, told how his boat had drifted to Islands of the Sun somewhere near the east coast of Africa. Other Greek writers claimed acquaintance with the happy Hyperboreans and the men of Ultima Thule on the edge of the European continent. ... throughout the Middle Ages new lands were constantly being incorporated into the utopian mappamundi from the seas to the west of Europe and Africa.[32]

Although utopic worlds like Plato's Kallipolis, St. Augustine's Eternal Jerusalem in his *City of God* (426 AD), the mythical land of Cockaigne, and Christine de Pisan's City of Ladies in *La Cité des Dames* (1405) set forth what their authors considered to be ideal places, the most influential early utopic writing was St. Thomas More's *Concerning the Best State of a Commonwealth and the New Island of Utopia* (1516), otherwise known as *Utopia*. The book was supposedly the recorded discourse of one Rafael Hythlodaeus, who traveled to Utopia, lived there five years, and then returned to Europe to tell about it. *Utopia* is also important from the point of view of the development of imaginary worlds. First, it is one of the earliest worlds to appear along with a map; the first edition (1516) had one drawn by an unknown hand, and the 1518 edition had one drawn by the Dutch painter Ambrosius Holbein (brother of Hans Holbein the Younger); both were woodcuts and contained an oblique view of the island. Other more realistic cartographic maps would come later, such as those by Abraham Ortelius around 1595 and Brian R. Goodey in 1970. An attempt to map Utopia is possible because More gives a detailed description of the shape of the island, complete with measurements in miles, though inconsistencies make a map following all his figures impossible.[33] The description of the urban plan shared by Utopia's 54 city-states, however, is consistent and practical, and amenable to mapping. But while Utopia's small-scale planning relates to its social design as a garden state, its large-scale design does not. As Goodey writes:

> "Utopia" was not written as a geography. The locale of More's society is almost incidental to the social structure that he describes, and as a result the maps included in the present paper are based on only a few sections of description. As Surtz suggests, a better title for the popular editions of the book might have been "The Best State of a Commonwealth"; for much of the work does not rely on the geography of the imaginary state of Utopia for its effect.[34]

Thus, More's *Utopia* is an early example of the inclusion of things beyond the immediate needs of the story (or in this case, the description of a culture and society). Some backstory is also given, for example, how the island was called "Abraxa" before it was renamed for King Utopus, and that Utopian civilization is more than 1,200 years old. Details about the neighboring countries of the Polylerites, the Macarians, the Achorians, and the Anemolians are given when comparisons are made between them and the Utopians. Ancillary materials included in the early editions of *Utopia* include a map (see Figure 2.2), letters written by More and others (which speak of Utopia as though it were a real place), and the Utopian alphabet and a quatrain written in the Utopian language (see Figure 3.4), making Utopia one of the first secondary worlds to have its own script and language sample. These last were apparently the work of Peter Giles, the author of one of the letters included and the recipient of several others, making Utopia, to a small degree, an early example of a collaboratively authored world.[35]

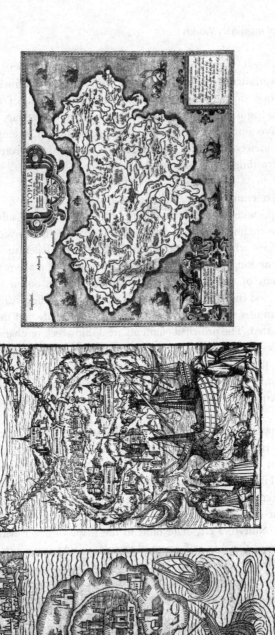

FIGURE 2.2 Maps of Thomas More's island of Utopia, from 1516 (left) and from 1518 (center), both attributed to Ambrosius Holbein; and from 1595, drawn by cartographer Abraham Ortelius (right).

Much of *Utopia*, especially Book II, is concerned with social and political structures, government, religion, education, customs, and routines of daily life, the content one now expects to find in the description of an imaginary society. *Utopia* inspired a host of imitators and began the literary genre of the same name, diverging from the travelers' tales genre in that its emphasis was on the imaginary society described, rather than the journey to or from the society's homeland. According to Manuel and Manuel:

> In the sixteenth and seventeenth centuries, descriptive works that imitated the Utopia were called utopias, with a miniscule, and they adhered more or less to the traditional literary devices that More himself received from Lucian of Samosata, who in turn had inherited them from Hellenistic novels, many of them no longer extant. The invention of printing made readily available translations of tales of this character from one European language into another, and they came to constitute an ever-expanding corpus, in which stock formulas and concepts can be traced historically and their modifications charted. The principal elements are a shipwreck or chance landing on the shores of what turns out to be an ideal commonwealth, a return to Europe, and a report on what has been remarked. If arranged in chronological order these works, considered "proper utopias" by bibliographers, form a sequence in which the imitation of predecessors is patent.[36]

Despite some positive advances, More's Utopia still had slavery, and many other utopias of the time also had aspects that would be considered dystopic today. Johann Eberlin von Günzburg's *Wolfaria* (1521), the first Protestant utopia, depicted a land in which everything was under governmental control, with harsh punishments like execution and drowning for such minor infractions as public drunkenness or saying the wrong prayers. Anton Doni's *I Mondi* (1552) introduced Mondo Nouvo, a city-state built in the shape of a star with 100 streets radiating out from the doors of a central temple, in which everyone's dress and meals are uniform, families are abolished, and women held in common. Women and children are both held in common in Tommaso Campanella's *The City of the Sun* (1623). Thus, the dividing line between utopic and dystopic depends on one's own desires and beliefs.[37]

As some of the descriptions mentioned above reveal, most utopias were dreamt up by men, and tended toward male chauvinism. However, the Renaissance also saw some of the first subcreated worlds made by women, for whom utopias were a way to imagine worlds which countered the male-dominated and misogynist attitudes of the time.[38] In 1405, Christine de Pisan wrote her utopian *La Cité des Dames* (*The City of Ladies*), an allegorical city composed of famous women from history. In 1659, Anne Marie Louise Henriette d'Orléans, Duchesse De Montpensier, wrote two short novels, *La Princesse de Paphlagonie*, about the kingdom of Misnie, and *Rélation de L'Isle Imaginaire*, about Imaginary Island, and both were published under the name of her secretary, Segrais. A year later, Madeleine De Scudéry, known for writing some of the longest novels of the time, included a map of Tendre, an imaginary land (see Figure 2.3), in her ten-installment novel *Clélie* (1654–1660). De Scudéry's detailed color map depicts a land of love, with such features as a Lac d'Indifference ("Lake of Indifference") and cities with names like Respect, Generosité, Grand Coeur, Probité, Billet Doux, and Exactitude. And finally, new worlds are proposed in two works by Lady Margaret Cavendish, Duchess of Newcastle; a set of utopian rules for a new society put forth in her essay, "The Inventory of Judgements Commonwealth, the Author cares not in what World it is established" in her collection, *The Worlds Olio* (1655), and her fictional work, *The Description of a New World, Called the Blazing-World* (1666) (described in the next section), which is sometimes included in lists of utopias though it is also considered to be early science fiction.

Throughout the seventeenth and eighteenth centuries, a variety of utopias appeared, ranging from those which were no more than a list of rules governing a society, to ones that more fully imagined the lands, culture, and history of their inhabitants. Among the latter, we can find examples in which some sense of an actual place is attempted. Tommaso Campanella's *The City of the Sun* (1602) begins with a lengthy description of his arrival on the island of Taprobane and a description of the city that he found there (the design of which reminds one of Tolkien's Minas Tirith):

> The greater part of the city is built upon a high hill, which rises from an extensive plain, but several of its circles extend for some distance beyond the base of the hill, which is of such a size that the diameter of the city is upward of two miles, so that its circumference becomes about seven. On account of the humped shape of the mountain, however, the diameter of the city is really more than if it were built on a plain.
>
> It is divided into seven rings or huge circles named from the seven planets, and the way from one to the other of these is by four streets and through four gates, that look toward the four points of the compass. Furthermore, it is so built that if the first circle were stormed, it would of necessity entail a double amount of energy to storm the second; still more to storm the third; and in each succeeding case the strength and energy would have to be doubled; so that he who wishes to capture that city must, as it were, storm it seven times. For my own part, however, I think that not even the first wall could be occupied, so thick are the earthworks and so well fortified is it with breastworks, towers, guns, and ditches.[39]

After giving the layout of the city, he goes on to describe the palaces and central temple, and their décor, before launching into an explanation of how their government is structured, urged on by the questions of the Genoese sea captain who is his interlocutor.

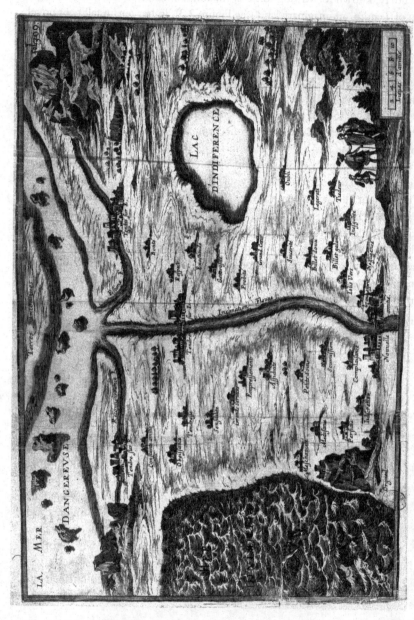

FIGURE 2.3 Map of Madeleine De Scudéry's Tendre, from 1654, which appeared with her novel *Clélie, Histoire Romaine* (1654–1660) and was designed by De Scudery and her friends, with the engraving of the final image attributed to François Chauveau.

Johann Valentin Andreæ's *Reipublicae Christianopolitanae Descriptio* (1619), otherwise known as *Christianopolis*, sets its walled utopian city-state upon an island called Caphar Salama. After his ship, *Fantasy*, is shipwrecked on the island, the book's main character, the pilgrim Cosmoxenus Christianus, is examined by the city's guardians and later shown the city. Christianopolis is small but meticulously planned out and described in 100 chapters, including a map drawn by Andreæ. According to Edward H. Thompson of Dundee University:

> The general description of Christianopolis is one of best-practice early modern accommodation: for example, the roofs are divided up by fire-walls at intervals, and the buildings are all constructed of baked bricks against the danger of fire; they have double windows "one of glass and one of wood, set into the wall in such a way that each may be opened or closed as desired", with lifting gear—presumably of the kind found to this day in Amsterdam—to hoist heavy items to the upper floors (Chapter 23). Pure spring water is channelled into the community, and divided up first into streets, then into houses, the outflow of a lake runs by subterranean channels through the sewers, to empty the houses of dirt each day (Chapter 95). In short, the domestic arrangements may be Spartan, but they are completely up-to-date for early modern Europe.[40]

Andreæ's architectural details and description gives his city-state a more concrete presence than the more dreamlike descriptions of prior utopias which focused more on social structures than physical ones.

Francis Bacon's *New Atlantis* (1626) involves a ship lost in the South Seas which chances upon the remote island of Bensalem. We are given detailed descriptions of the house where the ship's crew is quarantined right after arriving, and an elaborate backstory reaching over 3,000 years, which includes how a miraculous pillar and cross of light, along with a Bible and letter sent by St. Bartholomew, converted many of the islanders to Christianity; the early seafaring years and loss of Great Atlantis in a deluge; and the ancient King Salomana, their lawgiver, and the establishment of his house. At one point, one resident of Bensalem even says "I have read in a book of one of your men, of a feigned commonwealth," and goes on to make a specific reference to More's *Utopia*.

In many of these works, the author attempts to tell a tale that goes beyond the mere description of societal structures, and to create a world in which the story takes place. And, similar to the lands and islands of travelers' tales, the locations of utopias generally followed explorations of the day. According to Manuel and Manuel:

> For two hundred years thereafter the imaginary encounters of literary voyagers with stranger peoples kept close pace with the real adventures of their seafaring counterparts in America and Asia. Sometimes the utopias prophetically preceded rather than followed historical landings in new

places: Toward the latter part of the seventeenth century, at a time when the South Sea islands and Autralia were still unexplored, the utopians outstripped the sailors, and the Huguenots Gabriel de Foigny and Denise Vairesse situated kingdoms in the Mers Australes. For some, there was no longer enough wonderment attached to the coastline of the Americas. Happiness was where they were not, beyond the horizons. During the course of the next century ideal societies multiplied in a balmy region of the Pacific—in Tahiti and on the island of Nouvelle-Cythère—*rêves exotiques* bred by the real voyages of Captain James Cook and Louis Antoine de Bougainville in the same area. After 1800, the wilderness of the American West, opened to travelers, yielded up utopian worlds in hidden valleys and on the broad plains and plateaus. New territories were progressively annexed to utopia until the whole face of the earth was covered and men had to seek elsewhere.[41]

To explain why they were not on maps, some worlds, like Bacon's island of Bensalem, were said to be deliberately hidden from outsiders. Simon Tyssot de Patot's *Voyages et avantures de Jaques Massé* (1710), featured the monarchy of Satrapia, cut off from the outside world by mountain ranges, making it one of the first "lost world" novels. Moreover, works were starting to originate in the New World as well: Joseph Morgan's *The History of the Kingdom of Basaruah* (1715) appeared in New England, and was one of the first pieces of prose fiction to be written and published in America by an American.[42]

The eighteenth century saw increasing detail put into the design of utopian worlds, and their political aims changed as well. In her book *Journey Through Utopia*, Marie Louise Berneri writes:

> During the sixteenth and seventeenth centuries the dimly-known continents of America or Australia merely offered a setting into which London or Paris had been transplanted. In the eighteenth century these countries begin to have a life of their own and the customs of the people discovered there by travelers or missionaries are incorporated in the framework of the utopias. We find also that while utopias had tried to represent a society where complete equality was the rule, many of them are now concerned with building a free society. The inhabitants of Diderot's Tahiti, for example, do not know either government or laws. Utopias had provided sufficient food and clothing, comfortable houses and a good education, but in exchange they had demanded the complete submission of the individual to the state and its laws; they now sought above all these things freedom from laws and governments.[43]

Among the more narrative-based utopias, we find some descended from the travelers themselves, similar to Neville's Isle of Pines. For example, in Johann

Gottfried Schnabel's *Die Insel Felsenburg* (1731), two shipwreck survivors, Albertus and Concordia, marry and populate the island which Albertus rules over as his own ideal state; and in Francois Lefebvre's *Relation du Voyage de l'Isle d'Éutopie* (1711) the Eutopians are descended from a father with ten married children, whose descendents, after 250 years, number more than 40,000.

Another strategy for the presentation of an imaginary world is found in John Kirkby's *The History of Automathes* (1745). The main narrative, about the country of Soteria, is related in a manuscript from 1614 that the narrator finds washed up on the seashore. Such a device puts the imaginary world at one more remove from the reader, and reflects the experience of reading about an imaginary country within the story itself. Oddly enough, the narrator begins his own tale "During my abode in my native county of Cumberland," mentioning another fictional country which is never elaborated upon further; a curious addition, since the story could have been set in any real country bordering an ocean. Similarly, James Burgh's *An Account of the First Settlement, Laws, Form of Government and Police of the Cessares* (1764) is related in a series of nine letters dated 1620.

A printer who printed his own books, Nicolas-Edme Restif de La Bretonne authored around 200 volumes, among them a series of related utopias written between 1769 and 1789 which he collectively referred to as *Idées singulières*. These works, describing the laws and social structures of lands including Gynographe, Andrographe, and Thesmographe, are more concerned with politics and social reforms than with the concrete details and frame narratives that others used to make their countries seem like real places. In general, utopian writing could be seen as moving in two different directions. According to Manuel and Manuel:

> Toward the end of the eighteenth century, in a growingly de-Christianized Europe, even while the old isolated island and valley utopias and a newer type of awakened-dreamer utopia continued to be regurgitated, there came into greater prominence the branch of utopian thought that spurned any fictional backdrop, broke with the limitations of specific place, and addressed itself directly to the reformation of the entire species. ... By the early nineteenth century innovative utopian thought had all but lost its enclosed space. The novels portraying encapsulated and protected pictorial utopias, while they have continued to be sold in the millions of copies into our own time, were often in content residual and derivative, dependent on revolutionary utopian theory that others had propounded.[44]

The second group mentioned here, of course, is the one concerned with building secondary worlds. Derivative though they may have been politically, they sold their "millions" of copies and reached more people no doubt because of their narrative content and otherworldly settings; they were novels, not merely political manifestos or outlined programs of social reform. While communal movements of the nineteenth century and the rising interest in socialism led some of the latter to inspire actual communities that would attempt to live out their ideals, novelists sought to broaden utopian speculative potential while keeping it within a narrative framework. One author of the period, Félix Bodin, recognized the value of a secondary world in speculative fiction, and included criticism of the genre along with an unfinished novel in *Le Roman de l'Avenir* (1834) (also known as *The Novel of the Future*). Bodin felt that audiences were reached more effectively through imagination and a narrative world using novelistic techniques rather than through abstract utopian manifestos, and his work described the direction that science fiction would take decades later, even before the genre was fully codified.[45]

The nineteenth century saw an increase in the production of utopias, with over 300 published in the English language alone.[46] Socialist writings and the arrival of the Industrial Age with its abundance of new technology opened up possibilities, encouraging speculation and hopes that productivity and efficiency would be increased, while poverty could be eliminated, or at least reduced. Many utopias, however, also included an increased reliance on technology, reduced autonomy for individuals, and greater regulation and control by the state. For example, Etienne Cabet's *Voyage et aventures de Lord William Carisdall en Icarie* (1839) (later republished as *Voyage to Icaria*), which inspired a number of actual Icarian communities throughout the century, had streets that were all straight and wide, thousands of "street cars" for public transportation, and a State which planned everything including people's meal times, clothes, and curfews. In the story, Eugene, one of the book's characters, writes the following about Icarian dining in a letter to his brother Camille:

> The Committee which I have mentioned before has also discussed and indicated the number of *meals*, the time at which they should be eaten, how long they should last, the number of courses, their nature and the order in which they should be served, varying them continuously, not only according to the seasons and the months but also according to the days, with the result that every meal of the week is different from the other.
>
> At six o'clock in the morning, before they begin work, all the workers, that is to say all the citizens, eat a very simple breakfast in common at their workshops, prepared and served by the factory restaurant.
>
> At nine o'clock, they have a luncheon in the workshop, while their wives and children take theirs at home.
>
> At two o'clock, all the inhabitants of the same street eat together, in their *republican restaurant*, a dinner prepared by one of the *caterers* of the Republic.
>
> And every evening between nine and ten, each family has, in its own home, a supper prepared by the women of the household.
>
> At all these meals, the first TOAST is *to the glory of the good Icar, benefactor of the workers*, BENEFACTOR OF THE FAMILIES, BENEFACTOR OF THE CITIZENS.[47]

Many would hardly consider such strict conditions to be utopic, and some authors used their utopias to satirize existing conditions, like Benjamin Disraeli's *The Voyage of Captain Popanilla* (1828), a political satire in which England appears as the country of Vraibleusia; or Samuel Butler's *Erewhon: or, Over the Range* (1872), the bulk of which was a series of detailed descriptions of Erewhonian institutions and their operations which satirized their British counterparts. *Erewhon* eventually found enough success to warrant a sequel, *Erewhon Revisited Twenty Years Later, Both by the Original Discoverer and His Son* (1901).

Besides satirizing them, authors criticized conditions through the use of utopias gone wrong, places that look utopic at first glance, but are later revealed to be terrible, oppressive places, or places designed to suggest that if certain trends in society continue, undesirable conditions will result. In 1868, the term "dystopia" was introduced in a speech by John Stuart Mill in the British Parliament, and came to describe these negative utopias. Dystopic worlds had been around since Plato's discussion of a society's descent into a tyranny in his *Republic*, and could be found in the form of fictional countries like Nimpatan, the humorously bleak land of gold-worshipping Nimpatenese in John Holmesby's *The Voyages, Travels, And Wonderful Discoveries of Capt. John Holmesby* (1757) or the future Paris of Louis Hippolyte Mettais's *L'An 5865 ou Paris dans 4000 ans* (1865), even before the term created a separate category for them. Around the end of the nineteenth century, a new wave of utopian and dystopian literature began, with works like Anna Bowman Dodd's *The Republic of the Future* (1887), Elizabeth Corbett's *New Amazonia* (1889), William Morris' *News from Nowhere* (1890), Anna Adolph's *Arqtiq: A Story of the Marvels at the North Pole* (1899), and the distant future world of the Morlocks in H. G. Wells' *The Time Machine* (1895). The number of dystopias would increase sharply in the twentieth century, as industrial excess and growing reliance on technology, two world wars, depressed economies, fascist and totalitarian regimes, and eventually the invention of the nuclear bomb all conspired to make humanity's future appear disturbing and bleak. Such dystopic worlds include Aldous Huxley's *Brave New World* (1932), George Orwell's *Animal Farm* (1945) and *Nineteen Eighty-four* (1949), and the cinematic worlds of *THX 1138* (1971), *Blade Runner* (1982), and *The Matrix* (1999). The utopic tradition also continued throughout the twentieth century, producing a variety of worlds including a growing number of feminist utopias and ecological utopias that arose with and helped inspire parallel social movements and changes.

Throughout the nineteenth century, as the Age of Exploration gradually came to a close, utopias' locations, like those of travelers' tales, moved to other planets, or into the past or the future, where they could remain inaccessible and exotic. And just as the term "utopia" (literally, "no place") indicates an imaginary location, a story set in an imaginary time is sometimes referred to as a "uchronia", a term coined by Charles Renouvier in his novel *Uchronie* (1876). Uchronias can be set in a vague prehistoric time, in the future, or an unspecified or even fictional time period (the term is also sometimes used to include alternate history stories, since stories set in the future eventually become alternate histories).[48] Many uchronias of the nineteenth century were set far into the future, for example, Edward Bellamy's influential book *Looking Backward: 2000–1887* (1888), Mary Griffith's "Three Hundred Years Hence" (1836) (believed to be the first utopia or uchronia written by an American woman), Louis Sébastien Mercier's *L'An 2440, Rêve s'il en Fût Jamais* (1771) (published in 1795 in English as *Memoirs of the Year Two Thousand Five Hundred*); Paolo Mantegazza's *L'Anno 3000* (*The Year 3000,* 1897), with a good number of predictions that came true in the twentieth century; Emile Souvestre's *Le Monde tel qu'il sera* (*The World of the Future,* 1846) about the year 3000; Chauncey Thomas' *The Crystal Button; or, Adventures of Paul Prognosis in the Forty-Ninth Century* (1891); John Macnie's *The Diothas; or, A Far Look Ahead* (1883) about the sixty-ninth century, H. G. Wells' *The Time Machine,* part of which takes place in the year 802701, and his story "Man of the Year Million" (1893), set the farthest into the future that any nineteenth century author was willing to venture.[49]

By the end of the nineteenth century, a wide variety of authors had written works set in imaginary worlds; for example, James Fenimore Cooper's Vulcan's Peak and Leap Islands; Mark Twain's republic of Gondour; John Ruskin's Stiria; Herman Melville's Mardi Archipelago; the Brontë sisters' Gondal and Gaaldine; Alexander Pushkin's Land of Lukomorie; Anthony Trollope's Britannula; glimpses of worlds seen in the work of Edgar Allen Poe; Gilbert and Sullivan's Barataria, Titipu, and Zara's Kingdom; and composer Hector Berlioz's city of Euphonia. Occasionally, one could still find an imaginary world in the form of lost continents proposed in nonfiction works, like Lemuria, in Philip Sclater's 1864 essay "The Mammals of Madagascar" in *The Quarterly Journal of Science*; or Mu, described by Augustus Le Plongeon in *Queen Móo and the Egyptian Sphinx* (1896) as the land bridge across the Atlantic Ocean which allowed the ancient Mayans to cross over and become the founders of Egyptian culture. Utopias, dystopias, and uchronias would continue to be written, but from the end of the nineteenth century onward, the two literary genres that would see the most imaginary worlds were the newly-coalesced ones of fantasy and science fiction, which broadly encompassed past, future, interplanetary, and alternate worlds.

The Genres of Science Fiction and Fantasy

If travelers' tales brought audiences to imaginary worlds and utopias gave them some sense of how their inhabitants lived, the genres of science fiction and fantasy invited audiences to live in them vicariously. The main characters of these genres' stories could still be travelers from the Primary World, but as both genres developed, a growing number of main characters would be natives of secondary worlds instead of merely visitors. World information could still be introduced in long expository passages or monologues, but authors were finding ways to more smoothly integrate the new defaults and details their worlds introduced, easing the audience's transition into the subcreated world. And, over time, generic conventions codified and gave authors shortcuts to generating familiarity as audiences gained experience with the genres and expectations were formed. While science fiction and fantasy stories can be set in the Primary World, many of them propose secondary worlds, and the most elaborate imaginary worlds are now typically found in these genres.

The genres of science fiction and fantasy both coalesced during the Victorian era, due to a confluence of circumstances. The rise of newspapers, the establishment of publishing houses, and the growing literacy that came with mandatory education all encouraged the increasing output of literature during the nineteenth century. As the numbers of novels grew, classification grew in importance and new literary genres formed, claiming for themselves the works of past centuries that shared the common traits and elements that defined each genre. The Industrial Revolution and the development of scientific method promoted methodological investigation and technological speculation, and their influence would aid the separation of literature of the fantastic from so-called "realistic" literature toward the end of the century, with Romanticism challenged by Naturalist and Realist movements. Fantastic literature itself would eventually undergo a bifurcation into the genres of science fiction and fantasy, the former encompassing technologically speculative fiction, tales of space travel, and stories set in the future, while the latter included myth and legend, folklore, fairy tales, beast fables, chivalric romance, adventure stories, and stories of magic and the supernatural. During the twentieth century, elements of both genres would thoroughly intermix, creating subgenres like science fantasy and space opera, further blurring the boundaries between science fiction and fantasy. At the same time, however, the two genres, each with their own concerns and approaches, would remain the two major poles of fantastic literature.

Science Fiction

The main contributions of science fiction (and science in general) to the history of imaginary worlds is the locating of worlds outside of the earth, and the ability to speculate as to what those worlds might be like according to the use of physical laws and the extrapolation of earthly life and conditions. Although it did not always agree with science or use all the means it had available for world-building, science fiction followed closely on the heels of science, with the term "science fiction" first appearing in 1851, less than two decades after the term "scientist" was coined.[50]

Along with fantasy, science fiction was originally considered as a type of literature of the fantastic, and it was not until the twentieth century that it came to be seen as a separate genre by critics, scholars, and the publishing industry. Science fiction's roots also extend back into antiquity and precede the development of scientific method. Originating as a subset of imaginary voyages or travelers' tales, moon journeys can be found as far back as Lucian's *True History*, and begin to appear with regularity during the Renaissance; for example, in *Orlando Furioso* (1516), Johann Kepler's dream narrative *Somnium, seu Opus Posthumum de Astronomia Lunari* (1634), Francis Godwin's *The Man in the Moone; or A Discourse of a Voyage Thither* (1638), John Wilkins' *The Discovery of a World in the Moone* (1638), and David Russen's *Iter Lunare: Or, A Voyage To The Moon* (1703). Authors already known for their writing in other genres also wrote moon journeys; Cyrano de Bergerac wrote his *Voyage to the Moon* (1657), and Daniel Defoe wrote *The Consolidator: Or, Memoirs of Sundry Transactions From the World in the Moon* (1705), which, like his *Robinson Crusoe,* inspired a host of imitations and continuations.[51] As is usual in science fiction, stories mixed known facts about the moon and reasonable speculations with fantastic additions. For example, in George Tucker's *A Voyage to the Moon* (1827), characters travel to the moon in an airtight copper cube six feet long on a side, and relatively realistic descriptions of aerial views of the Earth are given, as well as speculations regarding the moon's origins; but his Morosofia, the country where they land on the moon, is as populous and cultivated as any city on Earth. One short story even anticipated satellites and space stations: Edward Everett Hale's short story "The Brick Moon" (1869) has its characters building and launching a 200-foot moon made of brick as an artificial satellite to aid navigation. The moon is accidentally launched with people aboard, and they continue living there, cultivating the brick moon and making it into their own little world where they raise their descendents.

But there was more in the cosmos than just the Earth–Moon system. As astronomy developed during the Renaissance, with improved telescopes and a shift to Copernican thinking, stars and planets were no longer thought of as points of light but as actual places, which demanded an entirely new conception of the universe. As astronomer Tilberg J. Herczeg describes it:

> The question of the habitable moon rested after Plutarch for almost 1,500 years. The problem of the plurality was centered on an entirely different idea: the simultaneous existence of "our world" and numerous, perhaps infinite, worlds in an infinite *cosmos*, with their planets and earths. This idea originated with the atomists, Democritus of Abdera and Leucippus of Miletos (5th century B.C.). According to this concept, each such cosmos was formed by *random aggregation* of a vast number of atoms. There was hardly a "debate" here: Aristotle strongly opposed the plurality of worlds and so did the medieval philosophers and theologians; the idea of atomism became even forbidden. The ideology of "our unique world", however, underwent drastic changes when, in the wake of the Copernican theory, the Englishman Thomas Digges (1576) and, probably under his influence, the unfortunate Giordano Bruno (1583 and later), constructed the magnificent, visionary picture that the stars are so many suns, possibly with planets around them, while our sun is a star.[52]

Although the sixteenth-century Italian philosopher and Dominican monk Giordano Bruno is often mentioned for his theory of the plurality of worlds in his *De l'Infinito Universo et Mondi* (*On the Infinite Universe and Worlds*, 1584), he was not the first with such ideas; during the thirteenth century, Etienne Tempier, the Bishop of Paris, argued that God could have created alien life forms on multiple worlds, and in the fifteenth century, Cardinal Nicholas of Cusa suggested the possibility of alien life on the sun and moon. The discussion was continued in later years by authors like Bernard le Bovier de Fontenelle, whose *Entretiens sur la Pluralité des Mondes* (*Conversations on the Plurality of Worlds*, 1686) discussed the possibility of life on other planets, opening the door for authors to begin considering them as settings for stories.

Imaginary worlds could be set on other planets, but transporting travelers to these worlds from the Primary World was another problem. Authors were used to having their travelers' tales told by narrators who had some link back to the Primary World; otherwise how could the story have come to the reader? A temporal version of the same problem would occur later regarding travel into the future. For serious scientific speculation regarding other worlds (or the future), fantastic literature itself had to develop further, to solve the new storytelling problems associated with faraway worlds. According to science fiction historian Brian Stableford:

> The adaptation of traditional narrative frameworks to the work of serious speculation laboured under several handicaps. Travelers' tales, even in their most utopian mode, were infected by a chronic frivolity that increased as the travels extended into regions inaccessible to ships and pedestrians. Literary dreams, even at their most gravely allegorical, were by definition mere phantoms of the imagination, demolished by reawakening. The transformation of moral fables into Voltairean *contes philosophiques* was hampered by the calculated artificiality of their traditional milieu and exemplary characters. These problems became more acute as the philosophy of progress made the future an imaginative realm ripe for exploration. Utopian speculation entered a "euchronian" mode once Louis-Sebastien Mercier had led the way in *L'An deux mille quarter cent quarante* (*The Year 2440*, 1771)—which soon prompted the production of more cynical accounts of futurity, such as Cousin de Grainville's *Le Dernier Homme* (*The Last Man*, 1805)—but the only obvious alternative to dreaming as a means of gaining access to the future was sleeping for a long time. This was no help to a contemporary narrator if the intelligence gained could not be returned to the present. The problem of designing and developing appropriate narrative frames for scientific *contes philosophiques* inevitably became acute during the nineteenth century and was not easily solved.[53]

Stableford also describes how some authors solved the problem by using dream-journeys or visions to accomplish the cosmic voyaging, as in Athanasius Kircher's

Iterarium Exstaticum (1656). But this would only allow the narrator to be an observer, and any worlds seen or described would lack the concreteness of those with which the narrator could interact. Trips could be done as satires, like Monsieur Vivenair's *A Journey lately performed through the Air, in an Aerostatic Globe, commonly called an Air Balloon, from this terraqueous globe, to the newly discovered Planet, Georgium Sidus* (1784), in which the narrator flies all the way to Uranus (Georgium Sidus) in a hot air balloon; but too much exaggeration erodes any Secondary Belief that the author might wish to evoke.

Several solutions appeared over the years, as science fiction slowly developed. One was to simply locate the foreign planet very close to Earth, hopefully in such a way that it would not be too noticeable or accessible. In Margaret Cavendish's *The Description of a New World, Called the Blazing-World* (1666), the other planet, the Blazing-World, hovers near the North Pole, so close to the Earth that it can be reached by boat. The description of how this works comes very early on in the story, when the heroine travels to the new world, the only survivor aboard a ship that has been blown into the Arctic Sea:

> Neither was it a wonder that the men did freeze to death; for they were not onely [*sic*] driven to the very end or point of the Pole of that World, but even to another Pole of another World, which joined close to it; so that the cold having a double strength at the conjunction of those two Poles, was insupportable: At last, the Boat still passing on, was forced into another World; for it is impossible to round this Worlds [*sic*] Globe from Pole to Pole, so as we do from East to West; because the Poles of the other World, joining to the Poles of this, do not allow any further passage to surround the World that way; but if any one arrives to either of these Poles, he is either forced to return, or to enter into another World: and lest you should scruple at it, and think, if it were thus, those that live at the Poles would either see two Suns at one time, or else they would never want the Sun's light for six months together, as it is commonly believed: You must know, that each of these Worlds having its own Sun to enlighten it, they move each one in their peculiar Circles; which motion is so just and exact, that neither can hinder or obstruct the other; for they do not exceed their Tropicks: and although they should meet, yet we in this World cannot so well perceive them, by reason of the brightness of our Sun, which being nearer to us, obstructs the splendor of the Sun of the other World, they being too far off to be discerned by our optick perception, except we use very good Telescopes; by which, skilful Astronomers have often observed two or three Suns at once.[54]

Cavendish's Blazing-World is a landmark achievement in the history of imaginary worlds for two reasons. First, it is the earliest story set on another planet, away from the Earth–Moon system, and a fictional planet at that, as opposed to known ones like Mars and Venus. Second, her story is the first to feature characters who build their own imaginary worlds; in other words, subcreated subcreators. The main character, who accidentally travels to the Blazing-World (as just described), becomes its Empress, and later brings the Duchess of Newcastle (the author, Cavendish herself) into her world to act as her scribe and seek her advice. The Duchess later wishes that she could be the Empress of a world, as is her friend, and laments the impossibility of it. The Immaterial Spirits, who aid the Empress, suggest an alternate way to rule a world:

> But we wonder, proceeded the Spirits, that you desire to be an Empress of a Terrestrial World, when as you can create your self a Celestial World if you please. What, said the Empress, can any Mortal be a Creator? Yes, answered the Spirits; for every human Creature can create an Immaterial World fully inhabited by Immaterial Creatures, and populous of Immaterial subjects, such as we are, and all this within the compass of the head or scull [sic]; nay, not onely [sic] so, but he may create a World of what fashion and Government he will, and give the Creatures thereof such motions, figures, forms, colours, perceptions, as he pleases, and make Whirlpools, Lights, Pressures, and Reactions, as he thinks best; nay, he may make a World full of Veins, Muscles, and Nerves, and all these to move by one jolt or stroke: also he may alter that World as often as he pleases, or change it from a Natural World, to an Artificial; he may make a World of Ideas, a World of Atoms, a World of Lights, or whatsoever his Fancy leads him to. And since it is in your power to create such a World, What need you to venture life, reputation and tranquility, to conquer a gross material World?[55]

The Empress and the Duchess subcreate their own worlds, and do so within the Blazing-World. Although their worlds are not entered into or described to the degree that the Blazing-World is, the act of world-building is performed and openly discussed in a way that had never been done previously.

Cavendish's Blazing-World was bold and unique but did not inspire imitators, although the next story to solve the question of interplanetary travel also used a nearby planet reachable through earthly transportation: Willem Bilderdijk's *Kort verhaalvan eene aanmerkelijke luchtreis en nieuwe planeetontdekking* (*Short account of a remarkable journey into the skies and discovery of a new planet*) which appeared in 1813. Bilderijk's narrator, who is also the main character, makes an accidental voyage in a hydrogen balloon to Selenion, a new moon between the earth and the known moon, called Luna. At one point, he even sees a line of other moons between Selenion and Luna.

Another nearby place to put a new planet, yet keep it out of sight, was inside the earth itself. Building on the tradition of underground realms, Ludvig Holberg put his new planet of Nazar, which he described as "scarcely six hundred miles in circumference", inside a hollow earth, in his book *Nicolai Klimii Iter Subterraneum*

(*Niels Klim's Underground Travels*) (1741). On his way down into the earth, Holberg's narrator falls through a cave and into open space, which he perceives to be a subterranean firmament. He continues falling and ends up orbiting the planet:

> I knew not but that I might be metamorphosed to a planet or to a satellite; to be turned around in an eternal whirl. Yet my courage returned, as I became somewhat accustomed to the motion. The wind was gentle and refreshing. I was but little hungry or thirsty; but recollecting there was a small cake in my pocket, I took it out and tasted it. The first mouthful, however, was disagreeable, and I threw it from me. The cake not only remained in the air, but to my great astonishment, began to circle about me. I obtained at this time a knowledge of the true law of motion, which is, that all bodies, when well balanced, must move in a circle.
>
> I remained in the orbit in which I was at first thrown three days. As I continually moved about the planet nearest to me, I could easily distinguish between night and day; for I could see the subterranean sun ascend and descend—the night, however, did not bring with it darkness as it does with us. I observed, that on the descent of the sun, the whole heavens became illuminated with a peculiar and very bright light. This, I ascribed to the reflection of the sun from the internal arch of the earth.[56]

The narrator falls to the planet's surface and continues his adventures there, visiting the kingdom of Potu, with its tree people, giving a description of their land, history, law, religion, customs, and education system, halting his narrative awhile in order to do so.

Another solution to space travel is to let the aliens do it, and come to Earth themselves. The first such story in which this occurs is Voltaire's *Micromégas* (1752), in which Micromégas, an inhabitant of a planet orbiting the star Sirius, comes to the Solar System, befriends a Saturnian, and together they come to Earth. The Sirian's height is 25 miles and the Saturnian's only a mile, and earthlings seem very tiny by comparison. The story continues as the visitors criticize human philosophy and point out its shortcomings, attacking the idea that mankind is the center point of the universe. While the story reveals a few facts about Voltaire's imaginary planet, none of the story takes place there, and as a result, it remains something just mentioned rather than described or depicted.

In 1854, readers could finally experience the first imaginary world set on another planet far away from Earth, in Charles Ischir Defontenay's *Star (Psi Cassiopeia): The Marvelous History of One of the Worlds of Outer Space*, which appeared in France. *Star* is the first story set entirely on other planets in outer space, and the device of a human traveler voyaging there is not used; no humans travel there from Earth, nor do any alien characters travel to Earth. The only part of the book that takes place on Earth is the opening sequence, which relates how the author discovered a metal chest housed in a meteorite that crashed in the Himalayas. Inside the chest are books written about, and written by, the occupants of the distant solar system of the planet Star. After the opening sequence, the remainder of the book is the author's translation of the Starian books, immersing the reader in the foreign cultures presented, and both he, and the audience, experience the Starian system the same way: through media.

Star was unusual for its time because its world, rather than a main character, is the central throughline connecting the various texts that make up the book; in a sense, the world *is* the main character. The story takes place over 4,200 years, the first work of fiction with a narrative covering such a vast time period. *Star* is divided into five parts, the first of which has no characters and consists only of the author's guided tour of the planet Star, four other neighboring planets (Tassul, Lessur, Rudar, and Élier), and the four suns of the Starian system. Lush descriptions of the flora, fauna, and subtle changes in lighting due to the four differently colored suns provide a background for the book's next four parts. The second part concerns the ancient history of Star's peoples, ending with their near-decimation by the slow plague, and includes Starian poetry about the plague. The third part follows the remaining survivors, as they travel to and colonize the four other planets of the Starian system, making *Star* the first story of interplanetary colonization. In the fourth part, descendents of the exiled Starians return to Star over 800 years later and reestablish their civilization there. The fifth part, entitled "Voyage of a Tassulian to Tasbar" occurs centuries after the fourth part, and is a description of Tasbar, Star's capital city, written by a traveler from Tassul. Included with his account are a play and historical prose poem, which together give an impression of Starian life and arts.

Even though *Star*'s various texts do not share the same characters or narratives, each section builds on the ones that came before it, requiring the reader to remember many of the world's details in order to get the most out of the stories which rely on them. Finally, after the last story, Defontenay includes an Epilogue of three poems: "The World of Dreams", "Regenerative Hopes", and "Farewell to the Reader", each of which discusses some aspect of the making of imaginary worlds. In many ways at least a half-century ahead if its time, *Star* achieves high degrees of immersion, absorption, and saturation, and is one of the most impressive works of subcreation to appear in the nineteenth century.[57]

The French astronomer Nicolas Camille Flammarion, who apparently read *Star* and disliked it,[58] probably because its emphasis fell more on the poetic than the scientific, wrote of the possibility of life on other planets in a number of scientific texts, starting with *La Pluralité des Mondes Habités* (*The Plurality of Inhabited Worlds*) in 1862, and *Les Mondes Imaginaires et Les Mondes Réels* (*Real and Imaginary Worlds*) in 1864. He also wrote several works of science fiction, including *Récits de l'Infini* (*Stories of Infinity*, 1872), *Uranie* (1889), and *La Fin du Monde* (*The End of the World*, 1893), which was adapted into a film by Able Gance in 1931. More than any other author, Flammarion popularized the idea of life on other worlds and brought it to public attention. Unlike Defontenay, however, Flammarion was more interested in the ideas behind his books than in world-building. His science fiction stories' characters travel with the aid of spirits or as disembodied spirits themselves, rather than in spaceships. Despite some detailed descriptions of terrain, his version of Mars is a much more spiritual place than any of the worlds of his predecessors:

> I learned too that on this planet, less material than our own, the constitution of the body resembles in nothing the constitution of the terrestrial body. Conception and birth take place there in an altogether different manner, which resembles, but in a spiritual form, the fecundation and blooming of a flower. Pleasure is without bitterness. They know nothing there of the heavy burdens we of the Earth bear, nor of the pangs of anguish that we suffer. Everything is more spiritual, more ethereal, more unsubstantial. One might call the Martians thinking and living winged flowers. But indeed there is nothing on Earth by means of a comparison with which we could form a conception of their form and mode of life.[59]

Flammarion's emphasis on the spiritual seems to foreshadow a comment C. S. Lewis would later make in reference to David Lindsay's *A Voyage to Arcturus* (1920), when writing about the value of planets in science fiction:

> He builds whole worlds of imagery and passion, any one of which would have served another writer for a whole book, only to pull each of them to pieces and pour scorn on it. The physical dangers, which are plentiful, here count of nothing: it is we ourselves and the author who walk through a world of spiritual dangers which make them seem trivial. There is no recipe for writing of this kind. But part of the secret is that the author (like Kafka) is recording a lived dialectic. His Tormance is a region of the spirit. He is the first writer to discover what "other planets" are really good for in fiction. No merely physical strangeness or merely spatial distance will realize that idea of otherness which is what we are always trying to grasp in a story about voyaging through space: you must go into another dimension. To construct plausible and moving "other worlds" you must draw on the only real "other world" we know, that of the spirit.[60]

Stories that ignore this sense of otherness run the risk of being little more than earthly stories transplanted to another planet, rather than something qualitatively different. Such otherness also runs counter to the similarities with the Primary World that an imaginary world's nature and culture must have for comprehensibility and character identification, challenging authors to find new ways to connect their worlds to their audiences.

One late nineteenth-century work notable for its innovative world-building is Edwin Abbott Abbott's *Flatland: A Romance of Many Dimensions* (1884). While the book reflects many of the social and cultural mores of its day, its originality and innovation lies in the structure of the world itself, which is the two-dimensional plane of Flatland. The experiences of characters living in two dimensions are explored, and the main character, A. Square, is visited by a higher-dimensional being (a sphere), and later visits Lineland, a one-dimensional world in which he himself is a higher-dimensional being. Through analogy, the book attempts to acclimate its readers to thinking about a fourth dimension and other dimensions beyond their own. The book is the first to present a world so fundamentally different from the Primary World (at least in its physical form), and one completely detached from our own universe; for the first time, no attempt is made to forge a connection to the Primary World, representing a new level of autonomy for imaginary worlds.

Other planets were not the only new location for the worlds of nineteenth-century science fiction. If the telescope could suggest locations for other worlds, so could the microscope. Since Robert Hooke's *Micrographia: or, Some Physiological Descriptions of Minute Bodies Made by Magnifying Glasses* (1665) had described and shown the detail of microscopic worlds, it was only a matter of time before imaginary worlds would appear under the microscope. Fitz-James O'Brien's short story "The Diamond Lens" (1858) told of a man who perfects a microscope only to find an alluring woman in a drop of water, whom he is unable to contact. Later, Raymond King Cummings' novelette of 1919, *The Girl in the Golden Atom* (later expanded into a novel and a sequel), took up the challenge of entering a microscopic world with a story about a chemist who looks at his mother's wedding ring under a microscope and finds a world there inhabited by a beautiful woman. He invents pills that can make his body shrink or grow in size (reminiscent of *Alice's Adventures in Wonderland* (1865)), and goes into the ring himself to find her. There he finds two nations made up of millions of people, the Oroids and the Malites, and there is even the suggestion that the atoms of their world contain even tinier inhabitants. Other microscopic worlds appeared, like those of R. F Starzl's "Out of the Sub-Universe" (1928), Festus Pragnell's *The Green Man of Kilsona* (1936), and Maurice G. Hugi's "Invaders from the Atom" (1937), and one story, G. Peyton Wertenbaker's "The Man from the Atom" (1926) even reversed the situation, by making Earth an atomic particle in another world.

Most imaginary worlds of the time, however, were still earthbound in the usual forms of islands, underground realms, mountain valleys, or uchronias set on future Earths. Jean Baptiste Cousin de Grainville's *Le Dernier Homme* (*The Last Man*) (1805) introduced what would come to be known as the "last man on Earth" subgenre, about Omegare, the only man left on a dying, sterile Earth. Jules Verne produced a number of imaginary worlds, including the Lindenbrock Sea and underground world of *Voyage to the Center of the Earth* (1864); Lincoln Island of *The Mysterious Island* (1874) (which would later inspire Myst Island in *Myst* (1993)); Ham Rock Island in *Le "Chancellor"* (1875); the underground Coal City in *Les Indes Noires* (1877); France-Ville in the Rocky Mountains and Stahlstadt near Pacific coast in *Les 500 Millions de la Bégum* (1879); Klausenburg County in Transylvania in *Le Château des Carpathes* (1892); and Standard Island, somewhere near New Zealand, in *L'Ile à Hélice* (1895). H. G. Wells wrote of Aepyornis Island in *The Stolen Bacillus and Other Incidents* (1894) and Moreau's Island in *The Island of Dr. Moreau* (1896), and George Griffith wrote of Aeria, a mountain valley in Northern Africa in *The Angel of the Revolution* (1893). Finally, one unusual underground world was that of the Vril-ya, a master race living in subterranean tunnels in Edward Bulwer-Lytton's *The Coming Race* (1871), which some readers believed to be true. The Vril-ya's substance of Vril, an energy source used both to destroy and to heal, even inspired a German "Vril Society" which would search for it.[61]

While imaginary worlds of science fiction tried to give a scientific basis to their worlds, secondary worlds in the twin genre of fantasy were also departing from the Primary World, but according to their magical or supernatural origins. Although the two genres would always remain closely related, it was during the late nineteenth century that their individual identities became distinct.

Fantasy

Fantasy finds its roots in myth and folklore traditions, and came to encompass older genres like the heroic romance, beast fables, and fairy tales. In the latter half of the nineteenth century, the work of a number of authors helped to define the genre. George MacDonald's 1893 essay "The Fantastic Imagination" analyzed certain aspects of how imaginary worlds functioned, and his fiction, including *Phantastes: A Faerie Romance for Men and Women* (1858), *At the Back of the North Wind* (1870), *The Princess and the Goblin* (1872), and *Lilith* (1895), influenced many twentieth-century fantasy authors. While some of these works are like fairy tales written for adults, the worlds they describe are nebulous fairylands, which some would argue fall short of being true secondary worlds. Referring to *Phantastes* and *Lilith* in his book *Imaginary Worlds: The Art of Fantasy*, Lin Carter writes:

> While the geography of the two romances is not of this world, the books do not quite make it as progenitors of the central imaginary-world tradition; they are vivid dreams, not stories, and the weird countries through which their characters move do not constitute serious, detailed attempts to construct an invented milieu that gives the illusion of genuine reality, which is a prerequisite of the genre. Still, they are profound and beautiful and strange: they make the mind to work, and they are indubitably fantastic.[62]

Another author's worlds combined the supernatural enchantment of fairy tales with the solidity of the lands of travelers' tales; William Morris, whose novels took elements of medieval romance and the details of historical novels, combining them into believable worlds. Together, his books *The Story of the Glittering Plain which has also been called the Land of the Living Men or the Acre of the Undying* (1891), *The Wood Beyond the World* (1894), *The Well at the World's End* (1896), and *The Water of the Wondrous Isles* (1897) represent a foundation for the fantasy genre. Morris was also innovative in that his stories' settings are among the first fantasy settings (along with Abbott's Flatland) to be completely disconnected geographically from the Primary World. Hallblithe travels to the Land of the Glittering Plain, but his story begins in the fictitious Cleveand by the Sea; likewise, in *The Wood Beyond the World*, Golden Walter travels to a faraway land, but his story begins in the fictitious Langton on Holm. Ralph, the main character of *The Well at the World's End* lives in the kingdom of Upmeads, and the real Upmeads in England, built in 1908, may even be named after Morris' kingdom.[63]

Two other world-builders of note were Henry Rider Haggard and Anthony Hope. Haggard helped develop the "lost world" subgenre of fantastic literature, and was best known for his Allan Quatermain series, which began with *King Solomon's Mines* (1885) set in the African country of Kukualand hidden away in the mountains, and for his "She" novels, beginning with *She: A History of Adventure* (1887) which takes place in the lost city of Kor. Hope's *The Prisoner of Zenda* (1894) was a popular novel in its day and its setting, Ruritania, gave its name to a subgenre of adventure novels, and entered as a word into the English Language and the dictionary, meaning "an imaginary country".

Another major literary development in the latter half of the nineteenth century that affected the building of imaginary worlds was the rise of children's literature. Child labor laws helped get children into schools and mandatory education helped to encourage the publication of fairy tales and stories for children, including reprints of earlier works like John Bunyon's *The Pilgrim's Progress* (1678), which featured an allegorical secondary world with locations like the Delectable Mountains, the Slough of Despond, the Hill of Difficulty, and the Valley of Humiliation. Like Bunyon's work and most nursery rhymes, many of the books written for children included another level within them for adults (such as allegory, satire, or narrative events and details that children would not understand but which were not necessary for their enjoyment of the tale). One of the first of these multi-level stories, which also helped inspire the revision of the Chimney-Sweep Act (keeping children from hazardous work), was Charles Kingsley's *The Water-Babies: A Fairy Tale for a Land-Baby* (1863).[64] The story is a moral fable set mainly in a secondary world beneath an English river, featuring characters with names like Mrs. Doasyouwouldbedoneby, Mrs. Bedonebyasyoudid, and Professor Ptthmllnsprts. The story mixed fairytale elements and nonsense with moral lessons and criticism of society, as well as the author's own prejudices against Americans, Jews, Catholics, and the French.

Similar to worlds designed for satire or humorous effects, Kingsley's world is not too concerned with verisimilitude and consistency, but instead delights in its own fantastic nature. Several other authors of the time are remembered for their nonsense stories; Edward Lear was known for his nonsense poetry in collections like *Book of Nonsense* (1846) and *Book of Nonsense and More Nonsense* (1862) before he invented the land of Gramblamble in "The History of the Seven Families of the Lake Pipple-popple", only months before Lewis Carroll's *Alice's Adventures in Wonderland* (1865) appeared (Lear's story later appeared in his *Nonsense Songs, Stories, Botany, and Alphabets* (1870)). Carroll's worlds of Wonderland, Looking-glass Land, and Snark Island are perhaps the best-remembered nonsense worlds, due to his combination of logic and humor that entertained both adults and children successfully, and served as inspiration for many twentieth-century authors.

Other imaginary worlds in children's literature of the time include Robert Louis Stevenson's Treasure Island in *Treasure Island* (1883) and Suicide City in his collection *New Arabian Nights* (1882); Carlo Collodi's Island of the Busy Bees in *The Adventures of Pinnochio* (1883); Edward Earle Childs' Mouseland in *The Wonders of Mouseland* (1901); and Edith Nesbit's island of "The Island of the Nine Whirlpools" (1900), the island kingdom of Rotundia in "Uncle James, or The Purple Stranger" (1900), and Polistarchia in *The Magic City* (1910). Of these, Nesbit's worlds were the most playful and inventive; in *Uncle James*, she even pauses her narrative of Princess Mary Ann and Tom the gardener's boy for a lengthy digression concerning the geography and natural history of Rotundia.[65] In *The Magic City*, Polistopolis, the capital city of Polistarchia, is a table-top city built by a boy, Philip, who suddenly finds himself put into the city where the people he has populated it with are all alive, another early instance of a subcreated subcreator. At one point, Mr. Noah, a figure from a Noah's Ark playset, tells Philip how the world works:

> "'It's a little difficult, I own,' said Mr. Noah. "But, you see, you built those cities in two worlds. It's pulled down in this world. But in the other world it's going on."
>
> "I don't understand," said Philip.
>
> "I thought you wouldn't," said Mr. Noah; "but it's true, for all that. Everything people make in that world goes on for ever."
>
> "But how was it that I got in?"
>
> "Because you belong to both worlds. And you built the cities. So they were yours."[66]

Nesbit's idea of a subcreated world possessing a kind of dual existence, one temporary and earthly and the other permanent and supernatural, linked the Primary World to a secondary world in a new way. It also suggested the importance of making and the creative urge, adding new implications and consequences to the subcreator's acts, ideas which J. R. R. Tolkien would take up later in his short story "Leaf by Niggle" (1947).

The last great fantasist who began working in the nineteenth century, Lyman Frank Baum, wrote plays and short stories in the 1880s and 1890s, as well as several collections of nursery rhymes for children. In 1900, two of his books were published. One was *A New Wonderland* (the book was originally named *Adventures in Phunnyland* and would later be renamed *The Surprising Adventures of the Magical Monach of Mo and His People* (1903)), which introduced the land of Phunnyland (later renamed Mo) in a collection of short stories that took place there, linked by a series of transnarrative characters. The other book of 1900 was *The Wonderful Wizard of Oz*. Baum would write 13 sequels to the Oz book, all of them with "Oz" in the title, making the Oz series the first major series linked by their world rather than by a main character. Most prior book series, like Rabelais' Gargantua and Pantagruel series, Carroll's Alice books, or Haggard's She series, centered around characters whose name appeared in the book titles, linking the series together (an exception being Samuel Butler's *Erewhon* (1872), which had a single sequel, *Erewhon Revisted* (1901)). The Oz series attracted its audience through the world it depicted, rather than a particular character.

The popularity of the series allowed Baum to develop his world to a far greater extent than the worlds that only appeared in a single book, and even his first book alone gave his world a solidity that many others lacked. In *Worlds Within: Children's Fantasy from the Middle Ages to Today*, Sheila A. Egoff described Baum's work writing:

> It is Baum's originality that must be saluted. *The Wizard of Oz* is not only the first Other World fantasy in American children's literature; it is the first fully created imaginative world in the whole of children's literature, all the more remarkable because in his own country there were few signposts to point Baum along "the yellow brick road." Charles Kingsley made use of a natural underwater setting in *The Water-Babies*, George MacDonald of a familiar folktale world in *The Princess and the Goblin*, and Carroll's *Alice* books are premised on artifices; but as Dorothy says at the end of *The Wizard of Oz*, when asked where she has come from, "From the Land of Oz." Oz was a place. It is true that the full cosmology of Oz did not develop until the later books (and is fully explained in Raylyn Moore's *Wonderful Wizard, Marvellous Land*), but there was sufficient detail in the first book to make one believe in Oz.[67]

Regardless of where one wishes to draw the line defining a "fully created imaginative world", it is undeniable that the stories about Oz and its surrounding lands comprised a secondary world of greater size, scope, and invention than most worlds of its time, even outside of children's literature.

The rise of the fantasy genre during the Victorian era, and especially children's fantasy, meant that a new generation of children would grow up reading it, and perhaps be inspired to create their own imaginary worlds. They, in turn, would become the authors of fantasy and science fiction in the twentieth century. For example, J. R. R. Tolkien (born 1892) and C. S. Lewis (born 1898) both wrote about their childhood reading and influences; Tolkien describes his early play with invented languages, while Lewis and his brother Warnie brought together imaginary lands they had created and invented a world they called Boxen, which appeared in the posthumously published *Boxen: The Imaginary World of the Young C. S. Lewis* (1986). Many other authors would cite works of Victorian fantasy as an influence on their own work, as would authors working in fantasy's generic twin, science fiction. Children would continue to develop their own detailed fantasy worlds into the twentieth century, a behavior that became so common that the term "paracosm" was coined in 1976 to describe it, resulting in the 1988 book *The Paracosm: A Special Form of Fantasy* by Robert Silvey and Stephen A. MacKeith, as well as a number of other books that discussed the phenomenon.

By the end of the nineteenth century, imaginary worlds had appeared all over the globe, underground, underwater, in outer space on the moon and other planets, in dreams, supernatural realms, other dimensions, in the distant past, the distant future, and in alternate histories, and a few even existed independently of the Primary World. More worlds began to achieve autonomy from the Primary World, appearing without frame stories or other links to the Primary World, though such devices would always remain in use. Main characters were now sometimes natives of the subcreated worlds, rather than merely travelers to them. And whereas travelers used as main characters had typically been merely observers or the passive recipients of explanations concerning the world being visited, more of them were now becoming active participants whose involvement and interaction often permanently changed the worlds into which they came, and the worlds themselves underwent growth and change instead of being static and fixed. A few early exceptions exist in which a traveling main character interacts with and changes the world being visited (as in Cavendish's *Blazing World* and Paltock's *Life and Adventures of Peter Wilkins*, as previously discussed), but these stand out from the norm of their times.

A good example of the "observer" role versus the "participant" role of the main character, and the audience preference for the latter, can be found in the works of L. Frank Baum. One year after publication of *The Wonderful Wizard of Oz* (1900), Baum published another novel, *Dot and Tot of Merryland* (1901). Merryland is discovered when the children, Dot and Tot, ride a boat through a tunnel and emerge in a valley hidden in the mountains. Merryland itself consists of eight valleys encountered along the river, each separated by a tunnel. The children pass through them one by one, and except for a time when the Queen of Merryland joins them for the ride, they do not interact with the world and leave it just as they found it. As Baum historian Michael O. Riley describes the book:

> Dot and Tot never feel the same pressing need to return home that Dorothy does. Also, no real obstacles are put in the way of their journey, and, except for their meeting with the queen, they do not become involved with any of the strange places and peoples of Merryland. The book has been described

as a travelogue, but it is also a stroll through a circus sideshow where the spectators move from one strange exhibit to another, looking, but never becoming personally involved.[68]

In contrast, when Dorothy arrives in Oz, her house lands on the Wicked Witch of the East, inadvertently making her a hero and irreversibly changing the world and politics of Munchkinland, all before she even leaves her house and sees Oz. Comparing the fates of the two books, it is interesting to note that while *The Wonderful Wizard of Oz* went on to become enormously successful and well known, few people have even heard of *Dot and Tot of Merryland*.

By the turn of the century, imaginary worlds had matured considerably and had established conventions and traditions of their own. While they could appear in any genre, they had found a receptive home in the new genres of science fiction and fantasy. Both genres would flourish in the twentieth century, a period in which more imaginary worlds would be produced than in all the centuries preceding it combined, and in a variety of different mass media forms.

The Rise of Mass Media

Before the twentieth century, imaginary worlds were largely a literary experience. Words were the building blocks from which worlds were made. In early works like those of Mandeville or Rabelais, and in many that followed, illustrations would sometimes accompany the text (for example, the 119 woodcut illustrations included with the 1481 edition of *The Book of Sir John Mandeville*), but these were more or less drawn from the descriptions in the texts themselves. Maps served as illustrations, and also provided additional information, of a geographical nature, that the written text did not. However, imaginary worlds that originated in imagery would take a much longer time to appear.

Unless one counts such things as murals of the netherworld found in Egyptian tombs or Greek depictions of Elysium (both considered real places at the time), early depictions of imaginary places included the *skenographia* of ancient Greece around the fifth century BC, stage plays like Aristophanes's *The Birds*, first-century Roman Empire walls painted to appear to have windows looking out onto imaginary vistas, and Filippo Brunelleschi's demonstrations of geometric perspective in the early fifteenth century and the *trompe l'oeil* tradition that followed, all of which extended actual spaces into fictional ones. Some paintings also depicted worlds already described in literary texts, like Pieter Bruegel the Elder's *Luilekkerland* (*The Land of Cockaigne*), painted in 1567, or imagined versions of heaven and hell, like Hieronymus Bosch's triptych *The Garden of Earthly Delights*, painted between 1503 and 1504. Large-scale paintings could depict imaginary places in detail, like Paolo Veronese's *Feast in the House of Levi* (1573), and from the late eighteenth century onward, panoramas (sometimes called cycloramas) increased the immersion of the viewer into the image, while dioramas produced small, dimensional scenes for onlookers to vicariously enter, and stereoscopic imagery, invented in 1840 by Sir Charles Wheatstone, added visual depth to flat imagery.

As time went on, illustrations designed to accompany texts began to provide additional information that the text did not; for example, Robert Paltock's *The Life and Adventures of Peter Wilkins* (1751) had accompanying woodcuts important enough to be described on the book's title page: "Illustrated with several CUTS, clearly and distinctly representing the Structure and Mechanism of the Wings of the Glums [*sic*] and Gawrys [*sic*], and the Manner in which they use them either to swim or fly." By the late nineteenth century, images were occasionally central to the depiction of an imaginary world, the best example of the period being the works of the French illustrator Albert Robida (see Figure 2.4). Robida, who would also draw illustrations for editions of Rabelais' works and *Gulliver's Travels*, produced a science fiction trilogy which depicted life in the twentieth century (*Le Vingtième Siècle* (1883), *La Guerre au vingtième siècle* (1887, first version in serial form, 1883), and *La Vie électrique* (1890)). Robida wrote and illustrated the novels, with series of highly detailed images of the machinery, inventions, and architecture of his future world. While some of his images were fanciful, others were predictive of actual developments, including the Telephonoscope (a prediction of television), microbe bombs, rotating architectural structures, flying cars, undersea tunnels, electric trains, and more. Another turn-of-the-century artist, the illustrator Louis Biedermann, was also known for highly detailed imagery of future cities full of skyscrapers and airships, and his work would inspire science fiction stories and imagery of the early twentieth century.

Imaginary worlds depicted in multiple images that were not based on or designed to accompany written texts, would first appear around the beginning of the twentieth century, in cinema and comic strips in newspapers, as imaginary worlds took their first steps into the new mass media forms. As the Age of Exploration drew to a close, descriptions and images of the Primary World's lands and countries gradually became more available through books, newspapers, magazines, and photographic media. More local events were also represented in mediated forms, as newspapers grew in importance while the century turned. All of these things, along with mandatory education and increasing literacy, media technologies like photography and halftone printing that allowed photographic images to be reproduced in newspapers, and growing media industries, resulted in a situation in which mediated knowledge began to displace firsthand knowledge to an unprecedented degree. People grew more accustomed to experiencing and forming a mental image of distant parts of the world through media representations, which often involved a wide range of sources of varying reliability. In this way, mass media helped to lessen the gap between real foreign countries which were experienced solely through media, and imaginary worlds, which could only be experienced through media.[69]

FIGURE 2.4 Albert Robida's detailed drawings helped to illustrate his novels, which were visions of what life would be like in the 20th century, including an aerial rotating house (left) and a restaurant and coffee-house atop an ironwork structure (right).

Of course, the similarity between the two had been exploited since the days of travelers' tales that copied real accounts of faraway places, but the rise of mass media made mediated experience far more common than it had been, and people's lives became more reliant on it as well, as the seeds of globalization began to be sown in the early twentieth century. With the addition of image and sound, the nature of mediated experiences also changed, as mass media brought its audience a far richer and more detailed version of the world than mediation had ever done previously. This heightened sense of reality found in the multi-mediated world of mass media was also a challenge to the builders of imaginary worlds, who over the next century would increase the detail and complexity of their worlds, as well as expand them into image and sound media, in an attempt to raise the verisimilitude of their worlds to match what was found in mass media. When successful, the illusion produced could be a pleasurable one; as Leonard Bacon wrote in the Introduction to Austin Tappan Wright's *Islandia* (1942):

> It was a strange experience to prowl among these records of the wholly imaginative expressed in terms so definite and concrete. One grew familiar with the physical geography of a dream. … And certainly there were several weeks when the reality of Islandia was at least as evident to me as the illusion of Kamchatka, the latter known only on a map by no means so exciting as these which grew under Austin Wright's cartographical hand.[70]

Worlds-builders would find ways to imitate nonfiction's use of new sound and image media, using them to bring their worlds to life in concrete ways that the printed word could only suggest. It is no accident that the increase in the popularity of secondary worlds coincided with the rise of the mediated Primary World; each encouraged the other, in a way, and the representation of the Primary World became a way to benchmark the representation of secondary worlds. But most of all, mass media were new venues in which imaginary worlds could grow, or even originate.

Early Cinema and Comic Strips

The first big steps taken by imaginary worlds into the realm of sequential imagery were in cinema and comic strips. Early film was often an extension of the stage, as performers would be filmed in an uninterrupted take, preserving their performances. Live theater and opera occasionally gave glimpses of secondary worlds, like Prospero's island in *The Tempest* (1610), Titipu and Barataria in Gilbert and Sulivan's musicals, or Wagner's Venusberg; but the restrictions of live stage productions limited what could be done; the German dream of the *gesamtkunstwerk*, combining all the arts, would be closer to being realized once motion pictures added sound. In early cinema, the filmmaker most responsible for bringing imaginary worlds to the screen was George Méliès, whose background in stage magic, love of technology, and innovative filmmaking would lead him to become the father of cinematic special effects. While others like Thomas Edison and the Lumiere brothers were filming nonfictional "actualities" shot on location, or short non-narrative performances like sneezing, dancing, or comic boxing, Méliès was creating films in which everything on screen was designed and built for the film, including sets, backdrops, vehicles, and everything needed to construct his on-screen worlds. In two of his early films, *A Trip to the Moon* (1902) and *The Impossible Voyage* (1904), he has scenes set on the moon and on the sun respectively, reminiscent of *True History*'s inhabited moon and sun. In addition to experimenting with visual compositing and inventing many of early cinema's in-camera effects, Méliès pioneered the intercutting of small-scale models sets and vehicles with full-scale versions of the same; vehicle cutaways revealing multiple interiors; three-dimensional sets that extend back into two-dimensional backdrops; and other visual effects techniques that could bring fantastic worlds to the movie screen.

Another type of moving imagery, animation, brought drawings to life, but many of the earliest worlds to appear in it would originate in another graphical medium of the age, the comic strip. Comic strips had been developing since the late 1880s, and were mostly character-centered, with scenery used mainly to fill in the background rather than create a coherent geography. One exception, however, was Winsor McCay's *Little Nemo in Slumberland*, which ran from 1905 to 1911 and was revived in 1924–1927 (and ran from 1911 to 1914 as *In the Land of Wonderful Dreams*). Not only did McCay's comic strip name its unique world and feature it in the strip's title, but it also foregrounded its highly detailed world of fantastic vistas and fanciful architecture in a way that no cartoonist had done before and that few have done since (see Figure 2.5). Slumberland, which Little Nemo travels to in his dreams, has its own logic, which Nemo discovers over the years. As comics historians Pierre Couperie and Maurice Horn describe it:

> On each of his nocturnal rambles, Little Nemo penetrates a little more deeply into the dream. One after another he meets those who are to be his companions and guides: Flip, the green, grimacing dwarf who involves him in increasingly dangerous escapades; Impy the cannibal, Slivers the dog, Dr. Pill, and the Princess and her father, King Morpheus. Under McCay's pen, Little Nemo undertakes a genuine methodological exploration of the dream; little by little he reveals to us its logic, its language, and its mythical landscapes. Under their influence Little Nemo changes imperceptibly; the timid, wonderstruck little boy becomes more assured, and grows in his own esteem as he enters into increasingly close intimacy with his universe. Ultimately, Little Nemo becomes ruler of his dream when he learns to be master of its powers and to interpret its laws.[71]

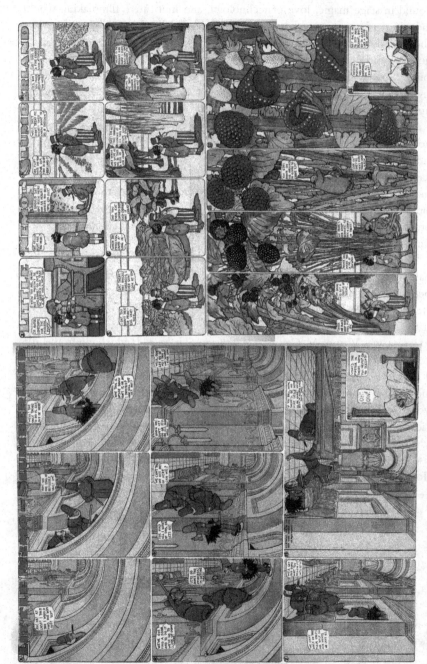

FIGURE 2.5 Typical pages from *Little Nemo in Slumberland*, including Befuddle Hall (left), which demonstrate McCay's attention to background detail and visual world-building.

But the complexity of Slumberland did not foster imitators. The majority of comic strips remained more character-centered (usually about family life) and set in the Primary World or thinly-veiled versions of Primary World places (like Superman's Metropolis or Batman's Gotham City). In a statistical study of comic strips covering the years 1900–1959, family-based strips were never less than 60 percent of the total, while fantasy and science fiction strips varied from 1 percent to 5 percent over the same period.[72] Only a few strips involved other planets, like Mongo in Alex Raymond's *Flash Gordon* (1934), or Superman's home planet of Krypton, which was already destroyed when Superman arrived on Earth. Some strips' worlds were set in the distant past, like the Kingdom of Moo in Vincent Hamiln's *Alley Oop* (1934), or the distant future, like René Pellos' *Futuropolis* (1937). Many had earthly locations for their distinctive settings, including Dogpatch in Al Capp's *Li'l Abner* (1934), Pharia of Bob Moore and Carl Pfeufer's *Don Dixon and the Hidden Empire* (1935), the Kingdom of Id in Johnny Hart and Brant Parker's *The Wizard of Id* (1964), or Grimy Gulch in Tom K. Ryan's *Tumbleweeds* (1965), although some, like Flyspeck Island in *Curtis* (1988), served only as places of characters' origins (like Krypton) and are talked about but rarely ever seen or used as destinations. Some places acquired a great deal of detail and history due to their longevity: *Gasoline Alley,* set in the town of the same name, began in 1918 and has continued to the present day; its characters have aged and two new generations, the children and grandchildren of the original characters, have grown up over the years. Other comic strips were extensions of worlds that had debuted in other media (such as those of Buck Rogers and Tarzan, both of which debuted in the comics on January 7, 1929), as worlds began to spread from one medium to another.

Oz: The First Great Transmedial World

As mass media grew more popular, not only did imaginary worlds appear in each of them, but individual worlds soon bridged across them, becoming transmedial, with new works in different media introducing new elements to those worlds. The first great multimedia world to appear was L. Frank Baum's Oz, which over the two decades of its development before Baum's death would encompass most of the existing media of the time. Even the first Oz book, *The Wonderful Wizard of Oz* (1900) had closely coordinated text and images. Instead of having illustrations added to an already completed text, the text and images of Baum's book worked together from the start to form a seamless whole, prompting Michael O. Riley to write that "the design for *The Wonderful Wizard of Oz* can only be described as *radically* innovative because there had never been anything like it, and few books since have equaled its amazing blend of story and pictures."[73] In some cases, the text is even printed over a background illustration, which, according to Riley, "results in the mind's receiving the picture that illustrates a portion of the text at exactly the same time as it is assimilating the meaning of the text."[74]

Baum's Oz was the most detailed imaginary world of its time, and from 1900 until his death in 1919, Baum wrote 14 Oz books: *The Wonderful Wizard of Oz* (1900), *The Marvelous Land of Oz* (1904), *Ozma of Oz* (1907), *Dorothy and the Wizard of Oz* (1908), *The Road to Oz* (1909), *The Emerald City of Oz* (1910), *The Patchwork Girl of Oz* (1913), *Tik-Tok of Oz* (1914), *The Scarecrow of Oz* (1915), *Rinkitink of Oz* (1916), *The Lost Princess of Oz* (1917), *The Tin Woodman of Oz* (1918), *The Magic of Oz* (1919), and *Glinda of Oz* (1920) (which was published posthumously). Baum had a lifelong interest in live theater, and in 1901 he completed a stage musical version of *The Wonderful Wizard of Oz*, which opened in Chicago in 1902 and went on to New York, where it had nearly 300 performances over a 2-year period before going on a national tour. It was still playing in 1911, making it one of the most successful stage musicals of its day. Baum's second Oz book, *The Marvelous Land of Oz*, was even written with the intention of turning it into a stage musical to follow up on the success of the previous Oz musical, though the book did much better than the play did.[75]

Oz quickly expanded into a variety of media. From August 28, 1904 to February 6, 1905, 26 short stories about Oz, known collectively as *Queer Visitors from the Marvelous Land of Oz*, ran in the comics section of newspapers accompanied by comic strip illustrations. Around the same time, from December 1904 to March 1905, Baum's first illustrator, W. W. Denslow, who shared the copyright with Baum, ran his own series of illustrated stories called *Denslow's Scarecrow and Tin-man*, based on the same characters. The *Queer Visitors* series also led to a short spin-off entitled *The Woggle-Bug Book* (1905) which was released along with a musical play of the same name, as well as other merchandise including Woggle-bug postcards, buttons, and an unauthorized card game from Parker Bros. In 1908, Baum released and starred in the multimedia show *The Fairylogue and Radio-Plays*, which combined a full orchestra, over two dozen live actors, 114 magic lantern slides and 23 film clips, both with hand-tinted color, together with Baum who would lecture and interact with characters onstage and on-screen. The show combined adaptations of his earlier Oz works, and one of the slides even presented the first map of Oz.[76]

The traveling show was too expensive to be a financial success, and his next planned musical extravaganza, based on Ozma of Oz, was not produced. In 1910, the world of Oz appeared on film in three motion picture productions, *The Wonderful Wizard of Oz*, *Dorothy and the Scarecrow in Oz*, and *The Land of Oz*, all written by Baum but filmed by William Nicholas Selig. And in 1913, Baum released *The Little Wizard Series* (which were six short books of Oz stories for children), and staged *The Tik-Tok Man of Oz*, his "fairyland extravaganza in three acts", which became the basis for the book *Tik-Tok of Oz* a year later. After moving to Hollywood, Baum started the Oz Film Manufacturing Company in 1914, and released a film version of *The Patchwork Girl of Oz*, and *The New Wizard of Oz*, which was a version of *His Majesty, the Scarecrow of Oz*, and served as the basis for the 1915 book. All this demonstrates that Oz did not simply originate in Baum's books and then get adapted to other media; new Oz stories could begin as books, musicals, comic strips, or plays and then be adapted across media, and those adaptations would often add new material, events, and characters as well, making Oz a truly transmedial world.

Oz also grew far beyond its original author. Besides additions to Oz from collaborators such as illustrators W. W. Denslow and John R. Neill who gave Oz a visual dimension, or all the people involved in the theater productions who brought the world to the stage, contributions would come from other authors commissioned by Baum's estate to continue writing Oz books after his death. Ruth Plumley Thompson would write a new Oz book every year from 1921 to 1939, writing more Oz books than Baum himself. MGM's film version of *The Wizard of Oz* (1939) renewed interest in Baum's world, and Oz novels appeared from other authors, including John R. Neill, Jack Snow, Rachel R. Cosgrove, Eloise Jarvis McGraw and Lauren McGraw Wagner, Dick Martin, and Baum's sons Frank Joslyn Baum and Kenneth Gage Baum. By the mid-1950s, Oz had grown so large that Jack Snow's *Who's Who in Oz* (1954) ran over 300 pages. Today, the International Wizard of Oz Club has thousands of members and new Oz stories continue to appear, as well as scholarship analyzing Baum's subcreated world.

Baum's world and its transmedial success would encourage other worlds to make the transition between media, once they had proven themselves and attracted a large enough audience in their medium of origin. With its unequalled malleability and low cost, print media would remain the main incubator for imaginary worlds into the twentieth century; however, books would be joined by an even less expensive print medium, in which dozens of new authors poured forth their stories and worlds to millions of readers every month.

Pulp Magazines

Evolving out of dime novels and penny dreadfuls, pulp magazines were one of the main venues for fantasy and science fiction from the late 1890s until the early 1950s. Pulp magazines aided the growth and spread of imaginary worlds in three main ways: they brought them to a large audience (in their heyday, an issue could sell as much as a million copies); they were an outlet for stories by new writers, many of whom would have prolific careers and build enormous worlds, the first glimpses of which would appear in the pulps; and they raised issues pertaining to world-building itself through the various approaches taken by different authors.

The broad audience reached by pulp magazines grew over the first few decades of the twentieth century. Early magazines included *The Black Cat* (1895–1922), which featured fantasy and science fiction stories, and Frank A. Munsey's *The Argosy*, the prototype adult adventure fiction pulp, which was converted from a boys' magazine in 1896, later merged with Munsey's *All-Story Magazine* (begun 1905) into *Argosy-All-Story Weekly* in 1920, and outlived the pulp era, finally ending in 1978. The 1920s and 1930s marked the heyday of the pulps, as well as the appearance of the most famous pulps, such as *Weird Tales* (1923–1954, and revived later), *Amazing Stories* (1926–2000, restarted 2004–2005), and *Astounding Stories* (begun in 1930, renamed several times, and presently called *Analog Science Fiction-Fact*). New magazines kept appearing, right up into the 1950s when the pulps died out. The boom in pulps occurred not only in the United States, but also in Britain, Australia, Italy, Mexico, the Netherlands, and Sweden.[77]

Pulp magazines brought a variety of imaginary worlds to a wide audience on a weekly or monthly basis, although the short stories or serialized novellas contained in them did not allow the same degree of world development as novels did. At the same time, the shortness of the stories, and their often more outlandish and exaggerated nature, allowed for more experimentation and innovation since development only needed to go so far. Some examples of the strange worlds introduced in pulp magazines include the Hall of Mist, where vast Brains of the far future gather to watch the end of the universe; the submicroscopic world of Ulm, entered with the aid of an Electronic Vibration Adjustor; the macroscopic world of Valadom in which our solar system is only an atom; the Pygmy Planet, a miniature artificial world created in a laboratory to test theories of evolution; Vulcan, a tiny planet whose orbit takes it closer to the sun than Mercury; Soldus, a planet located inside the sun; the planet Lagash, continually lit by its six suns, so that nightfall occurs only once every 2049 years; Logeia, a world without hyperbole or metaphor where everything is literal; the planet Hydrot, whose surface is almost entirely covered with water; the planet Placet, which can eclipse itself, due to the photon-decelerating Blakeslee Field through which it moves; and the planet Aiolo, where sentient plants have destroyed all animal life.[78]

Short stories and novellas gave glimpses of new worlds, which occasionally were compelling enough to interest their authors in exploring more of their possibilities. As a result, some of the worlds introduced in pulp magazines blossomed into larger and more detailed worlds and universes that became the settings for series of novels or even works in other media. Worlds and franchises that debuted in pulp magazines include Philip Francis Nowlan's twenty-fifth-century Earth of Buck Rogers; Clark Ashton Smith's Zothique (the last inhabited continent of a future Earth); Robert E. Howard's Hyborian Age; E. E. Smith's Lensman universe; Fritz Leiber's Nehwon (the world in which Fafhrd and the Gray Mouser have their adventures); Robert Heinlein's Future History universe; Isaac Asimov's Foundation universe and Galactic Empire universe; Ray Bradbury's version of Mars in his Martian Chronicles; Poul Anderson and John Gergen's Psychotechic League universe; L. Sprague de Camp's Viagens Interplanetarias universe; Cordwainer Smith's Instrumentality of Mankind universe; and H. Beam Piper's Terro-Human Future History universe, among others.[79]

The pulps were also known for their colorful cover images and fantastic interior illustrations, both depicting future cities and alien worlds. Following after Robida, graphic artists like Louis Biedermann, Frank R. Paul, and Elliot Dold imagined and drew detailed images of future cities, with elevated thoroughfares and flying cars docking at platforms atop skyscrapers, all massively scaled to breathtaking proportions. The sensationalist and often lurid imagery, combined with stories of aliens, robots, and monsters, also helped pulp magazines gain the reputation that they have today for being exaggerated and unrealistic. Yet, some in the industry cared deeply about verisimilitude and realism. As the founding editor of *Amazing Stories*, Hugo Gernsback, wrote in an editorial commentary in a 1932 issue of *Wonder Stories*:

> When science fiction first came into being, it was taken most seriously by all authors. In practically all instances, authors laid the basis of their stories upon a solid scientific foundation. If an author made a statement as to certain future instrumentalities, he usually found it advisable to adhere closely to the possibilities of science as it was then known.
>
> Many modern science fiction authors have no such scruples. They do not hesitate to throw scientific plausibility overboard, and to embark upon a policy of what I might call scientific magic, in other words, science that is neither plausible, nor possible. Indeed, it overlaps the fairy tale, and often goes the fairy tale one better.
>
> This is a deplorable state of affairs, and one that I certainly believe should be avoided by all science fiction authors, if science fiction is to survive.[80]

When the pocketbook-sized paperback came into popularity during the 1940s and 1950s, it brought about the end of the Golden Age of pulp magazines, and by the 1960s, according to science fiction historian David Kyle:

> The pulps were gone, dinosaurs which evolution had obliterated; they had been replaced by the smaller, tidier, subdued, digest-size periodicals. The carnage which commercial greediness had left was actually, in large measure, just resting, awaiting resurrection. The new, expanding market was now blazing—the paperback books. The old pulps with their insatiable demands had developed scores of writers and had left a strong and distinguished group which became the heart and soul of modern science fiction.[81]

The influence of pulp magazines was great and their spirit carried over into a variety of other media. In comics, for example, Alex Raymond's Flash Gordon traveled to the planet Mongo, and Bob Moore and Carl Pfeufer's Don Dixon found the Hidden Empire of Pharia. In 1940, Batman's Gotham City would appear, as well as what would come to be known as the DC Comics universe; in 1944 Wonder Woman would leave Paradise Island and begin her adventures; and in 1952, *Twin Earths*, by Okar Lebeck and Alden McWilliams, featured Terra, a planet orbiting the sun on the opposite side away from Earth and always hidden from view. As worlds begun in pulp magazines spread across media, the pulp sensibility would also carry over, into novels, movies, radio, and television.

Developments in Cinema and Theater

Movie serials, short subjects shown before features and broken up into chapters (usually 12 chapters of 20 minutes each), were the pulps of the silver screen, and many came from existing franchises in other media (like Flash Gordon, Tarzan, and Dick Tracy). A few, like Flash Gordon, visualized new worlds, but the serials' limited budgets restricted the amount of depth and detail that those worlds would have. Full-length feature films, however, were able to explore their worlds in more depth.

By the 1920s and 1930s, feature film production had the technology and budgets needed to do justice to bringing imaginary worlds to the screen. The theatrical stage, with all of its limitations, had produced a few worlds, including Toyland from Herbert and MacDonough's operetta *Babes in Toyland* (1903), Neverland from J. M. Barrie's *Peter Pan* (1904), Rossum's Island from Karel Čapek's *R. U. R. (Rossum's Universal Robots)* (1923), Caspo from Arnold Bennett's *The Bright Island* (1925), Grover's Corners from Thornton Wilder's *Our Town* (1938), Brigadoon from the Lerner and Loewe 1947 musical of the same name, the Grand Duchy of Lichtenburg from the musical *Call Me Madam* (1950), Anatevka[82] from the musical *Fiddler on the Roof* (1964), and adaptations of worlds from other media, like the Oz musical mentioned earlier; but the stage remained more the realm of dialogue and character development than world development. Cinematic representations had fewer restrictions, and films like *Metropolis* (1927), *King Kong* (1933), and *The Wizard of Oz* (1939) demonstrated the medium's ability to visualize worlds, and to some extent, even use them (along with special effects) to market the films in which they appeared. Especially when a story was already well known, as was the case with *The Wizard of Oz*, the depiction of its world on-screen could be a selling point. As the voiceover of the 1939 trailer for *The Wizard of Oz* proclaimed:

> Although *The Wizard of Oz* has captivated the children of four generations and fired the imagination of those youthful adults who have never grown old, although ten million copies have reached eager hands and eager hearts, no one has dared the towering task of giving life and reality to the Land of Oz and its people. Every delightful character of L. Frank Baum's classic is now reborn, every glorious adventure has been recaptured and painted with the rainbow; the celebration in Munchkinland, the flying monkeys, the rescue of Dorothy, the castle of the witch, the palace of Oz, and Dorothy's strange journey to the Emerald City to find the Wonderful Wizard of Oz himself.[83]

Yet most of the imaginary worlds visualized on film during the first half of the twentieth century were typically adaptations of worlds originating in other media; for example, the films *Alice in Wonderland* (1933), *Babes in Toyland* (1934), *She* (1935), *Lost Horizon* (1937), *Gulliver's Travels* (1939), *Pinocchio* (1940), *Call Me Madam* (1951), *Peter Pan* (1953), and *Brigadoon* (1954), expanded on or even changed the stories on which they were based, but still ultimately relied on existing source material for their worlds. It would not be until the second half of the twentieth century that the origination of imaginary worlds in film would become more common.

Radio and Television

Like comic strips and movie serials, broadcast media are usually episodic in nature and therefore require characters or worlds to link together multiple narratives. Before music and talk shows became the dominant forms of radio, dramatic series and comedies represented outlets for narrative; and since radio is a medium of voices and sound effects, characters became the usual link across a program's episodes (as evidenced by program titles, which typically included the name of the main character). Apart from adaptations, such as the BBC's dramatization of Tolkien's work or NPR's dramatization of the original *Star Wars* trilogy, there are relatively few secondary worlds on the radio, and even fewer originating there. Worlds making their debut on radio would include Euclidia from Perry Crandall's *Magic Island* (1936) about a technically-advanced island and its inhabitants; Five Points, a suburb of Chicago in which Irna Philips' soap opera *The Guiding Light* (1937–2009) first began; the Land of the Lost in Isabel Manning Hewson's *Land of the Lost* (1943–1948), about an underwater kingdom where lost objects go; and Borsetshire, a fictional county in England from *The Archers* (1951), a British program about rural life. Many radio shows transferred to television, and radio drama died away, although some shows continued to flourish; for example, after 19 years as a radio show, *The Guiding Light* finally moved to television in 1956, where it ran until 2009. The two best-known and most detailed secondary worlds to originate on radio in the latter half of the twentieth century are Lake Wobegon, from Garrison Keillor's *Prairie Home Companion* radio show which began in 1974 (and has since expanded into several novels, with the radio show itself spawning a feature film), and the Hitchhiker's Galaxy of Douglas Adams' *Hitchhiker's Guide to the Galaxy* which began as a radio drama in 1978 and expanded into several novels, a computer game, comic books, and a feature film.

At first, television's limitations were similar to those of theater, since early television programs had to be performed live. Budgets were also limited, so it is perhaps no surprise that most secondary worlds appearing on early television were adaptations of successful worlds from other media, rather than original ones created especially for television. These adaptations include the BBC's production of *Alice: Some of Her Adventures in Wonderland* (1946), *Toad of Toad Hall* (1946),

The Adventures of Alice (1960), *Alice* (1965), and *Alice in Wonderland* (1966), the British broadcast company Rediffusion's *The Adventures of Sir Lancelot* (1956) and *An Arabian Night* (1960), and NBC's *Peter Pan* (1955). Like stage adaptations, these works relied to some extent on the audience's prior knowledge of the works being adapted, and on conventions which helped viewers overlook their limitations.

During the 1960s and beyond, bigger budgets, expanded sets, and location shooting aided the creation of worlds, and new ones originating on television began to appear. Typically, these were in the form of towns, like Oakdale, Central City, Bay City, Salem, Collinsport, Llanview, Pine Valley, Genoa City, Hazzard, Corinth, Cabot Cove, Twin Peaks, Cicely, Capeside, and Harmony.[84] Some towns, like Mayfield, Mayberry, Hooterville, Port Charles, and Fernwood, even had multiple shows set in them.[85] A few shows were set on islands: the title island of *Gilligan's Island* (1964–1967), Tracy Island from *Thunderbirds* (1965–1966), Living Island from *H. R. Pufnstuf* (1969–1971), and the Island of Sodor from *Thomas the Tank Engine and Friends* (1984–present). Both Tracy Island and the Island of Sodor, as well as Titanica and Marineville from *Stingray* (1964–1965), were built as small-scale models inhabited by puppets, the size of which allowed for greater scope than the worlds of most live-action shows, or shows which mixed puppets with live actors (like the Neighborhood of Make-Believe of *Mister Rogers' Neighborhood* (1968–2001) and the eponymous street of *Sesame Street* (1969–present)). Animation also allowed more world-building to occur within a limited budget, as Bedrock (of *The Flintstones* (1960–1966)), Orbit City (of *The Jetsons* (1962–1963, 1984–1985, 1987–1988), and Springfield (of *The Simpsons* (1989–present)) can attest.

While the longest-running worlds on television tend to be those of soap operas, the worlds of broadest scope to originate on television are those of science fiction. The "Whoniverse" of *Doctor Who* (1963–1989, 1996, 2005–present), the universe of *Star Trek* (1966–1969), Moonbase Alpha of *Space: 1999* (1975–1978), the universe of *Babylon 5* (1993–1998), and the Uncharted Territories of *Farscape* (1999–2003) all are fairly broad in scope, with alien races and other planets. Several of these went on to start transmedial franchises, discussed later in this chapter. Other smaller-scale series also began franchises; *Twin Peaks*, for example, inspired a feature film, several books, an audio book, and a set of trading cards.

Apart from a few exceptions,[86] the early worlds of broadcast media brought with them few innovations regarding the form and structure of imaginary worlds, but what they did contribute was a new relationship between the worlds and their audiences. The worlds of radio and television were audiovisual worlds that people experienced in their own homes on a regular basis, returning to them week after week (or several times a week, for daily programs), over a period of time that could be decades long, especially in the case of soap operas. That imaginary worlds could attain such long-term, ongoing integration into the lives of their audiences was unprecedented; although novels could span hundreds of years, they did not take up nearly as much of their audience's time as long-running broadcast programs could. And actors could realistically age along with their characters over long periods of time; for example, in 2010, Susan Lucci and Ray MacDonnell began their fortieth year of playing the same characters on *All My Children* (occasionally actors can age naturally in a series of movies, like the young actors in the *Harry Potter* films released over an 11-year period). Another soap opera, *The Guiding Light* (later renamed *Guiding Light*), ran for 15,762 episodes over 72 years; as dedicated as the show's fans may be, it is unlikely that anyone can claim to have seen and heard every radio and television episode. Since they derive their support from advertising, which in turn relies on ratings, the episodic imaginary worlds of broadcast media are also very dependent on audience response for their continuation; so their makers are often very concerned about audience reaction and feedback, which can influence the direction further world-building takes, a situation encountered previously by writers of serialized literature. And literature, in general, also saw new advancements in world-building during the twentieth century.

Developments in Literature

Despite the wide range of new media appearing or coming to prominence in the first half of the twentieth century, books remained the main place where imaginary worlds were conceived and incubated, including those that spread to other media, and the first half of the twentieth century saw the publication of numerous novels whose worlds were uncharted islands, remote desert cities, lost worlds hidden away in mountains or jungles, underground realms, underwater worlds, future civilizations, and an increasing number of new planets (see the Appendix for a list of worlds). In addition to transmedial adaptation, popular worlds were now more likely to give rise to sequels and series, especially after the success of the Oz series. While most authors were content to write about their worlds in a single book, or develop a single series of books based on the same world, or both (like L. Frank Baum), Edgar Rice Burroughs was one of the first authors to produce multiple series of books, each of which was set in a different world.

Burroughs began his fiction-writing career in pulp magazines, where many of his novels would be serialized. In 1912, two of his series began this way: "Under the Moon of Mars" serialized in *All-Story* magazine, which would become the first entry of his Barsoom series (Barsoom was his version of the planet Mars); and "Tarzan of the Apes" serialized in *All-Story* later that year, introducing his Tarzan series. Burroughs went on to start several other series: the Pellucidar series, about a world inside the hollow earth, introduced in *At the Earth's Core* (1914); the Mucker series begun with *The Mucker* (1914), set on Yoka Island in the Pacific Ocean; the Caspak series beginning with *The Land That Time Forgot* (1918), set on the island of Caspak (also known as Caprona), an island of prehistoric animals;

and the Amtor series beginning with *Pirates of Venus* (1934), with Amtor as his fictional version of Venus. Of his six series, four of them, the Barsoom, Pellucidar, Caspak, and Amtor series, were world-based, with the book titles tying the series together in a manner similar to the Oz books (except that "Mars" and "Venus" were used in the titles instead of "Barsoom" and "Amtor"). While the Tarzan series is linked by the Tarzan character and does not form a coherent world, several novels in the series introduce imaginary worlds, including a number of African cities, countries, and kingdoms (such as Opar, Pal-ul-don, Alali, Castra Sanguinarius, Castrum Mare, Midian, Onthar, Thenar, and Ashair),[87] and Burroughs even has Tarzan visiting Pellucidar in the crossover novel, *Tarzan at the Earth's Core* (1930), retroactively linking the two series. Likewise, Burroughs wrote other standalone novels and stories introducing new worlds, like "Adventure on Poloda" (1942) which introduced his Omos solar system made up of the star Omos and 11 planets.[88]

Like Baum, Burroughs was a savvy transmedial author, and helped his creations spread to film, stage, comics, and radio. Burroughs even thought about television rights long before the medium appeared, writing in 1932:

> Since those simple days of twenty years ago, when I blithely gave away a fortune in rights that I did not know existed, many changes have taken place, bringing new rights with them. Today I am closing a radio contract covering the dramatic presentation of my stories over the air. What a far cry from second magazine rights. Within a year I have seen a television clause inserted in one of my motion picture contracts; and today I am watching my television rights with as great solicitude as I watch any of the others, for long before my copyrights expire television rights will be worth a fortune.[89]

Burroughs trademarked the Tarzan name and was probably the first author to incorporate himself, starting Edgar Rice Burroughs, Inc. in 1923 to handle the merchandising and licensing of his work, and after 1931, to publish his books. His multimedia empire flourished, and the company was passed down to his family after his death in 1950 and is still in business today.

As the twentieth century went on, more sequels and series also meant worlds of increasing size and complexity. Even some standalone novels of the time took place over vast timescapes, like William Hope Hodgson's *The Night Land* (1912), covering humanity's existence over millions of years; Olaf Stapledon's *Last and First Men* (1930), about 18 species of human beings evolving over 2 billion years; and Stapledon's *Star Maker* (1937), whose timeline spans billions of years and the entire history of the universe. *Last and First Men* included five "Time Scale" charts, each more vast in scope than the one before it, and *Star Maker* included "A Note on Magnitude", three "Time Scale" charts, and in some editions, a Glossary. Documenting a wide range of worlds and life forms, and the histories of societies and cultures arising from them, both books are overwhelmingly cosmic in scale and amazing feats of subcreation.

Since the addition of maps, secondary worlds had sometimes included additional materials beyond the story being told, which could add to the world and its verisimilitude without adding digressions to the narrative. For example, Robert Paltock's *The Life and Adventure of Peter Wilkins* (1751) included a glossary which listed 103 names and terms from the book. Other materials were written as backstory; Lord Dunsany (Edward John Moreton Drax Plunkett) wrote *The Gods of Pegāna* (1905), about his pantheon of gods, before writing legends of the lands where they were worshipped.[90] Dunsany's Pegāna inspired H. P. Lovecraft's Cthulhu mythology, and more than likely influenced Tolkien's writing of *The Silmarillion*, since Tolkien mentions Dunsany in his letters.[91] During the first half of the twentieth century, more worlds were being generated with elaborate histories and backstories, and along with the growing size and scope of these secondary worlds came more ancillary materials like maps, glossaries, timelines, genealogies, and so on, especially for larger-scale worlds or those spread over multiple volumes.

One of the largest worlds of its day, James Branch Cabell's *Biography of Manuel* series (launched with *Jurgen, A Comedy of Justice* (1919), although earlier works were later rewritten and incorporated retrospectively into the series) ran for 18 volumes[92] and spanned seven centuries, with a wide variety of imaginary lands worked into his world, the center of which is Poictesme, an imaginary province of France. Among these books is *The Lineage of Lichfield* (1922), a genealogy of the series' characters that shows how they are interrelated.

Other books with additional materials include Burrough's fourth Barsoom novel, *Thuvia, Maid of Mars* (1920), which contained a "Glossary of names and terms used in the Martian books" with 135 entries covering multiple books of the series, and E. R. Eddison's books, which had maps, timelines, lists of "Dramatis Personae", and genealogical tables to which readers could refer. Such material was helpful not only to readers, but to the authors themselves, whose world-building produced many such resources that were often never intended for publication. Nor were such ancillary works limited to worlds of science fiction and fantasy. In preparation for the writing of a series of five novels[93] set in the fictional U.S. midwestern state of Winnemac (see Figure 2.6), Sinclair Lewis drew detailed maps of the state and its capital, Zenith, in order to maintain geographic consistency throughout the novels. The 18 existing maps depict story locations at different scales, from floor plans of buildings, to city maps, to a map of the state of Winnemac. Drawn in the summer of 1921 while he was preparing to write *Babbitt* (1922), the maps were never published and were only discovered in 1961, 10 years after Lewis' death.[94]

Another work written for the sake of consistency and published posthumously is Robert E. Howard's essay "The Hyborian Age", about his fictional time period set around 20,000 BC to 9,500 BC, for his Conan the Cimmerian stories

FIGURE 2.6 A section of the map drawn by George Annand showing Sinclair Lewis's Winnemac, and where it is located in the American Midwest.

(and retrospectively for his Kull stories). Written sometime in the 1930s, the piece connects his world to the Atlantis myth and describes in detail the rise of the kingdoms of the Hyborians and their eventual downfall. The essay was found and published only months after Howard's death, and reprinted several times since then.

One of the most detailed worlds of the early twentieth century, of which nothing was published during the author's lifetime, was Austin Tappan Wright's *Islandia*, set mainly in the country of Islandia on the fictional Karain subcontinent. Wright was a Law Professor who had been developing Islandia as a hobby since his childhood. After his death in 1931 in an automobile accident, at the age of 48, his wife Margaret transcribed the 2,300 pages of Wright's longhand manuscript, which was later edited by his daughter Sylvia before being published in 1942. In an introduction published with the novel, Sylvia Wright described additional materials that her father had made:

> This novel represents only a part of the total Islandia papers. The original novel, containing close to six hundred thousand words, was so vast as to be virtually unpublishable, particularly during a wartime paper shortage. It was in this form, however, a manuscript contained in seven thick spring

binders, too heavy for me to carry by myself, that it was accepted by the publishers. ... With the intelligent and sensitive help of Mark Saxton, then an editor at Farrar and Rheinhart, I cut the novel by about a third. This is its form today. As I indicated in a note in the original edition, my father knew the exact lineaments of every scene that John Lang saw, down to its geological causes, and enjoyed describing such things. Much of the cutting was this sort of leisurely observation. ... My father knew the country so well because he had considered it and traveled around it in many guises. In one, he constructed its history, a scholarly work entitled *Islandia: History and Description*, by M. Jean Perier, whom readers will recognize as the first French consul to Islandia.

The document, of about 135,000 words, is the major part of the remainder of the unpublished Islandia papers. In addition, there are a large volume of appendices to the history, including a glossary of the Islandian language; a bibliography; several tables of population; a gazetteer of the provinces with a history of each; tables of viceroys, judges, premiers, etc.; a complete historical peerage; notes on the calendar and climate; and a few specimens of Islandian literature. There are also nineteen maps, one geological.[95]

At least a version of *Islandia* finally reached publication; some authors spend a lifetime developing imaginary worlds and ancillary materials without any public venue. Perhaps the best examples of these will remain unknown, though occasionally some gain publicity. For example, Henry Darger, a recluse who worked on his world for over five decades and died in 1973, was discovered to have written a 15-volume 15,145-page (single-spaced) novel *The Story of the Vivian Girls*, for which he produced several hundred paintings as illustrations. Since their discovery, Darger has become a cult figure in outsider art, books have been written about him, and his works hang in art museums, but his novel still remains unpublished.

During the twentieth century, more ancillary materials also appeared in the imaginary worlds of children's literature, particularly maps, like those of A. A. Milne's Hundred Acre Wood in his Winnie-the-Pooh stories, E. A. Wyke-Smith's detailed map showing where all the various adventures took place in *The Marvelous Land of Snergs* (1927), and C. S. Lewis' maps of Narnia and surrounding lands. Occasionally such materials could be quite elaborate; for their Railway series of books, begun with *The Three Railway Engines* (1945) and known for Thomas the Tank Engine, Reverend Wilbert Awdry and his brother George worked out the geography, history, industry, and language of their Island of Sodor; and these ancillary materials were later published in a separate book, *The Island of Sodor: Its People, History and Railways* (1987).

One interesting use of a map in a children's book appears in *365 Bedtime Stories* (1955) by Nan Gilbert (Mildred Gilbertson), a collection of 365 single-page stories, each with an illustration or two. All the stories revolve around the neighborhood of Trufflescootems Boulevard, otherwise known as What-A-Jolly Street, and the 22 children and their families and pets that live there. The book's endpapers provide a map of the street, with eight family homes, Mrs. Apricot's house, Mr. Gay's Store, and the School. Details that can be seen around the houses, like the creek, doghouse, and pony shed, appear in the stories, which all follow the map consistently, and although the individual single-page stories each have closure, there are larger story arcs extending through the book, sometimes linking consecutive stories, and sometimes returning weeks later and referring back to much earlier stories. While most of the stories are realistic, the children's pets and other neighborhood animals communicate with each other, and occasionally even inanimate objects like dolls, toys, a snowman, and the north wind become the stories' main characters, though none of the human characters ever see them interacting.

Amidst a growing number of children's books, one British book brought with it a glimpse of a world which its author continued expanding in the following decades, and its sequel became a turning point in the history of imaginary worlds, raising the bar and setting a new standard for all those that came after it. The book was J. R. R. Tolkien's *The Hobbit* (1937), and its sequel was *The Lord of the Rings* (1954–1955).

The Lord of the Rings and Tolkien's Influence

The first half of the twentieth century had seen a variety of imaginary worlds in literature: in addition to those mentioned in the last section, there were dystopias like those found in Aldous Huxley's *Brave New World* (1932) and George Orwell's *Animal Farm* (1945) and *Nineteen Eighty-Four* (1949); fantasy worlds like C. S. Lewis' Narnia and the planets of his Space Trilogy, H. P. Lovecraft's Dreamworld (also known as Dreamlands), and Mervyn Peake's Gormenghast; and the worlds of James Hilton's *Lost Horizon* (1933), A. E. van Vogt's *The Book of Ptath* (1943), and Herman Hesse's *The Glass Bead Game* (1943). However, it was J. R. R. Tolkien's Arda, in which Middle-earth is located, that would become one of the most beloved and influential imaginary worlds of all time.

Tolkien had always been interested in languages and had even made up his own imaginary languages as a child. He studied philology at Oxford University, and continued devising his own languages, influenced by the sound and structure of languages he was studying, including Finnish, Latin, Welsh, Icelandic, and other old Nordic and Scandinavian languages. Realizing that languages do not evolve in a vacuum, he decided to create the cultures from which his languages would come. While convalescing from trench fever in 1917, after serving in World War I, he began writing "The Fall of Gondolin", the story of Beren and Lúthien, and other connected tales that grew into his legendarium of the world he called Arda, which he called the "Silmarillion" (a version of which was edited and published by his son Christopher as *The Silmarillion* in 1977). Tolkien's children's story, *The Hobbit* (1937), was originally separate from this mythology but gradually became connected to it, and was later revised to be more consistent with his other works. Following the success of *The Hobbit*, Tolkien tried to get his Silmarillion mythology published, but it was turned down; the publishers wanted something with more hobbits in it instead. Therefore, Tolkien began writing a sequel, which would eventually become *The Lord of the Rings*.

Tolkien's Arda was unique, but not without its influences. Besides the older texts of his professional study like *Beowulf* and the *Kalevala*, Tolkien was familiar with the works of more contemporary writers, like George MacDonald, William Morris, Lord Dunsany, E. R. Eddison, E. A. Wyke-Smith, and his friend C. S. Lewis. While much of what Tolkien did, in terms of world-building, had already been done by others—a pantheon of gods, maps, timelines, glossaries, calendars, invented languages and alphabets—it was the *degree* to which he did them that gave his world its rich verisimilitude, and the *quality* of his work, with meaningful details integrated into an elaborate backstory, that set a new standard for world-building. As Humphrey Carpenter writes:

> Not content with writing a large and complex book, he felt he must ensure that every single detail fitted satisfactorily into the total pattern. Geography, chronology, and nomenclature all had to be entirely consistent. He had been given some assistance with the geography, for his son Christopher helped him by drawing an elaborate map of the terrain covered by the story. ... But the map in itself was not enough, and he made endless calculations of time and distance, drawing up elaborate charts concerning events in the story, showing dates, the days of the week, the hours, and sometimes even the direction of the wind and the phase of the moon. This was partly his habitual insistence on perfection, partly sheer revelling in the fun of "subcreation", but most of all a concern to provide a totally convincing picture.[96]

Tolkien wrote that "the ways in which a story-germ uses the soil of experience are extremely complex,"[97] and certainly his own background contributed to his writings, including his knowledge of medieval history and lore, his upbringing during the industrialization of the English countryside, and his war experience. As a professional linguist, his invented languages had a greater degree of development and a more realistic sound than most invented languages, and Tolkien even designed them to imitate the way real languages are related. His languages were even developed beyond what appears in the appendices to his books, and he considered including more of them in *The Lord of the Rings*, writing:

> A lot of labour was naturally involved, since I had to make a linkage with *The Hobbit*; but still more with the background mythology. That had to be rewritten as well. *The Lord of the Rings* is only the end part of a work nearly

twice as long which I worked at between 1936 and 53. (I wanted to get it all published in chronological order, but that proved impossible.) And the languages had to be attended to! If I had considered my own pleasure more than the stomachs of a possible audience, there would have been a great deal more Elvish in the book. But even the snatches that there are required, if they were to have a meaning, two organized phonologies and grammars and a large number of words.[98]

Like MacDonald and Lewis, Tolkien also theorized and wrote about what he was doing, coining the terms "subcreation" and "secondary world" in his essay "On Fairy Stories" in 1939, in which he explained the value of fantasy and the role of imagination. He expounded his ideas further in two other short works, the short story "Leaf by Niggle" (1947) and the poem *Mythopoeia* which he revised several times, as well as in a number of his letters. Nevertheless, it was the subcreation of Arda, in *The Hobbit* and especially in *The Lord of the Rings*, for which he became best known and which most influenced those who followed him.

While mainstream critics did not know what to make of *The Lord of the Rings*, readers responded enthusiastically. No other book imagined a fantastic world in such detail and beauty while ranging from low comedy to high drama and from rural homeliness to dark terrors and amazing wonders. Tolkien's story sold steadily after the last volume of it was published in 1955, and as Mike Foster summarized in the *J. R. R. Tolkien Encyclopedia*:

> But an unexpected party began in 1965, a long, loud boom in J. R. R. Tolkien's popularity in the United States that spread internationally and continues yet.
>
> Three factors contributed to this. One was the tenor of the times, the era of hippies, Vietnam, dissent, demonstrations, conscience, community: a homely ideal of benevolent, natural, ungoverned, mellow freedom like that of the Shire.
>
> Another factor was America's cultural Anglophilia. From the car radio to the movie theater to the fashion magazines, Britannia ruled pop culture from 1964 on.
>
> But the primary cause was an authorized paperback edition published by Ace Books, a New York science fiction firm, in June 1965.[99]

Ace Books had published an unauthorized paperback version of *The Lord of the Rings*, claiming that the work was public domain because American publisher Houghton Mifflin had failed to properly apply for an American copyright on the work. To counter Ace Books's inexpensive paperback edition, Houghton Mifflin asked Tolkien for revisions for a new edition, and put out the authorized paperback edition published by Ballantine Books, while fighting Ace's piracy of the book. In the end, Ace agreed to pay Tolkien royalties and cease publication.

The result of the controversy, however, was that *The Lord of the Rings*, as a relatively inexpensive paperback edition, became available to a much wider readership in the United States. The authorized 1965 edition of *The Lord of the Rings* included a new Foreword, an expanded Prologue, revisions of the text for consistency and additional detail, the correction of typographical errors, and an index (compiled by Nancy Smith). Tolkien continued making corrections and additions, which were added at various printings, with some first reaching publication as late as 1987.

Tolkien had begun work on his world around 1917 and was still adding to it and revising it when he died in 1973. Christopher Tolkien took on the editing and publishing of his father's manuscripts, including *The Silmarillion* (1977), *Unfinished Tales of Númenor and Middle-earth* (1980), and 12 volumes of *The History of Middle-earth* series, published over the years from 1983 to 1996, which gave readers a detailed inside look at how Tolkien created his legendarium, showing the evolution of his ideas and world over time. The same years saw the rise of a great deal of Tolkien scholarship including books, periodicals, and conferences dedicated to Tolkien's work, and adaptations of his work into theater, radio, film, television, board games, and video games. Likewise, Tolkien's influence extended beyond literature, to fantasy settings in film, television, and role-playing games such as TSR's *Dungeons & Dragons* (1974), which included hobbits, ents, and balrogs, until threats of copyright infringement caused the names to be changed. The fantasy adventure genre also provided settings for many text adventure games and graphical adventure video games during the early years of their development.

The popularity of Tolkien's work convinced Ballantine Books, who had released paperbacks of *The Hobbit*, *The Lord of the Rings*, and *The Tolkien Reader* (1966), that there was a growing audience for the fantasy genre, and they released paperback reprints of fantasy novels by E. R. Eddison, Mervyn Peake, David Lindsay, and Peter S. Beagle. In late 1968, Ballantine hired author Lin Carter as a consultant and together they began the Ballantine Adult Fantasy Series, which ran from 1969 to 1974 and consisted of 65 books, many of which were reprints of earlier works by authors including George MacDonald, William Morris, H. Rider Haggard, Lord Dunsany, William Hope Hodgson, James Branch Cabell, and others. Also in the series was Lin Carter's nonfiction *Imaginary Worlds* (1973), which looked at the history of fantasy and included chapters on world-building techniques, with examples from the other books.

Following Ballantine's lead, the Newcastle Publishing Company began the Newcastle Forgotten Fantasy Library, a series of reprints of 24 books by many of the same authors in Ballantine's series, released over the years 1973–1980. Both series reinvigorated interest in the fantasy genre, introduced it to a new generation, and encouraged a new crop of fantasy authors and world-builders, including Terry Brooks, Stephen R. Donaldson, Carol Kendall, Terry Pratchett, Anne McCaffrey, David and Leigh Eddings, Katherine Kerr, Robert Jordan,

Janny Wurts, Raymond E. Feist, and others, many of whose works were Tolkien-influenced in one way or another. Most of these authors, in addition to writing individual standalone novels, also produced series of novels each set in their own secondary world, and a number of their worlds became media franchises.

New Universes and the Rise of the Media Franchise

The idea of franchising, already present in business, boomed in the 1950s after the building of the interstate highway system, particularly in the area of restaurants and motels. Media franchising, which considers characters, settings, and stories as intellectual property to be used for licensing, had been around since the days of Baum and Burroughs, and an increasing number of worlds were being created with franchising possibilities already in mind. Multiple venues meant more rights and profits, turning the production of imaginary worlds into big business. During the first half of the century, most franchises were character-based (like those of Felix the Cat, Tarzan, Andy Hardy, and Ma and Pa Kettle) while only a few were world-based (like Oz, Barsoom, or Zothique); but the second half of the century would see a great increase in world-based franchises, and ones of growing size and scale. World-based franchises could be extended beyond the lifespan and experience of any individual character, which gave them an advantage over character-based franchises. The increased scale, size, and multimedia nature of these worlds would mean more worlds created by multiple authors (and their employees), and more worlds which were planned as a series of works from their very conception, as opposed to worlds that began as a single successful work which was then followed by one or more sequels that had not been planned in advance.

Other developments also helped spur the growth of imaginary worlds. As the second half of the century unfolded, pulp fantasy and science fiction passed from magazines into paperback fiction, allowing their stories and worlds to expand into series of novels. Many of these novels involved multiple planets and interstellar travel, so that the series' worlds widened from planets to galaxies or universes, making them broader in scope than those that had come before them (except for a few works of truly intergalactic scale, like Stapleton's *Star Maker*). The space race and the cold war nuclear threat provided the impetus for a new age of science fiction, and in the decade following the launch of Sputnik a vast number of new sci-fi universes appeared, including the Great Circle civilizations, the Technic History universe, the Childe Cycle universe, the Marvel Comics universe, the Noon universe, the Perry Rhodan multiverse, the Rim Worlds, the Imperium continuum, the Time Quartet universe, the Berserker universe, Michael Moorcock's Multiverse, the Whoniverse, the ConSentiency universe, the Demon Princes universe, the Hainish Cycle universe, the Known Space universe, the Dune universe, the Destination: Void universe, the Riverworld universe, the *Star Trek* galaxy, the World of Tiers universe, and the

Dumarest Saga universe.[100] Most of these would continue to expand into the 1970s and 1980s, and some are still growing today. The model that they provided, of series of novels or even series of series, continued to be followed by authors, especially in the genres of science fiction and fantasy, where series of books set in the same universe have become a standard strategy in book publishing.

In cinema, the growing use of animation and special effects during the postwar years (due in part to new technologies like the optical printer) helped bring these worlds to the screen, and a few films, like *Forbidden Planet* (1956), even introduced new worlds, instead of merely visualizing existing ones from other media. On television, effects-laden shows adapted worlds to the home screen, and brought new ones as well, including those seen on *Doctor Who* (1963), Gerry and Sylvia Anderson's *Stingray* (1964) and *Thunderbirds* (1965), and especially *Star Trek* (1966).

Doctor Who and *Star Trek* have both remained actively expanding worlds for over four decades, and each is composed of feature films, hundreds of hours of television episodes from multiple series and spin-offs, hundreds of novels, comic books and comic strips, dozens of games (card games, board games, role-playing games, pinball games, handheld electronic games, and video games (including arcade games, home console video games, and computer games (and for *Star Trek*, an MMORPG))), animated series, museum exhibitions, trading cards, action figures, and a variety of other merchandise. As each of these worlds is so vast, it is unlikely that anyone can claim to have experienced either world in its entirety, seeing every film and video, reading every book, and playing every game and so on; and these worlds' open and ongoing nature makes it less likely that anyone ever will. For example, as of mid-2012, the *Star Trek* universe had 11 feature films, six TV series with a combined total of 726 episodes, about 500 novels, and 69 video games. Even if one does not consider events in the video games to be canonical, that's still 23 days, 16 hours, and 7 minutes of continuous viewing along with several months of uninterrupted reading (depending on how long it takes to read 500 novels). These worlds, then, are not only quantitatively different from earlier ones, but qualitatively different, in that the audience has an experience of a world which, like the Primary World, not only achieves saturation of mind, but virtually exceeds the audience's ability to encounter it all in its entirety.

The one imaginary world most responsible for the rise of the media franchise in its modern form, with all its licensing and merchandising, made its first appearance during the mid-1970s. Inspired by the world-building in films like *2001: A Space Odyssey* (1968) and *Silent Running* (1972) and the television series *Space: 1999* (1975–1978), and having demonstrated his own world-building abilities in his film *THX 1138* (1971), George Lucas released *Star Wars* in May of 1977 (and to generate interest in it, preceded it with the novelization *Star Wars: From the Adventures of Luke Skywalker* in November of 1976). The *Star Wars* galaxy represented a milestone in the on-screen representation of imaginary worlds; not only was there great attention given to detail and design (see Figure 1.2), but locations and vehicles had a used and lived-in look, with all the scratches, dents, and wear-and-tear that made everything look as though it had a history. Lucas had taken the gritty realism of films of the late 1960s and 1970s, itself a cinematic descendent of postwar neorealism, and brought it into his imaginary world. Another way that he enhanced verisimilitude had to do with the freedom of camera movement that new special effects techniques provided, which changed the way the audience experienced the world of *Star Wars*. While other films like *2001* had used a locked-off camera for their special effects shots and spaceship shots, *Star Wars* was the first film to use computer-controlled cameras, allowing for special effects shots to be made with a dynamically moving camera that gave a more spacious and dimensional feel to the world.

Like Spielberg's *Jaws* (1975), *Star Wars* was an "event" picture released around the start of the summer season, and it proved that a film could become a blockbuster even though it was cast with mostly unknowns; instead of star power, it was the film's imaginary world itself, and the special effects that created it, that drew audiences. *Star Wars* also showed that more money could be made from merchandising than from box office receipts. Lucas understood the importance of merchandising early on; as a chapter on Lucas in *The Movie Brats* (1979) explained:

> From the start he [*Lucas*] was determined to control the selling of the film and its by-products. "Normally you just sign a standard contract with a studio," he says, "but we wanted merchandising, sequels, all those things. I didn't ask for another $1 million, just the merchandising rights. And Fox thought that was a fair trade." Lucasfilm Ltd., the production company George Lucas set up in July 1971, "already had a merchandising department as big as Twentieth Century-Fox has. And it was better. When I was doing the film deal, I had already hired a guy to handle that stuff."
>
> Lucas could argue, with reason, that he was protecting his own investment of two years' research and writing; and he was also protecting his share of the $300,000 from [*American*] *Graffiti*, which he and [*producer Gary*] Kurtz used as seed money for *Star Wars*. "We found Fox was giving away merchandising rights, just for the publicity," he says. "They gave away tie-in promotions with a big fast-food chain. They were actually paying these people to do this big campaign for them. We told them that was insane. We pushed and we pushed and we got a lot of good deals made." When the film appeared, the numbers become other worldly: $100,000 worth of T-shirts sold in a month, $260,000 worth of intergalactic bubble gum, a $3 million advertising budget for ready-sweetened *Star Wars* breakfast cereals. That was before the sales of black digital watches and Citizens [*sic*] Band radio sets and personal jet sets.[101]

Star Wars and its sequels and prequels did well at the box office, and even better in toy stores; by early 2010, licensing revenues for the franchise were estimated to be over US$12 billion.[102] Part of the reason was Lucas's timing; two innovations of the 1970s, cable television and commercial video cassette recorders (VCRs), extended a film's life cycle, allowing people who missed a film's theatrical release to catch up and join the audiences awaiting each new sequel (and buying the merchandise). And just as cable and VCRs made more repeat viewings possible, special effects became a reason for a repeat viewing. During the 1970s, more "Making of" documentaries came to be made, especially for films which pushed the boundaries of what special effects could do. Growing interest in the *Star Wars* galaxy also led to the publication of reference works which gave fans more information regarding the locations, vehicles, weaponry, creatures, minor characters, and other such minutiae present in the film's world.

The late 1970s and 1980s saw the franchising of older works (like *Star Trek*, which found new life in a series of feature films and new television series) as well as many new franchises, whose first appearances were in a variety of media, including books, film, television, video games, comic books and graphic novels, a card game (the planet Dominaria grew out of the card game *Magic: The Gathering* (1993)), and even a set of action figures; Flint Dille's *Visionaries: Knights of the Magical Light* (1987), set on the planet Prysmos, began as a set of Hasbro action figures and led to an animated television show and comic book series that told their story. By the mid-1980s, merchandising was so common that some worlds included their own commentary on the phenomenon; for example, Adrian Veidt, one of the superheroes in the graphic novel *Watchmen* (1986), is merchandising his superhero persona and even is shown with his own action figures, underscoring accusations that he has sold out. And by the 1990s, a number of how-to books on world-building in science fiction and fantasy, by authors like Orson Scott Card, J. N. Williamson, Matthew J. Costello, and others, were encouraging readers to subcreate their own worlds.

The growth of franchising and merchandising also aided the growth of world-based franchises. With an increasing number of media venues and merchandise, more money could be ventured in an attempt to establish a franchise, thus making world-based franchises more of a possibility. Character-based franchises set in the Primary World typically took less effort to produce, because they did not require a brand new world to be designed and developed around the characters to the degree that a world-based franchise did. The success of films like *Star Wars* (1977), *Alien* (1979), and *The Dark Crystal* (1982), and television shows like *Battlestar Galactica* (1978), encouraged more world-based franchises, which, at least in cinema, also decreased the dependence on stars, whose unavailability (or unwillingness) could end the continuation of character-based franchises centered on them, or at least require the audience to accept recastings (like the recasting of the role of Buffy when *Buffy the Vampire Slayer* moved from film to television, the recasting of the role of Dumbledore in the *Harry Potter* movies, or the multiply-recast role of James Bond).

The rise of franchising in the 1970s was also aided by a new medium that provided additional venues into which imaginary worlds could expand, and in which new ones would originate as well; the video game, which was a new development in tradition of interactive worlds.

Interactive Worlds

In one sense, the experiencing of imaginary worlds has always required the active participation of the audience, whose imaginations are called upon to fill gaps and complete the world gestalten needed to bring a world to life. However, such participation does not actively change the events occurring in the worlds imagined; stories have predetermined outcomes, and their worlds are experienced vicariously through the characters in those stories. Nevertheless, just as the role of stories' main characters changed from observer to participant, interactive worlds changed the audience member's role from observer to participant.

Interactive worlds can be traced back to children's play and games of pretend, either in role-playing situations or through the use of toys, like dolls and toy soldiers used as avatars through which children can vicariously enter the table-top worlds they created. Some adults also played with toy soldiers, for example, author Robert Louis Stevenson, who produced extensive written works and charts based on battles he staged with toy soldiers.[103] Toy soldier campaigns also prefigured the elaborate war board games that began to develop in the mid-seventeenth century.[104]

With the mass production of dollhouses in the nineteenth century and rise of model railroading in the early twentieth century, children's play gained more world-building tools, and both dollhouses and model railroads provided hobbies for adults as well. After World War II, dollhouses and their furnishing were mass-produced, making them more affordable and available as toys, but at the same time less detailed and simplified due to the demands of mass production. Other kinds of themed playsets appeared over the next few decades (most notably from the Marx Toy Company from the 1930s to the 1960s, and the Mego Corporation in the 1970s) and would become another venue for transmedial worlds as franchises began licensing them.[105]

Extending the age-old idea of building blocks, specialized building sets, like Meccano (1908), A. C. Gilbert's Erector Set (1913), the Tinkertoy Construction Set (1914), and Lincoln Logs (1916), allowed children to design as well as build, and encouraged the sale of additional building materials for even larger constructions. The most popular and successful of these began in the mid-twentieth century, when the LEGO Group's "Town Plan No. 1" set of 1955 introduced the LEGO System, the first "system" in the toy industry, in which every element can be connected to every other element, a fact which remains true more than 50 years and thousands of different building sets later. LEGO become another franchise outlet for several different worlds (including those of *Star Wars*, Harry Potter, and *The Lord of the Rings*), and the LEGO universe has itself expanded to include movies, comics, video games, and even a massively multiplayer on-line role-playing game (MMORPG).[106] Combining the best aspects of building sets and playsets, LEGO has become the most versatile world-building toy available.

Games became a new venue for worlds as early as the unauthorized Parker Bros. *Wizard of Oz* card game, and some board games, like Eleanor Abbott's *Candyland* (1949) or Klaus Teuber's *The Settlers of Catan* (1995), are set in imaginary lands. While few board games propose an imaginary world as a setting for game events, role-playing games typically do so. Building on the tradition of table-top war-gaming, game designer David Wesely developed the first role-playing game in 1967, a Napoleanic wargame set in the fictional German town of Braunstein. In earlier war games, players controlled whole armies, but in Wesely's game players controlled individuals and play was more open-ended.[107] A few years later in 1973, Wesely's friend and fellow wargamer Dave Arneson, along with Gary Gygax, started TSR (Tactical Studies Rules) Inc. to sell their *Dungeons & Dragons* (*D&D*) rule set, which was published as a game in 1974 and was inspired by the renewed interest in the fantasy genre. Like the building sets mentioned earlier, *Dungeons & Dragons*, using systems of rules and sets of dice, allowed players to create their own imaginary worlds and use them as game settings. TSR also published a number of games with ready-made settings that players could use, including Muhammad Abd-al-Rahman Barker's *Empire of the Petal Throne* (1974), Dave Arneson's *Blackmoor* (1975), and Fritz Leiber's *Lankhmar* (1976). TSR was not alone for long; another company, Chaosium, was started in 1975 by Greg Stafford to publish his game *White Bear and Red Moon* (1975) which introduced the world of Glorantha. TSR also published the Dragonlance series of novels written by Margaret Weis and Tracy Hickman, which grew out of a role-playing session and became a growing franchise itself. Other sets of role-playing rules have appeared, for example Steve Jackson's GURPS (Generic Universal Role-Playing System) which can be adapted to any gaming environment. Role-playing also left the tabletop as players got into character, with the rise of live-action role-playing (LARP) games in which players act out their characters in costume.

Just as a novel's author guides readers along, role-playing games often required one player to act as "Dungeon Master" (or DM), the controller of game world events and referee, and games could only run smoothly if all players consented to the DM's decisions. The control and regulation of the game world's events, however, would soon be able to be taken over by computer technology, allowing all players to have equal status under an automated referee, as role-playing games joined the ranks of video games.

The first video game that can arguably be said to depict an imaginary world (albeit a minimal one), was *Spacewar!* (1962), developed on the PDP-1 mainframe computer by students at MIT. The game takes place in a starfield in which two ships, the "needle" and the "wedge", attempt to shoot each other while avoiding the gravitational pull of a nearby star. Two mainframe games, Steve Colley's *Maze War* (1974) in which players wander about in a maze, looking for other players to shoot, and Jim Bowery's *Star Trek*–influenced *Spasim* (1974), short for "space simulator", which featured spaceships and bases in three-dimensional space, were the first video games to use a first-person perspective, giving players a point of view from within the game's world, rather than a third-person perspective looking in from outside the world. Several mainframe games attempted to bring *Dungeons & Dragons* to the computer, using *D&D* features such as hit points, experience points, monster levels, and mazes of dungeon rooms: Rusty Rutherford's *PEDIT5* (1975); Gary Whisenhunt and Ray Wood's *DND* (1975); Don Daglow's *Dungeon* (1975); *Oubliette* (1977); and *Rogue* (1980) by Michael Toy, Glenn Wichman, and Ken Arnold, which inspired many imitators.[108]

Most mainframe games used a combination of text and simple graphics, but one built its world using text alone, allowing players to type commands, use tools, and enter magic words as responses. Programmer Will Crowther, an avid *Dungeons & Dragons* player, wrote *Colossal Cave Adventure* (1976), based on part of the Mammoth Cave system in Kentucky. The game provided verbal descriptions of the player's location, and players explored by typing commands like "north" and "south"; a message at the beginning of the game read "I WILL BE YOUR EYES AND HANDS. DIRECT ME WITH COMMANDS OF 1 OR 2 WORDS." Later, Don Woods, a graduate student and Tolkien fan, took Crowther's program and with his blessing added fantasy elements, after which the game came to be known simply as *Adventure*. The game spread and spawned many imitators, which together became the game genre known as text adventures (which are sometimes included in the term "interactive fiction"). Crowther and Woods' *Adventure* inspired other games that led to the incorporation of companies to sell them: Scott Adams wrote *Adventureland* (1978), the first commercial adventure game, and began Adventure International in 1979 to sell it; Marc Blank, Dave Lebling, and others wrote *Zork* (1979) (the game was released commercially in three parts from 1980–1982) and started Infocom, which became the largest producer of text adventure games during the 1980s; and Roberta and Ken Williams began On-Line Systems (later Sierra On-Line) and their first game, *Mystery House* (1980), was one of the first to add graphical illustrations to the game's text.

Crowther and Woods' *Adventure* also inspired the first all-graphical adventure game, Warren Robinett's *Adventure* (1979) for the Atari 2600 (see Figure 2.7). With 30 screens worth of imagery through which players could move, Robinett's *Adventure* was the first game to cut cinematically from one screen to the next as the player–character moved from place to place, applying film conventions to a video game world. It also provided the player with a number of objects that could be carried and used (the chalice, sword, bridge, magnet, gold key, black key, white key, and the dot), though only one item could be carried at any given time, adding to the game's difficulty. The game world also contained four computer-controlled characters, three dragons and a bat, which interacted with the player–character.

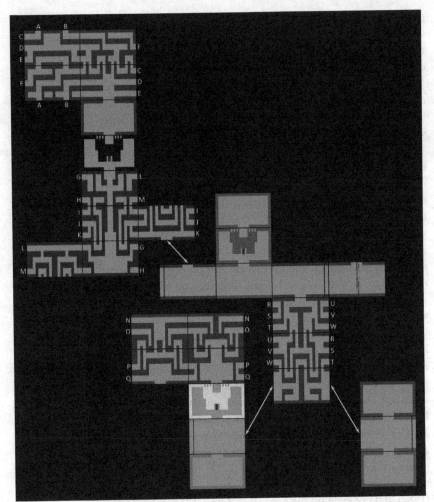

FIGURE 2.7 Warren Robinett's *Adventure* (1979) for the Atari VCS 2600 was the first video game that cut screen to screen as the player-character moved through the game's world.

As video games moved from mainframe computers to more public venues and became commercial products, the most elaborate video game worlds continued to appear in the adventure game genre, and were made for home consoles or home computers instead of for the arcade, where fast action, short games, and high rates of player turnover were more profitable than slower-paced games involving lengthy exploration and problem-solving. Only a few arcade games introduced elaborate worlds; for example, *Gravitar* (1982) was made of four "universes" each of which had three solar systems that each had four or five planets, and each planet had its own unique terrain to navigate. Early home console games, on the other hand, were cartridge-based and had limited memory, restricting the size and detail of their worlds, but still a few appeared on them: for example, the Atari 2600 had Robinett's *Adventure* (1979), an adaptation of *Superman* (1979) which also used Robinett's system of screen-to-screen movement, and *Dragonstomper* (1982), while the Nintendo Entertainment System (NES) introduced *The Legend of Zelda* (1986) and *Final Fantasy* (1987), both of which launched growing franchises.

Home computer role-playing games finally reached a wide audience with the release of Richard Garriott's *Ultima* (1980).[109] After the success of his Tolkien-inspired *Akalabeth: World of Doom* (1979), Garriott designed and wrote a larger, more detailed game and game world. Instead of using room-by-room graphics, Garriott (with the help of Ken Arnold who had helped design *Rogue*) used a system of tiled graphics that allowed four-way scrolling, recentering the graphics as the player moved. *Ultima*'s overhead-view graphics, combined with first-person perspective mazes, and the overall size of Sosaria, the game's world, helped make the game a success, and *Ultima* would go on to be become a franchise, with each game in the series including new advancements in graphics, character interaction, and overall world-building.

Throughout the 1980s, video game worlds would grow in size and interactivity. New programming techniques and programs like Lucasfilm's SCUMM engine, written for *Maniac Mansion* (1987), would increase the vocabulary of recognized words, and better graphics and faster processing speeds led to greater detail and more animation. Interaction increased as well, and games like Don Daglow's *Utopia* (1981), Will Wright's *SimCity* (1989), and Peter Molyneux's *Populous* (1989), allowed players to build their own individualized worlds directly, and began the genre now referred to as "god games", in which players create and manage miniature worlds. The CD-ROM provided far more storage capacity than any cartridge had, and the first game to use a CD-ROM, Cyan's *The Manhole* (1987), did not even fill the entire disc. CD-ROM technology also made possible Cyan's *Myst* (1993), which set new standards for the detail, size, and interactivity found in single-player adventure games, and went on to start the *Myst* franchise. However, the biggest changes in the imaginary worlds found in video games would come in the mid-1990s, when advances made in single-player games would be applied to multiplayer games.

As the worlds of graphical adventure games were developing during the late 1970s and 1980s, text adventure games were becoming multiplayer. In 1978, Roy Trubshaw and Richard Bartle, students at Essex University, wrote what they called a *MUD* (Multi-User Dungeon) on a PDP-10 mainframe computer; an all-text adventure world in which multiple players could participate in real time. During the 1980s, MUDs would expand along with the worlds they depicted. Among the first commercial MUDs, Alan Klietz's *Sceptre of Goth* (1983) allowed 16 users to call in remotely and play simultaneously, and Kelton Flinn and John Taylor's *Island of Kesmai* (1984) was run on Compuserve in 1985, allowing for up to 100 players. Lucasfilm's *Habitat* (1986) was a graphical virtual world made up of spaces in which users could see each other's avatars and speak to each other using displayed text. Richard Skrenta's *Monster* (1988) was a text-based MUD that allowed on-line creation, in which players could help edit *Monster*'s on-line world from within the world itself, making objects and location, and creating puzzles for other users to solve. Finally, Archetype Interactive's *Meridian 59* (1995) (see Figure 2.8), with three-dimensional graphics, was released with a flat-rate monthly subscription rate, as opposed to the usual method of charging by the hour or by the minute. More than 25,000 players took part in the beta version of the game before its commercial launch, and today it is considered the first MMORPG (massively multiplayer on-line role-playing game). Since then, many MMORPGs have followed; *Ultima Online* (1997), *The Longest Journey* (1999), *Asheron's Call* (1999), *EverQuest* (1999), *Motor City Online* (2001), *Star Wars Galaxies* (2003), *World of Warcraft* (2004), *Star Trek Online* (2010), and *LEGO Universe* (2010).

As imaginary worlds, MMORPGs and other non-game virtual worlds like *Second Life* (2003) and *Entropia Universe* (2003) are vast in geographical size, have millions of subscribers, and are persistent worlds which run continuously, often for years. The size and complexity of these worlds are such that one can never experience or even be aware of more than a tiny fraction of all the events occurring in the world, and even exploring such a world is a never-ending endeavor due to their ever-expanding and dynamic nature. Thus, their vast size and unrepeatable nature make MMORPGs the first imaginary worlds that run in real time and cannot be seen or experienced exhaustively, making them even more like the Primary World, of which only a tiny fraction can be known and experienced during one's lifetime.

A world's persistence also affects the audience's investment in that world. Many users have a great deal of time and money invested in the worlds of MMORPGs, whose virtual economies can affect actual economies in the Primary World. As secondary worlds, these worlds enjoy an ontological status unlike secondary worlds of the past. While not "real" in a physical sense like the Primary World, their persistent and interactive nature make them qualitatively different from the fictional worlds of novels, film, and television; they are ongoing and unrepeatable, they exist virtually as code and intricate mathematic models, they are social networks incarnated in intangible communities. Users do not experience them vicariously through an author's characters, but rather directly, though avatars, albeit still in a virtual sense. Users actively participate in the building of these worlds, shaping them and making them their own, within the confines set by the companies that keep them running. Whereas knowledge of a world's infrastructures and world logic is important for the audience's understanding of noninteractive worlds and their stories, such knowledge gains new importance in an interactive world, where it can be used directly by the player who is a participant in the world whose goals and objectives often cannot be completed without that knowledge.

FIGURE 2.8 *Meridian 59* (1995) came packaged with a map (top) and featured a first-person view (bottom), and today is considered the first MMORPG.

Participation in an MMORPG is collaborative, and differs from the creation of fan fiction, video game level modding, and other such activities in which fans change or add onto an existing world without affecting the world, as it is experienced by others; to an extent, everything that happens within an on-line virtual world is automatically a part of that world, rather than merely an independent fan production. This kind of large-scale ongoing collaboration is itself one of the fruits of the use of the computer in the building of imaginary worlds.

Into the Computer Age

In the latter half of the twentieth century, no other tool advanced the building of imaginary worlds as much as the computer. The four main ways that the computer aided subcreative efforts are through *interaction, automation, visualization,* and *organization.* The first three are different aspects of *simulation* which is, in a sense, always involved in the creation of an imaginary world, and the first of these, interaction, has already been covered in the previous section.

Automation is the computer's ability to take over the control of the events of an imaginary world; the most common example of this being the running of a video game world. The computer controls non-player characters, game events including physics simulations (everything from bouncing balls to car crashes to fluid mechanics), and even the changing position of the implied camera. Interaction makes automation necessary, since there must be some mechanism to deal with the user's input. Automation is another way that an author's ideas are embedded in an imaginary world; the algorithm is the guiding hand that regulates the experiences of the world's visitors and controls its inhabitants according to its author's design. Yet the algorithm is less fixed than the words and images of linear, noninactive media like novels or film; the algorithm is more contingent, even potentially self-adapting, and is able to generate replies and reactions to a variety of user responses. In addition to single-player and multiplayer games, computerized automation controls the enormous amount of data processing needed to run MMORPGs in real time, bringing worlds to life that would otherwise not be possible.

Automation is also used for world-building in noninteractive media. Filmmakers use programs like Weta Digital's Massive to automate crowd behaviors in scenes or grow the plants of a jungle. Fluid simulation programs like RealFlow create water that looks and behaves realistically, and other programs mimic other kinds of events and the physics affecting them. These programs bring real-world physics and behaviors into imaginary worlds, adding to their verisimilitude, as well as giving filmmakers greater control over what can be done in their worlds. Automation can even lead to unplanned events which arise wholly from the complex sets of rules governing a world's events, making characters appear autonomous. For example, while working on the battle scenes for the *Lord of the Rings* films, Peter Jackson and programmer Steven Regelous (who created Massive) encountered trouble when automated soldiers did the unexpected. According to an article in *Popular Science*:

> In another early simulation, Jackson and Regelous watched as several thou-
> sand characters fought like hell while, in the background, a small contingent

of combatants seemed to think better of it and run away. They weren't programmed to do this. It just happened. "It was spooky," Jackson said in an
interview last year.[110]

Stories exploring the idea of using computer technology to create an automated virtual world have themselves grown into a kind of subgenre of science
fiction, and include such imaginary worlds as the eponymous city of Daniel F.
Galouye's *Simulacron-3* (1964), Delmark-O of Philip K. Dick's *A Maze of Death*
(1970), The Other Plane in Vernor Vinge's short story "True Names" (1981),
the world inside the ENCOM computer in *Tron* (1982), Cyberspace in William
Gibson's *Neuromancer* (1984), the Metaverse in Neal Stephenson's *Snow Crash*
(1992), the Autoverse in Greg Egan's *Permutation City* (1994), and the Matrix in
Larry and Andy Wachowski's *The Matrix* (1999), just to name a few. These stories also helped to establish certain tropes of the subgenre: simulations that become
autonomous agents within their respective virtual worlds; characters who enter
these worlds and confuse them with the Primary World; and secondary worlds
which are internally indistinguishable from the Primary World, which has also
become a popular philosophical topic of discussion.[111]

Even more broadly than interaction and automation, computer graphics technology has been used for the *visualization* of imaginary worlds. Computer imag-
ing and digital special effects have been used to enhance the depiction of imaginary
worlds in every type of digital media, including the entire worlds of video games,
and worlds in feature films, like that of *Tron* (1982). In recent times, computer
animation has developed far enough that a wide stylistic range of depiction is
possible, from photorealistic worlds, like James Cameron's Pandora in
Avatar (2009)) to highly stylized ones, like Radiator Springs of *Cars* (2006) or
the eponymous planet of *Planet 51* (2009). Entire television series have been
computer animated along with their imaginary worlds, like Cube Town of
Naomi Iwata's *Pecola* (2003) and Kippernium of Martin Baynton's *Jane and the
Dragon* (2005).

Computer-based imaginary worlds also promote the production of sequels,
since the digital models developed and built for the original works can be end-
lessly reused in subsequent works set in the same world. Discussing *Avatar* sequels,
James Cameron stated in an interview:

> It just makes sense to think of it as a two-or-three-film arc, in terms of the
> business plan. The CG plants and trees and creatures and the musculoskeletal
> rigging of the main characters—that all takes an enormous amount of time
> to create. It'd be a waste not to use it again.[112]

Digital model-making and computer animation have decreased the cost involved
in building a world visually, and have opened up the scope and scale of what

is possible. Software advances and growing markets have also made powerful computer modeling and animation programs commercially available, bringing new world-building tools to the general public. Other tools, like YouTube and the World Wide Web itself, give world-builders outlets to display their worlds, whether they are novels, movies, comics, or video games. Even novel writing has become easier with computers, since tasks like character and place name changes can be done with simple search-and-replace commands.

Finally, computers have aided the building of imaginary worlds as a tool used for *organization*. Huge worlds generate vast amounts of data, which authors must keep straight in order to maintain consistency. In the past, authors have sometimes compiled "bibles" of their worlds or other such works, like timelines and glossaries, only some of which is ever published as ancillary materials. Such reference works become even more important as the number of people working on a collaborative world grows, and because the worlds themselves have grown to include thousands of characters, places, objects, events, and other details. The size of these databases is such that they would be difficult to manage or even search without computer assistance; for example, the *Star Wars* Holocron kept by Lucas Licensing continuity database administrator Leland Chee contains over 30,000 entries covering characters, planets, weapons, and other data of the *Star Wars* galaxy, and Chee spends three-quarters of his usual workday updating or using the database.[113] Some worlds have their own fan-created databases on-line, such as those for the *Star Wars* galaxy, *Star Trek* universe, and Tolkien's Arda, and there are databases for lesser-known worlds, like the Andromeda Wiki for the Systems Commonwealth universe or the HallaWiki for D. J. MacHale's Halla universe. Databases can even be the main medium in which a world exists; for example, the Galaxiki galaxy started by Jos Kirps and the Galaxiki Project (at http://www.galaxiki.org) is an editable galaxy to which anyone can contribute. Users are invited to start their own solar systems and write about them.

Moving beyond databases merely for storage, the Preserving Virtual Worlds project, begun in 2008, seeks to preserve entire virtual worlds for posterity. The project is a joint effort by the Library of Congress, the Graduate School of Library and Information Science at the University of Illinois at Urbana-Champaign, the University of Maryland, Stanford University, the Rochester Institute of Technology, and Linden Lab to "develop basic standards of metadata and content representation" and "Investigate preservation issues through a series of archiving case studies representing early games and literature, as well as later interactive multiplayer game environments" so as to save virtual worlds from the technological obsolescence that threatens the hardware on which they run.[114]

The use of computer technology, in all of the areas described in the preceding text, also advanced another imaginary-world tradition with a long history, and one which found its greatest expansion in the latter half of the twentieth century; the use of imaginary worlds as art and thought experiments.

Worlds as Art and Thought Experiments

Since Plato's *Republic*, imaginary worlds have existed for their own sake, not merely as narrative settings. At first, they were created for the purpose of either satire, or social thought experiments, in the form of utopias and dystopias. Such worlds are designed as models or arguments, and when one of them does contain a narrative, it usually serves as little more than a vehicle for world exploration and explanation, with many expository passages regarding the workings of the world. Most often, such secondary worlds are set in opposition to the Primary World, with the resulting differences highlighted and discussed to suggest alternative ways of seeing, living, and organizing societies, and put forth in the hopes of changing the Primary World.

Some worlds function as experiments within the stories in which they appear, like Io-Phoebe, the "brick moon" that is built, launched into orbit, and developed into a world of its own in Edward Everett Hale's "The Brick Moon" (1869), or the worlds used by their makers to imprison the human main characters in *Dark City* (1998) and *The Matrix* (1999). Characters often are aware (or become aware) of the imaginary status of the world they inhabit, like the characters in Edith Nesbit's Polistarchia in *The Magic City* (1910), the characters who enter the world King Mezentius creates at dinner in E. R. Eddison's *A Fish Dinner in Memison* (1941), the characters who enter the worlds they read about in books (like Bastian Balthasar Bux, who enters the land of Fantastica in Michael Ende's *The Neverending Story* (1979)), or the aforementioned main characters of *Dark City* and *The Matrix*.

Other authors experiment with the very nature and structure of the worlds themselves. Lewis Carroll's two *Alice* stories both play with logic and present strange worlds that function very differently from ours (for example, the scene in which Alice and the Red Queen must keep running to stay in the same place). Going even farther, Edwin Abbott's two-dimensional Flatland and one-dimensional Lineland were worlds quite unlike any that had gone before them, and unique in the manner in which they were unlike the Primary World. Abbott's book inspired what could now be seen as a traditional of lower-dimensional worlds, including those of C. H. Hinton's *An Episode of Flatland* (1907), Dionys Burger's *Sphereland* (1965), A. K. Dewdney's *The Planiverse* (1984), and Ian Stewart's *Flatterland* (2001). Postulations of other worlds can be found in science, too, where the development of quantum physics in the early twentieth century led to Hugh Everett's "relative state" formulation, later renamed the "many-worlds interpretation" of quantum physics, which proposes that all possible alternative futures and histories exist, and that each takes place in alternate realities branching off from each other, tracing out all possible events.

In the twentieth century, various strands of experimental literature took on the exploration of literary form and fictionality itself, and among them were authors whose work involved imaginary worlds. As literary theorist Thomas Pavel notes:

Much later, a new playful fictionality made its appearance under the sign of modernity. It took various forms, ranging from the spontaneous, sometimes naïve attempts of the surrealists to the elaborate fictional mechanisms of Borges and the postmodern writers. What these undertakings have in common is the construction of fictional worlds for the sake of laying bare the properties of fiction and exploring its virtualities. Borges fills his stories with impossible objects and contradictory situations, so that no return to the metropolis is possible after "The Aleph" or "The Library of Babel." The purpose of establishing these fictional spaces is less to increase the trade in conventional wisdom than to expand our perception of fictional possibilities. Fictional colonies established as bases for traveling back and forth to the actual world must therefore be distinguished from fictional settlements founded for the sake of adventure and investigation, after the burning of the ships.[115]

Jorge Luis Borges creates or at least hints at worlds in several short stories. In "Tlön, Uqbar, Orbis Tertius" (1940), Borges and his friend Bioy find an encyclopedia entry for the country of Uqbar, which appears to be a part of a larger encyclopedia being written about a world called Tlön, which may or may not be imaginary, and which has an unusual epistemology all its own. "The Library of Babel" (1941) is set in an infinite library of endless rows of hexagonal chambers containing all possible books, and describes the humans and librarians who live and wander there. The hero of "The Immortal" (1949), after a harrowing search, reaches the City of the Immortals, only to find it far different than he expected. And in "Undr" (1975) we are introduced to the nation of the Urns, whose poetry is the poetry of a single word. But these brief descriptions barely sketch the worlds Borges invents and fail to do justice to the experience of reading about them.

Perhaps inspired by Borges, other authors have constructed entire books from series of glimpses of strange worlds whose designs bear metaphorical and metaphysical significance. Set within a frame story in which Marco Polo relates his travels to Kublai Khan, Italo Calvino's *Invisible Cities* (1972) has 55 descriptions of exotic cities which explore the nature of cities and how they are experienced. Another frame story, of Albert Einstein dreaming during the days when he is working on his theories of relativity, structures Alan Lightman's *Einstein's Dreams* (1992), a series of impressionistic vignettes that investigate what life would be like in various universes where time operates differently. In one such universe, time stops at its center:

As a traveler approaches this place from any direction, he moves more and more slowly. His heartbeats grow farther apart, his breathing slackens, his temperature drops, his thoughts diminish, until he reaches dead center and stops. For this is the center of time. From this place, time travels outward in concentric circles—at rest at the center, slowly picking up speed at greater diameters.

Who would make the pilgrimage to the center of time? Parents with children, and lovers.

And so, at the place where time stands still, one sees parents clutching their children, in a frozen embrace that will never let go. The beautiful young daughter with blue eyes and blonde hair will never stop smiling the smile she smiles now, will never lose this soft pink glow on her cheeks, will never grow wrinkled or tired, will never get injured, will never unlearn what her parents have taught her, will never think thoughts that her parents don't know, will never know evil, will never tell her parents that she does not love them, will never leave her room with the view of the ocean, will never stop touching her parents as she does now.[116]

Literary works were not the only ones to encourage innovations. From the 1970s onward, experimental world-building even appeared in traditional narrative science fiction literature. Worlds were set in Dyson spheres (Bob Shaw's Orbitville and Frederik Pohl and Jack Williamson's Cuckoo), on a neutron star whose surface gravity is 67 billion times that of Earth (Robert Forward's Dragon's Egg), planets shaped like a ring (Larry Niven's Ringworld) or a disc (Terry Pratchett's Discworld) or designed to be a giant shopping mall (Somtow Sucharitkul's Mallworld).[117] In Bob Shaw's *The Ragged Astronauts* (1986) and its sequels, the twin planets Land and Overland orbit a center of gravity close enough to share an atmosphere, making interplanetary travel possible with hot-air balloons and wooden spaceships. The world of the Cavity in Barrington J. Bayley's "Me and My Antronoscope" (1973) reverses the idea of material planets in empty space by having its inhabitants live in a hollow cavity in a universe of solid rock, with "spaceships" that burrow through the rock, filling the tunnels left behind them as they go in search of other cavities.

Some authors built worlds using narrative elements, but without a traditional narrative structure to tie their novels together: George Perec's *Life: A User's Manual* (1978) is designed like a literary jigsaw puzzle, with interconnected series of stories of the residents of an apartment building in Paris, which is described in intricate detail, room by room; while Ursula K. LeGuin's *Always Coming Home* (1985) is a collection of poems, tales, histories, charts, maps, and music from the valley of the Kesh, a people who "might be going to have lived a long long time from now in Northern California."[118] Nonnarrative collections of information about imaginary countries were used as humor in the series of phony traveler's guidebook parodies produced by Tom Gleisner, Santo Cilauro, and Rob Sitch, which include books on an Eastern European country, *Molvanîa: A Land Untouched by Modern Dentistry* (2003); a country in Southeast Asia, *Phaic Tăn: Sunstroke on a Shoestring* (2004), and a Latin American country, *San Sombrèro: A Land of Carnivals, Cocktails and Coups* (2006).

Another world worth noting for its experimental nature, as well as its use as therapy, is artist Mark Hogancamp's Marwencol, a meticulously detailed one-sixth-scale World War II–era town built as a form of therapy after a brutal attack and beatings robbed Hogancamp of his memories. Hogancamp began photographing the narratives that he played out in Marwencol, in which he and people he knew were represented by costumed dolls. His photographs were later discovered and appeared in the art magazine Esopus in 2005, which led to the feature-length documentary *Marwencol* (2010).

Two extreme examples of worlds composed mainly of images, that do not rely on text or narrative content, are the unnamed world depicted in Luigi Serafini's *Codex Seraphinianus* (1981) (see Figure 1.1), and Naohisa Inoue's Iblard, which first appeared in his paintings and the book *The Journey Through Iblard* (1983). Probably inspired by the enigmatic Voynich Manuscript, *Codex Seraphinianus* is an illustrated, encyclopedic book of several hundred pages showing the peoples, flora, fauna, machines, physics, chemistry, history, language, and more of a bizarre imaginary world, all in rich and colorful detail. Text accompanies some of the images, but the entire book is written in the language of the world, without any means of deciphering it provided (although the book's page numbers hint at a numbering system). Drawn by the Italian artist and designer Luigi Serafini during the late 1970s and printed in 1981 and several times since then, the book has attained a cult following and copies now sell for hundreds of dollars apiece.

Iblard is the world of Naohisa Inoue, a Japanese painter who has been painting images of his world since the 1970s, and publishing books and CD-ROMs of the images since the early 1980s. His colorful, impressionistic paintings of Iblard number in the hundreds, and have been the subject of several exhibitions (some images can be found on-line). Both Inoue's and Serafini's worlds are visually captivating and stylistically unique, and demonstrate the possibility of designing worlds as art for their own sake, apart from any narratives that are set within them.

Many video game worlds also contain a minimum of text and narrative, relying mainly on visuals; but the addition of interactivity, especially at the scale allowed by MMORPGs, means that instead of creating worlds merely as thought experiments, the worlds can become laboratories in which actual experiments in the social sciences can be performed. Discussing the study of common-resource pool problems and macro-level behavioral trends using virtual worlds, telecommunications researcher Edward Castronova and his team write:

> By their nature, synthetic worlds are ideal tools for this research method. In order to allow for vast, persistent worlds, the servers on which such environments are stored must keep track of an innumerable amount of data. Among many other variables this includes player ability statistics and assets, auction inventory and market prices, resource depletion, and the randomized appearances of rare goods. Additionally, besides tracking information on the state of the world and players, databases may also be used to monitor nearly all of the social interactive content of the synthetic world. This includes components such as chat logs and player emotes (commands

for the visual display of emotive avatar animations). All of this information can be stored, and later, mined for aggregate trends in player behavior. ... In addition to tracking and storing vast amounts of behavioral data, synthetic worlds also permit the experimenter a great deal of control. All manner of methods by which players interact with the environment and each other (including exchange rates, rates of resource renewal, communication channels, and market locations) may be manipulated, allowing for a wide range of potential experimental variables. In controlling for world conditions, experimenters may then observe the dependent effect on participant behavior. We argue that these observations are significant because of the inherent complexity of the social environments in which they occur.[119]

Although human participants can be used, the simulations using Massive mentioned earlier demonstrate that algorithmically-controlled agents can also be usefully employed in experiments involving emergent behavior. In addition, with other simulated features like physical interactions and biological growth, imaginary worlds will be able to model increasingly detailed and complex phenomena, simulating more and more of the Primary World.

From their inception as imaginary geographical places in unexplored regions to elaborate persistent universes collaboratively created and populated by millions, imaginary worlds have developed enormously in the last three millennia, growing in size, complexity, and their ability to engage an audience. As secondary worlds subcreated within the Primary World, they are both a reflection of the world in which we live and those of which we dream. They are the *gesamtkunstwerk* that unite all arts, the culmination of human imagination, the first drafts of the future that humankind will inhabit, and the dreamworlds we already inhabit today. Although they can be everything from escapist fantasy to lenses that help us see our own world more clearly, imaginary worlds are more than art, entertainment, games, tools, dreams, nightmares, experiments, or laboratories; they are nothing less than the fulfillment of humanity's subcreative vocation.

3
WORLD STRUCTURES
AND SYSTEMS OF RELATIONSHIPS

Avidly, I searched some passages of the books for anything I could relate to my everyday life; always interpreting, always translating, I found no mention of mankind or anything from this world. There was no evocation of sciences, customs and details of our world. What I was unraveling, through my studies, was the history and knowledge of a world to which ours appeared unknown.

—Charles Ischir Defontenay, *Star (Psi Cassiopeia)*[1]

I now held in my hands a vast and systematic fragment of the entire history of an unknown planet, with its architectures and its playing cards, the horror of its mythologies and the murmur of its tongues, its emperors and its seas, its minerals and its birds and fishes, its algebra and its fire, its theological and metaphysical controversies—all joined, articulated, coherent, and with no visible doctrinal purpose or hint of parody.

—Jorge Luis Borges, "Tlön, Uqbar, Orbis Tertius"[2]

Secondary worlds are interesting because of the parallels that can be drawn between them and the Primary World; it is through these parallels that we can relate to them and imagine what it would be like to inhabit them. As discussed in Chapter 1, secondary worlds use Primary World defaults for many things, despite all the defaults they may reset. If an author wants an audience to understand and empathize with the characters of a world, Primary World defaults become important for making connections to the audience's own lived experience and establishing some degree of emotional realism; worlds too removed from the Primary World will be unable to do either. As Tolkien writes:

> Probably every writer making a secondary world ... wishes to be a real
> maker, hopes that he is drawing on reality: hopes that the peculiar quality

of this secondary world (if not all the details) are derived from Reality, or are flowing into it. If he indeed achieves a quality that can fairly be described by the dictionary definition: "inner consistency of reality", it is difficult to conceive how this can be, if the work does not in some way partake of Reality.[3]

Besides Primary World defaults which still hold true in a secondary world, similarities with the Primary World can be found in the kinds of infrastructures that provide a framework in which to locate information about a secondary world. These are the structures by which we make sense of a story or a world, whether in fiction or lived experience, and which place individual facts and details into the larger contexts needed for them to be fully understood. It is through the completeness and consistency of these structures that world gestalten are able to occur. Without these structures, worlds would fall apart and become little more than a collection of data and information, and they would cease to be worlds.

Secondary World Infrastructures

You can spend your entire life perfecting a new world when you create its every piece.

—George Lucas, from a 1977 interview in *Ecran*[4]

Early worlds, which grew out of the stories told in them or about them, depended on those stories for their structure; only the elements needed to tell the story appeared. But more developed worlds grew beyond the needs of narrative, and transnarrative worlds have an even greater wealth of detail to organize. What, then, are the frameworks and infrastructures that help both authors and audiences to organize all the pieces of information about a world and give a coherent or even consistent existence to the whole?

Naturally, *narrative* is the most common form of structure, and the one that usually determines which elements in a world are most defined and developed, or at least mentioned. As there is much to say about narrative and its relationship to world-building, narrative will be considered separately in Chapter 4.

The first three structures to be discussed in the following sections arise from the three basic elements needed for a world to exist: a space in which things can exist and events can occur; a duration or span of time in which events can occur; and a character or characters who can be said to be inhabiting the world, since defining "world" in an experiential sense requires someone to be the recipient of experiences. Each of these has its organizational tools, examined in the following sections: *maps* structure space and connect a world's locations together;

timelines organize events into chronological sequences and histories which show how they are temporally related; and *genealogies* show how characters are related to each other (the term can be applied more broadly than merely biological kinship). These three structures are almost always found to some degree in an imaginary world, since the places, events, and characters of an imaginary world are fictional.

The next five structures to be discussed are the various systems which build upon each other and comprise the world itself, from the physical to the philosophical. The first of these is *nature*, which is not only the flora and fauna of a world, but also all of its materiality down to even its laws of physics, which may differ from those of the Primary World. *Culture* is built atop nature by a world's inhabitants, and is partly determined by what nature provides, as well as the culture's own history in the world. *Language* arises from culture and contains a culture's worldview embedded within it, since it regulates what can be expressed and how it can be expressed, and gives communicable form to the way in which the members of a culture collectively conceptualize their world. *Mythology* emerges from a combination of the previous layers and is how a culture understands, explains, and remembers its world. And finally, *philosophy* is the set of worldviews arising from the world itself, which includes not only the ideas and ideologies of the world's inhabitants, but also those which the author is expressing through the world's structure and events.

Of course, depending on their purpose, worlds have these structures to varying degrees, and less developed worlds can lack some of them altogether. Learning the ways in which a secondary world differs from the Primary World, and learning how a world works, is often a large part of the enjoyment of experiencing an imaginary world. Thus, how world information is doled out to the audience is an important part of world-building and design. Subcreators can imply these structures by giving the audience information and letting them assemble it, or describe these structures directly through maps, timelines, glossaries, charts, dictionaries, encyclopedias, and other such materials. Some ancillary materials, like maps or casts of characters, are usually placed at the start of a book, so that they can be used to orient a reader immediately, while other materials, like timelines and glossaries, are usually placed at the end, since they might reveal story information too soon if read before the main narrative. Worlds can even be designed to frustrate the organization of data into world infrastructures; for example, the *Codex Seraphinianus* (1981) gives us an abundance of pieces but leaves us guessing as to how to fit them together into world infrastructures. Most worlds, however, are designed to make sense and the oldest and perhaps most common tool used to introduce a world and orient an audience is the map.

Maps

If you're going to have a complicated story you must work to a map; otherwise you'll never make a map of it afterwards.

—J. R. R. Tolkien[5]

Maps relate a series of locations to each other, visually unifying them into a world. They provide a concrete image of a world, and fill in many of the gaps not covered in the story; gaps between locations, at the world's edges, and places not otherwise mentioned or visited by the characters. As such, they are one of the most basic devices used to provide structure to an imaginary world.

Maps of imaginary worlds appeared as early as the one printed with More's *Utopia* (1516), which was more pictorial than geographical. Woodcut maps were added to works, like the double-paged map of Macaria Island in Caspar Stiblinus' "Commentariolus de Eudaemonensium Republica" in *Coropaedia, sive de moribus et vita virginum sacrarum* (1555). Sometimes a map was considered important enough to be mentioned in a subtitle; when Le Père Zacharie de Lisieux's *Relation du pays de Jansénie, où il est traité des singularitez qui s'y trouvent, des coustumes, Moeurs et Religion des habitants. Par Louys Fontaines, Sieur de Saint Marcel* (1660) was translated into English in 1668, its title was changed to *A relation of the country of Jansenia, wherein is treated of the singularities founded therein, the customes, manners, and religion of its inhabitants: with a map of the countrey.* During the 1500s, maps were already appearing in printed Bibles, which may have encouraged the inclusion of more maps of imaginary worlds. Some maps were intimately tied to story events, like the detailed allegorical map entitled "A Plan of the Road from the City of Destruction to the Celestial City" found in John Bunyan's *The Pilgrim's Progress from This World, to That Which is to Come* (1684). Others, like the maps found in *Gulliver's Travels* (1726) and *Treasure Island* (1883) (the story of which originated from a map Stevenson had drawn), had less narrative detail but looked more like the kind of maps found in atlases.

Maps became more important with the development of the fantasy genre, in which travel is often a central part of a story's events, and in which geography plays a large role, especially if simultaneous journeys have to be coordinated. Maps give the reader a sense of scale early on, and may range from the *Star Wars* galaxy map to maps of archipelagoes, continents, or countries, to smaller scale maps like the map of Yoknapatawpha County that William Faulkner included in the back of *Absalom, Absalom!* (1936). Some maps are of areas as small as neighborhoods or estates; these were commonly found during the 1940s, when over 500 Dell paperback books, known as "mapbacks", featured maps on their back covers which were related to their stories. Maps also give a sense of how locations are related to one another spatially and topographically, giving story locations a context, since places are affected and defined by what lies around them. Remoteness, inaccessibility, and isolation are all expressed in this way, as well as their opposites. Maps can convey the spaces and great distances needed for journeys, allowing such journeys to be ellipsized in the text, as well as giving them a concreteness they would not otherwise have. Maps can also encourage an author to remain consistent from one book to another. Michael O. Riley describes L. Frank Baum's manipulation of distances, before he codified the map of Oz:

> One important way in which Baum modified Oz to accommodate more stories is evident in *The Patchwork Girl:* he restored to Oz the sense of vast size that exists in *The Wizard*, but is somewhat ambiguous in the subsequent books. Dorothy's journeys in that book take days to accomplish, except when she has the assistance of the Winged Monkeys, but in The Marvelous Land [*of Oz*], Glinda reaches the desert from the Emerald City in an hour, and in Ozma [*of Oz*] the journey from the desert to the capital takes less than a day of leisurely walking. But here, once again, Oz is a land of great distances, and it is "a day's journey from the Emerald City" to Jack Pumpkinhead's house and "a two days' journey from Jack Pumpkinhead's house to the edge of the Quadling Country."
>
> This sense of space was necessary for the modification that Baum made to enable a seeming paradise to include the necessary obstacles and struggles that would generate plots.[6]

Discussing one of Baum's later Oz books, *The Lost Princess of Oz* (1917), Riley states that, "The map of Oz he had drawn, while eliminating the flexibility he had utilized in the earlier books to fit the country to his stories, had the effect of causing him to treat Oz in a more consistent manner. There are no major changes or reinterpretations of that fairyland in *The Lost Princess*, but there are several refinements."[7] Maps are initially designed to fit a story, but later stories must be fit to existing maps. A map, then, can restrict stories as well as generate them.

In the Fantasy genre, the use of maps has become so common that their conventions can be parodied. Diana Wynne Jones' book *The Tough Guide to Fantasyland* (1996), a faux travel guide to the generic fantasyland found in so many novels, begins with a parody of a map. After summarizing some cartographical clichés, she writes, "Find your STARTING POINT. ... You will find it down in one corner on the coast, as far away from anywhere as possible." And right before that, "If you take this Tour, you are going to have to visit every single place on this Map, whether it is marked or not. This is a Rule."[8] Both criticisms, while true of many novels, point out phenomena that have explanations which relate to mapmaking and world-building. When mapping the main character's journey, an author will often want to create a map that shows the entirety of the lands traveled, while also showing as much detail as possible. These goals are balanced by cropping the map around the plot of the journey, assuring that the map can be blown up as much as possible while keeping the whole journey within it. Inevitably, since most journeys do not involve spiral trajectories, the starting point will naturally end up somewhere along the border of the map.

Narratively speaking, having the main character come from a marginal region also naturalizes expository passages, since the main character is learning about the world along with the audience. The object of the second criticism, the journey which visits every place depicted on the map, is sometimes referred to as a "Cook's Tour" (after the extensive tours of English travel agent Thomas Cook). This is the result of an author producing a map, lazily perhaps, with the minimum needed for the story; the author has only mapped the places visited by the characters, rather than creating a robust and detailed map of regions reaching far beyond what is seen in the story. This is one example of why world-building should go beyond the story's needs and suggest a world much broader and more detailed than what the story gives the audience, since areas appearing on a map that do not appear in the story encourage speculation and imagination.

Another common convention involves the content of maps. Whereas regions of the Earth (and perhaps other planets as well) usually have large areas of fairly homogeneous terrain, many fictional maps will contain a wide variety of geological features; mountains, deserts, forests, oceans, archipelagoes, meadowlands, volcanoes, rivers, marshes, and so on, sometimes all within relatively close proximity. In the case of Fantasy, varying terrain makes for more interesting journeys, which, since they are typically on foot or by horse, must place a variety of features with a limited area if they are to be reached within a given timeframe (usually days or weeks). On the other hand, science fiction, with its high-speed modes of travel (even faster-than-light travel) will typically put each location on a separate planet of its own, with characters crossing the gulfs of space between them in spaceships or teleportation of some sort. And instead of juxtaposing multiple types of terrain within a small area, entire planets often represent a single type of terrain; for example, in the *Star Wars* galaxy, there is a desert planet (Tatooine), an ice and snow planet (Hoth), a jungle planet (Dagobah), a city planet (Coruscant), and so on. Even when planets have multiple types of terrain, there is usually some geographical or geological feature or combination of features that makes the planet unique and distinct from other planets. Likewise, planets will often be limited to a single dominant culture, which considers the planet its home world and gives the planet its name. Dozens of examples of these can be found in the *Star Wars* and *Star Trek* universes. When Earth is included among these planets, humans are usually grouped together as Earthlings, downplaying racial and cultural differences, implying that these are slight variations when compared to planetary differences. Planets, then, function much the way that countries do in single-planet narratives or worlds.

Each location's uniqueness and distinctiveness not only helps audiences keep from confusing locations, but also aids the stories set within them by giving each place a sense of character and even personality. The design and terrain of a location often corresponds to the events that take place there and to the worldviews of its inhabitants; desolate, barren wastelands are usually not happy places, dark places often are dangerous, while sunlit meadows full of birdsongs and blooms typically do not contain villains' lairs. Tolkien's Middle-earth contains numerous examples of such places: the blasted wasteland of Mordor; the bucolic Shire; grim, austere Orthanc; mysterious and beautiful Lothlórien; the dark, subterranean halls of Moria; and so on. Tolkien also uses design, characters, and events to make his four forests, Mirkwood, The Old Forest, Lothórien, and Fangorn, all distinct from each other. Elves inhabit both Mirkwood and Lothórien, but they are quite different from each other; the former are more primitive and build on the ground and underground, while the latter are more cultured and live on platforms high up in the trees. The Old Forest and Fangorn are both treacherous places for foreigners and both contain sentient tree-like beings, but whereas the Old Forest's Old Man Willow is immobile and remains provincial in his interests, the Ents of Fangorn recognize the interdependence of the Free Peoples of Middle-earth and decide to leave the woods and participate in battle. Places can also change along with the prevailing rulers of lands; Narnia is a snowy land under the power of the White Witch, but the enduring winter ends along with her reign.

Not only do maps unify the locations of a story or of a world, they also allow authors to join multiple worlds together into one. Perhaps the earliest example of this is when L. Frank Baum decided to combine his worlds. As Michael O. Riley describes it:

> In *The Road to Oz*, Baum had drawn all his imaginary countries together into the same Other-world, but he had given no information about their geographical relationships. Now he actually shows the reader how they are connected. The fact that their positions on the map do not always agree with the textual descriptions is overridden by the centrality of Oz and the interconnectedness of Baum's entire Other-world.
>
> Besides the reality given to Oz by being set in a detailed map, the country also gains in richness by being set among so many other exotic countries, most of them with their own histories and special ambiences. These other countries also gain from being placed around Oz. In fact, it becomes extremely difficult for a reader who has followed Baum to this point in his career to go back to the first part of the Oz series or to those earlier individual fantasies and divorce any of them from Baum's entire Other-world; all his various creations have become too firmly a part of one great fantasy world. The appearance of these maps is, in fact, the culmination of Baum's proclivity, evident as far back as 1901, to draw his various worlds together.[9]

The tendency to combine worlds is especially great in science fiction, where planets can become part of the same universe very easily, because they are not physically connected, and because there is no limit to the number of planets that can be added. Just as islands lay separated from each other in the ocean, making them the most popular sites for imaginary worlds before the twentieth century, planets reside in space in the same manner, separated from each other, often by vast distances and set in uncharted regions (and traveled to in space*ships*). As discussed in Chapter 2, from the 1950s onward, many authors began joining their stories and planets into larger configurations. A number of them also include Earth in their universes, even if the planet is only mentioned and never visited (as in the Dune universe), and in some cases, Earth is abandoned, almost forgotten, or even destroyed (as in the Foundation universe).

When worlds are set on Earth, however, the relationship of secondary world maps to Primary World maps can become an issue which can intrude on consistency; therefore some worlds go out of their way to suggest why they do not appear on standard maps. In More's *Utopia* (1516), the reason is given within a letter from More's friend Peter Giles, in which he describes how he and More talked to Raphael Hythloday, the adventurer whose tales of Utopia are supposedly the source of the book:

> As for More's difficulties about locating the island, Raphael did not try in any way to suppress the information, but he mentioned it only briefly and in passing, as if saving it for another occasion. And then an unlucky accident caused both of us to miss what he said. For while Raphael was speaking of it, one of More's servants came in to whisper something in his ear; and though I was listening, for that very reason, more intently than ever, one of the company, who I suppose had caught cold on shipboard, coughed so loudly that some of Raphael's words escaped me. But I will never rest till I have full information on this point, not just the general position of the island, but its exact latitude—provided only our friend Hythloday is safe and alive.[10]

Some places are deliberately hidden from outsiders, like Francis Bacon's island of Bensalem in *The New Atlantis* (1626) which had laws of secrecy for travelers; or more recently, the island on the television series *Lost* (2004–2010). Other worlds were naturally hidden by geographical barriers, like the monarchy of Satrapia in Simon Tyssot de Patot's *Voyages and Adventures of Jaques Massé* (1710), which was cut off from the outside world by mountain ranges, beginning a tradition of "lost world" novels. Political reasons could also be used for a world's obscurity; everything about the land of Archaos in Christiane Rochefort's *Archaos ou Le jardin étincelant* (1972) is said to have been removed from history books, because the country was such a threat to its neighbors.[11] And a place's absence on standard maps can be an occasion for humor; in Garrison Keillor's *Lake Wobegon Days* (1985), Keillor takes a full three pages to explain how Mist County, the location of Lake Wobegon, was "omitted from the map due to the incompetence of surveyors", and describes the political maneuvering that has kept it off the map since.[12] Authors can even chide the audience for wanting to know where their lands are located. In George Barr McCutcheon's *Graustark: A Story of a Love Behind a Throne* (1903), Miss Guggenslocker scolds another character at the end of Chapter 3:

> "Mr. Lorry has offended us by not knowing where Graustark is located on the map," cried the young lady, and he could see the flash of resentment in her eyes.

"Why, my dear sir, Graustark is in—" began Uncle Caspar, but she checked him instantly.

"Uncle Caspar, you are not to tell him. I have recommended that he study geography and discover us for himself. He should be ashamed of his ignorance."[13]

In many cases, authors do not provide any map at all, but if a place is developed enough, an audience can compile information from an author's works and create a map of their own. One of the earliest works to receive such attention was Dante's *Inferno*, which inspired many to map his version of Hell. According to historian Ricardo Padrón:

> During the fifteenth century, a Florentine architect by the name of Antonio Manetti decided that one could gather the information presented in these passages and extrapolate from it to map out precisely the size, shape, and location of Dante's Hell. Manetti's work would not make it into print for some time, but his ideas would be popularized in summary form by many others, fueling what John Kleiner (1994, 24) has called the "heyday of infernal cartography," stretching roughly from 1450 to 1600. Italian intellectuals, particularly Florentines, debated, questioned, and refined Manetti's "Dantean cosmography," and even converted his argument to maps that accompanied their own editions of Dante's poem and their commentaries on it. Dantean cosmography became an intellectual fad that attracted the attention of some leading thinkers, including no less than a figure than Galileo Galilei ..."[14]

Maps can be constructed from verbal descriptions, but also from visual information collected from images of the place in question. For his book *TV Sets: Fantasy Blueprints of Classic TV Homes* (1996), Mark Bennett mapped out the homes from 34 television series, the towns of Hooterville and Mayberry (see Figure 3.1), and Gilligan's Island, by watching the shows and establishing the relationships of spaces from what was shown (and in some cases, filling in gaps, like bathrooms, which he says are rarely shown). Some maps are used by authors or companies to ensure consistency during production, and may only appear some time afterwards in ancillary materials; for example, maps were made of the Podrace course in *Star Wars* Episode I and the area of Coruscant in which the speeder chase takes place in Episode II, but they were not publicly released until several years later in *Creating the World of Star Wars: 365 Days* (2005).[15]

Tolkien's world in particular has inspired mapmaking by others, and apart from Tolkien's own sketches and official authorized maps produced by his son Christopher in the 1950s and later by Pauline Baynes in the late 1960s, one can find published maps of Middle-earth by an "M. Blackburn", Richard Caldwell, Barbara Strachey, Karen Wynn Fonstad, Shelly Shapiro, James Cook, and

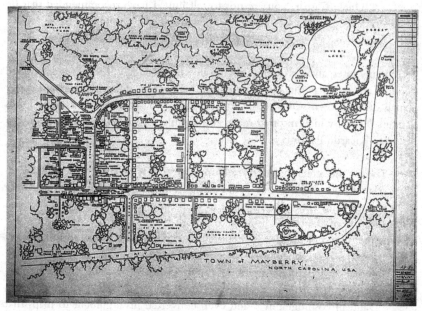

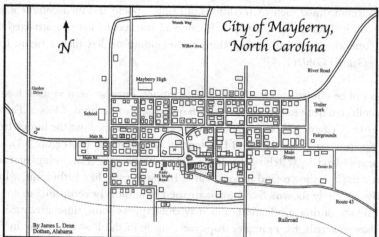

FIGURE 3.1 Two very different maps of Mayberry, North Carolina, by Mark Bennett (top) and James L. Dean (bottom), extrapolated from the visual information provided on *The Andy Griffith Show*. (Mark Bennett, *Town of Mayberry*, 1997, Lithograph on Rives BFK paper, 24.25 × 36.25 inches, Courtesy of the artist and Mark Moore Gallery) (Map of Mayberry courtesy of James L. Dean).

John Howe.[16] The maps are drawn in a variety of styles with varying degrees of detail. The most detailed of these were the maps produced by cartographer Karen Wynn Fonstad, who also produced atlases of other authors' worlds from the information provided in their books, including atlases of Anne McCaffrey's Pern, Stephen R. Donaldson's the Land, Krynn (the world of the *DragonLance* novels), the world of TSR's Forgotten Realms, and Tolkien's Middle-earth. As a cartographer, Fonstad was interested in more than just the landforms of these worlds; in *The Atlas of Middle-Earth*, which even came out in a second edition, she included maps with troop movements, the borders of kingdoms, landforms, climate, vegetation, population, and languages, all extrapolated from what is described or implied within Tolkien's writings and the maps that accompany them. That enough of an audience exists for such an atlas to be published (as well as a revised second edition) is testament to the importance that maps have as guides to secondary worlds, even when they are unauthorized.

Finally, some worlds exist only as maps, without accompanying stories or text. In 1999, Artist Wim Delvoye compiled his maps of an imaginary world in a catalog entitled *Atlas*, the images depicting all the roads, cities, and geological features that one finds in atlases of Primary World maps. Another artist, Adrian Leskiw, not only draws maps of his imaginary worlds, but some of them, like those of his Nation of Breda, have been edited or redrawn to represent different times in the country's history (see Figure 3.2). Leskiw describes the process at his website:

> I began this map series in 2003 with three pencil drawings and then proceeded to scan these. After digitizing the 2003 map of the Isle of Breda I created a unique map for each year before, until 1979, and after, until 2024, by editing the base map and each subsequent new map, ending up with 46 unique maps (and possibly more in the future)! In the interest of saving space I have selected an assortment of 10 maps from this 46-year span in order to illustrate the development of the island's highway network. After finishing the 2024 map I began making multiple updates without going to the trouble [*of*] creating a new map for each subsequent year and have tentatively labeled this iteration as the 2035 map.[17]

The multiple versions of the map, showing changes over time, adds a temporal dimension to the world depicted and combines cartography with another device often used to structure imaginary worlds: the timeline.

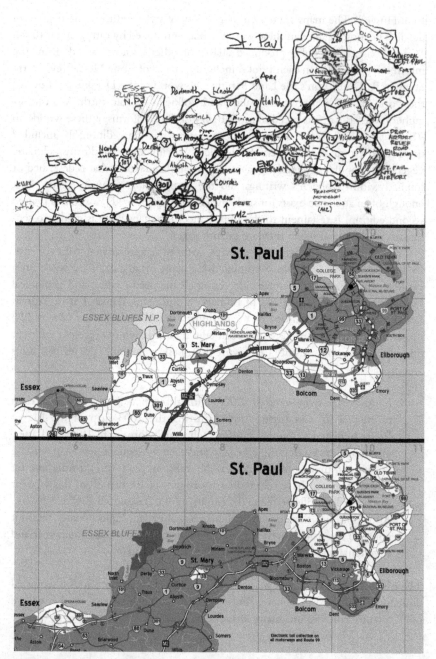

FIGURE 3.2 A detail of the Capital Region from Adrian Leskiw's map of the Isle of Breda, as it changed over time. The top image represents the land in 2002, the middle image in 2004, and the bottom image in 2040. The top and middle images were created in 2003, and the bottom one in 2005. (Images courtesy of Adrian Leskiw.)

Timelines

Timelines and chronologies connect events together temporally, unifying them into a history. They can be used to chart the cause-and-effect relationships between events, explain and clarify their motivations and maintain consistency, and give local events a context within larger movements of historical events. Timelines tie backstory into a story's current events and help an audience to fill in gaps, such as characters' ages or travel times, or their participation in events described in broader scale. Timelines also allow simultaneous strands of actions, narratives, or other causal chains to be compared alongside each other, providing both synchronic and diachronic contexts for events.

Unlike maps, timelines usually appear at the back of a book rather than the front, if they appear at all. Although they are often used by authors for the sake of organization and consistency, they are less likely to appear than maps, and are placed in the back of a book, because they usually contain spoilers and other story information that would ruin narrative surprise and suspense. Timelines may vary from short lists of events in an appendix to book-length chronologies of hundreds of pages (like those written for the *Star Wars* universe, the *Star Trek* universe, and Tolkien's Arda[18]), and can be provided by an author or assembled by third parties who analyze an author's works and compile references and inferences from which temporal structures can be reconstructed.

Timelines also vary considerably in scale. On one end of the spectrum are detailed minute-by-minute chronologies and those covering the events of a single day, like the on-line timelines covering individual seasons of the television show *24* (2001–2010), or the book-length chronology of James Joyce's *Ulysses* (1922) compiled by John H. Raleigh.[19] However, even these need not be limited to the time of the story's action; Raleigh's book, for example not only covers the single day (June 16, 1904) in which the main narrative of *Ulysses* takes place, but also over a century of backstory events which are referred to in the story. Since most stories are built around a main character's life or a portion thereof, most timelines cover a timespan measured in days, weeks, months, or years, or perhaps longer for backstory material. Other narratives built around the history of a people, a civilization, or a multigenerational family may use timelines extending hundreds of years, and in the case of fantasy and science fiction, sometimes thousands of years. Such timelines and narratives have to contend with social, cultural, and technological changes, and often include migrations, the establishment of countries, and the catastrophic events that decimate them. Finally, at the broadest scale are the timelines of books like Olaf Stapledon's *Last and First Men* (1930) with its timeline of millions of years, and Stapledon's *Star Maker* (1937) with its timeline of billions of years covering the entire history of the universe. In these stories, humanity itself becomes the main character, as one type of men evolves into the next, and these versions of humanity interact with vast and ancient empires on a galactic scale.

Timelines may use conventional calendars or ones unique to their worlds, like the Shire calendar used by Tolkien's hobbits, for which translated dates are also given. Timelines and changes in date can also be implied through such things as characters' ages, diurnal cycles, seasonal changes, phases of the moon, constellation positioning, and a wealth of other time-related details, which the audience can use to reconstruct the temporal order of events. For example, in 2008, using story information from Homer's *Odyssey* such as the position of Venus and a total eclipse, scientists Marcelo O. Magnasco and Constantino Baikouzis determined that the most likely date of Odysseus' return home was April 16, 1178 BC.[20] Other world devices can be used to imply the presence of history and an ancient past, like ruins and traces of long-lost civilizations, cultures and societies layered with palimpsests that suggest a deep history, or old sage-like characters who act as purveyors of backstory. All of these can help to create what author John Clute calls a "time abyss":

> TIME ABYSS   Either a phenomenon, or more interestingly, a moment of perception. As a perception it is closely analogous to the Sense of Wonder in science fiction, which may be defined as a shift in perspective so that the reader, having been made suddenly aware of the true scale of an event or venue, responds to the revelation with awe. The analogue in fantasy is the discovery by the reader that there is an immense gap between the time of the tale and the origin of whatever it is that has changed one's perspective on the world.[21]

Whereas timelines usually help an audience fill the gaps in the temporal range covering a world's events, a time abyss instead calls attention to itself as a gap, its enormity raising more questions than it answers, generating speculation, specifically as to how the world moved from the former state to the current one. Whether or not an abyss is used, the creation of historical depth and a sense of origins allow an author to comment on history and society through analogy or allegory and reflect upon how civilizations change and the causes of those changes. In *The Lord of the Rings*, the Human Men are a fallen race, and mortal, while the Elves are an unfallen race and thus immortal; the thousands of years covered in *The Silmarillion* chart the histories of both races and how their natures affect them. Just as traditional novels connect the actions and consequences of their characters to convey a certain worldview, subcreated worlds allow the stories of entire peoples over centuries to be devised according to an author's ideas.

Timelines can be synchronic as well as diachronic, tracing simultaneous strands of action as they interweave and interact. One extreme example of this can be found in Georges Perec's *Life: A User's Manual* (1978), which takes place at the moment of its protagonist's death, shortly before 8 PM on June 23, 1975. Perec moves room to room in the apartment building of the novel, describing each resident's experience of the moment, although there are backstories and other story information that expand the book's timeline beyond the moment described, and the book even includes an appendix with a timeline beginning in 1833. In most cases, simultaneous events requiring adherence to a timeline are the result of interlace narratives, the events of which include nodal points where multiple storylines converge and diverge. What has come to be known as the "interlace technique" or medieval interlace is similar to the structure used by Tolkien in *The Lord of the Rings*, and Tolkien scholar Richard C. West sums up the technique by comparing it to the "organic unity" type of structure, writing:

> Organic unity seeks to reduce the chaotic flux of reality to manageable terms by imposing a clear and fairly simple pattern upon it. It calls for a progressive and uncluttered narrative line in which there is a single major theme to which a limited number of other themes may be related so long as they are kept subordinate. The main theme grows from a clear-cut beginning through a middle which develops naturally ("organically") from the beginning to a resolution which is the product of all that preceded it. It is considered preferable to have a limited number of characters and to have no more than one or two dominate the action. Any single work should be self-sufficient, containing within itself everything that is necessary to it and excluding everything that is not necessary. In other words, the organic work is indivisible in itself but divided from everything else. … Interlace, by contrast, seeks to mirror the perception of the flux of events in the world around us, where everything is happening at once. Its narrative line is digressive and cluttered, dividing our attention among an indefinite number of events, characters, and themes, any one of which may dominate at any given time, and it is often indifferent to cause and effect relationships. The paths of characters cross, diverge, and recross, and the story passes from one to another but does not follow a single line. In addition, the narrator implies that there are innumerable events that he has not had time to tell us about; moreover, no attempt is made to provide a clear-cut beginning or end to the story. We feel that we have interrupted the chaotic activity of the world at a certain point and followed selection from it for a time, and that after we leave, it continues on its own random path. The author, or someone else, may perhaps take up the threads of the story again later and add to it at beginning, middle, or end.
>
> Yet, the apparently casual form of the interlace is deceptive; it actually has a very subtle kind of cohesion. No part of the narrative can be removed without damage to the whole, for within any given section there are echoes of previous parts and anticipations of later ones.[22]

It is apparent from this description that the interlace structure is best suited for the task of world-building, emphasizing as it does the narrative fabric of a world (discussed in detail in Chapter 4) and the context surrounding the storylines taking place there. And the simultaneity of an interlace structure means that some form of timeline to coordinate concurrent events is almost a necessity, at least for the author if not for the audience as well.

Timelines also help to manage temporal structures of worlds where time flows differently than in the Primary World, or at varying rates, as in the example from Alan Lightman's *Einstein's Dreams* (1992) given near the end of Chapter 2. One of the earliest examples of a world with a time differential is the country referred to in the title of George MacDonald's *At the Back of the North Wind* (1870):

> "Have you been sitting here ever since I went through you, dear North Wind?" asked Diamond, stroking her hand.
>
> "Yes," she answered, looking at him with her old kindness.
>
> "Ain't you very tired?"
>
> "No; I've often had to sit longer. Do you know how long you have been?"
>
> "Oh! Years and years," answered Diamond.
>
> "You have just been seven days," returned North Wind.
>
> "I thought I had been a hundred years!" exclaimed Diamond.
>
> "Yes, I daresay," replied North Wind. "You've been away from here seven days; but how long you may have been in there is quite another thing. Behind my back and before my face things are so different! They don't go at all by the same rule."
>
> "I'm very glad," said Diamond, after thinking a while.
>
> "Why?" asked North Wind.
>
> "Because I've been such a long time there, and such a little while away from mother. Why, she won't be expecting me home from Sandwich yet!"[23]

Not only can the speed at which time passes be different from the Primary World, but also the rate itself may even vary over time. For example, time in Lewis's Narnia seems to move at a variable rate and does not consistently correspond with that of the Primary World. According to Walter Hooper's timeline of the series, the period in England from 1900, when Digory Kirke, as a boy, first visits Narnia, to 1949 when the British railway accident mentioned in *The Last Battle* (1956) occurs, is concurrent with a period in which Narnia undergoes its entire history from its creation to its final dissolution, a period of 2555 years.[24] Hooper's timeline shows, however, that while 1900 in England coincides with Narnia year 1, the year 1930 coincides with Narnia year 300; 1932 with Narnia year 302; 1940 with Narnia year 1000; 1941 with Narnia year 2303; and 1949 with Narnia year 2555, just to list a few points of known correspondence. Lewis deliberately highlights the varying flow of time in his world to underscore its disconnect from the Primary World, since there is no system to relate the passage of time in one world compared to the other. An author can even include varying timeframes within a single secondary world; for example, residents of Fred Saberhagen's Azlaroc live in their own unique timeframes. As Brian Stableford describes it:

> Time worked in strange ways on Azlaroc, both objectively and subjectively. Local time was marked by the continual but irregular fall of "veils" of transformed matter which isolated sets of contemporary phenomena from those which had gone before, so that the apparatus of the past became vague to the eye and insubstantial to the touch by discrete degrees. Once caught by a veilfall, visitors to Azlaroc were marooned forever within their "year-group," assimilated to the local time-scheme.[25]

Taking Einstein's theories into account, characters in science fiction can also alter their own timeframes through the relativistic time dilations involved with high-speed travel and intense gravitational forces. The *Star Trek: The Next Generation Technical Manual* even includes a section entitled "Relativistic Considerations" which describes how *Star Trek* technology and protocol attempts to circumvent timeframe-related problems, while a chapter on "Warp Propulsion Systems" describes how faster-than-light travel is attained.[26] In addition to the pseudo-scientific discourse that makes up the bulk of the book, there is italicized extradiegetic commentary by the authors that addresses the world-building they are doing, which in the Warp Propulsion chapter reveals the need for timeline calculations:

> Figuring out how "fast" various warp speeds are was pretty complicated, but not just from a "scientific" viewpoint. First, we had to satisfy the general fan expectation that the new ship was significantly faster than the original. Second, we had to work with Gene's [*Roddenberry*] recalibration, which put Warp 10 at the absolute top of the scale. These first two constraints are fairly simple, but we quickly discovered that it was easy to make warp speeds TOO fast. Beyond a certain speed, we found that the ship would be able to cross the entire galaxy within a matter of just a few months. (Having the ship too fast would make the galaxy too small a place for the *Star Trek* format.)[27]

Worlds that involve time travel narratives (as *Star Trek* does, from time to time) have even more need to attempt to establish temporal order as events are recontextualized and revisited. In 2009, the makers of *Star Trek* even tried to tie in the rebooting of the franchise by suggesting that the *Star Trek* movie of 2009 actually took place in an alternate timeline diverging from the already-established timeline.[28] With both Zachary Quinto playing a young Spock and Leonard Nimoy playing the old "Spock Prime", the two timelines are joined and the rebooting is given a diegetic explanation that keeps it from being separated from the older material, as reboots are in so many other franchises. As this example shows, along with time and space, it is characters and their relationships which link together narratives as well as worlds, and it is to these that we next turn.

Genealogies

Genealogies relate characters to one another, giving them a context within larger frameworks which are familial, ancestral, social, institutional, and historical. They include such things as family tree charts connecting ancestors and descendents, kinship diagrams of lineal and collateral kin, lineages of rulers and their heirs, and hereditary systems which pass on knowledge, experience, titles, and property down from one generation to another. Genealogies can appear in authorized ancillary works such as charts and lineages, or be implied through a series of connections mentioned throughout the works making up a world. They act as world infrastructures, linking a world's stories together and extending characters by placing them in broader contexts and tying them into history. Even sequels written by others can make use of genealogy as a device to link their stories to the works they follow; for example, the main characters of both Dionys Burger's *Sphereland* (1965) and Mark Saxton's *The Islar, Islandia Today: A Narrative of Lang III* (1969) are the grandsons of the main characters of the stories that inspired them (Abbott's *Flatland* (1884) and Wright's *Islandia* (1942), respectively). Appreciation of subtleties in a text can also rely on the audience's knowledge of characters' genealogies; Tom Shippey describes how an insult directed at Elu Thingol in *The Silmarillion* can only be fully understood through detailed knowledge of Elven genealogy.[29]

Genealogies function as extensions of characters, which in turn provide continuity across a world's eras. Many worlds begin as the background to the story of a character's entire life; for example, the six *Star Wars* films at the core of the *Star Wars* universe tell the life story of Anakin Skywalker (Darth Vader) from childhood to death. Yet as a world grows temporally, it often passes beyond the lifespan of individual characters. One way around this is to have long-lived characters whose lives span many eras and thus allow for a greater degree of both character development and world development during their lifetime. Example of characters with great longevity who play a large role in their worlds include L. Frank Baum's Queen Zixi of Ix (who is 683 years old), George Lucas' Yoda (who lived to be over 800 years old), the Nemsédes in Defontenay's *Star* (1854) who are more than 1,000 years old, and the Dune universe's Duncan Idaho gholas, who are a series of clones carrying on the original's memories that extend the character over several millennia, making him the only character to appear in all six of Frank Herbert's *Dune* novels. Some characters may even be "immortals", like Swift's Struldbruggs of Luggnugg against whom special laws have been enacted limiting their rights after a certain age, Tolkien's Elves who are to remain in Arda until its end, Stephen R. Donaldson's Forestals who protect the forests of the Land, or the robots in many science fiction worlds. The consequences of immortality are also occasionally commented upon; for example, both Swift's Struldbruggs and Tolkien's Elves weary of the world and express their envy of mortals whose mortality gives them rest.

Ancestors and descendents are the most common way of temporally extending a character. Names and characteristics are often passed along from parent to child, as well as titles, property, and proprietary knowledge. Whole lineages of characters can share the same name, like the Dorns of *Islandia* (1942) and even objects can have their own lines (like the sequence of starships to bear the name *Enterprise* in the *Star Trek* universe), and sometimes objects and their history provide a throughline linking the works of a world together. Over a series of generations, biological descendents can grow to form a people, and their history can become the throughline of world at a larger narrative scale (similar to the way Jacob's descendents become the Israelites in the Old Testament).

Other relationships can function in a manner similar to biological descent; in the *Star Wars* universe, for example, both the Jedi and the Sith have partnerships of mentors and apprentices to pass their training along. Over the course of the six main films we discover that Anakin Skywalker was apprenticed to Ben Kenobi, Kenobi was apprenticed to Qui-gon Jinn, Jinn was apprenticed to Count Dooku, and Dooku was apprenticed to Yoda, linking them together almost like a series of fathers and sons.[30] Memories are sometimes passed along to keep a character's experiences alive even after their deaths; in the *Star Trek* universe Vulcans perform mind-melds, while in the Dune universe the Bene Gesserit pass on their memories genetically from mother to daughter.

Genealogies give characters context through structures of kinship and friendship, as characters are understood by the influence of ancestry, upbringing, and companionship. The deeds and failings of ancestors often provide a foreshadowing that colors their descendents' self-images and expectations. Sons carry the weight of their father's reputations, and are often expected to finish their projects or even correct their errors. As heir to the throne, Aragorn both fears failing in the same way that his ancestor Isildur did, and Aragorn's marriage to the Elf-maiden Arwen mirrors the romance of the human Beren and Elf-maiden Lúthien, from whom he is also descended. Ben Kenobi loses Anakin Skywalker to the Dark Side, and tries to make up for it by training Anakin's son Luke; and it is Yoda, much higher up the same chain of mentors, who finally completes Luke's training, allowing Luke to turn his father back to the side of good; when the chain of mentors is understood, one can see additional motivation that Yoda might have for helping Luke. In both cases, the audience does not need to know all the background connections in order to follow the story, but such knowledge does provide nuances enriching the audience's understanding of the situation.

Additional context can be given well beyond what is necessary for a story. For example, extensive family tree charts appear in the appendices of *The Lord of the Rings*, from the lines of Kings to various hobbit families. Whereas traditional novels like Tolstoy's *War and Peace* will sometimes have family trees linking the principal characters, charts made for secondary worlds often feature many names which do not appear in the story, but which nonetheless add to the experience and the verisimilitude of the world, and act as catalysts for speculation which heighten audience engagement and investment in a world.

Finally, genealogies can link stories together as each character's life history becomes another narrative thread in a world's narrative fabric (more on this in

Chapter 4). Even when unrelated characters cross paths briefly, with a main character from one story becoming just an extra in the background of another, such a transmedial appearance can be a powerful way to evoke the world extending beyond the confines of a particular story; and one can imagine that every minor character and extra passing through the background has as complete and detailed a life as the main character does.

Genealogies, timelines, and maps are the main infrastructures used in building a world's illusion of completeness, and the most basic and common areas in which invention occurs as well. The next five infrastructures examined—nature, culture, language, mythology, and philosophy—are often more backgrounded than the structures of space, time, and character that they serve, and may rely heavily on Primary World defaults; but even when invention occurs in them in small amounts, they can subtly and cumulatively create that feelings of differentness that make imaginary worlds so fascinating and attractive.

Nature

Imaginary worlds almost always have some kind of physical setting to them, or, in the case of supernatural worlds, laws and modes of being that operate in an analogous manner to a physically-based world, without which the world would cease to be relatable to an earthly audience. *Nature*, then, deals with the materiality of a world, its physical, chemical, geological, and biological structures and the ecosystems connecting them. Almost inevitably, worlds subcreated to this degree are less likely to be earthbound ones, since so many Primary World defaults have been changed. They also typically become, at some level, thought experiments about subjunctive worlds in which the consequences of changed Primary World defaults are explored and extrapolated.

The most common type of invention regarding an imaginary world's natural realm is that of new flora and fauna. Adding new plants and animals does little to disrupt the other defaults of the natural world, and even in the Primary World, new species continue to be discovered and studied. While such inventions appeared early on as sources of humor and satire, as in Lucian of Samosata's *True History* and Rabelais' Gargantua and Pantagruel series, they were also made in a more serious vein in the traveler's tales that described strange foreign lands and their inhabitants. In most of these worlds, new creatures were merely presented without any attempt to consider how they might fit into ecological systems or affect the structures built upon them (such as culture, language, philosophy, and so forth). Early utopias explored more of the effect they might have on these structures, but typically did not reinvent the natural realms of their worlds to any great degree. Underground worlds tended to connect invented flora and fauna to other structures of the world, usually by necessity, to explain how their inhabitants could meet the basic needs of food, water, shelter, and light. Robert Paltock's *The Life and Adventures of Peter Wilkins* (1751) was one of the first worlds to base a culture on its unique plants and animals, including the glumms and gawreys, the winged natives of Sass Doorpt Swangeanti; the crullmott tree whose fruit tastes like fowl; the padsi bush whose fruit tastes like fish; and sweecoes, which are insects that can glow and produce light. When invented flora and fauna are more than merely window-dressing or replacements for Primary World animals that serve a similar function (such as pets or beasts of burden), they are usually used to solve world-building problems: for example, Paltock's sweecoes are housed in wicker lamps to provide light while bioluminescent algae light the underground lake of the D'ni in the Myst universe; the babel fish of the Hitchhiker universe is inserted into one's ear and used as a universal translator to overcome language barriers; and the sandworms of Arrakis in *Dune* are used as a mode of transportation and a by-product of their life cycle is the spice melange needed for the guild navigators who use it to fold space and achieve faster-than-light travel. Occasionally an invented plant or animal even provides the impetus for a story, as any fantasy quest to defeat a dragon demonstrates.

Worlds that are subcreated to an even deeper level include new kinds of biology, ecosystems, and planets with unusual material compositions. For example, Koestler's Planet, from Barrington J. Bayley's "Mutation Planet" (1973), has organisms that can change their genetics and produce radically different offspring. The planet Sequoia, from Neal Barrett Jr.'s *Highwood* (1972) is a land of huge trees, and the planet Karimon, from Mike Resnick's *Purgatory: A Chronicle of a Distant World* (1993) consists of tall trees that are entire ecosystems. Some planets are metal-poor and their inhabitants must use other materials: on Lyra IV, the planet from Cyril M. Kornbluth's "That Share of Glory" (1952), technology is based on ceramics, while on Land and Overland from Bob Shaw's *The Ragged Astronauts* (1986) astronauts launch wooden spaceships to travel between the two planets, which orbit so close that they share an atmosphere. Some elaborate subcreations even have entire books devoted to their invented flora and fauna, for example, David Day's *A Tolkien Bestiary* (1979), Anne Margaret Lewis and R. K. Post's *Star Wars: The Essential Guide to Alien Species* (2001), and Dinah Hazell's *The Plants of Middle-earth: Botany and Sub-creation* (2007). Filmmaker James Cameron even assembled a 350-page *Pandorapedia* for his planet Pandora in *Avatar* (2009) and, according to *Wired* magazine:

> Every animal and plant received Na'vi, Latin, and common names. As if that weren't enough, Cameron hired Jodie Holt, chair of UC Riverside's botany and plant sciences department, to write detailed scientific descriptions of dozens of plants he had created. She spent five weeks explaining how the flora of Pandora could glow with bioluminescence and have magnetic properties. When she was done, Cameron helped arrange the entries into a formal taxonomy.[31]

At least one scientist has parodied this kind of scientific work; the German zoologist Gerolf Steiner, writing under the name Harald Stümpke, invented a fictitious order of mammals known as Rhinogrades or Snouters, which evolved in the imaginary Hi-Iay (or Hi-yi-yi) Islands along with a complete ecosystem, all described in detail in two books in the early 1960s.[32]

Among invented creatures, one often finds humanoid races, who range from those that are only slightly different from humans and treated like new nationalities, to races in which a subcreator has changed biological defaults in order to propose thought experiments designed to make an audience see Primary World biology in a new light. For example, many alternative sexual biologies can be found in imaginary worlds. In Defontenay's *Star (Psi Cassiopeia)* (1854), the natives of Tassul are hermaphrodites able to beget and give birth alone. The Gethen of Ursula LeGuin's *The Left Hand of Darkness* (1969) are neither male or female and have gender identities only once a month. Esthaa, the planet of James Tiptree Jr.'s "Your Haploid Heart" (1969) is inhabited by a race whose generations alternate reproductive methods, changing between asexual and sexual reproduction. Races with three sexes can be found in both Samuel R. Delany's Branning-at-Sea (where they are known as La, Le, and Lo) and in Isaac Asimov's para-Universe (where they are known as the Rationals, Emotionals, and Parentals). Melissa Scott's *Shadow Man* (1995), set on the planet Hara, has a race with five sexes (fem, herm, man, mem, and woman) and nine modes of sexual preference (bi, demi, di, gay, hemi, omni, straight, tri, and uni). In most cases, the main character's encounter with new sexes and the social norms and behaviors arising from them becomes a crucial part of the stories and worlds in which they appear.

Subcreating nature to an even deeper level, we find worlds in which the laws of physics are different from those of the Primary World; for example, in the world of Greg Egan's *The Clockwork Rocket* (2011), light has no universal speed. Some worlds introduce new colors, such as "jale" and "ulfire" (due to a blue sun in David Lindsay's *A Voyage to Arcturus* (1920)), "rej" in Philip K. Dick's *Galactic Pot-Healer* (1969), or "octarine", the "color of magic" in Terry Pratchett's Discworld universe. Some colors may not be given a name; as Raymond King Cummings writes in *The Girl in the Golden Atom* (1922), "Her lips were full and of a color for which in English there is no name. It would have been red doubtless by sunlight in the world above, but here in this silver light of phosphorescence, the color red, as we see it, was impossible."[33] Certain conventions of the science fiction genre, such as hyperspace, faster-than-light travel, wormholes, and so forth, already imply new laws of physics; but some worlds introduce new forces, like "noggox" in Brian Aldiss' "Legends of Smith's Burst" (1959), which keeps matter and antimatter from annihilating each other; or the gravitational forces of Linovection and Reticutriation in the Tryslmaistan universe of Jennifer Diane Reitz's *Unicorn Jelly* (2000). In his novel *Diaspora* (1998), Greg Egan invents new theories of physics including Kozuch Theory, which views elementary particles as six-dimensional wormholes; while Orson Scott Card invents "philotes", which are subatomic particles that allow for faster-than-light communication. Some video game worlds even let players experience alternative physical laws, like the negative gravity in some of the "universes" in *Gravitar* (1982), the non-Euclidean wraparound space of *Asteroids* (1979), or the user-generated spatial connections of *Portal* (2007).

Some worlds have characters who have the power to subcreate worlds, like the Thoans in the World of Tiers universe or the D'ni in the Myst franchise, and they can make worlds in which the laws of physics are different. For example, in *Myst: The Book of Atrus* (1995), Catherine's Age is a giant torus with a column of water that passes through the center, as a waterfall on one side and an enormous waterspout on the other. With most of the world's mass placed along the outer edge of the torus the water is pulled through the central hole and around the torus, to fall back as rain again on the other side. In many cases, "magic", as found in the genre of fantasy, often works according to a set of conventions or rules, and these could also be seen as implying new laws of physics, albeit indirectly. Virtual worlds set in computer-generated spaces also have their own rules, programmed by their makers, like the world inside the computer in *Tron* (1982), cyberspace in *Neuromancer* (1984), or the machine-created world of *The Matrix* (1999), in which the laws of physics can be bent or even broken.

While worlds have been built in many shapes, such as rings, discs, tiers, concentric shells, or even the negative curvature of a hypersphere (in Christopher Priest's *Inverted World* (1974)), the most extreme examples of changing the defaults of the natural world are those imaginary worlds with a dimensionality different from that of the Primary World. The first of these appears in Edwin Abbott Abbott's *Flatland: A Romance of Many Dimensions* (1884), which introduced not only the two-dimensional world of Flatland, but also the one-dimensional world of Lineland. One of the book's goals, besides satirizing the Victorian society of its day, was the introduction of four-dimensional mathematics to its general readership. The book begins with a detailed account of Flatland that builds the world and explains how it works over several chapters, and then the two-dimensional protagonist, A. Square, visits Lineland where he attempts to describe what the second dimension is like. Later, A. Square is visited by the Sphere, who attempts to describe to him what a third dimension is like, and through their discussion, a fourth dimension, and what four-dimensional entities might be like, are extrapolated from observations about the first three dimensions. Flatland was an exceptional work of subcreation for its time, and would go on to remain in print and to inspire an entire subgenre of worlds that experiment with dimensionality, as other authors' sequels took up where Abbott left off.

The first sequel to *Flatland* was C. H. Hinton's *An Episode of Flatland: Or, How a Plane Folk Discovered the Third Dimension* (1907), which recognized one of the faults of Abbott's original Flatland. The descriptions of Abbott's Flatland, along with his illustrations, give the impression of watching an overhead view of shapes moving around in Flatland, entering houses which are shown like floor plans, with the insides laid out like a diagram. Since Abbott's characters move around like figures over a background, there are really two layers to the world;

the background and what lies upon it, making it less than completely flat. Hinton indirectly acknowledges the need for a revisioning of Flatland in his Introduction:

> Placing some coins on the table one day, I amused myself by pushing them about, and it struck me that one might represent a planetary system of a certain sort by their means. ... And in this case considering the planets as inhabited worlds, confined in all their movements around their sun, to a slipping over the surface of the table, I saw that we must think of the beings that inhabit these worlds as standing out from the rims of them, not walking over the flat surface of them. Just as the attraction in the case of our earth acts towards the centre, and the centre is inaccessible by reason of the solidity on which we stand, so the inhabitants of my coin worlds would have an attraction proceeding out in every direction along the surface of the table from the centre of the coin, and "up" would be to them out from the centre beyond the rim, while "down" would be towards the centre inwards from the rim. And beings thus situated would be rightly described as standing on the rim.[34]

Hinton realized that a two-dimensional being could be more complicated than lines or triangles, and still be two-dimensional; though he does not go into detail as to what exactly their anatomy might be. After a brief review of the history of his world, which he calls Astria, most of his book is about the personal details of the character's lives, dinner parties, conversations, romance, and so forth, while Hugh Farmer, one of the principle characters, leads a crusade to convince the Unæans of Astria that the third dimension exists, a question which becomes a metaphysical controversy that shakes the foundations of their society. However, as far as world-building goes, most of the novel reads as though it were taking place in the Primary World, with relatively little examination of the consequences of making a world two-dimensional and only a few detailed descriptions of how their world operates differently than ours.

Dionys Burger's *Sphereland: A Fantasy about Curved Spaces and an Expanding Universe* (1965) is a book more along the lines of Abbott's work, and is a sequel, continuing the story of A. Square through his grandson, A. Hexagon. Burger's version of Flatland updates Abbott's with a relativistic worldview (as the book's subtitle reveals) that gives his two-dimensional universe a finite but unbounded space, in the shape of the surface of a sphere. Upon that surface, Flatland itself is a disc-shaped planet, much like Hinton's Astria, but the towns, homes, and forests are still laid out in overhead view, and they do not react to the gravity that pulls everything else toward the center of the world-disc. In a passage revealing the author's world-building difficulties, Burger seems aware of the awkwardness of combining the two approaches, writing:

Of course the question immediately arises why everything is not falling down. Solid objects such as houses and buildings, and plants such as single trees and the trees in forests, all stay put and do not show any inclination to sink. The answer is not so easy, and it might be best to just write it off to natural laws. This does not alter the fact, however, that scientific theories have been worked out to explain the phenomenon. I will be glad to touch on the matter in a few words, but this particular theory is so complicated that you need not worry if you do not understand it. Consider for a moment that all these solid objects are resting on a space parallel to our world—in other words, they are attached to a flat plane, directly beside the plane of our space. I admit that this hypothesis—it is no more than a mere supposition— is extremely difficult for a layman to grasp, even though it is not as difficult for a three-dimensional being as it is for us. Let us therefore simply note as fact that trees and houses *do* stay put, there being no question that they do.[35]

If the inhabitants of a two-dimensional disc-shaped world are to live on the surface of that world, they would have to be confined to the space above a curving line, resulting in only four directions; back and forth, and up and down. Hinton realized this but the consequences of it only occasionally figured into his story, whereas Burger keeps the two-dimensionality of his world always in mind; but, as the preceding passage shows, Burger had trouble keeping his design consistent. An amazing number of these problems were solved, however, in A. K. Dewdney's Planiverse in *The Planiverse: Computer Contact with a Two-Dimensional World* (1984).

In an amazing feat of subcreation, A. K. Dewdney describes Arde, a two-dimensional disc-shaped world with its own physics, chemistry, biology, plane-tary science, astronomy, creatures, cultures, and technologies, all of which are designed to work in a world of two dimensions. As a computer scientist and mathematician (and with the help of colleagues in other disciplines, credited in the acknowledgments), Dewdney considers how atoms, electromagnetic forces, light and sound waves, turbulence, and other physical phenomena would operate in two dimensions, and the implications these would have on the existence of Arde's inhabitants, the Nsana. He gives solutions and working designs for such things as doors, electrical wiring, hinges, gears, and other simple technologies that work differently in two dimensions, and provides descriptions and illustrations of more complex two-dimensional machines like clocks, printing presses, ground and air vehicles, and steam engines (see Figure 3.3). He also describes and illus-trates two-dimensional biological mechanisms including propulsion, digestion, cell division, and more. From all of these things arise the culture of the Nsana, with its own traditions and customs, for example, who passes over whom when two travelers meet who are traveling in opposite directions, or the order in which passengers board and disembark vehicles.

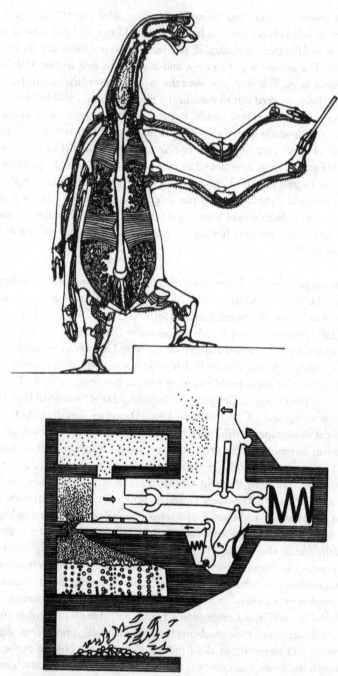

FIGURE 3.3 A Nsana (top) and a steam engine (bottom) from Arde, the two-dimensional world of A. K. Dewdney's *The Planiverse*. (Images courtesy of A. K. Dewdney.)

The book's story involves human computer science experimenters on Earth who, through their computer system, make contact with a Nsana named Yendred. The story is little more than a device to link together all the explanations of how things in the world works, but as is the case with so many subcreated worlds, narrative is only a single aspect of the world, and *The Planiverse* is worth reading as a brilliant piece of subcreation. So successful was Dewdney's subcreation, that some people actually believed the world was real. As Dewdney states in the "Preface to the Millennium Edition":

> When The Planiverse first appeared 16 years ago, it caught more than a few readers off guard. The line between willing suspension of disbelief and innocent acceptance, if it exists at all, is a thin one. There were those who wanted to believe, despite the tongue-in-cheek subtext, that we had made contact with a two-dimensional world. ... It surprised and worried the author that so many people believed the tale was factual. Subtext that should have implied a fantasy (albeit a highly detailed one) was missed by many.[36]

That some readers actually believed the world existed demonstrates the power of good subcreation, even when a secondary world is so far removed from our own.

Most secondary worlds, however, subcreate nature to a very limited degree, if they do so at all. Many will instead wish to ground their realism with Primary World defaults so far as nature is concerned. In the series bible for the rebooted *Battlestar Galactica* (2004–2009), there seems to be a sense of pride in the description of the show's science and how it does not partake of some of the usual conventions of science fiction:

> *Science.* Our spaceships don't make noise because there is no noise in space. Sound will be provided from sources inside the ships—the whine of an engine audible to the pilot for instance. Our fighters are not airplanes and they will not be shackled by the conventions of WWII dogfights. The speed of light is a law and there will be no moving violations.[37]

To whatever degree they use Primary World defaults or reset them, the natural realm provides the raw materials for civilizations and the production of the more commonly subcreated area of *culture*.

Culture

Culture links nature to history and is usually central to the unique situation that provides a story's conflict; and an invented culture can be more specifically tailored to the author's needs and does not come with the baggage of an existing culture. By providing a worldview that shapes the natural world's resources into such things as agriculture, architecture, clothing, vehicles, and artifacts, which in turn inform customs, traditions, language, and mythologies, culture grounds and connects the various productions of a people into a (hopefully) coherent structure through which characters see the secondary world.

As mentioned in Chapter 2, imaginary-world stories typically have the main character experiencing and learning about a new and foreign culture along with the audience; such was the basic structure of travelers' tales. The main character is often either someone from the Primary World who is a foreigner to the secondary world, or someone from a marginal area of the secondary world who journeys into an unfamiliar part of it. As early as More's *Utopia* (1516), culture became an important part of the story and world, with its proposal for a new way of living and inherent critique of existing culture; this became typical of utopias in general, since a cultural critique was usually one of the main reasons behind the writing of a utopia. Other works such as *Gulliver's Travels* (1726) even showed how its human protagonist appeared from the points of view of those in the foreign cultures encountered, attempting to make strange the author's own culture, by contrast.

Occasionally foreign cultures are presented directly in the form of documents from the cultures in question; for example, in Defontenay's *Star (Psi Cassiopeia): The Marvelous History of One of the Worlds of Outer Space* (1854), the chest that the narrator finds in the crashed meteor is full of Starian books, which make up the text of the novel. There is a description of the stars and planets of the Starian system, a book of ancient history, a poem related to the history, individual histories of each planet and their exploration, two plays, writings on philosophy, morality, and law, and the book-within-a-book entitled *The Voyage of a Tassulian to Tasbar* to which Defontenay adds, "I have preserved in the Tassulian's account two literary pieces which were found inserted, convinced that the reader will not be displeased to discover several samples of Tasbarite literature."[38] Though the range of texts is a disparate one, they are arranged in roughly chronological order and together present a coherent history of the Starian system and its peoples and cultures.

The development of fictional cultures, both in their depth as well as the quality and plausibility of the cultures generated, depends greatly on the ability and background of the author. The most complete and consistent imaginary world and culture of the first half of the twentieth century would have to be that of Austin Tappan Wright's *Islandia* (1942), written before the author's death in 1931. In it, main character and narrator John Lang leaves the United States to become consul to Islandia, which we discover and learn about along with him. The nation of Islandia, long closed off to foreigners and foreign trade, for the most part, is facing a time of internal debate as to whether the country should be opened up to the outside world. Lawyer that he was, Wright argues both sides of the issue, both explicitly in the speeches made by Lord Mora and Lord Dorn around the midpoint of the book, and implicitly throughout the entire book, and particularly at the end, where John Lang must decide where his destiny lies between the two cultures of Islandia and America.

The culture of Islandia is fleshed out to a great degree, and a variety of different scenes, settings, and discussions bring out its richness of detail. Many of the cultural concepts introduced are central to an understanding of the story, and though we do not get to see much of the Islandian language, these concepts are given Islandian terms since no exact equivalent exists in English. One such notion is that of *tanrydoon*, literally *soil-place-custom*, which means there is a room always reserved for you in a friend's home where you are welcome. The concept is first described to Lang by Perier, the French consul to Islandia:

> "Did you know that even the Islandian city man does not feel that the city is his home?"
>
> "In a way." I knew from Bodwin that city men usually had some relative in the country at whose place they were welcome.
>
> "More than that," he said. "*Every* city man has such a place. It is the same place for his grandfather that it is for his grandson; not only is he welcome but he has a right—a legal right—to go there and stay as long as he likes, though if he stays over a month he is expected to do some work. He may go and take all of his children. Good taste controls the actual working out."
>
> Perier was silent for a moment.
>
> "When you marry," he continued, "a month or so before your child is to be born you will put yourself and your wife on a boat bound for Doring, and you two will go to the house of Lord Dorn, and there you will find them expecting you and glad to see you. There your wife will stay until the child is weaned, and longer maybe, and you as long as and whenever you can. If the child becomes sickly or bored in The City here, back you will all go to Lord Dorn's. That, and a great deal more, is *tanrydoon*."[39]

While *tanrydoon* serves an important purpose in the story, even more important to the story are the four Islandian words for "love": *alia* (love of a place, specifically an ancestral home and land), *amia* (love of friends), *ania* (the desire for marriage and commitment), and *apia* (sexual attraction). These kinds of love, and the differences and relationships between them, are central to the book's romances and relationships and how they shape the narrative. The Islandian culture is carefully thought out and laid out in great detail, more so than any other fictional culture to appear before it. Through an interesting combination of elements, Wright achieves a new culture which is neither Eastern nor Western in outlook, and original enough that it does not feel like a thinly-veiled imitation of an actual existing earthly culture (as so often happens with fictional cultures), nor is it so primitive as to seem crude or undeveloped.

With the growth of archaeology and anthropology during the twentieth century, more fictional cultures, and more developed fictional cultures, began to appear as audiences became increasingly sophisticated in their expectations. In America, the growth of mass media, along with new possibilities for travel and tourism, and waves of immigrants arriving in the country, meant that most Americans had more contact with (or at least knowledge of) cultures outside of their own, and thus had more firsthand cross-cultural experience. Also, imaginary worlds that appeared in audiovisual media could not rely on mere verbal description as novels did; cultural design, in such areas as costume, architecture, vehicles, and so forth, had to be considered concretely, in the form of sounds and images, and had to be considered as an integrated whole, rather than as a collection of unrelated designs.

Whether on-screen or on the page, the fictional cultures of imaginary worlds often have one or more simple defining features to quickly establish and position them against other cultures (for example, in the *Star Trek* universe, the image of Klingons as warriors, Vulcans as logical, Ferengi as businessmen, and so forth). Just as entire planets often contain a single type of terrain, much like a single earthly location, quite often locations in secondary worlds are home to a single culture, regardless of whether those locations are cities, countries, or entire planets. In multi-planet worlds, planets that are the main home base of more than two or three cultures are relatively rare, since each culture can be given its own planet (unless the story requires otherwise). As mentioned earlier, in multi-planet worlds that include Earth, all of humanity is often grouped together under the same cultural umbrella (as "Earthlings" or "Humans"), with the implicit assumption that differences between human cultures on Earth are small compared to interplanetary cultural differences. Whatever the case, the lines dividing cultures are usually clearly drawn ones, and cultural differences are emphasized.

Cultures, then, provide important structural frameworks for the worlds into which they are integrated. Even with guides and mentors who are members of a culture and who provide explanations to main characters and the audience, new sets of cultural defaults, which may include different languages, artifacts, foods, customs, and so forth, often produce a great expository burden to be overcome. Besides maps, timelines, genealogical charts, and glossaries which convey structural information in a very direct way (but usually appear outside the narrative), some aspects of cultures can be conveyed through more indirect means. Elements may be introduced without explanation if there are Primary World analogs to which they can be compared, and if the meanings of the new elements can be obtained though the context in which they appear. In image-based media, elements of culture may appear visually but without explanation, leaving the audience to figure things out from context. For example, in video games like *Riven* (1997) or *Rhem* (2003), the player encounters machines the purposes of which are unexplained, and it is only after the player interacts with them and watches the consequences that their functions become apparent. Shaun Tan's graphical story of an immigrant family, *The Arrival* (2007), is a book-length example of learning a culture through context.

Cultural aspects that can be easily summarized or explained can be given in appendices as well. *Dune*, for example, includes appendices on the ecology of Dune, the religion of Dune, the Bene Gesserit and their motives and purposes, short biographies of characters, and a glossary in which we find that a baliset is "a nine-stringed musical instrument, lineal descendent of the zithra, tuned to the Chusuk scale and played by strumming. A favorite instrument of Imperial troubadors."[40] Since fictional cultures often are constructed or cobbled together from various aspects or aesthetics of existing real world cultures, it is not unusual to find a residue of connotations attached to them, which can be used by an author to aid explanations or create expectations (for example, *Dune*'s desert culture is patterned after Arab and Middle-Eastern cultures to some degree).

Like characters, fictional cultures often have stories of origins (involving the world's history), character arcs over the course of a story (cultural shifts and changes), and are often depicted during the turning points, power struggles, and decisive moments that determine their future paths. Quite often, this involves a world which is under the sway or at least the threat of evil powers; the main character learns about the evil power, joins the fight against it, and then plays a crucial role in fighting and defeating it (for example, Dorothy fighting the Wicked Witch in Oz, Frodo helping destroy the Ring and defeat Sauron, Luke Skywalker helping defeat the Empire, Tron helping to bring down the Master Control Program, or Neo helping to defend Zion against the machines). Usually, the decisive moment in the culture's history is an invasion or war, a debate as to whether or not to accept certain technologies or foreign influences, or its first encounter with another culture. Quite typically, cultural clashes are central to the stories being told, sometimes with a cross-cultural love story thrown in to personalize the conflict and add the friction so necessary to fictional romances. And, just as the end of a story will indicate the future direction taken by the main character, we are usually given enough information to assume the future direction in which the culture will be heading, which is usually a more peaceful and stable one.

Culture, as a means of structuring a world, not only helps to unite other structuring systems (like geography, history, nature, and so forth), but gives them a context that relates directly to the experience of its characters, and gives them meaning. Culture can be one of the most compelling ways that a world can exceed a story and spark the kind of speculation and conjecture that brings a secondary world alive in the imagination. And among all the various aspects of culture, *language* is one that immediately gives a sense of a culture's aesthetics and worldview.

Language

While there are numerous attempts to invent languages for international use or to try to avoid the supposed flaws of natural languages (Arika Okrent's book

In the Land of Invented Languages lists hundreds of them[41]), many imaginary worlds use constructed languages (or "conlangs") along with their invented cultures and peoples, usually without the desire that the language be used in the Primary World (although some of the more developed ones, like Quenya and Klingon, have a fan base that attempts fluency in them). Unlike "natural" languages, a constructed language is deliberately invented and designed, and typically only sketched out to the degree needed by the imaginary world in which it appears. Constructed languages are often divided into two groups, *a posteriori* languages that borrow or are based on elements of existing natural languages, and *a priori* languages that are not based on any real languages (although it is difficult to completely avoid the influence of real languages).

Invented languages serve several purposes in imaginary worlds. They can introduce new concepts, objects, or beings that otherwise have no words for them, or rename existing things so that the audience will consider them anew. The design of the sound of the language and its appearance in print, which can include invented alphabets, scripts, or pictograms, gives a culture or world an aesthetic flavor and emotional feeling. This, of course, depends a great deal on the original natural language in which the work appears, since it relies on connotations from that language, and even its aesthetics, to produce its own effect. Such connotations, however, may not have the same effect when a work is translated into other languages. For example, there is a tendency in English-language fantasy and science fiction to use letters that appear less frequently (like Q, X, and Z) when coining names that are intended to sound exotic.[42] Likewise, if invented words are too close to real words they may pick up other connotations inadvertently, so they are usually avoided, despite the fact that it is not unusual for independent languages to use the same words with different meanings (linguists refer to such words as "false friends", since they can be misleading).[43]

An invented language can also be used to generate names in a consistent manner that gives names meaning. For example, in Tolkien's Sindarin, "mor" means "black" or "dark", and is found in a number of names, such as Moria ("black chasm"), Morgoth ("dark enemy"), Morwen ("dark maiden"), and Mordor ("black land"). Even if no glossary of root words is provided, readers may be able to sense similarities and possibly even form expectations when encountering later names, based on the meanings inherent in the ones they have seen. Which concepts are given words and which ones are omitted, as well as the conceptual divisions that become codified in a vocabulary, will determine what can be expressed in a given language. For example, in Eunoia, the language devised by poet Christian Bök for the television program *Earth: Final Conflict* (1997), there is no past tense, and concepts and their polar opposites are embodied together (like "war" and "peace").[44]

Finally, besides organizing and connecting concepts and cultures in imaginary worlds, languages and words are also often a source of knowledge and power within their worlds. For example, George Orwell's *Nineteen Eighty-Four* includes an Appendix on the principles of Newspeak, the official language of Oceania which aims to limit thought by limiting vocabulary. The appendix even explains how word formation occurs, the rules of which limit coinages and new ideas, and impose certain attitudes on the speaker. The eleventh edition of the Newspeak dictionary is being edited at the time of the story, and Syme, a character who is working on it, describes it:

> "The Eleventh Edition is the definitive edition," he said. "We're getting the language into its final shape—the shape it's going to have when nobody speaks anything else. When we've finished with it, people like you will have to learn it all over again. You think, I dare say, that our chief job is inventing new words. But not a bit of it! We're destroying words—scores of them, hundreds of them, every day. We're cutting the language down to the bone. The Eleventh Edition won't contain a single word that will become obsolete before the year 2050. … "Don't you see that the whole aim of Newspeak is to narrow the range of thought? In the end we shall make thoughtcrime literally impossible, because there will be no words in which to express it."[45]

Besides their use for expressing concepts and formulating ideas (or limiting them), words can also have even more direct power. Like the Biblical "Fiat Lux" that begins Creation, certain words produce immediate effects in their respective worlds, like the "true names" of Earthsea, the written language of the D'ni culture (from the Myst franchise), and the magical spells, incantations, and passwords found in fantasy literature (see Chapter 5). As a result, knowledge of their use is often secret and guarded, and passed on only through the proper training and only to qualified individuals.

In early imaginary worlds, where main characters were mainly only observers of the secondary worlds they visited, there was less need for invented languages. Probably the first imaginary world to have its own language and alphabet was More's Utopia. The 1517 edition of More's book included a page of ancillary materials (attributed to either More or his friend, Peter Giles[46]) with the Utopian Alphabet and "A Quatrain in the Utopian Language", which was printed using the Utopian script as well as a transliteration using the Roman alphabet (see Figure 3.4). The language, however, is not used within the story itself, and some editions of the text do not even include Giles' page. A few years later, books in Rabelais' *The Histories of Gargantua and Pantagruel* series (1532–1551) used invented languages within them, but only in a few statements made for comic effect.

As worlds developed and there was more interaction between their natives and the travelers who visited them, the problem of a language barrier complicating communication began to be acknowledged and addressed. Although in some instances, the language barrier provided a source of misunderstanding that could fuel a story's conflict, more often it was seen as an inconvenience to be quickly

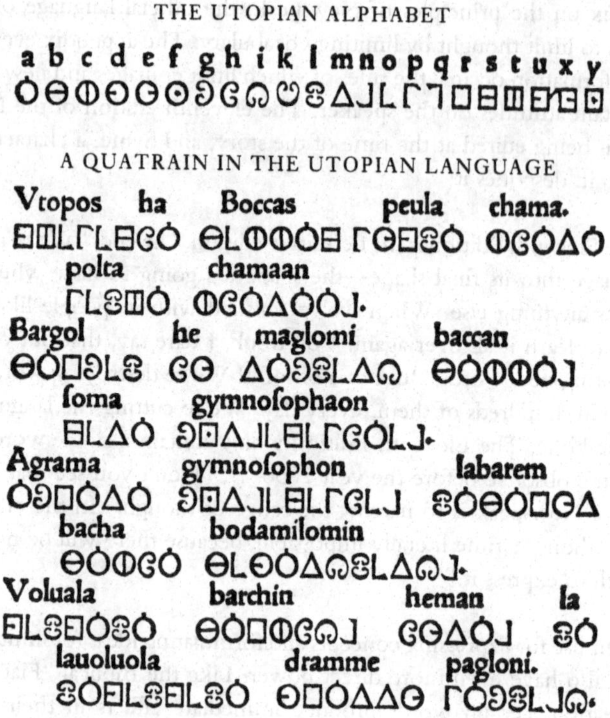

THE UTOPIAN ALPHABET

a b c d e f g h i k l m n o p q r s t u x y

ᴏⴄⴲⴊⴰⵀⴳⴄⴶⴄⴄⵁⴺⴺⴹⴰⴳⴼⵁⴲⴲⴴⴴⴳ

A QUATRAIN IN THE UTOPIAN LANGUAGE

Vtopos   ha   Boccas   peula   chama.

polta   chamaan

Bargol   he   maglomi   baccan

ſoma   gymnoſophaon

Agrama   gymnoſophon   labarem

bacha   bodamilomin

Voluala   barchin   heman   la

lauoluola   dramme   pagloni.

FIGURE 3.4 The Utopian alphabet and a quatrain in the Utopian language, from Thomas More's *Utopia.*

overcome so that the story could move along. In Margaret Cavendish's *The Description of a New World, Called the Blazing-World* (1666), the main character travels to the Blazing World sees the various animal men speaking in their own tongue (the world has a single language), and we are told that she "took courage, and endeavored to learn their language; which after she had obtained so far, that partly by some words and signs she was able to apprehend their meaning", after which she felt not only "safe, but very happy in their company".[47] The language learning appears to take place almost instantly, with no description of how it occurs; but the language barrier is at least acknowledged. Another solution was to allow time for the language to be learned, and then simply set it during an ellipsis; in Thomas Northmore's *Memoirs of Planetes, or a Sketch of the Laws and Manners of Makar* (1795), the main character traveling to Makar mentions (in first-person narration) how he lived with a family of natives for a month during which time he learned their language; but that is all we hear of the experience.

Another solution is to invent a device which can eliminate the language barrier instantly. Probably the earliest such device can be found in Crowder and Woodgate's *A Voyage to the World in the Centre of the Earth Giving an Account of the*

Manners, Customs, Laws, Government, and Religion of the Inhabitants, Their Persons and Habits Described with Several Other Particulars (1755), where the main character visiting the underground world is given a salve which allows him understand the native language. An even more powerful device appears in Benjamin Disraeli's *The Voyage of Captain Popanilla* (1828). In a sea chest washed up on shore, Popanilla finds a book, *The Universal Linguist, by Mr. Hamilton, or the Art of Dreaming in Languages*, which puts him to sleep as he reads it, and afterwards, upon waking, he is able to understand other languages. Later, when he encounters various peoples of Fantaisie and Vraibleusia, he is able to understand them as well, thanks to the Universal Linguist. The idea of a "universal translator" would eventually become a convention in science fiction; for example, the "universal translators" found in the *Star Trek* universe, or the Babel Fish in Douglas Adams' Hitchhiker's Galaxy, which lives in the user's ear and translates what it hears.

A variety of other methods attempted to speed up the learning of language. In Defontenay's *Star* (1854), the narrator learns the language of the Starian system by studying the Starian books found in a chest inside a crashed meteorite, despite the lack of any context in which to make a translation. L. Frank Baum's John Dough, from *John Dough and the Cherub* (1906) understands the animal's languages due to drinking an Elixir of Life; and in James Blish's "And Some were Savages" (1960), a technical process allows the user to learn a language "in about eight hours."[48] In cases where there are no characters from outside of the secondary world, a "common tongue" can be used (like Westron, in the case of Tolkien's Middle-earth) which most characters speak in addition to their own local languages. This common tongue is then translated into the natural language in which the story appears, so that readers can understand it as well, while still allowing the local languages to appear as foreign as the author wishes. In *The Lord of the Rings*, for example, Frodo's name in Westron is Maura Labingi and Sam's is Banazîr Galbasi, but these names are never used within the text of the story.

In some stories, the language barrier is addressed and learning of a language is not ellipsized so severely, for example, in Wright's *Islandia*, where the language barrier is considered thoughtfully and dealt with more realistically. In some cases, the overcoming of the language barrier can be the main conflict of a story; for example, the astronaut scientists of Stanisław Lem's *Solaris* (1961) struggle to communicate with the planet's sentient ocean, trying to bridge the gap between alien forms of understanding. However, since many stories set in new worlds start their action with the arrival of the main character, with neither the time nor the inclination to deal with the language barrier problem, many rely on established conventions to find a quick solution to allow communication and get on with the rest of their action.

With enough usage of an invented language in a story, difficulties can even arise for the reader, who is called upon to remember new words as they are used, resulting in the addition of a glossary. Probably the first imaginary-world story to include a glossary was Robert Paltock's *The Life and Adventures of Peter Wilkins,*

A Cornish Man (1751), which featured a two-page "Explanation of Names and Things mentioned in this Work" listing 103 terms.[49] Some definitions reference other terms (for example, a "filus" is defined as "a rib of the graundee"), enhancing the reader's immersion in the world through the interconnectedness of the world's terminology. Comparing terms in the glossary also reveals the consistency of the root structure of the language. We would expect to find the same root appearing in words with similar meanings, and we do: "Colamb" means "governor" and "Colambat" means "government"; while "Lask" means "a slave" and "Laskmett" means "slavery". Beyond such similarities, though, there is no overarching structure or logic to Paltock's language.

Some authors added to their invented language in a piecemeal way as their worlds grew (in *Thuvia, Maid of Mars* (1920), Edgar Rice Burroughs included a glossary for all the Barsoomian words that had accumulated over his four Mars novels), but this method makes it unlikely that the resulting language will be able to remain consistent. Other subcreators, like Cordwainer Smith (and later, George Lucas), were content to take words from languages other than English and use them as names, or like Samuel Butler, use anagrams or reversals of words.[50] However, language construction would reach a new level of sophistication when the author constructing the language had a background in how languages worked and developed.

During the twentieth century, linguists would sometimes be hired to develop languages for worlds (usually in cinema and television, where a budget existed for such things), and some literary authors were linguists as well. The most famous of these was of course J. R. R. Tolkien, for whom invented languages were the seeds from which his imaginary world grew. Tolkien's own personal history of inventing languages is the subject of his essay "A Secret Vice", where he describes early experiences with invented languages, including his friend's "Nevbosh" of which he was a speaker, and his own "Naffarin".[51] Tolkien created over a dozen invented languages of Middle-earth, of varying size and complexity. His Elven tongue, Quenya, is perhaps the most detailed (and some would say, the most beautiful) among them, and is influenced by Finnish and Latin. Based on a series of root words, Quenya is complete and detailed enough that linguist David Salo was able to extrapolate it for the translations of characters' lines in Peter Jackson's films of *The Lord of the Rings* (2001–2003).

Other linguists developing secondary world languages include Suzette Haden Elgin (who devised Láadan, a "woman's language" for her *Native Tongue* trilogy of novels, with words like *widazhad* (to be pregnant late in term and eager for the end) and *ásháana* (to menstruate joyfully)), Victoria Fromkin (who developed Paku for *The Land of the Lost* television series and the vampire language for *Blade* (1998)), Alan Garner (who developed languages for *The Dark Crystal* (1982)), Tom Shippey (who developed Marbak for Harry Harrison's *West of Eden* (1984)), Paul Frommer (who developed the Na'vi language for *Avatar* (2009)), and Marc Okrand (who designed Atlantean for *Atlantis: The Lost Empire* (2001) and Klingon for the *Star Trek* universe). Okrand's Klingon was developed beyond the films and television series, appearing in *The Klingon Dictionary* (1985), and it is supported by the Klingon Language Institute which features newsletters and other material in Klingon, including a translation of *Hamlet* (2000). With greater fan participation and communication due to the Internet, by the early twenty-first century, a community of constructed language inventors coalesced, as well as language construction tools like Mark Rosenfelder's *The Language Construction Kit*, which began on-line and was eventually published as a book in 2010; and in 2007, the Language Creation Society was formed, which sponsors an annual Language Creation Conference.

Invented languages, then, can range from hundreds of words, like Klingon, to a sampling of a language that may only be a few words (although some languages have very few words to begin with, like the language of Pierre Barton's subterranean Ogs, which has only two words, "og" and "glog").[52] Invented languages may be central to a story or world, or merely used to add flavor to the background. However, even when only well-constructed glimpses of them appear in a story, these languages add to the narratives and mythologies that they help to support.

Mythology

Mythologies structure secondary worlds by giving them a history and context for events, through legends and stories of origins that provide backstories for the current events and settings of a world. They often reveal how characters and ongoing problems came to be, so that story events seem more meaningful and perhaps even the completion of a long character arc or the resolution of an age-old conflict. Mythologies, then, provide historical depth, explanations, and purpose to the events of a world.

Inspired by Greek, Roman, or Norse mythology, authors like Dunsany, Lovecraft, and Tolkien produced hierarchical pantheons of godlike beings that oversee their subcreated worlds. Lord Dunsany's first book, *The Gods of Pegāna* (1905), contained a creation myth and a hierarchical pantheon of gods, which later provided a background when Dunsany wrote legends of the lands where they were worshipped. *The Gods of Pegāna* is a short book, with short chapters, and a form and style patterned after the Book of Genesis:

> When MANA-YOOD-SUSHAI had made the gods there were only the gods, and They sat in the middle of Time, for there was as much Time before them as behind them, which having no end had neither a beginning.
>
> And Pegāna was without heat or light or sound, save for the drumming of Skarl; moreover Pegāna was The Middle of All, for there was below Pegāna what there was above it, and there lay before it that which lay beyond.

Then said the gods, making the signs of the gods and speaking with Their hands lest the silence of Pegāna should blush; then said the gods to one another, speaking with Their hands; "Let Us make worlds to amuse Ourselves while MANA rests. Let Us make worlds and Life and Death, and colours in the sky; only let Us not break the silence upon Pegana."

Then raising Their hands, each god according to his sign, They made the worlds and the suns, and put a light in the houses of the sky.[53]

Dunsany followed up the book with *Time and the Gods* (1906), which begins with the preface "These tales are of the things that befell gods and men in Yarnith, Averon, and Zarkandhu, and in the other countries of my dreams." The stories include his pantheon of gods, this time interacting with men in the world.

Dunsany's work inspired H. P. Lovecraft, who developed his own mythology which he called his "pseudomythology", which would later be known as his "Cthulu Mythos" after one of the central figures of his pantheon. Unlike Dunsany's mythology, Lovecraft's was dark and disturbing, his "gods" (actually, extraterrestrials who are worshipped) malevolent and demonic, and his stories part of the horror genre. These powerful beings are harmful and indifferent to humanity, and their incarnate forms are similar to frogs, reptiles, gelatinous blobs, and clouds of shadow. They often are grotesque, with tentacles, horns, and detached eyes; but as interdimensional cosmic beings, their composition is different from that of physical matter. Lovecraft encouraged other writers who were friends of his to use his mythos in their stories, so as to increase the verisimilitude of his creation through intertextual references, which implied that the mythos was based on something real that was being alluded to by multiple authors.

Dunsany's pantheon was also an inspiration to J. R. R. Tolkien, who assembled an elaborate and carefully integrated legendarium of his own (most notably represented in *The Silmarillion* (1977) and *Unfinished Tales of Númenor and Middle-earth* (1980) among his works published posthumously). As a Roman Catholic, however, Tolkien did not want his mythology to contradict Christian theology, and so he attempted to devise his legendarium so as to fit into it, calling it a "monotheistic but "subcreational" mythology".[54] At the top of his hierarchy is God (Eru, which means "the One"), who creates the Valar, angelic-like created beings who take the place of "gods" but who are not deities, and serving under them are the Maiar. In his creation story, *Ainulindalë*, "The Music of the Ainur", one of the Valar, Melkor, sows discord and after a fall becomes the evil adversary that opposes the plans of the Valar. A number of mythological and supernatural issues, including the nature of evil, the definition of "magic", and the conception of death, changed over the decades as Tolkien worked on his legendarium and considered the theological implications of its design.

Tolkien could be a purist when it came to the construction of an invented mythology. His letters reveal his thoughts regarding his own mythology, including a critique of his ongoing work.[55] Although he liked *Out of the Silent Planet*

(1938), the first book of C. S. Lewis' Space Trilogy, Tolkien referred to the trilogy's mythology as "incipient and never fully realized"[56] and wrote, "I actively disliked his Arthurian-Byzantine mythology; and still think that it spoiled the trilogy of C. S. L. (a very impressionable, too impressionable man) in the last part."[57] Tolkien thought a mythology should be self-contained and disliked how Lewis's Narnia stories combined elements of various mythologies (including dwarves, dragons, and giants of Northern mythology; Bacchus, Silenus, fauns, and centaurs from Greek and Roman mythology; talking beavers; and Father Christmas), writing, "It is sad that 'Narnia' and all that part of C. S. L.'s work should remain outside the range of my sympathy, as much of my work was outside his."[58]

Not all authors go so far as to build their own legendarium, of course; but many use mythological elements for the historical depth and transcendental power that they bring to a text. As such, the Bible has been a strong influence and even an Ur-text for many world-builders developing their own mythologies, not just in literary style (as the Dunsany passage in the preceding text demonstrates), but also in structure, theme, and content. As Stephen Prickett states in his book on Victorian fantasy:

> It has often been noticed that Plato and the Bible are the two greatest philosophical influences on English Literature; it has less often been observed how great their influence has been specifically in the direction of fantasy. Nevertheless, their pull is obvious. Both suggest the existence of "other worlds" impinging on this, but of a greater reality, as part of a greater metaphysical and moral whole that is ultimately beyond man's understanding.[59]

The Bible contains a creation story, covers the rise of a people as they grow into a nation over thousands of years, follows the long struggle between good and evil on both natural and supernatural planes, and depicts an oppressed people looking for a prophesized savior (who is an outsider in some way); it then details the savior's growing conflict with the authorities which ends up in his self-sacrifice for the people, and through his help, the gaining of freedom or ascendancy as a new era is ushered in by the book's end. This pattern, or parts of it, can be found in a great many world-based stories (particularly that of a savior figure; for example, Peter Wilkins in Sass Doorpt Swangeanti, Dorothy in Oz, Aragorn in Middle-earth, Paul Atreides in Arrakis, Neo in the Matrix, Anakin Skywalker in the *Star Wars* galaxy, and so on).[60] Bibles also came to contain maps, timelines, and genealogies, first as descriptions within the text and later as ancillary materials that summed up its data in charts. The Bible is also a collection of multiple narratives woven together, with later books referencing earlier ones intertextually, as the stories of many large franchises do.

Along with gods and other supernatural beings, legendary figures from ancient times also abound in subcreated mythologies, their deeds shaping their worlds and their histories. War figures prominently in many stories, and is often a continuation of conflicts begun long before the main characters were born. *The Lord of the Rings*, for example, is really the culmination of the long struggle against Morgoth described in *The Silmarillion*, which is continued by his servant Sauron, whose spirit rules Mordor and the Nazgul even after his body is gone and whose power only ends when the One Ring is destroyed. Lines of kings and royal families also extend genealogical lines of characters, along with the conflicts they represent, from the past into the present. Other kinds of lines, like the mentor–apprentice pairings of the Sith and the Jedi in the *Star Wars* galaxy, can also carry on an opposition from one era to another, bringing about fresh revenge from long-simmering ancient disputes.

Mythology helps to create a sense of historical depth, connecting present characters and events with ancient ones, and the juxtaposition of the two eras may reveal differences which imply changes that have taken place in a world. The hierarchy of supernatural or mythical beings, as well as the models provided by ancient figures and the value placed on traditions of the past (or the lack of them), can also tell us something about the worldviews inherent in a secondary world, as mythology becomes an embodiment of philosophy.

Philosophy

A philosophical outlook can be embodied within a narrative in a number of ways: through an author's direct commentary on events; through characters' points of view; through statements made explicitly in dialogue or implicitly in characters' behavior and choices; through the way actions and consequences are connected, revealing a worldview concerning cause-and-effect relationships (for example, whether bad characters are punished for their crimes or get away with them); and through the author's overall attitude as to what is considered normal or unusual (which can be expressed by the norms within the diegetic world of the story itself). Depending on an author's skill and intent, philosophical messages and ideas can be overtly or covertly embedded to various degrees within a story, and inadvertent or conflicting messages or worldviews are also possible. Finally, the author's style and expectations of his or her audience can reveal something of a worldview (compare the lengthy meandering sentences of William Faulkner to the clipped staccato sentences of James Ellroy, or the lush, descriptive prose of E. R. Eddison to the telegraphic prose of Ernest Hemingway, and the demands each makes on the reader).

Secondary worlds often differ markedly from the Primary World, and it is precisely in these differences that philosophical ideas and points of view can be expressed in an even subtler manner. The subcreated world gives the author all the same opportunities to embed a worldview as traditional narrative, as well as new opportunities that occur during the process of world-building, in which a worldview's assumptions and implications are concretized and naturalized by the design of the world itself. Certain things can no longer be taken for granted, and history, geography, culture, language, and even ontology can all be designed to reflect ideas, systems, and beliefs about which the author wishes to make a point; a subcreator can change the laws of physics and metaphysics, alter the way actions result in consequences, propose new concepts that question or reconfigure traditional concepts that undermine our assumptions, or even change probabilities that suggest different boundaries of plausibility. If the author can present a world as a coherent whole with enough completeness and inner consistency so as to gain the Secondary Belief of the audience, the audience may be more receptive to the ideas being presented than they would be if the same ideas were stated directly in a more heavy-handed way. Once the conceit of the world is accepted, some ideas may even pass unnoticed as a part of the background and default assumptions. Sometimes even the mere presence of the world itself already makes a statement; if it is not intended as parody or satire, a utopia that is shown to be functional makes an inherent argument for its feasibility.

The many default assumptions that are reset can be used to introduce new ways of thinking, just as encountering a new culture can force one to see the world in a new way. Sometimes inventions and changed defaults are manifest even in a film's opening shot (as in *Star Wars* (1977) or *Blade Runner* (1982)), or a book's opening sentence: "In a hole in the ground there lived a Hobbit." (J. R. R. Tolkien, *The Hobbit* (1937)); "It was a bright cold day in April and the clocks were striking thirteen." (George Orwell, *Nineteen Eighty-Four* (1949)); "Composite image, optically encoded by escort-craft of the trans-Channel airship *Lord Brunel*; aerial view of suburban Cherbourg, October 14, 1905." (William Gibson and Bruce Sterling, *The Difference Engine* (1990)). Differences can provide an intriguing hook that pulls us into a world, but they must become naturalized to some degree for Secondary Belief to occur; at the same time, new terminology gives form to new ideas, like that of *tanrydoon* or *ania* described earlier. The interweaving of Primary World and secondary world material, and the way in which the new material is accepted and becomes part of the background assumptions, makes a subcreated world an effective vehicle for the delivery of philosophical ideas.

When a main character comes to a secondary world from the Primary World, there will inevitably be a comparison of worldviews between the secondary world and Primary World, or more specifically, the culture from which the main character (and usually also the author) comes. Not surprisingly, the author's own worldview usually comes through his or her secondary world, directly or indirectly; for example, the Roman Catholicism of Thomas More or J. R. R. Tolkien; the nihilism and cosmicism of H. P. Lovecraft; the atheism of Philip Pullman; or the Jungian and Taoist outlook of Ursula K. LeGuin. An author might not even be entirely aware of their influences until the revision stage. As Tolkien wrote of his own work:

> *The Lord of the Rings* is of course a fundamentally religious and Catholic work; unconsciously so at first, but consciously in the revision. That is why

I have not put in, or have cut out, practically all references to anything like "religion", to cults or practices, in the imaginary world. For the religious element is absorbed into the story and the symbolism.[61]

Likewise, a world's villains and evils are likely to represent a philosophy in direct opposition to the author's own worldview, and one which is equally "absorbed into the story and the symbolism", though it can appear overtly or even be given a name (like Nabakov's "Ekwilism" philosophy in *Bend Sinister* (1947)).

Sometimes competing philosophies can be played out through two characters who have similar origins but who take different paths through their choices and actions; in *The Lord of the Rings*, for example, Gandalf and Saruman both begin as Istari, the former remains good while the latter turns to evil through his lust for knowledge and power and unwillingness to serve; brothers Boromir and Faramir receive different treatment from their father and react differently when tempted with possession of the Ring; leaders Aragorn and Denethor approach their reign of Gondor very differently; and hobbits Bilbo and Gollum both possess the Ring for years but take different attitudes toward it, resulting in Bilbo's being able to let the Ring go and Gollum's obsession with reacquiring it.

Secondary worlds, then can embed and support philosophical ideas to an even greater extent than stories set in the Primary World, and can make use of all the structures holding a secondary world together to do so. Whether a philosophy comes naturally out of a subcreator's work or is the framework on which the subcreator builds a world, it can be seen as a structuring device that affects and determines much of the work, and in many cases, helps to pull various infrastructures together.

Tying Different Infrastructures Together

While each individual infrastructure needs to be complete and consistent within itself, all of the different infrastructures must also fit together consistently if world gestalten are to occur. Story events already act as points at which characters, places, and specific moments in time are tied together, automatically connecting maps, timelines, and genealogies. These three structures, which work the closest with narrative structures (the topic of the next chapter), also connect to the structures of nature, culture, language, mythology, and philosophy discussed in the preceding text, and fitting them all together often results in the need for adjustments and revisions as well.

Maps must be created with Nature and natural processes in mind, as Lin Carter points out in *Imaginary Worlds: The Art of Fantasy*:

Geography does not just *happen*—natural features are where they are due to certain causes. It behooves the would-be author of imaginary-world fantasy to think a little before sketching out his map.

You cannot really have a lush rainforest smack up against a parched desert of burning sands, you know; it pays to do a bit of reading into climatology so as to understand the interplay of forces that create deserts and rainforests, jungles and grasslands, and so on. Nor can you stick mountains on your map in a helter-skelter fashion; mountains have a good reason for being where they are, and a fantasy writer should know something about them.[62]

Even Tolkien, careful as he was, admitted that he did not pay enough attention to geology when designing Middle-earth, writing in one of his letters:

> As for the shape of the world of the Third Age, I am afraid that was devised "dramatically" rather than geologically, or paleontologically. I do sometimes wish that I had made some sort of agreement between the imaginations or theories of the geologists and my map a little more possible. But that would only have made more trouble with human history.[63]

Likewise, nature provides the raw materials from which culture arises, and thus determines much of what cultural artifacts and their societies will be like, which will in turn limit technologies and influence social structures. Subcreators must imagine how access to food, clothing, and shelter is obtained, and how they are found or made, considering the natural environment. In *The Tough Guide to Fantasyland*, Diana Wynne Jones satirically notes the lack of animals in fantasy genre fiction, and writes about animal skins:

> **Animal Skins** are much in use and are of four kinds:
>
> 1. Trappers' furs. These are occasionally brought south in bundles. As there appear to be no animals to be trapped, it is likely that these skins are either cunning manmade imitations or imported from another world.
> 2. Furs worn by NORTHERN BARBARIANS. It is possible that these are also false or imported. Another possibility is that the animals providing these furs are now extinct (see ECOLOGY) and that the famous fur loincloths are handed down father to son.
> 3. Leather for BOOTS, VESTS, etc. is again of mysterious origin. (See DOMESTIC ANIMALS.) There are not enough cows to go round, but the leather has to come from *somewhere*.
> 4. Skins of which the TENTS of the DESERT NOMADS are made. Here the source is obvious. Nomads breed HORSES: the Tents have to be made of horsehide. In fact, it is entirely probable that Horses provide all four kinds of Animal Skin.[64]

The discussion from Chapter 1, regarding food and water on Tatooine, is another example of how questions can arise when nature does not appear to completely support the cultures that live in it.

Language relies on both culture and nature, as words are needed for the objects encountered by the members of a culture in the place where they live. In linguistics, the Sapir-Whorf Hypotheses suggested that language shapes thought and culture through the way it allows certain concepts to be expressed, articulated, or even noticed, due to the available vocabulary and grammar of the language. Though the strong version of the Sapir-Whorf Hypothesis has been discredited, the discussion it engendered brought more attention to the ways in which language influences culture.

The invented languages of secondary worlds are often a large part of their cultures, and it is not unusual for the audience to receive only those words which present foreign concepts, since dialog and other uses of the language will likely be translated into the Primary World language understood by the audience. While there is a great deal of latitude in the connections made between language and culture, the two are often developed concurrently and together provide a specific flavor to the subcreated worlds in which they appear.

Language and mythology are also connected, since they help each other to continue and propagate, and they often share an aesthetic basis as well. For Tolkien, language was the starting point of his mythology; as he described the process:

> It was just as the 1914 War burst on me that I made the discovery that "legends" depend on the language to which they belong; but a living language depends equally on the "legends" which it conveys by tradition. (For example, that the Greek mythology depends far more on the marvelous aesthetic of its language and so of its nomenclature of persons and places and less on its content than people realize, though of course it depends on both. And vice versa. Volapük, Esperanto, Ido, Novial, are dead, far deader than ancient unused languages, because their authors never invented any Esperanto legends.) So though being a philologist by nature and trade (yet one always primarily interested in the aesthetic rather than the functional aspects of language) I began with language, I found myself involved in inventing "legends" of the same "taste".[65]

Mythology is often closely tied to nature, either through stories of origins and ancient beings associated with the nature elements (as in creation stories), or the *genius loci* connected with particular places. As mythology is also used to evoke a time abyss (as described earlier), it is frequently an important part of a world's timeline.

Although the careful integrating of secondary world infrastructures is necessary for the illusion of a complete and consistent world, deliberately not doing so can also be a way in which an author embeds a philosophical idea with a subcreated world. In an essay entitled "How to Build a Universe That Doesn't Fall Apart Two Days Later", author Philip K. Dick writes:

> So I ask, in my writing, What is real? Because unceasingly we are bombarded with pseudo-realities manufactured by very sophisticated people using very sophisticated electronic mechanisms. I do not distrust their motives; I distrust their power. They have a lot of it. And it is an astonishing power: that of creating whole universes, universes of the mind. I ought to know. I do the same thing. It is my job to create universes, as the basis of one novel after another. And I have to build them in such a way that they do not fall apart two days later. Or at least that is what my editors hope. However, I will reveal a secret to you: I like to build universes which *do* fall apart. I like to see them come unglued, and I like to see how the characters in the novels cope with this problem. I have a secret love of chaos. There should be more of it. Do not believe—and I am dead serious when I say this—do not assume that order and stability are always good, in a society or in a universe. The old, the ossified, must always give way to new life and the birth of new things. Before the new things can be born the old must perish. This is a dangerous realization, because it tells us that we must eventually part with much of what is familiar to us. And that hurts. But that is part of the script of life. Unless we can psychologically accommodate change, we ourselves begin to die, inwardly. What I am saying is that objects, customs, habits, and ways of life must perish so that the authentic human being can live. And it is the authentic human being who matters most, the viable, elastic organism which can bounce back, absorb, and deal with the new.[66]

However they may be used, and to whatever degree they occur, secondary world infrastructures help to suggest a larger world beyond the incomplete material available to an audience, by organizing it into shapes that can be extended by the imagination. Infrastructures provide the scaffolding by which a world logic can take shape, as well as a platform on which further extensions of a world can be devised and built. By far the most common infrastructure used to hold an imaginary world together, and the one to which most worlds can credit their existence, is that of *narrative*, the topic of the next chapter.

4

MORE THAN A STORY: NARRATIVE THREADS AND NARRATIVE FABRIC

> *May these stories drawn from another world have made you forget for a moment the miseries of this one.*
>
> —Charles Ischir Defontenay, *Star (Psi Cassiopeia)*[1]

Narrative is by far the most common structure found in imaginary worlds, and the reason that most of them exist in the first place. Quite often, a world is designed to fit a certain narrative, and expands along with that narrative as it grows. Eventually, as the amount of world information increases, secondary world infrastructures start to take shape, until enough information is present both to raise questions and suggest answers about the missing pieces in the world's history and organization. At that point, the author may begin adding material beyond that which is needed for the story, as the logic of the world begins to restrict how the gaps can be filled.

Conversely, as secondary world infrastructures grow, so does narrative. Mythologies are usually narrative in their organization, and as more events with causal relationships are added to timelines, narratives begin to form. Even maps can be used to imply narratives; for example, the presence of ruins suggests places that were built and then were destroyed or fell into disuse. As infrastructures are pieced together, world history emerges, as well as additional storylines from which future narratives set in the same world may grow. Thus, the extra-narrative material, through which a world exceeds the stories told in it, can become the seeds of new, connected stories, which in turn may extend the world even further. This chapter looks at how narrative operates within a world and helps to structure it, looking first at narratives within a work, narratives in separate works set in the same world, narratives that reach between worlds, and finally the extradiegetic narratives surrounding a world.

Narrative Threads, Braids, and Fabric

In narrative theory, the basic units of narrative have been conceptualized in a number of different ways, ranging from Vladimir Propp's functions, to the abstract units proposed by Gérard Genette, to the more concrete "kernels" and "satellites" proposed by Roland Barthes and Seymour Chapman.[2] The defining of narrative units differs according to the purpose for which they are used, and also by the defining of "narrative" itself. For this chapter, we can broadly define narrative as a series of events which are causally connected, and narrative units as the events themselves, each of which consists of some actor or agent taking part in some action (similar to the way that a noun–verb combination constitutes the minimum requirements for a complete sentence grammatically). Such a chain of events, often referred to as a *narrative thread*, typically revolves around the experiences of a particular character, place, or even an inanimate object (as in the film *The Red Violin* (1998), which follows the same violin over three centuries and multiple owners, with the violin's experiences as the main thread holding the film together), giving a sense of what happens to it over time. An audience typically will have some expectation that a narrative thread will lead somewhere, with some endpoint providing closure. For example, characters undergo changes leading some to endpoint of equilibrium, such as a stable condition, an achieved goal, or death; the overall change is referred to as a character arc, and often provides the reason for why the narrative thread begins and ends where it does.

While some stories are content to follow a single narrative thread, many stories, and storytelling traditions (like Icelandic sagas and medieval stories with interlace structures) bring together multiple narrative threads which run concurrently, with events that happen simultaneously in multiple threads. As multiple threads share the same diegetic materials, themes, or events, the individual threads can become tightly woven together into what we might call *narrative braids*. Here again, an audience will expect certain outcomes involving all the related threads within a braid, such as the working out of conflicts leading to interpersonal equilibrium, or the parting of the individual threads of the braid as characters depart and go their separate ways. Stories can follow a single braid, or they might follow multiple braids, alternating between them.

How tightly narrative braids are woven can also vary. Stories may have multiple narrative threads that have no connection to each other (and thus no braiding); they may have parallel threads that are thematically connected in order to compare and contrast characters and their situations, but with no direct diegetic contact between threads (which we could term *thematic braiding*); multiple threads which share the same locations, minor characters, and other details, but with no causal linkages between threads (*diegetic braiding*); and threads with causal linkages between them, in which the events of one thread have outcomes in other threads (*causal braiding*). Finally, it is possible that two or more characters are part of the same thread, for example, when they travel together and experience the same events and there is little to separate or differentiate the characters' experiences. Thus, as a story advances, narrative braids can tighten and loosen, sometimes separating entirely into a series of threads that then recombine in different ways to form new braids.

When an imaginary world is involved, we may be given extra information and events which fall outside of the main narrative threads and braids; for example, places on maps that are not visited, words in a glossary that do not appear anywhere else, historical events that are only alluded to, or additional characters who appear in genealogical charts but not within any of the main narrative threads. Places, objects, and incidental characters may have histories that are given in digressions, and since worlds often contain multiple stories, there may be other threads and braids that do not connect directly to each other in any way. Yet, because of all the secondary world infrastructures present, all this data and narrative together forms a coherent world; and in worlds that have accumulated a great amount of detail, it may be possible to assemble narrative threads for individual characters that have not been directly assembled by an author. For example, in the *Star Wars* galaxy, Han Solo appears in many separate narratives; in three films (Episodes IV, V, and VI); three novels by Brian Daley (*Han Solo at Star's End* (1979), *Han Solo's Revenge* (1979), and *Han Solo and the Lost Legacy* (1980)); three novels by Ann C. Crispin, which relate Han Solo's childhood and early years before the events of Episode IV (*The Paradise Snare* (1997), *The Hutt Gambit* (1997), and *Rebel Dawn* (1997)); and novels which take place after the events of Episode VI (including *The Courtship of Princess Leia* (1995), *Vector Prime* (1999), *Star by Star* (2001), and those of the *Legacy of the Force* series published between 2006 and 2008); and even in the *Star Wars Holiday Special* (1978). One could compile all of Solo's appearances in these works, resulting in a single narrative thread following the character's life. Besides characters, one can also often trace the histories of places and objects over long periods of time, resulting in new narrative threads that are implied by the information given throughout multiple works (provided that the world is complete and consistent enough). Given enough information, an audience can construct timelines to figure out all the events that are occurring simultaneously at a given moment in time within a world, forming a transverse thread that slices the world synchronically instead of diachronically (warp instead of woof). As more information is added, the narrative material of a world grows more complex than that of a set of braids, and becomes what we might call a *narrative fabric*.[3]

Narrative fabric can also be woven from nonfictional stories of the Primary World; for example, the collection of stories surrounding World War II, or the history of baseball, or the sinking of the Titanic, can each be seen as constituting a narrative fabric (to a certain extent, of course, all nonfiction narratives taking place in the Primary World can be seen as part of an immense narrative fabric about the history of human life on Earth). The seemingly limitless and inexhaustible amount of detail available regarding nonfictional Primary World narrative fabrics is the very thing that secondary world narrative fabrics attempt to imitate, through large amounts of information which exceed the saturation level of the audience (as described in Chapter 1). Fictional narrative fabrics can be set in the Primary World as well, but as a fabric grows, so does the amount of invention, which may eventually come into conflict with what the audience knows about the Primary World, possible affecting verisimilitude.[4] In secondary worlds, narrative fabric can be more freely created, because all aspects of the world can be designed to accommodate it.

By allowing the audience to assemble narrative threads from world material, narrative fabric greatly increases a world's illusion of completeness, as well as the audience's engagement in the world. Assembling narrative threads and looking for inconsistencies can become something of a fan pastime, as many Internet forums dedicated to such activities can attest. Thus, for larger worlds, world databases or "bibles" are often used by world-builders to monitor consistency, and also to standardize world-based facts and history when multiple authors are contributing to the same world. Although a narrative fabric can be created entirely by a single author, many larger worlds are the result of collaborative effort, and the multi-narrative nature of narrative fabric is ideally suited to collaboration since individual narratives within it can be created by separate authors. Many narrative fabrics expand well beyond the work of their originators, resulting in the concentric circles of authorship described in Chapter 7. Massively multiplayer on-line role-playing games (MMORPGs) are a good example of highly collaborative, open-ended narrative fabrics generated interactively by their audiences, while the overall shape, flow, and feel of a fabric is controlled by the company that provides the designs, updates, and large-scale narrative scenarios that keep the fabric a cohesive whole.

As mentioned earlier, a narrative fabric also allows the audience a synchronic way to slice the events of a world, since a dense fabric contains many simultaneous events.[5] These might be tethered together through the use of large-scale events that all the characters are reacting to, weather conditions that affect everyone simultaneously, or overarching activities like war efforts and other complex activities that require the timing of events involving many participants. We may see or experience the same event from a variety of points of view in different narratives, or within the same narrative; and again, if enough world information is present, we can speculate as to how things might look from points of view which are given only indirectly.

Since individual narrative threads within a fabric can share locations, events, and characters, it is worth examining how narratives within a world can be related to each other, and how their presence might affect those that are added after them. A common type of linkage can be found in nested stories, stories which are related within other stories; and these are typically used not so much to advance storylines as to ground them more fully in the world and its narrative fabric.

Such material often acts as backstory, which fills in the history of a world and its characters and events.

Backstory and World History

Stories set in secondary worlds may need to rely on backstory more than those set in the Primary World, since much Primary World history is already known, or at least accessible, to the audience. While initially backstory sets up the main action of a narrative and relates how the present situation (usually one of need or distress) came to be, as a world grows and more narratives take place in it, backstory and world history grow as well, as narratives are linked together in the world. From the first narrative set in the world, stories spread out into the future and into the past as sequels and prequels appear, and stories of origins become more important. Glimpses of larger structures first hinted at in backstories are opened up and explored, so the initial development of backstory becomes especially important for the further development of a world, since it plants the seeds of narratives that may later be expanded. For example, on pages 177–182 of *Myst: The Book of Atrus* (1995), Gehn tells Atrus the story of Veovis and the events surrounding the rebellion that Veovis started. These events would become *Myst: The Book of Ti'ana* (1996), a prequel that provides a context for the story of *Myst: The Book of Atrus* and the games *Myst* (1993) and *Riven* (1997) as well.

Backstories are also told with greater "narrative speed" than events of the main narrative, to use narratologist Gérard Genette's term. *Narrative speed* refers to the difference between the duration of story events versus the time needed to tell the events. If we make this concept independent of duration (which, in one sense, may vary depending on the intake capability of individual audience members (for example, people who read more slowly or quickly)), this becomes the measure of *narrative resolution* instead; that is, the amount of words, sounds, or images used to convey an event or other story information (*resolution* is used here to mean something like *granularity*, as in "graphical resolution"; as opposed to the use of "resolution" to mean the completion and closure of a narrative structure). Thus, a story told in high narrative resolution will relate events and information in great detail, with tight authorial control over the audience's experience, while stories told in low narrative resolution use more summary and synopsis, relying more on the imagination of the audience and narrative gestalten to complete the narrative details. Similarly, when an author turns an outline into a novel, or a treatment into a screenplay, the narrative increases in resolution.

Backstories are often told in the compressed form associated with low narrative resolution, and the histories of different locations in a world are often told to the story's main characters as they travel from one place to the next. For example, in *The Lord of the Rings*, the history of the Barrow-downs is given as a summary of what Tom Bombadil tells the hobbits about the place's history, resulting in a high degree of compression:

Suddenly Tom's talk left the woods and went leaping up the young stream, over bubbling waterfalls, over pebbles and worn rocks, and among small flowers in close grass and wet crannies, wandering at last up on to the Downs. They heard of the Great Barrows, and the green mounds, and the stone rings upon the hills and in the hollows among the hills. Sheep were bleating in flocks. Green walls and white walls rose. There were fortresses on the heights. Kings of little kingdoms fought together, and the young Sun shone like fire on the red metal of their new and greedy swords. There was victory and defeat; and towers fell, fortresses were burned, and flames went up into the sky. Gold was piled on the biers of dead kings and queens; and mounds covered them, and the stone doors were shut; and the grass grew over all. Sheep walked for a while biting the grass, but soon the hills were empty again. A shadow came out of dark places far away, and the bones were stirred in the mounds. Barrow-wights walked in the hollow places with a clink of rings on cold fingers, and gold chains in the wind. Stone rings grinned out of the ground like broken teeth in the moonlight.[6]

In film, such narrative compression might be conveyed by a montage sequence, as Peter Jackson does at the start of his film adaptation of *The Fellowship of the Ring* (2001), in which he gives the backstory of how the rings of power came to be. In either case, events are merely evoked impressionistically, leaving much gap-filling to be done by the audience.[7]

The looseness provided by low narrative resolution lets a subcreator sketch out the history of a world without having to commit to a high level of detail, allowing it to be determined later and leaving more options open. The fact that history is often given as character dialogue also leaves open the possibility that the character may be lying, mistaken, or simply uninformed about the history in question, should the author wish to change something without upsetting consistency with established material; by revealing that a narrator was unreliable, the world itself can remain consistent despite the conflicting information of earlier and later stories, since the blame for the inconsistency now falls on the character, not the author. The same applies if an entire work is given authorial attribution to a character within a world. An example of this occurred when Tolkien was revising *The Hobbit* to bring it more in line with *The Lord of the Rings*. In *The Lord of the Rings*, the Ring has gained powers and influence it did not originally have when *The Hobbit* was written, and the question arose as to why Gollum would give the Ring up so easily as he had in the original version of the story. This made the writing of *The Lord of the Rings* more difficult, so Tolkien rewrote the ending of Chapter 5 of *The Hobbit* (in which Gollum loses the Ring and Bilbo finds it) and sent it, along with other notes on the story, to his publisher. Three years later in 1950, the publisher had inserted the new material and asked Tolkien for an explanatory note to explain the changes in the new edition. Tolkien realized the two accounts were different enough to clash, and that this would be noticed by readers. Considering what to do, Tolkien wrote back to his publisher:

> I have now on my hands two printed versions of a crucial incident. Either the first must be regarded as washed out, a mere miswriting that ought never to have seen the light; or the story as a whole must take into account the existence of two versions and use it.[8]

Tolkien accepted the changes and figured out a way for the story to take them into account. In the "Introductory Note" for the new edition, he wrote:

> ... More important is the matter of Chapter Five. There the true story of the ending of the Riddle Game, as it was eventually revealed (under pressure) by Bilbo to Gandalf, is now given according to the Red Book, in place of the version Bilbo first gave to his friends, and actually set down in his diary. This departure from truth on the part of a most honest hobbit was a portent of great significance. It does not, however, concern the present story, and those who in this edition make their first acquaintance with hobbit-lore need not trouble about it. Its explanation lies in the history of the Ring, as it is set out in the chronicles of the Red Book of Westmarch, and it must await their publication.[9]

By attributing the textual discrepancies to Bilbo's authorship of the two accounts, Tolkien explains away the inconsistency and works it into his world, even turning it into "a portent of great significance".

Nested stories, then, are a common way of linking stories within an imaginary world, and indeed, diegetic storytelling itself has a long tradition (including Biblical dreams and parables, *The Arabian Nights*, Chaucer's *Canterbury Tales*, and Jan Potocki's *The Manuscript Found in Saragossa*, to name a few notable examples). Imaginary worlds, however, especially in recent times, are often transnarrative in scope, and have multiple stories occurring in them; not just nested stories, but separate stories that take place within the same world. While much has been written regarding intertextuality in narrative theory (for example, see Bakhtin, Barthes, Derrida, Doležel, and Kristeva), relatively little has been written about the relationships between stories set in the same imaginary world and how the creation of stories and worlds affect each other. In one sense, all the stories set in the same world can be seen as being nested within the overarching narrative of the history of the world itself; but unlike backstories, these stories can be conceived and created separately from one another, are sometimes made by someone other the author of the original, and do not always require knowledge of each other to be understood; thus their relationships differ from those of nested stories. The examination of how such stories relate to one another is something we could call internarrative theory.

Sequence Elements and Internarrative Theory

> At the same time I find it only too easy to write opening chapters—and for the moment the story is not unfolding. … I squandered so much on the original "Hobbit" (which was not meant to have a sequel) that it is difficult to find anything new in that world.
>
> —J. R. R. Tolkien, while writing The Lord of the Rings in 1938[10]

Worlds are built up as more and more stories are set in them, and if a world's consistency is to be maintained, each additional story to be added to a world must take into account all of the narrative material already present in a world. Often stories are related chronologically to each other and can be arranged in a sequence, fitting together the stories' events on the timelines of the world. Additional stories can also recontextualize the works that appear before them: new information can change our frame of reference; characters can be revealed to have different motivations or even to be lying; and different points of view can change how we understand characters and story events.

Considering additional stories as elements in a series that build up a world, we would probably find the most common sequence element to be the *sequel*. A sequel, as a story which takes place after an existing story, usually shares some common elements with the original story it follows, carrying them forward in time. A sequel is often able to take advantage of the existing popularity of the original, rather than having to rely solely on its own merits, at least initially. Sometimes this allows a work of lesser quality to be made, giving sequels a bad name, though this is, of course, not always the case; but audiences may still be less likely to experience a sequel if they have not experienced the original work first.

While they can rely on the success of their predecessors, sequels also face greater constraints than the original stories that precede them. Unless multiple stories set in the same world are planned simultaneously, quite often the relationship between the story and the world becomes reversed in the sequel; while the world is originally designed to accommodate the first story set in it, the world is already in existence when the sequel is made, and the sequel's story must be made to fit the world, rather than the other way around. A trade-off between novelty and familiarity occurs: the world is no longer new to the audience, but the burden of exposition is lessened by what has already been revealed of the world. One way that successful sequels restore a sense of novelty is by revealing new areas of the world not present in the original. For example, two very successful sequels, The Lord of the Rings (written as a sequel to The Hobbit) and The Empire Strikes Back (1980), both expand their worlds with new lands, characters, and storylines, while keeping strong links to the works that precede them. Another type of expansion jumps forward to a point in time where the world has changed considerably, as does *Star Trek: The Next Generation* (1987–1994) which takes place about a century after the original *Star Trek* (1966–1969) series, or each of Frank Herbert's five sequels to *Dune* (1965), the last of which takes place more than 5,000 years after the original story.

Since the rise of the sequel, authors and especially world-builders are more conscious of the fact that a successful world may result in a series of sequels, prequels, and other series elements, and may even keep this in mind while writing an original work that introduces a new world. However, this was not the situation faced by earlier authors, who either simply moved a popular character to another world or wrote entirely disconnected books set in different worlds; and before the nineteenth century, very few authors invented more than a single world. The most prolific world-builder of the turn of the twentieth century, L. Frank Baum, had written of the unconnected lands of Phunnyland and Oz in 1900 and had written stories set in three more unconnected lands (Merryland, Quok, and Yew) before writing the second Oz book, *The Marvelous Land of Oz* (1904); so returning to an existing land was new experience for him. As Michael O. Riley writes:

> It was not easy for Baum to return to a world that he had created almost five years earlier for a very different story; it was also against his inclinations. *The Marvelous Land of Oz* was his first attempt to fit a full-length story into a pre-existing background, and the first time he had to adapt and develop a background to accommodate a major new plot. Baum himself appears to have been uncertain just how to do this. The result is that in regard to the details of the imaginary world of Oz, *The Marvelous Land* is one of the more inconsistent books in the series, and the discrepancies make it difficult to sort out which alterations were the result of a change in his conception of Oz and which were the result of carelessness and hasty writing.[11]

Riley says that the later Oz novels were weaker because Oz was so established already, and he comments further on the growth of Oz as a world from book to book, writing:

> Not surprisingly, the development of Baum's great Other-world was not smooth and logical; very often, the changes created glaring inconsistencies from book to book, but that is because Oz did not grow organically from a central idea. Rather, it developed in successive versions, each enlarging while superseding the one before and each reflecting Baum's current idea of what constituted the most magnificent and alluring fairyland in the world.[12]

Series of sequels advance the overarching story of a world, but quite often this story grows into both the future and the past as more and more backstories and stories of origins are developed to explain characters, places, and conflicts. The second most common sequence element, then, is the *prequel*, a story that comes before an existing story, and acts as an expanded backstory for it. The term "prequel" is a relatively recent coinage, having come about in the latter half of the twentieth century, although the phenomenon itself is older, and can be found in traditional literature much earlier.[13] Imaginary-world prequels also precede the coining of the term. Five years and five books after *The Lion, the Witch, and the Wardrobe* (1950), C. S. Lewis wrote a prequel, *The Magician's Nephew* (1955), and E. R. Eddison's Zimiamvia Trilogy includes two prequels, with the second book, *A Fish Dinner in Memison* (1941), taking place before the first book, *Mistress of Mistresses* (1935), and the third (and unfinished) book, *The Mezentian Gate* (1958), taking place before the second book.

Prequels are constrained by the works which come before them, even more than sequels, since characters' fates and situations' outcomes, which appear in the original work, are already known; thus surprise can be lost, and the final ending state is more than predictable, it is already known for certain. We know which characters will not die, and we have some sense of how things will turn out in the end, unless we have not experienced the original work; and often a prequel will rely on the audience's knowledge of the original work, creating dramatic irony through the audience's knowledge of how things will eventually turn out and knowing what the characters do not know.

Much of what makes a prequel interesting has to do with how it provides a new starting point for a story the end of which is already known. Instead of following a character arc wondering where it will lead, we are given both ends of the arc first; the end at the start of the original work and the beginning at the start of the prequel. A prequel, then, is not so much about the destination, but about the journey to that destination, exploring how the beginning and end states of things are connected. Like characters, worlds are often younger and less developed in a prequel, with familiar places changed or even missing altogether. Also, like a sequel, a prequel may feature new locations and characters that have not appeared before, though they will usually include some links to the original work.

As worlds develop through multiple stories, a term is needed for works which come in between already-existing story materials. While these could be termed "midquels", there are two distinct types of them which are different enough to be considered separately, and which we could call *interquels* and *intraquels*.[14] An interquel is a sequence element that occurs between existing works in a series, while an intraquel is a sequence element that occurs during a gap within a single existing work. In both cases, the element's beginning and end points are known in advance, and the focus is on the transition between states, added detail, and revealed motivations that help to fill out an ellipsis, making character arcs and world arcs more complete.

Interquels appeared as early as the 1920s (within Hugh Lofting's Doctor Dolittle series of books), and perhaps the best-known examples of them would be *Star Wars* episodes II and III. Although episodes I, II, and III are collectively known as the "prequel trilogy", they appeared individually, making episodes II and III interquels, since they were released between episodes I and IV; and *The Clone Wars* (2008) would be an interquel as well, since it takes place between episodes II and III.

Most commonly, interquels are found in larger, well-developed worlds in which multiple authors are contributing works (such as novels) which are outside of the main series of works set in the world (such as films in the *Star Wars* galaxy, or movies and television series in the *Star Trek* universe). These works are often less canonical yet may use the main characters of the world, so their chronologies must be tucked into the ellipses of the main series to avoid conflict with the main series and its chronology. Sometimes works in a world's main series make reference to these interquels (as when Aayla Secura from the *Star Wars* "Expanded Universe" was given a cameo in Episode II), but it is more often the case that interquels reference more established works than the other way around.

Like prequels, interquels face constraints due to the fact that narrative material occurring before and after them is already established and known. How tightly the constraints limit what an interquel can do depends mainly on two factors; the size of the gap in which the interquel occurs, and how involved the interquel is with the narratives set before and after it. The larger the gap, the greater the amount of change is possible between the endpoints of the gap, resulting in more latitude for the interquel's story, and more change in the secondary world for the interquel to document. In the case of the *Star Wars* galaxy, George Lucas did not allow novels to be written about the 3-year period of the Clone Wars before the prequel trilogy was made, to keep more options open for the films.

An interquel may also be tightly involved or loosely involved with the narratives that surround it. Rather than merely filling in the events in the lives of main characters from the main series, interquels can give such characters background roles and concentrate their stories on new characters instead. The trade-off is one of newness versus connection to the other stories; the more an interquel introduces new characters and new material, the more original and less determined by existing stories it becomes, yet it also becomes less connected to those stories at the same time. Ties to the secondary world, then, grow in importance as narrative linkages between sequence elements decrease.

Sharing similar constraints and less common than interquels, *intraquels* fill gaps within a single work, usually an ellipsis in which little or nothing is said of intervening events. Intraquels usually face constraints even more restricting than interquels, due to the fact that the gap they fill resides within a work rather than between complete works in a sequence; such gaps are often smaller, and structures like character arcs that bridge a work may be less tolerant of interruption than the gaps between works. Intraquels also are likely to use both strategies that interquels use for dodging restrictions; that is, appearing in larger gaps and changing their focus to new characters. For example, Mario Puzo's novel *The Sicilian* (1984) is set during the time in *The Godfather* (1969) when Michael goes to Sicily, filling in the 2-month gap mentioned in the last paragraph on page 354 (at the end of Book VI): "But it was to be another month before Michael recovered from his injuries and another two months after that before all the necessary papers and arrangements were ready. Then he was flown from Palermo to Rome and from Rome to New York."[15] Michael Corleone appears in the novel, but most of the novel is concerned with the story of Salvatore Guiliano, a kind of Robin Hood-like bandit figure in the Sicilian countryside, and much of the story is told in flashback. In the *Chronicles of Narnia* series, *The Horse and His Boy* (1954) is an intraquel that takes place during *The Lion, the Witch, and the Wardrobe* (1950) and also focuses on new characters and places.

Unlike interquels, an intraquel can occur as the second sequence element in a series, serving a similar purpose as a sequel insofar as it gives the audience more of the same characters from a particular story or world. Several of Disney's direct-to-video movies are intraquels set within Disney's theatrically released films; for example, *Bambi II* (2006) takes place after Bambi's mother's death and before Bambi reaches adulthood, and was released 64 years after the original film *Bambi* (1942). Other such Disney videos, including *Belle's Magical World* (1998), *Tarzan II: The Legend Begins* (2005), and *The Fox and The Hound II* (2006), can also be considered intraquels.

While an intraquel fills a gap that occurs within a particular work, we can invert the relationship and suggest a sequence element that does just the opposite, one which includes an already-existing element (or elements) within itself, as if those preceding elements were filling gaps within it. Such an element, which would take place before, during, and after a previously-released sequence element (or elements), could be called a *transquel*. Such a work is typically broad in scope, setting other stories into a larger historical context and framework. Probably the best-known transquel would be the anthology of stories collectively known as *The Silmarillion* (1977), which together encompasses thousands of years of history, and condenses all the events of *The Lord of the Rings* down to a few paragraphs on two pages.[16] The events of *The Hobbit* and *The Lord of the Rings* take on new significance after one reads *The Silmarillion*, as they are the tail end of a long-running conflict between good and evil (since the Ring represents the last vestige of Sauron's power in Middle-earth, and Sauron is the last of Morgoth's servants to be vanquished, and Morgoth (originally Melkor) is the Valar who became evil and introduced discord into the music of the Ainur at the beginning of time).

Transquels are generally broad in scope, giving historical context to the works they encompass. They also tend to be told in low narrative resolution, and are concerned more with the histories of entire peoples rather than only individuals, due to the typically enormous timescales being covered. One of the most ambitious transquels ever written, Olaf Stapledon's *Star Maker* (1937) covers billions of years and has a timeline which includes his novel *Last and First Men* (1930). When used as a part of a series or franchise, a transquel provides a framework into which subsequent sequence elements can be fit, though it also closes off possibilities for the time period that it covers. Thus, transquels are the least likely kind of sequence element to appear, and often do so late in a franchise or series, if they appear at all.

The last kind of sequence element is one which runs in tandem (simultaneously) with an existing element or elements (or part of an element), which we might call a *paraquel*. Within works, the same events are sometimes seen from the perspectives of different characters; the paraquel is an entire work covering the same events or period in time from a different perspective. Paraquels can be developed together by the same author (like the four novels of Lawrence Durrell's *Alexandria Quartet* or the first three novels in E. E. Knight's *Age of Fire* series), or long after the sequence elements they parallel, and by a different author (like Alice Randall's *The Wind Done Gone* (2001), an unauthorized paraquel to Margaret Mitchell's *Gone With the Wind* (1936), told from a slave's perspective; or Kirill Eskov's *The Last Ringbearer* (1999), an unauthorized paraquel to *The Lord of the Rings*, told from the perspective of the residents of Mordor).[17] While many paraquels found in traditional literature set in the Primary World are unauthorized and noncanonical, authorized paraquels tend to be found mainly in series of works set in a secondary world, where the narrative fabric is broad enough to accommodate them.

Unlike individual stories in which the same events are told by different narrators, or time-travel stories within which past events are revisited and seen from a different perspective, or parallel works planned and created simultaneously, most paraquels are made *after* the sequence elements they parallel, which limits their events and outcomes the more closely related they are to existing sequence elements. Thus, they are more likely to introduce new characters and storylines and use the existing events of an imaginary world to set up suspense and provide a background structure. At the same, paraquels can reveal unseen events and provide motivation for events from a pre-existing sequence element, offering new explanations for known events. For example, *The Godfather* video game (2006) has scenes in which the player–character (whose default name is Aldo) helps Rocco Lampone into Jack Woltz's stable to decapitate the horse's head that ends up in Woltz's bed in the novel and film; a scene in which Aldo plants the gun in the bathroom that Michael Corleone uses during his dinner with Solozzo and McCluskey, which is going on at the same time in another room; and scenes pertaining to the hits carried out which, in the film, are intercut with the baptism of Carlo's son to whom Michael is Godfather. Familiarity with earlier sequence elements, then, is almost always required to make sense of paraquels.

Due to the variety of sequence elements, there are two orderings that are perhaps most typically experienced by the audience of an imaginary world; the order in which the individual sequence elements made their public appearance (the order typically experienced by contemporary audiences who experience each element as it appears), or chronological order (an order that later audiences can assemble once all the elements of a sequence are available).[18]

The order in which the sequence elements that make up a world are encountered greatly affects the way that the audience experiences them and the world in which they take place. Perhaps the most common example of this occurs with the *Star Wars* series of movies; the original trilogy (Episodes IV, V, and VI, which came out in 1977, 1980, and 1983), and the prequel trilogy (Episodes I, II, and III, which came out in 1999, 2002, and 2005). Audiences first encountering the movies in the twenty-first century have a choice; they can either see the movies in the order they were released, or in chronological order (I, II, III, IV, V, VI). Although the six films together are the story of Anakin Skywalker and how he becomes Darth Vader, the original trilogy, taken by itself, positions Luke Skywalker as the main character instead. Viewers watching the films in release order will experience the *Star Wars* universe along with Luke, learning about it as he does, from Ben Kenobi, Yoda, and others, without the background and context provided by the prequel trilogy; in doing so, identification with Luke and his emotional states are strengthened. Viewed in chronological order, however, the focus is on Darth Vader, and many of the surprises of Episodes IV, V, and VI are lost, after the prequel trilogy is seen: we already know Vader is father to Luke and Leia and creator of C3PO; we already know who Yoda is when Luke first meets him; and other characters like Jabba the Hutt have also already been introduced.

Viewing the films in release order has its disadvantages as well. Watching Episodes I, II, and III after seeing the original trilogy, we know that certain characters (like Anakin, Ben Kenobi, and the Emperor) will not die no matter what happens to them, so a certain amount of suspense is lost; and we know where everything has to end up by the end of Episode III, in order to set up Episode IV. On the other hand, irony can be generated since the outcomes are known in advance, and the films were designed with the assumption that audiences had already seen episodes IV, V, and VI. Of course, since the *Star Wars* universe has expanded into so many other media, there are many other possibilities for the way in which it can be experienced; in 2010, my sons Michael and Christian, at the ages of eight and six respectively, played the video game *LEGO Star Wars: The Complete Saga* (2007) on the Nintendo Wii, and as a result knew most of the characters and plotlines (down to details like the color of each character's lightsaber) before they ever saw any of the feature films (see Chapter 6 for more on the different ways that the works that make up a world can be encountered).

Thus, the context provided by surrounding sequence elements can change the way a particular element is understood, an effect that can even occur retroactively when more elements are added later as a world develops. Discussing how knowledge of earlier Oz books affects the reading of later ones, Michael O. Riley writes:

> *Ozma of Oz* is a transitional book. The story can stand alone without the section in Oz; the action is complete, and the place of safety and repose is reached in Ev. However, the visit to Oz at the end is the reward for both Dorothy and Baum's readers to whom the main point of the story is Dorothy's eventual return to Oz, but that return is not the main point of the plot. Only the readers' prior knowledge of Dorothy and of Oz as a desirable place gives Oz its dominant role and superimposes the larger, overarching goal onto the plot of the rescue of the royal family of Ev.[19]

Since an author's focus can vary from the story at hand to the larger world in which it occurs, some sequence elements may be weak as stand-alone stories when taken by themselves, yet still be important (and be enjoyed as such) for the world-building that they do. Riley points out that the fifth Oz book, *The Road to Oz* (1909), when considered by itself, seems to lack dangers and action, but that "in context, the serenity of and absence of violent and threatening incidents in *The Road to Oz* are assets. The very lack of a strong plot enabled Baum to concentrate more fully on the nature of Oz itself, and the book, in addition to clearing up more of the past confusion, contains a radical reinterpretation of Oz and of Baum's entire imaginary world."[20]

According to Riley, the growth of Oz was accomplished primarily through three methods: "the addition of information and details", "the alteration of previously given facts", and "the reinterpretations of the nature of Oz itself."[21] Riley gives an example of the third method by showing how the third Oz novel, *Ozma of Oz* (1907), "reversed the meaning and significance of Oz as it had first been created in *The Wizard*,"[22] writing:

> In *The Wizard* the strange and beautiful, but illusory, Land of Oz is the place of danger and trial, the ordeal through which Dorothy has to go to reach her goal of home. Baum subtly changed all that in *Ozma*; the illusion is made reality, and Oz becomes not the ordeal but the goal, the place of the heart's desire and, in a very real sense, Dorothy's true home because Ozma crowns her a princess of Oz, thus making her a part of that land.[23]

The last two methods Riley lists, the alteration of previously given facts and the reinterpretation of the world's nature, go beyond the mere growth of a world, bringing us to a discussion of retroactivity continuity (or retcon) and reboots.

Retroactive Continuity (Retcon) and Reboots

As a world grows over time, so does an author's conception of it. The author's creative abilities, and the tools used during world-building, may both mature and develop, making earlier works appear outdated or less sophisticated, causing an author to rethink and redesign his or her world. Such changes can be explained diegetically, especially if time has passed between when the older and newer sequence elements take place: like the new designs present in *Star Trek: The Next Generation* (1987–1994), which takes place almost a century after the original *Star Trek* series (1966–1969); or the redesigned Grid of *Tron: Legacy* (2010) which updates that of *Tron* (1982). The difference between new and old may be so great that the author may also want to go back and revise and update the earlier works; for example, *Myst Masterpiece Edition* (1999) and *realMyst* (2000) were both technologically-updated versions of *Myst* (1993) (see Figure 4.1). Or, it may be the case that larger story arcs require that earlier works be adjusted to fit into them better; for example, Tolkien's revising of *The Hobbit* to fit better with *The Lord of the Rings*, Lucas' *Special Edition* revision and re-release of the first *Star Wars* film trilogy, and Stephen King's revisions to *The Dark Tower: The Gunslinger* (original novel, 1982; revised version 2003), the first book in his *Dark Tower* series. Or, a universe may have grown so detailed and complex (especially those created by multiple authors over long periods of time) that it begins to collapse from increasing inconsistencies and contradictions, and needs to be reorganized and restarted, like the *Crisis on Infinite Earths* (April 1985–March 1986) and *Infinite Crises* (2005–2006) series of DC Comics that reset the continuity of the DC Comics Universe. Such alterations are now common enough to be referred to as "retroactive continuity" or "retcon", and are often controversial since the original versions of works, often the ones that established a particular series or franchise, are already well known and beloved by fans. The medium used matters as well; as Henry Jenkins has pointed out, fans of comics take a different attitude toward retcon than those of film and television franchises.[24]

Retconning is often disliked, because it changes already-established facts and even canonical material (canonicity will be discussed in Chapter 7). An author can reinterpret past events or make use of holes or audience assumptions to recontextualize events (for example, characters assumed to be dead but whose deaths were reported by unreliable characters, or the revelation of hidden motives and different points of view regarding the same events which lead to a new understanding of those events); but retconning, which directly contradicts established facts, can seem like cheating. When an author releases a work to the public, it is akin to the making of a statement or a kind of social contract with the audience; there is the tacit assumption that a work tells us something about the world in which it takes place, and that an author has committed to certain narratives, designs, and so forth. Retconning undermines this contract, destroying the integrity of the original work, possibly adding changes to it that audiences will consider degradations or at the very least, unnecessary. Retconning can make a work unstable, so that critiques and analyses of the work based on earlier versions may no longer apply to later ones. If a work is imbedded in cultural memory, retconning can damage the relationship that an audience has with a work; for example, after the already-revised

FIGURE 4.1 The view from the dock looking up the hill in *Myst* (1993) and in *realMyst* (2001). While *Myst* was made up of pre-rendered still images with 8-bit color, *realMyst* could render its images in 32-bit color in real time and allowed free movement through its three-dimensional space, allowing for greater interactivity in the exploration of the world's spaces.

versions of the original *Star Wars* film trilogy appeared on DVD with even more revisions, fans called for Lucas to release the original versions of the films on DVD (which he later did). In general, it seems that audiences typically would prefer that authors accept the creative challenge of working around the limitations imposed by earlier works rather than merely going back and changing them.[25]

On the other hand, there is the argument that living authors have the right to go back and revise their works, as their own outlooks, abilities, tools, and conceptions change. This attitude does not consider sequence elements as individual works standing on their own, but rather parts of greater whole, an imaginary world which is still a work in progress, changing as it grows. Whether or not fans like the way that a world is turning out, the author has the final say, and the world remains an open one until the author deems it finished or at least closed. Something similar to retconning goes on all the time during the creative process, in which the conception and details of a work or world evolve, but normally the audience does not see these stages of progress, only the final product. Retconning, then, reveals that it is the *world*, not any individual work set in it, that is the author's final product, reminding the audience that what they are witnessing are merely stages of development of a final form not yet attained.

Taken to an extreme, the replacement of existing ideas and details results in a complete reconception and redesign. Many franchises, such as Batman, James Bond, *Star Trek*, and Spider-man, have undergone such a rewriting, now called a "reboot" in fan communities. Taken from computer terminology, "reboot" suggests not only a restarting, but that something was no longer viable or had gone wrong to the point that such an extreme measure was required; thus it is not surprising that most reboots begin with a new "story of origins" for their main characters. The majority of the time, reboots appear in character-based franchises; they are done to update long-running franchises which have become dated over time, and they are usually done by people other than the original creators of the franchise (which naturally leads to discussions of canonicity). More often than not, reboots are done mainly to keep a franchise profitable and allegedly more appealing to a new generation of audience members, though such changes may alienate older audiences who still see the value of the original version.

Few authors, if any, reboot their own works, and world-centered franchises are far less likely to be rebooted than character-centered ones, due to the fact that a world's unique appearance is the reason for its popularity, and its design is either historically situated, or not so closely linked to the Primary World as to need updating. One notable exception is the *Star Trek* reboot that began with the film *Star Trek* (2009), which positioned itself as a kind of prequel, with a young Kirk, Spock, and McCoy beginning their Starfleet careers. The film also attempts to explain the reboot as an "alternate timeline", bringing in Leonard Nimoy to play the original version of Spock, who naturally meets his younger double, resulting in a kind of "passing of the torch" to the younger Spock played by Zachary Quinto.

The presence of Leonard Nimoy implies his own approval of the reboot, and also insures some participation from the older generations of audience members who may dislike the idea of a reboot but still will watch the film to see Nimoy as Spock. Unlike most reboots, which cannot be considered retcon, since they make no attempt to connect to the original versions they replace, *Star Trek*'s reboot attempts (though perhaps feebly) to connect it to the existing *Star Trek* universe, making it a form of retcon, depending on what one makes of the connection. In any event, such ambiguity shows the crisis that the *Star Trek* franchise finds itself in, as it attempts to reinvent itself while still trying to position new works as an extension of the original.

Worlds within worlds, made by subcreated subcreators, can also be rebooted; for example, in *The Matrix Reloaded* (2003), Neo learns from the Architect that the Machines have rebooted the Matrix several times; and in *Dark City* (1998), the Strangers rearrange buildings and implant new memories in their captives every night at midnight, which essentially reboots various situations in their constructed city, allowing new experiments to be run on the human beings imprisoned there.

Reboots and retroactive continuity change a world directly, by altering its contents, but worlds can also be changed through the context provided by their surroundings, with the appearance of crossovers and retroactive linkages, resulting in what are sometimes called "multiverses" or "metaverses".

Crossovers, Multiverses, and Retroactive Linkages

> "Is Elvis a Star Wars person?"
> —Christian Wolf, age 5

The two most common ways to link worlds together are transnarrative characters (or objects) and geographical (or spatiotemporal) linkages. The presence of transnarrative characters may imply a geographical linkage or some sort of spatiotemporal linkage between worlds, which enables characters to cross from one to the other, but the connection need never be explained or made explicit. Thus, the term "multiverse" is sometimes used, which describes the overall structure resulting from the connection of two or more universes that, though connected, still remain distinct and separate. "Crossovers" are beings or things that appear in two or more universes or worlds, suggesting a linkage, and "retroactive linkages" are what we might call the connections between two worlds which were conceived and made separately, and not originally intended to be connected. Retroactive linkages are most commonly found in the work of authors who have created two or more imaginary worlds and wish to bring them together into one larger creation, so they can be considered as a form of world-building, especially when care is taken to maintain consistency when the worlds are joined.

The last section of Chapter 1 has already described how secondary worlds are often linked in some way to the Primary World, and it is quite common for characters to pass from Primary World to secondary world and back. Occasionally, allusions to earlier secondary worlds appear in later ones; for example, Homer appears as a character in Lucian's *True History*, and More's *Utopia* is alluded to in Bacon's *New Atlantis* (when one of his characters says "I have read in a book of one of your men, of a Feigned Commonwealth"), but one rarely finds early crossovers from one secondary world to another except for characters who visit different worlds in different stories by the same author, like the stories in Rabelais' *Gargantua and Pantagruel* series, which do not make geographic connections between their worlds. The retroactive geographical linking of two separately conceived imaginary worlds, created by the same author, would have to wait until L. Frank Baum, who had developed several worlds in his children's stories and only afterward decided to connect them as neighbors on the same continent. This retroactive linking had an effect on the stories set in the linked lands. As Riley points out:

> Later when Baum finally drew all his imaginary countries together into one fantasy Other-world, Oz was, in general, the benefactor, gaining depth and reality. However, John Dough and the Cherub is the one non-Oz fantasy in which the benefits go the other way. When Baum later placed some of the countries from John Dough into a geographical relationship with Oz, he added a retroactive coherence to the book that was lacking in the story itself. Thus John Dough gains by being read after one is already familiar with Baum's total Other-world.[26]

The lands are joined, characters cross over into Oz from his other books, and the birthday party in *The Road to Oz* (1909) features characters from Baum's other non-Oz books. Since its appearance, Oz has been the subject of unauthorized crossovers and alternate versions, in the works of science fiction authors like Philip José Farmer, Robert Heinlein, L. Sprague de Camp, and Tad Williams, who continue the stories of Baum's characters and who bring their own characters into Oz.[27] Other books, like John Myers Myers' *Silverlock* (1949), have an original imaginary world but populate it with existing characters from history, mythology, and other works of fiction.[28]

Other examples of retroactive linkages between worlds would include Tolkien's linking of *The Hobbit* (1937) into his Legendarium, since both were initially conceived as separate projects. In the realm of comic books, there are crossovers in series set in the same universe (which are fairly common), retroactively-linked universes (like Jack Kirby's "Fourth World" series that was incorporated into the DC Comics Universe), and even crossovers between the universes of rival companies; for example, crossovers between the Marvel Comics Universe and the DC Comics Universe in which characters from both companies appear together in a story (like Superman meeting Spider-man, or Batman meeting Wolverine). One notable combination appears in the four-issue series known as *DC vs. Marvel* or *Marvel vs. DC*, depending on which issue you choose. In it, characters from both universes come together to fight, with the resulting multiverse called the "Amalgram Universe", for which the two companies created the fictional publisher Amalgam Comics, with its own backstory. Twenty-four issues of Amalgam Comics were published (half by Marvel and half by DC), which included characters that were combinations of characters from both companies: for example, Logan Wayne and his superhero persona Dark Claw was an amalgam of Batman (Bruce Wayne) and Wolverine (Logan); Hal Stark and his superhero persona Iron Lantern was an amalgam of Iron Man (Tony Stark) and Green Lantern (Hal Jordan); and Barbara Gordon Hardy and her superhero persona Black Bat was an amalgam of Batgirl (Barbara Gordon) and the Black Cat (Felicia Hardy). Often, however, such crossovers are explained away as alternate universes, "what if" scenarios, or dreams, and are either excluded from official timelines or considered noncanonical, to avoid the continuity problems that would otherwise arise. In *Who Framed Roger Rabbit* (1988), characters from numerous cartoon franchises come together in the same film, in what was the biggest crossover event in animation history up to that time, but there is relatively little continuity to disrupt since most animated characters rarely age or follow any kind of organized timelines at all. Likewise, the Disney video game *Kingdom Hearts* (2002) cobbles together its game world by linking original worlds of Disney films along with others taken from elsewhere, such as Alice's Wonderland, Winnie-the-Pooh's Hundred Acre Wood, and Peter Pan's Neverland.

Probably the most elaborate example of retroactive linkages resulting in a multiverse is the so-called Tommy Westphall Universe. Noting crossovers from one television show to another, fans in on-line forums have linked together 282 televisions shows, from *I Love Lucy* (1951–1957) to new programs still on television as of spring 2012, with lists and a chart demonstrating how all the shows are connected. One of the connected shows, *St. Elsewhere*, had a series finale that ended with a twist which suggests that the entire show may have taken place in the imagination of an autistic child named Tommy Westphall, which implies that all the other connected shows were also a figment of his imagination; hence the name "Tommy Westphall Universe".

For example, one can trace connections from *I Love Lucy* (1951–1957) to twenty-first century programming: *I Love Lucy*'s Lucy Ricardo also appears on *The Lucy-Desi Comedy Hour* (1957–1960), where the Ricardos briefly share a home with the Danny Williams family, and the Ricardos later visit them on *The Danny Thomas Show* (1953–1964). One episode of *The Danny Thomas Show* featured Buddy Sorrell from *The Dick Van Dyke Show* (1961–1966), who was a writer for the fictional show starring Alan Brady, who would later narrate a documentary directed by Paul Buchman, one of the two main characters of *Mad About You* (1992–1999). *Mad About You*'s regular guest character Ursula Buffay is the sister of Phoebe Buffay on *Friends* (1994–2004) (and played by the same actress, Lisa Kudrow), and other *Friends* characters, Chandler and Joey, interacted with characters from *Caroline and the City* (1995–1999). At the end of one episode of *Caroline and the City*, Niles Crane and Daphne Moon of *Frasier* (1993–2004) make an appearance, and in one episode of *Frasier*, John Hemingway of *The John Larroquette Show* (1993–1996) calls in to Frasier Crane's radio show. The bus station where *The John Larroquette Show* takes place is revealed to have been built by a company named Yoyodyne (manufacturer of parts of Federation Starships in the *Star Trek* universe)[29] which also happens to be a client of the law firm Wolfram & Hart on the television show *Angel* (1999–2004), which was a spin-off of the TV series of *Buffy the Vampire Slayer* (1997–2003). Spike of *Buffy the Vampire Slayer* smoked Morley cigarettes, the fictional brand also smoked by the Cigarette Smoking Man of *The X-Files* (1993–2002), as well as by characters on *ER* (1994–2009), *Lost* (2004–2010), *Medium* (2005–2011), *CSI: NY* (2004–), and over two dozen other television shows and movies.[30]

Of course, one might argue that a common brand of cigarettes, an industry in-joke and play on "Marleys" (Marlboros), is not enough to constitute a connection, nor perhaps use of the name "Yoyodyne", neither of which has the same crossover strength as a transnarrative character. Disagreeing with such connections, Brian Weatherson, a Cornell University professor of philosophy, wrote "Six Objections to the Westphall Hypothesis", looking at other interpretations and considerations that question the connections made. And inconsistencies also arise, when connections do not work the same way in both directions; *Petticoat Junction* (1963–1970) and *Green Acres* (1965–1971) were both set in the same town of Hooterville, and *Petticoat Junction* had many crossovers with *The Beverly Hillbillies* (1962–1971), while *Green Acres* treated *The Beverly Hillbillies* as a fictional program, and even had an episode in which the Hooterville Community Theater recreates an episode of the show as a play, and in a *Beverly Hillbillies* Thanksgiving episode, characters from all three shows share a meal together in Hooterville. Crossovers are often a source of humor, with many not considered canonical, if indeed consistency and a canon are even attempted.

Retroactive linkages, when taken seriously, are usually between different works or worlds by the same author, who wishes to consolidate his or her efforts into one larger, overarching world. Sometimes this can involve linking two or more secondary worlds, as with the L. Frank Baum example discussed earlier or it may mean connecting a secondary world to stories set in the Primary World, as Stephen King does with his multivolume *Dark Tower* novel (parts one through seven written 1970–2004) that incorporates many characters from his other books.[31] While retroactive linkages can be done for artistic reasons (like Tolkien's use of his developing Legendarium to provide background and history for a sequel to *The Hobbit*), it may also be done for commercial reasons, such as when an author hopes to tie his less successful books into a popular world he has created, hoping to increase their sales (which was Baum's motivation for doing so[32]). Whatever the case, retroactive linkages can alter the context and canonicity of a work, and change how an audience sees a particular world and the overarching narratives taking place within it; so it must be done carefully, if it is to be done at all. Another factor that can be introduced that influences all these things is that of interactivity, which gives the audience the ability to affect events in a world.

Interactivity and Alternate Storylines

All these diverse styles of image-making have one thing in common—they have the power to transport the viewer into fantastical otherworlds where the normal rules don't apply. It's like being offered a direct window into their creator's imagination. And in the case of computer games, it gets even more interesting because the audience actually has the opportunity to climb through the window and interact with this strange new world.

—Anthony Flack, independent video game developer[33]

The vicarious inhabitation of an imaginary world often goes hand-in-hand with the desire to interact within the world, from dollhouses and LEGO cities to video games and virtual worlds like *Second Life* (2003). And interaction most often gives way to narrative involvement, as one becomes engaged in a world. Interactivity, which is made up of choices, splits narrative threads into alternate storylines, each of which can be followed, depending on how decisions are made. And a world must account for these divergent strands.

Even in traditional, noninteractive worlds, the idea of alternate paths chosen by characters can be present. When two or more characters with similar backgrounds and abilities face the same choices but each goes a different way, we get a sense of how choices affect consequences. For example, as mentioned in Chapter 3, *The Lord of the Rings* contains many pairings of similar characters (like Gandalf/ Saruman, Faramir/Boromir, Aragorn/Denethor, and Bilbo/Gollum) who take diverging paths from similar decision points. Different sets of actions and consequences help an audience to more fully understand and appreciate a situation and what narrative possibilities exist. Likewise, interactive worlds, like those of video games, let the audience try out difference paths of action and see where they lead, and then start over again from the same starting point.

Much has been written about the problems and possibilities involved in the combination of narrative and interactivity.[34] Combining a *world* with interactivity, however, is a different proposition, since an interactive world does not require a predetermined narrative, and because the structure of a world is often more robust when it comes to user-led exploration. The worlds of MMORPGs are persistent and ongoing, and players can create their own narratives through their actions and interactions with the other inhabitants of the world, without an author providing events in a top–down fashion (such players could also be seen as collaboratively authoring world events). Video games can be designed with as much or as little narrative as an author wishes; from an open-ended multiplayer game to a very linear storyline that the user must find and follow, like the correct path through a maze (choices are made, but there is ultimately only one correct path).

The relationship between interactivity and immersion in a world depends greatly on the medium, the medium's conventions, and the audience's expectations of the medium. In traditionally noninteractive media, the presence of interactivity can make one more aware of the limitations of a world, and the limits of vicarious participation within it (as in "interactive movies"). The necessity of having to make choices and use an interface to indicate them may well distance an audience member and diminish immersion; for example, if a novel suddenly asks a reader to choose between alternate storylines, a reader could be thrown out of a story. On the other hand, in a video game, interactivity can help make a world seem more real, through one's ability to act within it rather than just observe it; and a video game player, who expects interactivity but finds none or very little of it (as in some early CD-ROM games like *Gadget* (1993) and *Star Trek: Borg* (1996)), may be frustrated and less likely to become immersed in a game. Highly interactive worlds, which range from ones using physical models (like a dollhouse, model train landscape, or city made of building blocks) to digital ones (like video games or virtual worlds), can be quite immersive due to the degree of interactivity they offer even when no predetermined narrative is present.

Imaginary worlds, however, often span multiple media. Some interactive settings are extensions of worlds which originate in other media, such as video games based on pre-existing world franchises or playsets based on characters and settings from movies or television shows. Transmedial expansion can also move in the other direction; a world which originates in an interactive medium can spawn extensions in noninteractive media. For example, the video game *Myst* (1993) was followed by a series of three novels, *Myst: The Book of Atrus* (1995), *Myst: The Book of Ti'ana* (1996), and *Myst: The Book of D'ni* (1997). Either way, changing media expectations and interactivity levels raise questions regarding the status of a world and the canonicity of events in that world.

Although all imaginary worlds are imaginary, they vary in their ontological status. Unlike a world present in a novel or a movie, a persistent on-line world like *Second Life* or an MMORPG has a continuing existence and real-time events, locations and objects represented by mathematical models, and characters which are avatars controlled by participants who together perform actions and make decisions that directly affect the world; therefore such a world is often said to be a *virtual* world in addition to being an *imaginary* world. In these worlds, which are usually not restarted or reset, one could argue that all events are canonical, since they occur diegetically within the world in question. Alternatively, one could argue that by a stricter definition, such worlds do not have canonical events apart from those "official" ones produced by the author of the world, such as those found in "expansions" and large-scale events which affect an entire world. Either way, worlds which appear in multiple media will likely have to adjust to the varying ontological possibilities offered by each medium.

Canonicity can also be affected by interactivity. A noninteractive world almost always has a set of *specific* canonical events, which helps define the world and the audience's experience of it: Frodo always takes the Ring to Mordor, Luke always becomes a Jedi, Neo always defeats Agent Smith, and so on; these events are fixed parts of their worlds' histories. An interactive world can also have specific canonical events; for example, in video games, the events taking place during cut-scenes that are the same every time and not altered by gameplay. Likewise, an interactive world can also have what we could think of as *general* canonical events: Inky, Pinky, Blinky, and Clyde always chase Pac-Man; the Qotile always shoots swirls of energy at enemy Yars; the Master Chief always is attacked by Covenant agents; and the Space Invaders always advance downward and eventually crush the player's cannon. While the specific details of these events vary with each game, they are still inevitable and always a part of the world. General canonical events often involve the main conflicts of interactive worlds, and thus are a constitutive part of the audience's experience of the world.

Interactive worlds with alternate storylines can also treat some endings as canonical and others as noncanonical. For example, in *Riven* (1997), out of ten possible endings, only the ending in which the player frees Catherine, allowing her to rejoin Atrus before Riven is destroyed, is canonical, since Catherine appears later in *Myst III: Exile* (2001). In such games, the player's challenge is to see to it that events play out as they should, resulting in the one set of events that is considered canonical; all interactivity amounts to merely exploring a world and keeping events going the way the author has predestined them to go. By keeping to a set storyline, however, such games can be more fully joined to their noninteractive counterparts in a world's history; thus, the events of *Riven* can occupy a central place in the franchise's overarching story.

In contrast, interactive branches of a transmedial world may only play with characters, locations, and situations, without adding any new events to a world's canon. The *LEGO Star Wars* video games, for example, feature LEGO versions of the franchise's characters and locations, and the game's cut-scenes are parodic versions of scenes from the films (although they contain enough information to advance the story along and give away plot twists). Player–characters engage in activities seen in the films, such as lightsaber fights and the piloting of vehicles and spaceships, but often in very different contexts and locations that mimic but do not reproduce those in the films; the games are essentially three-dimensional platform games dressed up in *Star Wars* attire.[35] In these kinds of games, canonical events from other media incarnations of a world are alluded to or even replayed, but no new canonical material is added to the world.

Interactive branches of a transmedial world, then, vary greatly in their relationships with their noninteractive counterparts, yet in all cases they provide the audience a new experience related to the world, and one which potentially can strengthen the world's bond with its audience. Even when an interactive setting is more or less detached from a world, its allusions, like the jokes in the

LEGO Star Wars cut-scenes, can serve to provide a sense of shared community among fans and perhaps even whet their appetite to re-experience the world in its other media incarnations. The same can be said for materials chronicling the behind-the-scenes making of an imaginary world.

The Story of the World: "Making Of" Documentation

Audiences who partake of imaginary worlds are often also interested in the extradiegetic narrative of their making, in subcreation as a process as well as a product. Since the 1970s, there has been a proliferation of "Making of" companion media, including such things as documentaries and featurettes (now most commonly found as DVD extras), books, magazine articles, websites, visual dictionaries and other reference works, interviews, TV specials, trading cards, and other kinds of "extras". These works usually provide information about the originator of a world and all the various assistants who worked on it, creating a story about the building of the world itself. Typically, these narratives contain such things as the origins and refinement of the artist's vision, difficulties in getting approval and backing, early versions of things which are radically different than the final product, the development of ideas and designs, the intricacies of production and attention to detail involved, troubles and changes encountering during production, later revisions and editing, early assumptions about a work's success, and the initial public reception of the work. Enjoyment of the "Making of" material, then, often brings an even greater appreciation of the world itself, and invites a revisiting of it within the context of the new knowledge gained.

"Making of" material can help to point out details that might otherwise be missed, with still photographs, design drawings, architectural plans, computer-generated models, and other imagery offering a better look at costumes, vehicles, creatures, sets and locations, props, and so forth. For example, an article on *Myst* in *Wired* magazine[36] describes views that many players do not find, as well as a mistake in the graphics, while John Knoll's *Creating the Worlds of Star Wars 365 Days* (2005) shows close-ups of control panel graphics and cluttered countertops that appear in the backgrounds of scenes, revealing details that cannot be seen as clearly in the films (one image of Watto's junkyard even reveals a two-armed pod that appears to be from the *Discovery* spaceship from *2001: A Space Odyssey* (1968)).[37] Documenting the design process, J. W. Rinzler's *The Making of Star Wars Revenge of the Sith* (2005) includes a behind-the-scenes discussion regarding the background of a concept design depicting a chase scene on Utapau:

> Indicating an Utapau interior, Lucas asks, "What is this signage for?"
> "Restaurant?" [*Concept Design Supervisor Ryan*] Church offers.
> "Where is the restaurant? Show me more—how does the restaurant fit in here?"

"We can be a little more literal."

"Yeah, because eventually we have to say where they eat and shop," Lucas says and then goes into more detail for an unusually long time—it's clearly important the artists get this right for next week. He pokes holes in the ceiling of an Utapau interior to allow for shafts of light. "We have to figure out how the city falls together. It's slightly organic, but they have cars."[38]

While attention to such minor details adds to the depth, verisimilitude, and completeness of a world, they are also worthy of attention precisely because of the "Making of" material which will ensure that fans are aware of these details; thus the presence of "Making of" materials can support world-building even in areas that would otherwise go largely unnoticed.

"Making of" materials can help demonstrate the consistency of a world as well, containing such things as explanations and motivations which add to an audience's knowledge of a world. For example, Knoll's *Creating the Worlds of Star Wars 365 Days* features an overhead map of the entire pod racing course from Episode I and a reference map of the section of Coruscant seen in the airspeeder chase from Episode II.[39] Both maps, the features of which are described in detail, show the overall spatial relationships and the care taken to connect everything together, even though no more than a small part of each is glimpsed in any given shot in either sequence. Even in cases where an entire design is not built, but only those parts needed for the areas shown, maps and layouts give a sense that the object in question (like a location, vehicle, or building) was still imagined and designed in its entirety, such that it could have been incarnated (or could be in a future installment of a world). A well-designed world already gives us glimpses and implies unseen areas, and the existence of designs, even behind-the-scenes ones, further provides a sense of completeness and consistency.

Finally, "Making of" material can also add new content (even canonical content) to a world.[40] Christopher Tolkien's 12-volume *History of Middle-earth* series, based on his father's manuscripts, is perhaps one of the most extensive "Making of" documentations in literature. Over the 12 volumes, the development of J. R. R. Tolkien's world is traced with writings from six decades, including additional poems, stories, drawings, etymological data, partial drafts, and revisions, many of which add to Tolkien's world, including *The New Shadow*, the start of a sequel to *The Lord of the Rings*. While the canonicity of such additions is debatable, since they were left unpublished (and many unfinished) at the time of the author's death, they add further depth and context and give some idea of what Tolkien might have done had he lived longer. Even in his letters (many of which could also be considered "Making of" material), one finds additional material which is arguably canonical, due to the fact that it was sent to someone (usually in answer to a question) and to the air of certainty that it often contains. For example, in a letter to a Mrs. Meriel Thurston in 1972, Tolkien writes:

I should be interested to hear what names you eventually choose (as individual names?) for your bulls; and interested to choose or invent suitable names myself, if you wish. The elvish word for "bull" doesn't appear in any published work; it was MUNDO.[41]

Of course, "mundo" eventually *did* appear in a published work, *The Letters of J. R. R. Tolkien* (1981). The notion that more material regarding an imaginary world exists in an unpublished state encourages the hope that it will one day see publication, and leads to speculation as to what else may remain hidden waiting to be discovered and made public, working against the idea that one has seen all there is to see of a world.

Narrative, then, holds a world together at different scales, as it structures individual works that make up a world, links different works set in a world, and occasionally, links separate worlds together into multiverses. Extradiegetically, there is also the "making of" narrative of the building of the world, which over time can include the revision and rebuilding of the world, in the form of retcon and reboots. Narratives about the building of imaginary worlds, however, can also occur within a diegesis, if characters within a story are themselves building an imaginary world. A story can be about subcreation, and about subcreators who themselves live within an imaginary world, which is the subject of the next chapter.

5

SUBCREATION
WITHIN SUBCREATED WORLDS

Why should you desire to be Empress of a Material World, and be troubled with the cares that attend Government? When as by creating a World within your self, you may enjoy all both in whole and in parts, without controle [sic] or opposition; and may make what World you please, and alter it when you please, and enjoy as much pleasure and delight as a World can afford you? You have converted me, said the Duchess to the Spirits, from my ambitious desire; wherefore, I'le [sic] take your advice, reject and despise all the Worlds without me, and create a World of my own.

—Margaret Cavendish, *The Description of a New World, Called the Blazing-World* (1666)[1]

The makers of subcreated worlds often reference or acknowledge their predecessors and the worlds that have gone before them: Lucian features Homer as a character in his *True History*; a character in Bacon's *New Atlantis* (1626) makes a reference to More's *Utopia*; Morpheus of *The Matrix* (1999) makes several allusions to *Alice in Wonderland*; a character in Arthur C. Clarke's *3001: The Final Odyssey* (1997) refers to "those old *Star Trek* Programs"[2]; and Henry Darger's story of the Vivian girls borrows from the works of a number of world-builders, including Dante, John Bunyan, Robert Louis Stevenson, Jules Verne, and L. Frank Baum. Some authors' works go even farther, including subcreation as a theme within an imaginary world, and these worlds feature characters who are themselves subcreators, giving an author an opportunity to comment on the nature of subcreation and what it means to make a world.

Quite often, subcreated subcreators are also able to enter their own subcreated worlds, sometimes resulting in convoluted ontological hierarchies. Subcreated subcreators have different motivations for making worlds, and some of their worlds' inhabitants are taken from the Primary World, voluntarily or involuntarily (occasionally these inhabitants do not even realize that they are in a secondary world). The abuse of subcreation, represented by evil subcreators, is also a theme one finds. This chapter, then, examines subcreation within subcreated worlds, and the reflections and explorations of the authors and diegetic characters who are involved in world-building activities.

Importance of the Word

> In the beginning was the Word ...
> —John 1:1

> Then God said, "Let there be light", and there was light.
> —Genesis 1:3

Like the *Fiat Lux* of Genesis, most subcreated worlds find their origins in words, whether as descriptive text, a novel outline, a screenplay treatment, lines of computer code, or even an invented language. In a sense, all storytelling, with its authoritative narration, calls narrative worlds into fictional existence in a similar way; writing about "World Construction as Performative Force", literary theorist Lubomír Doležel states:

> Where does the narrative's authentication authority originate? It has the same grounding as any other performative authority—convention. In the actual world, this authority is given by social, mostly institutional, systems; in fiction, it is inscribed in the norms of the narrative genre. Let us note that all discourse features of the authoritative narrative are negative: it lacks truth-value, identifiable subjective source (it is "anonymous"), and spatio-temporal situation (the speech-act is contextless). This annulling of all the typical features of natural discourse is a precondition for the performative force to work automatically. If this negativity reminds the reader of "God's word", so be it. It is precisely the divine world-creating word that provides the model for the authoritative narrative and its performative force.[3]

Words can have a performative force within diegetic worlds as well. In Tolkien's mythology, the world is sung into being through the Music of the Ainur (and words were the inspiration behind Tolkien's world itself, which was designed to provide a home for his invented languages and the cultures and mythology arising from them). In many fantasy worlds, magical incantations are used to bring things into being, and in science fiction worlds, words often have similar powers, whether as passwords that allow access or words of computer code that create, alter, or destroy, as the streams of computer code do in the *Matrix* films. The speaking of true names also holds power in folklore and in the worlds of

Vernor Vinge's "True Names", Andre Norton's *Witch World* series, Ursula K. LeGuin's *Earthsea* stories, and many others, where the knowing and using of someone's real name holds power over them.

Perhaps the best example of the performative force of the word within a subcreated world is the use of words in the Art of Writing of the fallen D'ni civilization found in the *Myst* franchise. The D'ni write Descriptive Books, which describe the details and structure of a world, or "Age" (the term has no temporal meaning, though it does invoke a sense of otherness and remoteness). Next they write associated linking books, each of which contains an image from the Age on the first page, a live, moving image that will transport the user to the Age described in the Descriptive Book if one places one's hand on the image. The entire D'ni civilization is based on these books, and the *Myst* stories revolve around their use. Early on when the *Myst* mythology was begun, the Miller brothers decided, taking a stance similar to Tolkien's idea of subcreation, that it would not be right to claim that the D'ni were creating *ex nihilo*, like God. Thus, the mythology was designed so that, instead of creating the worlds written in them, the Descriptive Books and linking books are said to connect to pre-existing worlds, which exist before the D'ni books describe them and link to them, bringing the *Myst* franchise's mythology more in line with Christian theology.

To explain the possible confusion between "created worlds" and "pre-existing worlds" diegetically, the Millers suggested that one of the central characters, Gehn, misconstrued what the books were actually doing. Both *Myst: The Book of Atrus* and the game *Riven* (1997) are about Gehn, a surviving D'ni who tries to revive the Art of Writing and believes he is creating the Ages the books describe (especially because he was able to develop his test Ages, very short books which linked to pre-existing Ages that matched his descriptions). He teaches his son Atrus the Art of Writing, but Atrus later realizes that his father is wrong about how the books work:

> The thought was one he had more and more often these past few months. A dangerous, unspoken thought.
>
> *And yet the more I discover about Writing, the more I challenge my father's view that we are creating the worlds we travel in.*
>
> What if they weren't so much *making* those worlds as linking to pre-existing possibilities?
>
> At first he had dismissed the notion as a foolish one. Of course they had created these worlds. They had to be! How else would they come into being in such precise and predictable forms? Besides, it was simply not possible that an infinite supply of different worlds existed out there, waiting to be tapped. Yet, the more he thought about it, the more he had come to question his father's simpler explanation.[4]

Even though the books link to pre-existing worlds, the words in them still have the performative force of opening a portal. Only a few phrases are enough to connect to a world.[5] And the text written in a book connects to the linked world so precisely, that Writing must be considered very cautiously. As Gehn tells Atrus:

> ... I do want you to begin to grip the relationship between the words that are written on the page and the complex entity—the physical, living Age—that results. You see, while our Art *is* a precise one, its effects are often quite surprising, owing to the complexity of the web of relationships that are created between things. The meaning of an individual phrase can be altered by the addition of other phrases, often to the extent that the original description bears no relation whatsoever to the resultant reality. That is why the D'ni were so adamant about contradictions. Contradictions can destroy an Age. Too often they simply make it break apart under the strain of trying to resolve the conflicting instructions.[6]

In the world of the D'ni, the written word has subcreative power beyond the power to invoke a secondary world, since the Ages involved can be physically traveled to by their subcreators, which also makes consistency even more important. Subcreators physically visiting the worlds they create is a theme frequently found in the imaginary-world tradition, and a form of self-reflexivity.

Self-reflexivity

When a world is fully imagined, the subcreative act takes a certain amount of effort and contemplation, so it is not surprising that it should itself be the inspiration behind some authors' works, providing ideas for their content and themes; thus the activities of diegetic subcreators sometimes mirror the processes of subcreation carried on by their authors. For example, the D'ni Art of Writing as described above is analogous to the computer programming done during the creation of the *Myst* games. Like the Descriptive Books within the games, the CD-ROMs containing the *Myst* games contain the computer code that both describes and calls into being the worlds of the games; and the above-mentioned quote of Gehn's, regarding contradictions, could equally be applied to the art of computer programming. Both the D'ni language and computer code are unlike spoken language, extremely precise in their phrasing, and must be free of contradictions in order to avoid strange results or unstable worlds. The point-and-click use of the mouse and cursor is similar to the placing of a hand on the linking image, and the games' cursor is actually shaped like a hand when the user uses it to click on a book's linking image within the games. The games' content imitates the form of the games and the interface they use, tying the user's experience more firmly into the secondary world along with more conventional means like direct address.

Likewise, the holodeck in the *Star Trek* universe functions as a portal to a subcreated world that one can physically enter; it is an empty room that can be programmed to simulate an environment that surrounds the user and allows interaction, through a combination of holography, force fields, tractor beams, and replicated matter (see Figure 5.1). People who write for the holodeck are known as holonovelists, a profession that one *Star Trek: Voyager* (1995–2001) character, Tom Paris, took up once the *USS Voyager* returned to Earth. Holodeck users can converse with simulated characters and interact with the imaginary world the holodeck presents, and as every *Star Trek* fan knows, the holodeck can malfunction, leaving characters trapped within it, sometimes with the safety protocols turned off, resulting in situations with real danger (for example, in "A Fistful of Datas" (Season 6, Episode 8) of *Star Trek: The Next Generation* (1987–1994), Worf suffers from a gunshot wound he receives in the holodeck).

When it is turned off, the holodeck is shown as an empty, rectangular room, with grids on the walls, floor, and ceiling. Apart from the grids, the large empty space is similar to a soundstage, which of course the holodeck set itself is. The spaces of both the soundstage and the holodeck temporarily become other places once the scenery and set pieces appear in them, and both spaces can be made to

FIGURE 5.1 Commander William T. Riker enters the holodeck during a jungle simulation in "Encounter at Farpoint" (Season 1, Episode 1) of *Star Trek: The Next Generation* (1987–1994).

include broad vistas that evoke a sense of much wider spaces than the room would actually allow. The space itself is also one of pretend for its participants, who dress in the appropriate costumes before entering, and yet that sense of pretend can still be interrupted by tragic real world events when something goes wrong (for example, actor Brandon Lee dying from a gunshot wound on the film set of *The Crow* (1994) when a prop gun fired at him during a scene was improperly prepared).

Other spaces, like the virtual places that the characters enter in *The Matrix*, are similarly shown to be constructs made from computer code, just like the computer-generated imagery used to fill in the greenscreen backgrounds behind actors. Like the holodeck, characters can face real dangers and even die within *The Matrix*'s computer-generated worlds, which seems to be a common ontological feature of many computer-generated worlds that characters can enter (characters can also die within the virtual worlds of *Tron* (1982), *The Lawnmower Man* (1992), *VR Troopers* (1994–1996), *Virtuosity* (1995), and others). The ability to enter virtual worlds within a diegesis open up narrative possibilities, but without the threat of possible death, narrative tension would be lost.

Another form of self-reflexivity is authorship attributed to characters within the text. Within Tolkien's Middle-earth, Bilbo is said to be the author of *The Hobbit*, and later, along with Frodo and Sam, the author of the fictional *Red Book of Westmarch*, which is, of course, *The Lord of the Rings* itself. As Verlyn Flieger describes it:

> Carrying the conceit about as far as it will go, Tolkien inserted his own name into the header and footer on the title-page of The Lord of the Rings (and thus into the history of the "book"), not as the author of the book but as its final transmitter/redactor. What appears to the first-time or untutored reader to be simply Tolkienian embellishment is in fact a running inscription in Tolkien's invented scripts of Cirth and Tengwar. It can be put into English as follows: "*The Lord of the Rings* TRANSLATED FROM THE RED BOOK [in Cirth] OF WESTMARCH BY JOHN RONALD REUEL TOLKIEN HEREIN IS SET FORTH THE HISTORY OF THE WAR OF THE RINGS AND THE RETURN OF THE KING AS SEEN BY THE HOBBITS [in Tengwar]." He is not inventing the story, the running script announces, he is merely translating and recording.[7]

Flieger goes on to compare the writing of the *Red Book of Westmarch* with the writing of *The Lord of the Rings*, looking at the various editions and its "traceable genealogy", and also points out that Tolkien, in a 1966 interview with Richard Plotz, suggested that *The Silmarillion* could be published as Bilbo's "research in Rivendell".[8]

The many and various self-reflexive moments in which Tolkien's characters reflect on or discuss the story they are in and the nature of such stories in general are examined in detail in Mary Bowman's essay "The Story Was Already Written: Narrative Theory in *The Lord of the Rings*"[9] so I will not enumerate them here. But the most self-reflexive figure within Tolkien's *oeuvre* regarding subcreation appears in his short story "Leaf by Niggle". Niggle, a painter, is working on a large painting of a tree, which is an allegory (a rare one, as Tolkien usually disliked allegory) of the subcreative process involved in the creation of Tolkien's own imaginary world. Tolkien describes Niggle's painting, writing:

> He had a number of pictures on hand; most of them were too large and ambitious for his skill. He was the sort of painter who can paint leaves better than trees. He used to spend a long time on a single leaf, trying to catch its shape, and its sheen, and the glistening of dewdrops on its edges. Yet, he wanted to paint a whole tree, with all of its leaves in the same style, and all of them different.
>
> There was one picture in particular which bothered him. It had begun with a leaf caught in the wind, and it became a tree; and the tree grew, sending out innumerable branches, and thrusting out the most fantastic roots. Strange birds came and settled on the twigs and had to be attended to. Then all round the Tree, and behind it, through the gaps in the leaves and boughs, a country began to open out; and there were glimpses of a forest marching over the land, and of mountains tipped with snow. Niggle lost interest in his other pictures; or else he took them and tacked them on to the edges of his great picture. Soon the canvas became so large that he had to get a ladder; and he ran up and down it, putting in a touch here, and rubbing out a patch there. When people came to call, he seemed polite enough, though he fiddled a little with the pencils on his desk. He listened to what they said, but underneath he was thinking all the time about his big canvas, in the tall shed that had been built for it out in his garden (on a plot where once he had grown potatoes).[10]

Niggle's painting of individual leaves and his desire to paint an entire tree is similar to Tolkien's love of myth and his desire to develop an entire mythology of linked stories; and the manner in which the tree begins and grows is also analogous to the gradual way that his legendarium developed, both in the way new tales grew out of existing ones ("sending out innumerable branches") and the way backstories grew to support his cultures ("thrusting out the most fantastic roots"). In his letters,[11] Tolkien mentions how characters sometimes appeared that he had not anticipated, like the Black Riders, Strider, Saruman, the Stewards of Gondor, and Faramir; these could be seen as the "strange birds that settled on the twigs and had to be attended to". The country that "began to open out" through glimpses in the "gaps in the leaves and boughs" could represent further details of the imaginary world being built around the story, the filling in of the background around it (quite the opposite of the "painter's algorithm", in which the background is done first and the foreground painted on top of it afterward). The pictures "tacked on" the edge of the great picture could allude to how works like *The Hobbit* (1937) and the poem *The Adventures of Tom Bombadil* (1934) were pulled into the mythology and made a part of it, and last two sentences quoted might be a description of how Tolkien himself was distracted by the creation of his world.

Self-reflexivity, whether it refers to the world or the world-building process, and ranging as it does from subtle analogy to thinly-veiled autobiography, allows an author to comment on the subcreative process and its relationship to the world it produces; and perhaps the greatest device for doing so (though it is often more reflexive than self-reflexive) is the presence of a subcreated subcreator.

Subcreated Subcreators and Diegetic World-building

Some subcreators appear as characters within the worlds they create; for example, in Henry Darger's book *The Story of the Vivian Girls*, Darger appears as a character and his book appears as well and is read by other characters in his world. Likewise, in Mark Hogancamp's one-sixth-scale town of Marwencol which he built in his yard and photographs, one of the dolls represents Hogancamp himself, and the end of Jeff Malmberg's documentary *Marwencol* (2010) shows that the Hogancamp doll is also building a one-sixth-scale town and photographing it. Nevertheless, most subcreated subcreators are not quite as self-reflexive, and are merely characters in the author's world.

Characters have always been writers, storytellers, and creators, and many have discussed hypothetical places or visited imaginary worlds; but the actual *making* of an imaginary world by a character was slower to develop. Socrates describes his Kallipolis in detail in Plato's *Republic* (c. 380 BC) and some nobleman make Sancho Panza the governor of the fictional island of Barataria (which is really a town) as a joke in the second part of *Don Quixote*, but in neither case does a character actually bring about an imaginary world that can be visited by that character or others. Probably the first instance of characters actually subcreating an imaginary world which they or other characters can visit is in Margaret Cavendish's *The Description of a New World, Called the Blazing-World* (1666), from which the opening quote of this chapter was taken. The story's characters make their own worlds and discuss the making of them as well, and the various possibilities open to them.

Although characters who are subcreators can tell stories set in imaginary worlds (like the town of Chewandswallow in *Cloudy with a Chance of Meatballs* (1978)) or simply imagine a world (like Deborah Blau's Kingdom of Yr, made to help her deal with her schizophrenia in *I Never Promised You a Rose Garden* (1964)), most subcreated subcreators make worlds that they, or other characters, can actually travel into, in one form or another. These types of worlds, and the means by which they are made, result in five additional types of subcreated subcreators: characters who build physical worlds using natural means; characters who build virtual worlds using natural means; characters who dream of worlds; characters who subcreate using supernatural tools; and characters who have inherent supernatural subcreative powers. The worlds produced by each of these have different limitations and sometimes different ontological dimensions, both of which need to be addressed in the stories that take place in and around them.

Characters who build physical worlds using natural means, a very literal and concrete approach to diegetic world-building, can be found as early as 1869, in Edward Everett Hale's short story "The Brick Moon". The story involves the building of an artificial satellite for navigational aid, a moon built from bricks. When the satellite launches, there are still people aboard it who accidentally get sent into space with it. However, since the moon takes an atmosphere with it, the people survive, and even begin a new world, which is described in a series of dispatches from the moon people. As the story's narrator writes about their growing world on the brick moon:

> Now, however, that it proved that in a tropical climate they were forming their own soil, developing their own palms, and eventually even their bread-fruit and bananas, planting their own oats and maize, and developing rice, wheat, and all other cereals, harvesting these six, eight, or ten times— for aught I could see—in one of our years,—why, then, there was no danger of famine for them. If, as I thought, they carried up with them heavy drifts of ice and snow in the two chambers which were not covered in when they started, why, they had waters in their firmament quite sufficient for all purposes of thirst and of ablution. And what I had seen of their exercise showed that they were in strength sufficient for the proper development of their little world.[12]

Hale's story begins a planet-building tradition in science fiction, in which artificial planets are made by civilizations with advanced technology and the ability to manipulate large masses of matter and construct gigantic structures, which often involve very different forms of planetary architecture. Such a civilization appears in Olaf Stapledon's *Star Maker* (1937):

> ...the Symbiotics ... armed with their highly developed physical sciences and with sub-atomic power, they were able to construct, out in space, artificial planets for permanent habitation. These great hollow globes of artificial super-metals, and artificial transparent adamant, ranged in size from the earliest and smallest structures, which were no bigger than a very small asteroid, to spheres considerably larger than the Earth. They were without external atmosphere, since their mass was generally too slight to prevent the escape of gases. A blanket of repelling force protected them from meteors and cosmic rays. The planet's external surface, which was

wholly transparent, encased the atmosphere. ... One very small and rather uncommon kind of artificial world consisted almost wholly of water. It was like a titanic bowl of gold-fish. Beneath its transparent shell, studded with rocket-machinery and interplanetary docks, lay a spherical ocean, crossed by structural girders, and constantly impregnated with oxygen. A small solid core represented the sea bottom...[13]

Other structures include a miniature tabletop planet created in a laboratory in Jack Williamson's "The Pygmy Planet" (1932), a ring-like planet that encircles the star it orbits in the *Ringworld* series by Larry Niven, and the five-layered world in the *World of Tiers* series by Philip José Farmer. The latter series goes beyond mere creation of planets to the making of "pocket universes" by the powerful Thoans, who can even create different laws of physics in each little universe they make.

As mentioned in Chapter 1, "world" need not refer to an entire planet, but rather the realm of a character's experiences, so diegetic world-building can occur on a smaller scale as well. In the novels *Time Out of Joint* (1959) and *Captive Universe* (1969) and the films *Dark City* (1998), *The Truman Show* (1998), and *The Village* (2004), town-sized worlds are physically built to house inhabitants who are not aware of the fact that they are in a small, artificial world set apart from the Primary World. The boundaries of these towns are made impassable to their trapped residents, who gradually discover their imprisonment and the fact that certain other inhabitants are aware of what is going on.

Although they are subcreations from the extradiegetic perspective of the audience, worlds that characters physically build by natural means are merely world-building projects from the characters' point of view, since they are not building a secondary world so much as they are reshaping a part of the Primary World. On the other hand, characters who build *virtual* worlds using natural means are performing an activity which could be considered subcreation even from within the diegetic world of the story. These kinds of worlds only appeared once a technology for creating them was available, namely the computer. Early examples of them include Delmark-O of Philip K. Dick's *A Maze of Death* (1970), the Other Plane of Vernor Vinge's short story "True Names" (1981), and the Grid from the film *Tron* (1982). In 1982, William Gibson's short story "Burning Chrome" introduced his on-line world of cyberspace, which would be the setting of his novel *Neuromancer* (1984), while "cyberspace" would become the term used to describe the on-line world in general. Other diegetic virtual worlds since then include *Star Trek*'s holodeck, and the on-line worlds of *eXistenZ* (1999) and *The Matrix* films, and Sapphire, a virtual planet in Greg Egan's short story "Crystal Nights" (2008) which, like Williamson's Pygmy planet, was designed to test theories of evolution. As mentioned earlier, these worlds, although virtual even within the diegesis, must be designed to pose real dangers in order to be narratively interesting. Thus, either characters must either be zapped electronically into the world (as in *Tron*), or go in virtually but face the real possibility of death (as in

The Matrix), or risk the virtual world inhabitants becoming sentient (as in *Star Trek: The Next Generation*) and escaping from their confines (as in "Crystal Nights"). One of *Star Trek*'s holodeck episodes, "Ship in a Bottle", even featured a holodeck character who appeared to be able to leave the holodeck, but he had in fact created a program that simulated the Enterprise within the holodeck, resulting in a holodeck-within-a-holodeck that fools the crew initially.

The need for the possibility of real danger within an imaginary world also occurs in the case of characters who dream worlds. The simplest way to create this possibility is to not reveal that the world is only a dream until the end of the story. One of the first examples of this strategy, *Alice's Adventures in Wonderland* (1865) by Lewis Carroll (Charles Lutwidge Dodgson), presented an imaginary world, Wonderland, which turns out to be Alice's dream; both the reader and Alice herself only realize this when she wakes up at the story's end. Technically speaking, an imaginary world made by dreaming can be considered a subcreated world, since it is the product of a character's imagination, though it is often not through a deliberate act; but it does solve all the problems regarding the visiting of a diegetically-subcreated world (we are led to believe that Alice physically enters Wonderland, but it turns out not to be the case; this device is also used in Carroll's sequel, *Through the Looking-Glass, and What Alice Found There* (1871)). Other imaginary worlds positioned as dreams from which the main character awakens include Winsor McCay's Slumberland and H. P. Lovecraft's Dreamworld (also known as Dreamlands), both of which are traveled to multiple times by their stories' protagonists (Little Nemo and Randolph Carter, respectively). However, some dream worlds have a more solid ontological status than others do. Although it is called a dream world, Lovecraft's world is not a *diegetically* subcreated world, insofar as his world (as it later turns out) does not appear to be merely the creation of Carter's slumbering mind; other humans like Richard Upton Pickman and King Kuranes, both of whom are Carter's friends from the Primary World, also travel or reside there, implying an existence of some kind outside of Carter's dreams.[14] Thus, a world can first appear to be something that one has dreamt, only to be revealed later as something that actually exists outside of the dreamer. In such cases, the dreamers are only finding portals to other worlds, not creating them.

A similar situation can exist among characters who subcreate using supernatural tools. The D'ni Art of Writing, discussed in the last section, is an example of characters using a subcreative technology they know how to use but do not fully understand; thus, it can exist as part of the world's premise without further explanation. Although it may be argued that when Atrus, Gehn, and others write Ages that they, like Lovecraft's dreamers, are not creating worlds but merely opening portals into them, certain moments in the stories (like when Atrus attempts to make changes to Riven to fix its instability) imply subcreative powers beyond merely that of a portal. As implied by Arthur C. Clarke's famous dictum, "Sufficiently advanced technology is indistinguishable from magic", sometimes it is difficult to tell whether advanced world-building technology is supernatural or not. Robert Wolff, the main character in Philip José Farmer's *The Maker of Universes* (1965), correctly suspects that the universe-building technology he encounters is scientific not supernatural, but he is not sure at first. Subcreational tools with a supernatural origin allow for the building of worlds which are more substantial than dream worlds or virtual worlds, and which are at the same time are not merely reshapings of the Primary World. The fact that the subcreational powers reside in the tools rather than their users means that the characters can remain ordinary humans (or something similar to ordinary humans), allowing the audience to identify with them more easily.

Characters who have inherent supernatural subcreative powers are perhaps among the rarest of subcreated subcreators, as they are typically supernatural beings or humans given supernatural abilities. The first such example of the latter can be found in Cavendish's *The Description of a New World, Called the Blazing-World*. The main character, the Lady, travels to an imaginary world, the Blazing-World, and marries the Emperor and becomes Empress. Later, she sends for the soul of the Duchess of Newcastle (the title held by Cavendish herself, though her own name does not appear in the story) who becomes her spiritual scribe. The Duchess later expresses her desire to be the Empress of a world, and is told that she need not conquer a world, but that she "can create an Immaterial World fully inhabited by Immaterial Creatures". The Empress and the Duchess then each set about creating their own imaginary worlds. The Duchess tries patterning her world after various philosophies, encountering problems with each one, until she finally decides to come up with the pattern herself:

> At last, when the Duchess saw that no patterns would do her any good in the framing of her World; she was resolved to make a World of her own Invention, and this World was composed of sensitive and rational self-moving Matter; indeed, it was composed onely [sic] of the Rational, which is the subtilest [sic] and purest degree of Matter; for as the Sensitive did move and act both to the perceptions and consistency of the body, so this degree of Matter at the same point of time (for though the degrees are mixt, yet the several parts may move several ways at one time) did move to the Creation of the Imaginary World; which World after it was made, appear'd so curious and full of variety, so well order'd and wisely govern'd, that it cannot possibly be expressed by words, nor the delight and pleasure which the Duchess took in making this World-of-her-own.
>
> In the mean time, the Empress was also making and dissolving several Worlds in her own mind, and was so puzled [sic], that she could not settle in any of them; wherefore she sent for the Duchess, who being ready to wait on the Empress, carried her beloved World along with her, and invited the Empress's Soul to observe the Frame, Order and Government of it. Her Majesty was so ravished with the perception of it, that her Soul desired

to live in the Duchess's World: But the Duchess advised her to make such another World in her own mind; for, said she, your Majesty's mind is full of rational corporeal motions; and the rational motions of my mind shall assist you by the help of sensitive expressions, with the best Instructions they are able to give you.[15]

Here we have not only the subcreation of a world that a character can enter into, but two subcreators who discuss world-building, examine each other's worlds, and, in a later section, discuss the Primary World in relation to the secondary worlds. The Duchess's world, however, is not described in detail, and the fact that it was made of the "purest degree of Matter" which can "move several ways at one time", with an appearance that "cannot possibly be expressed by words", left little room for further description or development.

Like the use of advanced technology, characters may exhibit magical subcreative powers without understanding them or controlling them. In Edith Nesbit's *The Magic City* (1910), Philip, a boy, builds two cities out of blocks and household objects, only to find himself later inside one of the cities:

He gazed on it [*the city*] for a moment in ecstasy and then turned to shut the door. As he did so he felt a slight strange giddiness and stood a moment with his hand to his head. He turned and went again towards the city, and when he was close to it he gave a little cry, hastily stifled, for fear some one should hear him and come down and send him to bed. He stood and gazed about him bewildered and, once more, rather giddy. For the city had, in a quick blink of light, followed by darkness, disappeared. So had the drawing room. So had the chair that stood close to the table. He could see mountainous shapes raising enormous heights in the distance, and the moonlight shone on the tops of them. But he himself seemed to be in a vast, flat plain. There was the softness of long grass round his feet, but there were no trees, no houses, no hedges or fences to break the expanse of grass. It seemed darker in some parts than others. That was all. It reminded him of the illimitable prairie of which he had read in books of adventure.

"I suppose I'm dreaming," said Philip, "though I don't see how I can have gone to sleep just while I was turning the door handle. However—" He stood still expecting that something would happen. In dreams something always does happen, if it's only that the dream comes to an end. But nothing happened now—Philip just stood there quite quietly and felt the warm soft grass round his ankles.[16]

Although Nesbit tells us that it is not a dream, little explanation is given, although in Chapter 2 a character says that "a sort of self-acting magic rather difficult to explain" is partly responsible, and gives us a glimpse of the cities' creation from the residents' point of view:

> As soon as the cities were built and the inhabitants placed here the life of the city began, and it was, to those who lived it, as though it had always been. The artisans toiled, the musicians played, and the poets sang. The astrologers, finding themselves in a tall tower evidently designed for such a purpose, began to observe the stars and to prophesy.[17]

The cities' past is thus created along with the present, yet at the same time, the speaker, a resident himself, seems aware of what happened. Nesbit's story never attributes its magic to a source, though earlier in the story, as Philip begins to build his cities, a supernatural one is hinted at:

> A bronze Egyptian god on a black and gold cabinet seemed to be looking at him from across the room.
> "All right," said Philip. "I'll build you a temple. You wait a bit."
> The bronze god waited and the temple grew, and two silver candlesticks, topped by chessmen, served admirably as pillars for the portico.[18]

In most cases, the only characters with inherent subcreative powers under their control are godlike beings, like the gods of Dunsany's Pegāna or Tolkien's Ainur. The Ainur are the angelic beings who receive themes of music from Eru Ilúvatar (God), and together fashion the themes into a great music, which Ilúvatar then shows them:

> But when they were come into the Void, Ilúvatar said to them: "Behold your Music!" And he showed to them a vision, giving to them sight where before was only hearing; and they saw a new World made visible before them, and it was globed amid the Void, and it was sustained therein, but was not of it. And as they looked and wondered this World began to unfold its history, and it seemed to them that it lived and grew.[19]

Some of the Ainur decide to go into the new universe, Eä, and become the Valar, the "Powers of the World". Once they do, they must subcreate Arda, the world itself:

> But when the Valar entered into Eä they were at first astounded and at a loss, for it was as if naught was yet made which they had seen in vision, and all was but on point to begin and yet unshaped, and it was dark. For the Great Music had been but the growth and flowering of thought in the

Timeless Halls, and the Vision only a foreshowing; but now they had entered in at the beginning of Time, and the Valar perceived that the World had been but foreshadowed and foresung, and they must achieve it. So began their great labours in wastes unmeasured and unexplored, and in ages uncounted and forgotten...[20]

After the Valar enter into the world, they reside in Valinor, a land that later becomes inaccessible to the Men of Middle-earth, and by the time of *The Lord of the Rings*, the Valar's role is an indirect one.

An example of more direct interaction with a diegetically-subcreated world can be found in E. R. Eddison's *A Fish Dinner in Memison* (1941), the second book in his Zimiamvia trilogy. The novel begins by intercutting chapters (and even parts of chapters) following two storylines; that of Edward Lessingham and Mary Scarnside on Earth, and the other of King Mezentius and his court in Zimiamvia. Edward and Mary's story is one of romance and marriage in tumultuous early twentieth-century Europe and of Edward's battle with despair after his wife's untimely death in a train crash, while the other storyline follows the political machinations and intrigues of Zimiamvia involving King Mezentius and his vassals and the Lady Fiorinda. The latter storyline ends with the fish dinner of the title, in which the Lady Fiorinda challenges King Mezentius to build a world according to her wishes:

> The King's hands, beautiful to watch in the play of their able subtle strength, were busied before him on the table. Presently he opened them slowly apart. Slowly, in even measure with their parting, the world of his making grew between them: a thing of most aery seeming substance, ensphered, glimmering of a myriad colours where the eye rested oblique on it, but, being looked to more directly, all mirk, darkling, and unsure. And within it, depth beneath depth: wherein appeared as if a seething and a churning together and apart continual of the dark and the bright.[21]

After discussing the nature of the lives and deaths of the people who will live in the King's world, Fiorinda proposes that she and the King go in and enter it, so as to know from within what it is like to live there. We soon find that the two storylines have merged, and that Edward and Mary are the lives taken on by the King and Fiorinda within the world, and that our world, the Primary World, is the world created at King Mezentius's fish dinner. Upon returning from the world, as the King is still recovering from his sorrow, "They looked for a minute at the unsure thing on the table before them. "Fifty more years, afterwards, I wrought there," said the King; "yet here, what was it? the winking of an eyelid..."[22] By not revealing the nested nature of the worlds until the end, the Lessinghams' story is all the more effective, and Edward's mourning carries more weight since we, like the characters, do not realize the true nature of the situation. Later, when the world is discarded, Fiorinda suggests that the King could always make a better one if he chose. He laughs and responds:

> "Doubtless I could. Doubtless, another day, I will. And," he said, under his breath and for that lady's ear alone, looking her sudden in the eye, "doubt-less I have already. Else, O Beguiler of Guiles, how came We here?"[23]

The notion that perhaps the Primary World itself is perhaps someone else's subcreated world goes back to the ancient Chinese philosopher Zhuangzi, who dreamed he was a butterfly, only to awaken and wonder if he was a butterfly dreaming he was a man. Apart from one other mention which is also only a speculation (*Through the Looking-Glass and What Alice Found There* (1872) ends with Alice considering whether she was a part of the Red King's dream), the narrative device of a character who slowly discovers that what appeared to be the Primary World is in fact a secondary world built to deceive him, is largely a twentieth-century development, perhaps a reflection on the growing degree of mediated experience and the rise of mass media. It is also a device often associated with another theme found within diegetic subcreation, the idea of an evil subcreator.

Evil Subcreators

> *I need Ages. Dozens of them. Hundreds of them! That is our task, Atrus, don't you see? Our sacred task. To make Ages and populate them. To fill up the nothing-ness with worlds. Worlds we can own and govern, so that the D'ni will be great again. So that my grandsons will be lords of a million worlds!*
>
> —Gehn in *The Book of Atrus*[24]

The figure of the evil subcreator is usually guilty of one or both sins; abusing his power and putting himself in the place of God, or using a subcreated world as a means of imprisoning or containing an individual or a community in order to further some project of his own. Examples of the abuse of power include Tolkien's Melkor, his satanic figure from *The Silmarillion*, and Gehn from the *Myst* franchise. Tolkien admitted that the temptation was inherent in subcreative power, writing:

> ... the creative (or should I say, subcreative) desire ... seems to have no biological function, and to be apart from the satisfactions of plain ordinary biological life, with which, in our world, it is indeed usually at strife. This desire is at once wedded to a passionate love of the real primary world, and hence filled with the sense of mortality, and yet unsatisfied by it. It has various opportunities of "Fall". It may become possessive, clinging to the things made as "its own", the subcreator wishes to be the Lord and God of his private creation. He will rebel against the laws of the Creator—especially

against mortality. Both of these (alone or together) will lead to the desire for Power, for making the will more quickly effective,—and so to the Machine (or Magic).[25]

The desire for power and the connection to the machine is especially apparent in those situations in which a world is not made for its own good, but rather as a tool used to dominate others or use them for its maker's own ends; which brings us to stories which use a subcreated world as a means of deception or imprisonment (or both).

Typically in these stories, we share the perspective of the main character who comes to discover that something is not right and that there are certain boundaries surrounding the world in which he or she lives that cannot be crossed. As such characters try to uncover the mysterious nature of their world and find a way to cross the boundaries being imposed on them, the fact that they are living in a world built to deceive them slowly becomes clear, as evidence accrues. The world-builders, who are usually also the guardians of the world, attempt to stop the main character's epiphany, but are unsuccessful, and eventually as the conflict escalates, the main character is somehow instrumental in bringing about an end to the world, or a rebuilding of it with a redistribution of power.

Even when the world-builders' intentions may be good (as in Margaret Peterson Haddix's *Running Out of Time* (1995) and M. Night Shyamalan's *The Village* (2004), in which some of the world-builders live and raise families within the world they made), the attempt to keep others from realizing the constructedness of the world results in the keeping of them in the world by force, turning it into a kind of prison. Others with evil intent not only use their worlds as prisons, but usually have other purposes as well for their worlds' unknowing inhabitants, as in *Time Out of Joint* (1959), *The Truman Show* (1998), *Dark City* (1998), and *The Matrix* (1999), to use a few more well-known examples.

In both *Time Out of Joint* and *The Truman Show*, a city is built with the sole purpose of providing an environment for one man whose life provides something for society at large, even while he is unaware of the true nature of his situation. In *Time Out of Joint*, Ragle Gumm plays a newspaper game entitled "Where Will the Little Green Be Next?" winning the cash prize week after week and managing to live off the proceeds; it is later revealed that his choices predict where enemy nuclear strikes will occur, and that this ability is being used against his will (he previously did the job consciously, until defecting to the other side, at which point he was stopped, his memory was erased, and he was placed in the phony town where the game was devised so that he would end up continuing his work without realizing it). In *The Truman Show*, Truman Burbank unknowingly lives his entire life as the subject of an ongoing reality TV show, providing entertainment for the show's audience, until he begins to realize how false his life is. In both cases, the unknowing victim around whom the world is built is allowed to function normally, and the world is constructed in such a way so that

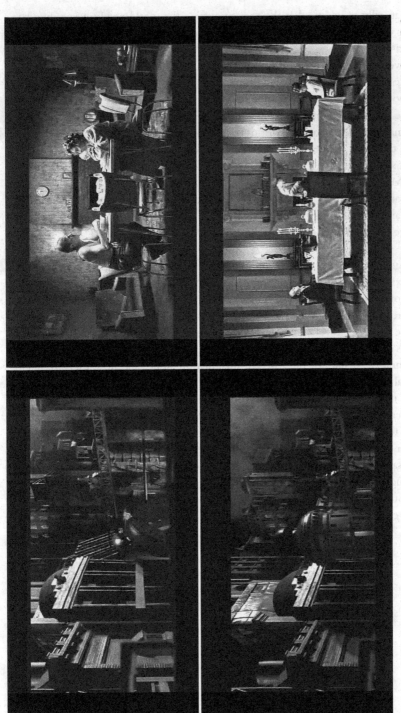

FIGURE 5.2 Nightly reshapings of the city performed by the Strangers in *Dark City* (1998): buildings shrink and grow into new forms (left, top and bottom), while the city's inhabitants have their memories reset and find themselves in new lives the next morning (right, top and bottom).

he naturally provides what the society outside the world needs; it is only when these worlds are tested that the main characters begin to realize they are in a kind of prison.

Even more sinister are the Strangers of *Dark City* and the Machines of *The Matrix*, who use the unknowing human inhabitants of their worlds for scientific purposes; the former studying human memory and identity (see Figure 5.2), while the latter use human bodies as a power source. Instead of merely escaping, the main characters in these worlds learn the powers of their inhuman captors and take them on directly, ending their rule of the subcreated world they have created. In both of these cases, however, the subcreated world is not destroyed; the Matrix is rebooted, with the Oracle and the Architect agreeing to free the humans that want to be freed, and at the end of *Dark City* Murdoch reshapes the city and creates his longed-for Shell Beach. Thus, the subcreative powers that create the worlds redeem them as well.

Subcreation, as a theme within a subcreated world, allows an author to reflexively examine the nature of subcreation, what it means to build a world, the uses of such worlds, and what it means to be in a world. The inclusion of diegetic subcreators in a world also has the potential for metaleptic twists, as characters move from one level of nested worlds to another, crossing between ontological levels of the diegesis. The way these worlds-within-worlds are made, whether by technology, magic, or the force of imagination alone, and how they are made, reveal some of the dreams that authors have harbored for some time: the autonomy of the inhabitants within a world; the making of worlds that become real and can be entered; and the completion of secondary worlds, the unreachable goal for Primary World authors who can only begin and expand a world but never complete it, no matter how much of their lives they may devote to it. At the same time, the ever-increasing number and variety of media windows, through which worlds can be experienced, are giving them unprecedented opportunities for transmedial growth and adaptation, which is the topic of the next chapter.

6
TRANSMEDIAL
GROWTH AND ADAPTATION

I would draw some of the great tales in fullness, and leave many only placed in the scheme, and sketched. The cycles should be linked to a majestic whole, and yet leave scope for other minds and hands, wielding paint and music and drama. Absurd.
—J. R. R. Tolkien, *Letters of J. R. R. Tolkien*[1]

At a certain point the length of a written work can change its nature completely. It ceases to be a book, or a piece of writing to be read. With words and images, and the accumulation of detail, not subdued to the task of communication, a different function is revealed: the creation of an alternate reality, a means of living for a lifetime in another world.
—John M. MacGregor, *Henry Darger: In the Realms of the Unreal*[2]

More and more, storytelling has become the art of world-building. ... The world is bigger than the film, bigger even than the franchise. ... World-making follows its own market logic.
—Henry Jenkins, *Convergence Culture*[3]

Many worlds extend beyond their work of first appearance, growing beyond the needs of the first story to be set in them, even when that story is the world's reason for existence. Not only do they become transnarrative in scope (as discussed in Chapter 4), they often also extend across multiple media, becoming *transmedial*. This can happen in two ways: *adaptation*, when a story existing in one medium is adapted for presentation in another medium, but without adding any new canonical material to a world (translation can be considered a type of adaptation); and *growth*, when another medium is used to present new canonical material of a world, expanding the world and what we know about it.[4] Of course, every adaptation adds something to the story or world within the work being adapted; even an audio book which is a straightforward reading of a written text may affect emphasis or pacing, or provide pronunciations of names that would otherwise be ambiguous in print. Whether or not additions can be considered *growth*, however, depends on the canonicity of the added material, and thus its authorship, topics which are discussed in the next chapter.

Both growth and adaptation assume pre-existing material which is being extended or modified in some way. The field of Adaptation Studies, arguably originating with George Bluestone's *Novels into Film* (1957), has typically been most concerned with how narratives change when they move from one medium to another. The growth and adaptation of a world, however, goes beyond narrative, and may even have very little to do with narrative. Some degree of a world's aesthetics (the sensory experience of a world) and a world's logic (how a world operates and the reasons behind the way it is structured) must be carried over from one work to another or from one medium to another. World infrastructures (discussed in Chapter 3) will have to be referred to or carried over to a recognizable degree, if the world is to retain some semblance to its appearance in its medium of origin, though sometimes only a few representative parts—characters, objects, or situations—are all that are carried over, for example in merchandising, where images of characters or objects from a world are used to tie just about any kind of product into a franchise.

Other factors also affect adaptation and growth. The budget allotted to a film adaptation, for example, and the technology available, may determine how faithfully a written work can be rendered; commercial pressures may attempt to move the world and its narratives into more action, sex, and violence; and extradiegetic information such as stars' personas and directors' reputations will influence the reception of a work. When *The Lord of the Rings* was adapted into a film, the romance between Arwen and Aragorn, which appeared mainly in Appendix A of the book, was expanded and foregrounded more in the movie, and Arwen's role was enlarged as well, due to studio's desire for more romance; and likewise many action scenes were prolonged and given greater emphasis than in the book. Peter Jackson's background as a director of horror movies, and his love of monsters, also colored his adaptation of the book (as he admits in the DVD extras for the films). Commercial forces naturally affect the originators of worlds as well; when a living author is still producing works set in a world while an audience is consuming them, the reception of those works will often influence the direction that the author takes in the further development of a world; for example, while writing *The Lord of the Rings* as a sequel to *The Hobbit*, Tolkien's publisher wanted more hobbits, a demand which determined the starting point for the writing of *The Lord of the Rings*.[5] And finally, another factor affecting transmedial growth and adaptation is the nature of transmediality itself.

The Nature of Transmediality

The notion of transmediality, the state of being represented in multiple media, suggests that we are vicariously experiencing something which lies beyond the media windows through which we see and hear it, since it posits an object that can be seen and heard through different windows, and one that is independent of the windows through which it is seen and heard, even though it exists only in mediated fashion. Transmediality implies a kind of independence for its object; the more media windows we experience a world through, the less reliant that world is on the peculiarities of any one medium for its existence. Thus, transmediality also suggests the potential for the continuance of a world, in multiple instances and registers; and the more we see and hear of a transmedial world, the greater is the illusion of ontological weight that it has, and experiencing the world becomes more like the mediated experience of the Primary World.

In order for a narrative or world to be transmedial, it must be able to be present in multiple forms of mediation (which contain and convey world information), such as text, imagery, sound, three-dimensional shapes, and interactive media. The range of different forms in which it can be present broadens the possibilities for transmedial growth and adaptation; for example, Dewdney's Planiverse, which is two-dimensional, can appear in text, image, and sound, but there will probably never be a LEGO playset based on the Planiverse, because of the three-dimensional form required for such an adaptation (there could, however, be a Colorforms playset based on it). Some worlds may appear in only one or two forms initially, but are expanded through adaptation to media involving other forms; in such cases, interpretations and additions to a world are inevitable, as information is generated for the new forms (as described in the next sections).

Transmedial worlds with sufficient growth in multiple forms and media can often be identified by a range of different elements even when they stand alone; sometimes a name, image, sound effect, or musical cue alone is enough to evoke the world in which it is found. One such world is George Lucas' *Star Wars* galaxy, which began as ideas that became a treatment and screenplay[6] that led to a theatrical feature film and a novelization, and which was followed by a holiday television special, trading card sets, toy sets with action figures, comic books, more feature films, film soundtracks, novels and novelizations, children's books, made-for-TV movies, radio plays, video games, websites, LEGO sets, animated TV shows, encyclopedias and a variety of other reference works, books about the LEGO adaptations, and a variety of other merchandise branded with *Star Wars* imagery and increasingly removed from the world itself. Many of these things only refer to or play with the world's elements, creating alternate or even parodic versions of them. The LEGO *Star Wars* video games, for example, greatly change the look and feel of all the world's visuals, simplifying and bowdlerizing them into a bright, cheery world where everything is comedic and no one dies (they just briefly fall to bouncing pieces). Yet, in these games, the world of *Star Wars* is referenced and evoked, even though we are experiencing virtual LEGO versions of characters, objects, locations, and situations which are loosely based on the "real" *Star Wars* galaxy. Other elements, like the *Star Wars* film soundtracks, occupy an interesting position; while much of the film's music is nondiegetic, and thus not a part of the diegetic world, the music is arguably still a part of the world insofar as the *audience's* experience of the world is concerned, as are other nondiegetic materials like the opening title crawl stretching into the distance or the custom font ("StarVader") used for the main title.

A discussion of transmedial growth should attempt to examine what occurs during the move across media. However, analyzing transmedial movements across every possible pairing of media would be a lengthy undertaking involving much overlap and repetition; a better approach is to look at each of the properties present in different media, their capabilities and peculiarities, and the process of using each as a window that reveals an imaginary world.

Windows on the World:
Words, Images, Objects, Sounds, and Interactions

Besides Doležel's observation that all imaginary worlds are inevitably incomplete (see Chapter 1), one thing that all imaginary worlds share in common is the fact that our experiences of them are always mediated experiences. And the medium in which a world originates will help determine the world's potential for growth and adaptation, due to such factors as the audience size and receptivity, the conventions and audience expectations that come with the medium, and most importantly, the medium's unique combination of properties available for the conveyance of the world and its stories.

To create their mediated experiences, every medium makes use of one or more basic elements: words, images, sounds, and interactions.[7] As windows on the world, we could also add *objects*, which tell us something about the world from which they come, through their design, appearance, and behavior, and even through their mere existence as well (for example, a piece of advanced technology suggests a culture with a certain amount of technological achievement). Objects may suggest much about the cultures and world from which they come, but like imagery and sound, the access to a world that they offer is necessarily indirect. Some things, such as playsets (like the LEGO sets based on *Star Wars* characters, vehicles, and locations) only *refer* to things in imaginary worlds, without being actual objects *from* those worlds (apart from in the imaginations of those who play with them). Likewise, even movie props (like Luke Skywalker's lightsaber), though they are the actual objects seen in the films, are at the same time *not* the objects of the imaginary world in another sense; Luke's lightsaber, for example, cannot produce a glowing blade the way it does in the film without the help of special effects. Stage props, though they are seen directly by the audience, also are stand-ins for other objects due to the imposition of theatrical conventions.

Such objects may *refer* to objects in an imaginary world, or stand in for them, but they cannot *be* those objects any more than actors are the characters they play, or people from an imaginary world can enter into the Primary World. Only within fiction itself is such dual citizenship in both Primary and secondary worlds possible, and perhaps this explains its popularity there.

While images and sounds are clearly sensory-oriented, working directly with the eye and ear, words and interactions are arguably more indirect and abstract. Although words become incarnate either graphically or sonically, they are concepts or ideas, able to engage an audience in complex ways, for example, through the description of a smell, taste, or emotion, or the internal thoughts of a character. Though they function more indirectly in the representation of a sensory experience than do images and sounds, they are also more flexible in the kinds of experiences they are able to represent. Interactions, likewise, tell us about the behaviors of things, the way things react and interact when prompted by someone. Like words, interactions are conceptual in nature and rely on graphic and sonic means for their expression. Words, images, objects, sounds, and interactions, then, are the five elements that make up the windows through which we experience imaginary worlds.

Media use these five elements in different ways to construct their windows, and there is much overlap as well between media: novels use the written word (though they may include maps); visual media like photography and film can include the written word within their images; aural media like radio can include the spoken word along with music and sound; audiovisual media can include word, image, and sound together; interactive media like video games can include words, images, sounds, and interactions; and playsets can incorporate all of these along with their objects. These overlaps make transmedial growth and adaptation easier, since the same elements may be present in different media; voices, visual designs, names, and so forth often carry over from one medium to another, strengthening transmedial ties. At the same time, however, differences between media impose limits and constraints during the process of transmedial expansion.

Transmedial Expansion

The work in which a world debuts usually must be able to stand on its own, since it introduces its world and because it will be judged on its own merits rather than by the reputation of a predecessor (though a work may receive attention due to an author's or company's reputation). Narrative often plays a part in a world's first appearance, since the reason most worlds are made is to serve and support a particular story that the author wants to tell, a story which for some reason cannot simply be set in the Primary World alone. Once the world is crafted to fit the initial story or stories, all later works set in the world will have to take into consideration the pre-existing aspects of the world set up by works that preceded them (which explains why some sequels are not as good as the stories they follow). Narrative extensions of the original story, covering the further adventures or backstories of characters, the exploration of new areas of a world, and so forth, have already been discussed in Chapter 4; how these extensions make the leap from one medium to another will be examined here.

During the move from one medium to another, forms of mediation may be lost or gained, causing the material of a story or world to be changed. These processes also occur as the world itself comes into being, moving from a conception in the author's mind to an incarnation in mediated form; thus even a work that is not transmedial undergoes at least one of these transformations. Looking at the list of media windows from the last section, we can describe processes of transformation involving each of them: *description* (adaptation into words), *visualization* (adaptation into images or objects), *auralization* (adaptation into sounds), *interactivation* (adaptation into interactive media), and *deinteractivation* (adaptation moving from interactive media to noninteractive media).[8] While all of these processes also occur in the transmedial adaptation of stories set in the Primary World, the problems encountered within them are especially heightened when they are applied to the adaptation of secondary worlds, because the use of Primary World defaults are not relied upon to the same degree (since so many of them are reset), leading to greater challenges but also to new possibilities.

Description

As discussed in Chapter 5, worlds often originate in words, because they are the fastest, easiest, most malleable, and most inexpensive elements to use when world-building. Words can describe conceptual ideas that have no perceptual forms; unshowable things like the inner states and unexpressed emotions of characters, and impressionistic experiences which the author describes in terms of how they make someone *feel*, instead of just what is seen and heard. In *The Lord of the Rings*, for example, Treebeard's eyes and Saruman's voice are described in such a way that we do not so much get a physical description of how they look and sound respectively, but rather the effect that they have on those who perceive them:

> But at the moment the hobbits noted little but the eyes. These deep eyes were now surveying them, slow and solemn, but very penetrating. They were brown, shot with a green light. Often afterwards Pippin tried to describe his first impression of them.
>
> "One felt as if there was an enormous well behind them, filled up with ages of memory and long, slow, steady thinking; but their surface was sparkling with the present: like sun shimmering on the outer leaves of a vast tree, or on the ripples of a very deep lake. I don't know but it felt as if something that grew in the ground—asleep, you might say, or just feeling itself as something between root-tip and leaf-tip, between deep earth and sky had suddenly waked up, and was considering you with the same slow care that it had given to its own inside affairs for endless years."[9]

Interestingly, Tolkien even mediates the description through Pippin's words, which are of course Tolkien's own as well. Saruman's voice receives a similar treatment, with a description of its effect rather than merely its sound:

> Suddenly another voice spoke, low and melodious, its very sound an enchantment. Those who listened unwarily to that voice could seldom report the words that they heard; and if they did, they wondered, for little power remained in them. Mostly they remembered only that it was a delight to hear the voice speaking, all that it said seemed wise and reasonable, and desire awoke in them by swift agreement to seem wise themselves. When others spoke they seemed harsh and uncouth by contrast; and if they gainsaid the voice, anger was kindled in the hearts of those under the spell. For some the spell lasted only while the voice spoke to them, and when it spoke to another they smiled, as men do who see through a juggler's trick while others gape at it. For many the sound of the voice alone was enough to hold them enthralled; but for those whom it conquered the spell endured when they were far away, and ever they heard that soft voice whispering and urging them. But none were unmoved; none rejected its pleas and its commands without an effort of mind and will, so long as its master had control of it.[10]

Both Treebeard's eyes and Saruman's voice would be hard to incarnate into image and sound without losing the powers that Tolkien can attribute to them in a written description. Words can also control the level of vagueness that an author desires, and they can easily be manipulated to hide ellipses, helping them to go unnoticed in a text. Finally, they allow anyone to produce as elaborate and epically-scaled a world as one can imagine for no more than the cost of pencil and paper, making them the most common elements used in world-building.

On the other hand, words are also the most provocative and connotative of world-building elements, relying upon the audience's experiences and world gestalten to produce their effects. As Tolkien puts it:

> The radical distinction between all art (including drama) that offers a *visible* presentation and true literature is that it imposes one visible form. Literature works from mind to mind and is thus more progenitive. It is at once more universal and more poignantly particular. If it speaks of *bread* or *wine* or *stone* or *tree*, it appeals to the whole of these things, to their ideas; yet each hearer will give to them a peculiar personal embodiment in his imagination. Should the story say "he ate bread", the dramatic producer or painter can only show "a piece of bread" according to his taste or fancy, but the hearer of the story will think of bread in general picture it in some form of his own. If a story says "he climbed a hill and saw a river in the valley below", the illustrator may catch, or nearly catch, his own vision of such

a scene; but every hearer of the words will have his own picture, and it will be made out of all the hills and rivers and dales he has ever seen, but especially out of The Hill, The River, The Valley which were for him the first embodiment of the word.[11]

In the making of his works, Tolkien takes on the role of architect, art director, costume designer, set decorator, and more, giving detailed verbal descriptions of all the sensory aspects of his world, using words to evoke a range of experiences, skillfully playing upon his readers' connotations while reining them in when necessary.

The connotative nature of words, however, becomes a problem when adaptation from other media occurs. The subtleties of a sunset, the vast visual spectacle of a landscape overrun by warring armies, the sound of a Beethoven symphony, the vertiginous changes in perspective during a cinematic chase scene, or even a cleverly composed set of panels filling a page of a graphic novel, is difficult, if not impossible, to translate into mere words. The rhetorical device of *ekphrasis* (the literary attempt to describe a visual work of art) has been around since Ancient Greece, but it can only go so far in evoking its subject, and may, like the examples given above, resort to describing the experience of perception as much as the object being perceived, in order to achieve its effect.

The connotative meanings of words can also come into play in invented languages, where linguistic aesthetics may play a part in generating meaning or at least the language's appeal. Similar to the linguistic "false friends" mentioned in Chapter 1, invented words may carry different connotations or meanings to speakers of different languages, or the invented words may even have meaning in another language. Discussing an invented language in *Star Wars*, Paul Hirsch recalled, "Ben Burtt came up with the language for Greedo. But one of the words he had was actually Spanish slang. He didn't know and so he changed the word. Actually, all the words had to be checked to make sure they were okay."[12] There is also the question of how invented languages should be translated or if they should be translated at all. Regarding the translation of *The Lord of the Rings*, Tolkien allowed English-based names to be translated (such as "Brandywine"), but wanted his invented words left as they were (the Swedish translation of *The Hobbit* had substituted *Hompen* for *Hobbit*, much to Tolkien's displeasure).[13]

Description, then, is especially useful for transmedial expansions of worlds that already exist in visual media (like the dozens of *Star Trek* and *Star Wars* novels), since audiences will have visual imagery to reference as they read verbal descriptions of the world's contents. Even if the written works introduce new characters, locations, and objects, the style and aesthetics of the existing visual imagery will still be able to carry over and influence how the new material will be envisioned in the imagination of the audience. And, as audiences imagine what they read, they take part in another process which many world-builders use: visualization.

Visualization

Visualization gives a concrete and visible form to things which are conceived in words (or sounds), adapting them into still images, moving images, or three-dimensional objects or models (physical or virtual) which are used in the production of still and moving imagery. Images can do many things that mere words cannot; they are sensually richer and more immersive, they can present a great deal of detail or information simultaneously and use complex compositions, and they have a more immediate effect on the audience's emotions, from foregrounded dramatic action to subtle effects involving atmosphere and mood. Although visual media are sometimes faulted for their failure to exercise the imagination the way reading does, seeing things does not reduce the need for imagination; it merely makes different use of it, especially where the revelation of worlds is concerned. While the written word may require the reader to imagine how things look and sound, imagery can present scenes of rich detail, visuals which suggest much and present many more gaps where information and explanation need to be filled in, encouraging extrapolation and speculation; for example, complicated machinery that challenges us to figure out its workings (see Figure 6.1), dense cityscapes that suggest the ongoing lives of millions of inhabitants, or background details which may provide narrative clues and hints of other events occurring simultaneously.[14] Such visual material is often not explained explicitly, and may require multiple viewings in order to be understood (or even noticed); likewise, background details and events may even take on great significance only in retrospect. Visualization may answer the question as to how things look, but it often raises many other questions regarding the purpose, functioning, usage, and history of what is depicted, especially in the depiction of secondary worlds in which Primary World defaults have changed.

Visualizations adapted from written works may range widely based on artists' interpretations. For example, Tolkien's work has been adapted into visual form by a variety of artists such as Alan Lee and John Howe (whose designs were an influence on Peter Jackson's film versions of Tolkien's works), Pauline Baynes, Ted Nasmith, Michael Hague, Ralph Bakshi, and dozens of other artists, including Tolkien himself who illustrated many scenes from his works. Douglas A. Anderson's *The Annotated Hobbit* also gives samples of illustrations from foreign language editions of *The Hobbit* from around the world, demonstrating a wide range of graphical styles.[15]

A visualization not only depicts events, but necessarily does so from a particular vantage point, which means that point of view and composition can be used to further comment on the scene, enhance aspects of it, and suggest a certain attitude towards what is portrayed. When applied to the depiction of a world, multiple angles and varying points of view are necessary to give the world a dimensional, fully-realized feel. Such visual world-building can be done with sketches, requiring some artistic talent, or with photorealistic imagery, which can

FIGURE 6.1 Examples of machinery encountered in *Myst III: Exile* (2001) which players learn about through examination and interaction.

be a costly venture and place demands on a world-builder's budget. *Star Trek* television series episodes, for example, often begin scenes with establishing shots of cityscapes on foreign planets which are matte paintings or models with minimal movement (an occasional vehicle or monorail car passing through), only to complete the rest of the scene with interiors shot in the studio. With a higher budget, more can be done to give a world's imagery an even more fully-realized appearance; for example, the planetscapes of the *Star Wars* movies, which feature three-dimensional fly-throughs of cities and locations seen from multiple angles and under varying lighting and weather conditions, and even at different scales.

The process of visualization in cinema has developed over time into a set of techniques. Storyboards first developed with the planning of animated films, and then were used by live-action filmmakers like Alfred Hitchcock. *Star Wars* (1977) went beyond storyboards to motion graphics, using World War II aerial fighter plane footage to demonstrate how its spaceships would move, and later *Star Wars* films used animatics, moving storyboards that allow shot dynamics like compositional movement and temporal length to be planned out in advance of production. This phase of production has come to be known as "pre-visualization" or "pre-viz", with the "pre" prefix indicating that it takes place before the visualization that occurs when the footage is actually shot or composited, although "pre-visualization" is certainly a form of visualization as well.

Of course, adaptation into visual form presents problems as well. The "normalizing tendency" discussed in Chapter 1, in which an audience adjusts their imagination according to Primary World defaults, suggests that a literal adaptation into visual form may not always be the best one; recall the example of Gandalf's eyebrows extending beyond the brim of his hat. Although Tolkien gives this description, seeing it all the time would produce an almost comic effect; thus in nearly every visual interpretation, Gandalf's eyebrows do not extend so far, even when they are shown as bushy. A further example is C. S. Lewis' *Perelandra* (1943), in which characters are naked for most of the story; easy to do in print, but far more distracting in a movie (it's one thing to *know* that someone is naked, and another to *see* it all the time).

Adaptation into visual form, even when the end result is two-dimensional imagery, usually requires adapting verbal descriptions into three-dimensional designs, especially for media with moving imagery or multiple images which view things from multiple angles, and even single images which use perspective will need to be conceived in three dimensions (some exceptions exist, like the two-dimensional worlds of Abbott's Flatland, Dewdney's Planiverse, and two-dimensional video games). These three-dimensional designs may remain designs drawn on paper, become virtual objects seen on a computer screen, or become actual, physical objects constructed for a stage play, film set, or playset.

The oldest kind of adaptation into three-dimensional form is visualization for the stage, going back to the plays of ancient Greece that depicted imaginary worlds like Aristophanes's Cloudcuckooland. The limitations of the stage, however, make for the harshest kind of adaptation, especially when it comes to the fantastic. While J. R. R. Tolkien was not against a film version of *The Lord of the Rings*, he was critical of the attempt to bring fantasy to the stage, writing:

> In human art Fantasy is a thing best left to words, to true literature. In painting, for instance, the visible presentation of the fantastic image is technically too easy; the hand tends to outrun the mind, even overthrow it. Silliness or morbidity are frequent results. It is a misfortune that Drama, an art fundamentally distinct from Literature, should so commonly be considered together with it, or as a branch of it. Among these misfortunes, we may reckon the depreciation of Fantasy. ... Drama is naturally hostile to Fantasy. Fantasy, even of the simplest kind, hardly ever succeeds in Drama. Fantastic forms are not to be counterfeited. Men dressed up as talking animals may achieve buffoonery or mimicry, but they do not achieve Fantasy. This is, I think, well illustrated by the failure of the bastard form, pantomime. The nearer it is to "dramatised fairy-story" the worse it is. It is only tolerable when the plot and its fantasy are reduced to a mere vestigiary framework for farce, and no "belief" is required or expected of anybody. This is, of course, partly due to the fact that the producers of drama have to, or try to, work with mechanism to represent either Fantasy or Magic. I once saw a so-called "children's pantomime", the straight story of *Puss-in-Boots*, with even the metamorphosis of the ogre into a mouse. Had this been mechanically successful it would have either terrified the spectators or else have been just a turn of high-class conjuring. As it was, though done with some ingenuity of lighting, disbelief had not so much to be suspended as hung, drawn, and quartered.[16]

Tolkien's comments, however, were not directed at film or animation, nor could he have envisioned the degree to which cinematic special effects would be able to appear photorealistic in their appearance and behavior.

The process of film production can involve the rendering of things mentioned in the script into visible form first as two-dimensional drawings (storyboards and sketches of costumes, sets, props, characters, and so forth), and then those drawings are adapted into three-dimensional forms, making such visualization a two-step process. Here, too, problems can occur with the change in dimensionality; unclear notes can lead to objects the wrong size on the set (for example, during the making of *Star Wars Episode III: Revenge of the Sith* (2005), a table that was supposed to be 10 feet wide was 16 feet wide due to a misread digit[17]), and designs must accommodate other considerations such as the human actors (during the making of *Star Wars Episode II: Attack of the Clones* (2002), costumes were drawn and made into maquettes (small, physical models) that had unrealistic body shapes and dimensions and had to be redesigned to fit the actresses[18]). Likewise, translation between physical models and digital models of the same things can present design challenges (like getting the digital version of Yoda to match the physical puppet version that audiences were already familiar with[19]).

Although visualization is usually a multi-step process as designs move across media and the different technologies used to create them, it can also occur directly from a conception into a three-dimensional form, provided the necessary tools are available. Computer animation programs allow three-dimensional models to be created directly in the computer, and physical processes like sculpting also begin in three dimensions. Another method for building three-dimensional models directly is through assemblage. Designer Joe Johnston describes the building of the speeder bikes in *The Return of the Jedi* (1983):

> The rocket bikes were built entirely in three dimensions. There were some preliminary sketches done, but once the final design was set, it was all done in model, you know, kit bashing. You'd take model kits, and you'd chop them off, and you'd get the pieces and use them to build the bikes. There're a lot of different pieces on the bikes; there's a space shuttle nose that is part of the exhaust flaring at the back; there's a part of a formula car that's up front; there's a Ferrari engine as part of the rocket engine, etc. … So in a way the rocket bikes were pretty unique because the design was determined more in three dimensions than it was on paper.[20]

This process also is amenable to collaborative efforts; according to Jody Duncan, "Throughout the design process, [*George*] Lucas would often break off parts from one model and attach them to another to create an entirely new design."[21] The use of computer graphics also allows designs to be made, and edited, directly in three dimensions, and the resulting computer models can be used by multiple departments, ensuring better communication and design consistency.[22]

Considering that most imaginary worlds begin in the realm of words and find their way across media, visualization is perhaps the most common process occurring during transmedial adaptation. As worlds are planned to be transmedial from their very conception, more of a world's look can be designed from the beginning, and more tools exist now than ever before to aid in the visualization process. Alongside visualization is another process that often occurs with it and which influences it as well: sound design.

Auralization

While much has been written about visualization, its sister process, auralization, or adaptation into sound, is far less discussed. After words, sound is the most inexpensive element to work with because of its flexibility and ease of manipulation. Sound is naturally immersive, surrounding the listener in space, providing atmosphere and evoking emotional responses; it can imply large spaces and a world through ambience and sound effects. Secondary worlds, with their invented languages, new creatures, vehicles, weaponry, and fantastic locations are often strongly associated with the sounds devised for them, and these sounds can be used across a variety of media to bind an imaginary world together even when the visual styles of works in different media vary considerably. Like imagery, sounds often cannot be described in words; for those who have seen the *Star Wars* films, the familiar sounds of a lightsaber's swooping hums, TIE fighters screaming through space, or Chewbacca's throaty roar will instantly bring to mind images from the films with a directness that text can only try to suggest. Sound designers, then, must envision (en*audition?*) sounds that are appropriate and capture the personality and feel of the visual designs, hopefully making as memorable an impression.

Apart from sound design, auralization can also involve turning words or imagery into sounds, or translating story material into voices, sound effects, music, and ambience. To look at the process of transmedial auralization here, it might be useful to compare three worlds being presented solely through sound; radio adaptations of *The Lord of the Rings* (adapted from a novel), the *Star Wars* radio plays (adapted from movies), and Garrison Keillor's Lake Wobegon (which originated as a radio program). In all three, there is, as one would suspect, a heavy dependence on the spoken word (particularly character dialogue) with sound effects filling in narrative information; but as each has a different medium of origin, the end results vary widely. Consider, for example, differences in length, resulting from compression and expansion of the original material.

The first adaptation of *The Lord of the Rings* was produced by Terence Tiller for the BBC in 1955–1956, an American adaptation by The Mind's Eye for National Public Radio appeared in 1979, and another BBC adaptation, by Brian Sibley and Michael Bakewell, appeared in 1981. The first BBC adaptation was the only one made during Tolkien's lifetime, and he was understandably displeased with it; the BBC allotted 3 hours for *The Fellowship of the Ring*, but then decided to only allot 3 hours more for the story's completion, rather than 3 hours for *The Two Towers* and another 3 hours for *The Return of the King*. (In the end, 6 hours proved to be too short and demanded such omissions and compression that the recording was evidently not valued enough to be preserved, since no copies of the broadcast are known to have survived.) The American adaptation made in 1979 was 12 hours long, and the second BBC one that followed shortly after it in 1981 was around 13 hours and 20 minutes long. While the 1981 version has received the most praise, it was also still quite abridged when one considers that the unabridged audio book of *The Lord of the Rings* read and performed by Rob Inglis in 2002 was 55 hours long.

Since *The Lord of The Rings* began as a book, voice casting of the characters had some latitude, since the character's voices had never been heard before. At the same time, they would have to be distinct enough to become recognizable after a short time, although those familiar with the book could tell who was speaking through context. Sound effects, likewise, might require additional explanation as some of the sounds would not be instantly understood and connected with things in the book; for instance, the sounds of various fictional creatures, or the ambient sound of different locations, might not be recognizable out of context.

By contrast, the *Star Wars* radio plays, were *longer* than the films from which they were adapted; the original film version of *Star Wars* (1977) was 2 hours and 1 minute long, while the radio version was 5 hours and 51 minutes; *The Empire Strikes Back* (1980) was 2 hours and 9 minutes in theaters but 4 hours and 15 minutes on radio; and *Return of the Jedi* (1983) was 2 hours and 16 minutes on film, and 3 hours on the air. Although both films and radio plays included Ben Burtt's sound effects, the radio plays added expository dialogue, and opened up the storyline, adding scenes that further explained what was going on and providing more back-story and additional conversations and events. Audiences familiar with the films may have naturally expected the film actors to voice their characters, and some did, including Mark Hamill, Anthony Daniels, and Billy Dee Williams; but some were replaced by other voices; Princess Leia was played by Ann Sachs, Han Solo by Perry King, Darth Vader by Brock Peters, Yoda by John Lithgow, and Jabba the Hutt by Ed Asner. To further frustrate expectations, although Mark Hamill voiced Luke Skywalker in the radio plays of the first two films, Joshua Fardon voiced Luke Skywalker for the third. While the *Star Wars* stories were more complete than the adaptations of Tolkien's work, the use of different voice actors was an unexpected change which also demanded audience adjustment. Audiences who had seen the films before listening to the radio plays, however, had a guide to visualization, even for the added scenes and dialogues in the radio plays.

Finally, Keillor's Lake Wobegon stories, appearing on his long-running radio program *A Prairie Home Companion*, are conceived and written for the air as radio programs, avoiding issues of compression and additions and audience expectations based on other media. The world of Lake Wobegon has successfully expanded into several novels, but as the characters and locations are so well established in the minds of listeners, it seems unlikely that there will ever be a movie about Lake Wobegon exploring it visually (in 2006 a movie was made about *The Prairie Home Companion* show, but this should not be confused with the Lake Wobegon stories themselves). The Lake Wobegon stories' reliance on Keillor as voiceover narrator, and voice actors who are not film actors, make radio the best medium for the world to appear in.[23]

Auralization also applies to interactive sound, which functions differently from noninteractive sound due to the game player's need to continually make decisions based on changing game information. In addition to aesthetic concerns like those described earlier, sounds are designed to provide orientation as well as exposition. According to Miles Griffiths, Senior Designer at SCI Games:

> All we have to do is present the player with as much information to process as possible. Given that the player can only look at one thing at a time, the best way to do this is with sound. First off, a good ambient track sets the tone. The distant thump and crackle of explosives and gunfire give the

illusion that combat is occurring over a wide area. On top of this, every foregrounded gunshot, scream, garbled radio message, and vehicle engine contributes to an illusion of great activity. Positional sound can make a player feel like he is in the middle of a huge cauldron of action, turning a small-scale skirmish into just one fragment of a huge battle.[24]

All of the same considerations in noninteractive media—mood and atmosphere, the feel and emotion evoked by the sound, the quality of the sound and its perspective, and so on—are present in the design of sound for interactive media as well, along with the additional considerations as to how sound can be used to aid orientation and navigation. Sound can introduce things at a distance before they are seen, lure the user in a particular direction, or warn the user from moving in a particular direction. The use of sound in interactive media brings us to the next transmedial adaptation process, that of making something interactive, which we might call *interactivation* (in the same way that "activation" means "to make something active").

Interactivation

Interactivity cannot be present by itself; it requires words, images, sounds, or physical objects (like a playset), or some combination of them, in order for interactivity to be possible. As such, some description, visualization, or auralization is required as a prerequisite to interactivation. A model of the world (or a copy of the world itself, in the case of a world originating in digital form) must be constructed which can be interacted with by the user, which usually includes the exploration of the world's spaces, the witnessing of events in the world, and interaction with other characters in the world. This can be done using only description (as in a text adventure game), but more likely it involves visualization and auralization of the world's assets.

The interactivation of a world differs from the interactivation of a narrative insofar as a world already implies multiple paths of action that a visitor can take. As discussed in Chapter 4, a world may contain a set of canonical stories that take place within it, but the degree to which these are included in an interactive work will vary considerably, and may even depend on the user whose choices will set events in motion or keep them from occurring. Either way, the world, as a set of locations, objects, and characters, can still be depicted and offered for exploration.

As a process of transmedial adaptation, interactivation usually requires that a world be simplified in order for interaction and exploration to be possible, since the larger and more detailed a world is, the more interactive possibilities arise. While the worlds of print, film, and television can selectively use locations and other world assets, needing only glimpses or even just mentions of some areas, users who cannot freely explore all the areas of a world may become more aware of the world's constraints and limitations, which in turn may damage a world's illusion of completeness. As Owain Bennalack, editor of the video game magazine *Develop*, puts it:

> The problem a game designer has, compared to a novelist or a filmmaker, is the "What's behind the door?" conundrum. ... If there are doors that can't be opened, then the player is going to step back from really being there. It breaks the spell. On the other hand, if any door can be opened, the world is going to have to be pretty straightforward—or else it's not going to have many doors![25]

Thus, many video game worlds are careful to have diegetic explanations that help make their world's boundaries seem natural, keeping their worlds from feeling confined. For example, some games or game levels are set aboard space stations (like the first level of *Halo* (2001)), in buildings that the player is trying to escape from (as in *Doom* (1993)), on islands (like *Myst* (1993), *Riven* (1997), and *Alida* (2004)), or in cities where only a few roads lead out of town (like the cities of the *Grand Theft Auto* series). To help add a feeling of expansiveness to these worlds, there are two types of boundaries, those prohibiting movement (like walls and shorelines), and beyond them, those prohibiting visibility, where vistas stretch into the distance to the horizon or into outer space, making the world appear vaster than it is.

While a world adapted into a game is usually simplified, narrative material is often expanded during the transmedial move to interactivity, allowing more possibilities to open up to the player's choices. Neil Randall and Kathleen Murphy describe the adaption that occurred in *The Lord of the Rings Online* (2007):

> Players need to be able to step into the world of the adapted story and spend a significant amount of time in that world, exploring its many locations and engaging with the characters and objects drawn from or even simply suggested by the source text. In addition, to meet the same requirement of long-term immersive player involvement, videogame adaptations must expand the scope of the original story, allowing players to meet added characters performing added tasks and fitting into added plots and subplots. They must allow players to explore what is happening in that world beyond the scope of the storyline presented in the source.[26]

Worlds adapted into games from other media come with audience expectations based on their source material, making it harder for them to succeed than games whose worlds originate within them and are thus designed with interactivity in mind. In the case of games adapted from feature films, a host of other factors, including tight production schedules, changing story information as the project passes through production and postproduction, and conflicting demands from the various constituencies (administrative, financial, marketing, technical, and so on) that have a stake in the production of a game, also make it more difficult for games adapted from movies to succeed.[27]

Game worlds adapted from worlds originating in noninteractive media are often not so much an extension of those worlds, as they are alternate versions of them. For example, the massively multiplayer on-line role-playing games (MMORPGs) *Star Wars Galaxies* (2003–2011) and *The Lord of the Rings Online* both are designed after their respective worlds from other media, but exist alongside them as separate worlds with their own separate histories that accrue as players play them. Since the events of the *Star Wars* films have already occurred, they can at best only be reenacted in *Star Wars Galaxies*, as they, and their outcomes, are already well known. One solution to the question of how to treat existing canonical events is to set the interactive world in another time period, long after the events from other works set in the world, the way the MMORPG *Uru: Ages Beyond Myst* (2003) takes place long after the events of the Myst games and novels that came before it, placing their canonical events in the past so that consistency and continuity can remain undisrupted. Another solution, as discussed in Chapter 4, is to have one "correct" set of events leading to the "right" ending which the player must achieve in order to win, so that only one course of events remains canonical.

The interactivation of a world presents continuity problems which are not faced by worlds which originate in interactive media and are designed with interactivity in mind, but these problems can be solved by the boundaries placed on interactivity. As more worlds are planned in advance as transmedial worlds, their interactive works can be designed to occupy either time periods left open by their noninteractive works, allowing audience participation to determine events, or they could also be set during the events occurring in the noninteractive works, but be limited spatially or narratively to events outside of the mainstream of canonical events in such a way that the player's deeds will not affect them. When interactive worlds make transmedial moves into noninteractive media, continuity is much easier to control, although the move must also deal with deinteractivation.

Deinteractivation

Worlds making transmedial moves are subject not only to gains and additions, but to losses and reductions as well. In this sense, description and visualization are complementary processes, insofar as one involves moving from image to word and the other from word to image; the same can be said of the relationship between description and auralization. Likewise, as interactivation occurs during the move from noninteractive media to interactive media, *deinteractivation*, the removal of interactivity, occurs when a world moves in the other direction, from interactive media to noninteractive media; for example, when worlds originating in video games are adapted into films, television shows, or books.

Deinteractivation usually involves the addition of narrative material, since the removal of interactivity often requires substituting a fixed series of events for the series of events that would otherwise occur as a result of the choices made by the user.[28] Even a speedrun video made from a video game will contain a fixed series of events which are not necessarily the same as what a player will encounter. The adaptation of a video game into a movie usually requires a large amount of additional narrative material, particularly when it is lacking in the game (for example, the adaptation of *Super Mario Bros.* (1985) into the 1993 movie of the same name or the adaptation of *Pac-Man* (1980) into the 42-episode television series *Pac-Man: The Animated Series* (1982–1983), as opposed to the adaptation of more cinematic games which already have three-dimensional worlds and more thoroughly-developed narratives). Just as movies that "open up" theatrical plays often differ from their source material, there is always the chance that the added material and change of medium and conventions will considerably alter the original world. At the same time, player interaction is the main reason for most games to exist, and without it, there may be little to interest an audience. It may be possible to exchange one type of interactivity for another (which occurs in the Pokémon card game or the board games based on *Pac-Man* and *Myst*), but the change from one type of interactivity to another can itself involve some degree of deinteractivation (for example, imagine the loss of direct action if *Pac-Man* was adapted into a text adventure (see www.pac-txt.com)).

The process of deinteractivation also removes the player's close identification with their avatar (which is usually the game's main character). Instead of being a surrogate for the player, the move to a noninteractive medium means that the audience must now watch as the character acts independently and makes its own decisions. In the case of first-person perspective games, where the point of view is that of the main character who is rarely seen directly, the loss of interactivity will be even more noticeable. Little can compensate directly for this loss of character identification since it is qualitatively different from the third-party character identification found in film and literature; and the shift from one to the other may also underscore the latter's noninteractive nature. In exchange for the control of the main character, the move to noninteractive media will usually mean a more developed world, often with a higher degree of realism and characters who are presented with more depth, and situations with more complexity and nuance. Whether or not these tradeoffs are acceptable to the audience will determine the success of the transmedial expansion, and perhaps even the future of the franchise in the new medium.

Like interactivation, the process of deinteractivation is easier if the new work is set in a different part of the world than its interactive counterparts. When the Myst franchise expanded into three novels, the novels were set in time periods before and after the action of the games. The first novel, *Myst: The Book of Atrus* (1995), set the stage for the action occurring in *Myst* (1993); the second novel, *Myst: The Book of Ti'ana* (1996) expanded the backstory of the first novel; and the third novel, *Myst: The Book of D'ni* (1997) was set some time after the events of *Riven* (1997). While the events of the games are central to the franchise, they do not contradict the events of the novels, which for the most part can stand on their own, narratively speaking.

The experience of deinteractivation, from the point of view of the audience, can even apply to transmedial worlds that begin in noninteractive media and move to interactive media, if the audience encounters the interactive works of the world first and the noninteractive works afterward. This, however, leads us to the next section, which considers the order in which the audience encounters the various works set in a particular world.

Encountering Transmedial Worlds

How an audience first enters into an imaginary world, and the sequence in which the various works making it up are experienced, can greatly shape the audience's experience of the world. While in the past worlds began in one medium and, if they found success there, made their way into other media, worlds have recently become more transmedial from their very inception, making the question of the ordering and timing of works in different media all set in the same world something which is considered from the start and shapes the world-building process thereafter. As Danny Bilsen, Executive Vice President of Core Games for THQ describes it:

> Finally, we are finding that the ultimate challenge for delivering transmedia experiences is one of production and timing. How can these pieces be built, how often on different systems and at different costs and how can they be delivered in the most rewarding sequence to the fans? For instance, a film may take a year or two to produce; a video game may take three years; and a graphic novel six months. Getting these to arrive in the most dramatic sequence is a new challenge that transmedia producers only now are having the privilege of facing. But it still all starts and ends with a robust and consistent world, created and managed by inspired visionaries, who are themselves its biggest fans.[29]

Since the first works to appear will introduce the imaginary world to the audience, setting the tone and expectations, an early failure could have the effect of producing a negative image of the world, making it more difficult for other works set in the same world to find backing and an audience (imagine, for example, if the old Marvel *Star Wars* comics and 1978 holiday TV special appeared first and their success determined whether or not the films would be made). From a practical standpoint, some media are easier to use or less expensive to produce, and more likely to be used to introduce a world; thus more worlds are debuted in novels than in feature films or television series. However, even though authors may take care to produce and release works in a particular order, audience members may still experience those works in an altogether different sequence.

Although a series of works can be experienced in any order, there are six types of orderings that are most likely to occur, each of which changes one's experience of a world: order of public appearance, order of creation, internal chronological order, canonical order, order of media preference, and age-appropriate order. Probably the most common of these is order of public appearance, which contemporary audiences, who experience the works as they appear, are most likely to follow. Series of works set in a world are almost always designed to be experienced in order of public appearance, and even when worlds are planned in advance, release order is the most likely order to be experienced. Once several works set in the same world have been released, though, later audiences will have more of a choice, and can enter into a world or franchise through any of its works, determining for themselves the order in which the works will be experienced.

Another common way that works are experienced is in the order of creation, which is usually the same as the order of public appearance. By experiencing works in this order, one can watch a world grow as the author develops it, and also experience the suspense and surprises built into the narrative structures; as discussed in Chapter 4, watching the *Star Wars* episodes in the original order they were made (IV, V, VI, I, II, III) is quite different from watching them according to their internal chronological order (I, II, III, IV, V, VI). The order of creation, however, can vary from the order of public appearance; for example, the order of publication of the seven Narnia books was *The Lion, the Witch and the Wardrobe* (1950), *Prince Caspian* (1951), *The Voyage of the Dawn Treader* (1952), *The Silver Chair* (1953), *The Horse and His Boy* (1954), *The Magician's Nephew* (1955), and *The Last Battle* (1956), while the order in which the books were actually completed runs *Wardrobe, Caspian, Treader, Horse, Chair, Battle,* and *Nephew* (and by internal chronological order, the books run *Nephew, Wardrobe, Horse, Caspian, Treader, Chair, Battle*). When the order of creation differs from the order of public appearance, it is often because the author is working on multiple works simultaneously, or because different teams may be working on works in different media designed to be released together (for example, the movie *The Matrix Reloaded* and the video game *Enter the Matrix* were developed simultaneously and were both released on May 15, 2003), a situation referred to as "co-creation" in the industry.[30] In cases of co-creation and simultaneous releases, both order of creation and order of public appearance will give way to other kinds of sequencing.

Internal chronological order is also a common way of experiencing a series of works, since following a world's internal chronology reveals the world's diegetic history and development, the arcs of its characters, and the resolution of its conflicts. While internal chronological order often matches order of public appearance for the most part, the fact that prequels are now a common sequence element means that chronological order is often not the best way to experience a series of works, since prequels are often made with the assumption that the audience is already familiar with worked released prior to them. Experiencing a prequel before the works that precede it can destroy enigmas by explaining them too soon; by revealing causes before their effects, by revealing secrets that drive suspense, or by giving the backstory of characters who are supposed to remain mysterious for awhile to achieve a certain effect in the narrative (for example, when Aragorn, Yoda, and Morpheus are first introduced in their respective worlds, other characters do not know who they are and neither is the audience supposed to know who they are at that point). Internal chronological order, then, is more useful once one is familiar with the works set in the world already, allowing one to get a better sense of how events relate to each other, as well as to test the consistency of a world's cause-and-effect structures. Internal chronological order is often provided by timelines and chronologies of a world's events, although transquels and simultaneous events can complicate the arrangement of a set of works into chronological order.

For larger worlds, another type of ordering is what we could call canonical order, in which the most canonical material is experienced first, with less canonical material experienced later. Since the most canonical material is usually what constitutes the core of the world, and what makes it popular if it is popular, it makes sense to begin there; and if one enjoys the world and wants more of it, one then moves to the spin-offs and derivative works next, rather than begin with ancillary works (it seems very unlikely that someone would read multiple *Star Wars* novels without ever having seen the feature films). For many worlds, canonicity is associated with quality and how true a work is to the world's subcreator's vision, thus the best material is often also the most canonical, with less canonical material dropping off somewhat in quality or varying from the author's original ideas.

Transmedial worlds, especially those which have already spread to a variety of media, allow the audience to experience the world in still another order, the order of media preference. People who have never read *The Lord of the Rings* might see the movies instead, since they require less time commitment, and then read the book later if they enjoyed the movie. Transmedial adaptation can make this a strange sequence; for example, there is a 256-page novelization of the movie *Great Expectations* (1998) which is itself based on the much longer Dickens novel of the same name; so someone could begin with the short novelization, see the movie, and then read the full-length Dickens original. The order of media preference may be determined by the investment each medium requires in terms of length, amount of time needed, the cost to purchase or experience a work, and individual media biases. Media preference could also be limited by what media are available, or allowed, leading to the next type of ordering, age-appropriate order.

Children are entering into franchises and worlds at younger and younger ages, making age-appropriate order the way many of them encounter a transmedial world. For example, all of the movies of the *Pirates of the Caribbean* franchise are PG-13, yet there are several LEGO sets based on the films which are designed for children under 13. Age-appropriate works can introduce worlds and the narratives in them through sanitized, simplified, and child-friendly versions of other works set in a world. The LEGO *Star Wars* video games, for instance, feature dozens of cut-scenes which recapitulate the plots of the six feature films, but use LEGO versions of characters in wordless parodies of the film scenes, often including slapstick comedy and leaving out violence or replacing it with some alternative representation (LEGO people falling to pieces rather than being executed realistically). These cut-scenes reveal storylines to children before they have seen the films, yet at the same time, as parody, they are quite different from the actual films. These early experiences, while they undoubtedly generate interest in a franchise or world, also may influence or even spoil the first-time film viewings that come later, ruining surprises and suspense, and giving dramatic scenes humorous connotations as the cut-scenes are recalled. Even reference works like encyclopedias or atlases may give away story information that could affect one's experience of other works. Thus, by courting younger and younger audiences, world-builders may be changing the ways their worlds are experienced and remembered.

Transmedial growth and adaptation enrich an imaginary world beyond what any single medium could present, and also make the world less tied to its medium of origin, giving it greater independence as more media windows are available through which to experience it. Authors can now design worlds for multiple media from their inception, and older worlds may gain new audiences as new interpretations of them in other media appear. Due to the use of multiple media, and the often wide scope and size of the worlds appearing in them, the authorship of such worlds often extends beyond the originator of the world, expanding into concentric circles of authorship, which are the subject of the next chapter.

7

CIRCLES OF AUTHORSHIP

It's strange, especially for a director, to find out you are not the creator. You are instrumental in creating something, but even if you fancy the idea that you pulled it out of yourself, you have to acknowledge that you could not have done it alone.
—Wim Wenders, from an interview in the journal *IMAGE*[1]

Suddenly he said: "Of course you don't suppose, do you, that you wrote all that book yourself?" … I think I said: "No, I don't suppose so any longer." I have never since been able to suppose so. An alarming conclusion for an old philologist to draw concerning his private amusement. But not one that should puff any one up who considers the imperfections of "chosen instruments", and indeed what sometimes seems their lamentable unfitness for the purpose.
—J. R. R. Tolkien, *The Letters of J. R. R. Tolkien*[2]

Despite attacks on them and proclamations of their death, the notions of authorship and the author have endured and show no signs of falling out of use. What has changed, however, is the idea of the author as a lone figure producing a work in isolation, for whom influences and potential consequences play no role in the shaping of a work. The notion of authorship has expanded out to include a variety of roles and acknowledged contributions that make a work what it is, while still maintaining the need for attribution. As Jack Stillinger writes in *Multiple Authorship and the Myth of Solitary Genius*:

> For practical purposes, the single most important aspect of authorship is simply the vaguely apprehended *presence* of human creativity, personality,

and (sometimes) voice that nominal authorship seems to provide. Just as it would be unthinkable for a visitor to an art museum to admire a roomful of paintings without knowing the names of the individual painters and for a concertgoer to sit through a program of symphonies and concertos without knowing the names of the individual composers, so it is impossible to imagine any presentation of writings (even of writings in which Barthes and Foucault contest the existence of authors!) that does not prominently refer to authorship. ...

Obviously, the myth of single authorship is a great convenience for teachers, students, critics, and other readers, as well as for publishers, agents, booksellers, librarians, copyright lawyers—indeed, for everyone connected with the production of books, starting with the authors themselves. The myth is thoroughly embedded in our culture and our ordinary practices, including the ordinary practices of criticism and interpretation, for which, I would argue, it is an absolute necessity. The countering reality of multiple authorship is no threat to the continuing existence of the myth, nor, except for deconstructionist theorists, is there any compelling reason for wanting the myth to cease to exist. Although a deconstructivist approach to interpretation might take comfort in the idea of a plurally altered text, the behavior of deconstructionists as authors of their own texts shows that the myth is in no danger from that quarter.[3]

While Stillinger writes mainly about literature and film, this is especially true of imaginary worlds; the larger they are, the more likely it is that they are the work of many people, not just as influences on an author, but also as workers who contribute new assets and storylines to a world. Imaginary worlds are often not only transmedial and transnarrative, but transauthorial as well.

Authorship, then, can be conceptualized as a series of concentric circles extending out from the world's originator (or originators), with each circle of delegated authority being further removed from the world's origination and involving diminishing authorial contributions, from the originator and main author to estates, heirs, and torchbearers; employees and freelancers; the makers of approved, derivative, and ancillary products that are based on a world; and finally to the noncanonical additions of elaborationists and fan productions. A world's expansion into these circles may occur early on, as transmedial demands require specialized work in different media, or later, as the world continues growing after its originator has retired or died. A world's author or owner, however, can decide to what extent authorship will be delegated, or if it will be at all, determining whether a world will remain open or closed, as well as what material will be considered canonical. Before we examine the different circles, then, we must first consider issues of canonicity, beginning with whether a world is open or closed.

Open and Closed Worlds

An "open" world is a world in which canonical material is still being added; such a world is still growing and developing, as it accrues more information, detail, and narrative. In an open world, an author is also free to change material or the canonical status of material, for example, when retconning occurs. An author can also arrange for a world to remain "open" even after his or her death, passing on the authorial power over the world to some successor along with whatever intellectual property rights may come with it. A "closed" world, on the other hand, is one which its author has declared "finished", meaning that no more canonical material will be added to it. A world may also become closed when an author dies without having passed on the authority to add canonical material to a world, or when someone to whom the author has passed such authority declares that no more canonical material will be added to the world.

Closed worlds can still make transmedial moves, but these will be interpretations instead of true additions (which is to say, none of the added material will be canonical). Thus, a closed world can continue growing as various interpretations and derivative material (like merchandise) appear for it, even after the author is done with it, as the various rights and ownership of the world are passed along to a custodian of the author's choosing. After a time, worlds fall into public domain; today anybody could write and publish a story set in More's Utopia or Butler's Erewhon, but these would still fail to contribute material that everyone would accept as canonical on the same level as the original stories by More and Butler. Both worlds, though public domain, would still remain closed.

Perhaps the most famous *closed* world would be Tolkien's Arda. Although Tolkien wanted to "leave scope for other minds and hands, wielding paint and music and drama",[4] he clearly intended this to mean transmedial interpretation, not additional stories written by others, as is evident in a letter written to his publisher.[5] Christopher Tolkien, chosen as his father's literary executor, has since published much of his father's writings posthumously, but it does not seem likely that he or the Tolkien estate will ever go against his father's wishes and allow stories written by others to add to the tales of Middle-earth (nor would fans be likely to accept new stories written by others as canonical, anyway).

An example of an *open* world would be the *Star Wars* galaxy, which, as of 2012, is still being added to by George Lucas and his employees. The longer a world remains open, the more likely we are to find its authorship spread out over the concentric circles of authorship described in this chapter; and the world of *Star Wars* provides excellent examples of them, as well as a good example of a world with material occupying multiple levels of canonicity.

Levels of Canonicity

The idea of canon, that certain things are "true" for an imaginary world (that characters, locations, and objects exist, and that events have happened within that world), demonstrates the desire for authenticity from the point of view of the audience, who are often concerned with demarcating what is "official" for a world or franchise. Part of this is due to the importance given to authorship; the author is considered the true source of world material, the creative vision that makes it a unified experience. Or at least one hopes it is unified; if others are authorized to contribute to a world, it also becomes a question of what an author is willing to accept, and how much authority has been delegated.

Canonicity is more than just a question of determining whether something is canonical or not. Just as there are circles of authorship, there are differing degrees of canonicity, and purists may accept less material as canonical than will a casual audience member with less interest in (and less knowledge of) a particular world. For example, one could accept only the *Dune* novels written by Frank Herbert, and not those written by his son Brian, even though some of them were developed out of the elder Herbert's notes. Those who view worlds as works of art may not accept anything beyond what was initially produced by the world's originator, recognizing only that which comes from their original artistic vision (which itself may vary over time) as authentic; even retcon performed by the world's originator may be rejected.

Some worlds have very well-defined levels of canonicity. The *Star Wars* Holocron (the franchise's database), managed by Leland Chee, is organized into five levels of canonicity: G-canon (the most recent versions of films Episodes I–VI, the scripts, movie novelizations, radio plays, and Lucas' statements), T-canon (the *Star Wars: The Clone Wars* television show and the live-action *Star Wars* television series); C-canon (the Expanded Universe elements); S-canon (a secondary canon including the role-playing game *Star Wars: Galaxies*); and N-canon (noncanonical material, such as the *Star Wars: Infinities* series of stories). And hierarchies exist even within canon levels; for example, in G-canon, the films are more canonical than the novelizations, and the more recent versions of films are considered more canonical than the older versions of them.[6] Different levels of canon can also disagree on points; for example, while Lucas considers Boba Fett to have died in *Return of the Jedi*, in the Extended Universe (EU) he survives and goes on to further adventures.

To complicate things further, noncanonical works are produced not only by fans, but sometimes by the world's own author or others authorized to produce them; for example, the Energizer battery commercial in which Darth Vader appears with the Energizer Bunny (see Figure 7.1), or the four commercials for Georgia Coffee in which characters from *Twin Peaks* appear. Thus, for a work to be canonical requires that it be declared as such by someone with the authority to do so; authorship alone is not sufficient to determine the work's status. Those works, however, that typically possess the highest degree of canonicity are those which come from the innermost circles of authorship, which surround the originator and main author of a world.

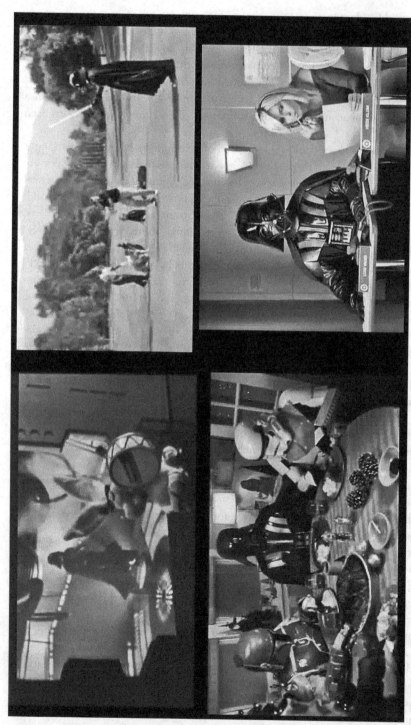

FIGURE 7.1 Some of the noncanonical appearances of Darth Vader allowed by Lucasfilm: in a 1994 Energizer battery commercial (top, left); in a 2009 promotional ad for *Star Wars* on the Space Channel (bottom, left); on the golf course in a 2008 *Star Wars* ad on the Spike Channel (top, right); and in a 2004 ad for Target (bottom right).

Originator and Main Author

The person who conceives of a world, the originator, is usually also the main author responsible for the first work or works appearing in the world; however, it is possible that the two roles are separate, as in the case of some shared worlds in which authors write works set in a world devised by someone else (for example, the planet Uller, invented by John D. Clark and used as the location for three novellas ("The Long View" by Fletcher Pratt, "Uller Uprising" by H. Beam Piper, and "Daughters of Earth" by Judith Merril) which were published together as *The Petrified Planet* (1952)). More often than not, though, the originator and main author are the same. The author, then, invents the world, determines its bounds, and usually builds some of its infrastructures (as discussed in Chapter 3). When the world makes its first public appearance, the author's name becomes associated with it as the source of the world and the authority behind it.

Levels of canonicity may exist even within the main author's own works. If an inconsistency occurs between a major work and a minor work in an author's oeuvre, the major work will likely be considered the more canonical of the two. Likewise, early works or later works may be given greater canonical status. Authors who change their work will undoubtedly prefer the later versions to the early ones (or else the changes would not be made). When those changes amount to retconning, the later work can be seen as preferable, because retconning usually ties earlier works more firmly into the author's world, eliminating inconsistencies. Nevertheless, if the works have existed a long time in their original, earlier form before the retconning, they may have become known and loved by an audience who will prefer the earlier versions and not want to see them changed; for example, fans who prefer the original versions of *Star Wars* Episodes IV–VI to the retconned Special Edition versions. These fans may consider the earlier versions canonical, disagreeing with what Lucas himself deems canonical. Tolkien was well aware of this kind of reaction when he retconned *The Hobbit* to bring it in line with *The Lord of the Rings*, doing so quietly and even finding a way to cleverly make *both* versions canonical; the older version is said to be the story that Bilbo told, but a distortion of the truth, while the newer "corrected" version tells the story as it really was. Thus, both versions can remain within Tolkien's mythology simultaneously, with their disagreement explained in diegetic terms.

Unpublished work also raises the question of canonicity. A work may remain unpublished due to not being finished, not being polished to a desired degree of quality, or simply because the author died before getting around to publishing it. If a work's authorship is unquestioned and the work appears to be complete, it may be considered canonical; on the other hand, without the author's final approval, one can ask whether the work in question actually reached the final stage of revision that the author would have wanted before it was released to the public (although even released works can later be retconned). A range of examples exists within J. R. R. Tolkien's posthumously published works edited by his son Christopher. The stories of *The Silmarillion* (1977) existed in various forms for decades and many of them feel complete and even polished in the published book; although he continued changing it until his death, Tolkien had tried to get a version of *The Silmarillion* published during his lifetime, so he must have considered much of it complete and ready to go. By contrast, other texts appearing in *Unfinished Tales* (1981) and the 12-volume *History of Middle-earth* series (1983–1996) range from ones that are nearly done to partial drafts and sketches. Multiple versions of the same stories occur at differing levels of narrative resolution, and conflicts arise between them as well. For example, Tom Shippey has pointed out that there are at least nine different versions of "The Legend of Beren and Lúthien" ranging in length from two pages to two hundred pages, and that "authors tend not to begin with Grand Designs which they then slowly flesh out, but with scenes and visions, for which they may eventually find intellectual justification."[7]

An author can even play with noncanonical material within a canonical work. Nine years after Miguel de Cervantes published the first part of his *Don Quixote* (1605), an unauthorized sequel appeared under the pseudonym Alonso Fernández de Avellaneda. In the second part of *Don Quixote* (1615), Cervantes confronted Avellaneda's unauthorized sequel by having his characters talk about it and ridicule it, and at one point, they even meet Don Alvaro Tarfe, a character from Avellaneda's book. By bringing Tarfe into his novel, Cervantes has turned a character who was originally noncanonical (since he only appeared in the false sequel) into a canonical one (since he appears in Cervantes' own Part II). (Of course, one could argue that Cervantes' use of Tarfe is itself an unauthorized act, making Cervantes' use of Tarfe noncanonical from the point of view of Avellanda's book; but it would be something of a stretch to regard Avellanda's book as having a canon of its own.) In any event, the audience's desire to see certain works and worlds continue does not end with a character's death or even the author's.

Estates, Heirs, and Torchbearers

The threat of unauthorized sequels persists after an author's death, so it is not unusual for a popular world to be handed over to a caretaker who will continue to manage the world, whether it is open or closed. If the world is closed, the new owners can collect income from the world, allowing adaptations and licensing merchandise and so on, without adding to the world. If the author leaves the world open, the author is granting permission to continue expanding the world, and the world's new owner may then oversee further world-building. Sometimes an author's worlds would not even reach an audience, were it not for the caretakers who manage and promote them (like the worlds invented by Thomas Williams Malkin, Austin Tappan Wright, and Henry Darger, each of which gained public recognition only after the author's death). Such caretakers include estates, heirs, and torchbearers.

If a world is left open, an author's estate, represented by an executor, usually determines how it will be passed on and to whom (unless the author has already dictated to whom it will go). As with the inheritance of physical property, there may be a direct heir, for example, Frank Herbert's son Brian who continued the *Dune* series of novels, or Christopher Tolkien, who took on the editing and publication of his father's unpublished work. If there is no direct heir, a torch-bearer can be granted the right to continue building a world. For example, after L. Frank Baum's death, his wife Maud Baum along with William Lee, vice president of L. Frank Baum's publisher, chose Ruth Plumy Thompson to continue writing Oz novels. Mark Saxton helped Sylvia Wright edit her father's manuscript for *Islandia* (1942), and then went on to write three Islandia novels of his own, using Austin Tappan Wright's notes. Some torchbearers even finish works begun by an author, for example, when Brandon Sanderson finished Robert Jordan's *A Memory of Light*, the last novel in his *Wheel of Time* series (the novel was broken into three books, *The Gathering Storm* (2009), *Towers of Midnight* (2010), and *A Memory of Light* (2012)). A torchbearer differs from an heir in the sense that a torchbearer's role is assigned by an estate, and could be revoked; whereas an heir, usually a widow, son, or daughter, has a natural right to inherit property due to familial ties or connections, or because the heir was specifically appointed by the author before his or her death (for example, H. P. Lovecraft named Robert Hayward Barlow as his literary executor, since Barlow had collaborated with him and Lovecraft was his friend and mentor).

Before 1900, few worlds extended beyond a single book, much less a single author. Baum's Oz was the first world to continue after the author's death in an official manner, with an authorized torchbearer. As the new "Royal Historian of Oz", Thompson ended up writing more canonical Oz novels than Baum did (19 to Baum's 14). Since then, the L. Frank Baum Family Trust has continued to name other "royal historian" torchbearers, with the most recent one (as of 2012) being Sherwood Smith. The flow of authorized novels, then, continues even though all of Baum's original novels have entered into public domain, which demonstrates that while individual works set in a world can become public domain, the world itself does not (canonically speaking), and Oz currently holds the record for the world remaining officially "open" the longest, with canonical additions having been made from 1900 to 2006.

Since heirs and torchbearers are given creative control of a world, can they retcon the originator's material that preceded them? Retconning is controversial enough even when performed by the work's original author, so even greater objections usually arise when someone else makes such changes. Torchbearer retconning occurs most often in film, television, and other media where high production costs make it more likely that a world is a corporation's intellectual property. While franchise ownership gives a company the legal right to control or change a franchise's works, critics and audiences will naturally object to alterations that destroy or degrade the artistic integrity of a work (such as Turner Entertainment's controversial colorization of *Casablanca* (1942)). Yet, while fans, critics, and historians may prefer the older, original versions of works, commercial pressures to "update" works for contemporary audiences can still prevail.

Although Gene Roddenberry originated *Star Trek*, the original television series was produced by Desilu, and after various acquisitions, mergers, and splits, CBS Paramount Television obtained the rights to produce *Star Trek* television shows, while Paramount Pictures produced the movies, licensing them from CBS Paramount Television.[8] When the original *Star Trek* episodes were remastered in high definition in 2006, CBS Paramount Television retconned the series as well: special effects shots were replaced with computer graphics versions, matte backgrounds were redone, scenes were recomposed, actors were added into shots, and the opening music was re-recorded in digital stereo. (And, in 2009, J. J. Abrams' *Star Trek* movie retconned the characters of the original series, though an attempt was made to tie the changes into the franchise's continuity through the use of time travel and an alternate reality.) In such cases, retconning is motivated not by the desire for world continuity, but rather by the desire to keep older works palatable to newer audiences, which is often the motivation behind remakes and reboots as well.

While torchbearers work for the author's estate or the franchise's corporate owners, they are more than just employees, since they fill the role vacated by the world's main author, actively setting the direction and the course of the growth of the author's imaginary world. However, other writers may be commissioned for books as well, and work on storylines given to them but without the control that a torchbearer has in the further development of a world.

Employees and Freelancers

Often a world, especially a transmedial one, will become too much for a single person to produce alone, so the author (or an estate, heir, or torchbearer) will hire employees and freelancers (who, unlike regular employees, come and go, working on a project-to-project basis) to aid in the construction of a world and the works set in it. Employees and freelancers differ from heirs and torchbearers in that they are unable to initiate new works, perform retconning, or add new canonical material without permission from the author, heir, or torchbearer; they are hired hands who are assigned tasks and paid for them. On the high end of this spectrum are writers commissioned to write novels set in an author's world, and screenwriters and directors making films set in the author's world (for example, screenwriter Leigh Brackett and director Irving Kershner both worked on *The Empire Strikes Back* (1980) for George Lucas). Since the work they do is for someone else's world, they usually do not own any of the intellectual property that they work on for the world. In the literary world, this practice of work-for-hire is known as "sharecropping". According to Walter Jon Williams, a writer of tie-in novels:

> Many of these invented universes proved enormously popular with the reading public, and commercial publishers were not slow to perceive the opportunity that lay within that popularity. When the author was

unavailable or not inclined to write further installments in the series, other writers were commissioned to pen "authorized" sequels. The background of Isaac Asimov's popular robot stories, for example, provided the framework for the *Robot City* novels of the late 1980s.

This is a practice known in the industry as "sharecropping," and as with sharecropping in the agricultural sector, the greatest benefit is gained by the owner of the (in this case literary) property, and much less by the workers toiling on that property. Typically, the original creator is given a large advance, usually with the expectation of doing little or no work on the project. The sharecropper receives a much smaller share of the money. ... The sharecropper is often a new writer whose profile would be raised by having his or her name associated with that of a best-selling author—the *Robot City* novels, for example, were written by Michael Kube-McDowell and William F. Wu, both relative newcomers.

Sharecropping is a practice with a venerable history. Many of the works of Alexandre Dumas père, as an example, were written in large part by his stable of collaborators—this includes all three Musketeers books as well as *The Count of Monte Cristo*. Unlike modern sharecroppers, however, Dumas' collaborators were rarely, if ever, credited for their works.[9]

The prestige connected with working on a well-known world, then, is often the main compensation received by the sharecropper. World-based franchises seem to be particularly prone to sharecropping; according to writer Carol Pinchefsky:

> Media tie-ins are not the sole domain of the speculative fiction genre. *Sweet Valley High*, *Little House on the Prairie*, and *CSI* have all been tied-in. However, tie-ins are a mainstay of speculative fiction, and bookstores are devoting an increasingly larger portion of bookshelf space to them. Why is this happening to science fiction and fantasy, but not other genres?
>
> In a genre based on speculation, the interviewees can only speculate. Margaret Weis (*Mistress of Dragons*) says, "I think because readers become so involved in the world itself. With fantasy and science fiction, [the readers] are interested in the whole exotic alien world, which is so different than ours. In a romance [the readers] care about the characters more than the world." In other words, fans become so smitten with a certain universe, they crave stories placed there.[10]

Employees and freelancers may be given varying degrees of artistic license and responsibility, and their creative contributions can shape a world to a large extent; consider Ben Burtt's sound design work and the graphic design work of Ralph McQuarrie and Doug Chiang which defined the sound and look of the *Star Wars* films. Those who work on a well-established world will be beholden to follow the world's "bible" and make sure their contributions remain consistent with it, which can be more difficult than inventing something new, due the restrictions imposed by existing material. Creative contributions of employees and freelancers can range from great to small, down to the contributions of movie extras who fill in the backgrounds of crowd scenes, and technicians whose work may go unnoticed in the finished product. Extending the circles of authorship even farther, we come to the licensing and merchandising of imaginary worlds, and other properties made from their data.

Approved, Derivative, and Ancillary Products

The most commercially successful imaginary worlds are those whose assets are instantly recognizable; iconic characters, places, vehicles, and other objects which evoke the world and are used to promote a variety of licensed merchandise, which bear their images and forms. Merchandised items, then, usually add little or no canonical material to a world, since they rely on the popularity of existing assets that have already appeared elsewhere. Occasionally, however, they can be used to reveal world information that does not appear in other sources. For example, designer Ralph McQuarrie made an uncredited cameo appearance in *The Empire Strikes Back* (1980) as an unnamed extra walking through the background of a shot. Later, an action figure of "General McQuarrie", made in his likeness, appeared, revealing the character's name. Such information, minimal as it is, has no real bearing on the film's story, but is the kind of trivia that fans enjoy knowing as "inside information" about a world.

While toys, games, and other merchandise contribute little or nothing in the way of canonical material, some ancillary products, like encyclopedias and atlases, organize existing data and sometimes provide new data that has not appeared in any other work but merely fills in gaps in various world infrastructures. When such reference works are officially commissioned by the world's owner, these additions may be given canonical status. Often, however, such works are compiled and assembled from existing material; cartographer Karen Wynn Fonstad, for example, was known for her atlases of imaginary worlds, including *The Atlas of Pern* (1984), *The Atlas of the Land* (1985), *Atlas of the Dragonlance World* (1987), *The Forgotten Realms Atlas* (1990), and two editions of *The Atlas of Middle-earth* (1981 and 1991). Other reference works filled with data about individual imaginary worlds, such as chronologies and encyclopedias, have been assembled and even published without the permission of the authors' estates. Yet, estates can hold back scholarship that discusses and involves an author's unpublished material; for example, the Tolkien Estate has not allowed publication of scholarly analysis of Tolkien's unpublished Quenya manuscripts.[11]

Approved, derivative, and ancillary products may add not to a world's canon, but they can change the way that a world and its assets are experienced. For example, encountering Darth Vader first as a LEGO minifigure or as bobble-head toy will reduce the air of menace that he had in his original appearance in *Star Wars* in 1977. Likewise, glancing through atlases like Fonstad's *Atlas of Middle-earth* or Barbara Strachey's *The Journeys of Frodo* (1992) or chronologies like Michael W. Perry's *Untangling Tolkien* (2006) or Daniel Wallace's *The New Essential Chronology to Star* Wars (2005), will reveal much of the stories and their plots to those who have not read the books or seen the films. The aggressive marketing behind certain worlds, especially in toy stores, can risk revealing too much about a world before its audience is old enough to experience its original core works.

While the production of world-based merchandise needs approval from the owners of a world, scholarly work which analyzes, discusses, or compiles information about a world can often avoid the need for authorization and approval. Whether it praises, critiques, or both, scholarly analysis calls attention to a world and usually provides a new context in which to view it, so it, too, can change the way an audience experiences a world. The fact that authorization is usually not required for such discussion of a world means that scholarship bridges the gap out to the next circle of authorship, that of elaborationists and fan productions.

Elaborationists and Fan Productions

Fan productions set in other authors' worlds have been around since early unauthorized sequels, like those made for *Orlando Innamorato* (1495) and *Don Quixote* (1605). In a sense, fan productions can be seen as an extension of what audiences do all the time while experiencing a world; filling in gaps as world gestalten occur. As Henry Jenkins describes it:

> The encyclopedic ambitions of transmedia texts often results in what might be seen as gaps or excesses in the unfolding of the story: that is, they introduce potential plots which cannot be fully told or extra details which hint at more than can be revealed. Readers, thus, have a strong incentive to continue to elaborate on these story elements, working them over through their speculations, until they take on a life of their own. Fan fiction can be seen as an unauthorized expansion of these media franchises into new directions which reflect the reader's desire to "fill in the gaps" they have discovered in the commercially produced material.[12]

"Fanon" is a term sometimes used to describe the theories and gap-filling ideas that many fans think are canon, when they actually are not.[13] Writers of fan fiction, whom Anthony Burdge and Jessica Burke refer to as "elaborationists",[14] go beyond the unconscious filling of gaps to consciously devising stories and world material that elaborate upon and extend the narratives and characters of a world. (While much can be said about fan fiction, machinima, and other such user-created additions to imaginary worlds, these kinds of additions are almost always noncanonical, and thus a detailed analysis of them is beyond the scope of this chapter.)

The material created by fans rarely becomes official canon, and in the rare cases that it does, it is usually only accepted at a lower level of canon. For example, the fan "Tawnia Poland" suggested the name "Darth Caedus" and won the "Darth Who" contest which asked fans to name a new Sith character who would appear in Karen Traviss's book *Sacrifice* (2007) from the *Legacy of the Force* series of *Star Wars* novels, which reside in *Star Wars* C-canon. Also more rare are those elements that move up levels of canon as well: Lucas liked the planet name "Coruscant" first used in Timothy Zahn's Expanded Universe (EU) novel *Heir to the Empire* (1991), and used it in *The Phantom Menace* (1999); and the character Aayla Secura first appeared in several EU novels and comics before Lucas put her in *Attack of the Clones* (2002); in both cases, an element from C-canon was moved up to G-canon.[15]

Although fan productions almost never become canon themselves, they can affect canon in a number of ways. Authors producing ongoing worlds often are aware of fans' reactions, through fan productions, fan mail, Internet forum discussions, and sales figures, and these reactions will influence the creation of later works set in the world. For example, Boba Fett, who was originally a minor character in *The Empire Strikes Back* and *Return of the Jedi*, became so popular with fans that he was given more backstory in *Attack of the Clones*.[16] Likewise, the negative reaction of fans to Jar Jar Binks in *The Phantom Menace* led to a much-reduced role in *Attack of the Clones* and *Revenge of the Sith* (2005).[17] Authors may also consider fan theories (fanon) regarding solutions to problems or directions that a story may go, and end up using them in the actual continuation of a story (a situation referred to as the "Sure, Why Not?" trope at *TVtropes.org*); Piers Anthony, for example, is known for using fans' suggestions for his Xanth series.[18] Thus, fan reactions (and the commercial success or failure that they can represent), can influence the design of works and worlds, potentially taking them in a different direction than an author's original intentions.

Fans who are serious about contributing canonical material to a world can become employees or freelancers, or in some cases, even the torchbearers assigned to continue a world (as is the case with lifelong *Doctor Who* fan Steven Moffat, who eventually became the head writer and executive producer of *Doctor Who*).[19] However, relatively few fans have the means and opportunity to devote their careers to working on their favorite worlds. And while some worlds employ hundreds of people in their ongoing creation, the majority of them are on the lower end of the hierarchies of authorship, with perhaps only a few near the top who have the power to decide what will become canon. There are, however, worlds in which the circles of authorship reach outward to fans much sooner, and where large numbers of people can add to a world's canon, albeit in limited form; we might refer to such worlds as *participatory worlds*.

Participatory Worlds

Many worlds are shared worlds, built from the work of multiple contributors; so such worlds can be said to be participatory at least in one sense. Some worlds, however, allow participation by world's audience, blurring the distinction between author and audience. The world is still originated by an author, who determines what the world will be like initially and what rules will be followed by the participants and inhabitants within it; so the role of an author is still present, even though it may be filled by a team rather than an individual. A participatory world, however, allows an audience member to participate in the world and its events, and make permanent changes that result in canonical additions to the world. Such additions may be the actions of an avatar who is a part of the diegesis and takes part in diegetic events (as in an MMORPG), a player–character in a tabletop game or MUD who can actively build and change the world from within the world, or a player who institutes changes from outside of the world, negotiating the world's shape and future with others.

Participatory worlds are a subset of interactive worlds, since while all participatory worlds are inherently open and interactive, not all interactive worlds allow the user to make permanent changes to the world, sharing in its authorship. The worlds of single-player video games, for example, allow interaction, but nothing the player does will result in a permanent change in the world's canon; individual play experiences may differ, but the world remains fixed (the copy of the game that the player owns is only an instance of the world).[20] In most MMORPGs, on the other hand, the player's avatar can make changes to the world that other players can note, and that become part of that world's history, even if those changes are relatively small within the scope of the world. Other worlds, like *Second Life* (2003) and *Galaxiki* (2007) are not games but also allow users to build, name, and edit their own properties.

Acts of authorship by players in participatory worlds can range from changes made diegetically from within a world (when characters battle opponents or build structures) to those made from without (when players contact the game makers and demand changes to the game). While typical player activities in a MUD or MMORPG will generate events which other players can observe (or observe the effects of), some on-line worlds allow players to actively reshape and change the world itself more directly and profoundly. Since Richard Skrenta's *Monster* (1988), some MUDs have "on-line creation" capabilities, allowing players to edit spaces, create and delete objects, and change the game world from *within* the game world. A world's rules can also be changed from within; in the MMORPG *A Tale in the Desert* (2003), social connections are important as players can organize petitions requesting various changes to the game world, which are granted if they have enough signatures of other players, integrating the ability to change the world into the legal system of the game.

Changes to a world can be categorized according to which infrastructures they affect, and the degree to which players can affect them. Maps may be altered when a character builds a house, or builds the land mass on which a house can be placed, or generates the space itself into which land can be placed, or perhaps even the rules governing how spaces can be edited or added in the world. Timelines, naturally, are built from events that occur, although many larger worlds like *Second Life* or most MMORPGs contain thousands of simultaneous events so that no practical timeline can be made to include all of them, although some large-scale events can affect the world as a whole, whether in-game or behind-the-scenes. Genealogies are determined by characters and their relationships, and though most on-line worlds do not introduce new avatars through the procreation of existing ones (though in theory they could), characters can be long-lived and can build social structures (like guilds), which often determine much of a user's experience of a world. The nature of a world can sometimes be changed internally or externally, as discussed earlier, and the culture of the world will often arise from player interactions, though many world elements, such as the objects or activities allowed within a world, may be seeded by the makers of the world. The culture of an on-line world can be suggested by the makers of the world, but it is the citizens of the world, the players and their avatars, who will either accept or reject cultural elements, becoming co-creators along with the makers of the world.

Culture in worlds like *Second Life* is largely produced by the world's inhabitants, and the building of virtual objects within on-line worlds, along with the selling of them for real currency, has become big business. Worlds like *Second Life* and *Entropia Universe* (2003) have in-world currencies that are interchangeable with real currencies, and in 2006, "virtual land baroness" Anshe Chung became the first person to become a millionaire in *Second Life*, all from a US$9.95 investment.[21] In the Entropia Universe, a virtual space station sold for US$330,000 in 2009; and in 2010, a virtual resort there sold for US$635,000.[22] In 2009, the *Second Life* economy was estimated to be worth US$567 million, about a quarter of the entire U.S. virtual goods market.[23] The building of participatory worlds, and the changing of their infrastructures, increasingly effects social and economic structures in the Primary World, as these secondary worlds grow more closely linked to the Primary World.

The most participatory kind of imaginary world is, of course, the one you create yourself. Since the appearance of "how-to" books on world-building for fantasy and science fiction authors in the 1990s, many tools for subcreators have appeared, from Bill Appleton's *World Builder* (1986) for the Macintosh, to Mark Rosenfelder's *Language Construction Kit* (published in 2010, though versions of it have been available on the Internet since 1996) and *The Planet Construction Kit* (2010), to computer animation programs like *Bryce* (1994), *3DS Max* (1996), *Blender* (2002), *Autodesk MotionBuilder* (2009), and many others which allow the design and construction of three-dimensional landscapes, objects, and characters.

The act of world-building, with the myriad decisions, intricacies, and complexities it can involve, not only leads to a greater appreciation of well-built worlds, but perhaps also to greater contemplation of the Primary World itself.

Creation, Subcreation, and the *Imago Dei*

> To construct plausible and moving "other worlds" you must draw on the only real "other world" we know, that of the spirit.
>
> —C. S. Lewis, "On Stories" in *Of Other Worlds*[24]

> The virtual "worlds" we enter into offer us a means of escape, a mode of imagining, and a never-depleted well of possibility for imagining ourselves all-powerful, infinite, beautiful, desired, even worshipped. Virtual reality experiences such as video games and online worlds like Second Life are the most potent forms of world-building available today, even more so than cinema or novels, because the agency of the player is ramped up to such an extent that in many virtual worlds, it is up to the player–inhabitant to literally construct the world, or to single-handedly destroy his or her enemies, thereby symbolically bringing order to the world and "building" it anew. World-building, I argue, is patently a religious endeavor, one of the oldest ones on earth, practiced today in some of the newest of ways.
>
> —Rachel Wagner, *Godwired: Religion, Ritual, and Virtual Reality*[25]

> Will's idea, at this point, was that players were to directly experience the difficulty and frustration of making life in the universe, and appreciate the improbability that life exists at all.
>
> —Chaim Gingold, "A Brief History of *Spore*"[26]

> Nevertheless—and it is curious when one considers how individual is the world of each fantasy—there is a very definite and constant character to fantasy, and in nothing is it perhaps so markedly constant as in its devotion to wonder at created things, and its profound sense that that wonder is above almost everything else a spiritual good not to be lost.
>
> —C. N. Manlove, *The Impulse of Fantasy Literature*[27]

> Wonder, in the sense of miracle, mysticism, and faith, may well be the single most important contribution of virtual worlds to human experience.
>
> —Edward Castronova, *Exodus to the Virtual World*[28]

Subcreation, by its very nature, is a collaborative effort in which existing concepts are combined in new ways, and a secondary world is produced which is a variation on the Primary World. Creation, the Primary World, makes possible and provides the conceptual and material support for subcreation and secondary worlds, and subcreation can be seen as a reflection of Creation. Thus, we find that many authors writing about human creativity have interpreted Genesis 1:27, in which God creates human beings in His own image, the

Imago Dei, to indicate that our desire to create is part of what it means to be created in God's image, and, according to Bruce Mazlish, "one of humanity's deepest aspirations."[29] In his "Letter of His Holiness Pope John Paul II to Artists", Pope John Paul II wrote of an idea similar to subcreation, substituting "craftsman" for "subcreator":

> The opening page of the Bible presents God as a kind of exemplar of eve-ryone who produces a work: the human craftsman mirrors the image of God as Creator. This relationship is particularly clear in the Polish language because of the lexical link between the words stwórca (creator) and twórca (craftsman).
>
> What is the difference between "creator" and "craftsman"? The one who creates bestows being itself, he brings something out of nothing— *ex nihilo sui et subiecti*, as the Latin puts it—and this, in the strict sense, is a mode of operation which belongs to the Almighty alone. The craftsman, by contrast, uses something that already exists, to which he gives form and meaning. This is the mode of operation peculiar to man as made in the image of God. In fact, after saying that God created man and woman "in his image" (cf. Gn 1:27), the Bible adds that he entrusted to them the task of dominating the earth (cf. Gn 1:28). This was the last day of creation (cf. Gn 1:28–31). On the previous days, marking as it were the rhythm of the birth of the cosmos, Yahweh had created the universe. Finally, he created the human being, the noblest fruit of his design, to whom he subjected the visible world as a vast field in which human inventiveness might assert itself.[30]

Subcreation, though it relies on Creation, inherently asks us to imagine what possible worlds could exist beyond what is known to exist in the Primary World. It invites invention and experimentation, leading to an examination of the con-sequences resulting from the various structures and combinations of elements that a subcreator imagines, and perhaps even the difficulty in incarnating them into words, images, objects, sounds, and interactions. In doing so, we are able to sup-pose what things would be like if they were otherwise, and different from those of existing Creation. Writing to someone who suggested that a subcreator should not go beyond "those channels which he knows the creator to have used already", Tolkien responded:

> We differ entirely about the nature of the relation of subcreation to Creation. I should have said that liberation "from the channels of the creator is known to have used already" is the fundamental function of "subcreation", a tribute to the infinity of His potential variety, one of the ways in which indeed it is exhibited, as indeed I said in the Essay. I am not a metaphysician; but I should have thought it a curious metaphysic—there

is not one but many, indeed potentially innumerable ones—that declared the channels known (in such a finite corner as we have any inkling of) to have been used, are the only possible ones, or efficacious, or possibly acceptable to and by Him![31]

The act of world-building makes one consciously consider the various decisions involved in creating a world, and realize, at least to a small degree, perhaps, the difficulties involved. Besides material considerations, a subcreator can also play with philosophical possibilities in a world, speculating as to what effects changes would have on the inhabitants of a world; as Edward Castronova has suggested, "Much of the task of world-building involves implicit messaging about what kind of world is a good world".[32]

Such contemplation of the aspects of world-building can lead to the *wonder* discussed in the quotes given earlier, along with a greater appreciation for the Primary World itself. Interviewing Rand Miller, one of the creators of *Myst*, Jon Carroll wrote:

> In my notebook I had a question from Kevin Kelly, the executive editor of *Wired*. It was not a question I had planned to ask, but many unexpected things had happened. "How has designing a whole world changed your idea of God?"
>
> Rand puffed his cheeks and blew. "Well, we could talk about that for hours. We thought about it a lot. I guess the simple way is to say that we know how much work it took to create *Myst*, and how puny and unreal it is compared to the real world, and therefore how miraculous all of creation is. Matching our experience … it just makes us realize how great God is."[33]

Subcreative activity, then, can be a humbling experience when one considers the relative simplicity and incompleteness that is inevitable in all subcreated worlds, no matter how large and detailed they may be. Comparing secondary worlds to the Primary World (which human beings, even collectively, have only seen a tiny fraction of), can only lead to a sublime experience of the latter's unimaginable vastness and intricacy.

While making one's own world is undoubtedly the best way to experience the subcreative process, the contemplation involved in the experience of making a world is also present in the genre of video games known as "god games", in which the player builds a world within the context of the game. As Mark Hayse sums it up:

> God games also inspire some theorists to reflect upon the player–game phenomenon as a divine–human metaphor. Kevin Kelly imagines that the player's work of designing and directing an emergent video game

world reflects the ongoing divine activity of creation (1995). For example, Kelly observes that god games feature an evolving future in which players directly control global events such as the weather while only indirectly influencing the response of those simulated organisms which are affected by it. Kelly speculates that god game players come to feel interest and affection for the worlds that they make. Elsewhere, Kelly argues that technology can "advance our understanding of god-ness by experiencing the limits and powers of unfolding creations of our own" (1999, 392). Similarly, Steven Garner (2005) suggests that creative engagement with technology is an expression of the *Imago Dei*—the image of God within human beings. Garner reasons that just as God might create persons, so those persons might imitate God through creative acts of their own. However, Noreen Herzfeld (2005) argues that god games do not fairly reflect the creative *Imago Dei*. She maintains that the *Imago Dei* implies a kind of mutual relationship that god games cannot reflect. Instead, Herzfeld contends that god games foster playful experiences of power and control.[34]

Subcreators in art and science have both struggled to define the limits of subcreation, for example, in the desire to create a conscious, autonomous being with self-awareness, evident in works spanning millennia from Pygmalion's statue and Hephaestus' automatons in Greek mythology to the robots and artificial intelligence of the present day. Taken to an extreme, the desire for autonomous creations results in an entire imaginary world which exists and functions on its own, a secondary world separated from the Primary World.

Differing as it does from *ex nihilo* creation, subcreation is not a usurping of the Creator's role, but rather cooperation with it, and acknowledgement of it. The subcreative desire is a part of human nature that precedes our fallen state, and the action and contemplation that accompanies it are both a gift and part of a divinely-mandated vocation calling us to carry on the work that God has begun. Like any gift, it can be neglected or even abused, but it is given to each person as an inalienable right. As Tolkien explains it:

> Fantasy is a natural human activity. It certainly does not destroy or even insult Reason; and it does not either blunt the appetite for, nor obscure the perception of, scientific verity. On the contrary. The keener and clearer is the reason, the better fantasy will it make. If men were ever in a state in which they did not want to know or could not perceive truth (facts or evidence), then Fantasy would languish until they were cured. ... For creative Fantasy is founded upon the hard recognition that things are so in the world as it appears under the sun; on a recognition of fact, but not a slavery to it. ... Fantasy can, of course, be carried to excess. It can be ill done. It can be put to evil uses. It may even delude the minds out of which it came. But of what human thing in this fallen world is that not true? Men have

conceived not only elves, but they have imagined gods, and worshipped them, even worshipped those most deformed by their authors' own evil. But they have made false gods out of other materials: their notions, their banners, their monies; even their sciences and their social and economic theories have demanded human sacrifice. *Abusus non tollit usum.* Fantasy remains a human right: we make in our measure and in our derivative mode, because we are made: and not only made, but made in the image and likeness of a Maker.[35]

Subcreation and the building of imaginary worlds has been around as long as human imagination, but the opening of many new media windows during the twentieth century has made them more vivid and concrete, and vastly increased the number of worlds being produced. The addition of new tools like the computer and the Internet in the late twentieth century further refined their production and allowed audiences to reach into worlds and inhabit them vicariously, at the same time bringing them ever closer to the Primary World. Whatever their use, whether for the proposals of social, political, technological, and philosophical possibilities, or for escape, entertainment, satire, therapy, communication, speculation, or the pleasures of a good story, imaginary worlds have always been with us and interest in them has never waned; if anything, it has grown stronger over time as more possibilities become realized in the Primary World, many of which can trace their origins to secondary worlds.

Subcreation is not just a desire, but a need and a right; it renews our vision and gives us new perspective and insight into ontological questions that might otherwise escape our notice within the default assumptions we make about reality. Subcreated worlds also direct our attention beyond themselves, moving us beyond the quotidian and the material, increasing our awareness of how we conceptualize, understand, and imagine the Primary World. And the more aware we are of it, the better we can appreciate the Divine design of Creation itself and our place in it.

> *In my opinion, when we talk about God making man in His own image and likeness, we should understand that the likeness has to do with his essence, and this is creation. From this comes the possibility of evaluating a work and what it represents. In short, the meaning of art is the search for God in man.*
>
> —Andrei Tarkovsky, film director[36]

APPENDIX

Timeline of Imaginary Worlds

This list of imaginary worlds, while broadly inclusive, is still far from complete and is only a sampling of worlds, chosen either for their size, scale, degree of subcreation, complexity, popularity, fame, historical significance, or uniqueness, to give an overview of the history of imaginary worlds. The entries are arranged chronologically by year (and alphabetically when a year has multiple entries), and each entry is in the format of year, name of the world (in boldface), scale of world or type of world (in square brackets), author (with real name in square brackets, if a pseudonym was known to be used), and work of first public appearance (typically in italics).

This list is world-based rather than based by work or author, thus only the work in which a world made its first public appearance is listed; further works set in the same world do not appear, since such a list would be far longer than the present one. As a result, works that were not the first to be set in their respective worlds do not appear on the list; for example, *World of Warcraft* (2004) is not listed because Azeroth, the Warcraft universe, already appears in *Warcraft: Orcs & Humans* (1994), and Ursula K. LeGuin's *The Dispossessed* (1974) is not listed, because Annares, the planet on which it is set, is a part of the Hainish Universe first introduced in the short story "Dowry of the Angyar" in a 1964 issue of *Amazing Stories*. Likewise, *The Lord of the Rings* (1954–1955) is not listed, because Arda, the world in which Middle-earth is located, already appears in *The Hobbit* (1937), and the film *Star Wars* (1977) is not listed, because the *Star Wars* galaxy first appeared in the novelization of the film, *Star Wars: From the Adventures of Luke Skywalker* (1976), which preceded it by only a few months. Of course, one can go too far in this direction as well; several published poems written by Tolkien, such as "The City of the Gods" (1923) and "The Adventures of Tom Bombadil" (1934) are arguably set in Arda, but the glimpses they provide are so minimal and fleeting, and their links to the world so tenuous (the Bombadil poem, for example, was not initially set there, and was linked to Arda only retroactively), that one hardly feels that the world has been introduced, in comparison to *The Hobbit*; so some judgment in this vein has had to be applied regarding first appearances.

The years listed also represent the time of public appearance, not composition, since typically only the former can be known with certainty. For example, Philip K. Dick's Plowman's Planet first appeared in *Nick and the Glimmung* which was written in 1966 but was not published until 1988; therefore its appearance in *Galactic Pot-Healer*, which was published in 1969, is listed here as its first *public* appearance. Since worlds are listed by place name rather than by main character, some appear only as "Alternate Earth" or "Future Earth"—for example, the world of Buck Rogers, which first appeared in "Armageddon, 2419 A.D." in the August 1928 issue of *Amazing Stories*. As the world of Buck Rogers demonstrates, some of the worlds listed here are versions of the Primary World which are set either in a past or future distant enough to be foreign to the Primary World as we know it, and likewise versions of Primary World with alternate histories also appear here if the resulting world is unique and sufficiently different from our own, for example, the San Francisco of *Do Androids Dream of Electric Sheep?* (1968) (which later would become the Los Angeles of *Blade Runner* (1982)), or the New York of *Watchmen* (1986). Also, because worlds are location-based rather than character-based, there is no listing of the Buffyverse, as it is centered around a person, but there is a listing for Sunnydale, the city in which Buffy lives (the TV series is set there, but the movie that preceded it was not, so the series is listed as the first public appearance of the location).

Occasionally, worlds are retroactively linked into the same universe; for example, L. Frank Baum's *A New Wonderland* (1900, later retitled *The Surprising Adventures of the Magical Monarch of Mo and His People* when it was rereleased in 1903), introduces the land of Phunnyland, which was later renamed Mo. Years later in 1915, part of the ninth book in his Oz series, *The Scarecrow of Oz*, takes place in Mo, revealing that Mo and Oz reside in the same world. In such a case, both worlds are still listed separately, since they were conceived separately and were only tenuously linked long after both had been in existence for some time. Likewise, Henry Rider Haggard's novel *She and Allan* (1921) combined characters of his "She" series and "Allan Quatermain" series, both of which were begun in the 1880s. In the same way, two or more series can take place in a linked universe in such a tenuous way that, for all practical purposes, the series are considered separately; for example, Edgar Rice Burroughs's Barsoom series (about Mars), his Amtor series (about Venus), and his Tarzan series all arguably take place in the same universe, but each has a different main character and occurs on a different planet, with very little overlap between them, so each receives a separate entry in the list (supposed sequels, set in another world and written by a different author, like Dionys Burger's *Sphereland* (1960) written as a sequel to Edwin Abbott's *Flatland* (1884), also warrant separate entries).

Rabelais's Gargantua and Pantagruel series, Burroughs's Tarzan series, and Lofting's Doctor Dolittle series also pose a similar problem, in that multiple books within each series introduce different worlds, with only the characters linking the series; in these cases, despite the presence of internarrative characters, all the worlds of each series do not form a consistent whole, and thus they appear as separate entries. Another example of a classification problem is the planet Uller: at the invitation of Twayne Publishers, John D. Clark invented the planet Uller, which was then used as the location for three novellas ("The Long View" by Fletcher Pratt, "Uller Uprising" by H. Beam Piper, and "Daughters of Earth" by Judith Merril) and published together as *The Petrified Planet* (1952). Piper went on to include Uller in his Terro-Human Future History universe, and also wrote another story, "Ullr Uprising" (1953), set on an alternate version of Uller. Uller is included in the list along with the Terro-Human universe, since the Terro-Human universe was Piper's creation, rather than Clark's, even though Clark was the originator of Uller; while Ullr is not included since it is a part of the Terro-Human universe.

In the compiling of this list, several sources were very useful, including *The Dictionary of Imaginary Places* by Alberto Manguel and Gianni Guadalupi (which itself acknowledges Pierre Versins's *Encyclopèdie de l'Utopie, des Voyages extraordinaire et de la Science-Fiction* and Philip Goves's *The Imaginary Voyage in Prose Fiction*), *The Encyclopedia of Fantasy* by John Clute and John Grant, *The Encyclopedia of Science Fiction* by John Clute and Peter Nicholls, *The Dictionary of Science Fiction Places* by Brian Stableford, *Encyclopedia of Fictional and Fantastic Languages* by Tim Conley and Stephen Cain, *TV Towns* by Stephen Tropiano, *100 Years of American Newspaper Comics* edited by Maurice Horn, *The Visual Encyclopedia of Science Fiction* edited by Brian Ash, and lists from Wikipedia. Also, the complete texts of many of the works written before 1900 are now public domain, and full-text versions of them can be found on the Internet.

Ninth century BC **Aiaia, Aiolio, Cyclops Island, Fortunate Islands, Ogygia, Siren Island, etc.** [islands], Homer, *The Odyssey*
Fifth century BC **Land of the Arimaspi** [land in Africa], Herodotus, *Histories*
414 BC **Cloudcuckooland** [city in the sky], Aristophanes, *The Birds*
≈ 380 BC **Kallipolis** [city], Plato, *The Republic*
360 BC **Atlantis** [island], Plato, *Timaeus*
Fourth century BC **Meropis** [island], Theopompos of Chios, *Philippica*
Fourth century BC **Mount Kunlun** [mountain in China], Anonymous, *The Book of the Mountains and Seas*
Fourth century BC **Panchaïa** [island], Euhemerus, *Sacred History*
Fourth century BC **Thule** [island], Pytheas, *On the Ocean*
Third century BC **Mount Tushuo** [mountain in China], Anonymous, *The Compendium of the Deities of the Three Religions*

165–50 BC **Islands of the Sun** [islands], Iambulus, *Islands of the Sun*

First century BC **Hsuan** [continent], Tung-fang Shuo, *Accounts of the Ten Continents*

First century BC **Southwest Wilderness** [region in China], Tung-fang Shuo, *Book of Deities and Marvels*

First century AD **Basilisk Land, Blemmyae Land, Ear Islands, etc.** [various places], Pliny the Elder, *Naturalis Historia*

Second century **Blessed Island, Cabbalussa, Cork Island, Dionysus's Island, Dream Island, Empi Archipelago, etc.** [islands], Lucian of Samosata, *True History*

≈Third century **Anostus** [island], Claudius Aelianus, *Varia Historia*

426 **Eternal Jerusalem** [city], St. Augustine of Hippo, *City of God*

Eighth century **Brissonte** [riverland], **Polyglot** [island], Anonymous, *Liber Monstrorum de Diversis Generibus*

Twelfth century **(Unnamed island)** [desert island], Ibn Tufail, *Hayy ibn Yaqzān*

Thirteenth century **(Unnamed island)** [desert island], Ibn al-Nafis, *Al-Risalah al-Kamiliyyah fil Siera al-Nabawiyyah*

Thirteenth century **Cockaigne** [country], Anonymous, *Le Dit de Cocagne*

Thirteenth century **Torelore** [kingdom], Anonymous, *Aucassin et Nicolette*

≈Fourteenth century **City of Brass, Irem Zat El-Emad, Waq Archipelago, etc.** [various places], Anonymous, *The One Thousand and One Nights (The Arabian Nights)*

c. 1321 **Hell, Purgatory, Heaven** [versions of metaphysical places], Dante Alighieri, *The Divine Comedy*

1325 **Hy Brasil** [island] Angelinus Dalorto, *L'Isola Brazil*

c. 1357 **Amazonia, Bragman, Calonack, Chana, Dondun, Lomb, Mabaron, Mancy, Nacumera, Silha, Tracoda, etc.** [various lands and islands], Sir John Mandeville (thought to be a pseudonym), *The Book of Sir John Mandeville*

1405 **City of Ladies** [city], Christine de Pisan, *La Cité des Dames*

1424 **Antillia, Devil's Island, etc.** [islands], Zuane Pizzigano, Pizzigano Chart of 1424

1485 **Avalon** [island], **Camelot** [castle], Sir Thomas Malory, *Le Morte d'Arthur*

1495 **Albracca** [city], Matteo Maria Boiardo, *Orlando Innamorato*

1508 **Devil's Island, Fixed Isle, Mongaza, Infante Island, etc.** [islands], Anonymous, *Amadís de Gaula*

1516 **Alcina's Island** [island] **Ebuda, Nubia, etc.** [lands], Ludovico Ariosto, *Orlando Furioso*

1516 **Utopia** [island], **Macarenses, Achora, Polyleritae** [lands], St. Thomas More, *Concerning the Best State of a Commonwealth and the New Island of Utopia*

1521 **Wolfaria** [land], Johann Eberlin von Günzburg, *Wolfaria*

1532 **Aspharage** [country in a giant's mouth], François Rabelais, *Les horribles et épouvantables faits et prouesses du très renommé Pantagruel Roi des Dipsodes, fils du Grand Géant Gargantua*

1534 **Abbey of Thélème** [Abbey in France], François Rabelais, *La vie très horrificque du grand Gargantua, père de Pantagruel*

1538 **Brigalaure, Fortunate Islands, etc.** [islands], François Rabelais, *Le voyage de navigation queue fist Panurge, disciple de Pantagruel, aux isles incognues et éstranges de plusiers choses merveilleuses et difficiles á croire, qu'il dict avoir veues, dont il fait narration en ce présent volume, et plusiers aultres joyeusetez pour inciter les lecteurs et auditeurs á rire*

1552 **Chaneph Island, Cheli, Clerkship, Savage Island, Sneak's Island, etc.** [islands], François Rabelais, *Le quart livre des faicts et dicts du bon Pantagruel*

1552 **Un Mondo Nuovo** [country in Central Europe], Anton Francesco Doni, *I Mondi*

1555 **Macaria** [island], Caspar Stiblinus, "Commentariolus de Eudaemonensium Republica" in *Coropaedia, sive de moribus et vita virginum sacrarum*

1558 **Estotiland, Drogio, Fislandia, etc.** [islands], F. Marcolini, *Dello scoprimento dell'Isole Frislandia, Eslanda, Engrovelanda, Estotilanda e Icaria, fatto sotto il Polo Artico dai due fratelli Zeno, M. Nicolo e M. Antonio*

1564 **Island of Charges, Island of Ignoramuses, Entelechy, Out, etc.** [islands], François Rabelais, *Lecinquiesme et dernier livre des faicts et ducts du bon Pantagruel, auquel est contenu la visitation de l'Oracle de la dive Bacbuc, et le mot de la bouteille; pour lequel avoir est enterpris tout ce long voyage*

1564 **Lamiam, Parthalia, Taerg Natirb** [islands], William Bullein, *A Dialogue both Pleasant and Pitiful, wherein is a Goodly Regimente against the Fever Pestilence, with a Consolation and Comfort against Death*

1572 **Sea of Giants** [Arctic region], Tommaso Porcacchi, *Le isole piu' famose del mondo*

1596 **El Dorado** [city in South America], Sir Walter Raleigh, *The Discoverie of the lovlie, rich and beautiful Empyre of Guiana with a relation of the great and golden City of Manoa (which the Spaniards call El Dorado) And the Provinces of Emerria, Arromania, and of other countries, with their rivers, adjoyning.*

1602 **Taprobane** [island], Tommaso Campanella, *La Città del Sole*

1605 **Terra Sancta, Lavernia, Viragynia, Variana, Lyperia, etc.** [lands in Antarctic region], Joseph Hall, *Mundus alter et idem, sive Terra Australis ante hac semper incognita*

1614 **Calemplui** [island], Fernão Mendes Pinto, *Peregrinação*

1615 **Barataria** [island], Miguel de Cervantes Saavedra, *El ingenioso hidalgo Don Quixote de La Mancha Part II*

1616 **Antangil** [island], Anonymous (though the initials I.D.M.G.T. are given as the author), *Histoire du grand et admirable royaume d'Antangil Inconnu jusques à*

présent à tous Historiens et Cosmographes: composé de six vingts provinces trés-belles &
trés fertile

1619 **Caphar Salama** [island], Johann Valentin Andreæ, *Reipublicae Christiano-*
politanae Descriptio (Beschreibung des Staates Christenstadt)

1623 **Prospero's Island** [island], William Shakespeare, *The Tempest*

1626 **Bensalem** [island], Francis Bacon, *The New Atlantis*

1634 **The Moon** [moon], Johannes Kepler, *Somnium*

1638 **The Moon** [moon], John Wilkins, *The Discovery of a World in the Moone*

1641 **Macaria** [kingdom, unknown location], Attributed to Samuel Hartlib but
now thought to have been written by Gabriel Plattes, *A Description of the*
Famous Kingdom of Macaria: shewing its Excellent Government, wherein the
Inhabitants Live in Great Prosperity, Health and Happiness; the King Obeyed, the
Nobles Honoured and All Good Men Respected; Vice Punished and Virtue Rewarded,
as an Example to Other Nations; in a Dialogue between a Scholar and a Traveller

1648 **Nova Solyma** [city in Israel], Samuel Gott, *Novae Solymae libri sex*

1654 **Animal Republic, Island of Poetry, Pyrandria** [islands], Jean Jacobé
de Frémont d'Ablancourt, *Supplément de l'Histoire Véritable de Lucien*

1656 **Oceana** [islands], James Harrington, *The Commonwealth of Oceana*

1657 **The Moon** [moon], Cyrano de Bergerac, *Voyage to the Moon*

1657 **The Marvellous Islands** [islands], Charles Sorel, *La Maison des Jeux*

1659 **Imaginary Island** [island], Anne Marie Louise Henriette d'Orléans,
Duchesse De Montpensier, *Rélation de L'Isle Imaginaire*

1659 **Misnie** [kingdom], Anne Marie Louise Henriette d'Orléans, Duchesse De
Montpensier, *La Princesse de Paphlagonie*

1654 **Tendre** [country], Madeleine De Scudéry, *Clélie, Histoire Romaine*
(published in ten volumes, 1654–1660)

1660 **Jansenia, Calvinia, Libertinia, Despairia** [lands], Le Père Zacharie de
Lisieux, *Relation du pays de Jansénie, où il est traité des singularitez qui s'y trouvent,*
des coustumes, Moeurs et Religion des habitants. Par Louys Fontaines, Sieur de Saint
Marcel

1666 **Blazing-World** [planet], Margaret Cavendish, *The Description of a New*
World, Called the Blazing-World

1668 **Centrum Terrae** [underground kingdom], Hans Jakob Christoffel von
Grimmelshausen, *Der abenteuerliche Simplicissimus Teusch*

1668 **Isle of Pines** [island], Henry Neville, *The Isle of Pines, or, A late discovery of*
a fourth island near Terra Australis incognita, by Henry Corneius van Sloetten

1673 **Floating Island, Savoya, Ursina, Vulpina, etc.** [islands in the North
Atlantic Ocean], Richard Head, *The Floating Island or A New Discovery Relating*
the Strange Adventure on a late Voyage from Lambethana to Villa Franca, Alias
Ramallia, to the Eastward of Terra Del Templo: By Three Ships, viz. the "Pay-naught",
the "Excuse", and the "Least-in-Sight" under the conduct of Captain Owe-much:
Describing the Nature of the Inhabitants, their Religion, Laws and Customs

1675 **Sevarambi** [country], Denis Vairasse D'Allais, *Histoire des Sevarambes, peuples qui habitent une partie du troisième continent, communement appelé la Terre Australe*

1676 **Terre Australe** [continent], Gabriel Foigny, *Les Aventures De Jacques Sadeur Dans La Découverte Et La Voyage De La Terre Australe, contenant les coutumes et les moeurs des Australiens, leur religion, leurs études, leurs guerres, les animaux particuliers à ce pais et toutes les raretez curiesses qui s'y trouvent*

1678 **Oroonoko Island** [island in the West Indies], Aphra Behn, *Oroonoko, or the Royal Slave*

1684 **Christian's Country** [country], John Bunyan, *The Pilgrim's Progress from This World, to That Which is to Come*

1696 **Noland** [land], Anonymous, *The Free State of Noland*

1700 **Calejava** [island], Claude Gilbert, *Histoire de Calejava ou de l'Isle des Hommes Raisonnables, avec le Paralelle de leur Morale et du Christianisme*

1703 **The Moon** [moon,] David Russen, *Iter Lunare: Or, A Voyage To The Moon. Containing Some Considerations on the Nature of that Planet. The Possibility of getting thither. With other Pleasant Conceits about the Inhabitants, their Manners and Customs*

1703 **Naudely** [island], Pierre de Lesconvel, *Idée D'Un Regne Doux Et Heureux, Ou RelationDu Voyage du Prince de Montberaud dan l'Ile de Naudely*

1704 **Formosa** [island near Philippines (not to be confused with Taiwan, which was formerly named Formosa)], **Xternatesa** [city], George Psalmanazar, *Description de l'isle Formosa*

1705 **The Moon** [moon], Daniel Defoe, *The Consolidator: Or, Memoirs of Sundry Transactions From the World in the Moon*

1708 **Fonseca** [island near Barbados], Anonymous, *A Voyage to the New Island, Fonseca, Near Barbados*

1708 **Krinke Kesmes** [island near Terra Australis], Henryk Smeeks, *The Mighty Kingdom of Krinke Kesmes*

1709 **Atalantis** [island], Delarivier Manley, *Secret Memoirs and Manners of Several Persons of Quality, of both Sexes, From The New Atalantis*

c. 1710 **Bustrol** [island], **Satrapia** [empire], Simon Tyssot de Patot, *Voyage et Avantures de Jaques Massé*

1711 **Éutopia** [island], François Lefebvre, *Relation du Voyage de l'Isle d'Éutopie*

1715 **Basaruah** [kingdom], Joseph Morgan, *The History of the Kingdom of Basaruah Containing A Relation of the most Memorable Transactions, Revolutions and Heroick Exploits in that Kingdom, from the first Foundation thereof unto this present time. Collected from the most Antient Records of that Country, and translated into our Language, not only for Delight, but for the abundant Instruction that may be learned there-from, in these Remote Parts. Written in Discharge of the Trust reposed in the Author by his Majesty, for the Discovery of Foreign things. By a Traveller in Basaruah*

1718 **Isle de la Pierre Blanche** [island in straits of Malacca], Dralsé de Grandpierre, *Relation De Divers Voyages Faits Dans L'Afrique, dans L'Amerique, & aux Indes Occidentales*

1719 **Crusoe's Island** [island near South America], Daniel Defoe, *The Life and Strange Surprizing Adventures of Robinson Crusoe, of York, Mariner*

1719 **Paradise Island, Vendchurch's Island** [islands in the Pacific Ocean], Ambrose Evans, *The Adventures, and Suprizing Deliverences, of James Dubordieu, And His Wife: Who were taken by Pyrates, and carried to the Unihabited-Part of the Island of Paradise*

1720 **New Athens** [country], Thomas Killigrew the Younger, "A Description of New Athens in Terra Australis Incognita", in *Miscellanea Aurea, or, The Golden Medley*

1720 **Rufsal** [underground country near the North Pole], Simon Tyssot de Patot, *La Vie, Les Aventures, & le Voyage de Groenland Du Révérend Père Cordelier Pierre De Mesange*

1724 **Alca** [island], Daniel Defoe, *A New Voyage Round the World, By a Course Never Sailed Before*

1724 **Hermaphrodite Island** [island drifting near Lisbon, Portugal], Thomas Artus, *Déscription de L'Isle des Hermaphrodites nouvellement découverte, contenant les Mouers, les Coutumes et les Ordonnances des Habitans de cette Isle, comme aussi lle Discours de Jacophile à Linne, avec quelques autres piéces curieuses*

1726 **Lilliput, Luggnagg, Laputa** [islands], **Brobdingnag** [peninsula off the California coast], Jonathan Swift, *Travels Into Several Remote Nations Of The World, In Four Parts, By Lemuel Gulliver, First a surgeon and then a Captain of several Ships*

1727 **Cacklogallinia** [island], Samuel Brunt, *A Voyage to Cacklogallinia: With a Description of the Religion, Policy, Customs and Manners of the Country*

1727 **Quarll Island** [island off the coast of Mexico], Peter Longueville, *The Hermit: Or, the Unparalleled Sufferings and Surprising Adventures of Mr. Philip Quarll, An Englishman*

1730 **Babilary, Doctor's Island, Foollyk, Greedy Island, etc.** [islands], Abbé Pierre François Guyot Desfontaines, *Le Nouveau Gulliver ou Voyage de Jean Gulliver, Fils du Capitaine Gulliver, Traduit d'un Manuscrit Anglois, par Monsieur L. D. F.*

1730 **Cantahar** [island], De Varennes de Mondasse, *La Découverie De L'Empire De Cantahar*

1730 **Schlaraffenland** [country], Matthäus Seutter, *Accurata Utopiae Tabula*

1731 **Drexara** [region in North America], **Land of Nopandes** [land], Abbé Antoine François Prévost, *Le Philosphe anglois, ou Histoire de Monsieur Cleveland, fils naturel de Cromwell, par l'autuer des Mémoires d'un Homme de qualité*

1731 **Genotia** [continent], Louis Adrien Duperron de Castera, *Le Theatre Des Passions Et De La Fortune Ou Les Avantures Surprenantes de Rosamidor & de Theoglaphire. Histoire Australe*

1734 **World of Truth** [country], Pierre Carlet de Chamblain de Marivaux, "Voyage au Monde Vrai" in *Le Cabinet du Philosophe*

1735 **Abdalles, Amphicléocles** [kingdoms in Africa], **Trisolday** [underground kingdom], **Island of the Sylphides** [island], Charles Fieux de Mouhy, *Lamékis, ou le voyages extraordinaires d'un Egyptien dans la terre intérieure avec la découverte de l'Isle des Silphides, enrichi des notes curieuses*

1735 **Groenkaaf, Manghalour** [islands], Louis Rustaing de Saint-Jory, *Les Femmes Militaires*

1735 **Romancie** [walled kingdom], Guillaume-Hyacinthe Bougeant, *Voyage Merveilleux du Prince-Fan-Férédin dans la Romancie; Contenant Plusiers Observations Histoiriques, Géographiques, Physiques, Critiques et Morales*

1736 **Autonous's Island** [island], Anonymous, *The History of Autonous, containing a Relation how that Young Nobleman was accidentally left alone, in his Infancy, upon a Desolate Island; where he lived nineteen years, remote from all Humane Society, 'till taken up by his Father*

1737 **Jumelles** [islands, near New Zealand], de Catalde, *Le Paysan Gentilhomme, Ou Avantures De M. Ransay: Avec Son Voyage Aux Isles Jumelles*

1737 **Mezorania** [kingdom, in east Africa], Simon Berington, *The Memoirs of Sigr. Gaudentio di Lucca: Taken from his Confession and Examination before the Fathers of the Inquisition at Bologna in Italy; Making a Discovery of an unknown Country in the midst of the vast Deserts of Africa*

1739 **Meillcourt** [island in the Indian Ocean], Jean Baptiste de Boyer, Marquis d'Argens, *Le Législateur Moderne, Ou Les Mémoires Du Chevallier De Meillcourt*

1740 **Argilia** [country], Johann Michael Freiherr von Loën, *Der redliche Mann am hofe, oder die Begebenheiten des Grafen von Rivera*

1740 **The Moon** [moon], Pythagorlunister, *A Journey to the Moon*

1741 **Ferdinand's Island** [island in the West Indies], Johann Michael Fleischer, *Der Nordische Robinson*

1741 **Nazar** [underground country], Baron Ludvig Holberg, *Nicolai Klimii Iter Subterraneum Novam Telluris Theoriam Ac Historiam Quintae Monarchiae Adhuc Nobis Incognitae Exhibens E Bibliotheca B. Abelini*

1745 **Soteria, Cumberland** [countries], John Kirkby, *The Capacity and Extent of the Human Understanding; Exemplified In the Extraordinary Case of Automathes; A Young Nobleman, Who was Accidentally left in his Infancy, upon a desolate Island, and continued Nineteen Years in that solitary State, separated from all Human Society. A Narrative Abounding with many surprizing Occurrences, both Useful and Entertaining to the Reader*

1747 **Goat Land** [empire in India], **Mask Island** [island], Charles Fieux de Mouhy, *Le Masque de Fer, ou les Aventures Admirables du Pere et du Fils*

1748 **Banza** [city], **Thermometer Island** [island], Denis Diderot, *Les Bijoux Indiscrets*

1750 **Frivola** [island in the Pacific Ocean], Abbé Gabriel François Coyer, *A Discovery of the Island Frivola*

1750 **Land of Parrots** [island in the South Seas], Pierre Charles Fabiot Aunillon, Abbé Du Guay de Launay, *Azor, ou Le prince enchanté; histoire nouvelle, pour* *servir de chronique à celle de la terre des perroquets; traduit de l'anglois du sçavant Popiniay*

1751 **Philos** [island], Comte de Martignay, *Voyage d'Alcimédon, ou Naufrage qui conduit au port*

1751 **Providence Island, Anderson's Rock** [islands], Ralph Morris, *A Narrative of the Life and Astonishing Adventures of John Daniel, A Smith at Royston in Hertfordshire for a Course of Seventy Years.*

1751 **Sass Doorpt Swangeanti** [island], Robert Paltock, *The Life and Adventures of Peter Wilkins, A Cornish Man. Taken from his own Mouth, in his passage to England, from off Cape Horn, in the ship "Hector".*

1752 **Dumocala** [island kingdom], Stanisław Leszczyński (Stanisłas I, King of Poland), *Entretien d'un européen avec un insulaire du Royaume de Dumocala*

1752 **Planet around the star Sirius** [planet], Voltaire [François Marie Arouet], *Micromégas*

1753 **Bingfield's Island** [island], William Bingfield, *The Travels and Adventures of William Bingfield, Esq.*

1753 **Floating Islands** [islands], Etienne-Gabriel Morelly, *Naufrage des isles flottantes ou Basiliade du célèbre Pilpai, poème héroïque traduit de l'indien*

1753 **Isle of Birds** [island], Eléazar de Mauvillon, *Le Soldat Parvenu Ou Mémoires Et Aventures De Mr. De Verval Dit Bellerose Par Mr. De M****

1754 **Gala** [country in Asia], André-François de Brancas-Villeneuve, *Histoire ou Police du royaume de Gala, traduite de l'italien en anglais, et de l'anglais en français*

1755 **(Unnamed world)** [underground world], Anonymous, published by S. Crowder and H. Woodgate, *A Voyage to the World in the Centre of the Earth Giving an Account of the Manners, Customs, Laws, Government, and Religion of the Inhabitants, Their Persons and Habits Described with Several Other Particulars: In Which Is Introduced the History of an Inhabitant of the Air, Written by Himself, with Some Account of the Planetary Worlds.*

1755 **Laïquhire, Waferdanos** [islands in the North Atlantic], Anonymous, *Voyage Curieux d'un Philadelphe dans des Pays nouvellement Découverts*

1756 **Albino Land** [country], Voltaire [François Marie Arouet], *Essai sur l'histoire générale et sur les moeurs et l'esprit des nations depuis Charlemagne jusqu'à nos jours*

1757 **Nimpatan** [island in the South Atlantic], John Holmesby, *The Voyages, Travels, And Wonderful Discoveries of Capt. John Holmesby*

1760 **Giphantia** [island in the West African desert], Charles-François Tiphaigne de la Roche, *Giphantie*

1764 **Cessares Republic** [country in South America], James Burgh, *An Account of the First Settlement, Laws, Form of Government and Police of the Cessares: A People of South America, in nine Letters From Mr. Vander Neck, one of the Senators of that Nation, to his Friend in Holland, with Notes by the Editor*

1765 **Galligenia** [island], Charles François Tiphaigne de la Roche, *Histoire Des Galligénes, Ou Mémoires De Duncan*

1766 **Indian Island, Learding's Island** [islands near Cape Horn], André Guillaume Contant d'Orville, *La Destinée Ou Mémoires Du Lord Kilmarnoff, Traduits De L'Anglois De Miss Voodwill, Par M. Contant Dorville*

1766 **Leonard's Land** [land in Patagonia, South America], **Kingdom of the One-eyed** [land in West Africa], Jean Gaspard Dubois-Fontanelle, *Aventures Philosophiques*

1767 **Winkfield's Island, Idol Island** [islands in the Atlantic by North American], Unca Eliza Winkfield, *The Female American: Or, the Adventures of Unca Eliza Winkfield*

1768 **Gangaridia** [kingdom on the River Ganges], Voltaire [François Marie Arouet], *La Princess de Babylone*

1768 **Island of the Ajaoiens** [island], attributed to Bernard Le Bovier de Fontenelle, *La République des philosophes ou Histoire des Ajaoiens*

1768 **Isle of Boredom** [island], **Castora, Futura, etc.** [countries], Marie Anne de Roumier Robert, *Les Ondins*

1771 **Land of Goat Worshippers** [land in southeast Russia], Abbé H. L. Du Laurens, *Le Compère Mathieu ou les bigarrures de l'esprit humain*

1776 **Yluana** [island], Charles Searle, *The Wanderer: Or, Memoirs of Charles Searle, Esq.: Containing His Adventures by Sea and Land. With Many remarkable Characters, and interesting Situations in Real Life; and a Variety of surprizing Incidents*

1777 **Gynographe** [country], Nicolas-Edme Restif de la Bretonne, *Les Gyno-graphes, ou Idées de deux honnêtes femmes sur un problème de réglement proposé à toute l'Europe pour mettre les femmes à leur place, et opérer le bonheur des deux sexes*

1778 **Carnovirria, Taupiniera, Olfactaria, Auditante, Bonhommica, Luxo-volupto** [countries], Attributed to John Elliott, *The Travels of Hildebrand Bowman, Esquire, Into Carnovirria, Taupiniera, Olfactaria, and Auditante, in New Zealand; in the Island of Bonhommica, and in the powerful Kingdom of Luxo-volupto, on the Great Southern Continent. Written by Himself; Who went on shore in the Adventure's large Cutter, at Queen Charlotte's Sound New Zealand, the fatal 17th of December 1773; and escaped being cut off, and devoured, with the rest of the Boat's crew, by happening to be a-shooting in the woods; where he was afterwards unfortunately left behind by the Adventure*

1781 **Metapatagonia** [archipelago between Tierra del Fuego and Antarctica], Nicolas-Edme Restif de la Bretonne, *La Découverte australe Par un Homme-volant, ou Le Dédale français; Nouvelle très-philosophique: Suivie de la Lettre d'un Singe, & ca.*

1782 **Andrographe** [country], Nicolas-Edme Restif de la Bretonne, *L'andrographe ou Idées d'un honnête homme sur un projet de réglement proposé à toutesles nations de L'Europe pour opérer une réforme générale des moeurs, et par elle, le bonheur du genre humain avec des notes historiques et justificatives*

1784 **Georgium Sidus** [the planet Uranus], Monsieur Vivenair, *A Journey lately performed through the Air, in an Aerostatic Globe, commonly called an Air Balloon, from this terraqueous globe, to the newly discovered Planet, Georgium Sidus*

1784 **Unknown Island** [island in the Indian Ocean], Guillaume Grivel, *L'Isle Inconnue, ou Mémoires du Chevalier de Gastines*

1785 **Cucumber Island** [island near Africa], Rudolph Erich Raspe, *Baron Munchausen's Narrative Of His Marvellous Travels And Campaigns in Russia*

1786 **Feather Island** [island in the Indian Ocean], Fanny de Beauharnais, *Rélation très véritable d'une isle nouvellement découverte*

1787 **Cannibal Island, San Verrado** [islands in the Carribean Sea], François Guillaume Ducray-Duminil, *Lolotte Et Fanfan, Ou Les Adventures De Deux Enfans Abandonnés Dans Une Isle Déserte*

1788 **Marbotikin Dulda** [island in the Indian Ocean], **New Britain Islands** [islands off the Cape of Good Hope], Pierre Chevalier Duplessis, *Mémoires De Sir George Wollap; Ses Voyages dans différentes parties due Monde; aventures extraordianaires qui lui arrivent; découverte de plusiers Contrées inconnues; description des moeurs & des coutumes des Habitans*

1788 **Protocosmos** [underground country on an island, entered underwater], Giacomo Girolamo Casanova di Seingalt, *Icosameron Ou Histoire D'Edouard, Et D'Elisabeth qui passérent quatre vingts un an chez les Mégamicres habitens aborginènes du Protocosme dans l'intérieur de notre globe*

1789 **Thesmographe** [kingdom], Nicolas-Edme Restif de la Bretonne, *Le Thesmographe, ou idées d'un Honêtte Homme sur une Projet-Règlement proposé à toutes la Nations de l'Europe pour opérer une Reforme Générale des Lois*

1790 **Fortune Island, Bear Island, Island of Chance** [islands near North American coast], **Philosophers' Island** [island near Tierra del Fuego], Abbé Balthazard, *L'Isle des Philosophes Et Plusiers Autres, Nouvellement découveries, & remarquables par leur rapports avec la France actuelle*

1792 **Empire of the Alsondons** [underground empire], Robert-Martin Lesuire, *L'Aventurier Français, ou Mémoires de Grégoire Merveil*

1794 **Spensonia** [island], Thomas Spence, *A Marine Republic, or A Description of Spensonia*

1795 **Butua** [kingdom in Africa], **Tamoe** [island in the Pacific Ocean], Donatien-Alphonse-François, Marquis de Sade, *Aline et Valcour, ou le Roman Philosophique*

1795 **Makar** [country], Thomas Northmore, *Memoirs of Planetes, or a Sketch of the Laws and Manners of Makar*

1796 **Hewit's Island** [island near Madagascar], Charles Dibdin, *Hannah Hewit: Or, The Female Crusoe*

1801 **Felicity Isle** [island in the Aegean Sea], Fanny de Beauharnais, *L'Isle de la Félicité ou Anaxis et Théone*

1802 **Lithconia** [country], John Lithcow, "Equality—A Political Romance" in *The Temple of Reason 2*

1802 **Palace of Arthur** [palace], Novalis [Georg Philipp Friedrich Freiherr von Hardenberg], *Heinrich von Ofterdingen*

1805 **Future Earth** [alternate Earth], Jean Baptiste Cousin de Grainville, *Le Dernier Homme*

1806 **Allestone** [land], Thomas Williams Malkin, The world's map and stories appear in Benjamin Heath Malkin's *A Father's Memoirs of His Child*

1808 **Harmonia** [colonies], Charles Fourier, *Théorie des Quatre Mouvements*

1812 **Eugea** [island in the Atlantic], Népoumucenè Lemercier, *L'Atlantiade, ou La Théogonie Newtonienne*

1812 **New Switzerland** [island in the East Indies], Johann David Wyss, *The Swiss Family Robinson*

1813 **Selenion** [a new moon located between the earth and the moon], Willem Bilderdijk, *Kort verhaalvan eene aanmerkelijke luchtreis en nieuwe planeetontdekking (Short Account of a Remarkable Journey into the Skies and Discovery of a New Planet)*

1817 **Goldenthal** [village in Switzerland], Johann Heinrich Daniel Zschokke, *Der Goldmacherdorf*

1820 **New Britain** [country in North America], G. A. Ellis, *New Britain: A Narrative of a Journey, by Mr. Ellis, To a Country So Called By Its Inhabitants, Discovered in the Vast Plain of the Missouri, in North America, and Inhabited by a People of British Origin, Who Live Under an Equitable System of Society, Productive of Peculiar Independence and Happiness. Also, Some Account of Their Constitution, Laws, Institutions, Customs and Philosophical Opinions: Together With a Brief Sketch of Their History from the Time of Their Departure from Great Britain*

1820 **Symzonia** [underground realm under Antarctica], Captain Adam Seabourn, *Symzonia, A Voyage of Discovery*

1821 **Pluto** [underground world inside the hollow Earth], Anonymous, *Voyage au centre de la terre, ou aventures de quelques naufragés dans des pays inconnus*

1822 **Hurlubiere** [empire in Western Europe], **Island of the Patagones** [island in the Atlantic Ocean], Charles Noldier, *Hurlubleu, Grand Manifafa d'Hurlubiére*

1826 **Imagination** [kingdom], Wilhelm Hauff, *Märchenalmanach*

1827 **Morosofia** [country on the moon], George Tucker, *A Voyage to the Moon: With Some Account of the Manners and Customs, Science and Philosophy, of the People of Morosofia, and Other Lunarians*

1828 **Isle of Fantaisie, Vraibleusia** [islands in the Indian Ocean], Benjamin Disraeli, *The Voyage of Captain Popanilla*

1830 **Micromona** [country], Karl Immerman, *Tulifänntchen, Ein Heldengedicht in drei Gesängen*

1831 **Apodidraskiana** [state of the United States], Thomas Love Peacock, *Crotchet Castle*

1832 **Mayda** [island], Washington Irving, *The Alhambra*

1834 **Future Earth** [alternate Earth], Félix Bodin, *Le Roman de l'Avenir*

1834 **Angria** [country], **Gondal** [island in the North Pacific Ocean], **Gaaldine** [island in the South Pacific Ocean], Emily, Anne, Charlotte, and Patrick

Branwell Brontë, (the islands appeared in various poems and prose, some now lost)

1835 **Leap Islands** [islands near Antarctica], James Fenimore Cooper, *The Monikins*

1835 **Tsar Dodan's Kingdom** [kingdom in Russia], Alexander Pushkin, *The Tale of the Golden Cockerel*

1835 **Viti Islands** [islands], Henry-Florent Delmotte, *Voyage pittoresque et industriel dans le Paraguay-Roux et la Palingénésie Australe par Tridacé-Nafé-Théobrôme de Kaou't'Chouk, Gentilhomme Breton, sous-aide à l'éstablissement des clysopompes, etc.*

1836 **Future Earth** [alternate Earth], Mary Griffith, "Three Hundred Years Hence" in *Camperdown; or, News from Our Neighborhood: Being Sketches*

1837 **Flora, Athunt** [countries], Ferdinand Raimund, *Die gefesselte Phantasie*

1837 **New Holland** [country in Australia], Richard Whatley, *Account of an Expedition to the Interior of New Holland*

1838 **Tsalal** [island near Antarctica], Edgar Allen Poe, *The Narrative of Arthur Gordon Pym of Nantucket*

1839 **Icaria** [country], Etienne Cabet, *Voyage et Aventures de Lord William Carisdall en Icarie*

1845 **Kingdom of Dolls** [kingdom entered through a wardrobe], Alexander Dumas (père), *Histoire d'une Cassenoisette*

1845 **Island of the Fay** [island], Edgar Allen Poe, "The Island of the Fay" in *Tales*

1845 **Silence** [land in Libya], Edgar Allen Poe, "Silence: A Fable" in *Tales*

1845 **Venusberg** [mountain realm], Richard Wagner, *Tannhäuser*

1845 **Vondervoteimittiss** [Dutch borough], Edgar Allen Poe, "The Devil in the Belfry" in *Tales*

1847 **Vulcan's Peak, The Crater, Rancocus Island, etc**. [various places], James Fenimore Cooper, *The Crater; or, Vulcan's Peak. A Tale of the Pacific*

1849 **Mardi Archipelago** [islands], Herman Melville, *Mardi, and A Voyage Thither*

1849 **Victoria** [town in England], James S. Buckingham, *National Evils and Practical Remedies, with a Plan of a Model Town*

1851 **Ejuxria** [country], Hartley Coleridge, *Poems by Hartley Coleridge, With a Memoir of His Life by His Brother* (by Derwent Coleridge)

1851 **Stiria** [land], John Ruskin, *The King of the Golden River or The Black Brothers, A Legend of Stiria*

1852 **Euphonia** [city in the mountains of Germany], Hector Berlioz, "Euphonie, ou la Ville Musicale, Nouvelle de l'Avenir" in *Les Soirées de l'Orchestre*

1854 **The Starian system** [solar system], Charles Ischir Defontenay, *Star (Psi Cassiopeia): The Marvelous History of One of the Worlds of Outer Space*

1855 **Aklis** [country], **Oolb** [city], George Meredith, *The Shaving of Shagpat*

1855 **Barsetshire** [county in England], Anthony Trollope, *The Warden*

1857 **Blackstaff, Paflagonia, Crim Tartary** [countries], M. A. Titmarsh [William Makepeace Thackeray], "The Rose and the Ring" in *Christmas Books*

1858 **(Unnamed world)** [microscopic world], Fitz-James O'Brien, "The Diamond Lens" in *Atlantic Monthly*, August 1858

1858 **Coral Island, Emo, Mango Island, etc.** [islands in the South Pacific], Robert Michael Ballantyne, *The Coral Island*

1858 **Fairyland** [country], George MacDonald, *Phantastes: A Faerie Romance for Men and Women*

1862 **Other planets** [planets], Nicolas Camille Flammarion, *La Pluralité des Mondes Habités*

1862 **Airfowlness, Land of Golden Asses, etc.** [lands], Charles Kingsley, *The Water-Babies: A Fairy Tale for a Land-Baby* (first serialized in *McMillan's Magazine*)

1864 **Lemuria** [lost continent], Philip Sclater, "The Mammals of Madagascar" in *The Quarterly Journal of Science*

1864 **Lindenbrock Sea** [underground], Jules Verne, *Voyage au Centre de la Terre, ou Aventures de Quelques Naufragés dans des Pays Inconnus*

1865 **Future Paris** [alternate Paris], Louis Hippolyte Mettais, *L'An 5865 ou Paris dans 4000 Ans*

1865 **Wonderland** [dream/underground below England], Lewis Carroll [Charles Lutwidge Dodgson], *Alice's Adventures in Wonderland*

1866 **Queen Island** [island near North Pole], Jules Verne, *Voyage et Aventures du Capitaine Hatteras*

1867 **Troll Kingdom** [land in the mountains of Norway], Henrik Ibsen, *Peer Gynt*

1868 **Forest Island, Island of the Wanderers** [islands], William Morris, *The Earthly Paradise, A Poem*

1869 **Fairyland** [land], Jean Ingelow, *Mopsa the Fairy*

1869 **Future Paris** [alternate Paris], Tony Moilin, *Paris en l'An 2000*

1869 **Io-Phoebe** [artificial moon], Edward Everett Hale, "The Brick Moon" serialized in *The Atlantic Monthly*, July 1869

1870 **Aphania** [kingdom], Tom Hood, *Petsetilla's Posy: A Fairy Tale*

1870 **Country at the back of the North Wind** [land], George MacDonald, *At the Back of the North Wind*

1870 **Gloupov** [town], Saltykov-Shchedrin [Mikhail Yevgrafovich Saltykov], *Istoriya Odnogo Goroda*

1870 **Mars** [planet], Annie Denton Cridge, *Man's Rights; or, How Would You Like It?*

1871 **Country of the Vril-ya** [underground country, under England], Edward George Earle Lytton Bulwer, Lord Lytton, *The Coming Race*

1871 **Gramblamble Land** [country], Edward Lear, "The History of the Seven Families of the Lake Pipple-popple" in *Nonsense Songs, Stories, Botany, and Alphabets*

1871 **Looking-glass Land** [dream/land], Lewis Carroll [Charles Lutwidge Dodgson], *Through the Looking-Glass, and What Alice Found There*

1871 **Mountain of the Spirits** [mountain], Gustavo Adolfo Becquer, "El monte de las animas" in *Leyendas*

1872 **Erewhon** [country], Samuel Butler, *Erewhon; or, Over the Range*

1872 **Wessex** [region in southwest England], Thomas Hardy, *Under the Greenwood Tree*

1874 **City of Night** [city], James Thomson, *The City of Dreadful Night*

1874 **Lincoln Island** [island in the Pacific Ocean], Jules Verne, *The Mysterious Island*

1875 **Gondour** [republic], Mark Twain [Samuel Langhorne Clemens], *The Curious Republic of Gondour, and Other Whimsical Sketches*

1875 **Ham Rock** [island in the Atlantic Ocean], Jules Verne, *Le "Chancellor"*

1875 **Nomansland** [kingdom], Dinah Maria Mulock Craik, *The Little Lame Prince and His Traveling Cloak*

1875 **Selene** [city near Belgrade, Yugoslavia], Paul Féval, *La Ville Vampire*

1876 **Hygeia** [town], Sir Benjamin Ward Richardson, *Hygeia, A City of Health*

1876 **Polar Bear Kingdom** [underground in ice, near Franz Josef Land], Jókai Mór, *20,000 Lieues sous les Glaces*

1876 **Snark Island** [island], Lewis Carroll [Charles Lutwidge Dodgson], "The Hunting of the Snark"

1876 **Uchronia** [alternate Europe], Charles Renouvier, *Uchronie: l'utopie dans l'histoire, esquisse historique apocryphe du développement de la civilisation européenne tel qu'il n'a pas été, tel qu'il aurait pu être*

1877 **Coal City** [underground city], Jules Verne, *Les Indes Noires*

1879 **Farandoulie** [kingdom in Australia], **Makalolo** [country in central Africa], Albert Robida, *Voyages Très Extraordinaires de Saturnin Farandoul dans les 5 ou 6 Parties du Monde*

1879 **Ville-France, Stahlstadt** [countries in the Pacific Northwest of North America], Jules Verne, *Les 500 Millions de la Bégum*

1880 **Mizora** [underground country], Mary E. Bradley Lane, *Mizora: A Prophecy. A Mss. Found Among the Private Papers of the Princess Vera Zarovitch, Being a true and faithful account of her Journey to the Interior of the Earth, with a careful description of the Country and its Inhabitants, their Customs, Manners and Government* (Originally published as "Narrative of Vera Zarovitch", with the same subtitle as that of the book, in the *Cincinnati Commercial* beginning November 6, 1880.)

1880 **Papefiguiera** [country], Béroualde de Verville, *Le Moyen de parvenir. Oeuvre contenant la raison de tout ce qui a esté, est et setra, avec démonstrations certaines et nécessaires selon la rencontre des effets de vertu*

1881 **Britannula** [island near New Zealand], Anthony Trollope, *The Fixed Period* (first serialized in *Blackwood's Magazine*)

1882 **Suicide City** [underground city east of Paris], Robert Louis Stevenson, *New Arabian Nights*

1883 **Future New York** [alternate New York], Ismar Thiusen [John Macnie], *The Diothas; or, A Far Look Ahead*

1883 **Future World of the 20th century** [world], Albert Robida, *Le Vingtième Siècle*

1883 **Island of the Busy Bees** [island], Carlo Collodi, *Le Aventure di Pinocchio*

1883 **Treasure Island** [island], Robert Louis Stevenson, *Treasure Island*

1884 **Flatland** [two-dimensional world], **Lineland** [one-dimensional world], **Spaceland** [three-dimensional world], Edwin Abbott Abbott, *Flatland: A Romance of Many Dimensions*

1884 **Malacovia** [city-fortress in the Danube], Amedeo Tosetti, *Pedali sul Mar Nero*

1885 **Agartha** [kingdom], Saint-Yves d'Alveydre, *Mission de l'Inde en Europe*

1885 **Kukuanaland** [land in central southern Africa on a plateau surrounded by mountains], Henry Rider Haggard, *King Solomon's Mines*

1885 **Titipu** [town in Japan], Sir William Schwenk Gilbert and Sir Arthur Sullivan, *The Mikado*

1887 **Alternate New York** [alternate New York], Anna Bowman Dodd, *The Republic of the Future: or, Socialism a Reality*

1887 **Coradine** [country in Northern Scotland], W. H. Hudson, *A Crystal Age*

1887 **Kor** [ruins of a city], Henry Rider Haggard, *She: A History of Adventure*

1887 **Zuvendis** [country in East Africa], Henry Rider Haggard, *Allan Quartermain*

1888 **Chairman Island** [island], Jules Verne, *Deux ans de vacances*

1888 **Future America** [alternate America], Edward Bellamy, *Looking Backward: 2000–1887*

1888 **Kosekin Country** [underground country under Antarctica], James De Mille, *A Strange Manuscript found in a Copper Cylinder*

1889 **Barataria**, [kingdom], Sir William Schwenk Gilbert and Sir Arthur Sullivan, *The Gondoliers*

1889 **New Amazonia** [country], Elizabeth Corbett, *New Amazonia*

1889 **Dogland** [land], Lewis Carroll [Charles Lutwidge Dodgson], *Sylvie and Bruno*

1889 **Pantouflia** [country], Andrew Lang, *Prince Prigio*

1889 **(Other planets)** [planets], Nicolas Camille Flammarion, *Uranie*

1890 **Freeland** [country in East Africa], Theodor Hertzka, *Freiland*

1890 **Future England** [alternate England], Lady Florence Dixie, *Gloriana, or the Revolution of 1900*

1890 **Future England** [alternate England], William Morris, *News from Nowhere (or, An Epoch of Rest)*

1890 **Future New York** [alternate New York], Ignatius Donelly, *Caesar's Column: A Story of the Twentieth Century*

1890 **Mars** [version of Mars], Robert Cromie, *A Plunge into Space*
1891 **The City of Tone** [city in the future], Chauncey Thomas, *The Crystal Button: or, Adventures of Paul Prognosis in the Forty-ninth Century*
1891 **Elisee Reclus Island** [island in the North Pacific], Alphonse Brown, *Une Ville de Verre*
1891 **Land of the Glittering Plain** [kingdom near Scotland], **Isle of Ransom** [island], William Morris, *The Story of the Glittering Plain which has also been called the Land of the Living Men or the Acre of the Undying*
1892 **Abaton** [city], Sir Thomas Bulfinch, *My Heart's in the Highlands*
1892 **Altruria** [island continent], William Dean Howells, *A Traveler from Altruria* (first serialized in *The Cosmopolitan*, November 1892)
1892 **Atvatabar** [underground country], William R. Bradshaw, *The Goddess of Atvatabar, being the History of the Discovery of the Interior World and the Conquest of Atvatabar*
1892 **Klausenburg County** [county in Transylvania], Jules Verne, *Le Château des Carpathes*
1893 **Aeria** [mountain valley in North African], George Griffith, *The Angel of the Revolution*
1893 **Isle of Feminine** [island in the Caribbean Sea], Charles Elliot Niswonger, *The Isle of Feminine*
1893 **Future Earth** [alternate Earth], Nicolas Camille Flammarion, *La Fin du Monde*
1893 **Zara's Kingdom** [island in the South Seas], Sir William Schwenk Gilbert and Sir Arthur Sullivan, *Utopia Limited; or, The Flowers of Progress*
1894 **Aepyornis Island** [island], H. G. Wells, "Aepyornis Island" in *The Stolen Bacillus and Other Incidents*
1894 **Boyberik** [town in Russia; later renamed "Anatevka" in *Fiddler on the Roof* (1964)], Sholem Aleichem, *Tevye and His Daughters*
1894 **Country of the People of the Mist** [country in central–southeast Africa], Henry Rider Haggard, *The People of the Mist*
1894 **Future Earth** [alternate Earth], H. G. Wells, *The Time Machine: An Invention* (first serialized in *New Review*)
1894 **Ruritania** [country in Europe], Anthony Hope [Anthony Hope Hopkins], *The Prisoner of Zenda*
1894 **The Wood beyond the World** [country], William Morris, *The Wood beyond the World*
1895 **Etidorhpa's Country** [underground country in a Kentucky cave], John Uri Lloyd, *Etidorhpa or the End of the Earth, the Strange History of a Mysterious Being and the Account of a Remarkable Journey as Communicated in Manuscript to Llewellyn Drury who Promised to Print the Same but Finally Evaded the Responsibility which was Assumed by John Uri Lloyd*
1895 **Raymangal** [island], Emilio Salgari, *I misteri della Jungla Nera*

1895 **Standard Island** [island somewhere near New Zealand], Jules Verne, *L'Ile à Hélice*

1896 **Noble's Isle** [island in the Pacific Ocean], H. G. Wells, *The Island of Dr. Moreau*

1896 **Mu** [continent], Augustus Le Plongeon, *Maya/Atlantis: Queen Móo and the Egyptian Sphinx*

1896 **Upmeads** [kingdom], William Morris, *The Well at the World's End*

1897 **Nu** [version of Mars], Kurd Lasswitz, *Auf zwei Planeten*

1897 **Wondrous Isles, Isle of Increase Unsought** [islands], William Morris, *The Water of the Wondrous Isles*

1898 **Adam's Country** [colony], Paul Adam, *Lettres de Malaisie*

1899 **The Arq** [city], Anna Adolph, *Arqtiq: A Story of the Marvels at the North Pole*

1899 **Avondale** [phalanstery], Grant Allen, "The Child of the Phalanstery" in *Twelve Tales*

1899 **Double Island** [island], George Maspero, *Les Contes Populaires de l'Egypte Ancienne*

1899 **Future London** [alternate London], H. G. Wells, *When the Sleeper Awakes: A Story of the Years to Come*

1900 **Cooperative City** [city in Maine], Bradford Peck, *The World, A Department Store, A Story of Life under the Cooperative System*

1900 **Island of the Nine Whirlpools** [island], Edith Nesbit, "The Island of the Nine Whirlpools" in *The Book of Dragons*

1900 **Phunnyland** [kingdom (later renamed **Mo**; retroactively linked to Oz)], L. Frank Baum, *A New Wonderland* (later renamed *The Surprising Adventures of the Magical Monarch of Mo and His People* when re-released in 1903)

1900 **Oz** [country], L. Frank Baum, *The Wonderful Wizard of Oz*

1900 **Rotundia** [island kingdom off the coast of Britain], Edith Nesbit, "Uncle James, or The Purple Stranger" in *The Book of Dragons*

1900 **Tryphême** [kingdom on the Mediterranean coast by Spain], Pierre Louÿs, *Les Aventures du Roi Pausole*

1901 **Bugville** [town], Gus Dirks, *The Latest News from Bugville*

1901 **Graustark, Axphain, Dawsbergen** [countries], George Barr McCutcheon, *Graustark: The Story of a Love Behind a Throne*

1901 **Merryland** [land (retroactively linked to Oz)], L. Frank Baum, *Dot and Tot in Merryland*

1901 **The Moon** [moon], H. G. Wells, *The First Men in the Moon*

1901 **Mouseland** [land], Edward Earle Childs, *The Wonders of Mouseland*

1901 **Neustria** [colony in South America], Emile Thirion, *Neustria, Utopie Individualiste*

1901 **Quok** [land (retroactively linked to Oz], L. Frank Baum, "The Queen of Quok" in *American Fairy Tales*

1901 **Riallaro Archipelago** [islands], Godfrey Sweven [John Macmillan Brown], *Riallaro, The Archipelago of Exiles*

1902 **Altneuland (Old Newland)** [country], Theodor Herzl, *Altneuland*

1902 **Cagayan Salu** [island], Andrew Lang, *The Disentanglers*

1902 **The Moon** [version of the moon], George Méliès, *A Trip to the Moon*

1903 **Toyland** [land], Victor Herbert and Glen MacDonough, *Babes in Toyland*

1903 **Yew** [island (retroactively linked to Oz)], L. Frank Baum, *The Enchanted Island of Yew*

1904 **Costaguana** [country in South America], Joseph Conrad, *Nostromo*

1904 **Country of the Blind** [country in the mountains of Ecuador], H. G. Wells, "The Country of the Blind" in *Strand Magazine*, April 1904

1904 **Neverland** [island], Sir James Matthew Barrie, *Peter Pan, or the Boy Who Wouldn't Grow*

1904 **The Sun** [version of the sun], George Méliès, *The Impossible Voyage*

1905 **Kaloon** [land], Henry Rider Haggard, *Ayesha, the Return of She*

1905 **Mandai Country** [underground country at the North Pole], Hirmiz bar Anhar, *Iran*

1905 **Pegāna** [home of the gods], Lord Dunsany [Edward John Moreton Drax Plunkett], *The Gods of Pegāna*

1905 **Slumberland** [kingdom], Winsor McCay, *Little Nemo in Slumberland*

1906 **Averon, Yarnith, Zarkandhu** [countries], Lord Dunsany [Edward John Moreton Drax Plunkett], *Time and the Gods*

1906 **Harmonia** [country, unknown location], Georges Delbruck, *Au Pays de l'Harmonie*

1906 **Isle of Phreex, Isle of the Mifkets, etc.** [islands], L. Frank Baum, *John Dough and the Cherub*

1906 **Kellecheura** [purgatorial place], R. H. Wright, *The Outer Darkness*

1906 **Kravonia** [country in Eastern Europe], Anthony Hope [Anthony Hope Hopkins], *Sophy of Kravonia*

1906 **Morrow Island** [island], Henri Chateau, *La Cité des Idoles*

1907 **Astria** [two-dimensional world], C. H. Hinton, *An Episode of Flatland: Or, How a Plane Folk Discovered the Third Dimension*

1907 **Expiation City** [city in Europe], P. S. Ballanches, *La Ville des Expiations*

1907 **Land of Paradise** [forest], L. Frank Baum, *Policeman Bluejay*

1907 **North Pole Kingdom** [underground country in the Arctic], Charles Derennes, *Le Peuple du Pôle*

1907 **Sargasso Sea, Land of Lonesomeness** [sea and land], William Hope Hodgson, *The Boats of the "Glen Carrig"*

1907 **Zvezdnym (Star City)** [city at the South Pole], Valery Briussov, "Respublika Yuzhnogo Kresta" in *Zemnaya Os*

1908 **Asgard** [city], Jack London, *The Iron Heel*

1908 **Dream Kingdom** [kingdom between Russia and China], Alfred Kubin, *Die Andere Seite: Ein Phantastischer Roman*

1908 **Penguin Island** [island], Anatole France [Jacques Anatole François Thibault], *L'Ile des Pingouins*

1908 **River Bank** [land], Kenneth Grahame, *The Wind in the Willows*

1908 **Terre Libre** [island in the Pacific Ocean], Jean Grave, *Terre Libre*

1909 **Alternate Earth** [alternate Earth], E. M. Forster, "The Machine Stops" in *The Oxford and Cambridge Review*, November 1909

1909 **Ardistan, Djinnistan** [countries], Karl Friedrich May, *Ardistan and Djinnistan*

1909 **Hoste** [island near Tierra del Fuego], Jules Verne, *Les Naufragés du "Jonathan"*

1909 **Grand Duchy of Grimmburg** [duchy in Germany], Thomas Mann, *Königliche Hoheit*

1910 **Polistarchia** [country], Edith Nesbit, *The Magic City*

1910 **Ponukele-Drelchkaff** [empire in North Africa], Raymond Roussel, *Impressions d'Afrique*

1910 **Roadtown** [city near New York City], Edgar Chambers, *Roadtown*

1911 **Amorphous Island, Cyril Island, Fragrant Island, etc.** [islands], Alfred Jarry, *Gestes et Opinions du Docteur Faustroll, Pataphysicien*

1911 **Future Earth** [future Earth], Hugo Gernsback, "Ralph 124C 41+: A Romance of the Year 2660" first serialized in *Modern Electrics*, April 1911

1911 **Kalomera** [community], William John Saunders, *Kalomera: The Story of a Remarkable Community*

1911 **True Lhassa** [underground city under Tibet], Maurice Champagne, *Les Sondeurs d'Abîmes*

1912 **Barsoom** [version of Mars], Edgar Rice Burroughs, "Under the Moons of Mars" in *All-Story Magazine*, February 1912)

1912 **Future Earth** [future Earth], William Hope Hodgson, *The Night Land*

1912 **Land of Wonder** [land], Isaac Leib Peretz, *Ale Verk*

1912 **Maple White Land** [land on a volcanic plateau in South America], Sir Arthur Conan Doyle, *The Lost World*

1913 **Flotsam** [island], Edgar Rice Burroughs, *The Cave Girl*

1913 **Maxon's Island** [island in the South China Sea], Edgar Rice Burroughs, *A Man Without a Soul*

1913 **Opar** [city in an African valley], Edgar Rice Burroughs, *The Return of Tarzan*

1914 **Lutha** [country in Southern Europe], Edgar Rice Burroughs, *The Mad King*

1914 **Pellucidar** [underground world inside the hollow earth], Edgar Rice Burroughs, *At the Earth's Core*

1914 **Yoka Island** [island in the Pacific Ocean], Edgar Rice Burroughs, *The Mucker*

1915 **Herland** [country], Charlotte Perkins Gilman, *Herland*

1915 **Plutonia** [underground world], Vladimir Obruchev, *Plutonia*

1915 **Toonerville** [town], Fontaine Fox, *Toonerville Folks*

1917 **Crotalophoboi Land** [country in North Africa], **Nepenthe** [island in the Tyrrhenian Sea], Norman Douglas, *South Wind*

1917 **Euralia, Barodia** [kingdoms], A. A. Milne, *Once on a Time*

1917 **Faremidoba** [land], Frigyes Karinthy, *Utazas Faremidoba*

1918 **Caspak** (also known as **Caprona**) [island], Edgar Rice Burroughs, *The Land That Time Forgot*

1918 **Gasoline Alley** [town], Frank O. King, *Gasoline Alley*

1918 **Meccania** [country in Western Europe], Owen Gregory, *Meccania, the Super-State*

1918 **Orofena** [island in the South Pacific], Henry Rider Haggard, *When the World Shook, Being an Account of the Great Adventure of Bastin, Bickley and Arbothnot*

1919 **Animal Land** [land], Howard R. Garis, *Uncle Wiggily*

1919 **Agzceaziguls** [country], Charles Derennes, *Les Conquérants d'Idoles*

1919 **Beaulieu** [town], Ralph Adams Cram, *Walled Towns*

1919 **Blackland** [ruined city], Jules Verne, *L'Etonnante Aventure de la Mission Barsac*

1919 **The Oroid world** [microscopic world in a wedding ring], Raymond King Cummings, "The Girl in the Golden Atom" (novellette, later published in book form in 1922)

1919 **Poictesme, Targamon, etc.** [countries], James Branch Cabell, *Jurgen, A Comedy of Justice*

1919 **Spinachova, Demonia, etc.** [lands], E. C. Segar, *Thimble Theatre*

1920 **Dreamworld** (or **Dreamlands**) [world], H. P. Lovecraft, "Polaris" in *Philosopher*, December 1920

1920 **Gopher Prairie** [town in central Minnesota], Sinclair Lewis, *Main Street*

1920 **Green Meadows, Smiling Pool** [rural locales], **Carrotville** [town], Thornton W. Burgess, *Peter Rabbit*

1920 **Jannati Shahr** [city in Saudi Arabia, beyond mountains], George Allen England, *The Flying Legion*

1920 **Mag-Mell, Raklmani** [islands near Ireland], Maria Savi-Lopez, *Leggende del Mare*

1920 **Tormance** [planet], David Lindsay, *A Voyage to Arcturus*

1920 **Tutter** [town in Illinois], Leo Edwards [Edward Edson Lee], "The Cruise of the Sally Ann", *Shelby Daily Globe*, April 1920

1921 **Capellette, Alma** [planets], Homer Eon Flint, *The Devolutionist*

1921 **Capillaria** [underwater world], Frigyes Karinthy, *Capillaria*

1921 **Pal-ul-don** [kingdom in Zaire], Edgar Rice Burroughs, *Tarzan the Terrible*

1922 **Auspasia** [kingdom], Georges Duhamel, *Lettres d'Auspasie*

1922 **Demonland, Witchland, Zimiamvia, etc.** [lands (supposedly on Mercury)], E. R. Eddison, *The Worm Ouroboros*

1922 **Isles of Wisdom** [archipelago], Alexander Moszkowski, *Die Inseln der Weisheit Geschichte einer abenteuerlichen Entdeckungsfahrt*

1922 **Jolliginki** [country on the African coast near Mozambique], Hugh Lofting, *The Story of Doctor Dolittle*

1922 **Rootabaga country, etc.** [countries], Carl Sandburg, *Rootabaga Stories*

1922 **Utopia** [planet], H. G. Wells, *Men Like Gods* (first serialized in *The Westminster Gazette*, December 1922)

1922 **Venusia** [island in Atlantic Ocean near equator], Raymond Clauzel, *L'Ile des Femmes*

1922 **Winnemac** [midwestern U.S. state], Sinclair Lewis, *Babbitt*

1923 **Barnsville** [town], Augustus Daniel "Ad" Carter, *Just Kids*

1923 **Belesbat** [underwater city], Claire Kenin, *La Mer Mystérieuse*

1923 **Capa Blanca Islands** [islands], **Spidermonkey Island** [island off the coast of Brazil], Hugh Lofting, *The Voyages of Doctor Dolittle*

1923 **Cuffycoat's Island** [island], **Vichebolk Land** [land in the Arctic Circle], André Lichtenberger, *Pickles ou Récits à la Mode Anglaise*

1923 **Rossum's Island** [island], Karel Čapek, *R. U. R. (Rossum's Universal Robots)*

1923 **Yu-Atlanchi** [land in the Andes], A. Merritt [Abraham Merritt], "The Face in the Abyss", in *Argosy*, September 8, 1923

1924 **Alali** [village], **Minuni** [region], Edgar Rice Burroughs, *Tarzan and the Ant Men*

1924 **Candelabra, Hitaxia, Kleptomania, Nikkateena, Woopsydasia** [European kingdoms], **Costa Grande** [Latin American republic], Roy Crane, *Washington Tubbs II* (later known as *Wash Tubbs*)

1924 **Elfland, Erl** [kingdoms], Lord Dunsany [Edward John Moreton Drax Plunkett], *The King of Elfland's Daughter*

1924 **Fantippo** [kingdom in West Africa], Hugh Lofting, *Doctor Dolittle's Post Office*

1924 **Ladies' Island** [island], Gerhart Hauptmann, *Die Insel der Grossen Mutter oder das Wunder von Ile des Dames*

1924 **OneState** [country], Yevgeny Zamyatin, *We*

1924 **Orphan Island** [island in the Pacific Ocean], Rose Macaulay, *Orphan Island*

1924 **Sannikov Land** [underground world], Vladimir Obruchev, *Sannikov Land*

1925 **Caspo** [island kingdom], Arnold Bennett, *The Bright Island*

1925 **Ebony** [island], Salvador de Madariaga, *The Sacred Giraffe; Being the Second Volume of the Posthumous Works of Julio Arceval*

1925 **Edomite Empire** [empire], An-Ski [Solomon Samuel Rappaport], *Gesamelte Shriften*

1925 **Neutopia** [country], E. Richardson, *Neutopia*

1926 **(Unnamed world)** [macroscopic world], G. Peyton Wertenbaker, "The Man from the Atom", *Amazing Stories*, Volume 1, Number 1, April 1926

1926 **City of Sand** [city in the deserts of Syria], Jean d'Agraives [Frédéric Causse], *La Cité des Sables*

1926 **City of Shadows** [city under the Mediterranean], Léon Groc, *La Cité des Ténèbres*

1926 **Dorimare, Land of Faerie** [lands], Hope Mirrlees, *Lud-in-the-Mist*

1926 **The Hundred Acre Wood** [forest], A. A. Milne, *Winnie-the-Pooh*

1926 **Ishtar** [land], **Emakhtila** [island], A. Merritt [Abraham Merritt], *The Ship of Ishtar*

1927 **Articoles, Maïna** [islands in the Pacific Ocean], André Maurois, *Voyage au Pays des Articoles*

1927 **Atlanteja** [city], Luigi Motta, *Il Tunnel Sottomarino*

1927 **Electropolis** [city in the Australian outback], Otfrid von Hanstein, *Elektropolis*

1927 **Hall of the Mist** [place on the star Antares], Donald Wandrei, "The Red Brain" in *Weird Tales*, October 1927

1927 **The Marvelous Land of Snergs** [land], E. A. Wyke-Smith, *The Marvelous Land of Snergs*

1927 **Metropolis** [city], Thea von Harbou and Fritz Lang, *Metropolis*

1927 **Sunless City** [underground city under the Nubian desert], Albert Bonneau, *La Cité sans Soleil*

1927 **Zaroff's Island** [island in the Caribbean], Richard Connell, "The Most Dangerous Game" in *Collier's Weekly*, January 19, 1924

1928 **(Unnamed world)** [microscopic world], Roman Frederick Starzl, "Out of the Sub-Universe", *Amazing Stories Quarterly*, Summer 1928

1928 **Captain Sparrow's Island** [island], S. Fowler Wright, *The Island of Captain Sparrow*

1928 **Future Earth** [future Earth], Philip Francis Nowlan, "Armageddon, 2419 A.D." in *Amazing Stories*, August 1928

1928 **Hulak** [city in a crater in Brazil], T. C. Bridges, *The Mysterious City*

1928 **Osnome** [planet], E. E. Smith, *The Skylark of Space*, first serialized in *Amazing Stories*, August 1928

1928 **Purple Island** [island in the Pacific Ocean], Mikhail Bulgakov, *Bagrobyj Ostrov*

1928 **Xenephrine** [planet], Raymond King Cummings, *A Brand New World*

1929 **Castra Sanguinarius, Castrum Mare** [cities], Edgar Rice Burroughs, *Tarzan and the Lost Empire*

1929 **Mahagonny** [city in the desert by the ocean], Bertol Brecht, *Aufstieg und Fall der Stadt Mahagonny*

1929 **Paroulet's Country** [underground country], Maurice Champagne, *La Cité des Premiers Hommes*

1929 **Thuria** [continent], Robert E. Howard, "The Shadow Kingdom" in *Weird Tales*, August 1929

1929 **Toyland** [land], Enid Blyton, *Noddy Goes to Toyland*

1929 **The World Below** [underground world], S. Fowler Wright, *The World Below*

1929 **Yoknapatawpha County** [county in the southern United States], William Faulkner, *Sartoris*

1930 **Alternate Earth** [alternate Earth], Olaf Stapledon, *Last and First Men: A Story of the Near and Far Future*

1930 **Alternate United States** [alternate United States], Georges Duhamel, *Scènes de la Vie Future*

1930 **Averoigne** [province in Medieval France], Clark Ashton Smith, "The End of the Story" in *Weird Tales*, May 1930

1930 **Big Tooth Continent** [continent], Lev Kassil, *The Black Book and Schwambrania*

1930 **City of Beauty, City of Smoke** [cities], Miles J. Breuer, "Paradise and Iron" in *Amazing Stories Quarterly*, Summer 1930

1930 **Le Douar** [island off the coast of Brittany], J. H. Rosny [Séraphin Justin François Boex], *L'Enigme du "Redoutable"*

1930 **Evallonia** [country in Central Europe], John Buchan, *Castle Gay*

1930 **Fattipuff Kingdom, Thinifer Kingdom** [kingdoms], André Maurois, *Patapoufs et Filifers*

1930 **Green Sand Island** [island near Hawaii], Tancrède Vallerey, *L'Ile au Sable Vert*

1930 **Lothar** [underwater city], Jack Williamson, *The Green Girl* (first serialized in Amazing Stories, beginning March 1930)

1930 **Poseidonis** [last isle of Atlantis], Clark Ashton Smith, "The Last Incantation" in *Weird Tales*, June 1930

1930 **Theives' City** [city in the Klondike region], Maurice Level, *La Cité des Voleurs*

1930 **Ultimo** [underground city] John Vassos and Ruth Vassos, *Ultimo: An Imaginative Narration of Life Under the Earth*

1931 **Bimble Town** [town], K. Bagpuize [J. R. R. Tolkien], "Progress in Bimble Town (Devoted to the Mayor and Corporation)", in *The Oxford Magazine*, October 15th, 1931

1931 **Hyperborea** [Arctic continent], Clark Ashton Smith, "The Tale of Satampra Zeiros" in *Weird Tales*, November 1931

1931 **Lodidhapura** [city in the jungles of Cambodia], Edgar Rice Burroughs, *The Jungle Girl*

1931 **Seachild's City** [island in the North Atlantic], **Streaming Kingdom** [kingdom under the English Channel], Jules Supervielle, *L'Enfant de la Haute Mer*

1931 **Ulm** [microscopic world], S. P. Meek, "Submicroscopic" in *Amazing Stories*, August 1931

1932 **Azanian Empire** [island], Evelyn Waugh, *Black Mischief*

1932 **Bronson Beta** [planet], Edwin Balmer and Philip Wylie, *When Worlds Collide* (first serialized in *Blue Book*, beginning in September, 1932)

1932 **Buyan Island** [island], Karl Ralston, "Buyanka" in *The Songs of the Russian People*

1932 **Future England** [future England], Aldous Huxley, *Brave New World*

1932 **Hyborian Age** [Earth with an alternate history], Robert E. Howard, "The Phoenix on the Sword" in *Weird Tales*, December 1932

1932 **Junkville** [town], Earl Duvall, *Silly Symphonies* (comic strip)

1932 **Midian** [country in Africa], Edgar Rice Burroughs, *Tarzan Triumphant*

1932 **Onthar, Thenar** [lands in Africa], Edgar Rice Burroughs, *Tarzan and the City of Gold* (first serialized in *Argosy* magazine, beginning March 1932)

1932 **Phandiom** [planet], Clark Ashton Smith, "The Planet of the Dead" in *Weird Tales*, March 1932

1932 **The Pygmy Planet** [artificial, miniature world], Jack Williamson, "The Pygmy Planet" in *Astounding Stories*, February 1932

1932 **Venusberg** [city in the Baltic region], Anthony Powell, *Venusberg*

1932 **Yoh-Vombis** [city on Mars], Clark Ashton Smith, "The Vaults of the Yoh-Vombis" in *Weird Tales*, May 1932

1932 **Zothique** [continent], Clark Ashton Smith, "The Empire of the Necromancers" in *Weird Tales*, September 1932

1933 **Alternate Earth** [alternate Earth], H. G. Wells, *The Shape of Things to Come: The Ultimate Revolution*

1934 **Dogpatch** [village], Al Capp, *Li'l Abner*

1933 **Freedonia** [country in Europe], Leo McCarey, *Duck Soup*

1933 **Rampole Island** [island in the South Atlantic], H. G. Wells, *Mr. Blettsworthy on Rampole Island*

1933 **Shangri-La** [valley in Tibet], James Hilton, *Lost Horizon*

1933 **Skull Island** [island southwest of Sumatra], Merian Cooper and Ernest Schoedsack, *King Kong*

1933 **Xiccarph** [planet], Clark Ashton Smith, "The Maze of the Maal Dweb" in *The Double Shadow and Other Fantasies*

1934 **(Unnamed world)** [world], Mo Leff, *Peter Pat*

1934 **Alternate Universe** [alternate universe], Murray Leinster [William Fitzgerald Jenkins], "Sidewise in Time" in *Astounding Stories*, June 1934

1934 **Amtor** [version of Venus], Edgar Rice Burroughs, *Pirates of Venus*

1934 **Kingdom of Moo** [kingdom], Vincent Hamlin, *Alley Oop*

1934 **Lensman universe** [universe], E. E. Smith, *Triplanetary* (serialized in *Amazing Stories*, January–April, 1934)

1934 **Mongo** [planet], Alex Raymond, *Flash Gordon*

1934 **Valadom** [inhabited asteroid], Donald Wandrei, "Colossus" in *Astounding Stories*, January 1934

1934 **Storn** [island near the coast of Southern England], Victoria Sackville-West, *The Dark Island*

1935 **Fluorescente** [city], Tristan Tzara, *Grains et Issues*

1935 **Grande Euscarie** [underground country], Luc Alberny, *Le Mammouth Bleu*

1935 **Green Land** [underwater country in England], **Roncador** [country next to Paraguay], Herbert Read, *The Green Child*

1935 **Nivia** [colony on Saturn's moon Titan], Stanley G. Weinbaum, "Flight on Titan" in *Astounding Stories*, January 1935

1935 **Pharia** [empire], Bob Moore and Carl Pfeufer, *Don Dixon and the Hidden Empire*

1935 **Roman State** [underground country beneath England], Joseph O'Neill, *Land Under England*

1935 **Tabbyland** [land], Grace Dayton, *The Pussycat Princess*

1935 **Uncertainia** [kingdom], William T. McCleery and Ralph Briggs Fuller, *Oaky Doaks*

1936 **Austin Island** [island in the Pacific Ocean], Stanley G. Weinbaum, "Proteus Island" in *Astounding Stories*, August 1936

1936 **Euclidia** [island in the South Pacific], Perry Crandall, *Magic Island*

1936 **Foozland, Skoobozia** [countries], Gene Ahern, *The Squirrel Cage*

1936 **Great Garabagne** [country], Henri Michaux, *Voyage en Grande Garabagne*

1936 **Kilsona** [microscopic world], Festus Pragnell, *The Green Man of Kilsona*

1936 **Ixania** [country in Europe], Eric Amber, *The Dark Frontier*

1936 **Tanah Masa** [island], Karel Čapek, *War with the Newts*

1936 **Vulcan** [planet], Ross Rocklynne, "At the Center of Gravity" in *Astounding Stories*, June 1936

1937 **(Unnamed world)** [microscopic world], Maurice Gaspard Hugi, "Invaders from the Atom", *Tales of Wonder* #1, Winter 1937

1937 **Arda** [Earth during an imaginary time period], J. R. R. Tolkien, *The Hobbit*

1937 **Artificial planets** [planets], Olaf Stapledon, *Star Maker*

1937 **Five Points, Selby Flats, Springfield** [towns], Irna Phillips, *The Guiding Light* (later renamed *Guiding Light*)

1937 **Rhth** [planet], Don A. Stuart [John W. Campbell, Jr.], "Forgetfulness" in *Astounding Stories*, June 1937

1937 **Futuropolis** [future world], Martial Cendros [René Thévenin] and René Pellos [René Pellarin], *Futuropolis*

1938 **Ashair** [city], Edgar Rice Burroughs, *Tarzan and the Forbidden City*

1938 **Future Earth** [future Earth], Ayn Rand, *Anthem*

1938 **Grover's Corners** [town], Thorton Wilder, *Our Town*

1938 **Gyronchi, Jonbar** [cities], Jack Williamson, *The Legion of Time*

1938 **Ishmaelia** [country in northeast Africa], Evelyn Waugh, *Scoop, A Novel about Journalists*
1938 **Krypton** [planet], Jerry Siegel and Joe Shuster, "Superman" in *Action Comics*, June 1938
1938 **Rimrock** [town in south western Colorado], Fred Harman, *Red Ryder*
1938 **Space Trilogy solar system** [planets], C. S. Lewis, *Out of the Silent Planet*
1938 **Soldus** [planet inside the Sun], Nat Schachner, "The Sun-world of Soldus" in *Astounding Science-Fiction*, April 1938
1938 **Ultra-Earth** [planet], Nat Schachner, "Simultaneous Worlds" in *Astounding Science-Fiction*, November 1938
1938 **Urbs** [city], Stanley G. Weinbaum, *The Black Flame*
1939 **Arkham, Dunwich** [cities], H. P. Lovecraft, *The Outsider and Others*
1939 **Blitva** [country], Miroslav Krleža, *Banket u Blitvi*
1939 **Campagna, Great Marina** [countries], Ernst Jünger, *Auf den Marmorklippen*
1939 **Future History Universe** [universe], Robert Heinlein, "Life-Line" in *Astounding Science-Fiction*, August 1939
1939 **Karud** [planet], Raymond Z. Gallun, "The Shadow of the Veil" in *Astounding Science-Fiction*, February 1939
1939 **Nehwon** [world], Fritz Leiber, "Two Sought Adventure" in *Unknown* magazine, August 1939
1939 **Rose** [island], Mervyn Peake, *Captain Slaughterboard Drops Anchor*
1939 **Uuleppe** [planet], Stanton A. Coblentz, "Planet of the Knob-Heads" in *Science Fiction*, December 1939
1940 **Centropolis** [city], A. E. van Vogt, *Slan* (serialized in *Astounding Science-Fiction*, beginning in September 1940)
1940 **DC Comics universe** [universe], Gardner Fox, *All Star Comics #3*
1940 **Gotham City** [city], Bill Finger, *Batman #4*, Winter 1940
1940 **Leigh Brackett solar system** [version of the solar system], Leigh Brackett, "Martian Quest" in *Astounding Science Fiction*, February 1940
1940 **Tlön, Mlejnas, Uqbar** [countries], Jorge Luis Borges, "Tlön, Uqbar, Orbis Tertius" in *Sur*, May 1940
1940 **Tomainia** [country], Charles Chaplin, *The Great Dictator*
1940 **Villings** [island in the Pacific Ocean], Adolfo Bioy Casares, *La Invención de Morel*
1941 **Babel Library** [library], Jorge Luis Borges, "La Biblioteca de Babel" in *El Jardin de Senderosque se Bifurcan*
1941 **Lagash** [planet], Isaac Asimov, "Nightfall" in *Astounding Science-Fiction*, September 1941
1941 **Tantalus** [planet], P. Schuyler Miller, "Trouble on Tantalus" in *Astounding Science-Fiction*, February 1941

1942 **The Black Planet** [planet], Henry Kuttner, "We Guard the Black Planet" in *Super Science Stories*, November 1942

1942 **Foundation universe** [universe], Isaac Asimov, "Foundation" in *Astounding Science-Fiction*, May 1942

1942 **Hydrot** [planet], Arthur Merlyn [James Blish], "Sunken Universe" in *Super Science Stories*, May 1942

1942 **Karain subcontinent** [subcontinent in the Southern Hemisphere], Austin Tappan Wright, *Islandia*

1942 **Logeia** [world], Fletcher Pratt, *The Undesired Princess* (first serialized in *Unknown*, February 1942)

1942 **Mechanistria** [planet], Eric Frank Russell, "Mechanistria" in *Astounding Science-Fiction*, January 1942

1942 **The Omos solar system** [star and 11 planets], Edgar Rice Burroughs, "Adventure on Poloda" in *Blue Book*, January 1942

1943 **Carcasilla** [underground city], Henry Kuttner and C. L. Moore, *Earth's Last Citadel*

1943 **Castalia** [province in central Europe], Herman Hesse, *The Glass Bead Game*

1943 **Cyrille** [planet], C. L. Moore, *Judgment Night*

1943 **Gondwana** [supercontinent], A. E. van Vogt, *The Book of Ptath*

1943 **Island of Eight Delights and Bacchic Wine** [island], Stefan Andres, *Wir sind Utopia*

1943 **Land of the Lost** [underwater land], Isabel Manning Hewson, *Land of the Lost*

1943 **Stygia** [planet], Manly Wade Wellman, "Legion of the Dark" in *Super Science Stories*, May 1943

1943 **Symbiotica** [planet], Eric Frank Russell, "Symbiotica" in *Astounding Science-Fiction*, October 1943

1943 **Zavattinia** [village near Bamba, Italy], Cesare Zavattini, *Totò il Buono*

1944 **Bombardy** [country], Eric Linklater, *The Wind on the Moon*

1944 **Paradise Island** [island], William Moulton Marston, *Wonder Woman*

1945 **Animal Farm** [farm], George Orwell [Eric Arthur Blair], *Animal Farm: A Fairy Story*

1945 **Galactic Empire universe** [universe], Isaac Asimov, "Blind Alley" in *Astouding Science-Fiction*, March 1945

1945 **The Island of Sodor** [island in the Irish Sea], Rev. Wilbert Vere Awdry, *The Three Railway Engines*

1945 **Kingdom of King Clode** [kingdom], James Thurber, *The White Deer*

1945 **Mount Tsintsin-Dagh** [mountain in northern Tibet], Paul Alperine, *Ombres sur le Thibet*

1946 **Aiolo** [planet], Murray Leinster [William Fitzgerald Jenkins], "The Plants" in *Astounding Science-Fiction*, January 1946

1946 **Alternate world** [alternate world], Franz Werfel, *Stern der Ungeborenen* (Star of the Unborn)

1946 **Erikraudebyg** [settlement], Paul Alperine, *La Citadelle des Glaces*

1946 **Gormenghast** [castle], Mervyn Peake, *Titus Groan*

1946 **Hekla** [planet], Hal Clement [Harry Clement Stubbs], "Cold Front" in *Astounding Science-Fiction*, July 1946

1946 **Placet** [planet], Fredric Brown, "Placet is a Crazy Place" in *Astounding Science-Fiction*, May 1946

1946 **Sainte Beregonne** [hidden city quarter in Hamburg, Germany], Jean Ray, *Le Manuscrit Français*

1947 **Brigadoon** [town in Scotland], Alan Jay Lerner and Frederick Loewe, *Brigadoon*

1947 **Doodyville** [town], Robert E. "Buffalo Bob" Smith, *Howdy Doody*

1947 **Longjumeau** [city in France], Léon Bloy, "Les Captifs de Longjumeau" in *L'Oeuvre Compléte*

1947 **Mars (of The Martian Chronicles)** [planet], Ray Bradbury, "Rocket Summer" in *Planet Stories*, Spring 1947

1947 **Niggle's Parish** [region], J. R. R. Tolkien, "Leaf by Niggle" in *The Dublin Review*

1947 **Padukgrad, Sinisterbad** [countries], Vladimir Nabakov, *Bend Sinister*

1947 **Throon** [planet], Edmond Hamilton, *The Star Kings*

1947 **Wing IV** [planet], Jack Williamson, "With Folded Hands…" in *Astounding Science Fiction*, July 1947

1948 **Dalarna** [country], George U. Fletcher [Fletcher Pratt], *Well of the Unicorn*

1948 **Raintree County** [county], Ross Lockridge, Jr., *Raintree County*

1948 **Walden Two** [town], B. F. Skinner, *Walden Two*

1949 **Alternate United States** [alternate United States], George Stewart, *Earth Abides*

1949 **Candyland** [board game setting], Eleanor Abbott, *Candyland*

1949 **Chita** [island], Pierre-Mac Orlan, *Le Chant de l'Equipage*

1949 **City of the Immortals** [city], Jorge Luis Borges, "El Immortal" in *El Aleph*

1949 **Comarre** [city], Arthur C. Clarke, "The Lion of Comarre" in *Thrilling Wonder Stories*, August 1949

1949 **The Commonwealth of Letters** [land], John Myers Myers, *Silverlock*

1949 **Heliopolis** [city], Ernst Jünger, *Heliopolis*

1949 **Karres** [planet], James H. Schmitz, *The Witches of Karres*

1949 **Oceania, Eurasia, Eastasia** [continents], George Orwell [Eric Arthur Blair], *Nineteen Eighty-Four*

1949 **New Crete** [future Earth], Robert Graves, *Watch the North Wind Rise* (also known as *Seven Days in New Crete*)

1949 **Psychotechnic League universe** [Earth with an alternate history], Poul Anderson and John Gergen, "The Entity" in *Astounding Science Fiction*, June 1949

1949 **Shuruun** [city on Venus], Leigh Brackett, "The Enchantress of Venus" in *Planet Stories*, Fall 1949

1949 **Viagens Interplanetarias universe** [universe], L. Sprague de Camp, "The Animal-Cracker Plot" in *Astounding Science Fiction*, July 1949

1950 **Borsetshire** [county in England], Godfrey Baseley, *The Archers*

1950 **Curbstone** [artificial satellite], Theodore Sturgeon, "The Stars are the Styx" in *Galaxy Science Fiction*, October 1950

1950 **Dying Earth universe** [future Earth], Jack Vance, *The Dying Earth*

1950 **Grand Duchy of Lichtenburg** [duchy in Europe], Howard Lindsay and Russel Crouse, *Call Me Madam*

1950 **Instrumentality of Mankind future history universe** [universe], Cordwainer Smith [Paul Myron Anthony Linebarger], "Scanners Live in Vain" in *Fantasy Book* #6, 1950

1950 **Moominland, Daddy Jones's Kingdom** [kingdoms], Tove Jansson, *Kuinkas Sitten Kävikään*

1950 **Narnia** [country], C. S. Lewis, *The Lion, the Witch, and the Wardrobe*

1950 **Myopia** [kingdom], Jack Kent, *King Aroo*

1950 **Quivera** [country in South America], Vaughan Wilkins, *The City of Frozen Fire*

1950 **Skontar** [planet], Poul Anderson, "The Helping Hand" in *Astounding Science Fiction*, May 1950

1950 **United Planets universe** [universe], Mike Moser, *Space Patrol*

1951 **61 Cygni VII** [planet], Clifford D. Simak, *Time and Again*

1951 **Farghestan, Orsenna, Vezzano** [countries], Julien Gracq, *Le Rivage des Syrtes*

1951 **Jemal, Medral** [planets], Raymond F. Jones, "The Toymaker" in *The Toymaker: A Collection of Science Fiction Stories*

1951 **Kyril** [planet], Jack Vance, "Son of the Tree" in *Thrilling Wonder Stories*, June 1951

1951 **Ormazd** [planet], L. Sprague de Camp, *Rogue Queen*

1951 **Qylao** [inhabited planetoid], Fox B. Holden, "The Death Star" in *Super Science Stories*, April 1951

1952 **Alternate America** [alternate America], Kurt Vonnegut, Jr., *Player Piano*

1952 **Alternate Earth and Venus** [alternate Earth and Venus], Frederik Pohl and Cyril M. Kornbluth, "Gravy Planet" in *Galaxy Science Fiction*, June 1952

1952 **Asbefore Island** [island], Jacques Prévert, *Lettre des Îles Baladar*

1952 **Lyra IV** [planet], Cyril M. Kornbluth, "That Share of Glory" in *Astounding Science Fiction*, January 1952

1952 **Mount Analogue** [mountain island], René Daumal, *Le Mont Analogue*

1952 **Ozagen** [planet], Philip José Farmer, *The Lovers*, in *Startling Stories*, August 1952

1952 **Shandakor** [city on Mars], Leigh Brackett, "The Last Days of Shandakor" in *Startling Stories*, April 1952

1952 **Terra** [planet], Oskar Lebeck and Alden McWilliams, *Twin Earths*

1952 **Terro-Human Future History universe** [universe], H. Beam Piper, "Uller Uprising" in *The Petrified Planet*

1952 **Uller** [planet], John D. Clark, Fletcher Pratt, H. Beam Piper, and Judith Merril [Judith Josephine Grossman], *The Petrified Planet*

1952 **Unreturnable-Heaven** [city in Nigeria], **Wraith Island** [island in Nigeria], Amos Tutuola, *The Palm-Wine Drinkard and His Dead Palm-Wine Tapster in the Dead's Town*

1953 **Alternate America** [alternate America], Ray Bradbury, *Fahrenheit 451*

1953 **Baudelaire** [planet], Philip José Farmer, "Mother" in *Thrilling Wonder Stories*, April 1953

1953 **Devon** [town], Elliot Caplin and Stan Drake, *The Heart of Juliet Jones*

1953 **Helle** [planet], Bengo Mistral [Norman Lazenby], *The Brains of Helle*

1953 **Lithia** [planet], James Blish, *A Case of Conscience*

1953 **Maghrebinia** [vast realm], Gregor von Rezzori, *Maghrebinische Geschichten*

1953 **Mesklin** [planet], Hal Clement [Harry Clement Stubbs], *Mission of Gravity*

1953 **Shadow City** [city], A. E. van Vogt, *The Universe Maker*

1954 **(Unnamed island)** [island], William Golding, *Lord of the Flies*

1954 **Azor, Gemser, Halsey's Planet, Sunward, etc.** [planets], Frederik Pohl and Cyril M. Kornbluth, *Search the Sky*

1954 **Borovnia** [country], Pauline Parker and Juliet Hulme, (Christchurch, New Zealand newspaper reports of the murder of Honora Mary Parker)

1954 **Iszm** [planet], Jack Vance, *The Houses of Iszm*

1954 **Troas** [planet], Isaac Asimov and probably John D. Clark, "Sucker Bait" in *Astounding Science Fiction*, February 1954

1954 **Viridis** [planet], Theodore Sturgeon, "The Golden Helix" in *Thrilling Wonder Stories*, Summer 1954

1955 **Abatos** [planet], Phillip José Farmer, "Father" in *The Magazine of Fantasy and Science Fiction*, July 1955

1955 **Bartorstown** [post-apocalypse city in the Rocky Mountains], Leigh Brackett, *The Long Tomorrow*

1955 **Belly Rave** [New York suburb in an alternate future], Frederik Pohl and Cyril M. Kornbluth, *Gladiator-at-Law*

1955 **Eterna** [planet], Eric Frank Russell, "The Waitabits" in *Astounding Science Fiction*, July 1955

1955 **India** [island in Indian Ocean], C. S. Lewis, *Surprised by Joy*

1955 **LEGO System universe** [universe], The LEGO Group, *Town Plan No. 1*

1955 **Neverreachhereland** [land], André Dhôtel, *Les Pays où l'on n'arrive jamais*

1955 **Planet orbiting Proxima Centauri** [planet], Stanisław Lem, *Obłok Magellana*

1955 **Rigo** [town in alternate North America], John Wyndham, *The Chrysalids*

1955 **Sabria** [planet], Jack Vance, "The Gift of Gab" in *Astounding Science Fiction*, September 1955

1955 **Tranai** [planet], Robert Scheckley, "A Ticket to Tranai" in *Galaxy Science Fiction*, October 1955

1955 **Tylerton** [town], Frederik Pohl, "The Tunnel under the World" in *Galaxy Science Fiction*, January 1955

1955 **What-A-Jolly Street (Trufflescootems Blvd.)** [neighborhood in Iowa], Nan Gilbert [Mildred Gilbertson], *365 Bedtime Stories*

1956 **Altair IV** [planet], Fred M. Wilcox, *Forbidden Planet*

1956 **Aniara** [space station], Harry Martinson, *Aniara*

1956 **Bachepousse** [island], **Country of the Graal Flibuste** [country], Robert Pinget, *Graal Flibuste*

1956 **Caphad, Essur, Glome, Phars, etc.** [kingdoms], C. S. Lewis, *Till We Have Faces*

1956 **Diaspar** [city on future Earth], Arthur C. Clarke, *The City and the Stars*

1956 **Exopotamia** [country], Boris Vian, *L'Automne à Pékin*

1956 **Nidor** [planet], Robert Randall [Robert Silverberg and Randall Grant], *The Shrouded Planet*

1956 **Oakdale** [town in Illinois], Irna Phillips, *As the World Turns*

1956 **Peyton Place** [town], Grace Metalious, *Peyton Place*

1956 **Tropical Valley** [valley in the Northwest Territories, Canada], Pierre Berton, *The Mysterious North*

1956 **Xanadu** [planet], Theodore Sturgeon, "The Skills of Xanadu" in *Galaxy Science Fiction*, July 1956

1957 **Abyormen** [planet], Hal Clement [Harry Clement Stubbs], *Cycle of Fire*

1957 **Alternate United States** [alternate United States], Ayn Rand, *Atlas Shrugged*

1957 **Barnum's Planet** [planet], Avram Davidson, "Now Let Us Sleep" in *Or All the Seas With Oysters*

1957 **Big Planet** [planet], Jack Vance, *Big Planet*

1957 **Dante's Joy** [planet], Philip José Farmer, *Night of Light*

1957 **Darkover** [planet], Marion Zimmer Bradley, *Falcons of Narabedla*

1957 **Great Circle civilizations** [planets], Ivan Efremov, *Andromeda Nebula*

1957 **Home, Rathe** [planets], James Blish, "Get out of My Sky" in *Astounding Science Fiction*, January 1957

1957 **Leeminorr** [planet], Robert Silverberg, "Precedent" in *Astounding Science Fiction*, December 1957

1957 **Mayfield** [town], Joe Connelly and Bob Mosher, *Leave it to Beaver*

1957 **Sargon Empire** [planets], Robert A. Heinlein, *Citizens of the Galaxy*

1957 **Tyana II** [planet], Robert Scheckley, "The Language of Love" in *Galaxy Science Fiction*, May 1957

1957 **Wild Island** [island], Ruth Stiles Gannet, *My Father's Dragon*

1957 **Ygam** [planet], Stefan Wul, *Oms en Série*

1958 **Conniption** [town], Stan Lynde, *Rick O'Shay*

1958 **Duchy of Grand Fenwick** [country in Europe], Jack Arnold, *The Mouse that Roared*

1958 **Kakakakaxo** [planet], Brian Aldiss, "Segregation" (also known as "The Game of God") in *New Worlds*, July 1958

1958 **Kapetopek** [country], **Flathill Country** [region], Tatsuo Yoshida, *Mach GoGoGo* (first serialized in Shueisha's *Shōnen Book*, and later known as *Speed Racer*)

1958 **Lanador** [planet], Robert A. Heinlein, "Have Space Suit—Will Travel" serialized in *The Magazine of Fantasy & Science Fiction*, August 1958

1958 **New Cornwall** [planet], Richard McKenna, "The Night of the Hoggy Darn" in *Worlds of If*, December1958

1958 **Pao** [planet], Jack Vance, *The Languages of Pao*

1958 **Ragnarok** [planet], Tom Godwin, *The Survivors*

1958 **Technic History universe** [universe], Poul Anderson, *War of the Wing-Men*

1958 **Tenebra** [planet], Hal Clement [Harry Clement Stubbs], *Close to Critical* (first serializaed in *Astounding Science Fiction*, beginning in May 1958)

1958 **Thalassa** [planet], Arthur C. Clarke, "The Songs of Distant Earth" in *The Other Side of the Sky*

1958 **Veldq** [planet], Charles V. de Vet and Katherine MacLean, "Second Game" in *Astounding Science Fiction*, March 1958

1959 **Aocicinori** [galaxy], Scotlund Leland Moore, *The Galaxy of Aocicinori*

1959 **Cannis IV** [planet], Colin Kapp, "The Railways up on Cannis IV" in *The Unorthodox Engineers*

1959 **Central City** [city], Max Schulman, *The Many Loves of Dobie Gillis*

1959 **Childe Cycle universe** [universe], Gordon R. Dickson, *Dorsai!*

1959 **Glumpalt** [planet], Brian Aldiss, "Legends of Smith's Bursts" in *Nebula Stories*

1959 **Katroo** [country], Dr. Seuss, *Happy Birthday to You*

1959 **Land between the Mountains** [land], Carol Kendall, *The Gammage Cup*

1959 **Level Seven** [underground city], Mordecai Roshwald, *Level Seven*

1959 **Old Town** [town], Philip K. Dick, *Time out of Joint*

1959 **Topaz** [planet], Harlan Ellison, "Eyes of Dust" in *Rogue*, December 1959

1959 **Tralfamadore** [planet], Kurt Vonnegut, Jr., *The Sirens of Titan*

1959 **Village of the Smurfs** [village], Peyo [Pierre Culliford], *Les Schtroumpfs* (*The Smurfs*)

1960 **Abbey Leibowitz** [abbey in North American desert in a post-apocalyptic future], Walter M. Miller, *A Canticle for Leibowitz*

1960 **Bedrock** [town], William Hanna and Joseph Barbera, *The Flintstones*

1960 **Bellota** [planet], R. A. Lafferty, "Snuffles" in *Galaxy Magazine*, December 1960

1960 **Chronopolis** [city], J. G. Ballard, "Chronopolis" in *New Worlds*, June 1960

1960 **Eden** [planet], Mark Clifton, *Eight Keys to Eden*

1960 **Genoa, Texcoco** [planets], Mack Reynolds, "Adaptation" in *Astouding Science Fact & Fiction*

1960 **Klendathu** [planet], Robert A. Heinlein, *Starship Troopers*

1960 **Ledom** [planet], Theodore Sturgeon, *Venus Plus X*

1960 **Mayberry** [town in North Carolina], Sheldon Leonard and Charles Stewart, *The Danny Thomas Show*

1960 **Omega** [planet], Robert Sheckley, *The Status Civilization*

1960 **Pyrrus** [planet], Harry Harrison, *Deathworld*

1960 **The Runaway World** [planet], Frederik Pohl and Cyril M. Kornbluth, *Wolfbane*

1960 **Savannah** [planet], James Blish, "And Some Were Savages", *Amazing Stories*, November 1960

1960 **Sirius IX, Walonka** [planets], Chad Oliver, *Unearthly Neighbors*

1960 **Tharixan** [planet], Poul Anderson, *The High Crusade*

1960 **Warlock** [planet], Andre Norton, *Storm Over Warlock*

1961 **Amara** [planet], William F. Temple, *The Three Suns of Amara*

1961 **Andorra** [country (not to be confused with the real country of Andorra)], Max Frisch, *Andorra*

1961 **Chandala** [planet], James Blish, "A Dusk of Idols" in *Amazing Stories*, March 1961

1961 **Concordia** [country in Europe], Peter Ustinov, *Romanoff and Juliet*

1961 **Dara** [planet], Murray Leinster [William Fitzgerald Jenkins], "Pariah Planet" in *Amazing Stories*, July 1961

1961 **Dunia** [country in Africa], Anthony Burgess, *Devil of a State*

1961 **Ghrekh, Pittam, Speewry** [planets], Robert Lowndes, *Believer's World*

1961 **Hi-Iay Islands** (also called **Hi-yi-yi Islands**) [archipelago], Harald Stumke [Gerolf Steiner], *Bau und Leben der Rhinogradentia*

1961 **Kandemir** [planet], Poul Anderson, "The Day after Doomsday" in *Galaxy Magazine*, December 1961

1961 **Lilith** [planet], Geraldine June McDonald Willis, *The Light of Lilith*

1961 **Marvel Comics universe** [universe], Stan Lee, Jack Kirby, and Steve Ditko, *Fantastic Four #1*

1961 **Noon universe** [universe], Arkady and Boris Strugatsky, *Noon: 22nd Century*

1961 **Og** [underground world], Pierre Berton, *The Secret World of OG*

1961 **Orisinia** [country], Ursula K. LeGuin, "An Die Musik" in *Western Humanities Review 15* (1961)

1961 **Perry Rhodan multiverse** [multiverse], K. H. Scheer and Clark Darton, *Perry Rhodan*

1961 **The Rim Worlds** [planets], A. Bertram Chandler, *The Rim of Space*

1961 **Sirene** [planet], Jack Vance, "The Moon Moth" in *Galaxy Magazine*, August 1961

1961 **Solaris** [planet], Stanisław Lem, *Solaris*

1962 **(Unnamed world)** [interactive world], Steve Russell, J. M. Graetz, and others, *Spacewar!*

1962 **Big Slope** [mountain in future Earth], Brian Aldiss, *Hothouse*

1962 **Imperium continuum** [parallel worlds], Keith Laumer, *Worlds of the Imperium*

1962 **Jundapur** [state in India], **Manoba** [island near New Guinea], Paul Scott, *The Birds of Paradise*

1962 **Orbit City** [city], William Hanna and Joseph Barbera, *The Jetsons*

1962 **Pala, Rendang** [islands in the Indonesian Archipelago], Aldous Huxley, *Island*

1962 **Sako** [planet], Edmond Hamilton, "The Stars, My Brothers" in *Amazing Stories*, May 1962

1962 **Time Quartet universe** [universe], Madeleine L'Engle, *A Wrinkle in Time*

1962 **Wisdom Kingdom** [kingdom], Norman Juster, *The Phantom Tollbooth*

1962 **Zembla** [country], Vladimir Nabakov, *Pale Fire*

1963 **Aerlith** [planet], Jack Vance, *The Dragon Masters*

1963 **Argent** [planet], John Phillifent, *King of Argent*

1963 **Artemis** [planet], Evelyn E. Smith, *The Perfect Planet*

1963 **Berserker universe** [universe], Fred Saberhagen, "Fortress Ship" in *If*, Jan 1963

1963 **Birdwell Island** [island], Norman Bridwell, *Clifford the Big Red Dog*

1963 **Crabwall Corners, Hooterville, Pixley, Stankwell Falls, etc.**, [towns], Paul Henning, *Petticoat Junction*

1963 **Dune universe** [universe], Frank Herbert, *Dune World* (serialized in Analog magazine)

1963 **Eden** [planet], Stanisław Lem, *Eden*

1963 **Fruyling's World** [planet], Laurence M. Janifer, *Slave Planet*

1963 **Future Earth** [future Earth], Poul Anderson, "No Truce with Kings" in *The Magazine of Fantasy and Science Fiction*, June 1963

1963 **The Multiverse** [multiverse], Michael Moorcock, *The Stealer of Souls*

1963 **Neighborhood of Make-Believe** [kingdom], Fred Rogers, *MisteRogers* (Canadian program that preceded *Mister Rogers' Neighborhood*)

1963 **The Phyto Planet** [planet], Richard McKenna, "Hunter, Come Home" in *The Magazine of Fantasy and Science Fiction*, March 1963

1963 **Port Charles** [city in New York], Frank and Doris Hursley, *General Hospital*

1963 **Space Patrol universe** [universe], Roberta Leigh, *Space Patrol*

1963 **Soror** [planet], Pierre Boulle, *La Planète des Singes*

1963 **Tirellian** [city on Mars], Roger Zelazny, "A Rose for Ecclesiastes" in *The Magazine of Fantasy and Science Fiction*, November 1963

1963 **Weng** [village in Austrian Mountains], Thomas Bernhard, *Frost*

1963 **The Whoniverse** [universe], Sydney Newman, C. E. Webber, and Donald Wilson, *Doctor Who*

1963 **X** [city], Tibor Déry, *G. A. úr X.-ben*

1963 **San Lorenzo** [island in the Carribean Sea], Kurt Vonnegut, Jr., *Cat's Cradle*

1963 **Witch World** [world], Andre Norton, *Witch World*

1964 **Alpha III M2** [planet], Philip K. Dick, *Clans of the Alphane Moon*

1964 **Arkanar** [planet], Arkady and Boris Strugatsky, *Hard to be a God*

1964 **Azrael** [planet], John Brunner, "The Bridge to Azrael" in *Amazing Stories*, February 1964

1964 **Bay City** [town in Illinois], Irna Phillips and William J. Bell, *Another World*

1964 **Blue World** [planet], Jack Vance, "The Kragen" in *Fantastic Stories of Imagination*, July 1964

1964 **ConSentiency universe** [universe], Frank Herbert, "The Tactful Saboteur" in *Galaxy Magazine*, October 1964

1964 **Dapdrof** [planet], Brian Aldiss, *The Dark Bright Years*

1964 **Demon Princes universe** [universe], Jack Vance, *The Star King*

1964 **Earthsea** [archipelago], Ursula K. LeGuin, "The Word of Unbinding", *Fantastic*, January 1964

1964 **Gilligan's Island** [island in Pacific Ocean], Sherwood Schwartz, *Gilligan's Island*

1964 **Hainish Cycle universe** [universe], Ursula K. LeGuin, "Dowry of the Angyar" in *Amazing Stories*, September 1964

1964 **Id** [kingdom], Johnny Hart and Brant Parker, *The Wizard of Id*

1964 **iDeath** [town in rural United States], Richard Brautigan, *In Watermelon Sugar*

1964 **Known Space universe** [universe], Larry Niven, "The Coldest Place" in *If*, December 1964

1964 **Marineville** [city], **Titanica** [underwater city], Gerry and Sylvia Anderson, *Stingray*

1964 **Nihil** [planet], Martin Thomas, *Beyond the Spectrum*

1964 **Prydain** [country], Lloyd Alexander, *The Book of Three*

1964 **Rainbow** [planet], Arkady and Boris Strugatsky, *Far Rainbow*

1964 **The Reefs of Space** [universe], Frederik Pohl and Jack Williamson, *The Reefs of Space*

1964 **Regis III** [planet], Stanisław Lem, *The Invincible*

1964 **Shinar** [planet], Ben Bova, *Star Watchmen*

1964 **Simulacron-3** [virtual world], Daniel F. Galouye, *Simulacron-3*

1964 **Yr** [kingdom], Hannah Green [Joanne Greenberg], *I Never Promised You a Rose Garden*

1965 **Chelm** [city], Samuel Tenenbaum, *The Wise Men of Chelm*

1965 **Dare** [planet], Philip José Farmer, *Dare*

1965 **Drimonia** [country in Europe], Lia Wainstein, *Viaggio in Drimonia*

1965 **Ellipsia** [planet], Hortense Calisher, *Journal from Ellipsia*

1965 **Grimy Gulch** [town in the Old West], Tom K. Ryan, *Tumbleweeds*

1965 **Helior** [planet], Harry Harrison, *Bill the Galactic Hero*

1965 **Lemuria** [continent], Lin Carter, *A Wizard of Lemuria*

1965 **Lifeline** [city on Venus], Roger Zelazny, "The Doors of His Face, the Lamps of His Mouth" in *The Magazine of Fantasy and Science Fiction*, March 1965

1965 **Na** [planet], Robert Scheckley, "Shall We Have a Little Talk?" in *Galaxy Magazine*, October 1965

1965 **Pia 2** (also known as Ptolemy Soter) [planet], Avram Davidson, *Rork!*

1965 **Refuge** [planet], Joseph L. Green, *The Loafers of Refuge*

1965 **Salem** [town], Ted and Betty Corday, *Days of Our Lives*

1965 **Sphereland** [two-dimensional spherical world], Dionys Burger, *Sphereland: A Fantasy about Curved Spaces and an Expanding Universe*

1965 **Tracy Island** [island], Gerry Anderson and Sylvia Anderson, *Thunderbirds*

1965 **World of Tiers universe** [multiverse], Philip José Farmer, *The Maker of Universes*

1966 **Camiroi** [planet], R. A. Lafferty, "Primary Education of the Camiroi" in *Galaxy Magazine*, December 1966

1966 **Collinsport** [town in Maine], Dan Curtis, *Dark Shadows*

1966 **Destination: Void universe** [universe], Frank Herbert, *Destination: Void*

1966 **Proavitus** [inhabited asteroid], R. A. Lafferty, "Nine Hundred Grandmothers" in *If*, February 1966

1966 **Riverworld** [planet], Philip José Farmer, "Riverworld" in *Worlds of Tomorrow*, January 1966

1966 ***Star Trek* galaxy** [galaxy], Gene Roddenberry, *Star Trek*

1966 **Zygra** [planet], John Brunner, *A Planet of Your Own*

1967 **Altair** [planet], Edmund Cooper, *A Far Sunset*

1967 **Alternate Earth and Mars** [alternate Earth and Mars], William F. Noland and George Clayton Johnson, *Logan's Run*

1967 **Branning-at-Sea** [city in future Earth], Samuel R. Delany, *The Einstein Intersection*

1967 **Braunstein** [RPG setting], David Wesely, *Braunstein*

1967 **Chthon** [planet], Piers Anthony, *Chthon*

1967 **Dumarest Saga universe** [universe], Edwin Charles Tubb, *The Winds of Gath*

1967 **Gor** [planet], John Norman [John Frederick Lange, Jr.], *Tarnsman of Gor*

1967 **Hawksbill Station** [prison colony in the prehistoric past], Robert Silverberg, "Hawksbill Station" in *Galaxy Magazine*, August 1967

1967 **Macondo** [village in Columbia], Gabriel García Márquez, *One Hundred Years of Solitude*

1967 **Pern** [planet], Anne McCaffrey, "Weyr Search" in *Analog*, October, 1967

1967 **Sangre** [planet], Norman Spinrad, *The Men in the Jungle*

1967 **Unistam** [country], James Blish and Norman L. Knight, *A Torrent of Faces*

1967 **Urath** [planet], Roger Zelazny, *Lord of Light*

1967 **The Village** [seaside village], Patrick McGoohan and George Markstein, *The Prisoner*

1968 **Alternate solar system** [alternate solar system], Stanley Kubrick and Arthur C. Clarke, *2001: A Space Odyssey*

1968 **Alternate United States** [alternate United States], Philip K. Dick, *Do Androids Dream of Electric Sheep?*

1968 **Astrobe** [planet], R. A. Lafferty, *Past Master*

1968 **Beninia** [country in West Africa], John Brunner, *Stand on Zanzibar*

1968 **Gurnil** [planet], Lloyd Biggle, *The Still Small Voice of Trumpets*

1968 **Halla, Shundi** [kingdoms], Satyajit Ray, *Goopy Gyne Bagha Byne*

1968 **Ici** [ruins], Philippe Jullian, *La Fuite en Egypte*

1968 **Llanview** [city in Pennsylvania], Agnes Nixon, *One Life to Live*

1968 **Montefor** [planet], William F. Temple, *The Fleshpots of Sansato*

1968 **Nacre** [planet], Piers Anthony, *Omnivore*

1968 **Nevèrÿon** [world], Samuel R. Delany, "Time Considered as a Helix of Semi-Precious Stones" in *New Worlds*, December 1968

1968 **Novaria, Vindium, Zolon, Xylar, Othomae, etc.** [countries], L. Sprague de Camp, *The Goblin Tower*

1968 **Paradise** [planet], Joanna Russ, *Picnic on Paradise*

1968 **Región** [country], Juan Benet, *Volverás a Región*

1968 **Star Well** [inhabited asteroid], Alexei Panshin, *Star Well*

1968 **Sulwen's Planet** [planet], Jack Vance, "Sulwen's Planet" in *The Farthest Reaches* (edited by Joseph Elder)

1968 **Tschai** [planet], Jack Vance, *City of the Chasch*

1969 **Belzagor** [planet], Robert Silverberg, *Downward to the Earth* (first serialized in *Galaxy Science Fiction*, November 1969)

1969 **Doona** [planet], Anne McCaffrey, *Decision at Doona*

1969 **Esthaa** [planet], James Tiptree Jr. [Alice Bradley Sheldon], "Your Haploid Heart" in *Analog Science Fact & Fiction*, September 1969

1969 **Flora** [planet], John Boyd, *The Pollinators of Eden*

1969 **Gondwane** [continent], Lin Carter, *Giant of World's End*

1969 **Harlech** [planet], John Boyd, *The Rakehells of Heaven*

1969 **Kanthos, Sulmannon, Anzor** [countries], Alex Dain, *Bane of Kanthos*

1969 **Living Island** [island], Hollingsworth Morse, *H. R. Pufnstuf*

1969 **Mnemosyne** [planet], Bob Shaw, *The Palace of Eternity*

1969 **Plowman's Planet** [planet], Philip K. Dick, *Galactic Pot-Healer*

1969 **Quilapa, Zaachila** [villages], Harry Harrison, *Captive Universe*

1969 **Sesame Street** [street in New York City], Joan Ganz Cooney and Lloyd Morrisett, *Sesame Street*

1969 **The South Kingdom** [kingdom], John Bellairs, *The Face in the Frost*

1969 **Yarth** [planet], Gardner F. Fox, *Kothar: Barbarian Swordsman*

1969 **Zarkandu** [planet], Lin Carter, *Lost World of Time*

1970 **Amber universe** [universe], Roger Zelazny, *Nine Princes in Amber*

1970 **Bremagne, Gwynedd, Kheldour, Meara, etc.** [countries], Katherine Kurtz, *Deryni Rising*

1970 **Brodie's Land, MLCH Country** [country], Jorge Luis Borges, *El Informe de Brodie*

1970 **Clio** [planet], Andre Norton, *Ice Crown*

1970 **Delmark-O** [virtual world], Philip K. Dick, *A Maze of Death*

1970 **Esperanza** [planet], Ron Goulart, *The Sword Swallower*

1970 **Pine Valley** [town in Pennsylvania], Agnes Nixon, *All My Children*

1970 **Rominten** [reserve in Eastern Prussia], Michel Tournier, *Le Roi des Aulnes*

1970 **Strackenz** [duchy in Germany], George MacDonald Fraser, *Royal Flash*

1970 **Tome** [planet], John Jakes, *Mask of Chaos*

1970 **Urban Monads** [skyscrapers that each contain 25 cities], Robert Silverberg, "A Happy Day in 2381" in *Nova 1* (edited by Harry Harrison)

1970 **Urban Nucleus world** [future Earth], Michael Bishop, "If a Flower Could Eclipse" in *Worlds of Fantasy*, Winter 1970

1970 **Vandarei** [world], Joy Chant [Eileen Joyce Rutter], *Red Moon and Black Mountain: The End of the House of Kendreth*

1971 **(Unnamed world)** [underground city], George Lucas, *THX 1138*

1971 **Antares IV** [planet], George Zebrowski, "Heathen God" in *The Magazine of Fantasy and Science Fiction*, January 1971

1971 **Arab Jordan** [kingdom in 21st century New York City], Katherine MacLean, *The Missing Man*

1971 **Balbrigian and Bouloulabassian United Republic** [country], Max Jacob, *Histoire du roi Kaboul Ier et du marmiton Gauwain*

1971 **Borthan** [planet], Robert Silverberg, *A Time of Changes*

1971 **Dhrawn** [planet], Hal Clement [Harry Clement Stubbs], *Star Light*

1971 **Fourth World** [world], Jack Kirby, *The New Gods*

1971 **Misterland** [land], Roger Hargreaves, *Mr. Tickle*

1971 **Oceana** [island near Ireland], H. R. F. Keating, *The Strong Man*

1971 **Roland** [planet], Poul Anderson, "The Queen of Air and Darkness" in *The Magazine of Fantasy and Science Fiction*, June 1971

1971 **Viriconium** [city], M. John Harrison, *The Pastel City*

1971 **Watkinsland** [South American coastal area], Doris Lessing, *Breifing for a Descent into Hell*

1972 **Aglaura, Anastasia, Argia, Baucis, Catmere, etc.** [55 cities], Italo Calvino, *Le Città Invisibli (Invisible Cities)*

1972 **Archaos** [kingdom], Christiane Rochefort, *Archaos ou Le jardin étincelant*

1972 **Blokula, Broceliande, Elfhame, Elfwick, etc.** [kingdoms], Sylvia Townsend Warner, *Kingdoms of Elfin*

1972 **The Cemetery** [future Earth], Clifford D. Simak, *Cemetery World*

1972 **Humanx Commonwealth universe** [universe], Alan Dean Foster, *The Tar-Aiym Krang*

1972 **Kregen** [planet], Alan Burt Akers [Henry Kenneth Bulmer], *Transit to Scorpio*

1972 **Marilyn** [planet], Micheal G. Coney, *Mirror Image*

1972 **The Para-Universe** [universe], Isaac Asimov, *The Gods Themselves*

1972 **Parsloe's Planet** [planet], Kenneth Bulmer, *Roller Coaster World*

1972 **Sainte Croix, Sainte Anne** [planets], Gene Wolfe, *The Fifth Head of Cerebus*

1972 **Sequoia** [planet], Neal Barrett, Jr., *Highwood*

1972 **Thanator** [fictional version of Jupiter's moon Callisto], Lin Carter, *Jandar of Callisto*

1972 **The Valley Forge** [space station orbiting Saturn], Douglas Trumbull, *Silent Running*

1972 **Watership Down** [warren of rabbits], Richard Adams, *Watership Down*

1972 **Whileaway and other worlds** [alternate worlds], Joanna Russ, "When it Changed" in *Again, Dangerous Visions* (edited by Harlan Ellison)

1972 **Yan** [planet], John Brunner, *The Dramaturges of Yan*

1973 **Abbieannia, Angelinia, Calverinia, Glandelinia** [countries], Henry Darger, *The Story of the Vivian Girls, in What is known as the Realms of the Unreal, of the Glandeco-Angelinnian War Storm, Caused by the Child Slave Rebellion*

1973 **Aeneas** [planet], Poul Anderson, *The Day of Their Return*

1973 **Alastor Cluster** [star cluster], Jack Vance, *Trullion: Alastor 2262*

1973 **The Cavity** [cavity surrounded by solid rock], Barrington J. Bayley, "Me and My Antronoscope" in *New Worlds Quarterly 5*, 1973

1973 **CoDominium universe** [universe], Jerry Pournelle, *A Spaceship for the King*

1973 **Florin, Guilder** [countries], William Goldman, *The Princess Bride*

1973 **Genoa City** [city in Wisconsin], William J. Bell and Lee Philip Bell, *The Young and the Restless*

1973 **Kark** [continent], Miles Copeland and Michael Hicks-Beach, *The Game of Nations*

1973 **Koestler's Planet** [planet], Barrington J. Bayley, "Mutation Planet" in *Frontiers 1: Tomorrow's Alternatives*

1973 **Lituania** [country], Henri Guigonnat, *Démone en Lituanie*

1973 **Murdstone** [planet], Ron Goulart, *Shaggy Planet*

1973 **Omelas** [city], Ursula K. LeGuin, "The Ones Who Walk Away from Omelas" in *New Dimensions 3*, October 1973

1973 **Starmont** [planet], Terry Carr, "The Winds of Starmont" in *No Mind of Man* (edited by Robert Silverberg)

1973 **Three-O-Seven** [island in the Aleutian Archipelago], René Barjavel, *Le Grand Secret*

1974 **(Player-created worlds)** [RPG setting], Gary Gygax and Dave Arneson, *Dungeons & Dragons*

1974 **(Unnamed world)** [interactive world], Steve Colley, *Maze War*

1974 **(Unnamed world)** [interactive world], Jim Bowery, *Spasim*

1974 **Beklan Empire** [country], Richard Adams, *Shardik*

1974 **Calliur** [planet], Mildred Downey Broxon, "The Stones have Names" in *Fellowship of the Stars* (edited by Terry Carr)

1974 **Cathadonia** [planet], Michael Bishop, "Cathadonian Odyssey" in *The Magazine of Fantasy and Science Fiction*, September 1974

1974 **Charon** [planet], Joe Haldeman, *The Forever War*

1974 **Earth City** [world], Christopher Priest, *Inverted World*

1974 **Folsom's Planet** [planet], Barry N. Malzberg, *On a Planet Alien*

1974 **The Holdfast** [community in an alternate Earth], Suzy McKee Charnas, *Walk to the End of the World*

1974 **Ishtar** [planet], Poul Anderson, *Fire Time*

1974 **Koryphon** [planet], Jack Vance, *The Gray Prince*

1974 **Land of the Lost** [prehistoric land], Sid and Marty Kroft, *The Land of the Lost*

1974 **Mist County (location of Lake Wobegon)** [county in central Minnesota], Garrison Keillor, *A Prairie Home Companion*

1974 **Mote Prime** [planet], Larry Niven and Jerry Pournelle, *The Mote in God's Eye*

1974 **Shkea** [planet], George R. R. Martin, "A Song for Lya" in *Analog Science Fact & Fiction*, June 1974

1974 **Sigma Draconis III** [planet], John Brunner, *Total Eclipse*

1974 **Skaith** [planet], Leigh Brackett, *The Ginger Star*

1974 **Solatia** [country], Jane Yolen, *The Magic Three of Solatia*

1974 **Weinunnach** [planet], Gardner Dozois, "Strangers" in *New Dimensions IV* (edited by Robert Silverberg)

1974 **Zangaro** [country in Africa], Frederick Forsyth, *The Dogs of War*

1975 **(Unnamed world)** [interactive world], Gary Whisenhunt and Ray Wood, *DND*

1975 **(Unnamed world)** [interactive world], Don Daglow, *Dungeon*

1975 **(Unnamed world)** [interactive world], Rusty Rutherford, *PEDIT5*

1975 **Arachne** [planet], Michael Bishop, "Blooded on Arachne" in *Epoch* (edited by Roger Elwood and Robert Silverberg)

1975 **Bellona** [city], Samuel R. Delany, *Dhalgren*

1975 **Blackmoor** [RPG setting], Dave Arneson, *Blackmoor*

1975 **Borderland, Wasteland** [parallel universes], Clifford D. Simak, *Enchanted Pilgrimage*

1975 **Cuckoo** [Dyson sphere], Frederik Pohl and Jack Williamson, *Farthest Star*

1975 **Da-Dake, Na-Nupp, Vipp** [countries], Dr. Seuss [Theodore Seuss Geisel], *Oh, the Thinks You Can Think!*

1975 **Dokal, Shaltoon, Laborlong** [planets], Kilgore Trout [Philip José Farmer], *Venus on the Half-Shell*

1975 **Ecotopia** [country], Ernest Callenbach, *Ecotopia: The Notebooks and Reports of William Weston*

1975 **Glorantha** [world], Greg Stafford, *White Bear and Red Moon*

1975 **Moonbase Alpha** [moon], Gerry and Sylvia Anderson, *Space: 1999*

1975 **Nation of the Urns** [land], Jorge Luis Borges, "Undr" in *El Libro de Arena*

1975 **Orbitsville** [Dyson sphere], Bob Shaw, *Orbitsville*

1975 **Sinapia** [country], Anonymous, edited by Stelio Cro, *Description de la Sinapia, Peninsula en la Tierra Austral: A Classical Utopia of Spain* (translation of an unpublished Spanish manuscript thought to have been written in the late 1600s or 1700s)

1975 **Tékumel** [planet], Muhammad Abd-al-Rahman Barker, *Empire of the Petal Throne*

1975 **W** [island], Georges Perec, *W, Or the Memory of Childhood*

1975 **Where-Nobody-Talks** [country], Jean-Marie-Gustave Le Clézio, *Voyages de l'Autre Côté*

1975 **X513** [planet], Suzette Haden Elgin, "Modulation in All Things" in *Reflections of the Future* (edited by Russell Hill)

1976 **(Unnamed world)** [interactive world], William Crowther, *Colossal Cave Adventure* (text adventure program)

1976 **Alliance-Union universe** [universe], C. J. Cherryh, *Gate of Ivrel*

1976 **Blaispagal, Inc.** [planet], Michael Bishop, "In Chinistrex Fortronza the Peole Are Machines; or Hoom and the Homonuculus" in *New Constellations* (edited by Thomas M. Disch and Charles Naylor)

1976 **Cinnabar** [city], Edward Bryant, *Cinnabar*

1976 **Fernwood** [town in Ohio], Gail Parent, Ann Marcus, Jerry Adelman, and Daniel Gregory Browne, *Mary Hartman, Mary Hartman*

1976 **Florian** [planet], Brian Stableford, *The Florians*

1976 **Hed** [land], Patricia A. McKillip, *The Riddle-Master of Hed*

1976 **Hoep-Hanninah** [planet], Marta Randall, *A City in the North*

1976 **Ibansk** [town in Eastern Europe], Aleksandr Zinoviev, *Ziyayushchie Vysoty*

1976 **Mansueceria** [planet], Michael Bishop, *And Strange at Ecbatan the Trees*

1976 **Mattapoisett** [rural community of the future], Marge Piercy, *Woman on the Edge of Time*

1976 **Oerth** [planet], Gary Gygax, *The Gnome Cache* (serialized in *Dragon* magazine beginning June 1976)

1976 **Redsun** [planet], Vonda N. MacIntyre, "Screwtop" in *The Crystal Ship*

1976 **Schilda** [city-republic], Erich Kästner, *Die Schildbürger*

1976 **The Seven Kingdoms** [kingdoms], Richard Cowper [John Middleton Murry, Jr.], "The Piper at the Gates of Dawn" in *The Custodians*

1976 *Star Wars* **galaxy** [galaxy], George Lucas, *Star Wars: From the Adventures of Luke Skywalker* (novelization of the 1977 film *Star Wars*, ghostwritten by Alan Dean Foster from the screenplay by George Lucas)

1976 **Sweet Pickles** [town], Richard Hefter, Jacqueline Reinach, and Ruth Lerner Perle, *Me Too Iguana*

1976 **Triton** [moon of Neptune], Samuel R. Delany, *Triton*

1977 **Atlanton Earth** [planet], Neil Hancock, *Greyfax Grimwald*

1977 **Cirque** [city on an alternate Earth], Terry Carr, *Cirque*

1977 **Dextra** [planet], David J. Lake, *The Right Hand of Dextra*

1977 **Estarcion** [world], Dave Sim, *Cerebus*

1977 **Fantasy Island** [island], Gene Levitt, *Fantasy Island*

1977 **The Four Lands** [lands of a future Earth], Terry Brooks, *The Sword of Shanarra*

1977 **Galactic Center Saga universe** [universe], Gregory Benford, *In the Ocean of Night*

1977 **The Land** [land], Stephen R. Donaldson, *Lord Foul's Bane*

1977 **Nullaqua** [planet], Bruce Sterling, *Involution Ocean*

1977 **Terabithia** [kingdom], Katherine Paterson, *The Bridge to Terabithia*

1977 **Tezcatl** [planet], Michael Bishop, *Stolen Faces*

1977 **Tsunu** [kingdom], Richard A. Lupoff, *Sword of the Demon*

1977 **Turquoise** [planet], Ian Wallace [John Wallace Pritchard], *The Sign of the Mute Medusa*

1977 **Worlorn** [planet], George R. R. Martin, *Dying of the Light*

1977 **Xanth** [world], Piers Anthony, *A Spell for Chameleon*

1978 **11 Rue Simon-Crubellier** [apartment building in Paris], Georges Perec, *La Vie, mode d'emploi*

1978 **Adventureland** [interactive world], Scott Adams, *Adventureland*

1978 **All-World** [multiverse], Stephen King, *The Gunslinger* (serialized in *The Magazine of Fantasy and Science Fiction*)

1978 **Azlaroc** [world], Fred Sabehagen, *The Veils of Azlaroc*

1978 **Chewandswallow** [town], Judi Barrett and Ron Barrett, *Cloudy with a Chance of Meatballs*

1978 **Demea** [planet], Elizabeth A. Lynn, *A Different Light*

1978 **Dis** [underground city], Charles L. Harness, *Wolfhead*

1978 **Eshgorin** [land], Eleanor Arnason, *The Sword Smith*

1978 **Evarchia** [country in the Balkan peninsula], Brigid Brophy, *Palace without Chairs: A Baroque Novel*

1978 **Hitchhiker's Galaxy** [galaxy], Douglas Adams, *Hitchhiker's Guide to the Galaxy* (radio drama)

1978 **Ireta** [planet], Anne McCaffrey, *Dinosaur Planet*

1978 **Isis** [planet], Marion Zimmer Bradley, *The Ruins of Isis*

1978 **Lysenka II** [planet], Brian Aldiss, *Enemies of the System: A Tale of Homo Uniformis*

1978 **Maralia** [planet], Barrington J. Bayley, *Star Winds*

1978 **MUD (Multi-User Dungeon)** [interactive world], Roy Trubshaw and Richard Bartle, *MUD (Multi-User Dungeon)*

1978 **Parhan** [empire somewhere in the Middle East], Dominique Bromberger, *L'Itinéraire de Parhan au Château D'Alamut et Au-delá*

1978 **The Proteus Universe** [universe], Charles Sheffield, *Sight of Proteus*

1978 **Ramah** [planet], Lee Killough, *A Voice out of Ramah*

1978 **Terran Federation planets** [planets], Terry Nation, *Blake's 7*

1978 **Twelve Colonies** [planets], **Battestar Galactica** [space station], Glen A. Larson, *Battlestar Galactica*

1978 **Tyree** [planet], James Tiptree Jr. [Alice Bradley Sheldon], *Up the Walls of the World*

1978 **Victoria** [planet], Ursula K. LeGuin, "The Eye of the Heron" in *Millennial Women* (edited by Virginia Kidd)

1978 **World of Two Moons** [world], Wendy and Richard Pini, *Elfquest*

1978 **Xuma** [planet], David Lake, *The Gods of Xuma or Barsoom Revisited*

1978 **Zacar** [planet], Andre Norton, *Yurth Burden*

1979 **(Unnamed world)** [interactive world], Warren Robinett, *Adventure* (for the Atari 2600)

1979 **Akalabeth** [interactive world], Richard Garriott, *Akalabeth: World of Doom*

1979 **BoskVeld** [planet], Michael Bishop, *Transfigurations*

1979 **Canopus universe** [universe], Doris Lessing, *Shikasta*

1979 **Delayafam** [planet], Jayge Carr [Margery Ruth Morgenstern Krueger], *Leviathan's Deep*

1979 **Everon** [planet], Gordon R. Dickson, *Masters of Everon*

1979 **Fantastica** [land], Michael Ende, *The Neverending Story*

1979 **Gaea** [space station orbiting Saturn], John Varley, *Titan*

1979 **Gateway** [space station], Frederik Pohl, "The Merchants of Venus" in *The Gold at the Starbow's End*

1979 **Geb** [planet], Brian Stableford, *The Paradox of the Sets*

1979 **God's World** [planet], Ian Watson, *God's World*

1979 **Goss Conf** [planet], David Dvorkin, *The Green God*

1979 **The Great Underground Empire** [interactive world], Tim Anderson, Marc Blank, Bruce Daniels, and Dave Lebling, *Zork*

1979 **Hazzard County** [county in Georgia], Gy Waldron, *The Dukes of Hazzard*

1979 **Jem** [planet], Frederik Pohl, *JEM*

1979 **Little Belaire** [township in a future Earth], John Crowley, *Engine Summer*

1979 **Lodon-Kamaria** [planet], Barbara Paul, *Bibblings*

1979 **LV-426** [planet], Ridley Scott, *Alien*

1979 **Monsalvat** [planet], M. A. Foster, *The Day of the Klesh*

1979 **Pacifica** [planet], Norman Spinrad, *A World Between*

1979 **Pile** [city], Brian W. Aldiss and Mike Wilks, *Pile: Petals from St. Klaed's Computer*

1979 **The Planiverse** [two-dimensional universe], A. K. Dewdney, "Exploring the Planiverse", *Journal of Recreational Mathematics*, Vol. 12, No. 1, September 1979, pages 16–20.

1979 **Theives' World** [world], Robert Asprin, *Theives' World*

1979 **Treason** [planet], Orson Scott Card, *A Planet Called Treason*

1979 **Zanthodon** [underground country under Africa], Lin Carter, *Journey to the Underground World*

1980 **(Unnamed world)** [interactive world], Michael Toy, Glenn Wichman, and Ken Arnold, *Rogue*

1980 **4H 97801** [star system with planet], Ian Watson, *The Gardens of Delight*

1980 **Alternate America** [alternate America], L. Neil Smith, *The Probability Broach*

1980 **Alternate England** [alternate England], Russell Hoban, *Riddley Walker*

1980 **Bloom County** [county], Berkeley Breathed, *Bloom County*

1980 **Coimheadach** [island], Helen Wykham, *Ottoline Atlantica*

1980 **Dragon's Egg** [neutron star], Robert Forward, *Dragon's Egg*

1980 **Eran** [planet], David J. Lake, *The Fourth Hemisphere*

1980 **Majipoor** [planet], Robert Silverberg, *Lord Valentine's Castle*

1980 **Momus** [planet], Barry B. Longyear, *Circus World*

1980 **Mystery House** [interactive world], Roberta and Ken Williams, *Mystery House*

1980 **Reverie** [planet], Bruce Sterling, *The Artificial Kid*

1980 **Rubanis** [planet], Pierre Christin and Jean-Claude Mézières, *Métro Châtelet, Direction Cassiopeia*

1980 **Tew** [planet], Orson Scott Card, *Songmaster*

1980 **Tiamat** [planet], Joan Vinge, *The Snow Queen*

1980 **Ultima Universe** [interactive world], Richard Garriott, *Ultima*

1980 **Uplift universe** [universe], David Brin, *Sundiver*

1980 **Urth** [alternate Earth], Gene Wolfe, *The Shadow of the Torturer*

1981 **(Unnamed world)** [world], Luigi Serafini, *Codex Seraphinianus*

1981 **Aerlon** [planet], Charles L. Harness, *Firebird*

1981 **Aldo Cerise, Colmar, Farhome** [planets], Keith Laumer, *Star Colony*

1981 **Boomerang** [planet], Nicholas Yermakov, *The Last Communion*

1981 **Bypass** [town in North Carolina], Doug Marlette, *Kudzu*

1981 **Carlotta, Nearth** [planets], James Morrow, *The Wine of Violence*

1981 **Eternia** [planet], Mattel Corporation, *Masters of the Universe* "Mineternia" minicomic

1981 **Greater Island, Lesser Island** [islands], Jörg Müller and Jörg Steiner, *Die Menschen im Meer* (*The Sea People*)

1981 **God-Does-Battle** [planet], Greg Bear, *Strength of Stones*

1981 **Nyumbani** [Africa with an alternate history], Charles R. Saunders, *Imaro*

1981 **The Other Plane** [virtual world], Vernor Vinge, "True Names", in *Dell Binary Star #5*

1981 **Radix series Earth** [future Earth], A. A. Attanasio, *Radix*

1981 **Toontown** [town], Gary Wolf, *Who Censored Roger Rabbit?*

1981 **Tuna** [small town in Texas], Jaston Williams, Joe Sears, and Ed Howard, *Greater Tuna*

1981 **Utopia** [interactive world], Don Daglow, *Utopia*

1981 **Windhaven** [planet], George R. R. Martin and Lisa Tuttle, *Windhaven*

1981 **The Worlds** [space habitats], Joe Haldeman, *Worlds*

1982 **Aloria** [world], David Eddings, *Pawn of Prophecy*

1982 **Asgard** [planet], Brian Stableford, *Journey to the Center*

1982 **Aventine** [colony on a distant planet], Lee Killough, *Aventine*

1982 **Ballybran** [planet], Anne McCaffrey, *The Crystal Singer*

1982 **Chiron** [planet], James P. Hogan, *Voyage from Yesteryear*

1982 **Counter-earth** [planet], François Schuiten and Benoît Peeters, *Les Murailles de Samaris* (the first book in the *Les Cités Obscures* series, first serialized in the June issue of *(A Suivre)*, a French periodical)

1982 **Cyberspace** [virtual world], **The Sprawl** [future United States], William Gibson, "Burning Chrome" in *Omni*, July 1982

1982 **Geta** [planet], Donald Kingsbury, *Courtship Rite*

1982 **Gravitar** [interactive world], Mike Hally and Rich Adam, *Gravitar*

1982 **The Grid** [digital world inside a computer], Steven Lisberger, *Tron*

1982 **Grimace** [town in Texas], Jerry Bittle, *Geech*

1982 **Helliconia** [planet], Brian Aldiss, *Helliconia Spring*

1982 **Inquestor universe** [universe], Somtow Sucharitkul [also known as S. P. Somtow], *The Dawning Shadow: Light on the Sound*

1982 **The Kingdom** [console RPG setting], Stephen Landrum, *Dragonstomper*

1982 **Meirjain** [planet], Barrington J. Bayley, *The Pillars of Eternity*

1982 **Neo-Tokyo** [city], Katsuhiro Otomo, *Akira* (first serialized in *Young Magazine*)

1982 **Riftwar universe** [universe], Raymond E. Feist, *Magician*

1982 **Shaper/Mechanist universe** [universe], Bruce Sterling, "Swarm" in *The Magazine of Fantasy & Science Fiction*, April 1982

1982 **Thra** [planet], Jim Henson, *The Dark Crystal*

1982 **Walpurgis III** [planet], Mike Resnick, *Walpurgis III*

1982 **Wundle** [kingdom], Robert Siegel, *The Kingdom of Wundle*

1983 **Altair IV** [planet], Ben Bova, *The Winds of Altair*

1983 **Boldhome** [on-line RPG setting], Alan E. Klietz, *Scepter of Goth*

1983 **Camarand** [kingdom], Don Reo, *Wizards and Warriors*

1983 **Corinth** [town in Pennsylvania], Agnes Nixon and Douglas Marland, *Loving*

1983 **Demiplane of Dread** [RPG setting], Tracy and Laura Hickman, *Ravenloft*

1983 **Discworld** [world], Terry Pratchett, *The Colour of Magic*

1983 **Dragaera** [planet], Steven Brust, *Jhereg*

1983 **Fraggle Rock** [world], Jim Henson, *Fraggle Rock*

1983 **Fujimura, Nelson, Sidon** [settlements on Ganymede], Gregory Benford, *Against Infinity*

1983 **Hyperion Cantos universe** [universe], Dan Simmons, "Remembering Siri" in *Asimov's Science Fiction*, December 1983

1983 **Iblard** [world], Naohisa Inoue, *The Journey Through Iblard* (paintings appeared in exhibitions prior to the release of the book)

1983 **Klepsis, Emporion, Apateon** [planets], R. A. Lafferty, *The Annals of Klepsis*

1983 **Ntah** [country], John Brunner, *The Crucible of Time*

1983 **Orthe** [planet], Mary Gentle, *Golden Witchbreed*

1983 **Rabelais** [planet], Jayge Carr [Margery Ruth Morgenstern Krueger], *Navigator's Sindrome*

1983 **Tortall** [country], Tamora Pierce, *Alanna: The First Adventure*

1983 **Warhammer universe** [universe], Games Workshop, *Warhammer Fantasy Battle*

1984 **(Unnamed world)** [world], Glen Cook, *The Black Company*

1984 **Absu** [planet], James Morrow, *The Continent of Lies*

1984 **Alternate Earth** [alternate Earth], Harry Harrison, *West of Eden*

1984 **Alternate United States** [alternate United States], Suzette Elgin, *Native Tongue*

1984 **Aseneshesh** [planet], James Kelly, *Planet of Whispers*

1984 **Cabot Cove** [town in Maine], Peter Fisher, Richard Levinson, and William Link, *Murder, She Wrote*

1984 **Fionavar** [world], Guy Gavriel Kay, *The Summer Tree*

1984 **Frontera** [settlement on Mars], Lewis Shiner, *Frontera*

1984 **Hawkins Island** [island near Cape Cod], Hilbert Schenck, *A Rose for Armageddon*

1984 **Krynn** [world], Margaret Weis and Tracy Hickman, *Dragons of Autumn Twilight*

1984 **Mallworld** [planet], Somtow Sucharitkul [also known as S. P. Somtow], *Mallworld*

1984 **Mu Archipelago** [on-line RPG setting], Kelton Flinn and John Taylor, *Island of Kesmai*

1984 **The Territories** [alternate world], Stephen King and Peter Straub, *The Talisman*

1984 **Tigris** [planet], Timothy Zahn, *A Coming of Age*

1985 **Amaterasu** [planet], Walter Jon Williams, *Knight Moves*

1985 **Belshazzar** [planet], Norman Spinrad, *Child of Fortune*

1985 **Cascara** [island in the Carribean Sea], Dick Clement, *Water*

1985 **Sea Venture** (also known as **CV**) [city], Damon Knight, *CV*

1985 **Damiem** [planet], James Tiptree Jr. [Alice Bradley Sheldon], *Brightness Falls from the Air*

1985 **Dayworld** [planet], Philip José Farmer, *Dayworld*

1985 **Ethshar** [land], Lawrence Watt-Evans, *The Misenchanted Sword*

1985 **Gilead** [republic], Margaret Atwood, *The Handmaid's Tale*

1985 **Hav** [peninsular city-state in the Near East], Jan Morris, *Last Letters from Hav*

1985 **Ibis 2** [planet], Linda Steele, *Ibis*

1985 **Medea** [planet], Harlan Ellison and others, *Medea: Harlan's World*

1985 **Mutare** [planet], Cynthia Felice, *Downtime*

1985 **Valley of the Kesh** [valley in Northern California], Ursula K. LeGuin, *Always Coming Home*

1985 **Rocheworld** [double planet], Robert Forward, *Rocheworld*

1985 **Thundera** [planet], Tobias "Ted" Wolf, *Thundercats*

1985 **The Way universe** [universe], Greg Bear, *Eon*

1986 **Alternate New York** [alternate New York], Alan Moore and Dave Gibbons, *Watchmen*

1986 **Athos** [planet], Lois McMaster Bujold, *Ethan of Athos*

1986 **Boxen** [world], C. S. Lewis, *Boxen: The Imaginary World of the Young C. S. Lewis*

1986 **Brotherworld** [space station], Gregory Benford, "As Big as the Ritz" in *Interzone* #18, Winter 1986

1986 **Chameleon** [planet], Sheila Finch, *Triad*

1986 **Deverry** [kingdom], Katherine Kerr, *Daggerspell*

1986 **Habitat World** [on-line RPG setting], Randy Farmer and Chip Morningstar, *Habitat*

1986 **Hyrule** [interactive world], Shigeru Miyamoto, *The Legend of Zelda*

1986 **Ingary, Strangia, Sultanates of Rashpuht** [countries], Diana Wynne Jones, *Howl's Moving Castle*

1986 **Keléstia** [RPG setting], N. Robin Crossby, *HârnMaster*

1986 **Land, Overland** [planets], Bob Shaw, *The Ragged Astronauts*

1986 **Landover** [kingdom], Terry Brooks, *Magic Kingdom for Sale—SOLD!*

1986 **Lusitania** [planet], Orson Scott Card, *Speaker for the Dead*

1986 **Redworld** [planet], Charles L. Harness, *Redworld*

1986 **Rhomary** [planet], Cherry Wilder [Cherry Barbara Grimm], *Second Nature*

1986 **Shora, Valedon** [planets], Joan Slonczewski, *A Door into Ocean*

1986 **Vorkosigan Saga universe** [universe], Lois McMaster Bujold, *Shards of Honor*

1987 **Abeir-Toril** [RPG setting], Ed Greenwood and Jeff Grubb, *Forgotten Realms Box Set*

1987 **Alternate universe of The Culture** [universe], Iain M. Banks, *Consider Phlebas*

1987 **Destiny's Road universe** [universe], Larry Niven, Jerry Pournelle, and Steve Barnes, *The Legacy of Heorot*

1987 **Dimension X** [alternate dimension], Kevin Eastman and Peter Laird, *Teenage Mutant Ninja Turtles*

1987 **Empire of Videssos** [empire], Harry Turtledove, *The Misplaced Legion*

1987 **Enigma 88** [planet], Hal Clement [Harry Clement Stubbs], *Still River*

1987 **Ephar** [planet], Harry Turtledove, "Last Favor" in *Analog Magazine*, December 1987

1987 **Final Fantasy Universe** [universe], Hironobu Sakaguchi, *Final Fantasy*

1987 **Ilia** [planet], Sheila Finch, *The Garden of the Shaped*

1987 **Imakulata** [planet], Orson Scott Card, *Wyrms*

1987 **Kingdom of Kroz** [kingdom], Scott Miller, *Kingdom of Kroz*

1987 **Jubal** [planet], Sheri S. Tepper, *After Long Silence*

1987 **The Manhole** [interactive world], Rand and Robyn Miller, *The Manhole*

1987 **Maniac Mansion** [interactive world], Ron Gilbert and Gary Winnick, *Maniac Mansion*

1987 **Pennterra** [planet], Judith Moffett, *Pennterra*

1987 **Prysmos** [planet], Flint Dille, *Visionaries: Knights of the Magical Light*

1987 **Springfield** [city], Matt Groening, *The Simpsons* (shorts appearing on *The Tracy Ullman Show*)

1987 **Talislanta** [RPG setting], Stephen Michael Sechi and P. D. Breeding-Black, *Talislanta*

1987 **Velgarth** [continent], Mercedes Lackey, *Arrows of the Queen*

1988 **(Unnamed world)** [on-line RPG setting], Rich Skrenta, *Monster*

1988 **Alternate version of Deimos** [moon of Mars], Charles Harness, *Krono*

1988 **Cadwal** [planet], Jack Vance, *Araminta Station*

1988 **Cay Habitat** [space station], **Rodeo** [planet], Lois McMaster Bujold, *Falling Free*

1988 **Clarion** [planet], William Greenleaf, *Clarion*

1988 **Desolation Road** [town on Mars], Ian McDonald, *Desolation Road*

1988 **The Domination of Draka series world** [alternate Earth], S. M. Stirling, *Marching Through Georgia*

1988 **Elanthia** [on-line RPG setting], Simutronics, *GemStone II*

1988 **Flyspeck Island** [island], Ray Billingsley, *Curtis*

1988 **Osten Ard** [continent], Tad Williams, *The Dragonbone Chair*

1988 **Qom** [planet], Nancy Kress, *An Alien Light*

1989 **(Unnamed world)** [interactive world], Peter Molyneux, *Populous*

1989 **Artemis** [planet], Storm Constantine, *The Monstrous Regiment*

1989 **The Cylinder** [world], K. W. Jeter, *Farewell Horizontal*

1989 **Elyisium** [planet], Paul J. McAuley, *Secret Harmonies* (also known as *Of the Fall*)

1989 **Peponi** [planet], Mike Resnick, *Paradise*

1989 **Republic of Elbonia** [country], Scott Adams, *Dilbert*

1989 **SimCity** [interactive city], Will Wright, *SimCity*

1989 **Stohlson's Redemption** [planet], Hayford Pierce, *The Thirteenth Majestral*

1990 **Alifbay, Kahani, Moody Land** [countries], Salman Rushdie, *Haroun and the Sea of Stories*

1990 **Cicely** [town in Alaska], Joshua Brand and John Falsey, *Northern Exposure*

1990 **Darwin IV** [planet], Wayne Douglas Barlowe, *Expedition*

1990 **Erhal system** [planets], Sherwood Smith, *Wren to the Rescue*

1990 **The Heritage Universe** [universe], Charles Sheffield, *Summertide*

1990 **Htrae** [underground world], Rudy Rucker, *The Hollow Earth: The Narrative of Mason Algiers Reynolds of Virginia*

1990 **Isla Nublar** [island], Michael Crichton, *Jurassic Park*

1990 **Mêlée Island, Monkey Island** [islands], Ron Gilbert, *The Secret of Monkey Island*

1990 **Miranda** [planet], Michael Swanwick, *Stations in the Tide* (serialized in *Isaac Asimov's Science Fiction Magazine*)

1990 **Randland** [world], Robert Jordan [James Oliver Rigney, Jr.], *The Eye of the World*

1990 **Twin Peaks** [town in Washington State], David Lynch and Mark Frost, *Twin Peaks*

1990 **Veritas** [city], James Morrow, *City of Truth*

1990 **World of the Three Moons** [planet], Marion Zimmer Bradley, Julian May, and Andre Norton, *Black Trillium*

1991 **Alternate Earth** [alternate Earth], William Gibson and Bruce Sterling, *The Difference Engine*

1991 **Athas** [RPG setting], Timothy B. Brown and Troy Denning, *Dark Sun*

1991 **The Caves of Mr. Seudo** [underground world], Rand and Robyn Miller, *Spelunx and the Caves of Mr. Seudo*

1991 **Hydros** [planet], Robert Silverberg, *The Face of the Waters*

1991 **Lunaplex** [city on the moon], Charles L. Harness, *Lunar Justice*

1991 **Odern** [planet], Harry Turtledove, "The Great Unknown" in *Analog*, April 1991

1991 **Slowyear** [planet], Frederik Pohl, *Stopping at Slowyear*

1991 **United Socialist States of America** [alternate United States], Eugene Byrne and Kim Newman, "In the Air" in *Interzone #43*, January 1991

1992 **Alternate Worlds** [alternate worlds where time operates differently], Alan Lightman, *Einstein's Dreams*

1992 **The Continent** [continent], Andrzej Sapkowski, *Miecz Przeznaczenia* (*The Sword of Destiny*)

1992 **Dinotopia** [island], James Gurney, *Dinotopia: A Land Apart From Time*

1992 **Drakkar** [RPG setting], MPG-Net, *Kingdom of Drakkar*

1992 **Ferngully** [rainforest], Diana Young, *Ferngully*

1992 **Harmony** [planet], Orson Scott Card, *The Memory of Earth*

1992 **Kyrandia** [kingdom], Frank Klepacki, *The Legend of Kyrandia*

1992 **Meridian** [planet], Eric Brown, *Meridian Days*

1992 **Metaverse** [virtual world], Neal Stephenson, *Snow Crash*

1992 **Nou Occitan** [planet], John Barnes, *A Million Open Doors*

1992 **Pop Star** [planet], Masahiro Sakurai, *Kirby's Dream Land*

1992 **Quintaglio homeworld** [planet], Robert J. Sawyer, *Far-Seer*

1993 **Babylon 5 universe** [universe], J. Michael Straczynski, *Babylon 5*

1993 **Dominaria** [planet], Richard Garfield, *Magic: The Gathering*

1993 **D'ni and various Ages** [underground world and "Ages"], Rand and Robyn Miller, *Myst*

1993 **Future Earth, Venus, and Mars** [planets], Jeff Segal, *Exosquad*

1993 **Honor Harrington universe** [universe], David Weber, *On Basilisk Station*

1993 **Kaleva** [planet], Ian Watson, *Lucky's Harvest*

1993 **Karimon** [planet], Mike Resnick, *Purgatory: A Chronicle of a Distant World*

1993 **Mars** [version of Mars], Kim Stanley Robinson, *Red Mars*

1993 **Petaybee** [planet], Anne McCaffrey and Elizabeth Ann Scarborough, *Powers That Be*

1993 **Stratos** [planet], David Brin, *Glory Season*

1994 **Alternate Paris** [alternate Paris], Jules Verne, *Paris in the 20th Century* (originally written in 1863)

1994 **Autoverse** [virtual world], Greg Egan, *Permutation City*

1994 **Azeroth** (Warcraft universe) [RPG setting], Blizzard Entertainment, *Warcraft: Orcs & Humans*

1994 **Boohte** [planet], Connie Willis, *Uncharted Territory*

1994 **Caribe** [underwater city], Maureen McHugh, *Half the Day is Night*

1994 **Dinadh** [planet], Sheri S. Tepper, *Shadow's End*

1994 **Foreigner universe** [universe], C. J. Cherryh, *Foreigner*

1994 **Grandinsula** [island], Jill Paton Walsh, *Knowledge of Angels*

1994 **Island of the Day Before** [island], Umberto Eco, *The Island of the Day Before*

1994 **Mera** [planet], Alison Baird, *The Stone of the Stars*

1994 **Nirn** [RPG setting], Bethesda Softworks, *Elder Scrolls: Arena*

1994 **Planescape** [RPG setting], David "Zeb" Cook, *Planescape*

1994 **Skolian Empire** [planets], Catherine Asaro, "Light and Shadow" in *Analog Fiction and Fact*, April 1994

1994 **Solis** [city on Mars], A. A. Attanasio, *Solis*

1994 **Stargate universe** [universe], Roland Emmerich and Dean Devlin, *Stargate*

1994 **Worldwar world** [alternate Earth], Harry Turtledove, *Worldwar: In the Balance*

1995 **(Unnamed planet)** [planet], Brian Stableford, *Serpent's Blood*

1995 **Aebrynis** [RPG setting], TSR, Inc., *Birthright*

1995 **Bountiful** [planet], Kristine Kathryn Rusch, *Alien Influences*

1995 **Catan** [island], Klaus Teuber, *The Settlers of Catan*

1995 **City of Lost Children** [city], Jean-Pierre Jeunet and Marc Caro, *City of Lost Children*

1995 **Clifton** [town in Indiana], Margaret Peterson Haddix, *Running Out of Time*

1995 **Dark Town** [town], Kaja Blackley and Vanessa Chong, *Dark Town*

1995 **Hara** [planet], Melissa Scott, *Shadow Man*

1995 **His Dark Materials multiverse** [multiverse], Philip Pullman, *Northern Lights* (also published as *The Golden Compass*)

1995 **Meridian 59** [MMORPG setting], Archetype Interactive, *Meridian 59*

1995 **Moor** [town in Austria], Christoph Ransmayr, *Morbus Kitahara*

1995 **Stateless** [artificial island], Greg Egan, *Distress*

1995 **Tiangi** [planet], Amy Thompson, *The Color of Distance*

1995 **Toxicurare** [planet], William Moy Russell, *The Barber of Aldebaran*

1995 **Waterworld** [future Earth], David Twohy, Peter Rader, and Kevin Reynolds, *Waterworld*

1996 **Greenwood** [planet], David Drake, *Patriots*

1996 **Neverwhere** [underground land], Neil Gaiman, *Neverwhere*

1996 **Night Dimension** [world], Naoto Ohshima, *NiGHTS into Dreams …*

1996 **Night's Dawn Trilogy universe** [universe], Peter F. Hamilton, *The Reality Dysfunction*

1996 **Quidam** [world], Franco Dragone, *Quidam*

1996 **Rakhat** [planet], Mary Doria Russell, *The Sparrow*

1996 **The Realm Online** [on-line RPG setting], Sierra On-Line, *The Realm Online*

1996 **Sims Bancorp Colony #3245.12** [colony on a distant planet], Elizabeth Moon, *Remnant Population*

1996 **Westeros** [continent], George R. R. Martin, *A Game of Thrones*

1997 **Aarklash** [RPG setting], Rackham (now Rackham Entertainment), *Confrontation*

1997 **Anderran, Emelan, Sotat, etc.** [countries], Tamora Pierce, *Sandry's Book* (also published as *The Magic in the Weaving*)

1997 **Carter-Zimmerman Polis** [alternate Earth], **Orpheus, Swift** [planets], Greg Egan, *Diaspora*

1997 **Corona** [world], R. A. Salvatore, *The Demon Awakens: The DemonWars Saga Vol. I*

1997 **Deception Well** [planet], Linda Nagata, *Deception Well*

1997 **Hogwarts Academy** [school and surrounding area], J. K. Rowling, *Harry Potter and the Philosopher's Stone*

1997 **Eseveron** [land], Rob Lay, *A Fork in the Tale*

1997 **Future Earth** [future Earth], Luc Besson, *The Fifth Element*

1997 **Green Lawn** [town in Connecticut], Ron Roy, *The Absent Author*

1997 **The Isles** [islands], David Drake, *Lord of the Isles*

1997 **The Lexx universe** [universe], Paul Donovan, *Lexx*

1997 **Liberty City** [interactive city], Rockstar Games, *Grand Theft Auto*

1997 **Oddworld** [interactive world], Lorne Lanning and Frank Ryan, *Oddworld: Abe's Oddyssey*

1997 **Quibsh** [planet], Timothy Zahn, "The Art of War" in *Fantasy & Science Fiction*, March 1997

1997 **Stormhold** [kingdom], Neil Gaiman, *Stardust*

1997 **Sunnydale** [suburb in California], Joseph "Joss" Whedon, *Buffy the Vampire Slayer* (TV series)

1997 **Timeline-191 world** [alternate Earth], Harry Turtledove, *How Few Remain*

1997 **Vlhan** [planet], Adam Troy-Castro, "The Funeral March of the Marionettes" in *Fantasy & Science Fiction*, July 1997

1998 **Capeside** [town in Massachusetts], Kevin Williamson, *Dawson's Creek*

1998 **Dark City** [city], Alex Proyas, *Dark City*

1998 **Darwinia** [continent], Robert Charles Wilson, *Darwinia*

1998 **The Edge** [island in the sky], Paul Stewart and Chris Riddell, *Beyond the Deepwoods*

1998 **Gallinaco** [country], Yves Beauchemin, "The Banana Wars" in *The Ark in the Garden: Fables for Our Times* (edited by Alberto Manguel)

1998 **Golgot** [city on Venus], Alexander Jablokov, *Deepdrive*

1998 **Jean** [planet], Mark Stanley, *Freefall*

1998 **Sasania** [desert country], A. S. Byatt, *Elementals: Stories of Fire and Ice*

1998 **Seahaven** [town], Peter Weir and Andrew Niccol, *The Truman Show*

1998 **StarCraft universe** [RPG setting], Blizzard Entertainment, *StarCraft*

1998 **Tereille, Kaeleer** [realms], Anne Bishop, *Daughter of the Blood*

1999 **(Unnamed world)** [world], Wim Delvoye, *Atlas*

1999 **Arcadia, Stark** [MMORPG setting], Ragnar Tørnquist and Didrik Tollefson, *The Longest Journey*

1999 **Dereth** [MMORPG setting], Turbine Entertainment Software, *Asheron's Call*

1999 **Everworld** [planet], K. A. Applegate, *Everworld #1: Search for Senna*

1999 **Harmony** [town], James E. Reilly, *Passions*

1999 **The Matrix** [virtual world], Larry and Andy Wachowski, *The Matrix*

1999 **Mazalan** [empire], Steven Erikson, *Gardens of the Moon*

1999 **Moda-5, Rados** [planets], Joanna Barkan, *Barbie: Voyage to Rados*

1999 **Neopia** [planet], Adam Powell and Donna Williams, *Neopets.com*

1999 **Neopolis** [city], Alan Moore, Gene Ha, Zander Cannon, *Top 10*

1999 **Norrath** [MMORPG setting], Brad McQuaid, Steve Clover, Bill Trost, *EverQuest*

1999 **Silent Hill** [town in California], Keiichiro Toyama, *Silent Hill*

1999 **Smuggler's Cove** [village], Walter Wick, *I Spy: Treasure Hunt*

1999 **Tørrendru** [land near the Central Siberian Plateau], Izaak Mansk, *The Ride of Enveric Olsen*

1999 **The Uncharted Territories** [galaxy], Rockne S. O'Bannon, *Farscape*

1999 **World of the League of Extraordinary Gentlemen** [alternate Earth], Alan Moore and Kevin O'Neill, *The League of Extraordinary Gentlemen, Volume I*

2000 **(Unnamed island)** [island in the South Pacific], William Broyles, Jr. and Robert Zemeckis, *Castaway*

2000 **CrossGen universe (Sigilverse)** [universe], Mark Alessi, *CrossGenesis*

2000 **Deltora** [kingdom], Emily Rodda, *The Forests of Silence*

2000 **Genovia** [country in Europe], Meg Cabot, *The Princess Diaries*

2000 **Maginaryworld** [world], Hidenori Oikawa, *Sonic Shuffle*

2000 **Mejere, Taraak** [planets], Takeshi Mori, *Vandread*

2000 **Mouse Island** [island], Geronimo Stilton [Elisabetta Dami], *Lost Treasure of the Emerald Eye*

2000 **Nyeusigrube** [world], Amelia Atwater-Rhodes, *In the Forests of the Night*

2000 **Pndapetzim** [city in Asia], Umberto Eco, *Baudolino*

2000 **Revelation Space universe** [universe], Alastair Reynolds, *Revelation Space*

2000 **Systems Commonwealth universe** [universe], Gene Roddenberry and Robert Hewitt Wolfe, *Andromeda*

2000 **Tryslmaistan** [universe], Jennifer Diane Reitz, *Unicorn Jelly*

2001 **Aldrazar** [RPG setting], Jolly R. Blackburn, David Kenser, et al., *Hackmaster*

2001 **Ambergris** [city], Jeff VanderMeer, *City of Saints and Madmen: The Book of Ambergris*

2001 **Arcanis** [RPG setting], Paradigm Concepts, *Arcanis*

2001 **Bas-Lag** [world], China Miéville, *Perdido Street Station*

2001 **BookWorld** [world], Jasper Fforde, *The Eyre Affair*

2001 **Bubble Town** [town], Cinepix, *Cubix*

2001 **Chalion universe** [universe], Lois McMaster Bujold, *The Curse of Chalion*

2001 **Creation** [RPG setting], Robert Hatch, Justin Achilli, Stephan Wieck, Andrew Bates, Dana Habecker, Sheri M. Johnson, Chris McDonough, Richard Thomas, *Exalted*

2001 **Flatterland, Mathiverse** [worlds], Ian Stewart, *Flatterland: Like Flatland, Only More So*

2001 **Halo universe** [interactive world], Bungie, *Halo*

2001 **Jumpgate universe** [MMORPG setting], NetDevil, *Jumpgate: The Reconstruction Initiative*

2001 **Motor City** [MMORPG setting], Electronic Arts, *Motor City Online*

2001 **Nydus** [planet], Julia Gray, *The Dark Moon*

2002 **Alternate Earth** [alternate Earth], Kim Stanley Robinson, *The Years of Rice and Salt*

2002 **Banton, Renberg, Morlaw, Danver** [towns], Bob Gale, *Interstate 60*

2002 **Firefly universe** [universe], Joss Whedon, *Firefly*

2002 **Halla** [universe], D. J. MacHale, *The Merchant of Death*

2002 **Nyambe** [RPG setting], Chris Dolunt, *Nyambe: African Adventures*

2002 **Polyester** [planet in a parallel universe], Jim Davis, *Garfield's Pet Force: Book 1: The Outrageous Origin*

2002 **Seven Suns universe** [planets], Kevin J. Anderson, *Hidden Empire*

2002 **Spaceland** [four-dimensional world], Rudy Rucker, *Spaceland*

2003 **Alagaësia** [land], Christopher Paolini, *Eragon*

2003 **Alternate Earth** [alternate Earth], Max Barry, *Jennifer Government*

2003 **Celenheim** [country], Starbreeze Studios, *Enclave*

2003 **Cube Town** [town], Naomi Iwata, *Pecola*

2003 **Entropia Universe** [MMORPG setting], MindArk, *Entropia Universe*

2003 **Ga'Hoole world** [world], Kathryn Lasky, *The Capture*

2003 **Kaihapa, Kainui** [ocean planets], Hal Clement [Harry Clement Stubbs], *Noise*

2003 **Maple Island, Victoria Island, Ossyria, Masteria** [MMORPG setting], Wizet, *MapleStory*

2003 **Michisota** [U.S. state], Lisa Wheeler, *Avalanche Annie: A Not-So-Tall Tale*

2003 **Molvania** [country in Eastern Europe], Tom Gleisner, Santo Cilauro, and Rob Sitch, *Molvania: A Land Untouched by Modern Dentistry*

2003 **Muddle Earth** [planet], Paul Stewart, *Muddle Earth*

2003 **Nation of Breda** [country], Adrian Leskiw, *The Map Realm: The Fictional Road Maps of Adrian Leskiw*

2003 **Planetside universe** [MMORPG setting], Sony Online Entertainment, *Planetside*

2003 **Rhem** [interactive world], Knut Müller, *Rhem*

2003 **Second Life** [on-line world], Linden Research, Inc., *Second Life*

2003 **Shadowbane world** [MMORPG setting], Wolfpack Studios, *Shadowbane*

2003 **Shutter Island** [island], Dennis Lehane, *Shutter Island*

2004 **Akloria, Illumina** [worlds], Tuomas Pirinen, *Sudeki*

2004 **Aliwalas, Avila, Halconia, Hayuhay** [kingdoms], Don Michael Perez, *Mulawin*

2004 **Bhrudwo, Elamaq, Faltha** [continents], Russell Kirkpatrick, *Across the Face of the World*

2004 **Eberron** [RPG setting], Keith Baker, Bill Slavicsek, James Wyatt, *Eberron Campaign Setting*

2004 **The Emberverse world** (also known as the **Change World**) [alternate Earth], S. M. Stirling, *Dies the Fire*

2004 **Estrada-Blair** [planet], Suzette Haden Elgin, "We Have Always Spoken Panglish" in *SciFiction*, October 27, 2004

2004 **The Fourlands** [world], Steph Swainston, *The Year of Our War*

2004 **Gezeitenwelt** (also known as **World of Tides**) [world], Magus Magellan [Bernhard Hennen, Hadmar von Wieser, Thomas Finn, and Karl-heinz Witzko], *Das Geheimnis der Gezeitenwelt*

2004 **Globus Cassus** [future Earth], Christian Waldvogel, *Globus Cassus*

2004 **The Island** [island], Jeffrey Lieber, J. J. Abrams, Damon Lindelof, *Lost*

2004 **The Kingdom of Far Far Away** [kingdom], Andrew Adamson, *Shrek 2*

2004 **Lazy Town** [town], Magnús Scheving, *Lazy Town*

2004 **Nasqueron** [planet], Iain M. Banks, *The Algebraist*

2004 **Neptune** [town in California], Rob Thomas, *Veronica Mars*

2004 **Paragon City** [MMORPG setting], Cryptic Studios and Paragon Studios, *City of Heroes*

2004 **Phaic Tăn** [country in Southeast Asia], Tom Gleisner, Santo Cilauro, and Rob Sitch, *Phaic Tăn: Sunstroke on a Shoestring*

2004 **Scrapland** [interactive world], American McGee, *Scrapland*

2004 **The Village** [village], M. Night Shyamalan, *The Village*

2005 **Aldea** [RPG setting], Jeremy Crawford, Dawn Eliot, Stephen Kenson, and John Snead, *Blue Rose*

2005 **Alphaverse, Betaverse, Gammaverse** [parallel universes], Chris Roland and Robert Wertheimer, *Charlie Jade*

2005 **Aurelia, Blue Moon** [planet and moon], *National Geographic* and Blue Wave Productions, *Alien Worlds*

2005 **Eidolon** [country], Jane Johnson, *The Secret Country*

2005 **Kippernium** [kingdom], Martin Baynton, *Jane and the Dragon*

2005 **Marwencol** [town in Belgium], Mark Hogancamp, "Marwencol on My Mind" in *Esopus 5*, 2005

2005 **Rivet Town, Robot City** [cities], Chris Wedge and Carlos Saldanha, *Robots*

2006 **Atlantika** [undersea world], Jun Lana, *Atlantika*

2006 **Calaspia** [land], Suresh Guptara and Jyoti Guptara, *Conspiracy of Calaspia*

2006 **Code Geass world** [alternate Earth], Gorō Taniguchi and Ichirō Ōkouchi, *Code Geass: Lelouch of the Rebellion*

2006 **Daikūriku** [planet], Junji Nishimura, *Simoun*

2006 **Dreamland** [world], Scott Christian Sava, *The Dreamland Chronicles*

2006 **Erfland** [world], Rob Balder, http://www.erfland.com

2006 **The Named Lands** [world], Ken Scholes, "Of Metal Men and Scarlet Thread and Dancing with the Sunrise" in *Realms of Fantasy*, August 2006

2006 **Overside** [planet], Evan Dahm, *Rice Boy*

2006 **Radiator Springs** [town in western North America], John Lasseter and Joe Ranft, *Cars*

2006 **San Sombrèro** [country in Latin America], Tom Gleisner, Santo Cilauro, and Rob Sitch, *San Sombrèro: A Land of Carnivals, Cocktails and Coups*

2006 **Sera** [planet], Epic Games, *Gears of War*

2007 **(Unnamed world)** [countries], Shaun Tan, *The Arrival*

2007 **Andalasia** [land], Kevin Lima and Bill Kelly, *Enchanted*

2007 **Dingburg** [city], Bill Griffith, *Zippy the Pinhead*

2007 **Galaxiki** [galaxy], Jos Kirps and the Galaxiki Project, *Galaxiki*

2007 **Rapture** [interactive world], Ken Levine and Paul Hellquist, *Bioshock*

2007 **Terra** [planet], Aristomenis Tsirbas, *Terra*

2008 **Arbe** [planet], Neal Stephenson, *Anathem*

2008 **Axiom** [space station], **Future Earth** [future Earth], Andrew Stanton, *WALL·E*

2008 **Panem** [country in future North America], Suzanne Collins, *The Hunger Games*

2008 **Sapphire** [virtual planet], Greg Egan, "Crystal Nights" in *Interzone* #215, April 2008

2008 **User-generated worlds** [worlds], Will Wright, *Spore*

2008 **Wizard City, Krokotopia, Grizzleheim, Marleybone, Mooshu, Dragonspyre, Celestia, Wintertusk** [on-line worlds], KingsIsle Entertainment, *Wizard101*

2009 **Chester's Mill** [town in Maine], Stephen King, *Under the Dome*

2009 **Farm Town** [on-line world], Slashkey, *Farm Town*

2009 **FarmVille** [on-line world], Zynga, *FarmVille*

2009 **Pandora** [planet], Gearbox Software, *Borderlands*

2009 **Pandora** [planet], James Cameron, *Avatar*

2009 **Planet 51** [planet], Jorge Blanco and Joe Stillman, *Planet 51*

2009 **Sengala** [country in Africa] Jon Cassar, *24: Redemption*

2010 **CityVille** [on-line world], Zynga, *CityVille*

2010 **Forbidden Island** [island], Gamewright, *Forbidden Island*

2010 **FrontierVille** [on-line world], Zynga, *FrontierVille*

2010 **Limbo** [world], Christopher Nolan, *Inception*

2010 **New Austin, West Elizabeth** [U.S. border counties], **Nuevo Paraiso** [Mexican state], Rockstar Games, *Red Dead Redemption*

2011 **Minor Universe 31** [universe], Charles Yu, *How to Live Safely in a Science Fiction Universe*

2011 **Palm City** [city], Tom Wheeler, *The Cape*

2011 **Terra Nova** [alternate Earth], Kelly Marcel and Craig Silverstein, *Terra Nova*

2011 **Yalda's universe** [universe], Greg Egan, *Orthogonal, Book One: The Clockwork Rocket*

NOTES

Introduction

1. Oscar Wilde, *The Soul of Man Under Socialism*, 1895, first published in *The Fortnightly Review*, February 1891.
2. Gore Vidal, "The Oz Books" in Gore Vidal, *United States: Essays, 1952–1992*, New York, New York: Random House, 1993, page 1095.
3. David Lynch, as quoted in Ed Naha, *The Making of Dune*, New York, New York: Berkley Books, 1984, page 213.
4. As quoted in Norman Holland, *Literature and the Brain*, Gainsville, Florida: The PsyArt Foundation, 2009, pages 327–328. The two essays Holland is summarizing are Leda Cosmides and John Tooby, "Consider the Source: The Evolution of Adaptations for Decoupling and Metarepresentation" in *Metarepresentations: A Multidisciplinary Perspective, Vancouver Studies in Cognitive Science*, Dan Sperber, editor, New York, New York: Oxford University Press, 2000, pages 53–116; and John Tooby and Leda Cosmides, "Does Beauty Build Adapted Minds? Toward an Evolutionary Theory of Aesthetics, Fiction, and the Arts" in *SubStance* 94/95, Special Issue, H. Porter Abbott, editor, 2001, pages 6–27.
5. Michele Root-Bernstein, "Chapter 29. Imaginary Worldplay as an Indicator of Creative Giftedness" in L. V. Shavinina, editor, *International Handbook on Giftedness*, Dordrecht, The Netherlands: Springer Science+Business Media B.V., 2009, page 599, available at http://www.psychologytoday.com/files/attachments/1035/imaginary-worldplay-indicator-creative-giftedness.pdf (accessed September 23, 2011).
6. Michael O. Riley, *Oz and Beyond: The Fantasy World of L. Frank Baum*, Lawrence, Kansas: The University Press of Kansas, 1997, page 225.
7. See Marsha Kinder, *Playing with Power in Movies, Television, and Video Games: From Muppet Babies to Teenage Mutant Ninja Turtles*, Berkeley, California: University of California Press, 1991, pages 122–123.
8. See Janet H. Murray, *Hamlet on the Holodeck: The Future of Narrative in Cyberspace*, Cambridge, Massachusetts, and London, England: MIT Press, 1997, pages 254–258.
9. See Lev Manovich, *The Language of New Media*, Cambridge, Massachusetts: MIT Press, 2001, pages 225–227.
10. Technically, the term should be "*transmedial* storytelling", since an adjectival form is required; I have used this term instead throughout this book.

11. See Henry Jenkins, *Convergence Culture: Where Old and New Media Collide*, New York, New York: New York University Press, 2006, pages 95–96.
12. Ibid., pages 97–98.
13. Ibid., page 114.
14. Henry Jenkins, "Transmedia Storytelling 101", March 22, 2007, available at http://www.henryjenkins.org/2007/03/transmedia_storytelling_101.html (accessed September 28, 2011).
15. David Bordwell, *The Way Hollywood Tells It*, Berkeley, California: University of California Press, 2006, pages 58–59.
16. To varying degrees, many of the essays in the anthology *Third Person: Authoring and Exploring Vast Narratives* discuss world-building and the way narratives and worlds are related. See Pat Harrigan and Noah Wardrip-Fruin, *Third Person: Authoring and Exploring Vast Narratives*, Cambridge, Massachusetts: MIT Press, 2009.
17. Michael O. Riley, *Oz and Beyond: The Fantasy World of L. Frank Baum*, Lawrence, Kansas: The University of Kansas Press, 1997, pages 12–13.
18. See Louis Kennedy, "Piece of Mind: Forget about beginnings, middles, and ends. The new storytelling is about making your way in a fragmented, imaginary world", *The Boston Globe*, June 1, 2003, page N1.

1 Worlds within the World

1. Charles Ischir Defontenay, *Star (Psi Cassiopeia): The Marvelous History of One of the Worlds of Outer Space*, first published in 1854, adapted by P. J. Sokolowski, Encino, California: Black Coat Press, 2007, page 28.
2. From Andrew Wyeth, *The Helga Pictures*, New York: Harry N. Abrams, 1987, page 186.
3. From Thomas G. Pavel, *Fictional Worlds*, Cambridge, Massachusetts and London, England: Harvard University Press, 1986, page 74.
4. See David Lewis, "Anselm and Actuality", *Nous*, 4, pages 175–188; and *Counterfactuals*, Cambridge: Harvard University Press, 1973, pages 84–91; and *On the Plurality of Worlds*, Malden, Massachusetts: Blackwell Publishing, 1986.
5. See Thomas G. Pavel, *Fictional Worlds*, Cambridge, Massachusetts and London, England: Harvard University Press, 1986, page 9.
6. Ibid., page 73.
7. See Lubomír Doležel, *Heterocosmica: Fiction and Possible Worlds*, Baltimore, Maryland: Johns Hopkins University Press, page 28.
8. Ibid., pages 22–23.
9. See Nelson Goodman, *Ways of Worldmaking*, Indianapolis, Indiana: Hackett Publishing Company, page 104.
10. See Marie-Laure Ryan, *Narrative as Virtual Reality: Immersion and Interactivity in Literature and Electronic Media*, Baltimore, Maryland: The Johns Hopkins University Press, 2001, page 91.
11. Ibid., page 91.
12. For a discussion of how the imagination was conceptualized before Coleridge, see John Spencer Hill, *Imagination in Coleridge*, Totowa, New Jersey: Rowman and Littlefield, 1978, pages 1–3.
13. From E. L. Griggs, editor, *Collected Letters of Samuel Taylor Coleridge*, 6 volumes, London and New York: Oxford University Press, 1956–1971, page 709.
14. From the 1795 "Lecture on the Slave-Trade", in Kathleen Coburn, general editor, and L. Patton, volume editor, *The Collected Works of Samuel Taylor Coleridge*, Vol. 1, London: Routledge and Kegan Paul; Princeton: Princeton University Press, 1969, page 235.

15. From Chapter xiii of *Biographia Literaria I*, in Kathleen Coburn, general editor, and James Engell and W. J. Bate, volume editors, *The Collected Works of Samuel Taylor Coleridge*, Vol. 7, London: Routledge & Kegan Paul; Princeton: Princeton University Press, 1969, page 304.

16. From "The Fantastic Imagination", the Introduction to George MacDonald's *The Light Princess and other Fairy Tales* (1893), reprinted in *The Heart of George MacDonald*, Rolland Hein, editor, Vancouver, British Columbia: Regent College Publishing, 1994, pages 424–425.

17. From Nikolai Berdyaev, *The Destiny of Man* (1931) as quoted in Dorothy L. Sayers, *The Mind of the Maker*, San Francisco, California: HarperCollins, page 61. Because the book and its 1937 English translation preceded Tolkien's writing of "On Fairy-stories", it is possible that Tolkien could have been influenced by Berdyaev's work, though there is no indication that he read it or even knew of it.

18. Tolkien used both "sub-creation" and "subcreation" in his writings; I have chosen to use the more streamlined "subcreation" for this book.

19. From J. R. R. Tolkien, "On Fairy-stories", reprinted in Verlyn Flieger and Douglas A. Anderson, editors, *Tolkien On Fairy-stories*, London, England: HarperCollins, pages 41–42.

20. Ibid., page 52.

21. The subjective nature of autobiography also skews the image of the world depicted, and can arguably be seen as a form of fiction-making as well. For a typology of fictional worlds, see Chapter 2 of Marie-Laure Ryan's *Possible Worlds, Artificial Intelligence, and Narrative Theory*, Indianapolis, Indiana: Indiana University Press, 1991.

22. From the Prologue to L. P. Hartley's novel, *The Go-Between* (1953).

23. See Don Carson, "Environmental Storytelling: Creating Immersive 3D Worlds Using Lessons Learned from the Theme Park Industry", *Gamasutra*, March 1, 2000, available at http://www.gamasutra.com/view/feature/3186/environmental_storytelling_.php.

24. World richness depends on the *amount* of world data, the *variety* of world data (data in multiple media windows, as well as from a variety of world infrastructures), and the *interconnectedness* of the data (in order to promote world gestalten and suggest world infrastructures).

25. Michael O. Riley, *Oz and Beyond: The Fantasy World of L. Frank Baum*, Lawrence, Kansas: University Press of Kansas, 1997, page 13.

26. See Lubomír Doležel, *Heterocosmica: Fiction and Possible Worlds*, Baltimore, Maryland: Johns Hopkins University Press, page 31.

27. From Robert Heinlein's *Beyond This Horizon*, published as a two-part serial in *Astounding Science Fiction* in the April and May issues of 1942, and later as a novel in 1948.

28. From J. R. R. Tolkien, "On Fairy-stories", reprinted in Verlyn Flieger and Douglas A. Anderson, editors, *Tolkien On Fairy-stories*, London, England: HarperCollins, page 69.

29. Ibid., pages 60–61.

30. Tolkien wrote, "anything that Hobbits had no immediate use for, but were unwilling to throw away, they called a *mathom*." (J. R. R. Tolkien, *The Lord of the Rings*, paperback one-volume edition, Boston and New York: Houghton Mifflin Company, 1994, page 5); while Dick wrote, "Kipple is useless objects, like junk mail or match folders after you use the last match or gum wrappers or yesterday's homeopape. When nobody's around, kipple reproduces itself." (Philip K. Dick, *Do Androids Dream of Electric Sheep*, (originally published in 1968), New York: Ballantine Books, 1990, page 57).

31. Although genetic engineering seems to have breached the third realm, along with selective breeding and Mendelian hybridization experiments in cross-breeding. Humans have the desire to subcreate in the third and fourth realms not only in their fiction, but also in the Primary World as well.

32. Fictional countries can be used to test people's geographical knowledge. For example, two articles by Lester Haines in *The Register* revealed that in 2004, 10 percent of poll

respondents in Britain believed "Luvania" was going to join the European Union, and in 2007, two-thirds of all Hungarians polled would not grant asylum to people from "Piresia". (From "Brits welcome Luvania to EU", *The Register*, April 29, 2004, and "Hungarians demand ejection of Piresan immigrants", *The Register,* March 21, 2007, as mentioned at http:www.wikipedia.org/wiki/Fictional_country (accessed May 20, 2009).)

33. Lubomír Doležel, *Heterocosmica: Fiction and Possible Worlds,* Baltimore and London: The Johns Hopkins University Press, 1998, page 169.
34. Tom Shippey, *The Road to Middle-earth,* Revised and Expanded Edition, Boston, and New York: Houghton Mifflin Company, 2003, page 74.
35. Earlier versions of the *Star Wars* script had characters carrying the "Aura Spice" instead of the Death Star plans as the McGuffin, and Han Solo being paid in spice instead of money; and in an early version of the *Return of the Jedi* (1983) script, Chewbacca and Lando were to give Jabba a "phony spice extractor" in exchange for Han. See Laurent Bouzereau, *Star Wars: The Annotated Screenplays,* New York, New York: Ballantine Books, 1997, pages 87, 91, 241, and 243.
36. This short story appeared in Kevin J. Anderson, editor, *Tales from Jabba's Palace,* New York: Bantam Spectra, 1995.
37. From the *Wookieepedia* entry for "gorg", at http://starwars.wikia.com/wiki/Gragra (accessed December 16, 2008).
38. Of course, the *Star Wars* universe is vast and growing, therefore, by the time you read this, there may be more of an explanation available. Also, more on the question can be found on *Wookieepedia*, The *Star Wars* Wiki, which lists 34 different forms of non-sentient life on Tatooine, and states that:

> Tatooine was once a lush world that had large oceans and a world-spanning jungle inhabited by the native and technologically advanced Kumumgah. Sometime in its history, the Rakatan Infinite Empire invaded the planet and conquered and enslaved its native inhabitants. After a terrible plague weakened the Rakata, the Kumumgah eventually rebelled and managed to drive the Rakata off the planet. In response, they subjected the planet to an orbital bombardment that "glassed" (that is, fused the silica in the soil into glass, which then broke up over time into sand) the planet and boiled its oceans away. It is possible that the Kumumgah's excessive production started this drastic climatic change before the Rakata arrived. Nonetheless, this change split the indigenous Kumumgah into two races: the Ghorfas and the Jawas.

From the "Tatooine" page of Wookieepedia, available at http://starwars.wikia.com/wiki/Tatooine#cite_ref-EP4NOVEL_4-0 (accessed December 9, 2011).

39. From a draft of a 1971 letter to Carole Batten-Phelps, in *The Letters of J. R. R. Tolkien,* edited by Humphrey Carpenter, Boston, Massachusetts: Houghton Mifflin Company, 1981, page 412.
40. From a 1963 letter to Colonel Worskett, in *The Letters of J. R. R. Tolkien,* edited by Humphrey Carpenter, Boston, Massachusetts: Houghton Mifflin Company, 1981, page 333.
41. For more on the Klingon augment virus, see http://memory-alpha.org/en/wiki/Klingon_augment_virus (accessed September 3, 2008).
42. From "Secrets of the *Millennium Falcon*", by Pablo Hidalgo with Chris Reiff and Chris Trevas, October 26, 2008, http://www.starwars.com/vault/books/feature20081026.html?page=2 (accessed October 28, 2008).
43. See "Retroactive Continuity" at http://en.wikipedia.org/wiki/Retconned (accessed September 3, 2008).
44. See Christopher Tolkien, "Foreword", in J. R. R. Tolkien, *The Silmarillion,* edited by Christopher Tolkien, (Boston, Massachusetts: Houghton Mifflin Company, 1977), pages 7–8.

45. From a draft of a letter to A. C. Nunn, in *The Letters of J. R. R. Tolkien*, edited by Humphrey Carpenter, Boston, Massachusetts: Houghton Mifflin Company, 1981, page 290.

46. A similar challenge exists for the audience of murder mysteries, who must piece together a series of what appear to be unconnected facts and events in order to solve the mystery.

47. Though the media-related meaning of the term is new enough that it does not appear in the Second Edition of the *Oxford English Dictionary* from 1989.

48. Of course, newspaper stories can describe other places or worlds, and radio drama is capable of creating a world through dialogue, sound effects, and ambience, but these are exceptions which are far from being the typical experience that most users have with these media.

49. Ryan divides "absorption in the act of reading" into four degrees: concentration, imaginative involvement, entrancement, and addiction. See Marie-Laure Ryan, *Narrative as Virtual Reality: Immersion and Interactivity in Literature and Electronic Media*, Baltimore, Maryland: The Johns Hopkins University Press, 2001, pages 98–99.

50. Norman Holland, *Literature and the Brain*, Gainesville, Florida: PsyArt Foundation, 2009, page 48.

51. This should not be confused with Doležel's use of the term "saturation" to denote an intensional function; see Lubomír Doležel, *Heterocosmica: Fiction and Possible Worlds*, Baltimore, Maryland: Johns Hopkins University Press, pages 169–184.

52. The count was made using the Second Edition of the book that appeared in 1999.

53. Terry Eagleton, *Literary Theory: An Introduction*, 3rd Edition, Minneapolis, Minnesota: University of Minnesota Press, 2008, page 66.

54. See Steven Lehar, *The World in Your Head: A Gestalt View of the Mechanism of Conscious Experience*, Mahwah, New Jersey: Lawrence Erlbaum Associates, 2002; and Norman Holland, *Literature and the Brain*, Gainesville, Florida: PsyArt Foundation, 2009.

55. See David Bordwell, *Narration in the Fiction Film*, Madison, Wisconsin: The University of Wisconsin Press, 1985, page 54.

56. See Douglas A. Anderson, *The Annotated Hobbit*, Second Edition, Boston, Massachusetts: Houghton Mifflin Company, 2002.

57. Martin Gardner and Russell B. Nye, *The Wizard of Oz and Who He Was*, East Lansing, Michigan: University of Michigan State Press, 1957, page 30, referenced in Michael O. Riley, *Oz and Beyond: The Fantasy World of L. Frank Baum*, Lawrence, Kansas: University Press of Kansas, 1997, page 194.

58. From a draft of a letter to a Mr. Thompson, in *The Letters of J. R. R. Tolkien*, edited by Humphrey Carpenter, Boston, Massachusetts: Houghton Mifflin Company, 1981, page 231.

59. From a 1944 letter to Christopher Tolkien, in ibid., page 79.

60. The use of Primary World defaults to fill gaps is especially evident in "overlaid worlds" that rely on so many Primary World defaults that they have a very low degree of secondariness; for example, the world of Spider-man, which takes place in a New York City very similar to the real one, except for the super-villains that continually plague it, or the other thinly-veiled versions of New York City found in Batman's Gotham City or Superman's Metropolis (the story of Superman does involve the fictional planet of Krypton, but only in its backstory).

61. See Kendall Walton, *Mimesis as Make-Believe: On the Foundations of Representational Arts*, Cambridge, Massachusetts and London, England: Harvard University Press, 1990.

62. See Marie-Laure Ryan, "Fiction, Non-Factuals and the Principle of Minimal Departure", *Poetics* 8, 1980, page 406.

63. From the "Sound in Space" section of the *Star Wars Technical Commentaries: Astrophysical Concerns* webpage by Dr. Curtis Saxton, available at http://www.theforce.net/SWTC/astro.html#sound (accessed November 19, 2008).

64. See Irvin Rock, *The Logic of Perception*, Cambridge, Massachusetts: MIT Press, 1983, pages 240–282.
65. From a draft of a letter to Carol Batten-Phelps, in *The Letters of J. R. R. Tolkien*, edited by Humphrey Carpenter, Boston, Massachusetts: Houghton Mifflin Company, 1981, page 412.
66. J. R. R. Tolkien, *The Hobbit*, New York: Ballantine Books, 1965, page 17.
67. Tolkien writes that "Frodo also showed signs of good 'preservation': outwardly he retained the appearance of a robust and energetic hobbit just out of his tweens." From J. R. R. Tolkien, *The Fellowship of the Ring*, New York: Ballantine Books, 1965, page 71.
68. See Douglas A. Anderson, *The Annotated Hobbit*, Second Edition, Boston, Massachusetts: Houghton Mifflin Company, 2002, page 207.
69. As quoted in Richard Ellmann, *James Joyce*, New Revised Edition, London, England: Oxford University Press, 1983, page 521.
70. From a letter to Naomi Mitchison, in *The Letters of J. R. R. Tolkien*, edited by Humphrey Carpenter, Boston, Massachusetts: Houghton Mifflin Company, 1981, page 174.
71. From a 1965 letter to Miss A. P. Northey in *The Letters of J. R. R. Tolkien*, edited by Humphrey Carpenter, Boston, Massachusetts: Houghton Mifflin Company, 1981, page 354.
72. See Chris Baker, "Master of the Universe", *Wired* 16.09, September 2008, page 141.
73. From John Keats' letter of 1817 to his brothers George and Thomas, reprinted in *The Complete Poetical Works of John Keats*, edited by Harry Buxton Foreman, published by H. Frowde, 1899, page 277, and also available at http://www.mrbauld.com/negcap.html (accessed September 22, 2008).
74. The question as to whether balrogs (mythical beasts in Tolkien's works) have wings is debatable, because while they seem to be suggested in the descriptions Tolkien provides, there is no clear evidence one way or the other; although the fact that the Balrog falls into the abyss with Gandalf when the bridge breaks seems to suggest either no wings or at least no functional wings.
75. Or a span of time, providing a temporal separation from the Primary World; being set in the future or distant past makes a world inaccessible to us as well.
76. From J. R. R. Tolkien, "On Fairy-stories", reprinted in Verlyn Flieger and Douglas A. Anderson, editors, *Tolkien On Fairy-stories*, London, England: HarperCollins, page 83.
77. From C. S. Lewis, "On Science Fiction" in *Of Other Worlds: Essays and Stories*, edited by Walter Hooper, New York and London: Harcourt Brace and Company, 1966, pages 64–65.

2 A History of Imaginary Worlds

1. From the "Prooemium" section of Philostratos the Younger, *Imagines*, third century AD, translated by Arthur Fairbanks, available at http://www.theoi.com/Text/PhilostratusYounger.html (accessed January 23, 2009).
2. Margaret Cavendish, "To the Reader" in *The Description of a New World, Called the Blazing-World*, printed by A. Maxwell in London, 1666.
3. Published histories of these areas often value and emphasize different things from those that are useful to an analysis of world-building. Thus, some of the texts that are important to those histories will not be important to the analysis in this chapter, while other works that are important to a history of world-building may not meet their criteria for importance.
4. Diskin Clay, "The Islands of the *Odyssey*", *Journal of Medieval and Early Modern Studies*, 37:1, Winter 2007, pages 141–161.
5. Herodotus, *Histories*, Book III, translated by George Rawlinson, from *The Internet Classics Archive*, available at http://classics.mit.edu//Herodotus/history.html (accessed January 26, 2009).

6. James Patrick, *Renaissance and Reformation*, Tarrytown, New York: Marshall Cavendish, 2007, page 384.
7. From the end of the "Introduction" of Lucian of Samosata, *The True History*, translated by H. W. Fowler and F. G. Fowler, Oxford, England: The Clarendon Press, 1905, availableat http://www.sacred-texts.com/cla/luc/wl2/wl211.htm (accessed January 27, 2009).
8. From S. C. Fredericks, "Lucian's True History as SF", *Science Fiction Studies*, No. 8, Volume 3, Part 1, March 1976, available at http://www.depauw.edu/sfs/backissues/8/fredericks8art.htm (accessed January 27, 2009).
9. David Marsh, *Lucian and the Latins: Humor and Humanism in the Early Renaissance*, Ann Arbor, Michigan: University of Michigan Press, 1999.
10. See http://en.wikipedia.org/wiki/Hayy_ibn_Yaqdhan and http://en.wikipedia.org/wiki/Ibn_al-Nafis#Theologus_Autodidactus (both accessed February 2, 2009).
11. From the "Introduction" of Rosemary Tzanaki, *Mandeville's Medieval Audiences: A Study on the Reception of the Book of Sir John Mandeville (1371–1550)*, Surrey, England: Ashgate Publishing, 2003, page 1.
12. Ibid., page 6.
13. As quoted in John Ashton, editor, *The Voiage and Travayle of Sir John Maundeville*, Knight, London, England: Pickering and Chatto, 1887, page vii.
14. From the "Introduction" of Rosemary Tzanaki, *Mandeville's Medieval Audiences: A Study on the Reception of the Book of Sir John Mandeville (1371–1550)*, Surrey, England: Ashgate Publishing, 2003, page 7.
15. Andrew Hadfield, *Literature, Travel, and Colonial Writing in the English Renaissance 1545–1625*, Oxford, England: Oxford University Press, 1999.
16. François Rabelais, *Les horribles et épouvantables faits et prouesses du très renommé Pantagruel Roi des Dipsodes, fils du Grand Géant Gargantua*, "Chapter XXXII. How Pantagruel with his tongue covered a whole army, and what the author saw in his mouth", translated by Sir Thomas Urquhart of Cromarty and Peter Antony Motteux, available online at http://en.wikisource.org/wiki/Pantagruel/Chapter_XXXII (accessed February 10, 2009).
17. See "Antillia", http://en.wikipedia.org/wiki/Antillia, and "Isle of Seven Cities", http://www.nationmaster.com/encyclopedia/Isle-of-Seven-Cities (both accessed February 26, 2009).
18. Nathalie Hester, *Literature and Identity in Baroque Italian Travel Writing*, Ashgate Publishing, 2008, page 3.
19. Percy G. Adams, *Travelers and Travel Liars, 1660–1800*, Berkeley and Los Angeles: University of California Press, 1962, pages 17–18.
20. Philip Babcock Gove, *The Imaginary Voyage in Prose Fiction: A History of Its Criticism and a Guide for Its Study, with an Annotated Checklist of 215 Imaginary Voyages from 1700 to 1800*, London, England: The Holland Press, 1961, pages 124–125.
21. Ibid., page 136.
22. Daniel Defoe, *Robinson Crusoe*, New York: Greenwich House Classics Library, distributed by Crown Publishers, Inc., 1982, page 71.
23. From Part One, Chapter Four of Jonathan Swift, *Gulliver's Travels*, 1726, reprinted by Sandy Lesberg, editor, New York: Peebles Press International, Inc., page 62.
24. From Book V, Chapter xii, of Hans Jacob Christoffel von Grimmelshausen, *Der Abenteurliche Simplicissimus Teutsch*, 1668, available at http://web.wm.edu/history/rbsche/grimmelshausen/bk5-chap12.html (accessed March 4, 2009).
25. A number of "Hollow Earth" theories are collected and summarized at http://en.wikipedia.org/wiki/Hollow_Earth (accessed March 6, 2009).
26. According to Peter Fitting, editor, *Subterranean Worlds: A Critical Anthology*, Middleton, Connecticut: Wesleyan University Press, 2004, page 8.
27. As quoted in Paul Burns, *The History of the Discovery of Cinematography*, available at http://www.precinemahistory.net/1750.htm (accessed March 12, 2009).

28. The case of Neo in *The Matrix* (1999) even reverses this idea, as he must leave the secondary world in order to be made aware of it; and the Primary World that we know is revealed to be only a secondary world within the ruined and rebuilt "real world" controlled by the machines.

29. Percy G. Adams, *Travelers and Travel Liars, 1660–1800*, Berkeley and Los Angeles: University of California Press, 1962, page 131.

30. Ibid., page 224.

31. Philip Babcock Gove, *The Imaginary Voyage in Prose Fiction: A History of Its Criticism and a Guide for Its Study, with an Annotated Checklist of 215 Imaginary Voyages from 1700 to 1800*, London, England: The Holland Press, 1961, page 159.

32. Frank E. Manuel and Fritzie P. Manuel, *Utopian Thought in the Western World*, Cambridge, Massachusetts: The Belknap Press of Harvard University Press, 1979, page 21.

33. See Brian R. Goodey, "Mapping "Utopia": A Comment on the Geography of Sir Thomas More", *Geographical Review*, Vol. 60, No. 1, January 1970, pages 15–30.

34. Ibid., page 18.

35. See the edition of More's *Utopia* in the *Cambridge Texts in the History of Political Thought* series, edited by George M. Logan and Robert M. Adams, New York and Cambridge: Cambridge University Press, 1975.

36. Frank E. Manuel and Fritzie P. Manuel, *Utopian Thought in the Western World*, Cambridge, Massachusetts: The Belknap Press of Harvard University Press, 1979, pages 1–2.

37. Thus, any division that one could attempt to make between utopias and dystopias would reveal particular beliefs and agendas; the only solution is to consider them both together as potential social structures.

38. Some worlds were guilty of female chauvinism; Marie Anne de Roumier Roberts's *Les Ondins* (1768) features the country of Castora, ruled by a queen, from which all men have been banished. Any visiting men who stay longer than a day are sacrificed to the goddess Pallas, the Protectoress of Castora.

39. Tommaso Campanella, *The City of the Sun*, 1602, available from Project Gutenberg at http://www.gutenberg.org/files/2816/2816-h/2816-h.htm (accessed April 9, 2009).

40. Edward H. Thompson, "Christianopolis—The Human Dimension", paper presented at the Table Ronde "Publicists and Projectors in 17th-Century Europe" at the Herzog August Bibliothek, Wolfenbüttel, February 1996, and available at http://homepages.tesco.net/ eandcthomp/andpro.htm (accessed April 16, 2009).

41. Frank E. Manuel and Fritzie P. Manuel, *Utopian Thought in the Western World*, Cambridge, Massachusetts: The Belknap Press of Harvard University Press, 1979, page 22.

42. See the discussion of the sale of one of the only four remaining copies of Morgan's book at http://antiques-collectibles-auction-news.com/2008/02/27/14th-century-work-of-art-by-the-italian-painter-allegretto-nuzi-1315-1373-soars-to-295000-at-philip-weiss-auctions-multi-estate-sale-held-feb-23-24-2008/ (accessed April 17, 2009).

43. Marie Louise Berneri, *Journey Through Utopia*, Berlin, Germany, and New York, New York: Schocken Books, 1950, page 177.

44. Frank E. Manuel and Fritzie P. Manuel, *Utopian Thought in the Western World*, Cambridge, Massachusetts: The Belknap Press of Harvard University Press, 1979, page 3.

45. See the entry "Bodin, Félix" by Paul K. Alkon in Samuel L. Macey, editor, *Encyclopedia of Time*, New York: Routledge Press, 1994, pages 67–68.

46. According to Lyman Tower Sargent, who claims there were "160 utopias published between 1800 and 1887" and "the same number of utopias written between 1888 and 1895 as in all the previous 87 years." From Lyman Tower Sargent, "Themes in Utopian Fiction in English Before Wells", *Science Fiction Studies*, Number 10,

Volume 3, Part 3, November 1976, available at http://www.depauw.edu/sfs/backissues/10/sargent10art.htm (accessed April 21, 2009).

47. From Etienne Cabet, *Voyage to Icaria*, reprinted in Marie Louise Berneri, *Journey Through Utopia*, New York: Schocken Books, 1950, page 229.

48. A list of over 2900 uchronias can be found online at "Uchronia: The Alternate History List" at http://www.uchronia.net/ (accessed April 28, 2009).

49. The next century would see even more distant uchronias, like Olaf Stapledon's *Last and First Men: A Story of the Near and Far Future* (1930) which covers about 2 billion years, and his *Star Maker* (1937) which covers even more.

50. The term "science fiction" appeared in Chapter 10 of William Wilson's *A Little Earnest Book upon a Great Old Subject* (1851). "Scientist" was a deliberate coinage, appearing in print in 1840, and it appears to have been first suggested, along with "science", in the 1830s, according to Raymond Williams's *Keywords: A Vocabulary of Culture and Society*, Oxford, England: Oxford University Press, page 279.

51. See Philip Babcock Gove, *The Imaginary Voyage in Prose Fiction: A History of Its Criticism and a Guide for Its Study, with an Annotated Checklist of 215 Imaginary Voyages from 1700 to 1800*, London, England: The Holland Press, 1961, page 205.

52. Tilberg J. Herczeg, "The Habitability of the Moon", in G. Lemarchand and K. Meech, editors, *A New Era in Bioastronomy, ASP Conference Series*, Vol. 213, 2000, page 594.

53. See Brian Stableford, "Science fiction before the genre" in Edward James and Farah Mendleson, editors, *The Cambridge Companion to Science Fiction*, Cambridge and New York: Cambridge University Press, 2003, page 18.

54. Margaret Cavendish, *The Description of a New World, Called the Blazing-World*, printed by A. Maxwell in London, 1666. Also available at http://digital.library.upenn.edu/women/newcastle/blazing/blazing.html (accessed June 4, 2009).

55. Ibid.

56. Baron Ludvig Holberg, "Chapter I. The Author's Descent into the Abyss" from *Nicolai Klimii Iter Subterraneum* (1741), available at http://www.archive.org/stream/nielsklimsjourne00holb/nielsklimsjourne00holb_djvu.txt (accessed June 4, 2009).

57. All titles of poems and section headings are taken from the DAW Books translation that appeared in C. I. Defontenay, *Star (Psi Cassiopeia): The Marvelous History of One of the Worlds of Outer Space*, Encino, California: Black Coat Press, 2007.

58. According to Pierre Versins's "Introduction" to the 1975 reprint of *Star*, that also appeared in the 2007 reprint cited earlier.

59. From Part III, Chapter III of Camille Flammarion's *Uranie*, translated from the French by Mary J. Serrano, available at http://fiction.eserver.org/novels/uranie/default.html (accessed July 9, 2009).

60. From C. S. Lewis, "On Stories" in *Essays Presented to Charles Williams*, Oxford, England: Oxford University Press, 1947, and reprinted in *Of Other Worlds: Essays and Stories*, edited by Walter Hooper, New York and London: Harcourt Brace and Company, 1966, page 12.

61. See the "Vril" page of Wikipedia, available at http://en.wikipedia.org/wiki/Vril (accessed July 10, 2009).

62. Lin Carter, *Imaginary Worlds: The Art of Fantasy*, New York: Ballantine Books, 1973, page 19.

63. See "Upmeads", http://manchesterhistory.net/edgarwood/upmeads1.html (accessed May 28, 2009).

64. According to Sheila A. Egoff, *Worlds Within: Children's Fantasy from the Middle Ages to Today*, Chicago and London: American Library Association, 1988, page 45.

65. The 596-word digression reads thus:

In old, old, olden times, when all our world was just loose earth and air and fire and water mixed up anyhow like a pudding, and spinning around like mad trying to get the different things to settle into their proper places, a round piece of earth got loose and went spinning away by itself across the water, which was just beginning to try to get spread out smooth into a real sea. And as the great round piece of earth flew away, going around and around as hard as it could, it met a long piece of hard rock that had got loose from another part of the puddingy mixture, and the rock was so hard, and was going so fast, that it ran its point through the round piece of earth and stuck out on the other side of it, so that the two together were like a very-very-much-too-big spinning top.

I am afraid all this is very dull, but you know geography is never quite lively, and after all, I must give you a little information even in a fairy tale—like the powder in jam.

Well, when the pointed rock smashed into the round bit of earth the shock was so great that it set them spinning together through the air—which was just getting into its proper place, like all the rest of the things—only, as luck would have it, they forgot which way around they had been going, and began to spin around the wrong way. Presently Center of Gravity—a great giant who was managing the whole business—woke up in the middle of the earth and began to grumble.

"Hurry up," he said. "Come down and lie still, can't you?"

So the rock with the round piece of earth fell into the sea, and the point of the rock went into a hole that just fitted it in the stony sea bottom, and there it spun around the wrong way seven times and then lay still. And that round piece of land became, after millions of years, the Kingdom of Rotundia.

This is the end of the geography lesson. And now for just a little natural history, so that we may not feel that we are quite wasting our time. Of course, the consequence of the island having spun around the wrong way was that when the animals began to grow on the island they all grew the wrong sizes. The guinea pig, as you know, was as big as our elephants, and the elephant—dear little pet—was the size of the silly, tiny, black-and-tan dogs that ladies carry sometimes in their muffs. The rabbits were about the size of our rhinoceroses, and all about the wild parts of the island they had made their burrows as big as railway tunnels. The dormouse, of course, was the biggest of all the creatures. I can't tell you how big he was. Even if you think of elephants it will not help you at all. Luckily there was only one of him, and he was always asleep. Otherwise I don't think the Rotundians could have borne with him. As it was, they made him a house, and it saved the expense of a brass band, because no band could possibly have been heard when the dormouse was talking in his sleep.

The men and women and children in this wonderful island were quite the right size, because their ancestors had come over with the Conqueror long after the island had settled down and the animals grown on it.

From Edith Nesbit, "Uncle James, or The Purple Stranger" in *The Book of Dragons* (1900), reprinted by Chronicle Press, 2001, pages 25–26. Also available at http://www.online-literature.com/edith-nesbit/book-of-dragons/2/ (accessed June 1, 2009).

66. From Edith Nesbit, *The Magic City*, London: MacMillan and Company, 1910, page 84. Also available at http://www.gutenberg.org/files/20606/20606-h/20606-h.htm (accessed June 2, 2009).
67. Sheila A. Egoff, *Worlds Within: Children's Fantasy from the Middle Ages to Today*, Chicago and London: American Library Association, 1988, page 73.
68. Michael O. Riley, *Oz and Beyond: The Fantasy World of L. Frank Baum*, Lawrence, Kansas: The University Press of Kansas, 1997, page 62.
69. In some cases, stories were presented as being already mediated; for example, John Kirkby's *The History of Automathes* (1745) is itself being read from a manuscript by the narrator.

70. Leonard Bacon, "Introduction" in Austin Tappan Wright, *Islandia*, New York and Toronto: Farrar & Rinehart, Inc., 1942, page viii.
71. Pierre Couperie and Maurice C. Horn et al, *A History of the Comic Strip*, translated from the French by Eileen B. Henessy, New York: Crown Publishers, Inc., 1967, pages 27–28.
72. Ibid., page 155. The study discussed was conducted by F. E. Barcus.
73. Michael O. Riley, *Oz and Beyond: The Fantasy World of L. Frank Baum*, Lawrence, Kansas: The University Press of Kansas, 1997, page 42.
74. Ibid., page 47.
75. Ibid., pages 98–99.
76. Ibid., page 150.
77. David Kyle, *A Pictorial History of Science Fiction*, London and New York: Hamlyn Publishing Group Limited, 1976, page 117.
78. The Hall of the Mist is from Donald Wandrei's "The Red Brain" in *Weird Tales*, October 1927; Ulm is from S. P. Meek's "Submicroscopic" in *Amazing Stories*, August 1931; Valadom is from Donald Wandrei's "Colossus" in *Astounding Stories*, January 1934; the Pygmy Planet is from Jack Williamson's "The Pygmy Planet" in *Astounding Stories*, February 1932; Vulcan is from Ross Rocklynne's "At the Center of Gravity" in *Astounding Stories*, June 1936; Soldus is from Nat Schachner's "The Sun-world of Soldus" in *Astounding Science-Fiction*, April 1938; Lagash is from Isaac Asimov's "Nightfall" in *Astounding Science-Fiction*, September 1941; Logeia is from Fletcher Pratt's novel *The Undesired Princess*, first serialized in *Unknown*, beginning in February 1942; Hydrot is from Arthur Merlyn's "Sunken Universe" in *Super Science Stories*, May 1942; Placet is from Fredric Brown's "Placet is a Crazy Place" in *Astounding Science-Fiction*, May 1946; and Aiolo is from Murray Leinster's "The Plants" in *Astounding Science-Fiction*, January 1946.
79. Philip Francis Nowlan's future Earth first appeared in "Armageddon, 2419 A.D." in *Amazing Stories*, August 1928; Zothique first appeared in Clark Ashton Smith's "The Empire of the Necromancers" in *Weird Tales*, September 1932; Robert E. Howard's Hyborian Age first appeared in "The Phoenix on the Sword" in *Weird Tales*, December 1932; the Lensman universe first appeared in E. E. Smith's *Triplanetary* (serialized in *Amazing Stories*, January—April, 1934); Nehwon first appeared in Fritz Leiber's "Two Sought Adventure" in *Unknown* magazine, August 1939; the Future History Universe first appeared in Robert Heinlein's "Life-Line" in *Astounding Science-Fiction*, August 1939; the Foundation universe first appeared in Isaac Asimov's "Foundation" in *Astounding Science-Fiction*, May 1942, while his Galactic Empire universe first appeared in "Blind Alley" in *Astouding Science-Fiction*, March 1945; Ray Bradbury's version of Mars first appeared in "Rocket Summer" in *Planet Stories*, Spring 1947; the Psychotechnic League universe first appeared in Poul Anderson and John Gergen's "The Entity" in *Astounding Science Fiction*, June 1949; the Viagens Interplanetarias universe first appeared in L. Sprague de Camp's "The Animal-Cracker Plot" in *Astounding Science Fiction*, July 1949; the Instrumentality of Mankind future history universe first appeared in Cordwainer Smith's "Scanners Live in Vain" in *Fantasy Book* #6, 1950; and the Terro-Human Future History universe first appeared in H. Beam Piper's "Uller Uprising" in *The Petrified Planet* (1952).
80. Hugo Gernsback, "Reasonableness in Science Fiction", *Wonder Stories*, December 1932, reproduced in David Kyle, *A Pictorial History of Science Fiction*, London and New York: Hamlyn Publishing Group Limited, 1976, page 80.
81. David Kyle, *A Pictorial History of Science Fiction*, London and New York: Hamlyn Publishing Group Limited, 1976, page 147.
82. Anatevka was originally named "Boyberik" in Sholem Aleichem's fictional memoir *Teyve and His Daughters* (1894).

83. From the voiceover for the 1939 trailer for MGM's *The Wizard of Oz*. The trailer can be viewed at http://www.youtube.com/watch?v=VNugTWHnSfw (accessed October 14, 2011).

84. Oakdale, Illinois is from *As the World Turns* (1956–2010); Central City is from *The Many Loves of Dobie Gillis* (1959–1963); Bay City, Illinois is from *Another World* (1964–1999); Salem is from *Days of Our Lives* (1965–present); Collinsport, Maine is from *Dark Shadows* (1966–1971 and 1991); Llanview, Pennsylvania is from *One Life to Live* (1968–2011); Pine Valley is from *All My Children* (1970–2011); Genoa City, Wisconsin is from *The Young and the Restless* (1973–present); Hazzard County, Georgia is from *The Dukes of Hazzard* (1977–1985); Corinth, Pennsylvania is from *Loving* (1983–1995); Cabot Cove, Maine is from *Murder, She Wrote* (1984–1996); Twin Peaks, Washington is from *Twin Peaks* (1990–1991); Cicely, Alaska is from *Northern Exposure* (1990–1995); Capeside, Massachusetts is from *Dawson's Creek* (1998–2003); and Harmony is from *Passions* (1999–2008).

85. Mayfield appeared in *Leave it to Beaver* (1957–1963), *Still the Beaver* (1985–1986), and *The New Leave it to Beaver* (1986–1989); Mayberry, North Carolina appeared on *The Danny Thomas Show* in 1960, *The Andy Griffith Show* (1960–1968), and *Mayberry, R. F. D.* (1968–1971); Hooterville appeared in *Petticoat Junction* (1963–1970) and *Green Acres* (1965–1971); Port Charles, New York is from *General Hospital* (1963–present), *Port Charles* (1997–2003), and *General Hospital: Night Shift* (2007–2008); and Fernwood, Ohio is from *Mary Hartman, Mary Hartman* (1976–1977), *Forever Fernwood* (1977), and *Fernwood 2-Night* (1977–1978).

86. For example, the Neighborhood of Make-Believe in *Mister Rogers' Neighborhood* has an unusually elaborate geography for a children's program (including non-Euclidean spaces); characters that occupy a broad ontological spectrum; and in at least one episode, an intertextual reference referring to an event (the fire in Corney's factory) that occurred 21 years earlier on the show, which could only be remembered by adults who had seen the show during their own childhood.

87. The city of Opar appears in *The Return of Tarzan* (1913); Pal-ul-don, a kingdom in Zaire, in *Tarzan the Terrible* (1921); the village of Alali and the region of Minuni in *Tarzan and the Ant Men* (1924); the cities of Castra Sanguinarius and Castrum Mare in *Tarzan and the Lost Empire* (1929); the African country of Midian in *Tarzan Triumphant* (1932); the lands of Onthar and Thenar in *Tarzan and the City of Gold* (1933); and the city of Ashair in *Tarzan and the Forbidden City* (1938).

88. Other worlds of his include Maxon's Island in the South China Sea in *A Man Without a Soul* (1913); the island of Flotsam in *The Cave Girl* (1913); Lutha, a country in Southern Europe in *The Mad King* (1914); and Lodidhapura, a city in the jungles of Cambodia, in *The Jungle Girl* (1931).

89. From Edgar Rice Burroughs, "Protecting the Author's Rights", *The Writers 1932 Year Book & Market Guide*, reprinted in *Edgar Rice Burroughs Tells All* (Third Edition), compiled by Jerry L. Schneider, Amazon.com: CreateSpace, 2008, page 160.

90. According to Lin Carter, *Imaginary Worlds: The Art of Fantasy*, New York: Ballantine Books, 1973, page 44.

91. In letters 19 and 294 in J. R. R. Tolkien, *The Letters of J. R. R. Tolkien*, edited by Humphrey Carpenter, Boston, Massachusetts: Houghton Mifflin Company, 1981, pages 26 and 375, respectively.

92. In the Storisende edition published by McBribe, at least, in which several works can form a single volume; see http://en.wikipedia.org/wiki/The_Biography_of_Manuel for the list of books.

93. The state of Winnemac is the setting for *Babbitt* (1922), *Arrowsmith* (1925), *Elmer Gantry* (1927), *The Man Who Knew Coolidge* (1928), and *Dodsworth* (1929).

94. Helen Batchelor, "A Sinclair Lewis Portfolio of Maps: Zenith to Winnemac", *Modern Language Quarterly*, December 1971, Volume 32, Issue 4, pages 401–429. Another example of an American locale outside the realm of fantasy and science fiction is

William Faulkner's Yoknapatawpha County, Mississippi, which served as the setting for fourteen novels and several short stories, with Faulkner's hand-drawn map of it included in *Absalom, Absalom!* (1936).

95. From Sylvia Wright's "Introduction" in the 1958 edition of Austin Tappan Wright, *Islandia*, New York, New York: New American Library, pages v–vi.

96. Humphrey Carpenter, *Tolkien: A Biography*, Boston, Massachusetts: Houghton Mifflin Company, 1977, pages 194–195.

97. From Tolkien's "Foreword" to *The Lord of the Rings*, Boston, Massachusetts: Houghton Mifflin Company, 1966, page 5.

98. From a draft of a 1955 letter to W. H. Auden, in *The Letters of J. R. R. Tolkien*, edited by Humphrey Carpenter, Boston, Massachusetts: Houghton Mifflin Company, 1981, page 216.

99. Mike Foster, "America in the 1960s: Reception of Tolkien" entry in Michael D. C. Drout, editor, *J. R. R. Tolkien Encyclopedia: Scholarship and Critical Assessment*, New York, New York, and London, England: Routledge, 2007, page 14.

100. For the dates, creators, and works of first appearance of these worlds, see the Appendix.

101. From Michael Pye and Lynda Miles, *The Movie Brats*, Geneva, Illinois: Holt, Rinehart, and Winston (now Holt MacDougal), 1979, as reprinted in Sally Kline, editor, *George Lucas: Interviews*, Jackson, Mississippi: University of Mississippi Press, pages 79–80.

102. According to Alex Ben Block and Lucy Autrey Wilson, *George Lucas's Blockbusting: A Decade-by-Decade Survey of Timeless Movies Including Untold Secrets of Their Financial and Cultural Success*, New York, New York: HarperCollins Publishers, 2010, page 624.

103. See Matthew Kirschenbaum, "War Stories: Board Wargames and (Vast) Procedural Narratives" in Pat Harrigan and Noah Wardrip-Fruin, editors, *Third Person: Authoring and Exploring Vast Narratives*, Cambridge, Massachusetts: MIT Press, 2009, pages 357–358.

104. Some examples are Christoph Weickhmann's *New-Erfundene Große König-Spiel* (The Newly Invented Great King's Game) (1650), and Johann Christian Ludwig Hellwig's *Versuch eines aufs Schachspiel gebaueten taktischen Spiels von zwey und mehreren Personen zu spielen* (Attempt at a Tactical Game for Two and More Persons, Based on Chess) (1780), according to Rolf F. Nohr's "war" entry in Mark J. P. Wolf, editor, *Encyclopedia of Video Games: The Culture, Technology, and Art of Gaming*, Westport, Connecticut: ABC-CLIO/Greenwood Press, 2012.

105. Begun in 1919, the Marx Toy Company made metal playsets during the 1930s and 1940s, like the *Sunnyside Service Station* (1934) and the *Roadside Service Station* (1935). With the advent of plastics, production became easier and less expensive, and the number of playsets increased as did their popularity. In the 1950s, Marx produced more generic sets, like *Cowboy and Indian Camp* (1953) and *Arctic Explorer Play Set* (1958), as well as sets based on actual events like the Civil War and real places like *Fort Apache* (1951) and *Fort Dearborn* (1952). Other sets were adaptations of existing properties in other media, like the *Roy Rogers Ranch Set* (1952), *Lone Ranger Rodeo* (1952), *Walt Disney's Davy Crockett at the Alamo* (1955), and *Gunsmoke Dodge City* (1960). The transmedial nature of these sets, which played on the popularity of existing franchises, encouraged the sale of playsets in general.

106. Although many LEGO sets are based on other franchises (like *Star Wars*), the LEGO system universe has its own settings and narratives. For example, in the *LEGOLAND Idea Book* of 1980, we find:

This book is presented like a story. Just follow our two Mini-Figures™, Mary and Bill, as they build their LEGOLAND home and community and then move on to other adventures by car, on foot, and finally by spaceship. Along the way you'll find lots of ideas for building, designing and combining: how to build an airport, or a spaceship, how to put on a circus, how to light up your town at night.

(From the LEGOLAND *Idea Book*, Hamburg, Germany: Mühlmeister & Johler, 1980.)

The 82-page narrative, which is laid out between graphical building instructions of the models seen in the story, follows Mary and Bill as they build their home, go into town for the day, and return to find their house on fire, which is quickly extinguished by the fire department. They then travel to see a circus, stay overnight at a windmill, visit a seaside town where they have a new house and buy furniture for it, have their car towed and fixed near an airport, and take part in other activities. Later they go to a movie theater where a movie about astronauts is playing, and when they leave the theater at night, they don space helmets and air tanks and fly off in their own spaceship. They travel to a moon base, and with another astronaut, they go to answer an SOS signal, which turns out to be coming from a downed alien spaceship. They meet the aliens, tow their spaceship back to the moon base, and help repair it. The aliens leave and Mary and Bill follow them to the aliens' planet, where they see strange buildings, vehicles, and other varieties of aliens. After their stay, Mary and Bill fly off in their spaceship, returning to Earth, where they arrive at a medieval castle (implying that their journey involves time travel as well as space travel, though this is never stated explicitly). They are brought to the castle in a horse and carriage, explore it and meet another couple there (who appear to be the lord and lady of the manor), and together the two couples attend a jousting tournament (where, oddly enough, two spacemen wearing medieval helmets are sitting among the crowd). After a brief tour of another, smaller castle, Mary and Bill are off again in their spaceship, waving goodbye as they often do when leaving a location. On the last page, they are shown looking out of their spaceship and waving goodbye to the reader as well. On the front and back cover of the book, Mary and Bill are pictured back in a town, telling the townspeople about their adventure (images of which appear in dialogue balloons). On the back cover, however, the medieval castle can be seen just over the hill, implying nearby proximity.

107. According to the Wikipedia page on David Wesely found at http://en.wikipedia. org/wiki/David_Wesely (accessed January 29, 2010).

108. See "Historia de los CRPGs", *Meristation Zonafora*, at http://zonaforo.meristation. com/foros/viewtopic.php?p=15403838 (accessed February 1, 2010); Matt Barton, "The History of Computer Role-Playing Games Part 1: The Early Years (1980–1983)", *Gamasutra*, at http://www.gamasutra.com/features/20070223a/barton_pfv. htm (accessed February 1, 2010); and Rusty Rutherford, "The Creation of PEDIT5", *Armchair Arcade*, available at http://www.armchairarcade.com/neo/node/1948 (accessed February 1, 2010). Also see Matt Barton, *Dungeons and Desktops: The History of Computer Role-Playing Games*, Wellesley, Massachusetts: A. K. Peters, 2008.

109. Sources seem to vary (especially on the Internet) as to whether *Ultima* was released in 1980 or 1981; however, *The Official Book of Ultima* by Shay Addams, with a preface by Richard Garriott, says it was "published by California Pacific in 1980". See Shay Addams, *The Official Book of Ultima*, Radnor, Pennsylvania: COMPUTE! Publications, 1990, page 15.

110. Dan Koeppel, "Massive Attack: Fasten Your Seat Belts: Peter Jackson's Second Lord of the Rings Installment Will Feature One of the Most Spectacular Battle Scenes in Film History, a Product of the Digital Dark Arts", *Popular Science*, January 23, 2003, page 44.

111. For example, see the Wikipedia page for "Simulated Reality" at http://en.wikipedia. org/wiki/Simulated_Reality (accessed February 2, 2010).

112. As quoted in Benjamin Svetkey, "The New Face of Movies", *Entertainment Weekly*, #1086, January 22, 2010, page 34.

113. See Chris Baker, "Master of the Universe", *Wired* 16.09, September 2008, page 136.
114. See the "Preserving Virtual Worlds" page at http://pvw.illinois.edu/pvw/ and the Library of Congress's page http://www.digitalpreservation.gov/partners/pwv/pwv. html (accessed February 3, 2010).
115. Thomas G. Pavel, *Fictional Worlds*, Cambridge, Massachusetts and London, England: Harvard University Press, 1986, pages 84–85.
116. Alan Lightman, *Einstein's Dreams*, New York, New York: Warner Books, pages 71–72.
117. These worlds can be found in Bob Shaw's *Orbitsville* (1975), Frederik Pohl and Jack Williamson's *Farthest Star* (1975), Robert Forward's *Dragon's Egg* (1980), Larry Niven's *Ringworld* (1970), Terry Pratchett's *The Colour of Magic* (1983), and Somtow Sucharitkul's *Mallworld* (1984), respectively.
118. From "A First Note" at the beginning of Ursula K. LeGuin's *Always Coming Home*, New York and London: Bantam Books, 1985. Perec's apartment building may be too small to be considered an imaginary world by some, but I include it here (and in the Appendix) due to the high degree of development and detail that the building and its apartments are given (which is certainly more than such buildings receive in traditional literature), and the importance of the spaces to the narratives contained in the book.
119. Edward Castronova, Mark W. Bell, Robert Cornell, James J. Cummings, Matthew Falk, Travis Ross, Sarah B. Robbins and Alida Field, "Synthetic Worlds as Experimental Instruments", in Bernard Perron and Mark J. P. Wolf, editors, *The Video Game Theory Reader 2*, New York and London: Routledge, 2008, pages 284–285.

3 World Structures and Systems of Relationships

1. Charles Ischir Defontenay, *Star (Psi Cassiopeia): The Marvelous History of One of the Worlds of Outer Space*, first published in 1854, adapted by P. J. Sokolowski, Encino, California: Black Coat Press, 2007, page 24.
2. From the short story "Tlön, Uqbar, Orbis Tertius" in Jorge Luis Borges, *Fictions*, 1944, reprinted in Jorge Luis Borges, *Collected Fictions*, translated by Andrew Hurley, New York, New York: Penguin Books, 1998, pages 71–72.
3. From J. R. R. Tolkien, "On Fairy Stories", as reprinted in *Tree and Leaf*, Boston, Massachusetts: Houghton Mifflin Company, 1964, page 64.
4. George Lucas, from an interview by Claire Clouzot in *Ecran*, September 15, 1977, pages 33–41, and later translated from the French by Alisa Belanger and reprinted in Sally Kline, editor, *George Lucas: Interviews*, Jackson, Mississippi: University of Mississippi Press, 1999, where the quote appears on page 58.
5. J. R. R. Tolkien, as quoted in Humphrey Carpenter, *Tolkien: A Biography*, Boston, Massachusetts: Houghton Mifflin Company, 1977, page 195. The quote comes from a January 1971 radio interview by the BBC.
6. Michael O. Riley, *Oz and Beyond: The Fantasy World of L. Frank Baum*, Lawrence, Kansas: The University Press of Kansas, 1997, pages 176–177.
7. Ibid., pages 208–209.
8. Both quotes are from Diana Wynne Jones, *The Tough Guide to Fantasyland*, New York, New York: DAW Books, 1996, page 11.
9. Michael O. Riley, *Oz and Beyond: The Fantasy World of L. Frank Baum*, Lawrence, Kansas: The University Press of Kansas, 1997, pages 186–187.
10. Thomas More, *Utopia*, edited by George M. Logan and Robert M. Adams, New York and Cambridge: Cambridge University Press, 1989, page 125.
11. As described by Culley Carson-Grefe:

    The very novel we read takes its existence from a clever manipulation of the meaning of the word hole. The history of the land of Archaos—the book we read—has supposedly been reconstructed by searching out what was lacking in official history: everything that was missing was Archaos. Because Archaos represented such a threat to its neighbors, all references to it had been eliminated. ... This supposedly verifiable lacuna assumes a wholeness to history impossible to justify in other than fanciful terms. At the same time, the very idea of the hole takes on an entirely new meaning. No longer an emptiness, a mere absence, it is a cutting out, an extraction.

From Culley Carson-Grefe, "Hole Studies: French Feminist Fiction", available at: http://crisolenguas.uprrp.edu/Articles/Hole%20Studies%20French%20Feminist%20 Fiction.pdf.

12. See page 10 and pages 111–113 of Garrison Keillor, *Lake Wobegon Days*, New York, New York: Penguin Books, 1985.
13. George Barr McCutcheon, *Graustark: A Story of a Love Behind a Throne*, Chicago, Illinois: Herbert S. Stone & Company, 1903, page 61.
14. See Ricardo Padrón, "Mapping Imaginary Worlds" in James R. Akerman and Robert W. Karrow Jr., editors, *Maps: Finding Our Place in the World*, Chicago and London: The University of Chicago Press, 2007, page 261.
15. See John Knoll, with J. W. Rinzler, *Creating the Worlds of Star Wars: 365 Days*, New York, New York: Harry N. Abrams, Inc., 2005, days 167 and 200.
16. The maps by Pauline Baynes, "M. Blackburn", and Richard Caldwell can be found in Akerman and Karrow (see endnote 14), Barbara Strachey's maps in her book *Journeys of Frodo* (1981), Karen Wynn Fonstad's maps in the two editions of *The Atlas of Middle-Earth* (1991 and 2001), Shelly Shapiro's maps in certain reissues of Tolkien's books, James Cook's maps in Alberto Manguel and Gianni Guadalupi's *The Dictionary of Imaginary Places* (2000), and John Howe's maps in Brian Sibley's *The Maps of Tolkien's Middle-earth* (2003).
17. Adrian Leskiw, "Nation of Breda", in *The Map Realm: The Fictional Road Maps of Adrian Leskiw*, available at http://www-personal.umich.edu/~aleskiw/maps/breda.htm (accessed March 8, 2010).
18. See Michael W. Perry, *Untangling Tolkien: A Chronology and Commentary for The Lord of the Rings*, Seattle, Washington: Inkling Books, 2003; Kevin J. Anderson and Daniel Wallace, *Star Wars: The Essential Chronology*, New York, New York: Del Rey, 2000; and Michael and Denise Okuda, *Star Trek Chronology: The History of the Future*, New York, New York: Pocket Books, 1993 (first edition), 1996 (second edition).
19. John H. Raleigh, *The Chronicle of Leopold and Molly Bloom: Ulysses as Narrative*, Berkeley and Los Angeles: University of California Press, 1977.
20. Constantino Baikouzis and Marcelo O. Magnasco, "Is an eclipse described in the Odyssey?", *Proceedings of the National Academy of Sciences 105*, (June 24, 2008), page 8823, available at http://www.pnas.org/content/105/26/8823 (accessed March 23, 2010).
21. John Clute, entry for "Time Abyss" in John Clute and John Grant, editors, *The Encyclopedia of Fantasy*, New York: St. Martin's Griffin, 1999, pages 946–947.
22. Richard C. West, "The Interlace Structure of *The Lord of the Rings*", in Jared Lobell, editor, *The Tolkien Compass*, Chicago, Illinois: Open Court Publishing Company, 1975 (first edition), 2003 (second edition), page 76–77.
23. George MacDonald, *At the Back of the North Wind*, New York, New York: Schocken Books, 1978, page 88.
24. Walter Hooper, *C. S. Lewis: Companion & Guide*, New York, New York: HarperCollins Publishers, 1996, pages 420–423.
25. Brian Stableford, *The Dictionary of Science Fiction Places*, New York, New York: The Wonderland Press, 1999, page 34.
26. Rick Sternbach and Michael Okuda, *Star Trek: The Next Generation Technical Manual*, New York and London: Pocket Books, 1991. See "Relativistic Considerations" on page 78 and "Warp Propulsion Systems" on pages 54–74.

27. Ibid., page 55.
28. See for example the "*Star Trek* Universe Timelines" at http://img.trekmovie.com/ images/st09/stotimelines.jpg (accessed April 1, 2010).
29. See Tom Shipppey, *J. R. R. Tolkien: Author of the Century*, Boston Massachusetts: Houghton Mifflin Company, 2001, pages 243–244. Shippey quotes the insult and describes its context, concluding, "But the subtlety and the tension depend on carrying in one's head a string of distinctions between elvish groups, and a whole series of pedigrees and family relationships. The audiences of Icelandic sagas could do this, but readers of modern novels are not used to it, and easily miss most of what is intended." (page 244).
30. Although Dooku became the padawan of Master Thame Cerulian at the age of thirteen, he trained with Yoda before this and could still be considered an apprentice of Yoda's; Yoda even refers to Dooku as his old padawan in *Attack of the Clones* (2002).
31. Joshua Davis, "Second Coming", *Wired*, December 2009, page 192.
32. See Harald Stümpke, *Bau und Leben der Rhinogradentia* with preface and illustrations by Gerolf Steiner, Stuttgart, Germany: Fischer, 1961, and Harald Stümpke, *Anatomie et Biologie des Rhinogrades—Un Nouvel Ordre De Mammifères*, Issy-les-Moulineaux, France: Masson, 1962. Also see J. B. Post, *An Atlas of Fantasy*, revised edition, New York, New York: Ballantine Books, 1979, page 152.
33. Raymond King Cummings, "Chapter XIX. The City of Arite" of *The Girl in the Golden Atom* (1922).
34. C. H. Hinton, *An Episode of Flatland: Or, How a Plane Folk Discovered the Third Dimension*, Swan Sonnenschein & Co., Limited: Bloomsbury, England, 1907, pages 1–2.
35. Dionys Burger, *Sphereland: A Fantasy about Curved Spaces and an Expanding Universe*, New York, New York: Quill/HarperResource, 2001, page 61. *Sphereland* was originally published in Dutch in 1965.
36. A. K. Dewdney, *The Planiverse: Computer Contact with a Two-Dimensional World*, New York: Copernicus, an imprint of Springer-Verlag, 2001 (original edition 1984), pages ix and xi.
37. Ronald D. Moore, *Battlestar Galactica Series Bible*, 2003, page 2, available at http://leethomson.myzen.co.uk/Battlestar_Galactica/Battlestar_Galactica_Series_Bible.pdf (accessed March 8, 2011).
38. Charles Ischir Defontenay, *Star (Psi Cassiopeia): The Marvelous History of One of the Worlds of Outer Space*, first published in 1854, adapted by P. J. Sokolowski, Encino, California: Black Coat Press, 2007, page 167.
39. Austin Tappan Wright, *Islandia*, Bergenfield, New Jersey: Signet, 1942, page 62.
40. Frank Herbert, *Dune*, New York: Berkley Books, 1977 (originally published by the Chilton Book Company, 1965), page 514.
41. Arika Okrent, *In the Land of Invented Languages*, New York, New York: Spiegel & Grau, 2009.
42. Lin Carter devotes an entire chapter of his book *Imaginary Worlds* to a discussion of good and bad names and how they function; see Lin Carter, "A Local Habitation and a Name: Some Observations on Neocognomia", *Imaginary Worlds*, New York, New York: Ballantine Books, 1973, pages 192–212.
43. For lists of words with different meanings in different languages, see Adam Jacot de Bonoid, *The Meaning of Tingo: And Other Extraordinary Words from Around the World*, New York, New York: The Penguin Press, 2006. For example, "dad" in Albanian means "wet nurse or babysitter", "babe" in SiSwati means "father or minister", and "mama" in Georgian means "father" (page 81). Invented languages that combine invented roots to make words can inadvertently result in words with unwanted real-language connotations; for example, in Tolkien's work, the character Celeborn ("silver tree") has a name that in Telerin Quenya translates as "Teleporno".

44. See "Earth: Final Conflict" in Tim Conley and Stephen Cain, *Encyclopedia of Fictional & Fantastic Languages*, Westport, Connecticut: Greenwood Press, 2006, page 55.
45. George Orwell, *Nineteen Eighty-Four*, New York: Harcourt, Brace, and Company, 1949, pages 51 and 53.
46. Thomas More, *Utopia*, edited by George M. Logan and Robert M. Adams, New York and Cambridge: Cambridge University Press, 1989, page 123.
47. Margaret Cavendish, *The Description of a New World, Called the Blazing-World*, 1666.
48. Tim Conley and Stephen Cain, *Encyclopedia of Fictional & Fantastic Languages*, Westport, Connecticut: Greenwood Press, 2006, page 13.
49. The glossary can found on pages 289–295 of the text of the Second Volume of the 1751 edition, which is available at http://books.google.com/books?id=OpPRAAAA MAAJ&printsec=frontcover#v=onepage&q&f=false (accessed October 25, 2011).
50. For example, in the *Star Wars* galaxy, words taken from Primary World languages are often used as names; for example, Tatooine (from Tataouine (also transliterated "Tatooine"), the Arabic name of the capital of the Tataouine Governate in Tunisia, where *Star Wars* was filmed), Vader (Dutch for "father"), Yoda (similar to "Yoddha", Sanskrit for "great warrior"), Padmé (Sanskrit for "Lotus"), Amidala (a feminine form of the Buddha Amida), Leia (Assyrian for "royalty"), Dooku (similar to "doku", Japanese for "poison"), and so on. Lucas even takes names directly from existing English words (Bail, Bane, Coruscant, Mace, Maul, Rancor, Solo, and so forth) or makes names from obvious variations from them (Ephant Mon (from "Elephant Man"), Sidious (from "insidious"), or Tyranus (tyrannous, tyrant), and so on). While the use of foreign words can add meaning to names, names whose etymologies are too obvious, or call attention to their origins too blatantly, may run the risk of undermining the verisimilitude of a world.
51. J. R. R. Tolkien, "A Secret Vice", in *The Monsters and the Critics and Other Essays*, edited by Christopher Tolkien, London, England: HarperCollins Publishers, 1997 (originally published by George Allen & Unwin Ltd. in 1983), pages 198–223.
52. Pierre Berton, *The Secret World of OG*, Toronto, Ontario: McClelland and Stewart, 1961.
53. From Lord Dunsany, "Of the Making of the Worlds" in *The Gods of Pegāna* (1905).
54. From Letter 181 of Humphrey Carpenter, editor, *The Letters of J. R. R. Tolkien*, Boston, Massachusetts: Houghton Mifflin Company, 1981, page 235.
55. Ibid., see Letters 15, 25, 31, 109, 153, 154, 156, 163, 165, 200, 211, 212, and especially 131, 144, and 181.
56. Ibid., from Letter 276, page 361.
57. Ibid., from Letter 259, page 349.
58. Ibid., from Letter 265, page 352.
59. Stephen Prickett, *Victorian Fantasy*, Bloomington and London: Indiana University Press, 1979, page 229.
60. Other Bible stories are also used for inspiration: in Defontenay's *Star* (1854), when the Starians are wiped out, Ramzuel escapes in an abare (spaceship) with his family and later his descendents become the new Starian people; and Book IV is even named "Exodus and Deuteronomy".
61. From Letter 142 of Humphrey Carpenter, editor, *The Letters of J. R. R. Tolkien*, Boston, Massachusetts: Houghton Mifflin Company, 1981, page 172.
62. Lin Carter, *Imaginary Worlds: The Art of Fantasy*, New York, New York: Ballantine Books, page 180.
63. From Letter 169 of Humphrey Carpenter, editor, *The Letters of J. R. R. Tolkien*, Boston, Massachusetts: Houghton Mifflin Company, 1981, page 224.
64. Diana Wynne Jones, *The Tough Guide to Fantasyland*, New York, New York: DAW Books, Inc., 1996, page 20.
65. From Letter 180 of Humphrey Carpenter, editor, *The Letters of J. R. R. Tolkien*, Boston, Massachusetts: Houghton Mifflin Company, 1981, page 231.

66. Philip K. Dick, "How to Build a Universe That Doesn't Fall Apart Two Days Later", 1978, in Philip K. Dick, *I Hope I Shall Arrive Soon*, New York, New York: Doubleday, 1985, pages 4–5.

4. More than a Story: Narrative Threads and Narrative Fabric

1. Charles Ischir Defontenay, *Star (Psi Cassiopeia): The Marvelous History of One of the Worlds of Outer Space*, first published in 1854, adapted by P. J. Sokolowski, Encino, California: Black Coat Press, 2007, page 237.
2. For an overview of the conceptualization of narrative units, see Jan Christoph Meister, "Narrative Units", in *Routledge Encyclopedia of Narrative Theory*, edited by David Herman, Manfred Jahn, and Marie-Laure Ryan, London, England, and New York, New York: Routledge, 2005, pages 382–384.
3. Although this may be the first time the term "narrative fabric" is used, this extension of the metaphor of narrative threads has been suggested by others; for example, Eugène Vinaver described the alternating themes of interlace narrative as needing to "alternate like threads in a woven fabric, one theme interrupting another and again another, and yet all remaining constantly present in the author's and the reader's mind." As quoted in Carol J. Clover, *The Medieval Saga*, Ithaca, New York: Cornell University Press, 1982, page 143, which cites page 76 of Vinaver's *The Rise of Romance* (Gloucestershire, England: Clarendon Press, 1971) as the source of the quote.
4. Although it is often the *degree* of invention, rather than the amount, that creates conflicts; a narrative fabric could be woven, for example, about the intersecting lives of a hundred characters living in New York City over several decades, producing a dense and detailed narrative fabric which does not become a secondary world.
5. For a look at how simultaneity was dealt with in Icelandic and medieval sagas, see the "Simultaneity" chapter in Carol J. Clover, *The Medieval Saga*, Ithaca, New York: Cornell University Press, 1982, pages 109–147.
6. From J. R. R. Tolkien, "In the House of Tom Bombadil" in *The Fellowship of the Ring*, New York: Ballantine Books, 1965, page 181.
7. It should also be noted here that narrative resolution depends on the level of narrative we are considering; while the preceding passage is a very low-resolution version of the history of the Barrow-downs, the passage is at the same time also a summary of what Bombadil is telling the hobbits, which involves less compression.
8. From a letter to Sir Stanley Unwin, reprinted as Letter 129 in Humphrey Carpenter, editor, *The Letters of J. R. R. Tolkien*, Boston, Massachusetts: Houghton Mifflin Company, 1981, page 142.
9. From the "Introductory Note" in 1951 Second Edition of *The Hobbit*, as reprinted in Douglas A. Anderson, annotator, *The Annotated Hobbit*, Boston, Massachusetts: Houghton Mifflin Company, 1988, page 322.
10. From a letter to Sir Stanley Unwin, reprinted as Letter 24 in Humphrey Carpenter, editor, *The Letters of J. R. R. Tolkien*, Boston, Massachusetts: Houghton Mifflin Company, 1981, page 29.
11. Michael O. Riley, *Oz and Beyond: The Fantasy World of L. Frank Baum*, Lawrence, Kansas: The University Press of Kansas, 1997, page 104.
12. Ibid., page 133. Riley's comment that the later Oz novels were weaker appears on page 171.
13. For example, Jean Webster's novel *Just Patty* (1911) is a prequel to her earlier book *When Patty Went to College* (1903).
14. As Internet searches of the terms reveal, "interquel", "intraquel", and "midquel" have all been independently invented a number of times since the mid-1990s, with all three terms being used interchangeably to suggest the same thing. This is why I propose "midquel" as a more general term, and "interquel" and "intraquel" as two specific and different types of midquels.

15. Mario Puzo, *The Sicilian*, New York, New York: Random House, 1984, page 354 in the paperback edition.
16. Pages 303 and 304, to be precise. Technically speaking, *The Lord of the Rings* extends a bit beyond the events of *The Silmarillion*, if one includes the timeline in Appendix B, which gives two pages' worth of events into the Fourth Age.
17. Thanks to Sean Malone for calling my attention to *The Last Ringbearer*.
18. The order of first public appearance of sequence elements can also differ from the order in which an author created them; for example, C. S. Lewis's seven books that make up *The Chronicles of Narnia* have a different order of creation, order of publication, and order in which they take place (see Chapter 6).
19. Michael O. Riley, *Oz and Beyond:The Fantasy World of L. Frank Baum*, Lawrence, Kansas: The University Press of Kansas, 1997, page 141.
20. Ibid., pages 152–153.
21. Ibid., page 134.
22. Ibid., page 135.
23. Ibid., page 137.
24. Jenkins writes, "Television and film producers often express the need to maintain absolute fidelity to one definitive version of a media franchise, fearing audience confusion. Comics, on the other hand, are discovering that readers take great pleasure in encountering and comparing multiple versions of the same characters." From Henry Jenkins with Sam Ford, "Managing Multiplicity in Superhero Comics: An Interview with Henry Jenkins" in Pat Harrigan and Noah Wardrip-Fruin, editors, *Third Person: Authoring and Exploring Vast Narratives*, Cambridge, Massachusetts: MIT Press, 2009, page 307.
25. Although sometimes earlier works do not receive the retconning they clearly need. For example, in the novelization of *Star Wars* that came out in late 1976 before the movie, during the scene in which Ben Kenobi gives Luke his lightsaber, the text reads:

    "Your father's lightsaber," Kenobi told him. "At one time they were widely used. Still are, in certain galactic quarters."

    Since by the end of Episode III Kenobi, Yoda, Anakin, and the Emperor are the only ones left who have lightsabers, they cannot be "widely used" anywhere; this line of dialogue did not appear in the movie, but was part of the extra material added for the novelization. From the *Star Wars* novelization, credited to George Lucas (though ghostwritten by Alan Dean Foster), New York, New York: Ballantine Books, 1976, page 79.
26. Ibid., pages 123–124.
27. For examples and descriptions of what some authors have done with Oz and Baum's characters, see http://en.wikipedia.org/wiki/Land_of_Oz.
28. Some, though, like Philip Jose Farmer's Wold Newton Family stories or Alan Moore's *League of Extraordinary Gentlemen* series, combine characters from other sources but have their stories set in the Primary World or some version of it, rather than an original imaginary world.
29. The use of Yoyodyne as a background detail on *Star Trek: The Next Generation* (1987–1994) comes from the film *The Adventures of Buckaroo Bonzai Across the 8th Dimension* (1984), although the name itself originally comes from the fictional aerospace company in Thomas Pynchon's novels *V.* (1963) and *The Crying of Lot 49* (1966).
30. See http://en.wikipedia.org/wiki/Morley_(cigarette) for a list of shows in which Morley cigarettes have appeared. The list even includes *The Dick Van Dyke Show* (1961–1966), thought to be the earliest appearance of Morley cigarettes.
31. King's eighth *Dark Tower* book, *The Wind Through the Keyhole* (2012), is an interquel which takes place between books four and five of the series.

32. Regarding the retroactive linking of Baum's worlds, Riley writes about Baum's sense as a businessman:

    [*Baum's*] suggestion in 1915 to his publishers that their reissue of his "Laura Bancroft" book BABES IN BIRDLAND under his own name include the subtitle "An Oz Fairy Tale." In his opinion, this connection would give it the appeal of his Oz stories and lead to larger sales. Quite rightly, I believe, his publishers felt that this might be perceived as deceptive and that the connection to Oz could be made in the advertising of the books. Thus, Baum never then pulled his Bancroft world into his larger fantasy world.

    From an e-mail from Michael O. Riley to the author, March 5, 2012.
33. Anthony Flack, as quoted in Dave Morris and Leo Hartas, *The Art of Game Worlds*, New York, New York: HarperCollins, 2004, page 174.
34. See especially the work of Roger Schank, Marie-Laure Ryan, Jesper Juul, Brenda Laurel, Janet Murray, and Chris Crawford.
35. Other LEGO video games, like those based on the Indiana Jones and Batman franchises, are very similar in their activities—running, jumping, climbing, beating up enemies, picking up studs—to the *LEGO Star Wars* games, but in different attire.
36. Jon Carroll, "Guerillas in the Myst", *Wired* magazine, 2.08, August 1994, page 72.
37. See John Knoll, *Creating the Worlds of Star Wars 365 Days*, New York, New York: Harry N. Abrams, Inc., 2005, pages 123, 149, 146, 147 in particular.
38. J. W. Rinzler, *The Making of Star Wars Revenge of the Sith*, New York, New York: Del Rey Books, 2005, page 50.
39. Ibid., pages 167 and 200, respectively.
40. The same can be said for other extradiegetic material pertaining to a world, such as advertising, merchandising, and so forth. As Pat Harrigan and Noah Wardrip-Fruin point out, "Everyone of a certain age (and their parents) knows what an Ewok is, but the word Ewok is never used in *Return of the Jedi* (1983), the movie in which they appear; the information was transmitted via the spin-off toys, comics, cartoons, and books." From Pat Harrigan and Noah Wardrip-Fruin, editors, *Third Person: Authoring and Exploring Vast Narratives*, Cambridge, Massachusetts: MIT Press, 2009, page 23.
41. From letter 342, to Mrs. Meriel Thurston, on November 9, 1972, in Humphrey Carpenter, editor, *The Letters of J. R. R. Tolkien*, Boston, Massachusetts: Houghton Mifflin Company, 1981, page 422.

5. Subcreation within Subcreated Worlds

1. Margaret Cavendish, *The Description of a New World, Called the Blazing-World*, printed by A. Maxwell in London, 1666. Also available at http://digital.library.upenn.edu/women/newcastle/blazing/blazing.html (accessed February 24, 2011).
2. On page 152 of Arthur C. Clarke's *3001: The Final Odyssey* (New York, New York: Del Rey Books, 1997), Captain Dmitri Chandler says "Where have I heard that idea before? Of course, Frank—it goes back a thousand years—to your own time! 'The Prime Directive'! We still get lots of laughs from those old *Star Trek* programs." Having his characters laugh at *Star Trek* seems to place his own world on a higher, more realistic plane, which of course is debatable, especially considering some of the events of Clarke's own story.
3. Lubomír Doležel, *Heterocosmica: Fiction and Possible Worlds*, Baltimore, Maryland: Johns Hopkins University Press, 1998, page 149.
4. Rand and Robyn Miller with David Wingrove, *Myst: The Book of Atrus*, New York, New York: Hyperion, 1995, pages 203–204 (paperback edition).

5. According to Cyan programmer and official D'ni Historian Richard "RAWA" Watson, a kind of world gestalt occurs to fill in the missing details of a world if the description does not cover them:

> The majority of Gehn's Ages were very short as he tested the effects of various phrases that he was copying from other Books.
>
> As page 123 of *The Book of Atrus* explains, a Descriptive Book will [connect] to an Age once the very first word is written. It's just that the more detailed your description, the more the Age will match what you want. If you just write the word "island" and use the Book, you'll link to a complete Age, but the only thing you'll know about it before you get there is that it will have an island. Everything else will be filled in "at random", meaning the Book will just link to one of countless Ages that match your generic description. You don't even know if it will have oxygen or not. Not a good idea.
>
> So many of Gehn's Ages would have just been a few paragraphs to cover the safety kinds of things and the particular phrase he was trying to test. (Similar to the test Ages that Atrus writes at the end of *The Book of Atrus*.)
>
> Ironically, these shorter Ages of Ghen's are much more likely to have been stable, as they were too short to have many contradictions in them.
>
> To use the programming analogy for the Art, many of Gehn's Ages were simple, such as:
>
> 10 PRINT "Hello"
> 20 GOTO 10

From an e-mail from Richard A. Watson to the author, September 17, 2004. Watson must be referring to the hard cover edition of *Myst: The Book of Atrus*, as the passage he describes comes later than page 123 in the paperback edition.

6. Rand and Robyn Miller with David Wingrove, *Myst: The Book of Atrus*, New York, New York: Hyperion, 1995, page 212 (paperback edition).
7. Verlyn Flieger, "Tolkien and the Idea of the Book" in Harold Bloom, editor, *Bloom's Modern Critical Interpretations: The Lord of the Rings—New Edition*, New York, New York: Infobase Publishing, 2008, page 130.
8. Ibid., pages 132–133.
9. Ibid., pages 145–169.
10. J. R. R. Tolkien, "Leaf by Niggle", reprinted in *The Tolkien Reader*, New York, New York: Ballantine Books, 1966, pages 100–101.
11. The letters in question are #163, which mentions the appearance of Strider, Saruman, the Stewards of Gondor and others, while Faramir's appearance is mentioned in letter #66.
12. From "The Brick Moon" (1869) in "The Brick Moon and Other Stories by Edward Everett Hale" at Project Gutenberg, available at http://www.gutenberg.org/ebooks/1633 (accessed February 28, 2011).
13. Olaf Stapledon, *Last and First Men, & Star Maker: Two Science-fiction Novels*, Chelmsford, Massachusetts: Courier Dover Publications, 1968, pages 364–365.
14. Although it is clear in Lovecraft's work that his Dreamworld is something beyond the dreams of one individual, multiple Primary World characters appearing in the same dream could be explained by technology, as the dream-invading apparatus used in the film *Inception* (2010).
15. Margaret Cavendish, *The Description of a New World, Called the Blazing-World*, printed by A. Maxwell in London, 1666. Also available at http://digital.library.upenn.edu/women/newcastle/blazing/blazing.html (accessed February 24, 2011).
16. Edith Nesbit, *The Magic City*, London: MacMillan and Company, 1910, pages 14–15. Also available at http://www.gutenberg.org/files/20606/20606-h/20606-h.htm (accessed March 1, 2011).

17. Ibid., page 27.
18. Ibid., page 11.
19. J. R. R. Tolkien, *The Silmarillion*, edited by Christopher Tolkien, (Boston, Massachusetts: Houghton Mifflin Company, 1977), page 17.
20. Ibid., page 20.
21. E. R. Eddison, *A Fish Dinner in Memison*, New York, New York: Ballantine Books, 1969, page 266.
22. Ibid., page 308.
23. Ibid., page 312.
24. Rand and Robin Miller, with David Wingrove, *Myst: The Book of Atrus*, New York, New York: Hyperion, 1995, page 262 (paperback edition).
25. From Letter #131, to Milton Waldman, in *The Letters of J. R. R. Tolkien*, edited by Humphrey Carpenter, Boston, Massachusetts: Houghton Mifflin Company, 1981, page 145.

6. Transmedial Growth and Adaptation

1. From letter #131, to Milton Waldman, in Humphrey Carpenter, editor, *The Letters of J. R. R. Tolkien*, Boston, Massachusetts: Houghton Mifflin Company, 1981, page 145.
2. John M. MacGregor, *Henry Darger: In the Realms of the Unreal*, New York, New York: Delano Greenidge Editions, LLC, 2002, page 24.
3. Henry Jenkins, *Convergence Culture: Where Old and New Media Collide*, New York: New York University Press, 2006, page 114.
4. At what point can something no longer be considered an adaptation? How much narrative must be carried over? For example, when adapting *The Lord of the Rings* into a video game, we could have Frodo passing through mazes of forests, eating evenly distributed lembas wafers that lie in his path, while being chased by four black Nazgul—and end up with a game which is only *Pac-Man* (1980) with new graphics.
5. One can find Tolkien's concern for his publisher's wishes in a number of letters, for example, letter #35 to C. A. Furth, in which he discusses whether or not *The Lord of the Rings* is shaping up as a suitable sequel to *The Hobbit*. He adds in a footnote:

   > Still, there are more hobbits, far more of them and about them, in the new story. Gollum reappears, and Gandalf is to the fore: "dwarves" come in; and though there is no dragon (so far) there is going to be a Giant; and the new and (very alarming) Ringwraiths are a feature. There ought to be things that people who liked the old mixture will find to have a similar taste.

   From letter #35 in Humphrey Carpenter, editor, *The Letters of J. R. R. Tolkien*, Boston, Massachusetts: Houghton Mifflin Company, 1981, page 42.
6. For an examination of the how the screenplays evolved, see Laurent Bouzereau, *Star Wars: The Annotated Screenplays*, New York, New York: Ballantine Books, 1997.
7. Future media may be able to add a few more sensory registers. Developing technologies aim to bring experiences of smell and taste to audiences, but since these require physical contact with at least trace amounts of the objects being experienced, and have effects that linger, unlike image and sound which can be switched off or changed abruptly, it seems unlikely that they will play much of a part in mediated experiences of imaginary worlds. The sense of touch, likewise, could become involved with virtual reality hardware like force feedback gloves, but these, too, are not expected to reach the stage of sophistication necessary to reproduce experiences with a level of realism to match that of sight and sound.

8. While "auralization" does not appear in the current edition of the *Oxford English Dictionary*, I believe it is a sound coinage based on the relationship between "visual" and "visualization", and can therefore be used to refer to sound design and the process of making audible sound from a description of a sound. The word "auralization" is also already used in the more narrow sense of using a computer to calculate and reproduce sound waves in computer simulations of spaces; for example, see Michael Vorländer, *Auralization: Fundamentals of Acoustics, Modelling, Simulation, Algorithms and Acoustic Virtual Reality*, New York, New York: Springer, 2008.

9. J. R. R. Tolkien, *The Lord of the Rings*, one-volume edition, Boston, Massachusetts: Houghton Mifflin Company, 1994, page 452.

10. Ibid., page 564.

11. J. R. R. Tolkien, Endnote E of "On Fairy-Stories" in *Tree and Leaf*, London, England: George Allen & Unwin Ltd., 1964, page 67.

12. Laurent Bouzereau, *Star Wars: The Annotated Screenplays*, New York, New York: Ballantine Books, 1997, page 49.

13. Christina Scull and Wayne G. Hammond, *The J. R. R. Tolkien Companion and Guide: Chronology and Reader's Guide*, Boston, Massachusetts: Houghton Mifflin Company, 2006, pages 647–649.

14. For example, the kitchen of Dex's Diner in *Star Wars Episode II: Attack of the Clones* (2002) is seen only briefly through the Diner's order window in the film, yet photographs in *Star Wars Mythmaking: Behind the Scenes of Attack of the Clones* reveal all the piping, machinery, utensils, furnishings, and food of the cluttered set. See Jody Duncan, *Star Wars Mythmaking: Behind the Scenes of Attack of the Clones*, New York, New York: Ballantine Books, 2002, pages 74 and 107. The existence of so much detail that is barely, if at all, seen in the film can be justified by the fact that it can be revealed in "Making Of" books such as Duncan's, and at the same time helps to give fans more reasons to buy the books, since they can reveal more of the *Star Wars* universe.

15. Douglas A. Anderson, *The Annotated Hobbit*, Second Edition, Boston, Massachusetts: Houghton Mifflin Company, 2002.

16. J. R. R. Tolkien, "On Fairy-stories" in Verlyn Flieger and Douglas A. Anderson, editors, *Tolkien On Fairy-stories*, London, England: HarperCollins Publishers, 2008, pages 61–62.

17. J. W. Rinzler, *The Making of Star Wars Revenge of the Sith*, New York, New York: Del Rey Books, 2005, page 208.

18. Jody Duncan, *Star Wars Mythmaking: Behind the Scenes of Attack of the Clones*, New York, New York: Ballantine Books, 2002, page 48.

19. Ibid., page 40. The preceding page also notes how Yoda's role in the film changed because the digital model was able to do much more than the puppet model could (as in Yoda's lightsaber fight with Count Dooku).

20. Designer Joe Johnston, as quoted in Laurent Bouzereau, *Star Wars: The Annotated Screenplays*, New York, New York: Ballantine Books, 1997, page 279.

21. Jody Duncan, *Star Wars Mythmaking: Behind the Scenes of Attack of the Clones*, New York, New York: Ballantine Books, 2002, page 175.

22. David E. Williams, "The Politics of Pre-Viz", *American Cinematographer, Authoring Images, Part I*, May 2007, pages 8–13.

23. Some may question the inclusion of Lake Wobegon as an imaginary world, perhaps citing its lack of invention (claiming it is too similar to the Primary World) or its incompleteness (due to a lack of visualization of much of it). To this, I would respond by pointing out Keillor's book, *Lake Wobegon Days* (1985), which gives a detailed history of the town, as well as the abundance of Lake Wobegon stories in subsequent books and on the air over several decades, which develop the town and its inhabitants.

Lake Wobegon's degree of development, its self-containedness and disconnectedness from the areas around it, and regular cast of inhabitants, qualifies it for inclusion under a broad definition of imaginary worlds.

24. Matthew Miles Griffiths, Senior Designer at SCI Games, as quoted in Dave Morris and Leo Hartas, *The Art of Game Worlds*, New York, New York: HarperCollins, 2004, pages 112–114.

25. As quoted in Dave Morris and Leo Hartas, *The Art of Game Worlds*, New York, New York: HarperCollins, 2004, page 122.

26. Neil Randall and Kathleen Murphy, "*The Lord of the Rings Online*: Issues of Adaptation and Simulation" in Gerald Voorhees, Joshua Call, and Katie Whitlock, editors, *Dungeons, Dragons and Digital Denizens: Digital Role-Playing Games*, New York, New York: Continuum, 2012, page 121.

27. These reasons, and more, are described in detail in Trevor Elkington, "Too Many Cooks: Media Convergence and Self-Defeating Adaptations" in Bernard Perron and Mark J. P. Wolf, editors, *The Video Game Theory Reader 2*, New York, New York: Routledge, 2008, pages 213–235.

28. Although this is not always the case. For example, an encyclopedic work could be made about a video game world which merely describes its contents without adding any narrative to them.

29. Danny Bilsen, as quoted in "Building Transmedia Worlds", *Game Theory with Scott Steinberg*, September 29, 2010, available at http://gametheoryonline.com/2010/09/29/transmedia-video-game-toys-comics-films-movies-tv/.

30. See Chapter 4 in Henry Jenkins, *Convergence Culture: Where Old and New Media Collide*, New York, New York: New York University Press, 2006.

7. Circles of Authorship

1. Wim Wenders, "A Conversation with Wim Wenders", Wim Wenders interviewed by Scott Derrickson, *IMAGE: A Journal of the Arts and Religion*, Summer 2002, Number 35, page 47.

2. J. R. R. Tolkien, in a draft of a letter to Carole Batten-Phelps, in J. R. R. Tolkien, *The Letters of J. R. R. Tolkien*, edited by Humphrey Carpenter, Boston, Massachusetts: Houghton Mifflin Company, 1981, page 413.

3. Jack Stillinger, *Multiple Authorship and the Myth of Solitary Genius*, Oxford, England: Oxford University Press, 1991, pages 186–187.

4. J. R. R. Tolkien, from letter #131 to Milton Waldman, in *The Letters of J. R. R. Tolkien*, page 145.

5. Ibid., page 371. In letter #292, Tolkien complains of hearing from a fan who was writing a sequel, and asks the press to do what they can to stop him. On page 404, in letter #315, written to his son Michael in 1970, Tolkien does write "I should like to put some of this stuff into readable form, and some sketched for others to make use of." However, this, too, appears to be referring to usage that would bring in income, rather than expansion by other writers, since the sentence that follows refers indirectly to the literary income passing on to his children.

6. See the "*Star Wars* Canon" Wikipedia webpage, available at http://en.wikipedia.org/wiki/Star_Wars_canon; and Chris Baker, "Master of the Universe", *Wired* 16.09, September 2008, pages 134–141. For a discussion of the debates surrounding *Star Wars* canon, see http://www.canonwars.com/SWCanon2.html. These pages, however, were written before the release of the 3-D versions of the films, so it is unclear if they are considered more canonical than the original two-dimensional versions of the films.

7. Tom Shippey, *The Road to Middle-earth*, Revised Edition, Boston, Massachusetts: Houghton Mifflin Company, 2003, page 315. The list of nine versions appears on pages 313–314.

8. See the explanation provided by Turkano, Senior Member of the *Star Trek* Wiki, on the "Who Owns *Star Trek*?" webpage available at http://forums.startrekonline.com/showthread.php?t=77190.

9. Walter Jon Williams, "In What Universe?" in Pat Harrigan and Noah Wardrip-Fruin, editors, *Third Person: Authoring and Exploring Vast Narratives*, Cambridge, Massachusetts: MIT Press, 2009, page 27. Unlike what one might think, writing for an existing world is not necessarily easier than inventing one; on page 29 of the essay, Williams adds, "Tie-in novels are said to be easier than the original ones because the characters and settings are already established. As far as my *Star Wars* book went, it would have been a lot less work to have invented it all myself."

10. Carol Pichefsky, "Expanded Universes, Contracted Books: A Look at Tie-in Novels", *Wizard Oil* blog on *Orson Scott Card's Intergalactic Medicine Show*, available at http://www.intergalacticmedicineshow.com/cgi-bin/mag.cgi?do=columns&vol=carol_pinchefsky&article=010.

11. See the discussion, regarding how the Tolkien estate did not give permission to publish certain scholarship which contained analysis of Tolkien's unpublished work, in Erik Davis, "The Fellowship of the Ring: Wherein an Oxford don and his ragtag army of fans turn a fairy tale about hobbits into the ultimate virtual world. Can any movie ever do it justice?", *Wired* 9.10, October 2001, pages 130–131.

12. Henry Jenkins, "Transmedia Storytelling 101", March 22, 2007, available at http://www.henryjenkins.org/2007/03/transmedia_storytelling_101.html (accessed September 12, 2011).

13. See the "fanon" *TVtropes.org* webpage available at http://tvtropes.org/pmwiki/pmwiki.php/Main/Fanon (accessed September 15, 2011).

14. See Anthony Burdge and Jessica Burke, "Fandom" entry in Michael D. C. Drout, editor, *J. R. R. Tolkien Encyclopedia: Scholarship and Critical Assessment*, Boca Raton, Florida: CRC Press, 2007, pages 194–195.

15. For a list of other elements that started as unauthorized additions and became canon, see the "Canon Immigrants" *TVtropes.org* webpage, available at http://tvtropes.org/pmwiki/pmwiki.php/Main/CanonImmigrant (accessed September 15, 2011).

16. Techically, Boba Fett's popularity began even before *The Empire Strikes Back*, since he first appeared in the *Star Wars Holiday Special* (1978) as an animated character. Also, see "Confirmation Case: Boba Fett" on the "*Star Wars* Canon: Overview" webpage, available at http://www.canonwars.com/SWCanon2.html (accessed September 15, 2011).

17. For more on the controversy surrounding Jar Jar, see the "Jar Jar Binks" *Wikipedia* webpage, available at http://en.wikipedia.org/wiki/Jar_Jar_Binks (accessed September 15, 2011); and the "Hear the Critics Speak" webpage available at http://www.mindspring.com/~ernestm/jarjar/jarjarcritics.html (accessed September 15, 2011).

18. See the "Sure, Why Not?" *TVtropes.org* webpage at, available at http://tvtropes.org/pmwiki/pmwiki.php/Main/SureWhyNot (accessed September 15, 2011), which also has a list of examples from different media, including some from Anthony's Xanth series.

19. For a list of fans that became employees or freelancers, see the list at "Promoted Fanboy", *TVtropes.org* webpage, available at http://tvtropes.org/pmwiki/pmwiki.php/Main/PromotedFanboy (accessed September 16, 2011), and the "Running the Asylum" TVtropes webpage, available at http://tvtropes.org/pmwiki/pmwiki.php/Main/RunningTheAsylum (accessed September 16, 2011).

20. This is not to say that the player's actions cannot be integrated into the events of the canon; in *Riven*, for example, Catherine is able to continue as a character in

Myst III: Exile (2001) only because the "stranger" (the player's character) rescued her, provided that the "right" ending was chosen. At the same time, only one ending of *Riven* is considered canonical, and Catherine is present in *Myst III: Exile* even if the player does not choose the canonical ending; so the narrative assumes that the "right" ending occurred, and thus the world remains unchanged by the player's actions.

21. According to Robert D. Hof, "*Second Life*'s First Millionaire", *Bloomberg Businessweek*, November 26, 2006, available at http://www.businessweek.com/the_thread/techbeat/archives/2006/11/second_lifes_fi.html (accessed September 20, 2011).

22. See Mike Schramm, "Man buys virtual space station for 330k real dollars", *Joystiq*, January 2, 2010, available at http://www.joystiq.com/2010/01/02/man-buys-virtual-space-station-for-330k-real-dollars/ (accessed September 21, 2011), and "Planet Calypso Player Sells Virtual Resort for $635,000.00 USD", *PR Newswire*, November 12, 2010, available at http://www.prnewswire.com/news-releases/planet-calypso-player-sells-virtual-resort-for-63500000-usd-107426428.html (accessed September 21, 2011).

23. Kathryn Gibson, "*Second Life* economy totals $567 million US dollars in 2009—65 percent growth over 2008", *Helix*, February 4, 2010, available at http://www.helixvirtualworlds.com/blogs/secondlife/2009endofyearsecondlifeeconomy (accessed September 21, 2011).

24. C. S. Lewis, "On Stories" in *Of Other Worlds: Essays and Stories*, edited by Walter Hooper, New York, New York: Harcourt Brace & Company, 1966, page 12.

25. Rachel Wagner, from the book proposal for her book *Godwired: Religion, Ritual, and Virtual Reality*, January 2010, page 2.

26. Chaim Gingold, discussing Will Wright's *Spore* (2008), in Chaim Gingold, "A Brief History of *Spore*" in Pat Harrigan and Noah Wardrip-Fruin, editors, *Third Person: Authoring and Exploring Vast Narratives*, Cambridge, Massachusetts: MIT Press, 2009, page 131.

27. C. N. Manlove, *The Impulse of Fantasy Literature*, Kent, Ohio: Kent State University Press, 1983, page 156.

28. Edward Castronova, *Exodus to the Virtual World*, New York, New York: Palgrave MacMillan, 2007, page 201.

29. Bruce Mazlish, *The Fourth Discontinuity: The Co-evolution of Humans and Machines*. New Haven, Connecticut: Yale University Press, 1993, page 195.

30. From Pope John Paul II, "Letter of His Holiness Pope John Paul II to Artists", 1999, available at http://www.vatican.va/holy_father/john_paul_ii/letters/documents/hf_jp-ii_let_23041999_artists_en.html (accessed September 21, 2011).

31. J. R. R. Tolkien, in a draft of a letter to Peter Hastings, in J. R. R. Tolkien, *The Letters of J. R. R. Tolkien*, edited by Humphrey Carpenter, Boston, Massachusetts: Houghton Mifflin Company, 1981, pages 188–189. Quotes from Hasting's letter, including the one mentioned earlier, appear on pages 187–188.

32. Edward Castronova, *Synthetic Worlds: The Business and Culture of Online Games*, Chicago, Illinois: University of Chicago Press, 2005, page 262. I would like to thank Mark Hayse for bringing this quote to my attention.

33. Jon Carroll, "Guerillas in the Myst", *Wired* 2.08, August 1994, page 73.

34. From Mark Hayse, "god games" entry in Mark J. P. Wolf, editor, *Encyclopedia of Video Games: The Culture, Technology, and Art of Gaming*, Santa Barbara, California: ABC-CLIO/Greenwood Press, 2012. The works that Hayse cites in the quote are Stephen R. Garner, "Hacking with the Divine: A Metaphor for Theology–Technology Engagement", *Colloquium* 37, No. 2, 2005, pages 181–195; Noreen Herzfeld, "God Mode in Video Games", paper presented at the 2005 Conference on Violence and Religion, Vallendar, Germany, July 2005; Kevin Kelly, *Out of Control: The New Biology of Machines, Social Systems and the Economic World*, New York: Basic Books, 1995;

and Kevin Kelly, "Nerd Theology", *Technology in Society* 21, 1999, pages 387–392, available at http://www.kk.org/writings/nerd_theology.pdf (accessed September 21, 2011).

35. J. R. R. Tolkien, "On Fairy-stories" in Verlyn Flieger and Douglas A. Anderson, editors, *Tolkien On Fairy-stories*, London, England: HarperCollins Publishers, 2008, pages 65–66.

36. Andrei Tarkovsky, June 11, 1982, *Diari Martirologio*, pages 503–504, as quoted in *Instant Light: Tarkovsky Polaroids*, edited by Giovanni Chiaramonte and Andrey A. Tarkovsky, London, England: Thames & Hudson, 2004, page 86.

GLOSSARY

absorption The process that often follows immersion in a world. Absorption is a two-way process; the audience's attention and imagination is absorbed or "pulled into" the world, and at the same time, the audience also "absorbs" the imaginary world as well, bringing it into mind, learning or recalling its places, characters, events, and so on, constructing the world within the imagination the same way that that memory brings forth people, events, and objects when their names are mentioned. Thus, one is able to mentally leave (or block out) one's physical surroundings, to some degree, because details of a secondary world displace those of the Primary World while one is engaged with it.

aggregate inconsistencies Inconsistencies occurring in a story which are only noticeable when one takes into account multiple facts and considers them together collectively. For example, in *The Hobbit*, when Bilbo and Gollum meet, they are able to converse easily; yet, if one considers the hundreds of years Gollum lived alone under the mountain, the 1,650 years separating the Shire-folk (from which Bilbo came) from the Stoors (from which Gollum came), and the changes in both cultures and the attendant changes in language that one would expect over the same length of time, it seems that Bilbo and Gollum would have more difficulty communicating than they do. However, to notice this inconsistency requires the integration of information from *The Hobbit*, *The Lord of the Rings*, and *The Letters of J. R. R. Tolkien*; if *The Hobbit* is considered alone, no discrepancy appears to exist.

auralization The process of turning something into a sound, just as visualization is the process of turning something (like a description) into an image that can be seen. Radio dramas, for example, use background sound effects along with character dialogue to bring to life the stories they tell, while in cinema sound, designers must devise sounds for invented creatures, vehicles, and devices that seem appropriate for them.

causal braiding   The condition that occurs when multiple stories or narrative threads set in the same world have causal linkages between them, in which the events of one thread have outcomes in other threads. This interrelatedness of narrative threads can then be seen as braiding them together through the cause-and-effect events that link them.

completeness   The degree to which an imaginary world has all the necessary elements needed to be considered feasible, with enough detail present such that the audience can answer questions about the world, such as where the world's residents get their food and basic necessities, what their daily lives are like, and how their society is structured.

conlang   Short for "constructed language", a conlang is a language which is consciously and deliberately devised by an individual or group, as opposed to languages that develop naturally over time within a culture.

consistency   The degree to which world details support each other without contradiction. This requires a careful integration of details and attention to the way everything is connected together. Lacking consistency, a world may begin to appear sloppily constructed, or even random and disconnected.

deinteractivation   The removal of interactivity that occurs when a world or narrative makes a transmedial move from an interactive medium to a non-interactive medium.

diegesis   The fictional world in which a story takes place. The term is used to distinguish between the world of the characters and the world of the story's audience; for example, film credits and subtitles are nondiegetic, because they do not exist for the film's characters, whereas the scenery and the objects used by the characters are diegetic. A diegesis can be an imaginary or secondary world, or a fictionalized version of the Primary World.

diegetic braiding   The condition that occurs when multiple stories or narrative threads set in the same world share the same locations, objects, characters, and other details. This interrelatedness of narrative threads can then be seen as braiding them together through the diegetic elements and events that link them.

dystopia   John Stuart Mill's term for a negative form of a utopia, that is, a utopia gone wrong, usually one where the government has become repressive and controlling.

encyclopedic impulse   A tendency toward having explanatory interludes, during which the narrative of a work halts so that information about the world and its inhabitants can be given. Descriptions of landscapes, peoples, customs, backstories, and philosophical outlooks are given either by the main character directly to the audience (if a story is told in first person) or experienced by the main character and the audience together (with the main character as a stand-in for the audience) through expository passages in which other characters introduce lands and peoples.

environmental storytelling   Theme park designer Don Carson's term for the telling of stories by infusing narrative elements into a world in such a way so that they can be found and recombined by the world's audience, who discover these elements as they experience the world.

imaginary world   All the surroundings and places experienced by a fictional character (or which could be experienced by one) that together constitute a unified sense of place which is ontologically different from the actual, material, and so-called "real" world. As "world" in this sense refers to an experiential realm, an imaginary world could be as large as a universe, or as small as an isolated town in which a character resides.

immersion   A process which involves being surrounded or engulfed in something; within Media Studies, the term may refer to one of three different types of experiences. The first is the *physical* immersion of user, as in a theme park ride or walk-in video installation; the user is physically surrounded by constructed experience, thus the analogy with immersion in water. The second is the *sensual* immersion of the user, as in a virtual-reality-type of head-mounted display, which covers eyes and ears. While the user's entire body is not immersed, what the user sees and hears is part of the controlled experience. The third is *conceptual* immersion, which is the least physical and which relies the most on the audience's imagination; for example, engaging books like *The Lord of the Rings* are considered "immersive" if they supply sufficient detail and description for the reader to vicariously enter the imagined world.

interactivation   The process by which something noninteractive is made into something interactive. Adding interactivity usually means adding moments of choice for the user, the outcomes of which have some bearing on the future choices that the user will have to face later.

internarrative theory   Theory that examines how individual narratives can be related and interact with each other, including separate narrative threads or braids that occur within a single work, or the narratives of separate works which are set in the same world, or which have transnarrative characters or objects.

interquel   A narrative sequence element which fits chronologically in between two already-existing narrative elements in the same sequence. An interquel connects works together, filling in the events that happened in between them, and so interquels are thus usually about how one situation developed into another, since both the beginning and end points of the interquel's story are already known to the audience.

intraquel A narrative sequence element which fills in a narrative gap within an already-existing narrative sequence element. Like an interquel, it is usually more about how one situation developed into another, since both the beginning and end points of the intraquel's story are already known to the audience.

invention The act of producing fictional elements for a narrative or world, particularly those elements which vary considerably from their Primary World counterparts, or those that have no Primary World counterparts.

midquel A narrative sequence element which takes place between sections or sequence elements of already-existing narrative material, combining the functions of sequels and prequels. Midquels can be further usefully divided into *interquels* and *intraquels*.

narrative braid Narrative threads taking place within the same world which become grouped together due to the fact that they share the same themes, characters, objects, locations, events, or chains of cause-and-effect. Types of narrative braiding include *diegetic braiding*, *thematic braiding*, and *causal braiding*.

narrative fabric A structure that results when a narrative or world has enough detail and events such that one can trace all the events happening to individual characters or locations over time (constituting diachronic or vertical narrative threads) or all the simultaneous events occurring at each moment (constituting synchronic or horizontal threads). All these resulting narrative threads woven together result in what could be called a narrative fabric.

narrative gestalt A structure or configuration of details which implies a sequence of causally-linked events, constituting a story, for which the audience fills in ellipsized actions or details, based on the sequence's narrative logic. For example, if a character in a film drives off from one location and the film cuts to the character arriving at another location, we assume the character has driven from one place to the other.

narrative resolution The amount of words, sounds, or images used to convey an event or other story information (*resolution* is used here to mean something like *granularity*, as in "graphical resolution"; as opposed to the use of "resolution" to mean the completion and closure of a narrative structure). Thus, a story told in high narrative resolution will relate events and information in great detail, with tight authorial control over the audience's experience, while stories told in low narrative resolution use more summary and synopsis, relying more on the imagination of the audience and narrative gestalten to complete the narrative details.

narrative speed Narratologist Gérard Genette's term which refers to the difference between the duration of story events versus the time needed to tell the events. If we make this concept independent of duration (which may vary, depending on the intake capability of individual audience members (for example, people who read more slowly or quickly)), this becomes the measure of *narrative resolution* instead, that is, the amount of words, sounds, or images it takes to describe a particular event.

narrative thread A series of causally-linked events, which usually revolves around a character, object, or location, giving a sense of what happens to it over time. An audience typically will have some expectation that narrative threads will lead somewhere, with some endpoint providing closure.

normalizing tendency An unconscious tendency in which Primary World defaults "normalize" secondary world defaults to some degree, within an audience's imagination, especially in the case of word-based media that leave visualization of a world to the reader's imagination. In other words, if certain aspects of a character are exaggerated in their initial description, readers are likely to play this down in their imagination as time goes on, resulting in a more "normal" appearance. Any divergence from realism may be reduced this way, to make a world and its elements seem more realistic when an author's details seem to be exaggerations of what is likely or possible.

overlaid world A fictional diegesis in which an existing, Primary World location is used, with fictional characters and objects appearing it, but without enough invention to isolate it from the Primary World into its own separate secondary world.

paraquel A narrative sequence element which runs parallel, that is, simultaneously, with an already-existing narrative sequence element or elements, often covering known events from a different perspective. Most paraquels are made *after* the sequence elements they parallel, which limits their events and outcomes the more closely related to existing sequence elements they are. They are thus more likely to introduce new characters and storylines and use the existing events of an imaginary world to set up suspense and provide a background structure. At the same, paraquels can reveal unseen events and provide motivation for the events of a pre-existing sequence element, offering new explanations for known events.

participatory world A world in which audience members participate in the world and its events, making permanent changes that result in canonical additions to the world. Such additions may be the actions of an avatar who is a part of the diegesis and takes part in diegetic events, as in an MMORPG, or a player–character in a tabletop game or MUD who can actively build and change the world from within the world, or a player who institutes changes from outside of the world, negotiating the world's shape and future with others. Such worlds differ from a merely interactive world, in which interaction occurs but no canonical changes can be made to the world.

prequel A narrative sequence element that comes before an already-existing narrative sequence element, which usually shows how characters and situations came to be, and often provides backstory for them.

Primary Imagination Samuel Taylor Coleridge's term for the kind of imagination that allows us to coordinate and interpret our sensory data, turning them into perceptions with which we make sense of the world around us. This he opposed to what he called "Secondary Imagination", which he describes as being similar in kind to Primary Imagination, but differing in degree and mode; it uses and recombines ideas and concepts in order to create, rather than using and interpreting direct sensory data, making it the kind of imagination that allows us to picture what does not exist.

Primary World J. R. R. Tolkien's term for our world, the material, physical world, as opposed to the imaginary worlds made within it, which he called secondary worlds, borrowing from Coleridge's ideas of Primary and Secondary Imagination.

reboot A complete reconception and redesign of a franchise or world. Taken from computer terminology, "reboot" suggests not only a restarting, but also that something was no longer viable or had gone wrong enough to require such an extreme measure; thus it is not surprising that most reboots begin with a new "story of origins" for its main character or characters. The majority of reboots appear in character-based franchises; they are done to update long-running franchises which have become dated over time, and they are usually done by people other than the original creators of the franchise (which naturally leads to discussions of canonicity). More often than not, reboots are done mainly to keep a franchise profitable and allegedly more appealing to a new generation of audience members, though such changes may alienate older audiences who still see the value of the original version.

retcon Originating in the comic book community, "retcon" is short for "retroactive continuity", which is when an author alters established facts in earlier works in order to make them consistent with later ones.

retroactive linkage A joining of two independently-created worlds that previously had existed separately, usually through a transnarrative character who appears in both worlds, or by the revelation that the two worlds share a border or some other geographic linkage. Authors who develop multiple worlds will often link them retroactively, to compile their world-building efforts into a single large entity.

saturation The condition that occurs when there are so many secondary world details to keep in mind that one struggles to remember them all while experiencing the world, to the point that the details of the secondary world crowd out thoughts of the immediate Primary World. Saturation is the pleasurable goal of conceptual immersion; the attempt to occupy the audience's full attention and imagination, often with more detail than can be held in mind all at once.

Secondary Belief J. R. R. Tolkien's term for the audience's belief in the secondary world that occurs when the construction and presentation of the world is successful; he suggests that additional belief is what is occurring in such a situation, rather than the "suspension of disbelief" as suggested by Samuel Taylor Coleridge.

Secondary Imagination Samuel Taylor Coleridge's term for the kind of imagination that uses and recombines ideas and concepts in order to create, rather than using and interpreting direct sensory data; the kind of imagination that allows us to picture what does not exist. This he opposed to what he called "Primary Imagination", which allows us to coordinate and interpret our sensory data turning them into perceptions with which we make sense of the world around us.

secondary world J. R. R. Tolkien's term for imaginary worlds, used to distinguish them ontologically from the material, physical world we inhabit (which he calls the Primary World), borrowing from Coleridge's ideas of Primary and Secondary Imagination.

sequel A narrative sequence element which follows an already-existing narrative sequence element. A sequel usually shares some common elements with the original story it follows, carrying them forward in time. A sequel is often able to take advantage of the existing popularity of the original, rather than having to rely on its own merits, at least initially. Sometimes this allows a work of lesser quality to be made, giving sequels a bad name, though this is, of course, not always the case; but audiences may still be less likely to experience a sequel if they have not experienced the original work first.

subcreated world J. R. R. Tolkien's term for a world which is made through the process of subcreation. The term deftly sidesteps philosophical problems with terms like "real" and "imaginary" and the ways they overlap.

subcreation J. R. R. Tolkien's term for the building of imaginary worlds through the using and recombining of existing concepts and ideas, as opposed to the *ex nihilo* ("from nothing") creation that only God is able to do;

thus, he appends the "sub" prefix; "subcreation" literally means "creating under".

thematic braiding   The condition that occurs when multiple stories or narrative threads set in the same world are thematically connected in order to compare and contrast characters and their situations. This interrelatedness of narrative threads can then be seen as braiding them together through the themes that link them.

transmedia storytelling   Henry Jenkins's term for storytelling which involves narrative material spread across works appearing in different media, resulting in a narrative that spans multiple media.

transnarrative character   A character who appears in more than one story. The presence of the character in multiple stories suggests that the stories share the same diegesis or world.

transquel   A narrative sequence element which covers a time period before, during, and after an already-existing narrative sequence element or elements, as if those preceding elements were filling gaps within it. Transquels are usually broad in scope, setting other sequence elements into a larger historical context and framework.

uchronia   Charles Renouvier's term for an unspecified or fictional time period in which a story is set, usually in the far future or distant past. "Uchronia" means "no time", and the word is patterned after "utopia" which means "no place".

utopia   Thomas More's term, taken from Greek, meaning "no place" and used as the name of his fictional island. More broadly, the term is used to describe an ideal community or society with a perfect form of governance (or what some characters think is the perfect form of governance).

virtual world   A world which has an existence independent of its users, usually as a model within a computer memory which is algorithmically reconstituted and controlled by a computer program. Users are able to interact with objects, characters, and each other in a virtual world through an interface, and some virtual worlds, like those of MMORPGs, are persistent and events continue within them after the user leaves them.

world gestalt   A structure or configuration of details which together implies the existence of a world, and causes the audience to automatically fill in the missing pieces of that world, based on the details that are given. Usually, all the given pieces follow a certain logic, which helps dictate what the missing information might be like, allowing existing information to be extrapolated to fill in the gaps.

INDEX